NEW TESTAMENT COMMENTARY

NEW TESTAMENT COMMENTARY

by

WILLIAM HENDRIKSEN

Exposition
of the
Gospel According to Mark

BAKER BOOK HOUSE
GRAND RAPIDS, MICHIGAN

Library of Congress Catalogue Card Number: 54-924

ISBN: 0-8010-4114-7

Eighth printing, July 1989

PHOTOLITHOPRINTED BY CUSHING - MALLOY, INC.
ANN ARBOR, MICHIGAN, UNITED STATES OF AMERICA

TABLE OF CONTENTS

LIST OF ABBREVIATIONS vii

INTRODUCTION TO THE GOSPEL ACCORDING TO MARK 1
    I. Who Wrote This Gospel? 3
    II. When and Where Was It Written? 13
    III. Why Was It Written? 16
    IV. What Are Its Characteristics? 18
    V. How Is It Organized? 25

GENERAL THEME: *The Work Which Thou Gavest Him To Do* 26

    I. *Its Beginning or Inauguration* 1:1-13 29

    II. *Its Progress or Continuation*   14—10:52 53
        A. *The Great Galilean Ministry* 54
            Chapter 1:14-45 54
            Chapter 2 84
            Chapter 3 112
            Chapter 4 146
            Chapter 5 184
            Chapter 6 218
            Chapter 7:1-23 268
        B. *The Retirement Plus Perean Ministries* 292
            Chapter 7:24-37 292
            Chapter 8:1—9:1 308
            Chapter 9:2-50 336
            Chapter 10 372

    III. *Its Climax or Culmination* 11:1—16:8 427
        A. *The Week of the Passion* 428
            Chapter 11 428

Chapter 12 472
Chapter 13 510
Chapter 14 548
Chapter 15 626
    B. *The Resurrection* 676
Chapter 16 676

SELECT BIBLIOGRAPHY 695

GENERAL BIBLIOGRAPHY 697

LIST OF ABBREVIATIONS

The letters in book abbreviations are followed by periods. Those in periodical abbreviations omit the periods and are in italics. Thus one can see at a glance whether the abbreviation refers to a book or to a periodical.

A. *Book Abbreviations*

A.R.V.	American Standard Revised Version
A.V.	Authorized Version (King James)
Gram.N.T.	A. T. Robertson, *Grammar of the Greek New Testament in the Light of Historical Research*
Gram.N.T. (Bl.-Debr.)	F. Blass and A. Debrunner, *A Greek Grammar of the New Testament and Other Early Christian Literature*
Grk.N.T. (A-B-M-W)	*The Greek New Testament,* edited by Kurt Aland, Matthew Black, Bruce M. Metzger, and Allen Wikgren
I.S.B.E.	*International Standard Bible Encyclopedia*
L.N.T. (Th.)	Thayer's *Greek-English Lexicon of the New Testament*
L.N.T. (A. and G.)	W. F. Arndt and F. W. Gingrich, *A Greek-English Lexicon of the New Testament and Other Early Christian Literature*
M.M.	*The Vocabulary of the Greek New Testament Illustrated from the Papyri and Other Non-Literary Sources,* by James Hope Moulton and George Milligan
N.A.S.	New American Standard Bible (New Testament)
N.N.	*Novum Testamentum Graece,* edited by D. Eberhard Nestle, revised by Erwin Nestle and Kurt Aland
N.E.B.	New English Bible
N.I.V.	The New International Version
N.T.C.	W. Hendriksen, *New Testament Commentary*
R.S.V.	Revised Standard Version
S.BK.	Strack and Billerbeck, *Kommentar zum Neuen Testament aus Talmud und Midrasch*

S.H.E.R.K.	*The New Schaff-Herzog Encyclopedia of Religious Knowledge*
Th.D.N.T.	*Theological Dictionary of the New Testament* (edited by G. Kittel and G. Friedrich)
W.D.B.	*Westminster Dictionary of the Bible*
W.H.A.B.	*Westminister Historical Atlas to the Bible*

B. *Periodical Abbreviations*

BTr	*Bible Translator*
Exp	*The Expositor*
JBL	*Journal of Biblical Literature*
JR	*Journal of Religion*
JSS	*Journal of Semitic Studies*
TT	*Theologisch tijdschrift*
WTJ	*Westminster Theological Journal*

Please Note

In order to differentiate between the second person singular (see Mark 10:37: "... one at your right") and the second person plural (next verse: "Y o u do not know"), the letters in "you sing." are not spaced; those in "y o u pl." are spaced.

Introduction
to
The Gospel According to Mark

I. Who Wrote This Gospel?

According to the superscription and unanimous tradition the name of the author or composer was *Mark*. On the reasonable assumption that whenever this name is mentioned in the New Testament the same man is indicated, he is called *Mark* in Acts 15:39; Col. 4:10; Philem. 24; II Tim. 4:11; I Peter 5:13. To be exact, that was his name in the Greek-speaking Roman world; spelled *Markos* in Greek, *Marcus* in Latin. Of course, since he was a Jew (Col. 4:10, 11), *Mark* was his surname, his "other" name. His original or Jewish name was *John* (Acts 12:12, 25; 15:37).

The New Testament does not give us a complete biography or personal history of this man. Tradition with respect to him, though valuable, is not in agreement on all points. It fails to give us a definite and undivided answer to such questions as the following: When Mark wrote his Gospel was the influence of Peter upon him decisive and controlling, so that Mark was merely the apostle's secretary—"Peter speaking, Mark writing"—; or (far more reasonable!) was it moderate, Mark being the real author but having Peter as his chief but by no means only source? Did Mark complete his book while Peter was still alive or not until after his death? Was Mark the "man bearing a pitcher of water" (Mark 14:13)? Was he one of the seventy missionaries (Luke 10:1)? Was he literally "stump-fingered" or does this description apply only to his Gospel, which lacks an introduction and a conclusion similar to what is found in the other Gospels? Was Mark the founder of the Alexandrian church? Did he die a natural death or did he suffer martyrdom?

The events in the life of Mark of which we are sure or which are at least invested with a considerable degree of probability are as follows:

By no means certain but nevertheless probable is the identification of Mark with "the young man" whose interesting story is told by the evangelist himself (14:51, 52). It was the night before the crucifixion. Jesus and his disciples were leaving the Upper Room. Was this room part of the very house owned by Mark's mother Mary, the home where Mark also lived? If so, it is understandable that "the young man," having supposedly already fallen asleep—it may have been 11 P.M.; see N.T.C. on Matt. 26:31–, awakens. Had he previously fully surrendered his heart to the Savior? However that may

3

be, an inner compulsion to accompany Jesus overpowers him. Snatching and throwing around his body a linen cloth he rushes out in order to follow the Master. He is seized by temple police. He escapes however, while his would-be captors hold in their hand the linen cloth. Cf. Gen. 39:12. If this reconstruction is not too bold it would imply that even as a young man Mark, like his mother, was one of Christ's "followers," though he was not one of The Twelve, and may not even have had any personal conversations with Jesus. In agreement with many we ascribe to the incident reported in Mark 14:51, 52 the date early April, A.D. 30. For more detail see on 14:51, 52.

Jesus, soon to depart from earth to heaven, did not leave his disciples leaderless. In a very real sense Peter was appointed to be the leader. See N.T.C. on Matt. 16:18. On Pentecost of the very year of Christ's departure God used Peter's stirring message to bring no less than three thousand "sheep" into the fold (Acts 2:41). Is it not probable that also upon John Mark the preaching of Peter exerted a mighty influence? See I Peter 5:13.

Between the years 30 and 44 there is a wide gap. What happened to Mark is not reported in Scripture. The next reported incident that may well have been of significance to John Mark is related in Acts 12:12-17. The date is probably A.D. 44. Peter, miraculously delivered from prison, makes straight for the house of "Mary the mother of John whose surname was Mark, where many were gathered together and were praying." This Mary—to be distinguished from Mary the mother of Jesus, Mary Magdalene, Mary of Bethany, and Mary the mother of James and Joses—was a woman of means. Her house had a porch or vestibule, and also an upper room large enough to accommodate a rather numerous assembly. She had at least one maid, Rhoda. Not only was Mary rich, she was also generous, wholeheartedly devoted to Christ's cause, and therefore willing to make available her facilities whenever these were needed by the Christian community. It was of such a mother that John Mark was a son. But are we certain that Mark was in Jerusalem at this time? Not entirely, yet this seems probable, for it is definitely reported that shortly afterward Paul and Barnabas take with them from Jerusalem (to Antioch) "John whose surname was Mark" (Acts 12:25). On the assumption then that Mark was in Jerusalem at the time covered by Acts 12:12-17, Peter's wonderful deliverance from prison must have made a deep impression on the younger man. Since it is definitely stated that "many" were gathered at his "widowed" mother's home, it is safe to assume that Mark was acquainted with several of the early witnesses of the events centering in Jesus. As already indicated earlier, to what extent he was acquainted with Jesus himself is not known, and early "tradition" is not of much help with respect to this point. —After A.D. 44 there is no unified solid evidence for several years of any close connection between Mark and Peter. Toward the end of Peter's life the evidence reappears. For a little while, therefore, we shall leave Mark, to return to him later.

As for influential Peter, of him too no biography is given. Nevertheless several events of his life are recorded in the Gospels and the book of Acts. Those related in Acts 1–5 occurred in Jerusalem, probably in close succession, perhaps between the years 30 and 32 (inclusive). In or about the year 37 Paul, converted three years earlier, visits Peter in Jerusalem (Gal. 1:18). About this time Peter and John are by the apostles sent to Samaria, where they strengthen Christ's followers and rebuke Simon the sorcerer. They return to Jerusalem (Acts 8:14-25). This tour is followed shortly by Peter's visits to Lydda and Joppa (Acts 9:32-43). The very important mission of Peter to Caesarea, an experience that opened his eyes with respect to the wideness of God's mercy, is reported in Acts 10. Returned to Jerusalem, Peter defends the manner in which he had conducted himself in Caesarea, his "visiting with the uncircumcised and eating with them" (Acts 11:1-18). The reign of Emperor Claudius (A.D. 41–54) is not introduced until Acts 11:28. It may well be, therefore, that Peter's visit to Caesarea and return to Jerusalem did not extend beyond the year 41. The next recorded event in the life of Peter, namely, his imprisonment and marvelous liberation, already referred to in the preceding, also has attached to it what looks like a note of time. If that inference is correct, this incident which, as we have seen, may well have been meaningful also for Mark, must have occurred just previous to the death, in the year 44, of King Herod Agrippa I (Acts 12:23). There is one more reference to Peter in the book of Acts (15:7-11). This passage summarizes Peter's address delivered at the Synod of Jerusalem, generally agreed to have met about the year 50. From Jerusalem Peter must have traveled to Syrian Antioch just before the beginning of Paul's second missionary journey, dated 50/51–53/54.[1] It was at this place and time that Peter was "corrected" by Paul (Gal. 2:11-21). Did Peter remain for a while in Asia Minor, or did he perhaps return to this general region later on? However that may have been, his interest in the churches of Asia Minor is evident from I Peter 1:1.

In the book of Acts Peter is never again mentioned; that is, never after chapter 15. In fact, by and large that is true for the rest of the New Testament. The statements that some Corinthians were playing off Cephas (=Peter) against Paul (I Cor. 1:12, 22), that Cephas was in the habit of taking his wife along with him on his mission tours (I Cor. 9:5), and that Jesus soon after his resurrection had made an appearance to that apostle (I Cor. 15:5), do not in any way cancel the fact that the New Testament offers no hint as

---

1 For the evidence in support of these several dates see the author's *Bible Survey*, pp. 62-64, 70, 71; also N.T.C. on Gal. 2:1.

to the whereabouts of the apostle from about the year 50/51 until close to the end of his life, presumably A.D. 64. The Lord himself had predicted the manner in which Peter was going to seal his confession with his martyrdom (John 21:18, 19; see N.T.C. on that passage; cf. II Peter 1:14; I Clement V; Tertullian, *Antidote for the Scorpion's Sting* XV; Origen, *Against Celsus* II.xlv; and Eusebius, *Ecclesiastical History* III.i).

Accordingly, the theory that Peter reigned as pope in Rome for twenty-five years, from 42 to 67, lacks scriptural support. In fact, if that tradition upheld by the church of Rome were true, Peter would have been at the very acme of his reign in or about the year 58, when Paul wrote his epistle to the Romans. Yet in his lengthy list of greetings addressed to individual believers in Rome (Rom. 16:3-15) Paul never mentions Peter at all.

Now with respect to the presence of Peter in Rome there is no justification for going into either of two extremes. On the one hand, such ideas as Peter's twenty-five year Roman episcopacy and the discovery and identification of that apostle's tomb should be abandoned. On the other hand, so should also the claim that Peter was never in Rome at all. As to the latter, the conclusion to which some have arrived, namely, that according to Rom. 15:20—hence before the year 58—Peter can never have been in Rome, because Paul writes, "making it my ambition not to preach the gospel where Christ has already been named, lest I build on another man's foundation," is certainly fallacious. The church in Rome had been established long ago, as this very epistle clearly indicates. It probably derived its origin from the return to their homes, with glowing reports, of the "visitors from Rome, both Jews and proselytes" who had listened to Peter's Pentecost sermon delivered in Jerusalem (Acts 2:10b, 14ff.). As to the meaning of Rom. 15:20, it was in *Spain*, which Paul intended to visit by way of Rome, that the gospel had not yet been preached (see Rom. 15:24). So Peter, to whom Jesus, in building his church, had assigned a very significant role (Matt. 16:18), may very well have made an early visit to Rome, especially with a view to the Jewish Christians there. As we have already noticed, there are various gaps in the story of Peter as recorded in the New Testament. We are not told where he was during the years 33 through 36; 42 and 43; 45 through 49; or 52 through 62. That he was not in Rome during the years of Paul's first Roman imprisonment (probably 60 through 62) is clear from Col. 4:11 (cf. Philem. 23, 24), for certainly Paul could not have written Col. 4:11b had Peter been in Rome at that time. But this still makes allowance for many years, from 33 on, during which Peter may have been strengthening the church in Rome by his presence, prayers, preaching, and pilotage. This brings us finally to a time close to the end of Peter's life and of Paul's life, when evidence for the intimate relation between *a.* Peter and Mark and *b.* Paul and Mark is furnished once again. About this a little later.

6

After the year 44, to which we last referred in connection with Mark, we find him in the company not of Peter but of Barnabas and Paul. It will be recalled that these two men, who had been sent on a relief mission to Jerusalem, had taken Mark with them to Syrian Antioch. When, prompted by the Holy Spirit, the church commissioned Barnabas and Paul to begin what was subsequently called *Paul's first missionary journey* (Acts 13:1-3), these men took Mark with them as their "attendant" (13:5). It is clear that Mark's position with respect to the other two was one of subordination. He was a helper. Exactly what was included in this role is not stated. Various possible tasks naturally occur to the mind; such as, serving as a kind of business manager and therefore arranging the details pertaining to the plan of the journey, making provision for food and lodging, sending messages, and perhaps above all, serving as a catechist, that is, taking up where the other two left off: telling the story of Christ's sojourn on earth and its triumphant ending, driving home once more the central lesson of Christ's life and teaching, asking and answering questions, etc. If Mark had already written his Gospel, he may all the more have been considered the right man in the right place for the performance of the task of a teacher or catechist.

For other reasons too Mark seemed to be the logical person to serve as helper. Was he not the son of ever hospitable Mary? Is it not natural to assume that Barnabas and Paul, on their charitable errand in Jerusalem (Acts 11:29, 30; cf. 12:25), had lodged at her house and had therefore communed with both mother and son? Besides, was not Barnabas an older cousin of Mark (Col. 4:10)? Is it not possible that Mark and his parents (at a time when perhaps the father was also still living?) had moved from Cyprus to Jerusalem, as was true with respect to Barnabas (Acts 4:36, 37)? Besides, was not John Mark bilingual, and were not also his superiors bilingual or even in a sense multilingual?

Via Seleucia, the seaport of the city of Antioch on the Orontes (Acts 3:14), the three missionaries crossed over to Cyprus. Having preached the Word of God in the Synagogues of Salamis, the men went through the entire island until they came to Paphos on the southwestern shore. From here, having smitten with blindness the false prophet or *magos* Bar-Jesus, who opposed them and unsuccessfully tried to keep the proconsul Sergius Paulus from accepting the gospel, they headed for Asia Minor. Then something unexpected happened: when they came to Perga in Pamphilia *Mark left them and returned to Jerusalem* (Acts 13:13; cf. 15:36-41)! The date may have been the year 47. Just why it was that Mark deserted the others is not explained. Was it because he was displeased with the fact that his cousin Barnabas had lost the leadership to Paul? Contrast *"Barnabas* and Saul" (11:30; 12:25; 13:2, 7), with "Saul who is also called Paul" (13:9), "Paul" (13:16), and *"Paul* and Barnabas" (13:43, 46, 50, etc.). Was it homesickness? Anxiety for his mother's safety? Misgivings about the offer of salvation to Jew and Gentile alike and on the same basis? All of these answers have been suggested. Or was it perhaps the difficulty of the task that lay ahead in this strange land, the rigors of this mountainous region, its terrors and dangers? Cf. II Cor. 11:26. To the present author it would seem that if any answer is at all possible, the last one is the most reasonable. According to Acts 15:38 Paul looked upon Mark as a deserter, one whose heart inexcusably quailed because of "the work" which confronted him. And does not Acts 15:40 imply that if any "sides" were taken in this dispute, the church chose the side of Paul? The inspired account, at any event, does not leave the impression that Mark was *wholly* without fault when he left Paul and Barnabas in the lurch and headed for home.

When, sometime later, after the completion of the first missionary journey and of the Jerusalem Conference, Barnabas wanted to take along Mark on the second journey, Paul adamantly refused to agree. So "Barnabas took Mark with him, and sailed away to Cyprus" (Acts 15:39b). After Acts 15:39 Luke never again mentions Mark, nor even "our beloved Barnabas" (15:25).

This means, then, that as far as the book of Acts—and, in fact, the New Testament as a whole—is concerned, with respect to *two lengthy periods covering respectively the years 31 through 43 and 52 through 59 no definite information is given or even implied about Mark.* We simply do not know where he was or what he was doing. The incidents that have been briefly described pertain entirely to the years 30, 44-47 50/51. And the only references so far are Mark 14:51, 52 (probably); Acts 12:12, 25; 13:5, 13; 15:37-39.

Does extra-canonical "tradition" furnish any reliable information about Barnabas and Mark after they had landed on the island of Cyprus? Not really, for *The Acts of Barnabas,* ascribed to Mark (!), a writing of much later date, is spurious. According to it, after Barnabas suffers martyrdom in Cyprus, Mark plants the banner of Christ in Alexandria. Sources in the same category state that he became the first bishop of the Alexandrian church—a rather common tradition—and retained this position until the eighth year of Nero's reign. Since Nero ruled from 54 to 68, the eighth year would be 61. On the other hand, the renowned Alexandrian fathers Clement and Origen say nothing at all about any activity or even presence of Mark in Alexandria.

Returning now to Scripture, the only truly reliable source, all it clearly implies with respect to Barnabas—i.e., implies in addition to what can be learned from the reports covering earlier years (see Acts chapters 4, 9, 11-15; and Gal. 2)—is that when, perhaps about the year 57, Paul wrote I Cor. 9:6, Mark's older cousin was obviously still alive. To be sure, the name "Barnabas" is also found in Col. 4:10, but only to indicate his relation to Mark: the two were cousins.

About the very time mentioned above, namely, "the eighth year of Nero's reign," or perhaps a year later, Paul is writing the epistles known as Colossians and Philemon. One of the men who are with him is Mark, who has fully re-established himself in Paul's confidence. The apostle, during this first Roman imprisonment commenting on those who were "of the circumcision," that is, those who were Jews, writes: "Aristarchus, my fellow-prisoner . . . Mark, the cousin of Barnabas, . . . and Jesus who is called Justus . . . are the only co-workers for the kingdom of God who have been a comfort to me" (Col. 4:10, 11; cf. Philem. 24; see N.T.C. on these passages). Mark, once rejected (in a sense) by Paul, has become a comfort to him, a valuable, highly esteemed, and warmly loved co-worker!

When Paul is released from his imprisonment and is traveling to various congregations of his farflung spiritual domain (see N.T.C. on I and II Timothy and Titus, pp. 39, 40), Peter is in Rome. He is writing the letter that came to be known as "the first epistle of Peter," having addressed it to "the elect who are sojourners in Pontus, Galatia, Cappadocia, Asia, and Bithynia" (1:1). In the closing salutation he is saying to them all: "The church [literally *she*] that is in Babylon, elect together with y o u, greets y o u, *and so does Mark my son*" (5:13). The date is perhaps about the year 63. It cannot have been later than 64, since it was probably in the latter part of that year that Peter became the victim of Nero's wrath. Does not this very term "my son" indicate that Peter's fatherly instruction and supervision was of long standing? Is it not distinctly possible that even before Peter wrote this there had been frequent contacts between him and John Mark? Is it not true that Peter was exactly the one who knew *by experience* that there was hope for those who had in one way or another succumbed to the temptation of failing to remain completely loyal to Christ and his cause? It would appear, then, that sovereign grace, making use of "the kindly tutelage of Barnabas" (F. F. Bruce), the stern discipline of Paul, and the potent influence of Peter, had triumphed in the life of Mark.

It has become clear therefore that for several years—probably 61 to 63 or 64—Mark is carrying on his ministry in the world's capital. After Peter's martyrdom Mark seems to have become *Paul's* assistant once more. At Paul's request and in co-operation with Timothy he is making a tour of the churches in Asia Minor. He is still there when, possibly in the year 66, Paul, shortly before his death, is writing the final letter that has come down to us from him. In it he exhorts Timothy, who at that time was probably in Ephesus (see N.T.C. on I and II Timothy and Titus, p. 43), as follows: "Pick up Mark and bring him with you, for he is *very useful to me for (the) ministry*" (II Tim. 4:11b). Over against Demas, who was the man who stayed away (II Tim. 4:10a) stands Mark, the man who came back!

Who, then, was Mark? Not a great leader but rather a follower, not a master-builder but a helper, not flawless but one who fought against and overcame his weakness, not a stay-at-home but a great traveler, not pre-eminently a man of quiet contemplation but a man of action, one who delighted to picture Christ in action for the salvation of sinners to the glory of God.

Though it is true that Mark wrote the shortest Gospel, one that never became as popular as did the other three, and was never quoted as frequently as they were, we must be careful not to sell it short. In the early church it became a custom to associate the four Gospels with the four faces—man, lion, calf, eagle—of the cherubim described in Ezek. 1:6, 10; cf. Rev. 4:7. The "man" symbol was frequently (not always) associated with Matthew, the "calf" with Luke, the "eagle" with John. As to Mark, the authorities could not agree. While none failed to discover also in this Gospel a true picture of the Christ, some on reading it were reminded of the swiftly flying eagle, some of the powerful lion, some of the lowly man, and some of the sacrificial calf.[2] In a sense, all were right!

Evidence in support of the assertion that it was indeed Mark who wrote the shortest Gospel is the following:

Writing at the beginning of the fourth century A. D. Eusebius, *op. cit.*, II.xiv.6-xv.2, states: "Close upon him [i.e., upon Simon the sorcerer] in the same reign of Claudius [A.D. 41-54], the Providence of the universe in its all-goodness and love toward men guided to Rome, as against a great corrupter of life [i.e., as against this Simon the sorcerer who had fled to Rome where a statue was erected in his honor] the great and mighty Peter, who because of his virtue was the leader of all the other apostles. And he, like a noble general of God, clad in divine armor, brought the costly merchandise of the light from the east to those in the west, preaching the gospel of the light itself, the word that saves souls, the proclamation of the kingdom of heaven.

"Thus, then, when the divine word had made its home among them, the power of Simon [the sorcerer] was extinguished and immediately perished, as did also the fellow himself.

"And so great a light of religion shone upon the minds of the hearers of Peter that they were not satisfied with a single hearing or with the unwritten teaching of the divine proclamation [kerygma], but with all kinds of entreaties urged Mark, whose gospel is extant, seeing that he was a follower of Peter, to leave them in writing a record of the teaching transmitted to them orally; nor did they cease until they had prevailed upon the man; and so they became responsible for the Scripture that is called The Gospel according to Mark. And they say that the apostle, knowing by the revelation

---

[2] See H. B. Swete, *The Gospel according to St. Mark*, London, 1913, pp. xxxvi-xxxviii.

10

of the Spirit to him what had been done, rejoiced because of their zeal, and ratified the Scripture for study in the churches. Clement quotes the story in the sixth book of the *Hypotyposeis* and the bishop of Hierapolis, Papias by name, confirms him. He also says that Peter mentions Mark in his first epistle, and that he composed this in Rome itself. And they say that he [Peter] indicates this, referring to the city metaphorically as Babylon, in the words [I Peter 5:13], 'The church that is in Babylon, elect together with y o u, greets y o u, and so does my son Mark.' "

Living a little earlier Origen (fl. 210-250) is quoted by Eusebius, *op. cit.,* VI.xxv.5, as follows: "Secondly, the [Gospel] according to Mark, who wrote it in accordance with Peter's instructions, whom also Peter in the general epistle acknowledges as his son, saying . . . [then follows I Peter 5:13] ."

From Origen we can go back still farther, to his teacher, Clement of Alexandria (fl. 190-200). From the latter's *Hypotyposeis* Eusebius VI.xiv.6, 7 quotes these words: "The occasion for writing the Gospel according to Mark was: After Peter had publicly preached the word in Rome and by the Spirit had proclaimed the gospel, those present, being many, urged Mark, as one who had followed him for a long time and remembered what he had spoken, to write down what he had said. He did this and distributed the Gospel among those who had asked him [for it]. When Peter learned about it, he neither strongly forbade it nor promoted it."

Tertullian (fl. 193-216), in his treatise *Against Marcion* IV.5, states: "The Gospel which Mark published may be affirmed to be Peter's whose interpreter Mark was."

Earlier by a few years, but still for a long time a contemporary of Clement of Alexandria and of Tertullian, was Irenaeus. In his work *Against Heresies* III.i.1 (quoted in part by Eusebius, *op. cit.,* V.viii.3) he writes: ". . . Peter and Paul went westward and preached and founded the church in Rome. After their *departure* [death? moving from one place on earth to another?] Mark, the disciple and interpreter of Peter, himself also handed down to us in writing what had been preached by Peter."

The Muratorian Fragment, an incomplete list of New Testament books, written in poor Latin and deriving its name from cardinal L. A. Muratori (1672-1750) who discovered it in the Ambrosian Library at Milan, may be assigned to the period 180-200. It is of importance for the history of the New Testament canon. Though regrettably it is merely a "fragment," hence incomplete, and in its survey of New Textament books has lost whatever was in the original with respect to Matthew, it definitely implies the existence and recognition of four Gospels. With respect to the second of these (Mark), the line-fragment that remains and *now* marks the beginning of the list reads: ". . . at which nevertheless he was present, and so he placed it." In view of all the other testimonies (Eusebius, Origen, Clement of Alexandria, Tertullian,

Irenaeus, etc.) it would certainly be rash to maintain that the author of this list of books was not here referring to the Gospel according to Mark.

About the middle of the second century A.D. Justin Martyr writes, *Dialogue with Trypho* CVI: "And when it is said that he changed the name of one of the apostles to Peter, and when this as well as the fact that he changed the names of two other brothers to Boanerges, meaning sons of thunder; this was an announcement of the fact, etc." This clearly shows that Justin had read Mark's Gospel, for that is the only place where the term Boanerges occurs, and where the surnaming of Simon and of James and John is mentioned in immediate succession (Mark 3:16, 17).

Probably as early as A.D. 125 the four Gospels were assembled into a collection for use in the churches and were given titles. "According to Mark" was the title of the shortest of the four.

Papias, a disciple of "the presbyter John"—in all probability *the apostle John*—seems to have been born between A.D. 50 and 60, and to have died shortly after the middle of the second century. In making inquiries concerning Christ's sojourn on earth he was far more interested in "the living voice," that is, in the oral testimony of those of the earliest witnesses who were still alive, than in written accounts (see Eusebius, *op. cit.*, III.xxxix.1-4). Based, then, on what Papias claims to have learned from John, Eusebius a little further (III.xxxix.15) quotes Papias as saying: "When Mark became Peter's interpreter, he wrote down accurately, although not in order, whatever he remembered of what was said or done by the Lord. For he had not heard the Lord nor had he followed him, but later, as I said, he followed Peter, who used to frame his teaching to meet the needs [of his hearers], but not composing, as it were, an orderly account of the Lord's oracles, so that Mark made no mistake [or: did no wrong] in thus writing down certain things as he remembered them. For to one thing he gave careful attention, namely, to leave out nothing of what he had heard and to falsify nothing."

There is therefore no justification whatever for denying the verdict of tradition, namely, that it was John Mark, cousin of Barnabas, who wrote the shortest of the four widely recognized Gospels. The evidence spans several centuries, from Eusebius all the way back to Papias. It comes from every region. From Asia, Africa, and Europe; that is, from the East (Papias of Hierapolis, Eusebius of Caesarea); the South (Clement of Alexandria, Tertullian of Carthage); and the West (Justin Martyr and the author of the Muratorian Fragment of Rome). Sometimes two regions are represented by one witness: the East and the West (Irenaeus of Asia Minor, Rome, and Lyons); the South and the East (Origen of Alexandria and Caesarea). Orthodox and heterodox, ancient Greek texts and early versions add their weight to the same conclusion.

Though it is certainly true that there are points with respect to which tradition varies—for example, the exact role of Peter in connection with the composition of Mark's Gospel, and the time when that Gospel was written (on which see section II)—all witnesses agree that the preaching of Peter at Rome figured significantly in the production of this work. It is reasonable to believe that Mark consulted many sources, probably both oral and written, but it remains true that according to a tradition which we have no reason to reject he was "Peter's interpreter." Moreover, the contents of the book confirm this conclusion. Peter's sins and weaknesses are recorded faithfully, but the praise which he received elsewhere (for example in Matt. 16:17) is omitted from Mark. Again, at times Mark mentions Peter by name (5:37; 11:21; 16:7) when Matthew does not. Mark's Gospel, moreover, is character- ized by a certain vividness, rapidity of movement, and attention to detail, which characteristics are easily associated with active, vivacious, enthusiastic Peter. See, for example, 1:16-31; 35-38; 5:1-20; 9:14-29; 14:27-42, 54, 66-72. In 1:36 the disciples are referred to as "Simon and those who were with him."

If we had nothing more than Mark's Gospel, it would be impossible to arrive at the conclusion that it was written as a result (at least to a considerable extent) of *Peter's* preaching. On the other hand, on the basis of the testimony of tradition telling us that this was indeed how it came to be written, it is possible, as has been shown, to find in the Gospel itself corroborating evidence in support of this conclusion.

II. When and Where Was It Written?

Let us consider first the "Where?" and then the "When?"

What has just been said with respect to the relation of Mark's Gospel to *Peter* holds also with reference to its connection with *Rome*. Here too this Gospel, though nowhere definitely indicating and proving its place of origin, confirms the statements of Eusebius, Clement of Alexandria, Irenaeus, etc., that it was written in Rome and for the Romans.

That it was composed for a non-Jewish public would seem to follow from the fact that such Semitic terms and expressions as *boanerges* (3:17), *talitha cumi* (5:41), *corban* (7:11), *ephphatha* 7:34), and *Abba* (14:36) are by Mark translated into Greek. Moreover, the author explains Jewish customs (7:3, 4; 14:12; 15:42). And as to this Gospel's origin in *Rome* note that at times Mark renders Greek into Latin. He mentions that the two *lepta* ("copper coins") which the poor widow cast into the offering box amounted to one Roman *quadrans* ("penny," 12:42), and that the *aulē* ("palace") into which the soldiers led Jesus was *the praetorium* (the governor's official residence, 15:16).

Mark is also the only Gospel that informs us (15:21) that Simon of Cyrene was "the father of Alexander and Rufus," who were evidently well-known in Rome (see Rom. 16:13).

To all this should be added the fact that the manner in which Mark pictures the Christ, namely, as an active, energetic, swiftly moving, warring, conquering King, a Victor over the destructive forces of nature, over disease, demons, and even death, would be of interest especially to Romans, people who, in their lust for and exercise of *power,* had conquered the world. To them Mark pictures a King who excels any earthly conqueror. His kingdom is far more extensive, his armor far more effective, and his rule far more enduring than anything originating here below. His victories, moreover, are far more honorable, for he causes the conquered to share in the glory of the conquest. Mark's King is the Savior-King. He is the Victor who does not gloat over the suffering of the conquered but suffers in their place and with a view to their everlasting welfare (10:45).

More difficult to answer is the question, *When* was this Gospel written? It is probably safe to state that it must have been composed within the period beginning fifteen years before and ending fifteen years after the middle of the first century A.D. Before the year 35 Mark may well have been too young to undertake such a task. After the year 65 Peter was probably no longer alive and could therefore not have ratified this book "for study in the churches."[3]

Beginning with the latter half of the period in question—hence, 50-65—, it has already been shown that Peter and Mark were together in Rome about the year 63. That would therefore seem to be an ideal date for the composition of Mark's Gospel. Nevertheless, the date is not without difficulty. As has been shown in N.T.C. on The Gospel according to Matthew—see the section on The Synoptic Problem—Mark was probably written before Matthew, and Matthew before Luke. Luke's Gospel, in turn, was followed by Acts. The question may well be asked whether, on the basis of this chronology, some of this literary activity is not thus pushed too far forward, perhaps into the terrible period of the Jewish War against the Romans, accompanied

---

[3] It is true that according to a rather common interpretation of the words of Irenaeus quoted above (p. 11) Mark wrote his Gospel after Peter's death. However, aside from the fact that Irenaeus confirms the well-nigh unanimous tradition according to which this Gospel was written in Rome by "Peter's interpreter," the words of this witness are too controversial to shed much light on the date of the book. Many questions arise: Is Irenaeus summarizing when he states that "Peter and Paul went westward"? How is it possible that they "founded" the church in Rome, or is this witness using the word "founding" in a sense other than the usual? Just what does he mean by "after their departure"?

by bitter strife between the various Jewish factions. Neither Luke nor Acts indicates that anything of the kind was actually occurring when these books were written.

The late fifties have been suggested. Our historical summary of important events in the lives of Peter and of Mark has shown that from the side of Scripture there is no objection to supposing that sometime between the years 52 and 59 Peter and Mark were together in Rome (exception, as has also been indicated, the year 58, when Peter was clearly not in that city).

Of late, however, the attention is being riveted upon the possibility that in our attempt to fix the date of Mark's Gospel we must look away from 50-65 and settle on 35-50, even better 40-50. Considerations that would seem to favor this view are the following:

First, according to the statement of Eusebius, quoted above, it was during the reign of Claudius (A.D. 41-54) that "the Providence of the universe guided to Rome . . . the great and mighty Peter" whose "follower" Mark, at the request of "the hearers of Peter" composed a record of Peter's teaching, this record being The Gospel according to Mark.

Secondly, the subscriptions of many of the later uncials (manuscripts with large and separate letters) and cursives (running-hand manuscripts) inform us that the Gospel according to Mark was written in the tenth or twelfth year after Christ's ascension, hence sometime between the years 39 and 42.

Thirdly, the small papyrus scrap found in cave #7 near Qumran, and deciphered by the Spanish priest Father O'Callighan as being part of Mark 6:52, 53, belonged to material to which upon discovery the date approximately A.D. 50 had been ascribed. This scrap would therefore seem to point back to a considerably earlier (than 50) date for the actual composition of that Gospel. Therefore a date somewhere in the beginning of the reign of Emperor Claudius might not be far from the truth. Besides, it has been shown that Peter and Mark may well have spent some time together in Rome at that time.

The discovery and identification of the papyrus scrap containing the keystone Marcan passage has created great interest among New Testament scholars. The comments range all the way from "nothing has changed" to "the mathematical probabilities that Dr. O'Callighan is right are astronomical." I would especially recommend the reading of the excellent articles by William White, Jr., "O'Callighan's Identifications: Confirmation and Its Consequences" *WTJ*, 35 (Fall 1972), pp. 15-20, and "Notes on the Papyrus Fragments from Cave 7 at Qumran" *WTJ*, 35 (Winter 1973), pp. 221-226.

Conclusion: When was Mark 1:1—16:8 written? Answer: sometime between A.D. 40 and 65, *with the balance of evidence now favoring the earlier part of this period.* It is too early to speak more definitely. Rushing to conclusions is never wise (Isa. 28:16b). As to Mark 16:9-20 see on that section.

The objection may be raised: "But if thus early, then Mark was still somewhat immature spiritually when he wrote, for the act of deserting his partners Paul and Barnabas occurred some years later. Does not this situation lower our estimate of the value of Mark's book?"

However, if we apply this criticism to The Gospel according to Mark we should apply it all around. Are we ready to reject David's early psalms because when he wrote them his sin with respect to Bathsheba and his subsequent repentance were still many years away? Shall we look askance upon Peter's powerful and very effective Pentecost sermon because a good twenty years later the man who had preached it "stood condemned" at Antioch (Gal. 2:11-21)? Must we discard an epistle written by a brother of the Lord, because its author had to confess, "In many respects we all stumble" (James 3:2)? And shall we throw out of the window the book of Revelation because when John received these visions he was still making mistakes in his personal behavior (Rev. 19:10; 22:8)? Certainly not! What applies to all books of the Bible holds also for Mark: we do not ascribe perfection to the men who wrote them, but we do ascribe plenary inspiration to the products which, under the guidance of the Holy Spirit, they produced.

Room should be left, therefore, for the possibility that this Gospel was written during the earlier part of the A.D. 40-65 period. This early date is by no means certain. See P. Garnet, "O'Callighan's Fragments: Our Earliest New Testament Texts?" E. Q. XLV, No. 1 (Jan.-March 1973), pp. 6-12. When did Mark write his Gospel? A safe answer is "sometime during the period A.D. 40-65."

III. Why Was It Written

As has been shown—see Chapter I above—according to tradition this Gospel was composed to satisfy the urgent request of the people of Rome for a written summary of Peter's preaching in that city. However, this cannot mean that the information found in this book must be withheld from everybody living outside of the city limits of the capital. As is clear from 1:37; 10:45; 12:9; 13:10; and even 16:15 (whatever be its authenticity), this Gospel was intended to reach the entire Greek speaking world: its message was, is, and is going to be meaningful for everybody.

A closely related question is: In writing it did Mark intend merely to supply *information* or also to bring about *transformation?* Was it his purpose, as some maintain, merely to record a *narrative,* or in so doing to furnish an *incentive* for living to the glory of God? To phrase it differently, How did he view Jesus? Merely as a very interesting personage, the story of whose mighty deeds must be related because it is fascinating and satisfies people's curiosity? Or did he primarily regard Jesus to be the mighty and conquering Savior King, to whom all men should turn in humble faith? Surely the latter! It must ever be borne in mind that Mark was "Peter's interpreter." Now whenever Peter preached he urged repentance. His predication amounted to, at least reached a climax of, exhortation (Acts 2:36-40; 10:43), in order that through repentance and faith men might be saved, to God's glory (Acts 11:18). Now if that was true with respect to Peter, it must also have been true with respect to Mark. Mark's Gospel, accordingly, does have a definitely doctrinal and thoroughly practical aim. It is a narrative, to be sure, but a narrative with a most noble purpose (Mark 10:45; 12:28-34; 16:16).

Now a person's willingness to surrender himself to Jesus depends upon how he views him; in other words, faith always implies doctrine. Even narrative is not without its doctrinal implications. The Christology implied throughout in Mark's Gospel is that, to begin with, Jesus is thoroughly human. He eats (2:16) and drinks (15:36). He becomes hungry (11:12). He touches people (1:41) and is touched by them (5:27). He becomes grieved (3:5) and indignant (10:14). He falls asleep from fatigue and is awakened (4:38, 39). He asks that a boat be provided for him, so that he may not be crushed (3:9). He (for a while) plies a trade; he has a mother, brothers and sisters (6:3). Viewed as a man, his knowledge is limited (13:32), so that he turns around to see who has touched him (5:30), and walks up to a fig tree to see whether it has edible fruit (11:13). He has a human body (15:43) and a human spirit (2:8). He even dies (15:37)!

However, this same Jesus of Mark's Gospel is also thoroughly divine. The "Son of man" (2:10, 28; etc.) is also "Son of God" (1:1; 3:11; etc.). The One whom Mark describes reigns supreme in the realm of *disease, demons, and death.* As such he heals diseases of every variety, casts out demons (1:32-34), cures the blind, the deaf, etc. (8:22-26; 10:46-52), cleanses the leper (1:40-45), and even raises the dead (5:21-24, 35-43). He exercises power over the domain of nature in general; for he stills winds and waves (4:35-41), walks on water (6:48), causes a fig tree to wither (11:13, 14, 20), and multiplies a few rolls so that they suffice to satisfy the hunger of thousands (6:30-44; 8:1-10). His knowledge of the future is so detailed and comprehensive that he predicts what will happen to Jerusalem, to the world, to his disciples (chapter 13), and to himself (8:31; 9:9, 21; 10:32-34; 14:17-21). He knows what is in men's hearts (2:8; 12:15), and knows their circumstances (12:44). His authority is so outstanding that he pronounces pardon in a manner befitting God and no one else (2:1-12, especially verses 5 and 6). The climax of his majesty is revealed in this that when he is put to death he rises again (16:6)!

As to whether Mark pictures this Jesus as the object of faith, this question, too, must be answered with a vigorous affirmative, really already implied in the foregoing. "Jesus Christ, the Son of God," is immediately introduced as the Lord whose coming, in accordance with prophecy, demands a herald or way-preparer (1:1-3). He is the One to whom the angels minister (1:13). His blood is a ransom for many (10:45; cf. 14:24). He baptizes with the Holy Spirit (1:8), is Lord even of the sabbath (2:28), appoints his own ambassadors (3:13-19), has a right to be accepted *in faith* even by those of "his own country" (implied in 6:6), has authority to bid men follow and receive him (8:34; 9:37), is the very One whom David called "Lord" (implied in 12:37), and is coming again in the glory of his Father (8:38), in clouds with power and great glory, when he will send forth the angels to gather his elect (13:26, 27).

According to this evangelist the two natures, human and divine (to use later terminology), are in perfect harmony. This is a fact which, in studying certain passages, one can hardly fail to detect (4:38, 39; 6:34, 41-43; 8:1-10; 14:32-41; etc.).

Mark's aim is that men everywhere may accept this Jesus Christ, "Son of man" and "Son of God," this conquering King—see Chapter II above—, as their Savior and Lord.

IV. What Are Its Characteristics?

The three most obvious ones are *compactness, vividness, and orderliness.* By *compactness* is meant that this Gospel is much shorter than any of the others. In the Bible lying before me Luke covers approximately 40 pages, Matthew 37, John 29, and Mark only 23. Luke has about 1147 verses, Matthew 1068. Mark (1:1–16:8) has only 661. Mark contains only one parable not found elsewhere, that of The Seed Growing in Secret (4:26-29). In addition it shares three parables with Matthew and Luke: The Sower (Mark 4:3-9, 18-23), The Mustard Seed (4:30-32), and The Wicked Tenants (12:1-9). Compare this with Matthew's ten parables that are peculiar to that Gospel, six that it shares with Luke, and three along with Mark and Luke; hence, nineteen parables in all. Luke has eighteen parables all its own. This number added to the nine already implied makes no less than twenty-seven parables for Luke.[4] Since some of the parables are rather lengthy this means

---

[4] However, parables can be counted differently. See N.T.C. on Matthew, p. 22-24.

that, other things being equal, Mark by omitting so many of them would be considerably shorter than the other Gospels.

What is just as important in this connection is that of the six great discourses found in Matthew only one—the sixth, on The Last Things (Matt. 24 and 25; cf. Mark 13)—is found also in Mark, and even then in shorter form. Of the other discourses only remnants, frequently scattered, are reported in Mark. See, however, also Mark 4.

All this means that Mark's brevity relates especially to *the words of Jesus*. Nevertheless, the number of verses in Mark *that contain such words* (some verses have only one or two of them) is not small: 278. They occur especially in chapters 2, 4, 7, 9, 10, and 12. Luke has 588 verses containing dominical words, Matthew 640. Accordingly, while such words are found in approximately 60% of Matthew's 1068 verses, and in about 51% of Luke's 1147, they occur in only about 42% of Mark's 661. Mark is definitely the *action* Gospel. It is understandable that because of the omission of so much *sayings* material there was room even in this short Gospel for a series of *miracle* stories almost as long as in the much larger Matthew. Each of Mark's first eleven chapters contains at least one miracle account (1:21-28, 29-31, 32-34, 39, 40-45; 2:1-11; 3:1-6; 4:35-41; 5:1-20, 21-43; 6:30-44, 45-52, 53-56; 7:24-30, 31-37; 8:1-10, 22-26; 9:14-29; 10:46-52; and 11:12-14, 20, 21). Those recorded in 7:31-37; 8:22-26 are peculiar to Mark. Moreover in several cases Mark's coverage is more detailed and graphic than is that of the other Synoptics.

This leads to the second characteristic of this Gospel, namely, its *vividness*. Mark's style[5] sparkles. Was he not the interpreter of vivacious, highly emotional, colorful Simon Peter?

---

[5] As to the vocabulary and style of the original note the following:

a. The *words* used in Mark's Gospel are listed in H. B. Swete, *op. cit.*, pp. 409-424. Those preceded by an asterisk are not used elsewhere in the New Testament. There are approximately 80 of these, not counting proper names.

b. As to *style*, in general it can be stated that Mark's is not only the most diffuse but also the most vivid; Matthew's is more succinct and polished; Luke's is the most versatile of the three.

c. The graphic character of Mark's manner of writing appears from the following: his description of Christ's looks on various occasions (3:5, 34; 10:23; 11:11); the latter's acts and gestures (8:33; 9:35, 36; 10:16, 32); emotions and feelings (3:5; 6:34; 7:34; 8:12, 33; 10:14, 21; 11:12); and the persons near him (1:29, 36; 3:6, 22; 11:11, 21; 13:3; 14:65; 15:21; 16:7). Sometimes Mark mentions the *number* of the persons, animals, etc. present, where the other Gospels either omit any reference to it or express it in a different manner (5:13; 6:7, 40; 14:30). Place and time indications abound in this Gospel (1:16, 19, 21, 32, 35; 2:1, 13, 14; 3:1, 7, 13, 20; 4:1, 10, 35; 5:1, 20; 7:31; 12:41; 13:3; 14:68; 16:5, to give but a few examples).

d. Frequent change of tenses is another characteristic that adds to the vividness of Mark's style. Mark also frequently uses a tense that differs from the one found in Matthew and/or Luke. Examples: ἐγγίζουσιν (they approach, Mark 11:1) versus ἤγγισεν (he approached, Luke 19:29); in the same verse ἀποστέλλει (he sends) versus ἀπέστειλεν

Having therefore studied the Gospel according to Matthew, one cannot afford to skip Mark, thinking, "This book contains hardly anything that has not already been said by the publican turned author." To be sure, of wholly new material—material not paralleled at all either in Matthew or in Luke—there is very little. Only 31 Marcan verses are generally mentioned in this connection (1:1; 2:27; 3:20, 21; 4:26-29; 7:3, 4; 7:32-37; 8:22-26; 9:29; 9:48, 49; 13:33-37; 14:51, 52). On the other hand, it is also true that in ever so many passages or paragraphs Mark presents lively little touches that are not found elsewhere. These touches (in addition to the ones already included in the immediately preceding list: 1:1, etc.) enliven the account. The following are examples:

In the wilderness where he was tempted Jesus was "among the wild beasts" (1:13). John the Baptist's preaching was not exclusively negative: he did not merely tell his audience to repent. He added "and believe the gospel" (1:15). When the fishermen James and John in order to follow Jesus left their father in the boat, they did not overburden him: they left him "with the hired men" (1:20). In healing Simon's mother-in-law Jesus not merely

---

(he sent). So also φέρουσιν (they bring, Mark 11:7) versus ἤγαγον (they brought, Luke 19:35); in the same verse ἐπιβάλλουσιν (they throw on) versus ἐπιρίψαντες (a synonym: having thrown on). In general it may be said that in many instances where Mark uses the present tense Matthew and Luke use the aorist or the imperfect. See J. C. Hawkins, *Horae Synopticae*, pp. 143-153.

e. Another striking difference between Mark, on the one hand, and Matthew and Luke, on the other, is the latter two's preference for the particle δέ over against Mark's strong leaning toward the use of καί. Thus, in the paragraph from which examples showing difference in tense were just cited (Mark 11:1-8 compared with Luke 19:29-35) Luke uses καί five times to introduce a clause or phrase, Mark a dozen times. In these same seven verses Luke uses δέ three times (also once in verse 36 and once in verse 37); Mark only once (also once in verse 8). On this point see also Mark 16:9-20.

f. In connection with Mark's generous use of καί it should also be mentioned that it is characteristic of Matthew and Luke that they frequently substitute a participle for Mark's finite verb with καί. In such cases the two favor subordination, where Mark co-ordinates.—On Semitic influence in Mark see Gram. N.T., pp. 106, 118, 119; also Gram. N.T. (Bl.-Debr.), *par.* 321, 353. And see on 13:19, 20.

g. A characteristic that adds to Mark's sparkling mode of expression is the frequent use of the adverb εὐθύς: *at once, immediately* (about forty times: 1:10, 12, 18, etc.). In line with this is also his use of direct (instead of indirect) discourse: "Hush. Be still!" (4:39); "Unclean spirit, come out of the man!" (5:8); "What is your name?" (5:9); "Send us into the swine so that we may enter them" (5:12).

h. In view of all that has been mentioned it is not strange that Mark's style is emphatically vernacular. Here is a common man speaking to common, mostly uneducated, people. He uses a style that attracts their attention, language that is both his and theirs. It is not surprising therefore that he makes frequent use of diminutives; such as θυγάτριον (5:23; 7:25); κοράσιον (5:41, 42; 6:22, 28); κυνάριον (7:27, 28); loves the popular double negative (1:44; 5:3; 16:8); is not afraid to employ a pleonastic phrase (τότε ἐν ἐκείνῃ τῇ ἡμέρᾳ, 2:20); and is fond of compound verbs (1:16, 36; 2:4; 5:5; 8:12; 9:12, 15, 36; 10:16; 12:17; 14:40; 16:4, etc.).

touched her; tenderly he "took her by the hand" (1:31). That evening at sundown "the whole town was gathered at the door" of Peter's house (1:33). "Very early the next morning Jesus . . . went to a lonely place, and there he prayed." It was here that Peter and his companions found him, telling him that everybody was looking for him (1:35-57).

The house where Jesus was proclaiming the message was filled to overflowing; in fact, "not even near the doorway" was there any room left (2:2).

At another occasion when Christ's enemies on a sabbath and in the synagogue were watching him with critical eyes to see whether on this day he would heal a man with a withered hand, Jesus "looked around at them with anger, being deeply disturbed by the hardness of their hearts" (3:5).

It was "evening" when the disciples took Jesus with them in the boat "just as he was" (4:35, 36). Soon he was "in the stern asleep on the cushion" (4:38). To the sea he said, "Hush! Be still!" (4:39). He asked his disciples, "Even now do y o u not have faith?" (4:40).

The story of the healing of the Gerasene demoniac is told with far more detail in Mark than in either Matthew or Luke. Mark devotes twenty verses to it (5:1-20); Luke fourteen (8:26-39); Matthew seven (8:28-34). For example, Mark relates that no one could keep this man in chains or subdue him. He adds, "And always, night and day, among the tombs and on the hillsides he was screaming and cutting himself with stones." All three Synoptics report that when Jesus gave the demons leave they came out of the man and went into the pigs, which thus possessed rushed down the cliff and into the sea. Mark adds that there were "about two thousand" pigs that drowned. What is true with respect to the cure of the demoniac holds also in the case of the woman who touched Christ's garment: the full story is told not in Matthew (three verses, 9:20-22), nor in Luke (six verses, 8:43-48), but in Mark (ten verses, 5:25-34). Notice particularly what *Mark* says—but "Dr." Luke does *not* say—about physicians! (cf. Mark 5:25 with Luke 8:43). Other details reported exclusively by Mark are found in 5:29b, 30. But though Mark was "Peter's interpreter" it is not Mark but Luke who brings Peter into the story (8:45).

In his home town Jesus "could not do any mighty work" (6:5). Herodias "had it in for [nursed a grudge against]" John the Baptist, and "wanted to kill him. But she could not, for Herod feared John . . . ' (6:19, 20). The apostles report to Jesus, who bids them, "Come away by yourselves to a quiet place and rest a while" (6:30, 31). In connection with the feeding of the five thousand the people sat down "by hundreds and by fifties" (6:40; cf. Luke 9:14). Jesus, having remained behind after he had told the disciples to go by boat to the opposite side, "saw them straining at the oars" (6:48; cf. Matt. 14: 24).

"Jesus entered into a home and did not want anyone to know about it"

(7:24). The Syrophoenician woman did not take her grievously afflicted daughter with her when she begged Jesus to take pity on her and to heal her child. Mark makes this clear by saying that the woman "went home and found the child lying in bed, the demon having gone out of her" (7:30).

When the Pharisees argued with Jesus and asked him to show them a sign from heaven, he "sighed deeply in his spirit" (8:12). The disciples "had only one bread-cake with them in the boat" (8:14; cf. Matt. 16:5).

The three disciples (Peter, James, and John) "discussed among themselves what this 'rising from the dead' could mean" (9:10, with reflection on Jesus' saying recorded in verse 9b). These same disciples, having descended from the mountain (of transfiguration), notice a great multitude surrounding the other nine disciples, "and scribes arguing with them" (9:14). Upon seeing Jesus, the crowd "is greatly amazed" (9:15). Mark presents a detailed description of the symptoms of epilepsy and of the manner in which the boy who was afflicted with it was healed (9:18-27). This evangelist also records the father's famous saying, "I believe; help my unbelief!" (9:24). At this particular time Jesus did not want his journeying through out-of-the-way places in Galilee to be publicized (9:30). Jesus asked the disciples what they were arguing about on the way. Answer: silence (9:33, 34; cf. Matt. 18:1; Luke 9:46, 47a). Jesus took the little child "in his arms" (9:36). To the reason recorded by Luke (9:49, 50), showing why an exorcist outside of Christ's company should nevertheless not be forbidden to continue doing what he was doing, Mark adds another (9:41; contrast Matt. 10:42).

The rich young ruler ran up to Jesus and knelt before him (10:17). "And Jesus looking upon him loved him" (10:21). When the young man was told what he should do "his countenance fell" (10:22; cf. Matt. 19:22; Luke 18:23). Jesus then "looked around" at his disciples, and when they were amazed repeated and clarified his saying about the difficulty which rich people experience in their attempt to enter the kingdom of God (10:23a, 24). The Master assures those who are willing to sacrifice their all for him that, among other things, they will receive "fields," though all these things "along with persecutions" (10:30). On the way to Jerusalem "Jesus was going ahead of them, and they were amazed" (10:32; cf. Luke 9:51b). It was not just *the mother* of James and John who made a selfish request (see Matt. 20:20), but so did these two disciples themselves (Mark 10:35). The name of the Jericho blind man who was healed was Bartimaeus. Moreover, not merely was he blind, he was "a blind beggar" (10:46). Mark 10:49, 50 presents vivid details regarding the manner in which Bartimaeus was encouraged and responded to this encouragement.

The disciples found "a colt hitched to a door outside near the street" (11:4). In connection with Christ's triumphant entry into Jerusalem the crowds shouted, "Blessed is the kingdom . . ." (11:10; cf. Matt. 21:9; Luke

19:38). Anent the temple cleansing Mark reports: "And he would not allow anyone to carry anything through the temple" (11:16).

"Hear O Israel, the Lord our God, the Lord is one" (12:29). The scribe wholeheartedly endorses Christ's summary of the law, for which approval the Lord commends him (12:32-34).

"Teacher look, what marvelous stones and what marvelous buildings!" (13:1; cf. Matt. 24:1; Luke 21:5). "Peter, James, John, and Andrew asked him privately . . ." (13:3, evidently an item Mark received from Peter). "And brother shall deliver brother to death, the father his child . . ." (13:12; more vivid than Matt. 24:10; Luke 21:16). "The desolating sacrilege" shall be "standing where he ought not" (13:14).

In connection with *a.*, the anointing at Bethany, Mark relates: "she broke the perfume bottle" (14:3); *b.* Christ's trial before the Sanhedrin: "their testimonies did not agree" (14:56); and *c.* Peter's denial: "And immediately for the second time a rooster crowed, . . ." (14:72; cf. Matt. 26:74b, 75; Luke 22:60).

Barabbas, the insurrectionist, was also "a murderer" (15:7). The people asked Pilate to release a prisoner (15:8). Pilate asked, "Then what shall I do with the man whom y o u call the King of the Jews?" (15:12; cf. Matt. 27:22). Simon of Cyrene was "the father of Alexander and Rufus" (15:21; cf. Rom. 16:13). It was on "Preparation-day, the day before the sabbath" that Joseph of Arimathea "boldly" went to Pilate and asked for the body of Jesus (15:42, 43; cf. Matt. 27:57, 58; Luke 23:50-52; John 19:38). What Pilate did before he granted the request is related in Mark 15:44.

It was on Saturday, after sunset, that Mary Magdalene, Mary the mother of James, and Salome, bought liquid aromatics with a view to anointing Christ's body (16:1; cf. Matt. 28:1). "And they were saying among themselves, 'Who shall roll the stone from the door of the tomb for us?' " (16:3). It was "a very heavy" stone (16:4). "They entered the tomb and saw a young man dressed in a white robe, sitting on the right side" (16:5). He said to the women, "Don't be alarmed. Y o u are looking for Jesus the Nazarene" (16:6). Go, tell his disciples "and Peter" (16:7, another reminder of the close connection between Mark and Peter; cf. Matt. 28:7). "They said nothing to anyone; for they were afraid" (16:8).

Finally, it would seem that in addition to compactness and vividness Mark's Gospel excels in chronological *orderliness*. From Mark 1:1—6:13 Mark and Luke run parallel to a considerable extent, so that when 3 (sometimes 4) is added to the number that indicates the chapter where Mark's narrative occurs, locating the corresponding story in the largest Gospel is easy. See N.T.C. on Matthew, pp. 12-14. It should be borne in mind however that Luke 7 contains no Marcan parallel (neither is Mark 7 duplicated in Luke).

Now the fact that Luke places Christ's rejection at Nazareth at the forefront of his report on the Galilean Ministry, even though the very story of that rejection (see Luke 4:23) presupposes that when it occurred Jesus had already been doing considerable work in Galilee, proves that this Gospel writer was not very interested in *chronological* order. Matthew (13:53-58) and Mark (6:1-6) do not relate this incident until they have almost reached the middle of their respective books. Similarly, in the middle section of Luke's Gospel various time references are so indefinite (see 11:1, 14, 29; 12:1, 13; 13:10, 18; 9:51 but see also 13:22; 17:11) that from this too it is clear that although Luke's account is certainly "orderly" (1:3) the arrangement of the material is chronological only in a very general sense. Finally, when Luke describes the pointing out of the betrayer (22:21-23) *after* the institution of the Lord's Supper (22:14-20; contrast Matt. 26:20-29; Mark 14:17-25; cf. John 13:30), it is clear that he does not arrange his material in a precise before-and-after order. And why should he? Luke had excellent reasons for telling his story exactly as he did. His thematically arranged narrative is just as inspired as is Mark's far more chronological story.

As to Matthew, it is very clear that he did not try to arrange Christ's early miracles (chapters 8 and 9; see N.T.C. on Matthew, pp. 27, 28) in the order of their occurrence. The cursing of the fig tree and the pointing out of the lesson that was to be drawn from this incident took place partly on Monday of the Passion Week, partly on Tuesday. Mark draws attention to this chronological fact (11:11, 12, 19, 20); Matthew does not. He wishes to tell the entire story all at once, in one connected and uninterrupted account (21:18-22). He was, of course, perfectly justified in doing so. But here again the conclusion is justified that if one is looking for chronological orderliness he should turn to Mark's Gospel rather than to Matthew or to Luke.

What is especially significant in this connection is the fact that in general when Matthew departs from Mark's order, Luke is still with him; and when Luke departs from it, Matthew remains with Mark. For proof see N.T.C. on Matthew, pp. 39-41.

Beginning with the story of the death of John the Baptist (Mark 6:14-29), followed immediately by that of the feeding of the five thousand (Mark 6:30-44), and extending all the way to the end of both Gospels, a definite pattern of relationship between Mark and Matthew is evident. See N.T.C. on Matthew, pp. 29, 30. A somewhat similar relationship exists between Mark and Luke, beginning with the account of Jesus welcoming the little children (Mark 10:13-16) and running from that point on to the close of these two books. See N.T.C. on Matthew, pp. 15, 16.

This does not mean, however, that every Marcan section has its parallel in Matthew or in Luke or in both. Of 62 sections into which Mark 6:14—16:8 can be divided, with separate heading for each, 5 have no real parallel in

Matthew (the Marcan sections being 7:31-37; 8:22-26; 9:38-41; 12:41-44; 14:51, 52). Of the 42 sections into which Mark 10:13—16:8 can be divided, 8 (Mark 10:35-45; 11:12-14; 11:20-25; 11:28-34—on this last one see N.T.C. on Matthew, p. 808, footnote 763—; 13:32-36; 14:3-9; 14:51, 52; 15:16-20) have no clear parallel in *Luke*. This still means that by far the most sections of Mark's Gospel, from 10:13 on, are paralleled both in Matthew and in Luke, the three accounts running side by side.

It is not claimed that the probably basic Marcan sections are by Mark always arranged in strictly chronological fashion. Here and there the Marcan connectives are indefinite as to time (10:13, 17; 12:1; 14:10). Besides, Mark has no nativity account. Also, it does not cover any Early Judean or any Later Judean Ministry. It was definitely not Mark's purpose to present any "Biography" or "Life" of Christ. Nor did he try to summarize Christ's discourses, referring to each of them in the order in which it was delivered.[6] All that is meant is that in emphasis on chronological arrangement Mark, rather than Matthew or Luke, has furnished us with a guide. Note the many definite time and place indications (10:32, 46; 11:1, 11, 12, 15, 19, 20, 27; 13:1, 3; 14:1, 3, 12, 17, 22, 26, 32, 43; 15:1, 22, 33, 42; 16:1, 2; these in addition to the ones found in the first nine chapters).

In conclusion, if one is looking for a Gospel chracterized by compactness, vividness, and chronological orderliness, he will find it especially in the Gospel according to Mark![7]

V. How Is It Organized?

The Gospel according to Mark contains no *birth-of-Jesus* narrative. However, its very first chapter gives expression to the *came-from-heaven* truth (see verse 38b). Not only was Jesus born, he *came*. There is no sound reason to believe that the thirty-eighth verse of Mark 1 has any other basic meaning than the thirty-eighth verse of John 6. Jesus came from heaven with a purpose. What that purpose was is plainly stated in Mark, namely, "to preach" (1:38), "to call sinners (to repentance)" (2:17), "to give his life a ransom for many" (10:45). With this may be compared "to save that which was lost" (Luke 19:10); "sinners to save" (I Tim. 1:15). Paul says, "He

---

[6] Therefore, even though the quotation from Papias (via Eusebius; see above, p. 12) is not entirely clear, it can be given an interpretation that is in harmony with the facts.

[7] The relative *priority* of Mark's Gospel as compared with Matthew and Luke has been discussed in N.T.C. on Matthew, pp. 36-42. In the same work see also the section on the three Synoptic Gospels viewed under the symbolism of three rivers, pp. 25-32.

became poor in order that through his poverty y o u might become rich" (II Cor. 8:9).

"The Father sent his Son into the world" with a task to perform, namely, to be "the Savior of the world" (I John 4:14). A good theme (see John 17:4b) for the story told in any or all of the Gospels is therefore:

The Work Which Thou Gavest Him To Do

The broad divisions would be the same for the three Synoptics, namely, this work (or this task):

I. Begun
II. Continued
III. Accomplished

Or, in slightly different phraseology:

I. Its Beginning or Inauguration
II. Its Progress or Continuation
III. Its Climax or Consummation

For the subdivisions of Mark, under each of these main headings, see Table of Contents and the Outlines at the opening of the chapters.

Commentary
on
The Gospel According to Mark

The Work Which Thou Gavest Him to Do

Its Beginning
or
Inauguration

Chapter 1:1-13

Outline of Chapter 1:1-13

Theme: *The Work Which Thou Gavest Him To Do*

1:1-8   The Ministry of John the Baptist
1:9-11   The Baptism of Jesus
1:12-13   The Temptation of Jesus in the Wilderness

CHAPTER I: 1-13

1 1 Beginning of the gospel of Jesus Christ, the Son of God. 2 As it is written in Isaiah the prophet,

"Behold, I send my messenger before thy face,
Who shall prepare thy way.
3 A voice of one crying in the wilderness:
Make ready the way of the Lord,
Make straight his paths."

4 So John the Baptist came, baptizing in the wilderness and proclaiming a baptism of conversion[8] for the forgiveness of sins 5 And there were going out to him all the land of Judea and all the people of Jerusalem. Confessing their sins they were being baptized by him in the Jordan River.

6 Now John was wearing a garment made of camel's hair, and a leather belt around his waist; and he was in the habit of eating locusts and wild honey. 7 He was preaching, saying, "After me comes One who is mightier than I, whose sandal straps I, bending down, am not fit to untie. 8 I have baptized y o u with water, but he will baptize y o u with the Holy Spirit."

1:1-8 *The Ministry of John the Baptist*
Cf. Matt. 3:1-12; Luke 3:4-18; John 1:6-8, 15-28[9]

Though in many respects the four Gospels resemble each other, each has a different point of departure. Matthew begins his story with an account of the ancestry, conception, birth, and naming of Jesus; Luke (after a dedicatory introduction), with a narrative of the birth of John the Baptist; John, with the reminder that "the Word," meaning Jesus Christ, already existed "in the beginning," that is, from all eternity, and became incarnate. What is Mark's starting-point, and why? It has already been indicated that Mark pictures Christ as an active, energetic, swiftly moving, warring, conquering King. Now when a king is about to arrive he is generally preceded by a herald. The herald's function is to prepare the way for the king and to

---

[8] Or: "of a complete turnabout in mind and heart." See the explanation.

[9] These cross references to the other Gospels are indicated merely for the purpose of comparison. The degree or amount of resemblance is not shown. So, for example, the cross references here given do not mean that the entire content of Mark 1:1-8 is paralleled or even reflected in the other Gospels.

proclaim his coming or arrival. It is not surprising, therefore, that Mark's Gospel starts out by picturing the herald, so that from the very outset the student of this writing may be impressed with the exalted character of the One who is being heralded or proclaimed.

1. Beginning of the gospel of Jesus Christ, the Son of God.

Although in the original the word "Beginning" is not preceded by an article, it probably permits the translation "The beginning" as well as "Beginning." More important is the question whether the words "Beginning [or: The beginning] of the gospel of Jesus Christ, the Son of God" must be *a.* construed independently, as the title of this entire Gospel, or *b.* regarded as being closely connected with what immediately follows, namely, "As it is written . . . Behold, I send my messenger before thy face who shall prepare thy way . . . So John the Baptist came. . . ."[10] In defense of the book-title theory it has been argued that according to Acts 1:1 Luke also viewed his "former treatise" as the *beginning* of the gospel. However, since Mark was probably not thinking of writing two books it is questionable whether this analogy holds. Arguments against the book-title theory and in favor of linking verse 1 with verses 2-4 are the following:

First, if 1:1 had been intended as a superscription or title for the entire Gospel, would not "The gospel of Jesus Christ, the Son of God" have been more natural than "*Beginning* of the gospel . . ."?

Secondly, does not the word "As" (in "As it is written . . .") indicate that verse 1 is closely connected with what immediately follows (in verses 2-4) with reference to prophecies that were fulfilled in John the Baptist?

Thirdly, it should be borne in mind that in all probability Mark was indeed "Peter's interpreter." Now when Peter proclaimed the good news in

---

10 In favor of the first position is Vincent Taylor, *The Gospel according to St. Mark*, London, 1953, p. 152. Also J. A. C. Van Leeuwen, *Het Evangelie naar Markus* (*Korte Verklaring*), Kampen, 1935, p. 20. From here on whenever Van Leeuwen's name is followed by *op. cit.* it is this volume of *Korte Verklaring* that is meant. Also endorsing the first position are G. C. Morgan, *The Gospel according to Mark*, New York, etc., 1927, p. 12; and R. C. H. Lenski, *The Interpretation of St. Mark's and St. Luke's Gospels*, Columbus, 1934, p. 15 of the first part of that volume. From here on *op. cit.* in connection with this author will be a reference to the Mark portion of the indicated volume in his commentary series. A. B. Bruce, *The Synoptic Gospels* (*The Expositor's Greek Testament*, Vol. I, the section on Mark, pp. 341-457 of that volume), Grand Rapids, no date, p. 341, also defends the idea that the words in question may best be taken as a superscription of the whole Gospel, though he regards their connection either with verses 2, 3, or with verse 4, as yielding a perfectly good meaning. Hereafter *op. cit.*, linked with A. B. Bruce, indicates this particular work. E. P. Groenewald, *Die Evangelie volgens Markus* (*Kommentaar op Die Bybel, Nuwe Testament*, Vol. II), Pretoria, 1948, p. 21, also favors the superscription ("opskrif") idea; and so do many others.

Very interesting is the view of C. R. Erdman, *The Gospel of Mark, An Exposition*, Philadelphia, 1945. He grants the possibility of the book-title theory (p. 19), but subsequently links the phrase with the John the Baptist sequel (bottom of p. 20).

the home of Cornelius he too traced its *beginning* to John the Baptist (Acts 10:37).[11]

And finally, did not Jesus also state that it was John the Baptist who had begun to proclaim God's royal rule in his Son? See Luke 16:16.

On the basis of all these considerations the most natural meaning of verse 1 would seem to be: "The good news about Jesus Christ, the Son of God, began with John the Baptist. It was John who, *as predicted*, prepared the way for Christ's coming."

There was a time when the word *euaggelion* (evangel, gospel) indicated a reward that was given for the bringing of good news. However, gradually it began to be used as a designation for the good news itself. This is obviously also the meaning here in Mark 1:1. The gospel is the message of salvation addressed to a world lost in sin. Not what *we* must do but what *God* in Christ has done is the most important part of that good news. For fuller explanation see N.T.C. on Philippians, pp. 81-85.

Now this gospel concerns "Jesus Christ, the Son of God." Mark, who writes this book, and John the Baptist, prophetically announced in verses 2, 3, have in common that they are ever directing the attention of the people away from themselves to their Lord. Thus Mark never mentions himself by name, not at the beginning of his writing nor anywhere else, not even in 14:51, 52. How closely his humility resembles that of the Baptist (John 3:30)!

Note the exalted title given to the Savior here in Mark 1:1. His name is Jesus, for "he will certainly save." See Matt. 1:21; 11:27-30; John 14:6; Acts 4:12. To this personal name *Jesus* is added the official name *Christ*, the Greek equivalent of the Hebrew *Messiah*, meaning *Anointed*. See Isa. 61:1; cf. Luke 4:16-21. It indicates that its Bearer was by the Holy Spirit anointed—hence, ordained: set apart (or commissioned) and qualified—as Prophet, Priest, and King, in order to carry out the task of saving his people to the glory of God Triune.

To "Jesus Christ" is added "the Son of God."[12] Not only is this designation applied to Jesus again and again in this Gospel (besides 1:1 see also 3:11; 5:7; 9:7; 14:61, 62; 15:39), but it is also in harmony with the fact that throughout his book Mark is constantly ascribing divine qualities and

---

[11] It has been pointed out that the scope of Peter's preaching, as shown in Acts 10:34-43, was almost the same as that of Mark's Gospel. See F. F. Bruce, *Commentary on the book of Acts* (*The New International Commentary on The New Testament*), Grand Rapids, 1964. p. 226.

[12] Though the words "the Son of God" are omitted by the very important manuscript Sinaiticus (or Aleph) and by some manuscripts of less significance, these words are found in the no less valuable uncial B (Vaticanus); also in Codex Bezae (D) and in fact in "the great mass of the manuscripts" (A. T. Robertson). There would seem to be no solid reason to omit them in the translation.

activities to Jesus, showing that the author regards the Savior as being indeed the Son of God in the full trinitarian sense. The rest of Scripture also confirms this fact (Isa. 9:6; Matt. 28:18; John 1:1-4; 8:58; 10:30, 33; 20:28; Rom. 9:5; Phil. 2:6; Col. 1:16; 2:9; Heb. 1:8; Rev. 1:8). For anyone to say that Jesus was both wise and good, and then to turn around and affirm that he was not uniquely the Son of God is inconsistent, for if he was not God his claims were false. If his claims were false he could not have been wise and good. The denial of the deity of Jesus destroys the very foundation on which the Christian's hope is built.[13]

The beginning, then, of the gospel—not meaning the book (Gospel) but the good news itself (gospel)—concerning Jesus Christ, the Son of God, was 2. **As it is written in Isaiah the prophet,**

> Behold, I send my messenger before thy face,
> Who shall prepare thy way.

Mark tells us that he is going to quote from Isaiah. He does exactly that, though not immediately. First, here in verse 2, he quotes Mal. 3:1; next, in verse 3, Isa. 40:3. The second reference is clarified by the first, for when the reader or listener, having first reflected on the quotation from Malachi, next rivets his attention on the words from Isaiah, he will know that the "voice" to which the latter passage refers is not an abstraction but the Lord's "messenger."

This method of quotation, namely, mentioning by name only one source when the reference is to two, is not peculiar to Mark. Matthew does this also, and again with good reason. See N.T.C. on Matt. 27:9, 10. Similarly, the quotation found in II Chron. 36:21, drawn from Lev. 26:34, 35 and Jer. 25:12 (cf. 29:10), is ascribed only to "Jeremiah." To those who would find fault with this we would put two questions: First, what right have we to impose our own method of citation upon the authors of Scripture? Secondly, when by implication Mark promises to give us *one* thing (Mark 1:2a), and then gives us *two*—a quotation from Mal. 3:1 and one from Isa. 40:3—, why should we complain?

As to the quoted words, "Behold, I send my messenger . . . who shall prepare . . ." (cf. Matt. 11:10; Luke 7:27), see the LXX rendering of Exod. 23:10.[14] This is also substantially what is found in the Hebrew original of Mal. 3:1. The meaning of Mal. 3:1 is in all probability: "Take note, I, Jehovah, send my messenger, to be the forerunner of thee, the Messiah." Moreover, in the final analysis the forerunner to whom reference is made

---

[13] On the subject of the denial of Christ's deity see also N.T.C. on Matthew, p. 57-61; and the record of the debate between J. R. Straton and C. F. Potter, *"Was Christ Both God and Man?"* (a volume in the Straton-Potter debates), New York, 1924.

[14] However, in the LXX the second line reads, "That he may guard thee in thy way."

functions in a spiritual sense. His task is to prepare the hearts of the people for the reception of their Messiah. Thus the forerunner "paves the way" for Messiah's *first* coming, but in view of the fact that the two comings are stages whereby God comes to his people in Immanuel, therefore in the Malachi context even that second coming is definitely included. In fact, as is common in the prophets, no clear distinction was as yet drawn between the two arrivals. Mark, however, as is clear from verse 4, very legitimately (see Matt. 11:13, 14) applies the prophecy especially to the first phase of the coming, or, to put it more simply, to the first coming.

Before mentioning the herald's name, Mark without any words of transition, according to his promise quotes from Isaiah (40:3):

> 3. **A voice of one crying in the wilderness:**
> **Make ready the way of the Lord,**
> **Make straight his paths.**

These words are found also, in that same form, in Matt. 3:3 and in Luke 3:4. The wording, though identical in the three Synoptics, differs from the form in which it occurs in the Hebrew Old Testament of Isa. 40:3 and from the way it was rendered in the LXX (Greek) translation. The explanation for their remarkable identity in Matthew, Mark, and Luke may well be that Matthew, the former publican, had made his own paraphrase of Old Testament passages fulfilled in the New, and that, together with other notes, this material had been distributed widely before any of our four Gospels had been written.[15]

Isa. 40:3-5 symbolically pictures the approach of Jehovah for the purpose of leading the procession of Jews who will be returning joyfully to their homeland after long years of captivity. In the Syrian desert, between Babylonia and Palestine, the way must be prepared for the Lord's coming. So, a herald cries out to the people,

> "In the wilderness make ready the way of the Lord,
> Make straight in the desert a highway for our God."

This figure of the herald is in the Gospels applied to John, as Christ's herald. The Baptist, by saying, "I am the voice . . ." shows that he agrees with this interpretation (John 1:23). So does Jesus himself (Matt. 11:10). This shows that the deliverance granted to the Jews when, in the latter part of the sixth century B.C. and afterward, they returned to their own country

---

[15] In the Gospels and in the considerably different Septuagint text the phrase "in the wilderness" modifies "of one crying," and not "make ready," as it does in the masoretic accentuation of the Hebrew text of Isa. 40:3, the latter construction being also supported by the parallelism: "in the wilderness make ready" and "make straight in the desert." However, this difference between the Gospels and the Hebrew text is unimportant, for it is natural to assume that the wilderness crier, as the mouthpiece of the One who sent him, wants a way to be cleared in the wilderness.

was but a type of that far more glorious liberation in store for all who accept Christ as their Savior and Lord. In other words, Isaiah's prophecy regarding the voice that cried out lacked *total* fulfilment until both Messiah's fore-runner and also the Lord himself had arrived on the scene.[16]

Though we know that in verses 2 and 3 Mark is referring to John the Baptist, he does not mention the herald's name until he reaches verse 4. **So John the Baptist came, baptizing in the wilderness. . . .**

The appropriate character of the application of Isa. 40:3 to John the Baptist is evident from the following: *a.* John was preaching in the wilder-ness (Mark 3:4); and *b.* the task assigned to him from the days of his infancy (Luke 1:76, 77), yes even earlier (Luke 1:17; Mal. 3:1), was exactly this, namely, to be Messiah's herald or way-preparer. He was to be the Lord's "voice" to the people, *all of* that but *not more than* that (cf. John 3:22-30.) As such he must not only announce Christ's approach and presence but also urge the people *to prepare the way* of the Lord, that is, by God's grace and power to effect a complete change of mind and heart. This implies that they must *make straight his paths,* meaning that they must provide the Lord with a ready access into their hearts and lives. They must *make straight* whatever was crooked, *not in line with* God's holy will. They must clear away all the obstacles which they had thrown into his path; such obstructions as self-righteousness and smug complacency ("We have Abraham as our father," Matt. 3:9), greed, cruelty, slander, etc. (Luke 3:13, 14).

John was preaching in "the wilderness" (Mark 1:4), "the wilderness of Judea" (Matt. 3:1), a term indicating the rolling bad lands between the hill country of Judea to the west, and the Dead Sea and lower Jordan to the east, stretching northward to about the point where the Jabbok flows into the Jordan. It is indeed a desolation, a vast undulating expanse of barren chalky soil covered with pebbles, broken stones and rocks. Here and there a bit of brushwood appears, with snakes crawling underneath. It is clear, however, from Matt. 3:5 (cf. John 1:28) that the terrain of John's activity extended even to the east bank of the Jordan. It is evident that, both in Isaiah and in John's preaching as recorded by Mark, "the wilderness" through which a path must be made ready for the Lord is in the final analysis the people's heart, inclined to all evil.

What is emphasized with respect to John is that he was the Baptizer or Baptist. Now what was new and startling was not that he baptized, for the

---

16 The fact that what is said of *Jehovah* in the Old Testament is referred to *Christ* in the New should cause no surprise. For similar instances of this transition from Jehovah to Christ see Exod. 13:21, cf. I Cor. 10:4; Ps. 68:18, cf. Eph. 4:8; Ps. 102:25-27, cf. Heb. 1:10-12; and Isa. 6:1, cf. John 12:41. It is in Immanuel that Jehovah comes to dwell with his people.

people were already acquainted with the baptism of proselytes, but rather that this rite, being the sign and seal (Rom. 4:11; cf. Col. 2:11, 12) of a fundamental transformation of mind, heart, and life, was required even of the children of Abraham! They too must be converted, for Mark continues: **and proclaiming a baptism of conversion.** . . . One could also say, "with a view to conversion" (Matt. 3:11). To be sure, a man must already be converted before he can properly receive baptism. However, it is also true that by means of baptism conversion is powerfully stimulated. How could devout reflection on the adopting, pardoning, and cleansing grace of God have any different effect?

The word which I have rendered "conversion"—"repentance" in A.V. and in many other translations—indicates a *radical change* of mind and heart leading to a complete turnabout of life. Cf. II Cor. 7:8-10; II Tim. 2:25. Repentance is certainly a basic element in conversion. Such a conversion is **for the forgiveness of sins.** When John baptized he called upon the people to confess their sins (Matt. 3:6). The law of God, conscience, the cleansing water, the words of the Baptist, all these impressed upon the people the need to confess and to be cleansed from their sins. The stepping down into the Jordan and later stepping up out of it reminded them that the old sinful self must be buried so that those baptized may rise to newness of life.

The word "forgiveness" means remission or sending away. It is a very comforting expression, reminding one of such passages as Lev. 16 (the two goats); Ps. 103:12 ("As far as the east is from the west, etc."); Isa. 1:18 ("Though y o u r sins be as scarlet . . ."); 44:22 ("I have blotted out, as a thick cloud your transgressions . . ."); 55:6, 7 (". . . for he will abundantly pardon"); and Mic. 7:18 ("Who is a God like thee, pardoning iniquity . . ."). The importance of this divine favor, apart from which life everlasting is impossible, is stressed also in many New Testament passages (Mark 3:29; Luke 24:47; Acts 2:38, 5:31; 10:43; 13:34, 38; 19:4; 26:18; Eph. 1:7; Col. 1:14). That removal of sin necessitated the shedding of the blood of the Lamb was taught by John the Baptist himself (John 1:29), in thorough harmony with the teaching of Christ and the apostles, as recorded by Mark and other New Testament writers (Mark 10:45; cf. 14:24; Matt. 20:28; 26:28; Luke 22:20; John 6:53, 56; Rom. 3:25; Heb. 9:22; I Peter 2:24; Rev. 1:5; 5:6, 9).

Though Mark informs us that "John came," he does not say when he made his first public appearance. Matthew's time designation is also very indefinite ("in those days"). For a more precise chronological note see Luke 3:1, 2. If John, like Jesus (Luke 3:23), was about thirty years of age when he made his first public appearance, then, since the Baptist was about six months older than Jesus (Luke 1:26, 36), and Jesus probably began his ministry about late A.D. 26,[17] it was likely during the summer of that same year that John began to address the multitudes and to baptize.

5. **And there were going out to him all the land of Judea and all the people of Jerusalem.** Multitudes went out to see and hear John. He did not withdraw himself from them. He was no hermit or recluse. He was entirely willing to have the crowds come out to see and hear him. In fact, he *wanted* to be of service to them. In this respect John differed from the men who belonged to the Qumran community, about which we have been hearing so much since the discovery of the Dead Sea Scrolls. To a considerable extent these men had withdrawn themselves from the public. The Baptist, on the other hand, welcomed multitudes, not only men but also women (Matt. 21:31, 32). He did not try to conceal his convictions.

Yet, even so, does not the record indicate a difference between John and Jesus? To be sure, multitudes—in fact, even greater multitudes (John 3:25-30)—were going to resort to *Jesus* (Mark 1:32; 2:1, 2, 13; 3:8; 4:1; 5:21; 6:33, 55, 56; 10:1). He, too, would welcome them, his heart going out to them (9:36). He would even call and invite men (Mark 8:34; 10:13, 14, 49; cf. Matt. 11:28). But even more, he would actually take the initiative and *go out to meet* the people (Mark 1:38; Matt. 14:14). Had he not come from heaven in order to seek and to save sinners (Luke 19:10)?

As to the multitudes that went to see and hear John, they are described here in somewhat figurative language. The expression "the land" may be considered *synecdoche,* a figure in which one object (here *the people*) is called by the name of another that is closely associated with it (here *the land*). Or, in view of the action ascribed to this "land" it might even be called *personification* (cf. Ps. 114:3, 4; Hab. 3:10). It is clear at least that "land" refers here to those who inhabit it (cf. Jer. 22:29); in the present case, the people of Judea. This harmonizes with "and . . . the people of Jerusalem." As to "all" ("all the land . . . all the people"), this is *hyperbole,* and as such entirely legitimate. Cf. Judg. 7:12; II Sam. 1:23; I Kings 14:23; Ps. 6:6.

Matthew adds, "and the whole Jordan neighborhood." Not only the inhabitants of Judea in general, including those of Jerusalem, but definitely also those living on either side of the Jordan, resorted to John. There must have been thousands upon thousands of people, one crowd replacing another, and then still another, and another, etc. The Baptist, too, did not always remain at exactly the same place, but beginning in the vicinity of the Dead Sea seems to have ascended the Jordan Valley until he reached

---

[17] For facts in support of this date see the author's *Bible Survey,* Grand Rapids, 1961, pp. 59-62, 69.

"Bethany beyond Jordan" (John 1:28), and a little later, "Aenon near Salim," having crossed the river, and thus having arrived at a place west of it, with seven springs, a spot within easy reach of people of four provinces: Galilee, Samaria, Decapolis, and Perea (John 3:23). It is not surprising, therefore, that some of Christ's earliest disciples who had evidently been baptized by John were living in Galilee (John 1:35-42). **Confessing their sins they were being baptized by him in the Jordan River.** See on v. 4.

A description of John's attire and mode of life is given in the words of verse 6. **Now John was wearing a garment made of camel's hair, and a leather belt around his waist; and he was in the habit of eating locusts and wild honey.** John's long, flowing garment, woven from camel's hair, reminds us somewhat of Elijah's mantle, though there is a difference in the description (cf. Matt. 3:4 with II Kings 1:8). Such rugged apparel may have been regarded as symbolic of the prophetic office. Zech. 13:4 (cf. I Sam. 28:14) seems to point in that direction. At any rate, such rough garb was fit for desert wear. It was durable and economical. Jesus makes special mention of the fact that John did not wear fine clothes (Matt. 11:8). The leather belt fastened at the waist not only kept the loose robe from blowing and tearing apart but also enabled it to be tucked up to facilitate walking. In this connection see also N.T.C. on Eph. 6:14.

John's food was as simple as was his clothing. He subsisted on locusts and wild honey, evidently such fare as could be found in the wilderness. Honey, the kind that is found in the wild, presents no problem. It was not just a sweetener (sugar, as we now know it, being then rather rare) but an article of food. In the wilderness it could be found under rocks or in crevices between the rocks (Deut. 32:13). The role which wild honey played in the stories of Samson (Judg. 14:8, 9, 18) and of Jonathan (I Sam. 14:25, 26, 29) is too well-known to need elaboration.

But *locusts!* It is entirely possible that one shudders to think of actually *eating* them, their legs and wings having been discarded, their bodies roasted or baked, a little salt added. Nevertheless, it is clear from Lev. 11:22 that the Lord *permitted*—and by implication *encouraged*—the Israelites to eat four kinds of insects which we in North America would popularly call "locusts." Even today certain Arabian tribes relish them. And why not? The Latin saying, "De gustibus non disputandum est" ("One should not argue about taste") still holds. Those who enjoy shrimp, mussel, oyster, and frog-leg should not find fault with those who eat the locust.

It is, however, not necessary to conclude that verse 6 gives us a complete summary of the Baptist's diet. The main point is that by means of his simple mode of life, evident with respect to both food and clothing, he was a living protest against all selfishness and self-indulgence, hence also against that frivolousness, carelessness, and false security with which many people were rushing toward their doom.

Of course all John could do was to urge upon his hearers the necessity of conversion. As to baptism, considered as a symbol of divine purification (Isa. 1:16-18; Ezek. 36:25), John was able to perform only the outward rite. To impart the thing signified required the power and the grace of One mightier than John. We are not surprised, therefore, that Mark continues: **7, 8. He was preaching, saying, after me comes One who is mightier than I, whose sandal straps I, bending down, am not fit to untie. I have baptized y o u with water, but he will baptize y o u with the Holy Spirit.** In these verses Mark informs us that John, Christ's forerunner, gave a twofold comparative description of Jesus, indicating *a.* the latter's superior majesty, "mightier than I" (verse 7), and *b.* his equally superior activity (verse 8). It was necessary for John to draw this contrast between himself and his Master, for soon the people were wondering whether perhaps the Baptist might not himself be the Christ (Luke 3:15; cf. John 1:19, 20; 3:25-36). Note how also in John 1:19-27 the herald unconditionally rejects this thoroughly erroneous and reprehensible notion. True, on life's pathway, not only in his birth but also in the beginning of his public ministry, Jesus had come behind John (Luke 1:26, 36; 3:23). But between Christ and the Baptist there was a qualitative difference as between the Infinite and the finite, the Eternal and the temporal, the Original Light of the sun and the reflected light of the moon (cf. John 1:15-17).

In order to emphasize this contrast between himself and his Superior, John uses an illustration borrowed from the custom prevailing at the time, namely, that when, weary of travel and with dusty sandals, a master would return home, his menial servant or slave would try in every way to make him comfortable. He would of course render this same service to his master's honored guests. Its omission would be cause for justified criticism (Luke 8:44-46). In the present instance one item of the service rendered is singled out, namely, that of untying or unlacing the honored person's dusty sandals and removing them. In the New Testament this figure occurs in forms which, though varying somewhat, in essence are the same. Whether one speaks of untying sandal straps (Luke 3:16; John 1:27), bending down (Mark alone adds this little detail) and untying these straps (Mark 1:7), untying sandals (Acts 13:25), or even removing sandals (Matt. 3:11), in each case the basic idea is that the underling stoops down in order to loosen the straps or laces of this footwear, and then brings it to the proper place and cleans it.

To appreciate more fully what depth of genuine humility is expressed when, with reference to Jesus, the Baptist says "whose sandal straps I, bending down, am not fit to untie" it should be borne in mind that according to an ancient Jewish tradition the difference between a "disciple" and a "servant" (or "slave") was this, that a disciple was willing to perform every service for his master that a menial servant would perform except to untie his sandals. So what may very well be implied here are three ascending degrees or stages of humility:

a. The disciple is willing to render almost every service.

b. The slave or humblest servant is willing to render every service.

c. The Baptist considers himself unfit or unworthy to render the service of untying his Master's sandal straps. In this connection see also N.T.C. on Phil. 2:3, 5-8, and on I Tim. 1:15.

John, moreover, baptizes with water; Jesus will baptize with the Spirit. He will cause his Spirit and the latter's gifts to come upon his followers (Acts 1:8), to be poured out on them (Acts 2:17, 33), to fall upon them (Acts 10:44; 11:15). Now it is true that whenever a person, having been drawn out of the darkness into God's marvelous light, is baptized, he is baptized with the Holy Spirit. However, according to Christ's own words (Acts 1:5, 8), remembered by Peter (Acts 11:16), *in a special sense* this prediction was fulfilled on the day of Pentecost and the era which it introduced. It was then that, through the coming of the Spirit, the minds of Christ's followers were enriched with unprecedented illumination (I John 2:20); their wills strengthened, like never before, with contagious animation (Acts 4:13, 19, 20, 33; 5:29); and their hearts flooded with warm affection to a previously unprecedented degree (Acts 2:44-47; 3:6; 4:32).

---

9 Now it happened in those days that Jesus came from Nazareth of Galilee and was baptized in the Jordan by John. 10 And immediately, as he was stepping up out of the water, he saw the heavens split open and the Spirit like a dove descending on him; 11 And a voice came from heaven, "Thou art my Son, the Beloved, with whom I am well pleased."

1:9-11 *The Baptism of Jesus*
Cf. Matt. 3:13-17; Luke 3:21, 22; John 1:32-34

9. Now it happened in those days that Jesus came from Nazareth of Galilee and was baptized in the Jordan by John. Though it often happens that Mark gives a more detailed account of an event than does Matthew, at times the opposite is true. So it is in the present case. Mark devotes only three verses to this incident and fails to say anything about the objection raised by John when Jesus presented himself to him to be baptized. Luke also omits this detail and uses only two verses to tell the story of Christ's baptism by John. For the full story we must turn to Matt. 3:13-17: five verses.

Mark's phrase "in those days" probably indicates "at the height of John's baptizing activity." Cf. Luke 3:21. Note the difference between Matthew

41

who states that Jesus, in making his first public appearance, came "from Galilee" (to the Jordan), while Mark is more specific and says, "from Nazareth of Galilee." It is possible that Mark does this because he was writing to Gentiles, people who were not well acquainted with Jewish terrain. But not too much can be made of this. The phrase "Nazareth of Galilee" is also found in Matthew (21:11). And in connection with the story of Christ's baptism Matthew did not have to add "from Nazareth" because that is where he had left Jesus a few verses earlier (2:22, 23, where both Nazareth and Galilee are mentioned). It was at Nazareth that Joseph, Jesus' legal father, had plied the carpenter's trade (Matt. 13:55). It was here that Jesus grew up to manhood, and became known as "the carpenter" (Mark 6:3). At the age of thirty (Luke 3:23) Jesus left Nazareth and proceeded on his way to the Jordan.

In very simple language Mark states that Jesus "was baptized in the Jordan by John." Did Jesus step down Jordan's bank into the water, so that his feet were covered with water, and did the Baptist then pour or sprinkle water on the Master's head? It has not pleased the Holy Spirit to give us any details in this connection as to the mode of baptism.

The question may be asked, however, "Since Jesus was sinless, and the water of baptism symbolized the necessity of the removal of filth, that is of sin, how then was it possible for the Sinless One to submit to baptism? Many answers have been given. The most simple one may well be the best. Jesus did, after all, have sin, namely *ours*. Is not this answer suggested by Isa. 53:6 ("All we like sheep have gone astray; we have turned every one to his own way; and Jehovah has laid on him the iniquity of us all"); and by the fact that not very long after John had baptized Jesus, the Baptist saw him approaching and exclaimed to his audience, "Look, the Lamb of God who is taking away the sin of the world" (John 1:29)? It would appear, therefore, that the demand of Jesus to be baptized by John signified his solemn resolution to take upon himself the guilt of those for whom he was going to die. In a sense, by means of baptism Jesus was fulfilling part of his task of laying down his life for his sheep. Cf. Matt. 20:28; Mark 10:45; John 10:11; II Cor. 5:21; I Peter 3:18. Moreover, apart from this voluntary self-surrender, symbolized by his baptism, would not all other baptisms have been meaningless? It was by means of the Savior's sacrifice of himself that the basis was established for the forgiveness of sins, a forgiveness signified and sealed by baptism for all those who sincerely confess their unworthiness and intended to pursue their further journey "in newness of life."

10, 11. And immediately, as he was stepping up out of the water, he saw the heavens split open and the Spirit like a dove descending on him; and a voice came from heaven, Thou art my Son, the Beloved, with whom I am well pleased. Gloriously the Trinity is here revealed. At the very moment when *the Son*, having been baptized, starts to step up out of the water, heaven suddenly opens wide and *the Spirit* descends on him. Jesus himself sees something resembling a dove, and representing the Spirit, coming lower and lower and going directly toward him. Though not all interpreters agree, it must be maintained that the pronoun "he" in "he saw the heavens . . ." refers to Jesus.[18] And *the Father,* as it were deeply impressed with the willingness of his Son to shoulder so heavy a burden—for, as has been pointed out, by means of submitting to this cleansing rite he confirmed his promise, made from eternity, to take upon himself and atone for the sin of the world (John 1:29)—proclaims, "Thou art my Son, the Beloved, with whom I am well pleased." Thus, very touchingly the doctrine of the Holy Trinity in action is set forth. That these three are One is the comfort of every believer.

As to the details a few more remarks are in order:

First, as to *the Son,* the question might be asked, "Was (and *is*) he not divine, and therefore not in need of the anointing of the Holy Spirit to qualify him for the carrying out of his task?" Answer: The divine Son at his incarnation adopted the human nature, which is in need of, and capable of, being strengthened. Thus qualified he, as divine *and human* Mediator, was enabled to function in his threefold office as Prophet, Priest, and King, for the salvation of God's people, to the glory of God Triune. With respect to this anointing see also Ps. 45:7; Isa. 61:1 ff.; 11:1, 2; Matt. 11:27; 28:18; Luke 4:18; John 3:34; Acts 10:38.

Secondly, as to *the Spirit,* "Why was the third person of the Trinity represented by an object in the shape of a dove?" Answer: Perhaps in order to indicate the purity, gentleness, peacefulness, and graciousness which characteristics mark the Holy Spirit, and are in popular opinion, as well as

---

18 Van Leeuwen, *op. cit.,* p. 25, favors the idea that this "he" refers to John the Baptist. Now it is true that John did indeed see all this happening (John 1:32; cf. Matt. 3:16). But here in Mark 1:10 "he" can very well point to its closest antecedent, Jesus.

As to the other passages, it is not easy to think of Jesus himself actually "seeing" the dove-shaped object *alighting* on himself and *remaining* in that position for a little while. That Jesus himself would see the "dove" descend is not hard to grasp, as is also the fact that someone who stood nearby—in the present case John the Baptist and probably others—saw the object not only descend but also settle on the head of Christ. It would seem, therefore, that *a.* the "he" in "and he saw the Spirit of God descending like a dove *and lighting on* him" (Matt. 3:16) is the "I" of John 1:32; hence, is John the Baptist; but *b.* the "he" of Mark 1:10 indicates Jesus himself. This double conclusion is also supported by the fact that the immediately following context in *Matthew* (see verse 17) introduces the Father as addressing not Jesus but *John* ("This is my Son, etc."); while, on the other hand, the immediately following context in *Mark* (see verse 11) represents the Father as speaking not to John but to *Jesus* ("Thou art my Son, . . ."). Of course, the difference is minor. In reality what occurred here was of significance not only for Jesus but also for John and for anyone else who may have been present.

even in Scripture (Ps. 68:13; Song of Sol. 6:9; Matt. 10:16), associated with the dove. Did the water of Jordan suggest the need of cleansing? The *Holy Spirit*, symbolized by a form resembling a dove and resting on the Son, could very well indicate that in and by himself Jesus, Spirit-indwelt, was pure and holy; not only that but also gentle and peaceful. The sins for which he was to die were not his own but had been *imputed* to him.

Thirdly, as to *the Father*, "Whose voice was it that exclaimed, 'Thou art my Son, the Beloved, with whom I am well pleased'?" The Speaker is not named.[19] Neither is this necessary, for the very phraseology ("my Son, the Beloved") identifies the Speaker as being, of course, the Father. Moreover, not only in his official Messianic capacity but also as Son by eternal generation, the One who fully shares the divine essence together with the Father and the Spirit, is he the Father's Beloved (John 1:14; 3:16; 10:17; 17:23). No higher love is possible than the love which the Father cherishes toward his Son. According to the verbal adjective (agapētos: beloved) here used, this love is deep-seated, thorough-going, as great as is the heart of God itself. It is also as intelligent and purposeful as is the mind of God. It is tender, vast, infinite![20]

In the original the words "My Son, the Beloved" are so constructed (literally "*the* Son my, *the* Beloved") that with this repetition of the article equal emphasis is placed on both the noun, "Son," and the adjective, "Beloved." In fact, the addition (after the noun) of the adjective, with repetition of the article, forms a kind of climax.[21]

In addition to possessing all the qualities already ascribed to this love it is also *eternal;* that is, it is timeless, raised far above all temporal boundaries. Though some disagree, the rendering "in whom *I am* well pleased" must be considered correct.[22] In the quiet recess of eternity the Son was the object of the Father's inexhaustible delight (cf. Prov. 8:30). The former's re-affirmation, by means of baptism, of his purpose to shed his blood for a world lost in sin did nothing to diminish that love. That is what the Father is telling his Son. That is what he is also telling John . . . and all of us.

How filled with comfort this paragraph, comfort not only for the Son and for John, but for every child of God, for it indicates that *not only the Son*

---

[19] In connection with the subject of *God's good pleasure* the present is by no means the only passage in which the One who exercises this good pleasure is not named; see, for example, also Luke 2:14; Phil. 2:13; and Col. 1:19. Eph. 1:5 makes very clear whose good pleasure is meant. So does the context in each of the other cases.

[20] On the difference between ἀγαπάω and φιλέω, and their respective derivatives see N.T.C. on John, Vol. II, pp. 494-500.

[21] See Gram. N.T., pp. 369, 370. Cf. in English "The House Beautiful" with "the beautiful house."

[22] This is an excellent example of the timeless aorist. See Gram. N.T., p. 837; thus also in Matt. 17:5; Mark 1:11; and Luke 3:22.

loves his followers enough to suffer the pangs of hell in their stead, but that also the Spirit fully co-operates by strengthening him for this very task, and that the Father, instead of frowning upon the One who undertakes it, is so very pleased with him that he must needs rend asunder the very heavens, that his voice of delightful approval may be heard on earth![23] All three are equally interested in our salvation, and the three are One.

---

12 And immediately the Spirit sent him out into[24] the wilderness. 13 And he was in the wilderness forty days, being tempted by Satan. He was among the wild beasts, and the angels were rendering service to him.

1:12, 13 The Temptation of Jesus in the Wilderness
Cf. Matt. 4:1-11; Luke 4:1-13

By means of his voluntary submission to baptism Jesus had signified his entire willingness to accomplish the task assigned to him, namely, to suffer and die in his people's stead. It is therefore logical that affliction, in the form of temptation, begins at once. Adam, when tempted, failed. So Christ, "the last Adam" (I Cor. 15:45) must now be tempted, in order that by his victory over the tempter he may, for all who believe in him, undo the results of the first Adam's failure.

That even Jesus, the Sinless One, could be tempted is a mystery incapable of being made perfectly clear. All we can say about it is that this temptation pertains, of course, to Christ's *human* nature, since *God* cannot be tempted (James 1:13). Since Jesus was not only God but also man, it should not be entirely surprising that after a fast of forty days (4:2 in Matthew and in Luke) the proposal to turn stones into bread was a temptation to him. This by no means solves every problem, for the very sensitive and searching mind of Christ must have discerned immediately that proposals coming to him from Satan were evil. The subject of the temptation of the perfect Savior is shrouded in mystery. But is not this true of doctrine in general?

That Christ's temptation experience actually occurred is taught not only here in Mark and its parallels but also in Heb. 4:15: "He was tempted in all points (or *in every respect*) as we are, yet without sin"; that is, without falling into sin. Heb. 4:15 cannot mean, however, that the psychological process involved in being tempted was exactly the same for Jesus as it is for men in general. For the latter, including believers, there is first, the tempting voice or inner whispering of Satan, urging them to sin. But there is also the inner desire ("lust") goading the tempted one to give heed to the devil's

---

23 On the entire subject of Christ's baptism read also the following: A. B. Bruce, "The Baptism of Jesus," *Exp*, 5th ser., 7 (1898), pp. 187-201; and W. E. Bundy, "The Meaning of Jesus' Baptism," *JR*, 7 (1927), pp. 56-71.

24 Or: impelled him (to go) into

prompting. Thus man, being "drawn away and enticed by his own evil desire" (James 1:14) sins. With Christ the case was different. The outward stimulus—*outward* in the sense that it did not originate in the Lord's own soul but was the voice of another—was there, but the *inner* evil incentive or desire to co-operate with this voice from without was not. Nevertheless the temptation—that is, the sense of need, the consciousness of being urged by Satan to satisfy this need, the knowledge of having to resist the tempter, and the struggle to which this gave rise—was real even for Christ.

For a far more complete account of the separate temptations see N.T.C. on Matt. 4:1-11. See also Luke 4:1-13. Mark's coverage of the temptation is so brief that it will hardly do to interpret Matthew's far more complete and chronological account in the light of certain first impressions one may receive from Mark's words. Neither Mark nor Luke gives us a step by step consecutive account. Matthew, on the other hand, does present a historical sequence, as is clear from 4:2 ("after"), 4:5, 10 ("then") and 5:11 ("then the devil left him . . .") and from the inner or thought connection between the first and second temptations.

It is in the light of these facts that we proceed now to the explanation of Mark's account, verse 12. **And immediately the Spirit sent him out into the wilderness.** Note the following:

"Immediately. . . ." There was no interval between the glory of Christ's baptism ("Thou art my Son, the Beloved") and the hardship of the temptation. As it was going to be in connection with Christ's transfiguration, so already here the narrative shows how Jesus, the King, to be sure, but also the Suffering Servant, proceeds at once from daylight to darkness, from the Father's approving smile to Satan's contemptuous wile.

" . . . the Spirit sent him out." Here others have "driveth him" (A.V.), "driveth him forth" (A.R.V.), "drove him out" (Williams, Beck), or something similar. And it is true that the verb used in the original frequently has the meaning *to drive out* or *expel*. In fact, in this very chapter (Mark 1) the word indicates the expulsion of demons (1:34, 39, 43). Also, Jesus drove or cast the merchants out of the temple (Matt. 21:12); and the wicked sharecroppers cast the heir out of the vineyard (Matt. 21:39). However, when the word is thus translated it is not easy to dissociate from it the idea of the use of external force in order to move an unwilling object. And certainly that cannot be the connotation in the present instance. It would be better therefore, either—with N.A.S.B. (N.T.)—to substitute the rendering *impelled* him (to go) *out,* filled him with an inner urge, moved him; or else, to take cognizance of the fact that the same Greek verb is also used in a somewhat weaker sense, namely, *released, sent out, put out* (John 10:4; Acts 16:37).

" . . . into the wilderness." The question has been asked, "But was not Jesus already in the wilderness when he was baptized? Was it not exactly in the wilderness that John was baptizing (Mark 1:4)?" It has been suggested therefore that "the wilderness" into which Jesus was now sent was more rugged and inhospitable than the one mentioned in verse 4. Though this is possible, and the presence of "wild beasts" (verse 13) might even lend some support to this theory, is it not more reasonable to find the solution in Luke 4:1? In other words, the meaning may simply be that *from the Jordan* Jesus was led *into the wilderness*. It is useless to venture a guess as to the location of the particular wilderness region where Christ fasted and was tempted. Was it a limestone height near Jericho? No one knows.

One fact must not be forgotten: the wilderness, though dreadful, especially when one spends at least forty days there without food, was also the place where nothing was able to separate Jesus from communion with his heavenly Father. It was also the place, therefore, of preparation for the performance of the mediatorial task! Cf. Mark 1:35; Luke 5:16.

13. **And he was in the wilderness forty days** .... The experience of Moses on Mount Horeb (Exod. 34:2, 28; Deut. 9:9, 18) and that of Elijah on the same height (I Kings 19:8) occur to the mind immediately. Not only for them but also for Jesus the period was one of fasting. It was in the wilderness that Jesus was **being tempted by Satan.** The verb here rendered "tempted" can have a favorable meaning: to put someone to the test in order to strengthen him spiritually. It was in that sense that Jehovah "tested" Abraham (Gen. 22:1-19; Heb. 11:17). See also John 6:6. But the addition of the phrase "by Satan" makes it clear that in the present case the sense is that the prince of evil tried hard *to entice* Jesus *to sin.* Mark says, "tempted by Satan"; Luke, "by the devil"; Matthew, "by the devil . . . the tempter." *Diabolos* means devil, slanderer, accuser (Job 1:9; Zech. 3:1, 2; cf. Rev. 12:9, 10) and (through the influence of the LXX) also *adversary* (I Peter 5:8), which, strictly speaking, is the meaning of *Satan.*

It is clear that Mark believed in the existence of a personal "prince of evil."[25] So did all the other New Testament writers: Matthew (4:1, 3, 5, 8); Luke (4:2, 3, 6, 13; 8:12); Peter (Acts 10:38; I Peter 5:8); Paul (Rom. 16:20; Eph. 4:27; 6:11); the author of Hebrews (2:14); James (4:7); John (Gospel 13:2, 27; I John 3:8, 10, 12; 5:18, 19; Rev. 12:9; 20:2, 7, 10); and Jude (see his epistle verse 9). So did also Jesus himself (Matt. 6:13; 13:39; 25:41; Mark 3:23, 26; 4:15; 8:33; Luke 4:8; 10:18; 11:18; 13:6; 22:3, 31; John 8:44). Many other references could have been added.

It is certainly fitting that it is exactly (though not alone) in Mark, which

---

25 However, he never uses the term *diabolos* (devil), always *Satan.* From the A.V. it might appear that Mark also used the term "devil" (5:15, 16, 18; 7:26, 29, 30), but in these passages this evangelist speaks about "demons" and of those who were "demon-possessed."

describes Jesus as the Conquering King, that the tempter is called Satan, that is Adversary. The battle, then, is going to be between the King and his Adversary.

The entire clause, "And he was in the wilderness forty days, being tempted by Satan" is by many interpreted to mean that *throughout the entire forty days* Jesus was being tempted by the devil. It is even argued that the Greek does not allow any other interpretation. Now when this clause is considered entirely by itself—that is, apart from the far more detailed and chronological account found in Matthew—it must be admitted that the language used in the original certainly *allows* it to be understood in that sense. At the same time it should also be stated that this is not the only possible view. At times this is even recognized by those who favor the forty days of temptation theory.[26] The argument in defense of *a forty day temptation* would be unassailable if the clause were as follows: "Forty days he was being tempted, being in the wilderness." As it actually stands, however, the original can mean: "Forty days he was in the wilderness, where he was being tempted."[27]

In favor of the second construction, rejecting the forty days of temptation, it can be argued that:

a. Matt. 4:2, 3, clearly teaches that the temptation by Satan began at the close of a forty day fast.

b. The greatly condensed account in Mark should be interpreted in the light of the full and chronological narrative found in Matthew; not vice versa.

But even if the forty day temptation theory is adopted one should be careful not to fill in this period with all kinds of products of the imagination. It should be borne in mind that if there was a lengthy series of temptations that preceded the familiar three, Scripture has given us no details.

As a further description of what happened while Jesus was in the wilderness Mark (alone) continues: **He was among the wild beasts. . . .** The Jordan valley and the adjacent wilderness have been known as the haunt of hyenas, jackals, panthers, and even lions, which at one time were by no means scarce in Palestine,[28] as is evident from the fact that lions are mentioned in two-thirds of the books of the Old Testament. The region where Jesus fasted and was tempted was therefore the scene of abandonment and peril, the very opposite of paradise, where the first Adam was tempted.[29]

Mark concludes the description of what happened to Jesus at this time by

---

[26] Thus, for example, A. B. Bruce states that Jesus was being tempted "presumably the whole time" (*op. cit.*, p. 343). The adverb "presumably" or "probably" leaves the door ajar for a different interpretation!

[27] The same holds with respect to Luke 4:1b, 2a, where the rendering offered by Phillips and by A.R.V. is to be preferred to that found in A.V.

[28] See J. G. Wood, *Story of the Bible Animals*, Philadelphia, no date, pp. 19-41.

[29] The idea of G. C. Morgan (*op. cit.*, p. 27) that the animals gathered about Jesus as a

writing: **and the angels were rendering service to him.** Rendering service in various ways is the function of these "ministering spirits" (Heb. 1:14). See N.T.C. on I and II Timothy and Titus, pp. 184, 185. In connection with the story of the temptation, just when was it that the angels rendered this service to Christ? Here also the answer is found in the more detailed and chronologically arranged account written by Matthew (4:11), "Then the devil left him, and behold, angels came and were rendering service to him." The service was evidently rendered when the devil had been thoroughly vanquished. Just what this service implied is not mentioned. The general statement that angels were sent by the Father to provide for the Son's needs, whatever these may have been, is perhaps the best. That this also included providing bodily nourishment would seem to be a reasonable inference.[30]

Mark does not make any statement about Christ's triumph over Satan. For this we are again dependent on Matt. 4:1-11; cf. Luke 4:1-13. But is not this triumph implied in the ministry of the angels, sent by the Father as a reward upon obedience?

We have noticed in these two verses: the action of *the Holy Spirit*, the obedience of *Christ*, the presence of *wild beasts*, the temptation by *Satan*, and at the close, the service rendered by *angels*. In the background—implied rather than expressed—we have become aware of *the total absence of any human helpers* and *the providential love and care of the Father*, who sent his angels to render service. The presence (and, in the case of human helpers, the absence) of these seven shows the majesty of the central figure, Jesus Christ, the great King who was at the same time the Suffering Servant.

The victory having been won, Christ's actual ministry of preaching, teaching, healing, and (last but not lacking in importance) casting out of demons, all this leading to the final triumph of death followed on the third day by a glorious resurrection, can now begin. A significant section of Mark's Gospel closes here.

Summary of Chapter 1:1-13

This first section of Mark's Gospel consists of three paragraphs and deals with three topics: *a.* the ministry of John the Baptist (1:1-8), *b.* the baptism

---

friend—cf. the experience of Fr. of Assisi with the birds—runs contrary to the context, which—note the words "wilderness," "tempted," and "wild beasts"—stresses the difficult and terrible conditions surrounding the Lord. It is true that μετά basically means *among, in the company of*, but the company is by no means always nice and friendly (Matt. 24:51; Luke 12:46).

[30] It is held by some that Mark drew this item about wild beasts and angels from Ps. 91:11-13, where the promise of victory over the lion and the adder follows immediately upon that of angelic protection. See S. E. Johnson, *A Commentary on the Gospel according to St. Mark*, London, 1960, p. 41. But is not this analogy rather far-fetched? Mark's account does not speak about angelic *protection* nor about *victory over the wild beasts*.

of Jesus (1:9-11), and *c.* the temptation of Jesus in the wilderness (1:12, 13).

John's ministry. Time: the first part of John's ministry, the part here in view, stretched from about the middle to the end of the year A.D. 26 (or a little later). *Place:* the wilderness of Judea and the Jordan River. John's ministry was in fulfilment of prophecy (Mal. 3:1 and Isa. 40:3; in Mark 1:2, 3 referred to in that order). The Baptist urged the people to undergo a basic spiritual change, that their sins might be forgiven. He also baptized, for baptism was a sign and seal of this forgiveness. In the light of verses 2-4 the meaning of verse 1 ("Beginning of the gospel of Jesus Christ, the Son of God") would seem to be: "The good news about Jesus Christ, the Son of God, began with John the Baptist. It was John who, *as predicted,* prepared the way for Christ's coming." His preaching consisted in proclaiming the necessity of genuine conversion and of faith in the One "whose sandal-straps," said John, "I, bending down, am not fit to untie." To show that he, the Baptist himself, was unable to supply what the people needed, he added, "I have baptized y o u with water, but he will baptize y o u with the Holy Spirit," uttering words which in a sense are realized whenever a sinner is brought from darkness to light, but are fulfilled especially during the dispensation beginning with the Spirit's outpouring on Pentecost.

The response to John's ministry was astounding: large multitudes from Judea, including Jerusalem, were constantly going out to hear John. Many of them confessed their sins and were being baptized in the Jordan River. The Baptist's simple manner of life—wearing a garment made of camel's hair, with leather belt around his waist; eating locusts and wild honey—, as well as the earnestness and directness of his appeal, must have contributed to this favorable result, whereby the way for the entrance of Christ's message into the hearts and lives of the people was being prepared.

Jesus' baptism. Time: probably about December of the year A.D. 26 (or shortly afterward). *Place:* the Jordan River, exact spot unknown. Jesus inaugurated his ministry by requesting John to baptize him. When he had been baptized the heavens opened and the Spirit like a dove descended on him. A voice spoke to him: "Thou art my Son, the Beloved, with whom I am well pleased."

It is true that the water of baptism indicated the necessity of the removal of sin. It is also a fact that Jesus was and is the Sinless One. How then could he be baptized? Answer: he did, after all, have sin, namely *ours* (Isa. 53:6; II Cor. 5:21).

Jesus' temptation. Immediately after the baptism the Spirit sent Jesus from the Jordan into the wilderness. Here he spent forty days, and was tempted by Satan. The region where the temptation took place was desolate and dangerous: Jesus was in the midst of the wild beasts. Yet he triumphed and was rewarded, as is indicated by the fact that the angels, sent by the Father, were rendering service to him.

By his voluntary submission to the rite of baptism and also by his equally voluntary obedience to the Father's will and the Spirit's direction when he was tempted by Satan, Jesus, as the last Adam, fulfilled the law which the first Adam had transgressed. By means of this obedience he was clearly indicating that he had taken upon himself and was taking away "the sin of the world." Cf. John 1:29. He was therefore ready to begin his ministry of teaching, preaching, healing, casting out demons, and overarching everything else, suffering and dying for all those lost "sheep" who would place their trust in him. See Isa. 53:6, 11; John 10:11, 14, 15, 27, 28.

The Work Which Thou Gavest Him to Do

Its Progress
or
Continuation

Chapter 1:14–10:52

Outline of Chapter 1:14-45

Theme: *The Work Which Thou Gavest Him To Do*

A. The Great Galilean Ministry

1:14, 15	Its Beginning
1:16-20	The Calling of Four Fishermen
1:21-28	The Healing of a Man with an Unclean Spirit
1:29-34	The Healing of Simon's Mother-in-law and of Many Others
1:35-39	Christ's Pre-dawn Prayer; Simon's Exclamation and Christ's Answer; Christ's Preaching and Demon-expulsions throughout All Galilee
1:40-45	A Leper Cleansed

CHAPTER I: 14-45

14 Now when John had been taken into custody, Jesus came into Galilee preaching the gospel of God, 15 and saying, "The time is fulfilled and the kingdom of God is at hand; be converted and believe the gospel."

1:14, 15 *The Beginning of the Great Galilean Ministry*
Cf. Matt. 3:2; 4:12; 11:2; 14:3-5; Mark 6:17-20;
Luke 3:19, 20; 4:14, 15; John 3:24; 4:1-3, 43, 44.

14. Now when John had been taken into custody, Jesus came into Galilee . . . .

A new section of Mark's Gospel begins here. Between Christ's baptism and temptation, on the one hand (1:9-13), and his arrival in Galilee, recorded here in verse 14, on the other, there may well have been a time interval of about a year.[31] But though thus separated in time from the earlier events reported by Mark, yet what the evangelist is about to report is closely related in thought to that which precedes. The preparation for, and inauguration of, the work which the Father had given his Son to do is ended. The beginning has been accomplished. Having been introduced to Israel by the herald, John the Baptist, Jesus by means of the baptism which he himself requested has reaffirmed his decision to take upon himself the sin of the world. Moreover, he has proved himself worthy, for in the wilderness he has triumphed over Satan. He has done this as his people's representative, the last Adam, succeeding where the first Adam failed. Therefore nothing can now prevent him from carrying forward the task assigned to, and voluntarily assumed by him.

The time of Christ's departure from Judea to Galilee (see John 4:1-3, 43) had something to do with the imprisonment of John the Baptist. When John had been taken into custody (Mark 1:14), and the Pharisees, with head-

---

31 I base this probability on the assumption that the departure for, and entrance into, Galilee, to begin the Great Galilean Ministry mentioned here in Mark, is the same as that to which John 4:3, 43 refers. In John it was followed soon afterward by what was probably the *second* Passover festival of Christ's public ministry (John 5:1); hence, the Passover of the year A.D. 28, preceded, a year earlier, by the *first* Passover mentioned in John 2:13, 23. See also N.T.C. on the Gospel according to John, Vol. I, pp. 36, 173, 188, 189; and my *Bible Survey*, pp. 61, 62, 69.

quarters in Jerusalem, had heard that Jesus was gaining and, through his disciples, was baptizing more disciples than John, the Master left Judea and started on his way to Galilee. He was aware of the fact that his own great popularity in the country region of Judea would bring about such keen resentment on the part of the religious leaders of the Jews that in the natural course of events this hatred would lead to a premature crisis. As soon as the appropriate moment for his death would arrive Jesus would voluntarily lay down his life (John 10:11, 14, 15, 18; 13:1). He was going to do this *then*, but not before then. Besides, Galilee, too, has lost sheep that must be brought into the fold.

So Jesus came into Galilee **preaching the gospel of God**, that is, heralding or proclaiming the good tidings of salvation as God's free gift to men, a salvation which from start to finish is God's work. To be sure, all of God's true servants tell the story, but God (in Christ) saw to it that there was a story to tell. It was he who provided the way of salvation, apart from which all men would have been everlastingly lost. This good news is therefore in truth "the gospel *of God*." What could be a better commentary than the following series of passages: John 3:16; Rom. 8:3, 32; II Cor. 5:20, 21; Gal. 4:4, 5; Eph. 2:8-10; Titus 3:4-7?

15. . . . **and saying, The time is fulfilled.** . . . Cf. Gal. 4:4; Eph. 1:10. The appropriate season or golden opportunity[32] for the fulfilment of God's redemptive promises and along with it for the promulgation of the gospel had arrived. The hour for the realization of Isa. 9:1, 2[33] had struck. Hence, Jesus continues: **and the kingdom of God is at hand.** Note "kingdom *of God*" where Matthew generally has "kingdom *of heaven*." Basically the meaning is the same. What Jesus is saying, then, is that God's reign in the hearts and lives of men would begin to assert itself far more powerfully than ever before. Great blessings were in store for all those who, by sovereign grace, would confess and forsake their sins and would begin to live to God's glory.

In its broadest connotation *the terms "the kingdom of heaven," "the kingdom of God,"* or simply *"the kingdom"* (when the context makes clear that what is meant is "the kingdom of heaven or of God") *indicate God's kingship, rule or sovereignty,* recognized in the hearts and operative in the lives of his people, and effecting their *complete salvation,* their constitution as a *church,* and finally a *redeemed universe.* Note especially the four concepts:

---

[32] Note, "Fulfilled (is) the καιρός." In distinction from χρόνος, καιρός here views *time* from the aspect of the opportunity it provides, and not simply as a change from the past into the present into the future, not mere *duration*. See R. C. Trench, *Synonyms of the New Testament*, Grand Rapids, 1948, par. lvii.

[33] See A.R.V., R.S.V., etc., but *not* the poor rendering of 9:1 in A.V.

a. God's kingship, rule, or recognized sovereignty. That may be the meaning in Luke 17:21, "The Kingdom of God is within you," and is the meaning in Matt. 6:10, "Thy kingdom come, thy will be done. . . ."

b. Complete salvation, i.e., all the spiritual and material blessings—that is, blessings for soul and body--which result when God is King in our hearts, recognized and obeyed as such. That is the meaning, according to the context, in Mark 10:25, 26, "It is easier . . . than for a rich man to enter the kingdom of God. And they . . . said, 'Then who can be saved?' "

c. The church: the community of men in whose hearts God is recognized as King. Kingdom of God and church when used in this sense are nearly equivalent. This is the meaning in Matt. 16:18, 19, " . . . and upon this rock will I build my church . . . I will give unto you the keys of the kingdom of heaven."

d. The redeemed universe: the new heaven and earth with all their glory; something still future: the final realization of God's saving power. Thus in Matt. 25:34, " . . . inherit the kingdom prepared for you . . . ."

These four meanings are not separate and unrelated. They all proceed from the central idea of the reign of God, his supremacy in the sphere of saving power. The *kingdom* or *kingship* (the Greek word has both meanings) of heaven is like a gradually developing mustard seed; hence, both present and future (Mark 4:26-29). It is present; study Matt. 5:3; 12:28; 19:14; Mark 10:15; 12:34; Luke 7:28; 17:20, 21; John 3:3-5; 18:36. It is future; study Matt. 7:21, 22; 25:34; 26:29.

Jesus spoke of the work of salvation as the kingdom or reign of heaven in order to indicate the supernatural character, origin, and purpose of our salvation. Our salvation begins in heaven and should redound to the glory of the Father in heaven. Hence, by using this term Christ defended the truth, so precious to all believers, that everything is subservient to God's glory.

Accordingly, when Jesus says, "The time is fulfilled and the kingdom of God is at hand" an excellent commentary would be Matt. 4:14-16; 11:4, 5; Luke 4:18-21. It is understandable that Jesus says "is at hand," for when these words were spoken Christ's work of preaching, teaching, and healing in and around Galilee was only just beginning.

Jesus continues: **be converted and believe the gospel.** Compare "Be converted, for the kingdom of heaven is at hand," spoken by the Baptist (Matt. 3:2; see also Mark 1:4), with "The kingdom of God is at hand; be converted. . . ," spoken by Jesus. The meaning is the same. In fact, in Matthew's Gospel the identical words are ascribed to both John (3:2) and Jesus (4:17). Basically, therefore, their gospel was the same. John was a true way-preparer.

Though the rendering found in many of our translations, namely, "Repent," which stresses only the negative aspect of the required change, is probably not the best, repentance is definitely demanded. Genuine sorrow for sin and an earnest resolution to break with the evil past is at times even emphasized (Luke 3:13, 14). But the word used in the original[34] looks forward as well as backward. It means "Be converted,"[35] "undergo a radical change of heart and life, a complete turnabout of life. The positive side of conversion is given further emphasis in the added words "and believe the gospel."[36] Such believing or faith implies knowledge, assent, and confidence. In the language of the Heidelberg Catechism, "True faith is not only a sure knowledge, whereby I hold for truth all that God has revealed to us in his Word, but also a firm confidence which the Holy Spirit works in my heart by the gospel, that not only to others, but to me also, remission of sins, everlasting righteousness and salvation are freely given by God, merely of grace, only for the sake of Christ's merits." A person accepts a message when he acts upon it.

---

16 While he was going along the Sea of Galilee he saw Simon and Andrew, Simon's brother, throwing a casting-net into the sea, for they were fishermen. 17 Jesus said to them, "Come, follow me, and I will make y o u become fishers of men." 18 And at once they left their nets and followed him. 19 And when he had gone a little farther he saw James the son of Zebedee and John his brother, who were in the boat mending their nets. 20 At once he called them. And they left their father Zebedee in the boat with the hired men and followed him.

1:16-20 *The Calling of Four Fishermen*
Cf. Matt. 4:18-22; and for Mark 1:17b
and Matt. 4:19b cf. Luke 5:10b.[37]

16-18. While he was going along the Sea of Galilee he saw Simon and Andrew, Simon's brother, throwing a casting-net into the sea, for they were fishermen. Jesus said to them, Come, follow me, and I will make y o u become fishers of men. And at once they left their nets and followed him.[38]

The wonderful gospel of the kingdom was not intended only for the men

---

34 μετανοεῖτε, sec. per. pl. present imperative of μετανοέω. The verb occurs five times in Matthew (3:2; 4:17; 11:20, 21; 12:41), twice in Mark (1:15; 6:12), nine times in Luke, five times in Acts, once in II Cor. (12:21), and eleven times in the book of Revelation. The cognate noun μετάνοια is also of frequent occurrence, beginning with Matt. 3:8, 11.

35 The Dutch *Statenbijbel* already had the correct translation: "Bekeert u." This has been retained in *Nieuwe Vertaling*.

36 I do not accept Lenski's reasoning (*op. cit.*, pp. 43, 44) that because πιστεύετε follows μετανοεῖτε, the latter refers only to contrition. A word is not so easily deprived of its basic meaning. The addition of πιστεύετε is for the sake of emphasis on the positive aspect of μετάνοια.

37 For the reasons showing why Luke 5:1-11 cannot in its entirety be regarded as a true parallel to Matt. 4:18-22 and Mark 1:16-20 see N.T.C. on Matthew, p. 246.

38 In phraseology Mark 1:16-18 and Matt. 4:18-20 are almost identical. The differ-

living during the time of Christ's earthly ministry. It was intended for the ages. It is not at all surprising, therefore, that at the very beginning of his ministry Jesus chose men who, by means of their testimony both oral and written, would perpetuate his work and proclaim his message. For a teacher to have not only a general audience but also a band of *close companions* or *disciples* was nothing new. Did not Socrates have disciples? Did not John the Baptist? The Pharisees? The rabbis? Christ's disciples were to become the links between himself and his church. Think, for example, of the importance of such men as Matthew, John, and Peter in the formation of the Gospels, which are our chief sources of information about Jesus Christ. Accordingly, while he was passing along the Sea of Galilee Jesus invites certain men to come to him.

It must be understood, however, that the call which Jesus extended to the four men mentioned here in Mark 1:18-22 was not the first one they received. A year earlier Andrew and an unnamed disciple, in all likelihood John, had been invited to "come and see" where Jesus lived and had become his spiritual followers. Andrew had brought his brother Simon to Jesus. John had probably rendered the same service to his own brother James. See N.T.C. on John 1:35-41.

So now, according to Mark 1:16-20, about a year later these same four disciples become the Lord's more steady companions, and are made more conscious than ever of the fact that they are being trained for apostleship, that is, for becoming "fishers of men."

The men who were chosen by Jesus to be his immediate companions needed to be trained for apostleship. Simon the fickle must become Peter the rock. Something similar was true with respect to all. When we first meet these men, and to a certain extent even much later, they manifest lack of deep spiritual penetration (Mark 4:10, 13; 8:4, 16-21, 32, 33; 9:10-13; 10:10, 24-27); of fervent sympathy (6:35, 36; 10:13, 14); of profound humility (9:33, 34); of the gladly forgiving spirit (10:41); of persevering prayerfulness (9:28, 29); and of an unflinching courage (14:50, 66-72). Nevertheless, on their part it required a degree of courage to become Christ's followers and thereby face the opposition of many, including the religious leaders. For further details on The Twelve see on 3:16-19a.

---

ences can be considered stylistic. Thus, Mark has "going (or: passing) along"; Matthew, "walking along"; Mark, "he saw Simon and Andrew, Simon's brother"; Matthew, "he saw two brothers, Simon called Peter and Andrew his brother". Matthew uses the noun "casting-net" where Mark's verbal form implies the noun. Matthew has, ". . . and I will make y o u fishers or men"; Mark, " . . . and I will make y o u become fishers of men." In verse 20 Matthew has οἱ δὲ εὐθέως, while Mark's corresponding verse 18 reads καὶ εὐθύς. Such close resemblance, yet slight difference, lends support to the theory that *a.* there is a literary connection between Mark and Matthew; *b.* each evangelist, nevertheless, has his own style.

In this connection one fact must not be ignored. *Their* decision to side with Jesus exhibits *his* greatness: the impelling force of his influence over the minds and hearts of men, so that when he calls they follow immediately. The breadth of his sympathy and the magnitude of his power are also shown here. Is it not marvelous that he was willing and able to take such common folk, four fishermen, etc., unschooled individuals, and, in spite of all their prejudices and superstitions, to transform them into instruments for the salvation of many; to make them leaders who, by means of their testimonies, would turn the world upside down?

The four mentioned in verses 16-20 are:

Peter, the impetuous (Matt. 14:28-33; Mark 8:32; 14:29-31, 47; John 18:10), who becomes the leader of The Twelve, and is mentioned first in every list of apostles (Matt. 10:2-4; Mark 3:16-19; Luke 6:14-16; and Acts 1:13).

Peter's brother Andrew, who is always bringing people to Jesus (John 1:40-42; 6:8, 9, cf. Matt. 14:18; John 12:22).

Zebedee's son James, the first of The Twelve to wear the martyr's crown (Acts 12:1, 2).

His brother John, who is called "the disciple whom Jesus loved" (John 13:23; 19:26; etc.). To be sure, the Lord loved all "his own" very intensely (John 13:1, 2), but between Jesus and John the tie of attachment and understanding was the tenderest.

A few more details now on verses 16-18. Jesus, passing along the Sea of Galilee, saw two men, Simon and his brother Andrew, throwing a casting-net into the sea. When such a net is cast over the shoulder it will spread out, forming a circle as it strikes the water. Then, because of the pieces of lead attached to it, it will quickly sink, capturing the fish underneath. These two brothers, then, were engaged in their daily occupation, for they were fishermen.

"They were fishermen." This is the type of people the Lord chooses in order that they may become the foundation of his church (Rev. 21:14, 19, 20). By worldly standards not many are wise or powerful or highborn. But God chose those whom men consider foolish, to shame the wise (I Cor. 1:26, 27).

It is important to note that the Lord by saying, "Come, follow me," exercises his sovereignty over Simon and Andrew. He shows that he has a right to claim them for service in his kingdom. They must be ready to follow immediately when he calls them.

Simon and Andrew hailed from Bethsaida (John 1:45), but Simon (i.e. Peter) had recently moved to Capernaum (Matt. 4:13; 8:5, 14, 15; Mark 1:21, 29, 30; Luke 4:31, 33, 38). By this time these men had come to know Jesus, because a year had elapsed since the unforgettable event recorded in John 1:35-42. Hence, when he now said to them, "Come, follow me, and I will make y o u become fishers of men," they at once left their nets and followed, encouraged by the promise of their Lord to train them for a task far superior even to the honorable one in which they were now engaged. Instead of catching fish for the table they would recruit men for the kingdom.

It must not escape us that by means of the promise, "I will make y o u become fishers of men" Jesus sets the seal of his approval upon the words of the inspired author of the Book of Proverbs, "He who wins souls is wise" (Prov. 11:30); confirms Dan. 12:3: "They that turn many to righteousness shall shine as the stars forever and ever"; adds his own authority to Paul's striking statement, "To all I became all, that in one way or another I may save some" (I Cor. 9:22); and anticipates his own glorious invitation, "Come to me, all who are weary and burdened, and I will give y o u rest" (Matt. 11:28).

Two other disciples of Jesus were given the same command and promise: **19, 20. And when he had gone a little farther he saw James the son of Zebedee and John his brother, who were in the boat mending their nets. At once he called them. And they left their father Zebedee in the boat with the hired men and followed him.** These two were not fishing, like Peter and Andrew (verses 16-18). They were not with the other two brothers but a little distance removed from them. James and John were with their father in his boat. Instead of fishing they were mending their nets, getting ready for the next attempt at catching fish. When Jesus saw these two he repeated what he had done a moment before in connection with the other two: at once he called them to follow him. Accordingly, also of them he demands that they enter into a closer relation to him; that is, that they, too, by means of a more constant presence with their Master, begin their training for the apostolate.

They immediately leave their father and begin to follow Jesus. Now this action of theirs, even though it had been prepared for by the event that had occurred a year earlier, requires more than passing notice. It was really very remarkable. In the spirit of Matt. 13:55; John 1:47; 6:42, they might have said, "Isn't he the son of the (late?) carpenter from nearby Nazareth? Isn't he himself also a carpenter? Why should we become *his* apprentices?" In fact, if the theory held by many and not to be lightly rejected is correct—see N.T.C. on John 19:25—, namely, that their mother Salome was a sister of Jesus' mother Mary, they might even have added, "And aren't James, Joseph, Simon, and Judas his brothers? Isn't he merely our cousin? Why then should we follow him?"—The fact that they say nothing of the kind but immediately leave their father and join Jesus is not only to their credit but also and *especially* shows the magnetic and majestic character of their Master!

The question might be asked, "But did not these men act rather rashly?

61

Were they not unkind to their father Zebedee in leaving him in the lurch?" Answer: *a.* At this particular stage in the increasing degree of association that was being established between these men and their Lord, helping their father by doing a little fishing now and then as long as Jesus had his headquarters in Capernaum is not excluded. *b.* Mark—not Matthew—informs us that James and John left their father in the boat "with the hired men." So, whenever Zebedee's sons were not able to be with him, these hired men could be depended upon to find ways in which to fill the gap. Provision has been made for every need. *c.* Overarching all other considerations is the fact that when Jesus calls there must be prompt obedience. The "but's" must be left to him. He has the solution.

As to Zebedee, though Mark mentions him also later in his Gospel (3:17; 10:35) as being the father of James and John, he is not heard from again as a man engaged in a fishing enterprise. Did he perhaps die soon afterward? And could this be the reason why in the story of the request of his sons (Mark 10:35) and of their mother (Matt. 20:20) no action is ascribed to him? This is possible, but it is clear from Mark's Gospel that our attention should be concentrated not on Zebedee, his wife Salome, their sons James and John, but on the Lord, on him alone and thus on his majesty, power, and love.

---

21 And they went to Capernaum; and immediately on the sabbath he entered the synagogue and began to teach.   22 The people were astonished at his teaching, for he taught them as one who had authority and not as the scribes.   23 Just then there was in their synagogue a man with an unclean spirit. He cried out,   24 saying, "Why do you bother us, Jesus of Nazareth? Have you come out to destroy us? I know who you are—the Holy One of God!"   25 But Jesus rebuked him, saying, "Be quiet and get out of him!"   26 And the unclean spirit threw the man into convulsions and with a loud shriek got out of him.   27 The people were all so dumbfounded that they began to ask each other, "What is this? A new (kind of) teaching! With authority! Even to unclean spirits he issues commands, and they obey him!"   28 And the news about him went out immediately everywhere, over the entire region of Galilee.

1:21-28 *The Healing of a Man with an Unclean Spirit*
Cf. Luke 4:31-37

In the desert of temptation Satan had been defeated (Mark 1:12, 13; cf. Matt. 4:1-11). So now it is not surprising that the prince of evil is going to attempt in every possible way to oppose Christ and his kingdom. Does the Anointed One seek entrance into the hearts of men? Satan sends out his servants, the demons, to take control of these hearts. In fact, he was already in the habit of doing this, but now more than ever. On the other hand, for the Conqueror this means that in many cases he would "cast out" these demons, thereby seriously binding, curtailing, or limiting the power of "the strong man, Beelzebul" (Mark 3:22-27; cf. Matt. 12:22-29; Rev. 20:1-3).

Thus hearts would be opened for the reception of the gospel. Mission activity, also clearly predicted in the preceding context (Mark 1:17), would replace Satanic deception.

After a couple introductory verses (1:21, 22) Mark now for the first time presents a demon expulsion narrative (verses 23-28). Luke follows the same procedure in 4:31, 32 (introductory), followed by verses 33-37.

21. And they went to Capernaum; and immediately on the sabbath he entered the synagogue and began to teach. It now becomes clear that the part of the shore on which Jesus was walking when he called his first four disciples was near Capernaum. It was customary for Jesus to attend the synagogue (Luke 4:16). Soon it also became customary for him to teach while there (John 18:20). So also at the present occasion, probably after the prescribed portion of the law had been read in Hebrew and translated into Aramaic, Jesus, having indicated his desire to speak and having gained permission to do so, while standing read from the prophets; then, seated, explained the portion read and applied it to the needs of the hearers. **22. The people were astonished at his teaching. . . .** While Jesus was speaking, and even after he had finished, the people were dumbfounded. They were literally "struck out of themselves," that is, "out of their senses" by amazement and wonder. It was a state that did not leave them immediately but lasted for a while.

What were some of the reasons for this reaction on the part of the audience? One of them may well have been that he, a carpenter (Mark 6:3), revealed such wisdom. But especially there was this: **for he taught them as one who had authority and not as the scribes.** Cf. Matt. 7:28b, 29. Consider the following points of contrast between Christ's method of teaching and that of the scribes.

a. He spoke the truth (John 14:6; 18:37). Corrupt and evasive reasoning marked the sermons of many of *the scribes* (Matt. 5:21 ff.).

b. He presented matters of great significance, matters of life, death, and eternity. *They* often wasted their time on trivialities (Matt. 23:23; Luke 11:42).

c. There was system in *his* preaching. As their Talmud proves, *they* often rambled on and on.

d. He excited curiosity by making generous use of illustrations (Mark 4:2-9, 21, 24, 26-34; 9:36; 12:1-11). *Their* speeches were often dry as dust.

e. He spoke as the Lover of men, as One concerned with the everlasting welfare of his listeners, and pointed to the Father and his love. *Their* lack of love is clear from such passages as Mark 12:40; etc.

f. Finally, and this is the most important, for it is specifically stated here, *he* spoke "with authority," for his message came straight from the very heart and mind of the Father (John 8:26), hence also from his own inner being, and from Scripture. *They* were constantly borrowing from fallible sources, one scribe quoting another scribe. *They* were trying to draw water from broken cisterns. *He* drew from himself, being "the Fountain of living waters" (Jer. 2:13).

23a. Just then there was in their synagogue a man with an unclean spirit. As is clear from Mark 1:32-34; 6:13; Luke 4:40, 41, it is not true that the New Testament writers, in common with all primitive people, ascribed all physical illnesses and abnormalities to the presence and operation of evil spirits. It is contrary to fact that demon-possession is simply another name for insanity or for dissociation. Fact is that demon-possession describes a condition in which a *distinct* and *evil* being (Mark: "an unclean spirit"; Luke 4:33, "the spirit of an unclean demon"), foreign to the person possessed, has taken control of that person. For more on this subject of demon-possession see N.T.C. on Matthew, pp. 436-438.

The theory according to which demon-possession has continued through the centuries and is present with us today is held by many. Origen (fl. A.D. 210-250) claimed that by calling on the name of Jesus *and the name of martyrs*(!) demons could be driven out. During the middle ages there were those who held that making the sign of the cross would be of help in expelling them. Many present-day advocates of this theory appeal to the often quoted work by H. W. White, *Demonism Verified and Analyzed.* W. P. Blatty's paperback *The Exorcist* ("a nightmare novel of demonic possession") has received high praise. And a certain newspaper reports a demon-expulsion resulting from five-hour directions by telephone!

That superstition plays its role in at least some of these claims is evident even on the surface. Besides, it is a question whether all those who believe in demon-possession as an actual present-day fact are scientifically equipped to draw the necessary distinction *a.* between certain abnormal mental conditions (for example "dissociation") and the invasion of the human personality by one or more of Satan's underlings; and *b.* between demonic *influence* and demon-*possession.* In the Roman Catholic Church before a priest is allowed to proceed with exorcism he has to make a thorough examination to see whether he is dealing with a real case of demon-possession, and even then he must receive authorization from his bishop before proceeding.

A man of high reputation, with thorough theological, medical, and psychiatric training, the late Dr. J. D. Mulder, in a series of articles on "Mental Disease and Demon Possession," wrote as follows, "For six years I have worked as medical missionary among the Navahos, a tribe of Indians still deeply steeped in fear of evil spirits, witchcraft, and related subjects, while the last ten years I was in daily contact with mentally disturbed of all types. . . . Daily conversations with these . . . patients, however, and careful delving into their inner thoughts have made me convinced that, whereas there might well be demoniacal *influence*, the picture of *possession*, as found in the New Testament, was always absent. I therefore fully agree with Prof. Schultze when he writes, 'I venture to suggest that demon possession was a phenomenon limited almost exclusively (if not entirely) to the period of special divine manifestations during the period in which the New Testament church was born.' "[39]

Mark continues: **23b, 24. He cried out, saying, Why do you bother us,[40] Jesus of Nazareth?** Literally the demon, making use of the wretched man's vocal organs, said, "What (is there) to us and you," meaning, "What have we in common?" and in the present context, "What have you to do with us?"; hence, "Why do you bother us?" See also Mark 5:7; cf. Matt. 8:29. Note "with *us*," the one demon speaking for them all, for he realizes that what will happen to him is going to be the lot of all his fellow-demons.

He calls the One who is about to expel him "Jesus of Nazareth," literally, "Jesus the Nazarene." Although being brought up in Nazareth spelled humble beginnings, and in the case of Jesus pointed to the Messiah's low estate (Matt. 2:23), and Nathanael by asking, "Out of Nazareth can any good come?" was moved either by town-rivalry or more probably was thinking of any good thing in the Messianic category, yet calling Jesus "the Nazarene" does not always or necessarily imply disdain. In fact Jesus even uses the term with respect to himself (Acts 22:8).[41]

That the form of address, "Jesus of Nazareth," used by the demon was simply the designation by which Jesus was generally known, and not a title indicating disrespect, is clear also from the added words: **Have you come to destroy us? I know who you are—the Holy One of God.** "Have you come" can hardly be taken to mean, "from Nazareth," for Jesus did not need to come from Nazareth to crush the power of Satan's emissaries. It is best taken to mean "Have you come from heaven into the world. . . ." The demon, accordingly, is asking whether the very One who had come *to seek and to save* the lost (Luke 19:10) had also come *to destroy* the demons, that is, now *already* (cf. Matt. 8:29) to hurl them into the abyss or dungeon where Satan is kept (Rev. 20:3).

---

39 *The Banner* (a weekly published by the Christian Reformed denomination, with headquarters in Grand Rapids, Mich.), the March 24 and April 7, 1933 issues. After his valuable experience as a medical missionary Dr. Mulder was for many years the superintendent of a mental institution, namely, Pine Rest Christian Hospital, Grand Rapids, Mich.

40 On τί ἡμῖν καὶ σοί see M. Smith, "Notes on Goodspeed's 'Problems of New Testament Translation,' " *JBL*, 64 (1945), pp. 512, 513.

41 The meaning is the same whether the word "Nazarene" or "man from Nazareth" is spelled Ναζαρηνός (Mark's usage; see, besides 1:24 also 10:47; 14:67; 16:6) or Ναζαραῖος (Matthew's spelling; see 2:23; 26:71; also John's; see 18:5, 7; 19:19). Luke has both forms.

When the demon declares, "I know" he is not telling a lie. There are certain things that are known to the prince of evil and his servants. See James 2:19. Moreover, some of this knowledge causes them to tremble, to be frightened. They know that for them there is no salvation, only dreadful punishment. The demon is thinking of this very fact, as he realizes that he is at this moment being confronted with his Great Opponent, whom he, again correctly, calls "the Holy One of God." He knows that holiness cannot brook sin. A demon . . . the Holy One of God, what a contrast! In connection with "Holy One" see also Luke 4:34; John 6:69; Rev. 3:7. Jesus was "holy" not only in the sense of being sinless in himself, filled with virtue, and the cause of virtue in others, but specifically also in this sense, that he had been anointed, hence set apart, separated, for the performance of the most exalted task (Isa. 61:1-3; Luke 4:18, 19; 19:10; John 3:16; 10:36; II Cor. 5:21).

When radicals deny Christ's deity they show less insight than the demons, for the latter are constantly acknowledging it. To be sure, they do not do this in the proper spirit. For reverence they substitute impudence; for joyfulness, bitterness; for gratitude, turpitude. But they do it all the same. They call Jesus "the Holy One of God" (here in Mark 1:24), "the Son of the Most High" (5:7), "the Son of God" (Matt. 8:29).

25. **But Jesus rebuked him, saying, Be quiet and get out of him!** Jesus does not accept an acknowledgment coming from a thoroughly corrupt demon. Besides, the demon had no business to interrupt. But see also on verses 34 and 44. So Jesus issues a terse, peremptory, two-fold command, "Be still and get out!"[42]

The demon obeys at once; that is all he could do. He obeys, though, as is evident, most unwillingly: 26. **And the unclean spirit threw the man into convulsions and with a loud shriek got out of him.** Here the A.V. has, "And when the unclean spirit had torn him." But this, besides being in conflict with "having done him no harm" (Luke 4:35), is also out of harmony with the fact that the same Greek word is used (Mark 9:26; Luke 9:39; and cf. Mark 9:20; Luke 9:42) in connection with an epileptic (see Matt. 17:15), in which case not lacerations but convulsions are in view. Therefore also here in Mark 1:26 no tearing is implied. The translation, accordingly, should be, ". . . threw the man into convulsions." Then, for the last time using the man's vocal organs, the demon "screaming with a loud scream" (thus literally), left him.

27. **The people were all so dumbfounded that they began to ask each**

---

42 φιμώθητι, 2nd per. sing. aor. imper. passive of φιμόω; hence, "Be silenced" or simply "Be silent," "Be still," "Be quiet." Cf. 4:39. And ἔξελθε, 2nd per. sing. aor. of ἐξέρχομαι.

other, What is this? A new (kind of) teaching! With authority! Even to unclean spirits he issues commands, and they obey him! The reaction of the people to all that had happened in the synagogue is graphically related here. The emotion described ("were . . . dumbfounded") is a synonym of that expressed in verse 22 ("were astonished"). When those who were present begin to ask each other, "What is this?" they were referring both to Christ's teaching and his demon-expulsion. As to the first, they realized that both as to contents and method (see on verse 22) the teaching which on this sabbath they had heard in the synagogue was different from that ever heard before at this place. And as to the second, the same authority and power exhibited in Jesus' teaching was shown also in the commands he issued to demons, so that the latter had to yield, were totally unable to resist. Note that although the account itself speaks only of one demon, the people immediately draw the correct conclusion that what had been done to one unclean spirit could be done to all.

What to make of all this the audience did not know. They were deeply impressed with the words and works of Jesus. What kind of person was he? They discussed this question among themselves, but as yet could not find the answer.

28. And the news about him went out immediately everywhere, over the entire region of Galilee. The happenings in the synagogue on this sabbath had been so astounding that without any delay one neighbor was telling another about it, and he still another, etc. The news could not be confined to Capernaum. In "no time at all," as we would say, the news was spreading all over Galilee; or, as Luke puts it, "the reports . . . went out into every place in the surrounding region" (4:37).

---

29 And immediately they[43] left the synagogue, and with James and John entered the house of Simon and Andrew. 30 Simon's mother-in-law was lying sick with a fever. And immediately they told him about her. 31 So he went up to her, took her by the hand and lifted her up. The fever left her and she began to wait on them. 32 That evening after sunset they were bringing to him all that were afflicted and the demon-possessed. 33 And the whole town was gathered at the door. 34 He healed many who were afflicted with various diseases, and he cast out many demons. But he was not allowing the demons to speak, because they knew who he was.

1:29-34 *The Healing of Simon's Mother-in-law and of Many Others*
Cf. Matt. 8:14-17; Luke 4:38-41

29. And immediately they [or: he] left the synagogue, and with James and John entered the house of Simon and Andrew. From the synagogue the walk was directly to Simon's (=Peter's) house. So much is clear (cf. Matt.

---

43 According to another reading: he.

8:14; Luke 4;38). Peter was a married man, and his mother-in-law was living with them. Mark, however, speaks of "the house of Simon *and Andrew*." Evidently then, Simon's brother Andrew must also have been living in the same house.

A difficulty arises, however, in connection with the subject of the sentence. Should it be "they" or "he"? We know that Jesus had attended the synagogue, had taught there, and had performed an astounding miracle (verses 21-28). May we not assume that Simon and Andrew, James and John, all of whom had just previously been called to become fishers of men (verses 16-20) and had entered Capernaum with Jesus, had also attended the services in Capernaum's synagogue? Now if that assumption is correct, then at first glance would it not seem that the word "they" in verse 29 refers to Jesus and these four disciples? However, a second look is necessary: the fact that they are said to have entered the house of Simon and Andrew "with James and John" makes this interpretation impossible. Among the solutions that have been offered the two that are probably the best are as follows:

a. Mark, being Peter's interpreter, is reproducing almost literally (with change from the first to the third person) what he had heard Peter say in a sermon or discourse. Peter had spoken somewhat as follows, "And immediately *we* [meaning Jesus, I myself and Andrew] left the synagogue, and with James and John went (to my) home." If this be the correct solution Mark's "they" would refer to Jesus, Simon, and Andrew.[44]

b. Instead of "they" the variant reading "he," which has considerable manuscript support,[45] should be adopted. That "he" refers to Jesus. It is he who, taking James and John with him, enters the home of Simon and Andrew.

Either way, however, we now find Jesus, Peter, Andrew, John, and James at the home of Peter and his brother. **30. Simon's mother-in-law was lying sick with a fever. And immediately they told him about her.** While Matthew and Mark report that the mother of Peter's wife was "laid up with fever" or "lying sick with fever," Luke, who was himself a physician (Col. 4:14), tells us that she was "in the grip of a high fever," or "was suffering from a severe attack of fever."[46] Without delay Jesus was informed about the situation, either on reaching the home or even before. Not only did the disciples—no doubt especially Peter and Andrew—*tell* Jesus about her, but, as Luke

---

44 This solution is suggested by Van Leeuwen, *op. cit.*, p. 33.

45 The reading ἐξελθὼν ἦλθεν is supported by uncial B, and with different word order also by D. It also has the support of a couple other uncials and of a number of rather important cursives. R.S.V. has adopted the "he" reading in its text. Swete regards the "they" reading as being "hardly tolerable."

46 See A. T. Robertson, *Luke the Historian in the Light of Research*, New York, 1923, pp. 90-102: "The Use of Medical Terms by Luke." ἦν συνεχομένη πυρετῷ μεγάλῳ (Luke 4:38).

mentions, they *asked* him to help her. **31. So he went up to her, took her by the hand and lifted her up.** It is very interesting to note how the different evangelists individually describe just what Jesus did. Matthew characteristically (8:3, 15; 9:29; 17:7; 20:34) states that Jesus "touched" the woman's hand. What a tender touch it was, and how powerful! See N.T.C. on Matt. 8:3. Mark, very graphically, having often listened to Peter as the latter with unrestrained emotion had described what happened, says, "He took her by the hand and lifted her up." *Dr.* Luke mentions what must have struck *him* especially, namely, that the position in which Jesus, the Great Physician, was standing was exactly that of the typical doctor: "So he *stood over* her. . . ." Had Luke himself done this many times while attending patients? Luke adds, "and rebuked the fever." Jesus bade the fever leave her. Fever, winds, waves, it made no difference to Jesus. He exercised complete control over them all. So here he speaks to the fever as he was going to speak to the wild winds and the boisterous billows, in the original using the same verb in each case (cf. Luke 4:39 with 8:24).

Result: **The fever left her and she began to wait on them.** Jesus had already lifted her up. But now of a sudden "the fever left her," as all three evangelists state. Moreover, she did not even say, "I'm rid of the fever, but completely exhausted." Nothing of the kind. On the contrary, one moment, just before Jesus had taken her by the hand and had rebuked the fever, there were still those flushed cheeks, that burning hot skin, profuse sweating, dryness in the throat—or else, depending on the kind of fever, there may have been violent shivering—; the next moment (see Luke 4:39, "at once she got up . . .") every fever symptom had vanished completely. Not only was the woman's temperature normal but such a surge of new strength was coursing through her entire being that she herself insisted on getting up. In fact, she actually got up and started to perform the duties of a busy hostess. She began to wait on all those present: Jesus, Peter, Andrew, James, John, and perhaps even on her daughter if she too was present, as is probable. Or, "mother" may have been ably assisting "daughter" in performing this act of hospitality.

So quickly did the news of the demon-expulsion (verses 23-26) and of the victory over a terrible attack of fever (verses 29-31) spread that people from all around regained hope of recovery for their dear ones. Result: **32. That evening after sunset they were bringing to him all that were afflicted and the demon-possessed.** Matthew has "when evening had come" (8:16); Luke, "when the sun was setting" (4:40). Mark has the genitive absolute, literally "evening having come," or, according to the modern idiom "that evening." He adds "after sunset," literally "when the sun did set."

According to the Hebrew way of speaking there were two evenings (see Exod. 12:6 in the original). The first began at 3 P.M., the second at 6 P.M.

So when Mark writes "that evening" and immediately adds "after sunset" we know that the people waited until the end of the sabbath before they "were bringing to him all that were afflicted . . ." or "were sick"; literally "all that had (it) badly." To this is immediately added "and the demon-possessed," clearly showing that a distinction is being made between *a.* sick people who were not demon-possessed, and *b.* demon-possessed individuals who may or may not have been physically ill. For demon-possession see above, on verses 23-26. That ever so many persons came, or were brought, to Jesus is clear from verse 33. **And the whole town was gathered at the door.** One might say: Peter's house was mobbed. "The whole town" refers, of course, to Capernaum (verse 21). That the multitude of the sick and the demoniacs, together with those who brought or accompanied those in need of help, was indeed huge is stressed also by Matthew (8:16) and Luke (4:40).

Christ's power to heal was never lacking. His love and sympathy never failed: **34. He healed many who were afflicted with various diseases, and he cast out many demons.** Mark is very brief here. In the light of the preceding context he conveys the thought that Jesus healed *all* (see verse 32; cf. Matt. 8:16; Luke 4:40) the *many* (verse 34) sick people that were brought to him, no matter what happened to be the nature of their illness. Luke, as we would expect of this doctor, pictures the procession of the sick being brought one by one to Jesus, who, paying due attention to, and lovingly placing his hands on, each in turn, healed them all (4:40). Mark, in harmony with Matthew and Luke, states that Jesus similarly cast out *many* demons. Matthew adds that it was "with a word," namely, the word of effective command, that the evil spirits were driven out (8:16).

When Mark now adds, **But he was not allowing the demons to speak, because they knew who he was,** this must not be interpreted to mean that the evil spirits never said anything at all. Luke explains what is meant. At first the demons cried out, "You are the Son of God." Cf. above, on Mark 1:24. Immediately they were rebuked by Jesus, and thus prevented from saying any more about this.

Now what these demons, by means of the vocal organs of the possessed, were saying was the truth. They actually "knew who Jesus was," namely, the Son of God, the long expected Messiah. Similarly, for example, the outcry of the demon-possessed girl described in Acts 16:17 was true; so true, in fact, that what she said ("These men are servants of the Most High God, who proclaim to y o u the way of salvation") has been used as the text for an ordination service; theme: "The word of the devil!" Nevertheless, two questions arise. The first one is: Why did these demons loudly proclaim this truth? Was this caused by an irresistible fascination which the person of Jesus cast upon them?[47] Was it due, rather, to a malicious and sadistic desire

---

[47] Cf. H. N. Ridderbos, *Zelfopenbaring en Zelfverberging*, Kampen, 1946, p. 52.

to get Jesus into trouble, since they may have known that if already at this time the truth with reference to Christ's identity were accepted by the masses, this would cut short Messiah's contemplated program and would bring him to death sooner than would have been the case otherwise? An *indisputable* answer has not been revealed. The second question is: Why did Jesus silence them? A *possible* answer has already been suggested, but see also on verse 44.

While Mark and Luke end their respective paragraphs with this prohibition addressed to the demons, Matthew (8:17) sees in the cures performed by the Master a fulfilment of the prophecy of Isa. 53:4, "Surely, our diseases he has borne, and our pains [or: sorrows] he has carried."

---

35 Very early in the morning, while it was still dark, Jesus got up, went out, and departed to a lonely place; and there he was praying. 36 Simon and those who were with him went in search of him, 37 and having found him said to him, "Everybody is looking for you!" 38 And he said to them, "Let us go elsewhere, to the next towns, that I may preach there also; because for this purpose I came forth." 39 So he traveled throughout all Galilee, preaching in their synagogues and casting out demons.

1:35-39 *Christ's Pre-dawn Prayer; Simon's Exclamation and Christ's Answer; Christ's Ministry of Preaching and Demon-expulsion throughout all Galilee*
Cf. Luke 4:42-44; and with Mark 1:39 cf. Matt. 4:23-25

After a long and strenuous day Jesus, who was and is not only divine but also human, felt the need of prayer. So, 35. **Very early in the morning, while it was still dark, Jesus got up, went out, and departed to a lonely place; and there he was praying.** Had he spent the night in Peter's home, and did that disciple, upon arising discover that the Master had already left? This is possible but we do not know. What we do know is that "very early while it was still night," that is, still dark,[48] and was just starting to get light (Luke 4:42), Jesus got up, left the house (whether his own or Peter's), and went off to a lonely or deserted spot, a quiet retreat. There he poured out his heart in prayer to his heavenly Father. It may well have been a thanksgiving for blessings already received and a petition for strength needed for the Galilean circuit that was about to begin.

Jesus attached great importance to prayer. He himself prayed when he was baptized (Luke 3:21); just before choosing the twelve disciples (Luke 6:12); in connection with, and after, the miraculous feeding of the five thousand (Mark 6:41, 46; cf. Matt. 14:19, 23); when he was about to ask his disciples an important question (Luke 9:18); on the mountain where he was transfigured (Luke 9:28); just before extending the tender invitation, "Come to

---

48 Note πρωΐ ἔννυχα λίαν = "early at night very" (cf. 16:2).

me all who are weary . . ." (Matt. 11:25-30; Luke 10:21); just before he taught the disciples the Lord's Prayer (Luke 11:1); at Lazarus' tomb (John 11:41, 42); for Peter, before the denial (Luke 22:32); during the night of the institution of the Lord's Supper (John 17; cf. 14:16); in Gethsemane (Mark 14:32, 35, 36, 39; cf. Matt. 26:39, 42, 44; Luke 22:42); on the cross (Luke 23:34;[49] Mark 15:34; Matt. 27:46; Luke 23:46); and after his resurrection (Luke 24:30). These references must be considered as being merely examples of a much more extensive life of prayer and thanksgiving.

A few quotations culled from the prayers of our Lord, as recorded in the Gospels, show how genuine, intimate, trustful, unselfish, and God-glorifying they were:

"I praise thee, Father, Lord of heaven and earth, that thou didst hide these things from wise and learned (people) and didst reveal them to babes . . ." (Matt. 25, 26).

"Father, I thank thee that thou hast heard me. I know that thou dost always hear me, but on account of the multitude that is standing around I said (this), in order that they may believe that thou has sent me" (John 11:41, 42).

"Father, the hour has arrived; glorify thy Son, in order that the Son may glorify thee" . . . "Holy Father, keep them in thy name" . . . "I make request that they all may constantly be one . . ." (John 17: Christ's highpriestly prayer, for himself, his immediate disciples, and the Church Universal).

"My Father, if it be possible, let this cup be spared me; nevertheless, not as I will but as thou wilt. . . . My Father, if it is not possible that this (cup) be spared me except I drink it, thy will be done" (Matt. 26:39, 42 and parallels in Mark and Luke).

"Father, forgive them; for they do not know what they are doing" . . . "Father, into thy hands I commend my spirit" (Luke 23:34, 46).

Jesus also urged prayer on his followers (Mark 9:29; 13:18, 33; 14:38; cf. Matt. 7:7-11; Luke 18:1-8), and showed them how to pray and how not to pray (Matt. 6:6-8). In this connection he also taught them what is known as "the Lord's Prayer" (Matt. 6:9-15).

Viewed in this context verse 35 becomes meaningful. **36, 37. Simon and those who were with him went in search of him, and having found him said to him, Everybody is looking for you.** If Jesus had spent the night at Simon's house, this might explain why Simon is mentioned so prominently: "Simon and those with him." But it is probable that almost from the beginning this man Simon—that is, Peter—was, on account of his very character 'or personality, considered a leader. "Those who were with him"; shall we say Andrew, James, and John? On the basis of verses 16-20 this would seem natural, but there may also have been others (see John 1:43-45).

---

[49] On the assumption that this passage is authentic.

These men, then, diligently, eagerly searched for Jesus. They were determined to find him.[50] Note the synonymous expression in II Tim. 1:17: "He [Onesiphorus] diligently searched for me and found me!" So also in the case of Simon and his fellow-disciples the search was successful. They found Jesus. Their intention was to bring him right back to Capernaum, where "everybody," that is, a large crowd of people—perhaps gathered again in front of Peter's house—was looking for Jesus. Excitedly the disciples inform Jesus about this.

The result, however, was surprising. Jesus is not going to allow the people in general, or even his disciples, to tell him where he should go. Besides, in his great love he wishes to distribute his favors among the many. Capernaum will see him again. It remains for a while his center of operations, his headquarters. But he does not wish to confine himself to that one city. Hence, there follows: **38. And he said to them, Let us go elsewhere, to the next town, that I may preach there also . . . .**[51] "Let us go" shows that Jesus wishes to have his disciples remain with him as he goes on this tour through the Galilean towns and villages. Are they not being trained for apostleship?

Jesus says nothing about performing miracles in these places. That he actually performed them is clear from verse 39b; cf. Matt. 4:23, 24. But he places all the emphasis on "preaching the good tidings" (Luke 4:43). The miracles served an ancillary purpose. They confirmed his message and showed who he was. But he stresses *the open proclamation* of the love of God revealed in the salvation of sinners and reflected in their lives. He underscores *the preaching* that men are saved apart from any burdensome obligation to obey all the rabbinical regulations; that they enter the kingdom solely on the basis of the blood that was to be shed (cf. Matt. 11:28-30; Mark 10:45). By means of such preaching Jesus was fulfilling the very purpose of the Savior's departure from heaven and coming to earth. Therefore, with respect to it he continues: **because for this purpose I came forth.**

---

[50] The prefix κατά is perfective. The verb καταδιώκω is often used in a hostile sense: *to pursue, hunt* or *track down,* but here: *to search,* with eager determination to find Jesus by all means.

[51] Ἄγωμεν = 1st per. pl. pres. subj. active of ἄγω. The basic meaning *to bring, lead, guide, conduct, drive, convey* develops into *convey oneself,* hence *go.* For this intransitive use see also Mark 14:42; John 11:7, 15, 16; 14:31. With ἀλλαχοῦ in the New Testament occurring only here, and meaning *elsewhere,* cf. πανταχοῦ (verse 28), meaning *everywhere.* The word ἐχομένας, acc. pl. fem. pres. middle participle of ἔχω, means *holding fast to, clinging to,* and so *next, neighboring.* (In the papyri οἱ ἐχόμενοι are *the neighbors.*) The same word can also have a temporal sense: *immediately following, next* (in time) Luke 13:33; Acts 13:44; 20:15.

The κωμόπολις is literally a *village-*(κώμη) *city* (πόλις); hence, *small town.* In the parallel passage Luke, however, uses the word *cities* (4:43).

Finally, κηρύξω is 1st. per. sing. aor. act. subj. of κηρύσσω; hence, "that I may herald, preach, proclaim."

"Came forth" not just from Nazareth, or from Capernaum, but definitely *from heaven*. See John 1:11, 12; 6:38; 8:42; 13:3; 18:37.

39. So he traveled throughout all Galilee, preaching in their synagogues and casting out demons. The logic is clear: "Let us go elsewhere" is here followed by "So he traveled throughout all Galilee"; and, "that I may preach," by "preaching in their synagogues and casting out demons." For demon-possession and expulsion see also on 1:21-28, 32-34; and N.T.C. on Matt. 9:32.

Striking is the expression "throughout all Galilee," the Galilee with its mixture of Jew and Gentile. Though healings are not mentioned, they may well be suggested by demon-expulsions, for the two often go together. And with respect to such deeds of mercy, we may well assume that nationalistic distinctions did not triumph in the end. The spirit of the Master is clearly set forth in such passages as Matt. 8:10-13; Mark 7:24-30; Luke 4:25-27. Truly he was, and is, "the Savior of the world" (John 4:42; I John 4:14).

Nevertheless, when specific mention is made of "preaching in their synagogues" the reference is, of course, to a distinctly Jewish institution. "To the Jew first, and also to the Greek" (Rom. 1:16) was the order of operation.

The Synagogue During New Testament Times

Exactly when it was that the synagogue had its origin is not known. It is clear, however, that during the days of the New Testament it was already considered an ancient and widely spread institution (Acts 15:21). Nevertheless not until the days of the Babylonian captivity did the synagogue attain a permanent place in the lives of the Jewish people. Some authorities believe that it did not come into being until *after* the captivity; hence, perhaps in the time of Ezra with his emphasis on the importance and sacredness of God's holy law. However that may be, both the destruction of the temple and for many people the great distance between their homes and the Jerusalem temple made the erection of synagogues a necessity. They appeared everywhere. Sometimes one city would have several synagogues. According to a statement in the Jerusalem Talmud, at the time of the destruction of Jerusalem (A.D. 70) there were 480 synagogues in Jerusalem—an exaggeration, of course.

What made the synagogue so important was the many services it rendered. First and most of all it was supposed to be the place where God's holy law was read and explained to the people. When this was done properly great blessings followed. But when misuse was made of this privilege, so that the explanation of the law deteriorated into a superimposition of hairsplitting rabbinical ordinances on that which God demanded, the blessing never arrived.

The existence of both temple and synagogue did not create any problem.

Though both offered facilities for teaching (John 18:20), yet in the temple the emphasis was on offerings, in the synagogue on teaching. That temple and synagogue were no competitors or rivals appears from the fact that before the destruction of the temple there was a synagogue on temple hill; and Theodotus functioned in a double capacity, being priest in the temple and ruler of the synagogue.

As to the form or shape of synagogues, this varied. Generally they were built of stone. Until recently it was thought that no synagogue dating from the first century A.D. had survived. It was well-known that what had remained of the one at Capernaum (Tel Hum) was of a later date, although the site may well have been the same as that of the synagogue in which Jesus taught.[52] However, under the leadership of the archaeologist Y. Yadin a synagogue has now been uncovered on the rock of Masada, near the western shore of the narrow part of the Dead Sea.[53] It is a rectangular structure, the roof resting upon two rows of columns. It dates from the time of the second temple.

What made the synagogue so important was that in addition to being a place where the regular worship services were held it also served many other purposes. It was a place to which a person could go to pour out his heart in prayer or thanksgiving. It was also an elementary school, had rooms that could be used for imparting instruction to the youth, or had a school attached to it. Often it was used by the rabbi as his study. Sometimes the building even provided lodging facilities for the rabbi and/or for strangers who were looking for shelter.

From the viewpoint of Christianity most important of all was what has been called "the freedom of the synagogue." What this means will become clear from a brief summary of the Order of Worship that prevailed. It was probably about as follows:

1. Thanksgivings or "blessings" spoken in connection with (before and after), the Sh*e*ma': "Hear, O Israel, the Lord our God, the Lord is One, and you shall love the Lord your God with all your heart, and with all your soul, and with all your might"

2. Prayer, with response of "Amen" by the congregation

3. Reading of a passage from the Pentateuch (in Hebrew, followed by translation into Aramaic)

4. Reading of a passage from the Prophets (similarly translated)

5. Sermon or word of exhortation

6. The Benediction pronounced by a priest, to which the congregation

---

52 For pictures of the ruins of the second or third century Capernaum synagogue see L. H. Grollenberg, *Atlas of the Bible*, New York, etc., 1956, p. 126, plates 365-367.

53 For location see E. G. Kraeling, *Rand McNally Bible Atlas, New York, etc., 1956, p.* 251.

responded with "Amen." When no priest was present a Closing Prayer was substituted for the Benediction.

For corroboration of this Liturgy, as far as this is possible from Scripture, see the following: Num. 6:22-27; Deut. 6:4, 5; I Chron. 16:36; Neh. 5:13; 8:6; Luke 4:16-27; Acts 13:15; and I Cor. 14:16. Talmudic passages and other Jewish sources, having been written at a later date, are valuable also but cannot always be relied upon to show exactly how the services were conducted during the days of Jesus and the apostles.

"The freedom of the synagogue" implied that any person present at the service, that is, anyone who was considered suitable by the ruler (or the rulers) of the synagogue, was privileged and even encouraged to deliver the sermon. See Luke 4:16, 17; Acts 13:15. It is easy to understand that this provision made it possible for Jesus and also later on for Paul and other Christian leaders to bring the gospel to the assembled congregation. The sermon preached by Jesus in Nazareth's synagogue is summarized in Luke 4:21-27; that preached by Paul in the synagogue of Pisidian Antioch is recorded in Acts 13:16-41. That Jesus took full advantage of this privilege is clear also from Matt. 4:23; 9:35; 13:54; Mark 1:21; 6:2; Luke 4:44; 13:10; John 6:59; 18:20. So did Paul. Besides Acts 13:15 see 9:20; 13:5; 14:1; 17:1, 10, 17; 18:4, 19. And so did Apollos; see Acts 18:26. Since not only Jews but also God-fearers from the Gentile world—people who had exchanged the idolatry and immorality of paganism for Judaism—attended the synagogues in the regions where Paul, etc. performed their missionary labors, it is clear that *the synagogue was used by God as one of the most important and powerful means for the spread of the gospel among both Jews and Gentiles!*

In order to understand more fully what it meant for Jesus to preach in the synagogues of Galilee (Mark 1:39) or anywhere else, a few more facts should be added. As the existing ruins clearly indicate, synagogues faced Jerusalem; that is to say, they were so built that the speaker, while addressing the audience, and also the man who at the close of the service was leaving the synagogue, would be looking toward the Holy City. Thus, the Galilean synagogues faced south; those east of the Jordan faced west; those south of Jerusalem, north; and those to the west of it faced east.

What this meant for Jesus was that in whatever synagogue he preached he was always, while speaking, facing the place where he was going to be crucified. It was impossible for him not to be thinking of the cross![54]

---

[54] For the arrangement of the furniture, the seating of the worshipers, the position of the reader and of the speaker, etc., see illustration in *Zondervan's Pictorial Dictionary*, Grand Rapids, 1963, p. 819, with accompanying article by W. W. Wessel. W. Schrage's articles on συναγωγή etc., Th.D.N.T., Vol. VII, pp. 798-852, are also very informative. So is the excellent treatise by the New Testament scholar H. Mulder, *De Synagoge in de Nieuwtestamentische Tijd*, Kampen, 1969.

40 And a leper came up to him, on his knees begging him, "If you will, you can cleanse me." 41 So, while his heart went out to him, he [Jesus] stretched out his hand, touched him, and said to him, "I will; be cleansed." 42 At once the leprosy left him and he was cleansed. 43 And he sternly warned him and immediately sent him away. 44 "Be sure not to tell anything to anybody," he said to him, "but go, show yourself to the priest and, for a testimony to them, offer what Moses prescribed for your cleansing." 45 Instead he went out and began to publish the matter, spreading the news around so widely that he [Jesus] could not enter any town openly but stayed outside in lonely places. Yet people came to him from everywhere.

1:40-45 *A Leper Cleansed*
Cf. Matt. 8:2-4; Luke 5:12-16

40. And a leper came up to him, on his knees begging him . . . . Exactly when and where the miracle here recorded occurred is not stated anywhere. Most natural, however, is the view that it took place on the Galilean circuit to which Mark has just now referred (verse 39). In support of this consider also "Let us go elsewhere, to the next towns" (verse 38); cf. "to the other cities" (Luke 4:43), followed by the statement that the cleansing of the leper occurred while Jesus was "in one of the cities" (Luke 5:12). If this conclusion is correct, the incident probably occurred before the calling of The Twelve to the apostleship (Mark 3:13-19; Luke 6:12-16) and before the preaching of the Sermon on the Mount (Matt. 5:1—8:1; Luke 6:12-16).[55]

In connection with "And a leper came up to him" there are those who deny the correctness of the rendering "leper" and "leprosy." They maintain that not leprosy proper (Hansen's disease) but vitiligo, leucoderma, and/or other skin sicknesses are meant. On the other hand Dr. L. S. Huizenga, having received both a theological and a medical training, and basing his conclusion upon a detailed study of all the pertinent biblical material and on his own experience with lepers, states: "I believe that Moses describes a definite disease—a disease which corresponds to what we today call leprosy, though the symptoms may not be the same" (*Unclean! Unclean!*, Grand Rapids, 1927, pp. 145, 146; see his entire argument, pp. 143-147). One matter must be made perfectly clear: Jesus did not hold anybody in low esteem for being a leper, not any more than for being blind, deaf, etc. He came into the world to help, to heal, and to save. The unkind and harsh judgment of those who ascribed individual physical afflictions to the particular wickedness of the person so afflicted—as if, for example, a physical leper would of necessity also be a moral leper—was condemned by him in no uncertain terms (Luke 13:1-5; John 9:1-7).

---

55 Matt. 8:2 is not in conflict with this view. It contains no time reference. Besides, the miracles recorded in Matt. 8:2—9:34 are arranged topically, not chronologically. For a different view with respect to the time when the cleansing of the leper occurred see Lenski, *op. cit.*, p. 57.

Moreover, the healing ministry of Christ should be an encouragement to all those persons and organizations that are genuinely involved in providing help and care for those in need: deacons and deaconates, relief workers and societies, medical missionaries, nurses, voluntary helpers in hospitals, etc. From this the inference must not be drawn that the responsibility for providing help and care rests only on certain groups of specialists; no, it rests on everyone, and certainly on every believer (Prov. 19:17; Matt. 10:8; 25: 31-46; Mark 9:41; II Cor. 8:8, 9; 9:7; Gal. 6:10; Eph. 4:32—5:2; Phil. 4:17; I Tim. 5:4).[56]

This leper "came up to" Jesus, up close enough to be touched by the Master. This is remarkable, especially in view of Lev. 13:45, 46: ". . . Alone shall he dwell; outside the camp shall be his habitation." With this compare "ten lepers who stood *at a distance*" (Luke 17:12). This man must have heard enough about Christ's deeds of power coupled with sympathy to understand that here was someone who could be hopefully approached. Of course, he did not know whether the help he craved would be given even to him . . . a man "full of leprosy" (Luke 5:12). But there was nothing wrong with asking. He does this in a most humble manner: he "drops to his knees" (thus Mark), then lowers his face to the ground ("fell on his face," Luke 5:12), begging, **If you will, you can cleanse me.** According to Matt. 8:2 he even addressed Jesus as "Lord." By this he must have meant far more than "Sir." Otherwise, how could he have made the confession that he made. "You can cleanse me," he says. Of this *power* on the part of Jesus he is sure. "*If* you will." Of this *willingness* he is not sure, but he submits himself to Christ's sovereign disposition. He does, however, beg or implore that he, too, may be the recipient of Christ's healing power and mercy.

41. **So, while his heart went out to him** . . . . It is Mark alone who mentions this. Literally, the translation would have to be "having been moved in his inner being" (his "entrails"). On this active sympathy of Jesus, a compassion that expressed itself in deeds, see also Matt. 9:36; 14:14; 15:32; 18:27; 20:34; Mark 6:34; 8:2; Luke 7:13. However, it is not enough to study only such passages in which the very same verb occurs. See also passages of similar import and at times synonymous phraseology; for example, "He has taken our infirmities upon himself and carried our diseases" (Matt. 8:17; cf. Mark 2:16; 5:19, 34, 36, 43; 6:31, 37; 7:37; 9:23, 36, 37, 42; 10:14-16, 21, 43-45, 49; 11:25; 12:29-31, 34, 43, 44; 14:6-9, 22-24 (!); 16:7. Similar passages could be added from Luke and John. One stands amazed at the number of times this compassion of Jesus, this tenderness or outpouring of his heart in words and deeds of sympathy, is mentioned in the Gospels. He is constantly taking the condition of the afflicted ones "to

---

[56] See I. Van Dellen, *The Ministry of Mercy,* Grand Rapids, 1946.

heart." Living in the midst of a people who were placing all the emphasis on legal trivialities, which was true especially of the leaders, he stands out as the One whose emphasis is on "the weightier matters of the law: justice, mercy, and fidelity" (Matt. 23:23). The sorrows of the people are his own sorrows. He dearly and intensely loves the burdened ones, and is eager to help them.[57]

. . . he [Jesus] stretched out his hand, touched him, and said to him, I will; be cleansed.[58] Repeatedly and in varying phraseology the Gospels speak of the healing touch of Christ's hands. To Mark 1:41 add 7:33; cf. Matt. 8:3, 15; 9:29; 17:7; 20:34; Luke 5:13; 7:14; 22:51. Sometimes, however, the sick touched Jesus (Mark 3:10; 5:27-31; 6:56). Either way the afflicted ones were healed. Evidently in connection with such physical contact healing power issued from the Savior and was transmitted to the person in need of it (Mark 5:30; Luke 8:46). This, however, was no magic! The healing power did not originate in his fingers or his garment. It came straight from the divine and human Jesus, from his almighty will and infinitely sympathetic heart. There was healing power in that touch because he was, and is, "touched with the feeling of our infirmities" (Heb. 4:15). It should not escape the reader that according to Mark 1:41 Jesus was "moved with compassion" when he stretched out his hand and touched the leper. The leper's need and faith found an immediate response in the Savior's eagerness to help. And this readiness was one in which his power and his love embraced each other.

It is sometimes said that between the words of the leper and those of Jesus there is perfect correspondence. This is correct in the sense that the two statements do not clash but are in full harmony, revealing even a partial identity of phraseology. One could also say, however, that the words of the Lord excel mere "correspondence." To be sure, the leper's "you can cleanse me" is answered by Christ's "I can, indeed!" implied in his act of healing. But the leper's "*if* you will" is superseded by the Master's swift and splendid "I will." Here the *will* joins the *power*, and the subtraction of "if" conjoined

---

57 Here in Mark 1:41, as well as in the list of passages beginning with Matt. 9:36, the verb is σπλαγχνίζομαι, of which σπλαγχνισθείς in the passage now under study is the nom. sing. masc. aor. participle. The ancients had just as much right to speak figuratively about the entrails (heart, liver, lungs), as we have about *one* of these, namely, the heart. Paul writes, "His heart goes out to y o u " (II Cor. 7:15); "The hearts of the saints have been refreshed by you" (Philem. 7); "my very heart" (Philem. 12). See also N.T.C. on Philippians, p. 58, footnote 39.

58 καθαρίσθητι = sec. per. sing. aor. imper. passive of καθαρίζω. It is the aorist, however, not because it refers to just one act. The aorist could still be used even if a hundred acts were involved. The point is not the number of acts, whether one or many, but *the view*: what Jesus orders here is the realization of a single *fact* or *condition*. See N.T.C. on John Vol. I, p. 125, footnote 64.

with the addition of "Be cleansed" transforms a condition of hideous disease into one of hardy health.

42. At once the leprosy left him and he was cleansed. Luke 5:13 refers to the departure of the leprosy; Matt. 8:3, to the cleansing; Mark has both. The healings brought about by Jesus were complete and instantaneous.[59] Peter's mother-in-law did not have to wait until the following day to be cured of her fever. The paralytic immediately begins to walk away, carrying his pallet. The withered hand is restored at once. The demoniac, wild a moment earlier, cutting himself with sharp stones, all at once is fully cured. The same holds with respect to the woman who touched Christ's garment. Even the dead daughter of Jairus is in one moment restored to life, so that she arises and starts walking. Let the healers of today imitate this! Let them cure every illness immediately. Yes, let them even raise the dead, for if their claim to be able to do what Jesus did and what he commanded his apostles to do, is valid, they should certainly also raise the dead (Matt. 10:8). So far, however, they have not succeded in doing this.[60] In fact, they have not even succeeded in getting rid of death by denying its existence.[61]

43, 44. And he sternly warned[62] **him and immediately sent him away. Be sure not to tell anything to anybody, he said to him, but go, show yourself to the priest and, for a testimony to them, offer what Moses prescribed for your cleansing.**

The verb "sternly warned (or: charged)" is interesting. Starting, perhaps, from the idea of the snorting of an impatient horse, or simply in general from the idea of making noise in anger, it is easy to see how readily this develops into "charge or warn sternly," as here and in Matt. 9:30; and into "reproached" or "scolded." In this manner the disciples rebuked Mary of Bethany when they failed to understand that the language of love is lavishness (Mark 14:5). In John 11:33, 38 the context indicates that a very broad meaning must be assigned to the verb: Jesus "was deeply moved in the spirit."

Jesus does not want the man to publicize how and by whom he was cleansed. The reason(s) for this prohibition have not been revealed. Perhaps one reason was that the Master wanted to be known as "a bringer of good tidings," not most of all as "a miracle worker." It is, after all, *the word,* the message, which, applied to the heart by the Holy Spirit, saves. See 1:38. Also, enthusiasm about Jesus as a miracle worker could have led to a

---

59 Is this refuted by Mark 8:23-25? See on that passage.

60 On Faith Healing read W. E. Biederwolf, *Whipping Post Theology,* Grand Rapids, 1934.

61 See A. A. Hoekema, *The Four Major Cults,* Grand Rapids, 1963, p. 188.

62 ἐμβριμησάμενος, nom. sing. masc. aor. participle of ἐμβριμάομαι. The verb means *to snort* (as a horse). It is probably a sound-imitation (onomatopoeia).

premature crisis. This, too, he wishes to avoid. He is going to die for his people. But the "hour" decreed for this has not yet arrived. So, what the man was ordered to do was to go to Jerusalem and show himself to the priest. This implied that he must bring the required offering (Lev. 14:1-7). That offering consisted of two clean, living birds. One had to be killed. In its blood the other bird had to be dipped and then released. The blood of the slain bird was also sprinkled over the healed man; in fact, seven times. He was then pronounced cured. When the priests hear that it was Jesus who had so completely and instantly cured this man, they will have received an irrefutable testimony to Jesus' power and love. They will also know that even though Jesus condemns human traditions that make void God's holy law, he does not disobey that law.

45. Instead he went out and began to publish the matter, spreading the news around so widely that he [Jesus] could not enter any town openly but stayed outside in lonely places.

" . . . began to publish." Is this "began" (26 times in Mark) a redundant auxiliary? Would not its *consistent* omission spoil Mark's graphic style? Cf., however, 6:7, footnote 233.

In verse 40 we saw the leper at his best. Now, in verse 45, we see him at his worst. By this act of inexcusable disobedience he deprived many towns of the blessings that might have come their way if Jesus could have entered. Cf. Luke 11:52b. **Yet people came to him from everywhere.** The work of Jesus did not suffer complete interruption. Men are divided into two groups: *a.* those who wait until the messenger comes to them; *b.* those who go out to find and hear the one who brings the message. From all around this latter group came to Jesus.

It is not the leper on whom our main attention should be riveted. Rather, it should be bestowed upon the Benefactor, who was willing to pour an inestimable blessing upon a man so unworthy.

Summary of Chapter 1:14-45

The material under this heading may be divided as follows:

a, The beginning of the Great Galilean Ministry (1:14, 15). Between Christ's baptism and temptation, on the one hand, and his arrival in Galilee, on the other, about a year may have elapsed, spent mostly in Judea. At the end of that year his popularity had become such that remaining any longer in and around Jerusalem, the headquarters of the Jewish religious leaders, would have been inadvisable. John the Baptist had been imprisoned. Even before that had happened the crowds following Jesus were already larger than those following John. So naturally, when John was completely removed, the only Leader commanding respect was Jesus. Result: huge crowds listening to the

Master, many believing in him; increased envy among scribes, Pharisees, priests; the decision of Jesus to leave for the north, that is, for Galilee. Arrived there, "The time is fulfilled and the kingdom of God is at hand," was his message. He announced that the reign of God in the hearts and lives of men would begin to assert itself more powerfully than ever before, with great blessings in store for many, especially for those who would turn to God and believe the gospel.

b. The calling of four fishermen (verses 16-20). Going along the Sea of Galilee, Jesus calls to himself Peter and Andrew, who were fishing when they heard Jesus say to them, "Come, follow me, and I will make y o u to become fishers of men." Immediately they obeyed. So did also James and John who, at a little distance away from the others, were mending their nets. They left their father Zebedee in the boat with the hired men, and followed Jesus. All four, though already acquainted with Jesus, now start training in earnest for apostleship.

c. The healing of a man with an unclean spirit (verses 21-28). In the synagogue at Capernaum Jesus teaches. The people are amazed about the content and the method of his teaching. In the synagogue that sabbath there was a man with an unclean spirit. "Why do you bother us?" said the demon, making use of the man's vocal organs. "Have you come to destroy us?" The evil spirit seemed to fear that even now Jesus would hurl him and his fellow-demons into the place where Satan is kept. Jesus commanded the demon to leave the man. Throwing him into convulsions and causing him to shriek loudly, the demon got out of him. Reaction on the part of the synagogue audience to Christ's teaching and demon-expulsion in the synagogue: utter amazement.

Curtailing the power of Satan ("binding the strong man") and opening the hearts of men for the reception of the gospel ("mission activity") are closely connected both in the Gospels and elsewhere (for example, Rev. 20:1-3).

d. The healing of Simon's mother-in-law and of many others (verses 29-34). We find Jesus, Peter, Andrew, James, and John at Peter's home. Simon's (=Peter's) mother-in-law is laid up with a high fever. The help of the Master has been requested. Jesus "stood over her" (Luke), "touched her" (Matthew), "took her by the hand and lifted her up" (Mark). At once the fever left her so completely that she began to wait on her guests. So quickly did the report of what Jesus had done in the synagogue and immediately afterward spread that at sabbath's close people started to bring to Jesus those that were sick and/or demon-possessed. To all those many people Jesus granted deliverance from their afflictions. Yet he did not allow the demons to speak. Why not? One reason may have been that he did not want to be known chiefly as a miracle-worker. He wanted the people to take to heart his *words* even more than to be amazed by his *works*.

82

e. Christ's pre-dawn prayer, etc. (verses 35-39). After such a long, strenuous day Jesus felt the need of quiet communion with his Father. Therefore very early in the morning he left the house (Peter's? His own?) and departed to a lonely place, where he prayed. The Gospels report that Jesus prayed on many occasions, urged prayer upon his followers, and even showed them how to pray. Christ's devotions, however, were interrupted by the exclamation of Peter (and company), "Everybody is looking for you!" Peter and the others wanted to take Jesus right back to Capernaum. But Jesus refused. He wanted to distribute his favors among the people of many towns and villages. Did he perhaps also wish to impress upon the citizens of Capernaum that those who had received should now begin to give? "Let us go elsewhere, to the next towns," he said, "that I may preach there also, because for this purpose I came forth," meaning: from heaven to earth. Preaching and demon-expulsions throughout Galilee followed.

f. A leper cleansed (verses 40-45). Probably while Jesus was on the Galilean circuit mentioned by Mark in verse 39 a leper came up to him. In spite of Lev. 13:45, 46 he came close enough to be touched by Jesus. Falling on his knees he begged the Master, "If you will, you can cleanse me." Mark's Gospel reports that the heart of Jesus went out to this sorely afflicted man. The Healer said, "I will; be cleansed." At once the leprosy left him and he was completely cured. Not only that, but Jesus even saw to it that the man's standing among the public and in the religious life of Israel would be completely restored. For that purpose he sent him to Jerusalem so that he might bring the offerings stipulated by the Mosaic law, might be pronounced cured, and would then be able to take his place in society without being shunned by anyone. This very cure would bear testimony to the priesthood with reference to Christ's greatness and his obedience to the divine law. Jesus, for reasons not stated, charged the man not to broadcast what had happened to him: how and by whom he had been healed. Upon the dark background of the cleansed leper's disobedience the mercy of Jesus stands out all the more triumphantly.

Outline of Chapter 2

Theme: *The Work Which Thou Gavest Him To Do*

2:1-12   The Healing of a Paralytic
2:13-17   The Call of Levi
2:18-22   The Question About Fasting
2:23-28   The Son of Man Asserting His Authority as Lord Even of the
          Sabbath; Picking Heads of Grain on the Sabbath

CHAPTER II

2 1 When he had re-entered Capernaum some days later, it was reported that he was at home. 2 And many were gathered together, so that there was no longer any room left, not even near the doorway; and he was speaking the word to them. 3 And they came, bringing to him a paralytic, carried by four men. 4 Being unable to get to him [Jesus] because of the crowd, they opened up the roof (above the place) where he was; and when they had dug an opening they lowered the pallet on which the paralytic was lying. 5 Now when Jesus saw their faith he said to the paralytic, "Son, your sins are forgiven." 6 But some of the scribes were sitting there, and reasoning in their hearts. 7 "Why does this fellow talk like that? He's blaspheming! Who can forgive sins but God alone?" 8 And immediately Jesus, perceiving in his spirit that they were reasoning thus within themselves, said to them, "Why are y o u reasoning thus[63] in y o u r hearts? 9 Which is easier, to say to the paralytic, 'Your sins are forgiven,' or to say, 'Get up, take up your pallet and walk'? 10 But in order that y o u may know that the Son of man has authority on earth to forgive sins" (he said to the paralytic) 11 "I say to you, get up, take up your pallet and go home." 12 He got up, and immediately took up his pallet and went out in full view of them all, so that they were all astonished and glorified God, saying, "Never have we seen anything like this."

2:1-12 *The Healing of a Paralytic*
Cf. Matt. 9:2-8; Luke 5:17-26

When one compares chapter 1 of Mark's Gospel with chapter 2 the contrast is striking. Chapter 1 is the chapter of glory; chapter 2, of opposition. To be sure, even in chapter 1 Jesus encountered opposition, but this was coming from the side of Satan and his demons (1:13, 23-26, 32, 34, 39), not from the side of men. The Spirit descends on Jesus (1:10), the Father calls him "my beloved Son" (1:11), and the people are filled with amazement because of his words and works (1:27).

As far as the human realm is concerned, the description of conflict begins in chapters 2 (see especially verses 6, 7, 16, and 24) and 3 (verses 2, 6, and 22). The struggle increases in intensity. At first the scribes merely "reason in their hearts" (2:6, 7) against Jesus. Next, they complain about him to his disciples (2:16). Afterward they become bolder and protest to Jesus himself; yet not immediately because of what *he* is doing but because of what he is

---

63 Or: harboring such thoughts

allowing his disciples to do (2:24). But in the third chapter they begin to scheme how they may destroy him (verse 6), and charge him with being in league with the devil (verse 22).

Of course, the conflict could not be avoided; for he stressed love, they legalism; he God's holy law, they law-burying tradition; he freedom, they bondage; he the inner attitude, they the outward act. How they hated to surrender to him their prestige, their hold on the public!

1. **When he had re-entered Capernaum some days later,**[64] **it was reported that he was at home.** Jesus has returned from his Galilean circuit (1:38, 39). He is back in "his own city" (Matt. 9:1). He is now "at home," or, as some interpret the phrase "in a house." In this connection some think of the house where—as they assume—Jesus, his mother Mary, and other members of the family, are now living. Here, however, one must be careful not to come into conflict with Matt. 13:54-56 (cf. Luke 4:16). Does the phrase refer, perhaps, to a Capernaum home which he himself now owned? The possibility cannot be ruled out. Matt. 8:20 (" . . . the Son of man has nowhere to lay his head"; see on that passage) does not necessarily render this view unreasonable. Does it refer to *Peter's* house, an interpretation that is rather popular?[65] But if Mark had been thinking of Peter's house, would not his reference to it have been more definite? See 1:29. The possibility should be considered that friends had provided Jesus with a home for his use while performing his task in and around Capernaum. However that may have been, in some real sense the house to which Jesus had come was "home" to him. And "everybody" had heard the report that he was home, for the news had quickly spread.[66]

2. **And many were gathered together, so that there was no longer any room left, not even near the doorway . . . .** In view of the amazement caused by Christ's words and works (1:21-34, 38-45) we can understand why it was that the house was filled. No doubt friends and disciples of Jesus were

---

[64] δι ἡμερῶν = "(some) days having come between" or "(some) days having inter-vened"; hence, "after some days," "some days later." See the interesting discussion on διά in Gram. N.T., pp. 580-584. The root meaning of διά is probably δύο, two. This develops into "by twos" or "between."

[65] See Vincent Taylor *op. cit.*, p. 193; A. B. Bruce, *op. cit.*, p. 350; A. Edersheim, *The Life and Times of Jesus the Messiah*, New York, 1897, Vol. I, p. 502. On the other hand, Lenski definitely opposes this view, *op. cit.*, p. 62.

[66] It is probably best to regard ἠκούσθη ("it was reported") as the main clause, and εἰσελθών ("when he had re-entered . . .") as its modifier. As to ὅτι ἐν οἴκῳ ἐστίν there are two possibilities: *a.* to regard this as indirect discourse, though we, in such a case, would use the past tense; *b.* to regard ὅτι as being recitative; hence in English represented by quotation marks, the direct discourse being retained (it was reported, "He is at home"). For the latter possibility see A. Plummer, *The Gospel according to Matthew* (*Cambridge Greek Testament for Schools and Colleges*), Cambridge, 1914, p. 80.

present in goodly numbers, with genuine interest in the truth. Also, there must have been many "rubbernecks" burning with curiosity to hear what Jesus would say and especially what he would do. Last but not least, there were straitlaced rabbis—Pharisees and doctors of the law (Luke 5:17)—, filled with envy, deeply disturbed about the large crowds Jesus was attracting. These "important" people had come from every village not only in Galilee but even in Judea and Jerusalem! Result: not even near the doorway was there any room left. Normally it was by the doorway that entrance was obtained into the house. Only the well-to-do had an extra "gate" and entrance hall. In the more modest homes the "door" opened directly to the street. But today this entrance was blocked. And there were no fire-marshals to open a path.

. . . and he was speaking the word to them. In his own unique manner (see on 1:22) Jesus was bringing the gospel to this audience. Cf. 4:14 ff., 33; 16:20. That, after all, was the purpose of his coming from heaven to earth (Mark 1:38), namely, to bring the message of cheer, liberty, salvation full and free. Cf. Luke 4:17-22. Words of grace, clear and simple, were falling from his lips.

Suddenly, however, there is an interruption, a noise overhead: 3. **And they came, bringing to him a paralytic, carried by four men.** Wretched indeed was this man. The disease that plagued him is characterized by extreme loss of power of motion, and is generally caused by inability of the muscles to function, due to injury in the motor areas of the brain and/or of the spinal cord. In addition to the parallels in Matthew and Luke see also Matt. 4:24; 8:5-13; Acts 8:7; 9:33. In the present case whatever may have been the parts of the body affected by paralysis and the point to which the sickness had progressed, one fact is clear: the stricken person was unable to move about. He had to be carried. Four men—relatives? friends?—performed this service for him, as Mark indicates.

4. **Being unable to get to him [Jesus] because of the crowd, they opened up the roof (above the place) where he was; and when they had dug an opening they lowered the pallet on which the paralytic was lying.** The courage and resourcefulness of the five, particularly also their faith in the success of their venture, hence ultimately their trust in Jesus, must be admired. If the house where the crowd had gathered had an outside stairway, then it was by means of it that the four and their precious cargo reached the roof. If it did not but the adjoining house had one, then, having reached the top of that other house, they crossed over from roof to roof. In one way or another they reached the place directly above the spot where Jesus was addressing the people.

Now to get through the roof! This outside cover of a house was generally flat. It had beams with transverse rafters, overlaid with brushwood, tree branches, etc., on top of which was a thick blanket of mud or clay mixed with chopped straw, beaten and rolled. Such a roof was not difficult to "unroof" (the very word used in the original: "they unroofed the roof").[67]

Having made an opening in the roof, the four *lowered* the pallet on which the paralytic was lying. Cf. the manner in which Paul was *let down* over the wall at Damascus (Acts 9:25; II Cor. 11:33). The "pallet" was a kind of poor man's bed, perhaps a thin, straw-filled mattress. Since there were four men who lowered the pallet, it is probably legitimate to imagine that ropes had been attached to the four corners of the bed. Thus it was that the sick man landed right in front of Jesus. The latter, looking down, saw this patient; and glancing up, took notice of the four "friends in need" who were proving to be "friends indeed."

We do not read that the four, from their position on top of the roof, shouted anything to Jesus. Nor does any of the evangelists report that the sick man himself said anything to him. As far as the paralytic is concerned, it is even possible that, due to his condition, he was unable to speak. But though the five did not talk, they trusted! And that was what really mattered. Their confidence touched the very heart of the Lord, so that we read: 5. **Now when Jesus saw their faith he said to the paralytic, Son, your sins are forgiven.** To infer from this that *Jesus* traced the man's sickness to his sin, as is often done,[68] is unwarranted, though it is true that among the Jews the notion, "A grievously afflicted individual must have been a grievous sinner" was not unusual (Job 4:7; 22:5-10; Luke 13:4; John 9:2). For a similar belief among non-Jews see Acts 28:3, 4. As the passages from the Gospels prove, Jesus combated this error. But as to this paralytic, all we really know is that he was deeply concerned about his sin. Whether even he himself thought that his sin had resulted in his sickness is not stated. Jesus knew, however, that this man's sins—the many ways in which by means of his attitudes, thoughts, words, and deeds he had missed the mark of living in harmony with God's will—grieved him deeply. According to Matthew, Jesus very tenderly addresses this man as *son* or *child*. He said to him (according to

---

[67] When Luke's "tiles" (5:19) are misconstrued and/or are regarded as having been placed in a sturdy framework of very small squares, a difficulty is unnecessarily created. Besides, the roof opening did not have to be as long as the man was tall! By means of skillful manipulation of ropes even a sick man of average size could be gently lowered through a rather small opening. "Where there is a will, there is a way." For the construction of a roof see article "House," I.S.B.E., Vol. III, p. 1437.

[68] See Vincent Taylor, *op. cit.*, p. 195; J. Schmid, *The Gospel according to Mark* (*The Regensburg New Testament*), English tr. 1968, New York, p. 59. In his very interesting and instructive comentary, *The Gospel of Mark* (*The Daily Study Bible*), Philadelphia, 1956, pp. 40, 41, W. Barclay argues that the man's own consciousness of sin may well have brought about the paralysis. But the text does not suggest this.

all three evangelists), "Forgiven[69] are your sins" (the order of the words in the original, placing all the emphasis on forgiving love).

Not only for the paralytic was this pronouncement of pardon an inestimable blessing, it was also a source of gladness for his benefactors. They must have rejoiced in his joy. More even, it was a lesson for the entire audience. All were made aware of the fact that *this* Physician regarded spiritual blessings above material, and claimed to possess "authority"—that is, *the right* and *the power*—to heal not only the body but also the soul.

Jesus never took sin lightly. He never told people, "Do y o u have a sense of guilt? Forget about it." On the contrary, he regarded sin as inexcusable departure from God's holy law (Mark 12:29, 30), as having a soul-choking effect (4:19; cf. John 8:34), and as being a matter of the heart and not only of the outward deed (Mark 7:6, 7, 15-23. But he also offered the only true solution. He was well aware of the fact that the advice, "Get rid of your guilt feelings; a little cruelty, promiscuity, infidelity is not so bad," creates more problems than it solves. He also knew that it was entirely impossible for a person to rid his soul of the sense of guilt by trying to offset his sins by good deeds. He knew that this philosophy would lead but to tragic failure and appalling despair. Instead, he had come to proclaim—no, not only *to proclaim* but first of all *to provide*—the one and only solution, namely *forgiveness,* and this on the basis of his own atonement for sin (10:45; 14:22-24). Cf. John 1:29. When he therefore now says to the paralytic, "Forgiven are your sins," he is not only *conveying* to this man the news of God's forgiveness, as Nathan had done to penitent David (II Sam. 12:13); he is also in his own right *canceling* the paralytic's debt. He blots out his sins completely and forever. Cf. Ps. 103:12; Isa. 1:18; 55:6, 7; Jer. 31:34; Mic. 7:19; John 1:9. Moreover, such forgiveness never stands alone. It is ever "pardon *plus.*" In Christ, God dispels the invalid's gloom *and* embraces him with the arms of his protecting and adopting love. Cf. Rom. 5:1.

6, 7. But some of the scribes were sitting there, and reasoning in their hearts, Why does this fellow talk like that? He's blaspheming! Who can forgive sins but God alone? A Dutch poet has called man's guilt "the root of all human problems." A British psychologist has called man's sense of having been forgiven "the most healing force in the world." And how often have not specialists informed us that many patients could be dismissed from mental institutions if they were only able to convince themselves that their

---

[69] Whether, among the variants, one adopts ἀφίενται, the present passive indicative, both for Mark 2:5 and for Matt. 9:2, or ἀφέωνται, the perfect passive indicative (Luke 5:20), the meaning remains about the same. This man's sins are at this very moment—and have been permanently—forgiven.

guilt had been blotted out! One would think, therefore, that everybody who heard Jesus say to the paralytic, "Son, your sins are forgiven" would have rejoiced with the pardoned man. But no, in the hearts of the scribes who had come here to find fault with Jesus there was no room for participation in the joy of this grievously stricken man who at this moment heard words of encouragement and cheer. In a highly derogatory manner these enemies are saying something decidedly unfavorable. However, they are not saying it out loud, only *within their hearts.* But hearts are very important. Are they not the mainsprings of dispositions as well as of feelings and thoughts? Does not a man's heart show what kind of a person he really is? See Mark 3:5; 6:52; 7:14-23; 8:17; 11:23; 12:30, 33; Eph. 1:18; 3:17; Phil. 1:7; I Tim. 1:5. Cf. Prov. 23:7 A.V.

In their hearts, then, the scribes are carrying on a *dialogue,* throwing thoughts back and forth. What they are saying is this, "Why does this fellow talk like that? He's blaspheming." He is claiming for himself a prerogative that belongs to God alone, and is therefore guilty of blasphemy, that is, of defiant irreverence. He is robbing God of the honor that belongs to no one else, for "Who can forgive sins but God alone?"

The scribes were right in considering the remission of sins to be a divine prerogative (Exod. 34:6, 7a; Ps. 103:12; Isa. 1:18; 43:25; 44:22; 55:6, 7; Jer. 31:34; Mic. 7:19). To be sure, there is a sense in which we, too, forgive, namely, when we earnestly resolve not to take revenge but instead to love the one who has injured us, to promote his welfare, and never again to bring up the past (Matt. 6:12, 15; 18:21; Luke 6:37; Eph. 4:32; Col. 3:13). But *basically,* as described, it is God alone who forgives. It is he alone who is able to remove guilt and to declare that it has actually been removed. But now the thinking of the scribes arrives at the fork in the road, and they make the wrong turn. Either: *a.* Jesus is what by implication he claims to be, namely, God; or *b.* he blasphemes, in the sense that he unjustly claims the attributes and prerogatives of deity. The scribes accept *b.*

Not only do they commit this tragic error, but, as the following context indicates, they compound it by reasoning somewhat as follows, "It is an easy thing for him to say, 'Your sins are forgiven,' for no one is able to disprove it, since no one can look into his neighbor's heart or enter the throne-room of the Almighty and discover his judicial decisions as to who is, and who is not, forgiven. On the other hand, to tell this man, 'Get up and walk' would be far more difficult, for if no cure results, as is probable, we are all here to witness his embarrassment." As they see it, therefore, Jesus is both blasphemous and flippant.

In what the Master now says and does he annihilates both of these false conclusions: **8-11. And immediately Jesus, perceiving in his spirit that they were reasoning thus within themselves, said to them, Why are y o u reasoning** thus [or: harboring such thoughts] in y o u r hearts? Which is easier, to say to the paralytic, Your sins are forgiven, or to say, Get up, take up your pallet and walk? But in order that y o u may know that the Son of man has authority on earth to forgive sins (he said to the paralytic)[70] I say to you, get up, take up your pallet and go home. Jesus perceived in his spirit what these scribes were thinking. Their inner deliberations were not concealed from him. Cf. Matt. 17:25; John 1:47, 48; 2:25; 21:17. Had he not been God he would not have been able to penetrate so deeply into their "secret" cogitations (Ps. 139; Heb. 4:13). By means of questioning these men—"Why are y o u reasoning thus?"—he sharply reprimands them. Their "dialogue" was wicked (cf. Matt. 9:4), for they were accusing him falsely. They themselves were the evil ones. Was it not in order to find fault with Jesus that they had come here today, with the ultimate purpose that they might destroy him (cf. Mark 3:6)? Let them then examine their own hearts.

As to which was easier to say to the paralytic, "Your sins are forgiven," or "Get up, take up your pallet and walk," do not both in an equal measure require omnipotent power? Jesus decides, however, that if, as the scribes reason, a miracle in the physical sphere is required in order to prove to them his "authority" (right plus power) in the spiritual realm, then let them see this miracle!

So to the paralytic he addresses the words, "I say to you, get up, take up your pallet and go home." Obedience to this command will prove that he, the humble yet all-glorious "Son of man" has the divine authority on earth—hence, before the door of grace is closed—to forgive sins.

Here, for the first time in Mark, the term "Son of man" is found. In all it occurs fourteen times in this Gospel: twice in the beginning (2:10, 28), seven times in the middle (8:31, 38; 9:9, 12, 31; 10:33, 45), and five times toward the end (13:26; 14:21; 14:41 twice; 14:61). It is Christ's self-designation, *revealing* something with reference to him, *concealing* even more, especially to those not thoroughly acquainted with the Old Testament. Use of the term led to the question, "Who, then, is this Son of man?" (John 12:34). The term characterizes Jesus as the Sufferer, the One who is going to be betrayed and killed (9:12; 14:21, 41), all of this in accordance with the divine decree, voluntarily, and vicariously (10:45). His willing sacrifice in the place of his people will, however, be rewarded (8:31; 9:31; 10:33, 34). Put to death he rises again. Having departed from the earth, one day he returns in glory, sitting at the right hand of the Almighty (14:62), fulfilling the prophecy of

---

[70] Does not the occurrence of very similar style, including even the mid-sentence parenthesis, in both Mark 2:10 and its parallels Matt. 9:6; Luke 5:24, point in the direction of literary dependence? See the discussion of the Synoptic Problem in N.T.C. on Matthew. For 2:8 "in his spirit" see on 8:12.

Daniel 7:13, 14. So intrinsically glorious is he that this glory reaches back, as it were, through his entire life on earth. In reality he is always—even in his suffering—the glorious Son of man. While yet on earth he has the right to forgive sin (2:10) and is Lord of all, including *even* the sabbath (2:28). For more on this subject see N.T.C. on Matthew, pp. 403-407.

The glory of the Son of man is clearly evident also in the present account. Jesus had commanded the paralytic to get up, etc. Result: 12. **He got up, and immediately took up his pallet and went out in full view of them all....** The man believed that the One who ordered him to get up, take up his pallet and go home would also enable him to obey the order. So "before"—here meaning "in full view of"—all the onlookers he at once obeyed the threefold command and went home (probably right here in Capernaum?). Effect on those who had heard what Jesus said and had taken note of the glorious transformation experienced by this man: **so that they were all astonished and glorified God, saying, Never have we seen anything like this.** Mark reports the people's astonishment. Never in all their past experience have they witnessed anything similar. According to Matthew the crowd was "awe-struck." Luke relates that all were "seized with astonishment . . . and filled with awe," causing them to exclaim, "We have seen strange things today." Common to these three Gospel writers is the remark that the people glorified God: "all" (thus Mark and Luke) ascribed to God the honor and splendor due to him. This "all," as often, is very general, and does not mean that scornful and fault-finding scribes suddenly experienced a genuine change of heart and mind. That men of this type remained hostile and became more and more hardened is clear from 2:16, 24; 3:2, 6, 22. Nevertheless, the response of glorifying God was sufficiently general to warrant the use of the word "all." And no doubt among the many who did exalt him there were those upon whom Christ's words and deeds had made a lasting and saving impression. Probably there were also others, people who in their excitement uttered loud words of praise to the Most High (cf. Dan. 4:34; 6:26, 27), but whose hearts remained unreborn. See Mark 7:6.

---

13 He went out again along the seashore; and all the people kept coming to him, and he was teaching them. 14 And as he was passing by, he saw Levi, the (son) of Alphaeus, sitting at the tax-collector's booth; and he said to him, "Follow me." He got up and followed him.

15 And as he was reclining at table in his [Levi's] house, many tax-collectors and sinners[71] were reclining with Jesus and his disciples; for there were many, and they were beginning to follow him. 16 And when the scribes who were Pharisees saw that he was eating with the sinners and tax-collectors, they said to his disciples, "Why does he eat with tax-collectors and sinners?" 17 Hearing this, Jesus said to them, "It is not those who are healthy that need a doctor, but those who are ill; I did not come to call righteous people but sinners."

---

71 Or: people of low reputation; and so throughout the Gospels. See the explanation.

2:13-17 *The Call of Levi*
Cf. Matt. 9:9-13; Luke 5:27-32

As Matt. 9:9 indicates, the healing of the paralytic was followed closely by the calling of the publican, Levi. **13. He went out again along the seashore; and all the people kept coming to him, and he was teaching them.** Again, as before when he had called the first four disciples (1:16), Jesus was walking along the Sea of Galilee. It is not surprising that out of an uncomfortably crowded house (2:2) the Master made his way to the pleasant and refreshing breezes of the shore. But as soon as the people knew where he was they started to gather around him again, and this process of gravitation toward Jesus continued for some time. He, in turn, did not ask them to leave but started to teach them, and is here pictured in the act of thus addressing them. The scene somewhat reminds us of the one described in 6:30-34. There, too, Jesus, seeking rest and refreshment for himself and his disciples, leaves the multitudes behind, only to find them regathered at the retreat he had selected. A *crowd*—or even a *person* (7:24)—in need always aroused Christ's sympathy. See Matt. 9:36. When Jesus had finished his teaching he resumed his walk along the shore. **14. And as he passed by, he saw Levi, the (son) of Alphaeus, sitting at the tax-collector's booth; and he said to him, Follow me. He got up and followed him.** Mark and Luke call this man Levi—for explanation of the name see Gen. 29:34—, but he calls himself Matthew (Matt. 9:9 ff.), meaning "gift of Jehovah." When was his name changed from Levi to Matthew? Did Jesus give him this new name when the tax-collector became a disciple, as the Lord had also changed Simon's name to Cephas (=Peter) when the latter joined the group (Mark 3:16; John 1:42)? It is, however, possible that from the beginning the man here described as becoming a disciple had two names, as may also have been true with respect to Thomas (John 11:16) and Bartholomew (Matt. 10:3; Mark 3:18; Luke 6:14; Acts 1:13; cf. John 1:45-49; 21:2).

The identity of Levi and Matthew can hardly be questioned, as a comparison of the three Synoptic accounts of this event proves. Moreover, Luke calls Levi a "publican" (5:27), and in the list of The Twelve as recorded in Matt. 10:3 there is mention of "Matthew the publican."

Levi's father's name was Alphaeus, not to be confused (as is sometimes done) with the man by the same name who was the father of James the Less and of Joses (Mark 3:18; cf. 15:40). If Levi or Matthew had had a brother who was also one of The Twelve, this fact would probably have been mentioned, as it was in the case of Peter and Andrew, and of James and John.

When Jesus, proceeding along the shore, saw Levi, the latter was sitting at (i.e., in or near the entrance of) the tax-collector's booth, the place where the tariff was collected on any merchandise that passed along the international highway between Syria and Egypt.

Levi, then, was a tax-collector or "publican." To gather the *public* revenue on exports and imports pertaining to a province, certain Romans, generally of equestrian rank, would pay a large sum of money into the Roman treasury. These "farmer-generals," as they have been called, were accustomed to sublet the privilege to district "chief publicans," like Zacchaeus (Luke 19:2), who then, in turn, appointed lower rank "publicans" to do the actual collecting. The term "publican," probably at first the equivalent of farmer-general, began to be used in a secondary sense to indicate tax collectors of whatever rank. In this part of the Roman empire the main tax booths were located at Caesarea, Capernaum, and Jericho.

Publicans generally charged whatever the traffic would bear, huge amounts. They acquired the reputation of being *extortionists*. In addition, Jewish publicans were regarded by other Jews as being *traitors,* unfaithful to their own people and to their own religion. Were they not in the service of the foreign oppressor, ultimately in the service of the pagan Roman emperor? Were they not filling his coffers? The low esteem in which publicans were held appears from passages such as the following: Mark 2:15, 16; cf. Matt. 9:10, 11; 11:19; 21:31, 32; Luke 5:30, 7:34; 15:1; 19:7. "Publicans" and "sinners" are at times mentioned in one breath. Yet it was to such a hated individual, such a *publican,* that Jesus now turns, in order to make him one of his disciples.

It should be borne in mind that by this time Jesus had already gathered around him the following disciples: Simon and Andrew, James and John (1:16-20); and according to John's Gospel also Philip and Nathanael (1:35-51). Whether or not any others had been called is not indicated. If not, then Levi (=Matthew) was Christ's seventh disciple. The calling of The Twelve as a group occurred a little later (cf. Mark 2:13, 14 with 3:13-19; Luke 5:27, 28 with 6:12-16), shortly before the delivery of the Sermon on the Mount (Luke 6:17-49), a sermon which Matthew, not following a chronological order, records in chapters 5—7.

When Jesus said, "Follow me," Levi immediately got up and followed him. In Matthew's own Gospel, as well as in Mark, the decisive and immediate obedience of the tax-collector is thus soberly reported. For more detail, with emphasis on the greatness of the sacrifice, we must turn to Luke 5:28, which informs us that Matthew "forsook all." He left his lucrative business and trusted that God would provide for his needs. It is clear that in doing so, his sacrifice was even greater than that of the four men mentioned in Mark 1:16-20. At this stage it was not impossible for Simon and Andrew, James and John to do a little fishing now and then. Matthew's sacrifice, on the other hand, was total.

His eagerness to join Jesus and his generosity are also clear from the fact that in his house he proved the sincerity of his act by honoring Jesus with a banquet.

In summary, Levi is described in the Synoptics as follows: He was:

M atthew, a Jewish tax-collector, in the service of Rome; and as such

A bhorred by the Jews, especially by the scribes. Nevertheless, he was

T rained in the Old Testament, which he quotes very often. He was also

T alented, an inspired writer, acquainted with Hebrew, Aramaic, and Greek;

H umble and **H** ospitable; see especially Luke 5:28, 29;

E cumenical, in the sense of Matt. 28:19, reflecting Christ's mind; and

W illing, ready, and eager to obey the Master's call.

It is in Levi's house that Mark pictures Jesus as a guest: **15. And as he was reclining at table in his [Levi's] house, many tax-collectors and sinners were reclining with Jesus and his disciples; for there were many, and they were beginning to follow him.** That it was indeed Levi who gave the banquet in his house is clear from Luke 5:29. It was in that house that "he," namely Jesus—the immediate antecedent ("followed *him*") at the close of verse 14 refers to no one else—was reclining at table, and that many tax collectors and sinners were reclining with the Master and his disciples. They were "reclining" on mattresses, couches, or divans around low tables, and resting on the left elbow, as was customary at least at festive occasions. Cf. Mark 6:26; 14:18; 16:14; and see N.T.C. on John 13:23.

Tax-collectors and sinners![72] As the Pharisees saw it, a "sinner" was one who refused to subject himself to *the Pharisaic interpretation* of God's holy law, the Torah. In that sense even Jesus himself and his disciples were sinners, that is, sinners as the Pharisees understood the term; for in several respects—not rinsing the hands before every meal, not observing various man-made sabbath regulations, based on sophistical reasoning—neither the Master nor his followers conducted themselves in accordance with the rabbinical interpretation of the law. In fact, we are not far from expressing the truth when we say that in the eyes of the Pharisees all non-Pharisees were "sinners": "But this rabble that does not know the law, accursed are they" (John 7:49). Actually, therefore, the man who by the Pharisees was called a "sinner" might be an individual upon whom God's favor rested, a true disciple of the Lord Jesus Christ.

However, here we must be very careful. The term as used in the Gospels must not be interpreted too favorably, as if all these "sinners" who were reclining with Jesus in Matthew's house were "saints" (in the sense of exceptionally virtuous people). Quite the contrary would probably be nearer to the truth. Not only the rabbinical interpretation of God's law but even

---

[72] On ἁμαρτωλός see K. H. Rengstorf, Th.D.N.T., Vol. I, p. 328.

that divine law itself was often grossly violated by these tax-collectors and sinners. Jesus does not justify or even condone their manner of life. He regards them as the sick who have to be healed (verse 17), as the lost who must be found (Luke 15:1-4; 19:10). He had come from heaven to deliver these people from their sins and miseries. Matthew understands this and honors Jesus with a banquet. He hopes, of course, that all of the despised tax-collectors and sinners will also, like himself, become the Lord's spiritual followers.

Although there are divergent explanations of the words at the close of verse 15, yet when they are read in the light of the context the true explanation does not appear to the present author to be very difficult. The key to the meaning is in all probability the repetition of the word "many." Note: ". . . *many* tax-collectors and sinners were reclining with Jesus and his disciples; for there were *many*, and they were beginning to follow him." The second *many* is probably resumptive, and means that "they, the publicans, and generally the people who passed for sinners, were many, and that they had begun to follow him" (Bruce). The word "for" can then be explained in this way: "It may seem strange that many tax-collectors and sinners, despised people, would be reclining at table with Jesus; nevertheless, it is the truth: they were reclining with him *because* they had begun to see in him a Friend (cf. Matt. 11:19; Luke 7:34), One whom they were beginning to follow."[73]

Continued: **16. And when the scribes who were Pharisees saw that he was eating with the sinners and tax-collectors, they said to his disciples, Why does he eat with tax-collectors and sinners?** Just as not every priest was a Sadducee (see on John 1:24), so also not every scribe was a Pharisee. Cf. Luke 5:30, "*their* scribes"; but in the present case we are definitely told that the critics were scribes by profession and belonged to the religious sect of the Pharisees.[74]

---

[73] The punctuation of the text—see Grk. N.T. (A-B-M-W)—so that καὶ ἠκολούθουν αὐτῷ has as its subject καὶ οἱ γραμματεῖς κτλ, yields a highly improbable sense, as if these enemies of Jesus were present at this banquet, and were following or beginning to follow Jesus! Vincent Taylor is right in rejecting this construction. If, thus construed, "following Jesus" is then interpreted favorably, a conflict with verse 16 results; if unfavorably, the answer would be that in about a score of instances in which ἀκολευθέω is used in Mark's Gospel it is never elsewhere used in any other than a favorable sense.

On the other hand, it seems to me that Taylor's own view—shared by Bolkestein, Groenewald, Van Leeuwen, in their respective commentaries—, namely, that the second "many" refers to the disciples of Jesus, as if Mark were calling the readers' attention to the fact that by this time Jesus had other disciples besides those already mentioned in 1:16-20, fails to do justice to the repetition of the word "many." In summary, I endorse the sentence structure and interpretation as found in such translations as the following: Berkeley Version, Phillips, Williams, N.A.S.; and in, among others, the following commentaries: Barclay, Bruce, Erdman, Cole. See Bibliography for titles.

[74] On Pharisees and Sadducees, their origin, mutual opposition, and co-operation against Jesus, see N.T.C. on Matthew, pp. 201-203.

In all probability it was when the banquet had ended and the guests were departing that these Pharisaic scribes, ever ready and eager to find fault with Jesus, but at times lacking courage to criticize him directly, approached his disciples with the question,[75] "Why does he eat with tax-collectors and sinners?" Does not eating with a person imply sweet fellowship? See N.T.C. on Matt. 8:11. And had not the rabbis laid down the rule, "The disciples of the learned shall not recline at table in the company of the *'am hā-'āreç*"? The term *'am hā-'āreç* was used by them to indicate "the people of the soil," "the rabble that does not know the law." See John 7:49.

What the critics, because of their unsympathetic, self-righteous attitude (Luke 18:9), failed to understand was that there are times when fellowship with publicans and sinners is entirely proper, so altogether right that lack of such fellowship would be highly improper. Jesus, by associating with these people of bad reputation, was meeting a need, as he himself now declares: **17. Hearing this, Jesus said to them, It is not those who are healthy that need a doctor, but those who are ill.** The criticism of the scribes had been duly noted by Jesus. He himself, by means of what may have been a current proverb, flings back a clinching answer. When he associates on intimate terms with people of low reputation he does not do this as a hobnobber, a comrade in evil, "birds of a feather flocking together," but as a physician, one who, without in any way becoming contaminated with the diseases of his patients, must get very close to them *in order that he may heal them!* Moreover, it is especially the Pharisees who should be able to understand this. Are not they the very people who regard themselves as being healthy, and all others as being sick? If, then, in the eyes of the Pharisees, publicans and sinners are so very sick, should they not be healed? Is it the business of the healer to heal the healthy or the sick? The sick, of course.

Jesus adds: **I did not come to call righteous people but sinners.** Substantially this is the reading also in Matthew and Luke, though in Matthew these words are preceded by a quotation from Hos. 6:6, and prefixed by "for"; while Luke adds the phrase "(sinners) to repentance."

The passage makes clear that the invitation to salvation, full and free, is extended not to "righteous people," that is, not to those who consider themselves worthy, but rather to those who are unworthy and in desperate need. It was sinners, the lost, the straying, the beggars, the burdened ones, the hungry and thirsty, whom Jesus came to save. See also Matt. 5:6; 11:28-30; 22:9, 10; Luke 14:21-23; ch. 15; 19:10; John 7:37, 38. This is in line with all of special revelation, both the Old Testament and the New (Isa. 1:18; 45:22; 55:1, 6, 7; Jer. 35:15; Ezek. 18:23; 33:11; Hos. 6:1; 11:8; Rom. 8:23, 24; II Cor. 5:20; I Tim. 1:15; Rev. 3:20; 22:17). It is a message full of comfort and "relevant" to every age!

---

[75] Here ὅτι is probably an ellipse for τί ὅτι; hence, "what (is it) that?" and so "why?" Cf. Matt. 9:11 and Luke 5:30 which have διὰ τί, that is, "because of what?" or "why?"

18 Now John's disciples and the Pharisees were fasting. And they[76] came and said to him [Jesus], "Why do John's disciples and the disciples of the Pharisees fast, but your disciples do not fast?[77]   19 Jesus said to them, "While the bridegroom is with them, is it possible for the bridegroom's attendants to be fasting? So long as they have the bridegroom with them they cannot fast.   20 But days will arrive when the bridegroom shall be taken away from them; then, on that day, they shall fast.   21 No one sews a patch, made of a piece of new cloth, on an old garment; otherwise the patch pulls away from it, the new from the old, and a worse tear results.   22 And no one pours new wine into old wine-skins—otherwise the wine will burst the skins; the wine is lost and so (are) the skins—but new wine (is poured) into fresh wine-skins.

2:18-22 *The Question About Fasting*
Cf. Matt. 9:14-17; Luke 5:33-39

18. Now John's disciples and the Pharisees were fasting. Mark's story lacks any specific reference to time or chronological order.[78] This is true both for the beginning and the close of his account. As to Matthew, it is not at all certain that the word "then" links this story with the immediately preceding, as if the two events—Matthew's banquet and the enquiry concerning fasting—followed each other in *immediate* succession.[79] Luke's conjunction "And" (5:33) is no more definite than Matthew's "then." There is, however, one clear chronological note. It is found in Matt. 9:18: "While he was still saying these things, look, a ruler came. . . ." The probability is that while Matthew's call and banquet took place *before* the choosing of The Twleve and the delivery of the Sermon on the Mount (see Mark 3:13-19; Luke 6:12-49), the question about fasting—followed shortly by the double miracle recorded in Mark 5:25-43—occurred *afterward,* that is, after that choosing, etc.

The law of God suggests only one fast in an entire year, namely, on the day of atonement (Lev. 16:29-34; 23:26-32; Num. 29:7-11; cf. Acts 27:9). In course of time, however, fasts (not always total; see the text in each instance) began to multiply, so that we read about their occurrence at other times also: from sunrise to sunset (Judg. 20:26; I Sam. 14:24; II Sam. 1:12; 3:35); for seven days (I Sam. 31:13); three weeks (Dan. 10:3); forty days (Exod. 34:2, 28; Deut. 9:9, 18; I Kings 19:8); in the fifth and seventh

---

76 Or: And some people
77 Or: "Why are John's disciples and the disciples of the Pharisees fasting, but your disciples are not fasting?"
78 Cf. N. B. Stonehouse, *Origins of the Synoptic Gospels,* Grand Rapids, 1963, p. 66.
79 Matthew uses the adverb of time τότε about ninety times. However, even when, as often, it indicates chronological succession, this does not always necessarily mean *immediate* succession. "Then" = afterward, but indefinite as to exact time (Matt. 3:13; 12:22); "then" = immediately afterward, thereupon (Matt. 2:7; John 13:27). For other uses see any good Lexicon; example, L.N.T. (A. and G.), p. 831.

month (Zech. 7:3-5); and even in the fourth, fifth, seventh, and tenth month (Zech. 8:19). The climax was the observance of a fast "twice a week,"[80] the boast of the Pharisee (Luke 18:12).

It is not surprising therefore that for some reason or other the Pharisees were once again keeping a fast. Their manner of fasting—looking glum, making their faces unsightly in order that everybody might see that they were fasting—was roundly condemned by Jesus (Matt. 6:16).

But why were the disciples of John also fasting? Various reasons have been suggested. John had probably made his first public appearance in the summer of the year A.D. 26. About the close of the year 27 he had been imprisoned. Jesus may have preached the Sermon on the Mount sometime during the spring to mid-summer of the year 28. Not long afterward—perhaps near the beginning of the year 29—John was put to death. It is therefore not impossible that the fasting of John's disciples was essentially a mourning for their master, whether for his imprisonment or for his death. It is not necessary to believe that the Pharisees and John's disciples were fasting for the same reason. But the opposite possibility—that both groups were indeed fasting for the same reason—must also be granted. It must be borne in mind that John was in a sense an ascetic (Matt. 11:18; Luke 7:33). He emphasized sin and the necessity of turning away from it. It is not inconceivable, therefore, that he may have encouraged fasting as an expression of mourning for sin, the very reason which the Pharisees probably also gave for much of their fasting (cf. Matt. 6:16).

And they came and said to him [Jesus], Why do John's disciples and the disciples of the Pharisees fast, but your disciples do not fast? As to "And they came," the question is, "To what group does the pronoun 'they' (implied in the Greek verb) refer?" Luke 5:33 is as indefinite as is Mark 2:18. In either case "And some people" might be subsituted for "And they." If a definite antecedent is indicated, then in Mark 2:18 it would be "the scribes who were Pharisees" (literally "the scribes of the Pharisees") of verse 16; and in Luke 5:33, "the Pharisees and their scribes" of verse 30. However, it is very questionable whether in either case we are dealing with a contextual antecedent. On the other hand, Matt. 9:14 clearly states that the questioners were "the disciples of John." Since not only they but also the Pharisees were fasting at this time, it is conceivable that the group of *enquirers* also included Pharisees.

With respect to those of whom it is predicated that they were fasting, the reference to "John's disciples" presents no further important difficulty. Even after John's imprisonment his disciples continued as a separate group, one that distinguished itself from the followers of Jesus. There was, however,

---

[80] On Mondays and Thursdays, according to *Didache* VIII.1.

a relation of friendship and co-operation between the two groups, as is clear from such passages as Matt. 11:2, 3; 14:12, and probably even from the passage now under study, Mark 2:18. A difficulty arises, however, in connection with the phrase "the disciples of the Pharisees" (see also Luke 5:33). Considered as a group "Pharisees" were not technically teachers, hence had no disciples. However, the difficulty may be more apparent than real. Mark, in writing "disciples of the Pharisees," may well have had in mind disciples of "the scribes who were Pharisees," as in 2:16. The main point is that John's disciples and presumably the disciples of these Pharisaic scribes were fasting, in harmony with the teaching and/or example of their leaders. Matt. 9:14 states that the Pharisees fasted "often." On the other hand, Christ's disciples did not join in observing these fasts. This striking contrast gave rise to the question.

In favor of these enquirers it must be said that they did not bypass Jesus but approached him directly and frankly. Also, their question, though perhaps not entirely free from a tinge of criticism, was probably rather an honest request for information than a veiled but bitter accusation.

In reality, however, there was no justification for this question. Had these men been better students of Scripture they would have known *a.* that, as has been indicated, the only fast that could by any stretch of the imagination be derived from the law of God was the one on the day of atonement, and *b.* that according to the teaching of Isa. 58:6, 7 and Zech. 7:1-10 it was not a literal fast but love, both vertical and horizontal, which God demanded.

19. Jesus said to them, While the bridegroom is with them, is it possible for the bridegroom's attendants to be fasting? In all three synoptics the question is so phrased that the answer must be "No." Mark, however, makes that answer explicit by reporting that Jesus continued: **So long as they have the bridegroom with them they cannot fast.** Jesus here compares his blessed presence on earth with a wedding-feast. Again and again Scripture compares the relationship between Jehovah and his people, or between Christ and his church, with the bond of love between bridegroom and bride (Isa. 50:1 ff.; 54:1 ff.; 62:5; Jer. 2:32; 31:32; Hos. 2:1 ff.; Matt. 25:1 ff.; John 3:29; II Cor. 11:2; Eph. 5:32; Rev. 19:7; 21:9). Verse 19 speaks about "the sons of the bridal chamber" (thus literally), meaning "the bridegroom's attendants." These were friends of the groom. They stood close to him. They had been invited to the wedding, were in charge of arrangements, and were expected to do everything possible to promote the success of the festivities.

Bridegroom's attendants fasting while the feast is in progress! How absurd, says Jesus as it were. Disciples of the Lord mourning while their Master is performing works of mercy and while words of life and beauty are dropping from his lips, how utterly incongruous!

Jesus adds, however, **20. But days will arrive when the bridegroom shall** be taken away from them; then, on that day, they shall fast. This is an early prediction of Christ's death on the cross. The prediction that the bridegroom, Christ, *shall be taken away* is found also in the parallels (Matt. 9:15; Luke 5:35). It strongly reminds one of Isa. 53:8, "By oppression and judgment he was taken away." It is remarkable how often in the Gospels *Jesus himself* quotes from (or at least alludes to passages from) Isaiah. Among the well-known are those found in Matt. 11:5 (cf. Isa. 35:5, 6); Luke 4:18, 19 (cf. Isa. 61:1, 2); and 22:37 (cf. Isa. 53:12).[81] In the Gospel according to Mark see also

Mark	cf.	*Isaiah*
4:12		6:9, 10
7:6, 7		29:13
11:17		56:7
12:1		5:1, 2
13:8		19:2
13:24, 25		13:10; 34:4

The present passage (Mark 2:20) is not even the only one containing at least an allusion to Isa. 53. See also Mark 9:12; cf. Isa. 53:3; and Mark 15:4, 5; cf. Isa. 53:7. Isaiah's expression "shall be taken away," and this "by oppression and judgment," refers, of course, to a violent death; note context: "He was oppressed . . . led to the slaughter . . . cut off (cf. Dan. 9:26) out of the land of the living." It is natural to assume that here in Mark the meaning is similar.

With reference to "days will arrive," followed by Mark's very striking "on that day" (contrast Luke's less definite "in those days" and Matthew's complete omission of anything similar), Jesus is saying that his approaching violent death will mean days of mourning for his disciples. Then, at that particular time ("on that day"), fasting as an expression of sorrow would be in order and would occur. That the mourning would not be of long duration is pointed out in John 16:16-22.

The important truth which Jesus here reveals and which makes the passage so practical and filled with comfort especially also for today is that for those who acknowledge Christ as their Lord and Savior the proper attitude of heart and mind is not that of sadness but that of gladness. If it be true that "God *with* us" (Immanuel) spells joy for believers, should not "God *within* us" (the situation on and after Pentecost) awaken in every child of God joy unspeakable and full of glory? It was in order to bring such abounding joy

---

[81] Well-known is also the virgin birth passage (Matt. 1:23; cf. Isa. 7:14; 8:8) but that is *Matthew's* quotation, not Christ's.

that Jesus came on earth and that he, through his sacrificial death, brought salvation full and free. See Luke 2:10: "good tidings of great joy"; 24:52: "they . . . returned to Jerusalem with great joy"; John 15:11: "that y o u r joy may be full"; 17:13: "that they may have my joy made full in themselves." The apostles learned that lesson (Rom. 5:11; 15:13; Gal. 5:22; Philippians, the entire epistle; I Peter 1:8; 4:13; I John 1:4; II John 12).

By two illustrations taken from daily life Jesus makes clear how inappropriate it would be for the disciples *now* to be fasting, as if with the coming of Christ a great calamity had descended upon them. The main lesson conveyed is that the new order of things which Jesus by his coming has ushered in, bringing healing to the sick, liberation to the demon-possessed, freedom from care to the care-ridden, cleansing to lepers, food to the hungry, restoration to the handicapped, and above all salvation to those lost in sin, does not fit into the old mold of man-ordained fasting. The first figure is as follows: **21. No one sews**[82] **a patch,**[83] **made of a piece of new**[84] **cloth,**[85] **on an old garment; otherwise the patch pulls away from it, the new from the old, and a worse tear results.** If a patch of unfulled wool or undressed cloth is placed on a garment that has seen better days, the result will be that, especially when this unshrunk piece becomes wet and shrinks, the bordering cloth of the badly worn piece of clothing will be pulled to pieces. "The new—strong, fresh—will pull away from the old," says Mark, and a worse rent results. The patch that was supposed to solve a problem creates a bigger problem.

The second figure reinforces the first: **22. And no one pours new wine into old wineskins—otherwise the wine will burst the skins; the wine is lost and so (are) the skins—but new wine (is poured) into fresh wineskins.** What Jesus means is that the salvation which he was bringing was out of line with joyless fastings. Old wineskins are no match for new, still fermenting, wine. Such wine would burst the skins, resulting in the loss of both skins and wine. Similarly the new wine of rescue and riches for all who are willing to accept these blessings, even for publicans and sinners, must be poured into new, that is, fresh, strong[86] wineskins of gratitude, freedom, and spontaneous service to the glory of God.

---

82 Mark writes ἐπεράπτει, "sews on," where Matthew and Luke have "puts on." Mark's word basically means *to stitch on.* Cf. "rhapsodist," one who strings or stitches songs together, a reciter of epic poetry.

83 In Greek the word ἐπίβλημα, *something put on,* hence, "patch," could also have the meaning bedspread, coat, robe, bandage, etc. For "robe" see Isa. 3:22 LXX.

84 The basic verb is κνάπτω, to card or comb wool, to full or dress cloth. Hence ἄγναφος (here ἀγνάφου, gen. sing.) means: not fulled, unsized, hence "new."

85 The word ῥάκος (here ῥάκους, gen. sing.) indicates a piece of cloth. At times it refers to a "rag," (cf. Jer. 38:11 = LXX 45:11), but the sound similarity between the Greek and the English word is purely accidental, has no etymological significance.

86 Note that both here and in the preceding verse ("the new from the old") the

23 Once, on a sabbath, when he [Jesus] happened to be passing through the fields of standing grain, his disciples began, as they went, to pick the heads of grain. 24 The Pharisees said to him, "See here, why are they doing what is not permitted on the sabbath?" 25 He said to them, "Have y o u never read what David did when he was in need, and he and those with him were hungry: 26 how, in the days of Abiathar the highpriest, he entered the house of God and ate the consecrated bread, which only the priests were allowed to eat, and also gave (some) to those who were with him?" 27 And he said to them, "The sabbath was made for man, not man for the sabbath. 28 Consequently, the Son of man is Lord even of the sabbath."

2:23-28 The Son of Man Asserting His Authority as Lord Even of the Sabbath, Picking Heads of Grain on the Sabbath Cf. Matt. 12:1-8; Luke 6:1-5

As has been indicated, Matthew's Gospel clearly states that the question with respect to fasting was followed by a double miracle: a. the revival to life of the ruler's daughter, and b. the healing of the woman who touched Christ's garment. Mark and Luke, having reported the enquiry concerning fasting, now as it were turn the clock back and relate two sabbath controversies. In all three Synoptics the two stories—a. on a sabbath plucking grain, and b. on another sabbath healing the man with the "withered" hand—are told in immediate succession.[87] Since neither Mark nor Luke indicates any chronological connection between the question concerning fasting and the story concerning the plucking of grain on the sabbath there is obviously no chronological conflict.

As to exactly when the sabbath controversies occurred, much remains uncertain. The four Gospels contain three of these narratives, recording events that may have been rather closely connected with respect to the time when they occurred. Worthy of consideration (first see John 5:1, 16; then Matt. 12:1; finally, Luke 6:11, 12) is the theory that the three took place in rather close succession during the spring to mid-summer of the year A.D. 28. I suggest that they may have followed each other in this order: a. the healing at the pool, about the time of the Passover (John 5:1-18), b. picking heads of grain (Matt. 12:1-8; Mark 2:23-28; Luke 6:1-5), and c. the healing of the man with the withered hand (Matt. 12:9-14; Mark 3:1-6; Luke 6:6-11). The last of these three controversies seems to have been followed by the choosing of The Twelve and the preaching of the Sermon on the Mount (see Luke 6:11-49; cf. Mark 3:6, 13-19).

---

original uses the adjective καινός, "new" with emphasis on quality; in contrast with νέος (as in "new wine"), "new" in respect of time.

[87] Mark's chapter division at this point (between 2:28 and 3:1) is unfortunate. Neither Matthew (12:1-14) nor Luke (6:1-11) have had this strange separation of that which belongs together superimposed upon them.

23. Once, on a sabbath, when he [Jesus] happened to be passing[88] through the fields of standing grain, his disciples began, as they went, to pick the heads of grain. Although no *chronological* connection between this and the immediately preceding paragraphs is indicated, Mark may well have had in mind a *logical* connection. He has just now described Jesus as emphasizing that those who are living in his very presence should be feasting instead of fasting, rejoicing rather than mourning. The evangelist now proceeds to picture the Master in the act of showing that this manifestation of gladness instead of sadness should characterize even the manner in which the sabbath is observed.

Grain was evidently ripening. This process, varying with the altitude, occurred during a period extending from the spring of the year until mid-summer. In Palestine's warm Jordan Valley barley ripens during April; in Transjordan and the region east of the Sea of Galilee wheat is harvested in August. *Exactly* when it was that Jesus and his disciples went through the fields of standing grain is not stated in the text. The place is even more indefinite than the time. A. T. Robertson's suggestion that the event took place "probably in Galilee on the way back from Jerusalem" may be as good a guess as any.[89] But it is no more than a conjecture.

The translation "fields of standing grain" leans heavily upon the context for its justification. Literally and etymologically the reference is simply to "that which was sown." However, the context shows that when the trip on a path through the grain fields occurred, harvest time had arrived or was soon to arrive.

Matthew reports that the disciples were hungry (12:1). What they did to relieve this hunger is reported variously in the Synoptics. Mark merely states that, in going through the fields, these men started to pick[90] the heads of grain. Matthew adds, "and to eat them." This eating is also implied in Mark 2:26. Luke, more complete on this point than either of the others, has, "His disciples began picking and eating the heads of grain, rubbing them with their hands." What they were doing was entirely legitimate. As long as the traveler did not thrust a sickle into a man's standing grain he was permitted to pick the heads or ears (Deut. 23:25).

Nevertheless, on the part of those who hated Christ and were trying to find some excuse for having him condemned there was an immediate adverse reaction, as is shown in verse 24. **The Pharisees said to him, See here, why are they doing what is not permitted on the sabbath?** The Greek particle,

---

88 For ἐγένετο αὐτὸν παραπορεύεσθαι (see L.N.T. (A. and G.), p. 158, first column, under 3 e.

89 *Harmony of the Gospels*, New York, 1930, p. 44.

90 The participle τίλλοντες expresses the main idea.

which must be rendered variously, according to the context in each case,[91] in the present instance expresses shocked disapproval of an action which, as the Pharisees see it, calls for immediate correction; hence "See here," or "Now look." In both Mark and Luke the Pharisees ask a question. In Luke 6:2 this question is addressed to the disciples themselves: "Why are y o u doing what is not permitted on the sabbath?" In Mark it is addressed to Jesus, "Why are *they* doing. . . ?" In both cases the question clearly implies a charge, an accusation. What is implied in Mark and Luke is plainly stated in Matt. 12:2, where the question form has been dropped and the Pharisees are reported to have made the bald statement, "Your disciples are doing what is not permitted on the sabbath." Since both Jesus and the disciples were certainly involved—the disciples were plucking the heads of grain, and Jesus approved of what they were doing—there is no real discrepancy here. The criticism directed against one, namely, Jesus, was also directed against the entire group.

The underlying reasoning of the Pharisees was as follows: Was not work forbidden on the sabbath day (Exod. 20:8-11; 34:21; Deut. 5:12-15)? Had not the rabbis drawn up a catalogue of thirty-nine principal works, subsequently subdivided into six minor categories under each of these thirty-nine, all of which were forbidden on the sabbath? In accordance with this list was not plucking heads of grain *reaping?*[92] And here were these disciples engaged in this forbidden activity, and Jesus was doing nothing about it! Obviously, what was happening was that Christ's enemies were burying the real law of God—which did not in any sense forbid what the disciples were now doing—under the mountain of their man-made, foolish traditions (Mark 7:8, 9, 12, 13; cf. Matt. 15:3, 6; 23:23, 24).

25, 26. He said to them, Have y o u never read what David did when he was in need, and he and those with him were hungry: how, in the days of Abiathar the highpriest, he entered the house of God and ate the consecrated bread, which only the priests were allowed to eat, and also gave (some) to those who were with him? "Have y o u never read?" As if to say, "Y o u pride yourselves in being the very people who uphold the law, and y o u r scribes deem themselves to be so thoroughly versed in it as to be able to teach others; yet are y o u yourselves unacquainted with the fact that even this very law allowed its ceremonial restrictions to be ignored in case of need [note: "what David did *when he was in need,*" the words in italics occurring

---

[91] Ἴδε calls special attention to whatever it introduces. The translation cannot always be the same, but must be determined by the context in each separate case; thus 2:24: see here; 3:34; 11:21; 16:6: here is (are); 13:1, 21: look!; 15:35: listen!; 15:4: you hear.

[92] See Shabbath 7:2, 4; S.BK., Vol. I, pp. 615-618; and A. T. Robertson, *The Pharisees and Jesus*, New York, 1920, pp. 87, 88.

only in Mark]? Have y o u not read about David and the showbread?" The reference is to consecrated bread, "bread of the Presence," in Hebrew *leḥ em happānîm* (Exod. 25:30), translated literally and accurately in Luke 6:4. This showbread consisted of twelve loaves placed on a table three feet in length, one and a half feet wide, and two feet, three inches high. The table was overlaid with pure gold, surrounded by a molding of gold, and equipped with four rings of gold, a ring at each corner, through which poles were passed, so that the table could be carried. The description of this article of tabernacle furniture is found in Exod. 25:23, 24. In ancient times this table was standing in the Holy Place, not far away from God's special dwelling-place: the Holy of Holies. The showbread was laid on the table in two rows. The twelve loaves represented Israel's twelve tribes and symbolized the constant fellowship of the people with their God. The Israelites were, so to say, guests at his table, were consecrated to him, and by means of the offering of these presentation loaves gratefully acknowledged their indebtedness to him.

Every sabbath the old bread was exchanged for fresh loaves (I Sam. 21:6). The old loaves were eaten by the priests. They were "for Aaron and his sons," that is, for the priesthood, definitely *not* for everybody (Lev. 24:9). Yet when, "in the days of Abiathar the highpriest" (see below), hungry David entered "the house of God" (see Judg. 18:31; cf. I Kings 1:7, 24), the (court of the) sanctuary in Nob, which was the shrine where the ark was kept (I Sam. 21:1; 22:9), he was given this consecrated bread. He shared it with his equally hungry companions. They all ate of it, even though by divine law it had been designated as food for the priests, for them alone. The point is this: if David had a right to ignore a *divinely ordained ceremonial provision* when necessity demanded this, then would not David's exalted Antitype, namely, Jesus, God's Anointed in a far more eminent sense, have a right, under similar conditions of need, to set aside *a totally unwarranted, man-made sabbath regulation?* After all, to a considerable extent the rabbinical sabbath regulations amounted to misapplications of God's holy law. That was true also in the present case.

Much has been made of the fact that Mark represents Jesus as saying that the event in connection with David and his men took place "in the days—or: at the time—of[93] Abiathar the highpriest," though according to I Sam. 21:1-6 it was Ahimelech, not Abiathar, who gave David the holy bread.

Proposed Solutions

1. The two names, Ahimelech and Abiathar, were borne by both father and son. Cf. I Sam. 22:20; II Sam. 8:17. In the first of these two passages

---

[93] The preposition ἐπί has this meaning at times. Cf. Matt. 1:11; Luke 3:2; 4:27; Acts 11:28, etc.

Abiathar is "one of the sons of Ahimelech"; in the second (see also I Chron. 18:16) Ahimelech is "the son of Abiathar."[94]

Evaluation. Though this may seem to solve the problem, it is doubtful that there would be this interchange of names in writings so closely related that in the Hebrew Canon what we now call I Samuel and II Samuel were one book. Besides, is it not possible that Ahimelech had a son by the name of Abiathar, who in turn had a son named Ahimelech?

2. The Hebrew text is confused (note contrast between I Sam. 22:20 and I Chron. 24:6).[95] The New Testament passage (Mark 2:26) may be a copyist's gloss.[96]

Evaluation. Although in our attempt to solve the problem room must be left for any solution that does not ascribe error to the original author, confusion in the Hebrew text has not been proved (see 1. Evaluation), and the variants in the text of Mark 2:26 (see textual apparatus) do not solve the difficulty.

3. Mark's statement may be a primitive error.[97]

Evaluation. If this means that Mark himself originated this error, or accepted it as the truth and repeated it, it must be rejected. In writing their books divinely inspired authors did not commit errors.

4. The father, Ahimelech, and the son, Abiathar, were both present when David came to Nob, and both gave the bread to David. Soon afterward the father was killed; the son became highpriest and recorded the facts.[98]

Evaluation. Though it is impossible to speak with any degree of finality, this proposed solution is the best I have come across. In support of it note the following:

An entire family of priests evidently co-operated at Nob (I Sam. 22:15). When King Saul heard that his enemy David had been given loaves of showbread and the sword of Goliath, his wrath was directed most of all against Ahimelech; not exclusively against him however, also against the entire priesthood in Nob (I Sam. 22:17). Eighty-five priests were slain. Abiathar escaped, fled to David (I Sam. 22:20), and became highpriest, subsequently functioning in that capacity along with Zadok. It is clear therefore that the man who here in Mark 2:26 is called "highpriest" was definitely alive and active when David entered the court[99] of the house of God. The action took place "in his time."

---

94 This solution, already proposed by some of the Fathers, has been suggested as a possibility by (among others) Lenski, *op. cit.*, p. 81; A. B. Bruce, *op. cit.*, p. 356; and A. T. Robertson, *Word Pictures in the New Testament*, Vol. I, 1930, p. 273.

95 J. A. C. Van Leeuwen, *op. cit.*, p. 42; E. P. Groenewald, *op. cit.*, p. 65.

96 This is one of the two solutions suggested by Vincent Taylor, *op. cit.*, p. 217.

97 Vincent Taylor's alternative suggestion, same page as above.

98 This is Lenski's alternative suggestion, *op. cit.*, p. 81.

99 I Sam. 21:1 would seem to imply that he proceeded no farther than this.

It is true that at the moment when the bread was given to David and his men and consumed by them, Abiathar was not as yet the highpriest. This, however, does not prove that Mark—really Jesus, for Mark is reporting *his* words—was in error when he said "in the days of Abiathar the highpriest." It is not at all unusual to designate a place or a man by a name which did not belong to it or to him until later. Thus Gen. 12:8 mentions "Bethel," though in the days of Abraham it was still called "Luz" (Gen. 28:19). We do the same thing even today. We say, "It happened in Marne (Michigan)," when we mean, "It happened in Berlin, which today is called Marne." Or, "The house was sold to Gen. Smith," though we know very well that at the time when Smith became the owner of the house he was not as yet a general. Scripture contains many examples of abbreviated expression—on which see N.T.C. on John, Vol. I, p. 206–, and so does our everyday conversation.

The suggested solution (No. 4) may therefore be the right one. Certainty in this matter is impossible.

When critics add, as they sometimes do, that Matthew and Luke were aware of Mark's error and therefore omitted it, the answer is that this is an unwarranted assumption. Fact is that under the guidance of the Spirit each Gospel writer made his own selection of materials. Exactly why it is that some material found in one Gospel is lacking in others is not always clear. That at times even one of the most precious sayings of our Lord is found in only one Gospel is proved by the passage which follows, recorded only by Mark: **27. And he said to them, The sabbath was made for man, not man for the sabbath.**

Not the sabbath but man was created first; then came the sabbath (Gen. 1:26–2:3). The sabbath was instituted to be a blessing for man: to keep him healthy, to make him helpful, hence happy, to render him holy, so that he might calmly meditate on the works of his Maker, might "delight himself in Jehovah" (Isa. 58:13, 14), and look forward with joyful anticipation to the sabbath rest that remains for the people of God (Heb. 4:9).

But by means of ever so many minute and often absurd requirements, vexing and burdensome restrictions—including the one that forbade men to still their hunger by picking heads of grain on that day—the rabbis were changing the sabbath into a cruel tyrant, and man into that tyrant's slave . . . as if God's intention had indeed been to make "man for the sabbath," instead of "the sabbath for man."

Jesus concludes by saying **28. Consequently, the Son of man is Lord even of the sabbath.** When Jesus said, "The sabbath was made for man," he implied that God had made it what it was. It was the Lord, no one else, who had laid down his principles for sabbath observance. And since all authority had been given to the Son (Matt. 11:27; 28:18), who is one with the Father (John 10:30), with whom the Father is well pleased (Mark 1:11), and who was sent into the world by the Father (Mark 1:38; 9:37), the connective "Consequently"—or, if one prefers, "So," "Thus," "Therefore"—makes excellent sense when it is followed by the words, "Lord is the Son of man even of the sabbath" (thus literally according to the original). Greater is he than the temple (Matt. 12:6); than Jonah (12:41); than Solomon (12:42), and thus also, than the sabbath!

For a detailed study of the term "Son of man" see on 2:10; and on Matt. 8:20. Surely, if Jesus, as the Son of man, is Lord over all, is he not then Lord *even* of the sabbath? Note the word "even," in this narrative found only in Mark. As sovereign Lord he possesses the authority to lay down principles governing that day. Therefore no one has any right to find fault with him when he allows his disciples to satisfy their hunger by picking and eating heads of grain!

Summary of Chapter 2

Well-nigh unforgettable is the arrangement of the contents of Mark's Gospel. This is evident already in chapter 1. The appearance and ministry of John the Baptist, Christ's baptism by John, and Christ's temptation are described in the first part of that chapter (1:1-13). Then, after a considerable lapse of time, Jesus has arrived in Galilee with the message, "The time is fulfilled and the kingdom of God is at hand; be converted and believe the gospel." Jesus calls his first four disciples, promising to make them fishers of men. A very busy sabbath day in the life of our Lord is pictured next: at a synagogue service he teaches; he also heals a demoniac. Immediately afterward he enters the home of Simon and Andrew, and cures Simon's mother-in-law of her fever. His fame spreads to such an extent that after sunset, hence on what *we* would call that same day, he cures ever so many afflicted people. It is not surprising that after such a long and strenuous day he feels the need of an extended period of communion with his Father. Thus, very early the next morning, engaged in prayer in a lonely place, he is discovered by Simon and his companions. They are anxious to take him right back with them to Capernaum; for, as Simon phrases it, "Everybody is looking for you." Christ's plans are different, however. Accompanied by his disciples, as many as have gathered about him by this time, he starts on a Galilean circuit. He travels from town to town, and from village to village, preaching in the synagogues and casting out demons. On this tour he also cleanses a leper (1:14-45).

As concerns memorization, chapter 2 is just as easy. The Galilean tour is over. Jesus re-enters Capernaum. In an over-crowded house he imparts blessing to the soul and body of a paralytic (verses 1-12). From the stifling atmosphere and tenseness (think of the Pharisees and their sinister designs) of the suffocatingly packed house the Master wends his way to the refreshing breezes along the Sea of Galilee. Levi's tax-collector's booth is in clear view. That "publican" becomes Christ's disciple and prepares a banquet for him. Many publicans are present. Jesus' close association with these despised people is adversely criticized by Pharisaic scribes. They hear the dominical reply, "It is not those who are healthy that need a doctor but those who are ill. I did not come to call righteous people but sinners." Though there is probably no close chronological connection between this *feasting* under Levi's hospitable roof and the question about *fasting* related next, the *logical* transition is very easy. Jesus points out that those who have the bridegroom with them do not fast. By means of a twofold illustration—a patch of new cloth will never do on an old garment; new wine is not poured into old wineskins—, Jesus points out that for those who have accepted him sadness has been replaced by gladness, fear by freedom. This also means, of course, that the old fear and worry brought about by rabbinical sabbath regulations must be cast aside. So, Mark closes this chapter with one sabbath controversy narrative (picking heads of grain on that day) to be followed immediately (3:1-6) by another similar section (the shriveled hand). Everything is arranged in a very natural—and in Mark, to a considerable extent even chronological—order.

The four sections of chapter 2 may be summarized as follows:

a. The healing of a paralytic (verses 1-12). Back in Capernaum from his Galilean circuit, Jesus is speaking the word in an over-crowded house. By four men a paralytic is lowered through the roof, landing in front of Jesus. The Sympathetic Physician for both soul and body, deeply touched by the faith of the five and realizing that what bothered the sorely afflicted person most of all was his guilt in the sight of God, pronounces his pardon, full and free. The scribes, bent on finding fault with their enemy, Jesus, in their hearts accuse him of blasphemy, for "who except God can forgive sins?" *Pronouncing* forgiveness is easy enough. Let him *do* something for the physically afflicted one. If he is unable to do this, his claim to bless the poor man's soul is false. So they reason.—By means of instantly and completely delivering the paralytic of his illness "the Son of man" proves his claim, to the astonishment of everybody.

b. The call of Levi (=Matthew), the "publican" or tax-collector (verses 13-17). Walking along the seashore Jesus is soon surrounded by a large crowd. He teaches them and afterward calls Levi to be one of his disciples. The call, "Follow me," is immediately obeyed. Not only that, but the publican, having sacrificed his lucrative position, even prepares a banquet in honor of Jesus. Many publicans are also present. In answering the criticism of the Pharisees, who had confronted the Master's disciples with the question, "Why does he eat with tax-collectors and sinners?" Jesus reminds them that it was exactly to call sinners, not (self-)righteous people, that he had come.

c. The question about fasting (verses 18-22). Once, while the disciples of John the Baptist were fasting, and the Pharisees were also keeping a fast, Jesus was asked how it was that *his* disciples did not fast. He answers that in their capacity as "bridegroom's attendants" it would be improper and impossible for them to fast. By means of a double illustration—a patch of new cloth is not placed on an old and badly worn garment; new wine is not poured into old, stiff and rigid, wine-skins—Jesus drives home the lesson that the new message which he is bringing—new as compared with the old, legalistic teaching of the scribes—requires a fresh reception, one of faith and freedom, not one of fear and fasting.

d. The Son of man asserting his authority as Lord *even* of the sabbath (verses 23-28). This same spirit of faith and freedom, of gladness instead of sadness, should also mark the sabbath. Therefore, when the Pharisees criticize Jesus for allowing his hungry disciples to pick (and eat) some heads of grain on that day, he answers that the sabbath was made for man, not man for the sabbath, and that "the Son of man" was and is Lord even of the sabbath. If, in time of need, it was permissible for David to ignore a divine statute (see Lev. 24:9; I Sam. 21:1-6), which under normal circumstances could not have been ignored with impunity, would not the Lord of the sabbath have the right to set aside a merely human sabbath regulation?

There is one significant feature with respect to chapter 2 that has not yet been emphasized. This happens to be the chapter in which, either directly or by clear implication, Jesus ascribes four names or titles to himself, designations or descriptions that are very meaningful. Also in some of the remaining chapters of Mark's Gospel the glory of the Son is enhanced by appellations which he uses with reference to himself. Beginning, then, with chapter 2, note the following:

The Son of man (2:10, 28; and see on 2:10), The Physician (2:17), The Bridegroom (2:19, 20), The Lord even of the sabbath (2:28), The One who binds Beelzebul, that is, Satan (3:22, 23), The Lord (5:19, 20; 11:3), The Prophet (6:4), The Compassionate One (8:2; cf. 1:41), The Christ (8:29, 30), The Father's Son (8:38), The Ransom for many (10:45), The Beloved Son of the Vineyard's Owner (12:6, 7), The Rejected Stone that becomes The Cornerstone (12:10), David's Son and Lord (12:35, 37), The Teacher (14:14), The Shepherd (14:27), The Son of the Blessed (14:61, 62), The King of the Jews (15:2).

111

Outline of Chapter 3

Theme: *The Work Which Thou Gavest Him To Do*

3:1-6   The Son of Man Asserting His Authority as Lord Even of
         the Sabbath (continued); the Shriveled Hand
3:7-12   By the Seaside Teaching and Healing Great Multitudes
3:13-19 Choosing The Twelve
3:20-30 Were Christ's Miracles Proof of Beelzebul's Dominion or
         of His Doom?
3:31-35 The Mother and the Brothers of Jesus

CHAPTER III

3 1 Again he entered the synagogue, and a man with a shriveled hand was there. 2 And in order that they might bring a charge against him [Jesus], they were watching him closely (to see) whether he would heal him on the sabbath. 3 He said to the man with the shriveled hand, "Rise and come forward." 4 And he [Jesus] asked them, "Is it right on the sabbath to do good or to do harm, to save life or to kill?" But they remained silent. 5 And when he had looked around at them in anger, being deeply grieved at the hardening of their heart, he said to the man, "Stretch out your hand." He stretched it out, and his hand was restored. 6 Then the Pharisees left, and immediately, in consultation with the Herodians, began to take counsel against him, how they might destroy him.

3:1-6 *The Son of Man Asserting His Authority as Lord*
Even of the Sabbath; The Shriveled Hand
Cf. Matt. 12:9-14; Luke 6:6-11

The story is found in all three (Matt. 12, Mark 3, Luke 6). They all report: *a.* that on a sabbath Jesus somewhere attended the synagogue (cf. "went to church") and noticed a man with a withered or shriveled hand; *b.* that present also were some Pharisees, who were aiming to bring a charge against Jesus; *c.* that the Lord told the man to stretch out his hand; *d.* that obedience to this command resulted in complete restoration; and *e.* that the Pharisees discussed what should be done about the situation.

As to further details, there is a very interesting variety of presentation, again showing that the Gospel writers were no mere copyists. There are no contradictions. Combining the various items mentioned in the three accounts, the following vivid and dramatic narrative results:

Another sabbath has arrived. Jesus has entered the synagogue. Here he teaches (Luke 6:6). Attending the service is a man with a shriveled hand. It is the *right* hand (Luke 6:6; cf. Col. 4:14). Opponents of Jesus, that is, Pharisees—and scribes (Luke 6:7)—are closely watching him (Mark 3:2; Luke 6:7), with the purpose of preparing a charge against him. He knows their thoughts (Luke 6:8), and makes them voice what they have on their minds. "Is it right to heal on the sabbath?" they ask (Matt. 12:10). Jesus turns to the man, telling him to rise and step forward (Mark 3:3; Luke 6:8). Then Jesus asks his adversaries, "Is it right on the sabbath to do good or to do

113

harm, to save life or to kill?" (Mark 3:4a; Luke 6:9). When they remain silent, Jesus looks around at them in anger, being grieved at the hardness of their hearts (Mark 3:4b, 5a). He continues, "What man of y o u, if he has a sheep and it falls into a pit on the sabbath, will not grab hold of it and lift it out? Of how much more value is a man than a sheep! Therefore it is right to do good on the sabbath" (Matt. 12:11, 12). [100] Jesus then says to the man, "Stretch out your hand." So complete was the restoration that the (right) hand was now "sound as the other" (Matt. 12:13). The opponents were furious (Luke 6:11). Having left the synagogue (Matt. 12:14; Mark 3:6), not only did they discuss among each other what they should do to Jesus (Luke 6:11b), but they also made contact with the Herodians (Mark 6:6a), so that a combined plot was hatched. The aim was to kill, to destroy Jesus (Matt. 12:14; Mark 3:6b).

Turning now to the story as found in Mark we read: 1. **Again he entered the synagogue, and a man with a shriveled hand was there.** The exact location of this synagogue is not indicated. Could it have been the one in Capernaum? In view of the fact that Mark and Luke relate this story in close connection with that of the choosing of The Twelve and the ascent up the mountain (Mark 3:13-19; Luke 6:12-49), a "mountain" or "hill" probably not far removed from Capernaum (Luke 7:1; cf. Matt. 8:5), it is at least possible that a synagogue somewhere in the vicinity of what was now Jesus' headquarters is meant. But we cannot be sure.

On this sabbath in walks a man with a lame hand. The apocryphal Gospel according to the Hebrews states that the man was a stonemason, who pleaded with Jesus to heal him that he might not have to spend his life as a beggar. Be that as it may, the point is that this is a sabbath, and though there may well have been a difference of opinion between the disciples of Shammai, with their stricter interpretation of sabbath observance, and those of Hillel, with their more lenient view—the more rigorous position prevailing in Jerusalem, the more lenient in Galilee—, the rule that only in such cases in which a man's life was actually in danger would it be permissible to heal him on the sabbath was widely endorsed. [101] Would Jesus dare to oppose this rule, by the Pharisees regarded as a well-established and basic principle which must not be violated?

It is useless to speculate how the man had come to have a hand that was paralyzed. There are those who think that the form of the word used in the original here in 3:1, and translated "shriveled" or "withered," indicates that the condition of the hand was not congenital, but the result of an injury

---

[100] This affirmative answer to his own question was, of course, already implied in the question.
[101] See S.BK., Vol. I, pp. 622-629.

caused by disease or accident. [102] This, however, may well be an over-refinement. It may be true but cannot be proved. Far more important is what follows in verse 2. **And in order that they might bring a charge against him [Jesus], they were watching him closely (to see) whether he would heal him on the sabbath.**

Secretly the opponents hope that Jesus may trample upon their rule with respect to the sabbath. Who were these opponents? According to Matt. 12:14 and Mark 3:6, the Pharisees; to which Luke, as was shown, adds "the scribes." It is with evil intent that they watch Jesus so closely, that they observe him so scrupulously. See also Luke 14:1; 20:20. [103] They wanted to see whether Jesus would actually heal this man on the sabbath. If so, they will be in a position to press charges against him for unnecessarily practicing medicinal therapy on that day.

Jesus, however, does not shrink from his purpose to show kindness to this man: **3. He said to the man with the shriveled hand, Rise and come forward.** The Lord clearly takes the offensive. He is opposed to all secret scheming and conniving, furtive watching and under-cover planning. Besides, he may have wished to elicit the sympathy of the audience for this handicapped person. So, he tells the man to get up and to stand where everybody can see him. **4. And he [Jesus] asked them, Is it right on the sabbath to do good or to do harm, to save life or to kill?** Were not the Pharisees and the scribes the very people who were always claiming that *they* knew what was "permitted," "lawful," and therefore "right"? Let them therefore give their expert opinion. Of course, the answer to Christ's question was so obvious that a child could have given it. If it is right *to do good*—for which see also Luke 6:9, 33, 35, I Peter 2:14, 15, 20; 3:6, 17; 4:19; III John 11—on any ordinary day of the week, would it not be right to do good on the sabbath? Besides, in the Old Testament was it not exactly *doing good,* both with respect to God—loving, serving, and delighting oneself in him—, and with respect to man—delivering him from bondage, feeding and clothing him—, which God had required and even emphasized? And this in a context of fasting and sabbath observance? How strange that these adverse critics had not recalled the clear and definite teaching of Isa. 56:6; 58:6-14! The Lord had urged Israel to use the sabbath for the very purpose for which Jesus was here, now, and always using it. Nevertheless, it was with *him* that men who were supposed to be experts in the law were finding fault.

---

[102] Thus, for example, Swete, *op. cit.,* p. 50; Robertson, *Word Pictures,* Vol. I, p. 275. But see Vincent Taylor, *op. cit.,* p. 221. The word ἐξηραμμένην, perf. pass. participle of ξηραίνω. Matt. 12:10 and Luke 6:6 use the adjective ξηρά. But so does Mark in 3:3.

[103] At a later date, at Damascus, the Jews were going to watch the gates of the city "day and night," again with sinister purpose (Acts 9:24), namely, to prevent Paul from escaping.

However, Jesus probed even more deeply. He exposed the perversity of the critics even more unequivocally; for not only did he ask whether it was permitted on the sabbath to do good and to save life; he added, "or to do harm and to kill?" Certainly, if it was improper to do harm and to kill on the other six days of the week, was it not very improper to engage in this sinister business on the day specifically set aside for honoring God and showing sympathy to man? Nevertheless this doing harm and killing was exactly what these enemies were right now engaged in! In their hearts they were doing harm to the Messiah, sent by the Father. They were engaged in killing him! For proof see verse 6; cf. Matt. 5:21, 22; I John 3:15. O that even now they had repented and confessed their wickedness. **But they remained silent.** [104]

5. **And when he had looked around at them in anger, being deeply grieved at the hardening of their heart, he said to the man, Stretch out your hand.** Mark's description is very vivid. He writes as if he were reporting the very words spoken by an eye-witness, which was probably what he was indeed doing, the eye-witness being Peter. [105]

Mark states that it was "in anger" that Jesus looked around at his critics. For this word "anger" or "wrath" see also 3:7 in both Matthew and Luke; further: Luke 21:23; John 3:36; and the many references to divine wrath in the epistles and in the Book of Revelation. Similarly, Jesus was going to be "moved with indignation" upon noticing that the disciples were trying to stop those who were bringing the little ones to him, that he might touch them (Mark 10:14).

It should not be necessary to point out that there was nothing wrong with such indignation, such intense horror and disapproval. Actually it was simply the necessary concomitant of love. What was happening, as recorded here in Mark 3, was that the Pharisees were esteeming man-made ritualism above God-ordained concern about a man's welfare. Strict adherance to a rabbinical rule evidently meant more to them than the happiness of a human being. Jesus, on the other hand, sympathized with this handicapped person. Hence, he was terribly displeased with those cold-hearted ritualists. But even his anger was tempered by grief: he was deeply grieved at the hardening of their heart, that is, at their spiritual obtuseness, insensibility, and obstinacy.

---

104 Note imperfect tense ἐσιώπων.

105 The expression used by Mark, καὶ περιβλεψάμενος αὐτούς, literally "and having looked around on them," is similar to that found in 3:34 and 10:23, in both instances referring to the manner in which Jesus looked at his disciples. In 5:32 the reference is to his looking around at the crowd in order to see who had touched him; and in 11:11 Jesus is described as having looked around at everything in the temple. On the Mount of Transfiguration the disciples "having looked around," saw no one with them but Jesus only (9:8). With the exception of 5:32 (the imperfect) Mark everywhere uses the aorist participle. Outside of Mark's Gospel this word, hence also this vivid reference to Christ's look, is found only in Luke 6:10a, where Luke parallels (probably borrows from) Mark.

Cf. Rom. 11:25; Eph. 4:18. Are we correct in saying that he "felt sorry" even for these rigid traditionalists? Cf. Luke 23:34. However that may be, it is significant that, according to the tenses used in the original, the angry look was *momentary*, the deep-seated grief was *continuous*, abiding. [106]

A chilling silence prevails in the ranks of the critics. With bated breath the rest of the people are also watching, wondering what will happen now. The atmosphere in the synagogue is surcharged with uneasiness on the one hand, expectancy on the other. The man with the "withered" hand is still standing there, in full view of the audience. Jesus is about to perform the miracle demanded by this situation. He must act *now*, not later. For him to have waited until the following day could easily have been interpreted as an admission on his part that deeds of healing, unless in a case of life or death, were after all wrong when performed on the sabbath. Such a delay would have compounded error. This must not be. Now is the appropriate moment. So, after the scrutinizing all-around look, Jesus says to the handicapped man, "Stretch [or: hold] out your hand." Immediately he obeys: **He stretched it out, and his hand was restored.** The cure was instantaneous and complete. Cf. I Kings 13:6. Subsequent treatments or check-ups were not required. In a manner too mysterious for any mortal to comprehend, the Savior had concentrated his mind on the plight of this poor man, and by means of his power and compassion, had willed and performed the cure; and this not "in a dark corner" but in the sight of everyone present.

The effect upon the legalists? Answer: **6. Then the Pharisees left, and immediately, in consultation with the Herodians, began to take counsel against him, how they might destroy him.** Not only did the Pharisees leave the synagogue; they left *in a huff*. They were furious (Luke 6:11). The fact that a handicapped man had been delivered of his serious impediment, did not affect them in the least. It did not make them feel happy for this man. And it did not make them kindly disposed toward the Healer. What riled them was that here, before the eyes of everybody, they and their traditionalism had suffered a humiliating defeat. What a vast difference between *Christ's* totally unselfish anger (Mark 3:5) and *their* thoroughly selfish resentment! Moreover, as the word "immediately" shows, these men lost no time in planning their opponent's destruction. At once they started their scheming, choosing as their co-plotters . . . of all people, the thoroughly unholy, worldly adherants of Herod Antipas and his family. A strange

---

106 As to the theory endorsed by several commentators, namely, that the phrase "in anger" was omitted by Matthew and Luke because they were unwilling to ascribe this emotion to Jesus, would not a more reasonable explanation for the difference between Matthew and Luke's account, on the one hand, and Mark's, on the other, be this, that the latter report, being the precipitate of the preaching of lively, dramatic Simon Peter, would naturally in many instances be the most detailed and animated?

117

coalition between the sanctimonious and the sacrilegious! See also 12:13 and Matt. 22:16.

Nevertheless, a little reflection may well lead to the conclusion that the unholy alliance was not so strange after all. The life and teaching of Jesus implied a denunciation of worldlimindedness; hence, of the mode of life that characterized, among others, the Herodians. Besides, as viewed by the Herodians, who were lovers of the political status quo, would not Christ's huge following appear to hold within its bosom the seeds of political rebellion and revolution? If, then, the Herodians are willing to be "in" on the plot to bring about the destruction of Jesus, their co-operation will be welcomed and appreciated by the Pharisees. Anything . . . yes, anything will do, to get rid of Jesus!

---

7 Together with his disciples Jesus withdrew to the seashore, and a large crowd from Galilee followed. 8 And many people, hearing all the things he was doing, came to him from Judea and from Jerusalem and from Idumea and the regions across the Jordan and around Tyre and Sidon. 9 So, because of the crowd he told the disciples that a small boat should be kept in readiness for him, to prevent the people from crushing him; 10 for he had healed so many that all those who were suffering from illnesses were crowding in upon him in order to touch him. 11 And whenever the unclean spirits saw him, they were falling down at his feet and were screaming, "You are the Son of God." 12 But he strictly forbade them to reveal who he was.

3:7-12 *By the Seaside Teaching and Healing Great Multitudes*
Cf. Matt. 12:15-21

7. Together with his disciples Jesus withdrew to the seashore, and a large crowd from Galilee followed. Up to this point Mark has recorded four clashes [107] —whether direct or indirect—between Jesus and the Pharisees (2:6-11; 2:15-17; 2:23-28; 3:1-6). The most bitter of these were the first, when the opponents in their hearts accused Jesus of blasphemy, and the fourth, when they began to scheme how they might destroy him. At the close of the first confrontation Jesus went to the seashore. It is not surprising, therefore, that now, too, after the fourth collision, he withdraws to the seashore. Both times it is from inside a building (crowded house, synagogue) that he retires to the shore; the first time, after healing a paralyzed man; now, after restoring a paralyzed hand. We must bear in mind also that the time for the decisive head-on confrontation with the religious authorities had not as yet arrived. According to the Father's time-clock Calvary is still some distance away. For the present therefore the seashore is better suited to the Master's purpose than the synagogue.

The disciples accompany Jesus to the seashore. From Mark's Gospel we

---

107 Some, however, say "five," for they would include 2:18-22.

know that Simon, Andrew, James, John, and Matthew had accepted the call to be Christ's disciples (1:16-20; 2:13, 14). According to John 1:35-51 Philip and Nathanael had also been added to the group. Were all of these present with Jesus at this time? Any others? Mark's five but not Philip and Nathanael? However that may have been, it is clear that The Twelve as a body had not yet been appointed. Since the Galilean Ministry was still continuing, we are not surprised that a large crowd from Galilee followed Jesus. It must be borne in mind that already many sick, demon-possessed, and handicapped persons had been blessed by Christ's healing, rescuing, and restoring power and love. See 1:29-34, 39-42; 2:1-12; 3:1-6. This was going to continue (see verses 10-12).

The good news with reference to what was taking place in Galilee kept on reaching other places both within and outside of the nation: **8. And many people, hearing all the things he was doing, came to him from Judea and from Jerusalem and from Idumea and the regions across the Jordan and around Tyre and Sidon.** The reports kept coming in, for Christ's deeds, too, were continuing. So, people came in great numbers and from several different places. They came from Judea—including Jerusalem—in the south. Also, from south of the borders of Palestine, that is, from Idumea, which by John Hyrcanus had been conquered and whose people had by him been forced "to observe the laws of the Jews" (Josephus, *Antiquities* XIII.257). They came also from the region across—that is, east of—the Jordan; hence, from Transjordan or Perea, stretching from beyond Machaerus in the south, almost to Pella in the north, a region "for the most part desert and rugged," but interspersed with "tracts of finer soil, productive of every kind of crop" (Josephus, *Jewish War* III.44-47). For this see also 10:1; Cf. Matt. 4:15, 25; 19:1; John 1:28; 3:26; 10:40. They even came from Phoenicia, the region around Tyre and Sidon, along the Mediterranean Sea, northwest of Galilee. Cf. 7:24, 31; see also I Chron. 14:1; 22:4; Ps. 45:12; 83:7; 87:4; Matt. 11:21, 22; Acts 21:3-7. It was mainly because of Christ's continuing miracles that people from everywhere, many of them seeking healing for themselves and/or for relatives, came to him.

The size of the crowd and the eagerness of the people to get close enough to Jesus to touch him caused a problem: **9, 10. So, because of the crowd he told the disciples that a small boat should be kept in readiness for him, to prevent the people from crushing him; for he had healed so many that all those who were suffering from illnesses were crowding in upon him in order to touch him.** Jesus had already healed many. Accordingly, the people were so thoroughly convinced of his power and readiness to deliver them from their "scourges" or illnesses (cf. 5:29, 34; Luke 7:21; and see the very comforting Heb. 12:6) that, unwilling to wait for Jesus to touch *them,* they were crowding (literally "falling") upon him, in order to touch *him.* For the significance of either touch see on 1:41; cf. 5:27-31; 6:56.

119

Therefore, for safety's sake, Jesus told the disciples to provide a boat for him. The original uses a diminutive. Mark makes frequent use of diminutives; see footnote 5 on p. 19f. The one here used is generally translated "a small boat." By no means is it true, however, that such diminutives always emphasize smallness in size, though in the present instance the vessel was probably small. But the "small boat" of 3:9 may have been equal in size to the "boat" of 4:1. [108] Whether in the present instance the emphasis is on size or on familiarity with the indicated object would be hard to determine. At any rate, by making use of such a boat moored offshore, *if* he found it advisable to do so, Jesus could when he deemed it necessary not only protect himself but also in an unhampered manner address large throngs on the beach. Jesus tells the disciples that such a vessel "should be kept in readiness" [109] for him, so that it could be used *if* and *when* needed. Whether at this particular time the Lord actually made use of the boat, as he was going to do in 4:1, is not indicated.

The passage about "the little boat" must not be passed by as if it were of no practical significance, as is often done. On the contrary, it is intensely practical. It shows that even Jesus, though divine as well as human, in his state of humiliation made wise use of precautions, measures taken beforehand against possible danger. In doing this, is he not teaching a lesson which everyone would do well to heed? This lesson is not always taken to heart. Think of the student heading for the ministry, but neglecting the study of Scripture in the original; of the would-be enthusiastic "missionary," preaching the gospel in his own native tongue on a busy street corner in a foreign land, to people who do not understand a word of what he is saying; and of the man who is down on medical care for himself and for his family, because (as he puts it) he "trusts wholly in God." Certainly Matt. 6:19-34; Phil. 2:13; 4:6, 7, must not be emphasized at the expense of Gen. 41:33-36; Isa. 38:21; Matt. 4:7; 10:16, 23; Mark 3:9; Luke 14:28-32; 16:8, 9; Phil 2:12.

---

108 As compared with Greek (definitely including also *modern* Greek), German, Dutch, French, Spanish, etc., the English language is rather poor in single word diminutives. "Boatlet" would sound queer. Contrast the Greek (both Koine and modern) πλοιάριον; the French *nacelle;* German *Schifflein;* South African *schuitjie;* Frisian *skipke;* and the Dutch *scheepje, bootje, schuitje.* Though such diminutives do at times indicate physical smallness, in other contexts the emphasis is rather on familiarity, attachment, endearment. Compare English "Sonny," at times used in addressing a six-footer! So also "Girlie" often indicates intimacy or affection, rather than size. Cf. Spanish "mamacita," "abuelita," etc.

109 προσκαρτερῇ = third per. sing. pres. subjunctive of προσκαρτερέω. In the present context the meaning "should be kept in readiness" or "should constantly wait on" is clear enough. Considerable difference of opinion prevails in connection with the meaning of the same verb in other New Testament passages (Acts 1:14; 2:42, 46; 6:4; 8:13; 10:7; Rom. 12:12; 13:6; Col. 4:2), as will become evident when one consults lexicons and commentaries.

When God created the human body he equipped it with many precautionary extras! At the particular occasion to which Mark 3:9 refers the small boat may not have been used. The point is: *it was there, always ready, ever available.* That little vessel teaches a big lesson!

Jesus not only healed all those many sick people; he also drove out demons: **11. And whenever** [110] **the unclean spirits saw him, they were falling down at his feet and were screaming, You are the Son of God.** For demon possession see on 1:23a. These spirits are called "unclean" because they are morally and spiritually filthy, evil in themselves, and because they urge those whom they inhabit to commit evil. "They"—here, of course, "those possessed by them, their helpless tools, the demoniacs"—kept falling down at his feet and screaming. It is pointless to argue that when these spirits yelled, "You are the Son of God," they were using the term "Son of God" in the sense of angel (Gen. 6:2), or Israel (Hos. 11:1), or child of God, believer (Rom. 8:17). Clearly, when they yelled "You are *the* Son of God," they were referring to Jesus as Son of God in a unique sense, God's *Son* as no one else ever was or will be. Cf. 1:24. Also the idea that this item is not historical but merely expresses Mark's theology must be rejected. **12. But he strictly forbade them to reveal who he was.** More literally, "But he kept on strictly warning [or: charging] [111] them not to make him known." Just why was it that Jesus refused to allow the demons to reveal his identity? Several answers may be suggested:

1. The person and the work of the Savior are so holy and exalted that it would not be fitting to allow corrupt, filthy demons to proclaim them.

2. The title "the Son of God" implied at least that Jesus was the long expected Messiah. However, most of the people conceived of the Messiah in a nationalistic sense: one who could deliver them from the yoke of the foreign oppressor. So, before publicly revealing himself as the Messiah, or allowing himself to be thus proclaimed, Jesus must first make clear the nature of his Messianic office: that he has to suffer and die for the sins of his people, etc. The time to proclaim this publicly, or to have it thus proclaimed, has not as yet arrived.

3. The scribes were telling the people that Jesus and the demons were allies (3:22). If, then, Jesus permitted himself to be advertised by demons, would he not seem to be confirming the allegation of these scribes?

---

[110] The description is very graphic. Note ὅταν followed by the imperfect ἐθεώρουν in the subordinate clause, here indicating repetition. The verbs in the main clause are also in the imperfect tense: they "were [or: kept] falling down" and "were [or: kept] screaming."

[111] Note ἐπετίμα from ἐπιτιμάω. Here *to warn*; with μή: *to warn not to*; hence, *to forbid.* Frequently this verb has the meaning *to rebuke* (1:25; 4:39; 8:32; etc.) Basically the meaning is: to award a τιμή (penalty) ἐπί (upon). The word πολλά is here used as an adverb. See also on 9:26.

Which of these reasons is the correct one? Or which combination of reasons? Or was there perhaps another reason? We simply do not know. The possible reasons that have been enumerated show at least that Christ's unwillingness to be proclaimed as "the Son of God" by demons need not be considered very surprising.

---

13 He went up into the mountain and called to himself those whom he wanted, and they came to him. 14 And he appointed twelve—whom he also named "apostles"—, that they might be with him, and that he might send them out to preach 15 and to have authority to expel demons. 16 He appointed these twelve: Simon—whom he named Peter—, 17 and James the son of Zebedee, and John the brother of James—them he named "Boanerges," that is, "sons of thunder"—, 18 and Andrew, and Philip, and Bartholomew, and Matthew, and Thomas, and James the son of Alphaeus, and Thaddaeus, and Simon the Cananaean, 19 and Judas Iscariot, who betrayed him.

3:13-19 *Choosing The Twelve*
Cf. Matt. 10:1-4; Luke 6:12-16

13. He went up into the mountain and called to himself those whom he wanted, and they came to him. The transition is again very natural. With so many sick to be healed, so many demoniacs to be set free, so much preaching needed (see 3:7-12, 14, 15), it was natural that Jesus would authorize some of his followers to have a share in the work he himself was doing, his own power and sympathy operating also in them. Moreover, the hostility of the religious leaders had become so bitter (3:6) that co-operation with them had become impossible: God's people must become separately organized. Also, from the start of Christ's earthly ministry death and (after resurrection) departure from this earth were staring him in the face. In fact, he had come for the very purpose of giving his life as a ransom for many (10:45). He felt the need therefore of appointing witnesses by means of whom, through his own work in them, the militant church could be gathered and guided, after his own physical departure.

So Jesus went up into "the mountain." Both in Matthew (see 8:1) and in Luke (6:12, 17) the description has so much local color, that a specific elevation—whether we today would call it a "mountain" or a "hill" is of no consequence—seems to be meant. Hence, the rendering "the mountain" would in this case seem to be better than "the hills." [112] It is true, nevertheless, that neither here nor in Matt. 5:1, where the same expression occurs, are we told which mountain is indicated. To the people of that day it was probably well-known, so that they understood exactly what the Gospel

---

[112] Thus also Lenski ("of course, a definite mountain"); and this or a very similar rendering in N.A.S.; L.N.T. (A. and G.), p. 586; Beck, Phillips, Williams, Dutch (Nieuwe Vertaling), etc.

writers meant by "the mountain." It seems to have been in the general vicinity of Capernaum. For more on this see N.T.C. on Matthew, pp. 259, 260. And for an introduction to the Sermon on the Mount preached here, see that same commentary, pp. 259-262.

So very important did Jesus consider the appointment of The Twelve and the preaching of the sermon to be that on this mountain he spent the entire preceding night in prayer (Luke 6:12). Thereupon he [113] called to himself those whom he wanted. His sovereign will prevails. They choose him only after he first had chosen them! In the night of his betrayal he was able to say to his disciples, "Y o u did not choose me, but I chose y o u and appointed y o u that y o u should go and bear fruit . . ." (John 15:16). See also I John 4:10, 19. Result: they came to him, leaving behind whatever had to be left behind. In fact, several of them (Mark 1:16-20; 2:13, 14; John 1:35-51) had already been closely associating with him, and even the rest must have been his followers, though in a more general sense (Luke 6:13).

14, 15. And he appointed twelve—whom he also named *apostles*—**that they might be with him, and that he might send them out to preach and to have authority to expel demons.** It is clear that Mark summarizes. The full content of the commission is found in Matt. 10: The Charge to the Twelve, which must be dated a little later. The disciples—all twelve of them—must have been in Christ's company a while before they could be sent out to proclaim the good tidings to others. As *Mark* relates, the task for which Jesus *appointed* (cf. I Kings 12:31; Acts 2:36; Heb. 3:2) these men was threefold: association and education, mission, and demon-expulsion. *Matthew* adds a fourth item.

Association and *Education*. He appointed them, first of all, to spend some time with their Master, seeing and hearing him, and learning whatever it was he wished to teach them. For them such association meant spiritual education.

Mission. Secondly, and in close connection with the preceding, he appointed them to be his heralds; hence, in that sense, to preach. Receivers must become givers. Disciples must become apostles. They must publish the message of salvation through Jesus Christ. In a sense they were invested with his authority. So real was this authority that Jesus was going to say, "He who receives y o u receives me, and he who receives me receives him who sent me" (Matt. 10:40). Cf. Mark 6:11; John 20:21-23. They were sent first to the lost sheep of the house of Israel (Matt. 10:5, 6); later, to all the nations (Matt. 28:19), into all the world (Mark 16:15).

---

[113] Even though we may not agree with those commentators who assign an intensive or emphatic meaning to αὐτός—"he himself"—, it remains true that not the disciples took the initiative but Jesus did.

Demon Expulsion. Thirdly, Jesus appointed them to have [114] authority (the right and the power) to expel demons. For demon possession see on 1:23.

Restoration of the body—both healing and bringing back to life—was also included, as Matt. 10:8 shows.

16-19. He appointed these twelve: Simon—whom he named Peter—, and James the son of Zebedee, and John the brother of James—them he named Boanerges, that is, sons of thunder—, and Andrew, and Philip, and Bartholomew, and Matthew, and Thomas, and James the son of Alphaeus, and Thaddaeus, and Simon the Cananaean, and Judas Iscariot, who betrayed him.

The very fact that Jesus appointed exactly twelve men, no more no less, indicated that he had in mind the new Israel, for ancient Israel had twelve tribes and twelve patriarchs. The new Israel was going to be gathered from among all the nations, Jews and Gentiles alike (Matt. 8:10-12; 16:18; 28:19; Mark 12:9; 16:15, 16; Luke 4:25-27; John 3:16, 10:16; Rev. 21:12, 14).

In the New Testament the names of The Twelve are listed four times (Matt. 10:2-4; Mark 3:16-19; Luke 6:14-16; Acts 1:13, 26). Acts 1:15-26 records the manner in which Judas Iscariot was replaced by Matthias. With that exception the twelve names undoubtedly indicate the same persons in each of the four lists.

With respect to the three lists recorded in the Synoptics note the following: If theoretically the twelve names are viewed as in each case consisting of three groups of four, the ones mentioned are the same in each group. They are, however, not always arranged in identical sequence. In the first group of four Mark, unlike Matthew and Luke, separates the names of the two brothers Simon (=Peter) and Andrew. Mark's order is: Simon, James, John, Andrew. Matthew's and Luke's is: Simon, Andrew, James, John. In the second group Luke's order agrees with Mark's: Philip, Bartholomew, Matthew, Thomas. In this group Matthew places Thomas before his own name; hence, Philip, Bartholomew, Thomas, Matthew. In the final group Matthew's order is the same as Mark's: James the son of Alphaeus, Thaddaeus, Simon the Cananaean, Judas Iscariot. Here Luke, reversing the middle two, has: James the son of Alphaeus, Simon the Zealot, Judas the (son) of James—this Judas, we may assume, is Thaddaeus—, Judas Iscariot.

Mark, it will be noted, does not arrange the twelve names in pairs, as Matthew does. He mentions them all in one long row. Just why it was that Mark separated the names of the two brothers, Simon and Andrew, is not clear. Suggestions: Does he group Simon, James, and John in immediate

---

114 The infinitive ἔχειν instead of ἵνα in the two preceding clauses makes no essential difference.

succession because frequently Jesus chose exactly these three, not the others, to be with him? Does he mention Andrew in immediate connection with Philip because there may well have been a close relationship between these two? See John 12:21, 22. Or is it possible that he separated the names of the brothers Simon and Andrew because he wanted to indicate that in Christ's family spiritual kinship was even more important than physical? See this very chapter (3:31-35). We simply do not know.

As to the twelve, considered individually, in the order in which Mark has arranged them, note the following:

Simon. He was a son of Jonas or John. By trade he was a fisherman, who with his brother Andrew first lived in Bethsaida (John 1:44), afterward in Capernaum (Mark 1:21, 29). Both Mark and Luke report that it was Jesus who gave Simon the new name Peter. For details of this event see John 1:42. This new name, meaning *rock,* was a description not of what Simon was when called, but of what by grace he was to become. At first, and for some time afterward, Simon was anything but a model of steadfastness or imperturbability. On the contrary, he was constantly swaying from one position to its opposite. He turned from trust to doubt (Matt. 14:28, 30); from open profession of Jesus as the Christ, to rebuking that very Christ (Matt. 16:16, 22); from a vehement declaration of loyalty, to base denial (Matt. 26:33-35, 69-75; Mark 14:29-31, 66-72; Luke 22:33, 54-62); from "By no means shalt thou wash my feet ever," to "Not my feet only but also my hands and my head" (John 13:8, 9). See also John 20:4, 6; Gal. 2:11, 12. Nevertheless, by the grace and power of the Lord this changeable Simon was transformed into a true Peter. For the significance of Peter in the post-resurrection church see N.T.C. on Matt. 16:13-20. Accordingly, when Jesus at this early date—for Mark 3:16 reflects John 1:42—assigned to Simon his new name, that was an act of love, a love that was willing to overlook the present and even the near future, and to look far ahead. Wonderful and transforming grace of our loving Lord!

Two New Testament books are by tradition accredited to this apostle: I and II Peter. As was shown earlier—see pp. 12, 13—, Mark has not unjustly been called "Peter's interpreter."

James the son of Zebedee, and John the brother of James. Mark mentions these two fishermen not only here and in 1:19, 20 (see on that passage) but also later on (9:2; cf. 10:35-45). There are also several references to them in the other Gospels. Probably because of their fiery nature Jesus called these two brothers Boanerges. This is an Aramaic word, which Mark, who is the only Gospel-writer to report this, for his non-Jewish readers interprets to mean "sons of thunder." The Hebrew name would be *b^{e}nē reghesh.* [115] That

---

115 The puzzle with respect to the vowels in Boa has not as yet been solved.

the two did indeed have a fiery nature may perhaps be inferred from Luke 9:54-56. Cf. Mark 9:38. James was the first of The Twelve to wear the martyr's crown (Acts 12:2). While he was the first to arrive in heaven, his brother John was in all probability the last to remain on earth. On the life and character of John, considered by many (I believe correctly) as being "the disciple whom Jesus loved" (John 13:23; 19:26; 20:2; 21:7, 20) see N.T.C. on the Gospel according to John, Vol. I, pp. 18-21. Five New Testament books have by tradition been assigned to John: his Gospel, three epistles (I, II, and III John), and the book of Revelation.

Andrew. It was he, also a fisherman, who brought his brother Peter to Jesus (see N.T.C. on John 1:41, 42). For other references to Andrew see above (on 1:16, 17, 29); also study Mark 13:3; John 6:8, 9; 12:22. See also below under Philip.

Philip. He was at least for a while a fellow townsman of Peter and Andrew, that is, he too was from Bethsaida. Having himself responded to the call of Jesus, he found Nathanael, and said to him, "The one about whom Moses wrote in the law and about whom the prophets wrote, we have found, Jesus, son of Joseph, the one from Nazareth" (John 1:45). When Jesus was about to feed the five thousand he asked Philip, "How are we to buy bread-cakes that these (people) may eat?" Philip answered, "Bread cakes for two hundred denarii would not be sufficient for them so that each might get a little something" (John 6:5, 7). Philip apparently forgot that the power of Jesus surpassed any possibility of calculation. To deduce from this incident the conclusion that Philip was a coldly-calculating type of person, more so than the other apostles, would be basing too much on too little. In the Gospels Philip generally appears in a rather favorable light. Thus, when the Greeks approached him with the request, "Sir, we would see Jesus," he went and told Andrew, and these two, Andrew and Philip, brought the enquirers to Jesus (John 12:21, 22). It must be admitted that Philip did not always immediately understand the meaning of Christ's profound utterances—did the others?—but to his credit it must be said that with perfect candor he would reveal his ignorance and ask for further information, as is also clear from John 14:8, "Lord, show us the Father, and we shall be content." He received the beautiful and comforting answer, ". . . He who has seen me has seen the Father" (John 14:9).

Bartholomew (meaning: son of Tolmai). He is clearly the *Nathanael* of John's Gospel (1:45-49; 21:2). It was he who said to Philip, "Out of Nazareth can any good come?" Philip answered, "Come and see." When Jesus saw Nathanael coming toward him he said, "Look, truly an Israelite in whom deceit does not exist." This disciple-apostle was one of the seven persons to whom the resurrected Christ appeared at the Sea of Tiberias. Of the other six only Simon Peter, Thomas, and the sons of Zebedee are mentioned.

Matthew. This disciple has already been discussed in some detail (see above on 2:14-17).

Thomas. The references to him combine in indicating that despondency and devotion marked this man. He was ever afraid that he might lose his beloved Master. He expected evil, and it was hard for him to believe good tidings when they were brought to him. Yet when the risen Savior in all his tender, condescending love revealed himself to him it was he who exclaimed, "My Lord and my God!" For more information on Thomas see N.T.C. on John 11:16; 14:5; 20:24-28; 21:2.

James the son of Alphaeus. By Mark (15:40) he is also called "James the Less," which by some is interpreted as meaning "James the younger," but by others as "James small in stature." About him we have no further positive information. It is probable, however, that he was the same disciple who is referred to in Matt. 27:56; Mark 16:1; and Luke 24:10. If this be correct, his mother's name was Mary, one of the women who accompanied Jesus and stood near the cross. See N.T.C. on John 19:25. It has already been shown that the Alphaeus who was the father of Matthew should probably not be identified with Alphaeus the father of James the Less. See above on 2:14.

Thaddaeus (called Lebbaeus in certain manuscripts of Matt. 10:3 and Mark 3:18). He is in all probability the "Judas not Iscariot" of John 14:22 (see on that passage); cf. Acts. 1:13. From what is said about him in John 14 it would seem that he wanted Jesus to show himself to the world, probably meaning: to get into the limelight.

Simon the Cananaean. "The Cananaean" is an Aramaic surname meaning enthusiast or zealot. In fact Luke calls him "Simon the Zealot" (Luke 6:15; Acts 1:13). In all probability this name is here given him because formerly he had belonged to the party of the Zealots, which party in its hatred for the foreign ruler, who demanded tribute, did not shrink from fomenting rebellion against the Roman government. See Josephus *Jewish War* II.117, 118; *Antiquities* XVIII.1-10, 23. Cf. Acts 5:37.

Judas Iscariot. This name is generally interpreted as meaning "Judas the man from Kerioth," a place in southern Judea. (Some, however, prefer the interpretation, "the dagger-man.") The Gospels refer to him again and again (Matt. 26:14, 25, 47; 27:3; Mark 14:10, 43; Luke 22:3, 47, 48; John 6:71; 12:4; 13:2, 26, 29; 18:2-5). He is at times described as "Judas who betrayed him," "Judas one of the twelve," "the betrayer," "Judas the son of Simon Iscariot," "Judas Iscariot, Simon's son," or simply "Judas." This man, though thoroughly responsible for his own wicked deeds, was an instrument of the devil (John 6:70, 71). While other people, when they felt that they

127

could no longer agree with or even tolerate Christ's teachings, would simply disassociate themselves from him (John 6:66), Judas remained, as if he were in full accord with him. Being a very selfish person he was unable—or shall we say "unwilling"?—to understand the unselfish and beautiful deed of Mary of Bethany, who anointed Jesus (John 12:1 ff.). He was unable and unwilling to see that the native language of love is lavishness. It was the devil who instigated Judas to betray Jesus, that is, to deliver him into the hands of the enemy. He was a thief; yet it was he who had been entrusted with the treasuryship of the little company, with the predictable result (John 12:6). When, in connection with the institution of the Lord's Supper, the dramatic moment arrived—forever commemorated in Scripture (Matt. 26:20-25; John 13:21-30) and emblazoned in art (Leonardo da Vinci, etc.)—in which Jesus startled The Twelve by saying, "One of y o u will betray me," Judas, though having already received from the chief priests the thirty pieces of silver as a reward for his promised deed (Matt. 26:14-16; Mark 14:10, 11) had the incredible audacity to say, "Surely not I, Rabbi?" Judas served as guide for the detachment of soldiers and the posse of temple police that arrested Jesus in the garden of Gethsemane. It was by means of perfidiously kissing his Master, as if he were still a loyal disciple, that this traitor pointed out Jesus to those who had come to seize him (Matt. 26:49, 50; Mark 14:43-45; Luke 22:47, 48). As to the manner of Judas' self-inflicted demise, see on Matt. 27:3-5; cf. Acts 1:18. What caused this privileged disciple to become Christ's betrayer? Was it injured pride, disappointed ambition, deeply entrenched greed, fear of being put out of the synagogue (John 9:22)? No doubt all of these were involved, but could not the most basic reason have been this, that between the utterly selfish heart of Judas and the infinitely unselfish and outgoing heart of Jesus there was a chasm so immense that either Judas must implore the Lord to bestow upon him the grace of regeneration and complete renewal, a request which the traitor wickedly refused to make, or else he must offer his help to get rid of Jesus? See also Luke 22:22; Acts 2:23; 4:28. One thing is certain: The shocking tragedy of Judas' life is proof not of Christ's impotence but of the traitor's impenitence! Woe to that man!

What points up the greatness of Jesus is that he took *such men as these,* and welded them into an amazingly influential community that would prove to be not only a worthy link with Israel's past but also a solid foundation for the church's future. Yes, he accomplished this multiple miracle with such men as these, with all their faults and foibles. Even when we leave out Judas Iscariot and concentrate only on the others, we cannot fail to be impressed with the majesty of the Savior, whose drawing power, incomparable wisdom, and matchless love were so astounding that he was able to gather around himself and to unite into *one* family men of entirely different, at times even opposite, backgrounds and temperaments. Included in this little band was Peter the optimist (Matt. 14:28, 26:33, 35), but also Thomas the pessimist (John 11:16; 20:24, 25); Simon the one-time Zealot, hating taxes and eager to overthrow the Roman government, but also Matthew, who had voluntarily offered his tax collecting services to that same Roman government; Peter, John, and Matthew, destined to become renowned through their writings, but also James the Less, who remains obscure but must have fulfilled his mission.

Jesus drew them to himself with the cords of his tender, never-failing compassion. He loved them to the uttermost (John 13:1), and in the night before he was betrayed and crucified commended them to his Father, saying:

"I have manifested thy name to the men whom thou gavest me out of the world; thine they were, and thou gavest them to me, and they have kept thy word. . . . Holy Father, keep them in thy name which thou hast given me, in order that they may be one, even as we are one. . . . I do not make request that thou shouldest take them out of the world, but that thou shouldest keep them from the evil one. They are not of the world, even as I am not of the world. Consecrate them in the truth; thy word is truth. Just as thou didst send me into the world, so have I also sent them into the world. And for thy sake I consecrate myself, in order that they also may be truly consecrated (John 17:6-19, in part)."

---

20 He came home; and again a crowd gathered, so that they were not even able to eat a meal. 21 Now when his friends [116] heard (about this), they went out to take charge of him, for they said, "He is out of his mind." 22 And the scribes who had come down from Jerusalem said, "He is possessed by Beelzebul" [117] and "It is by the prince of the demons that he is casting out the demons." 23 So he called them to himself and spoke to them in parables: "How can Satan cast out Satan? 24 If a kingdom is divided against itself, that kingdom cannot stand. 25 And if a house is divided against itself, that house will not be able to stand. 26 And if Satan has risen up against himself and is divided, he cannot stand—he is finished. [118] 27 On the contrary, no one can enter the strong man's house and carry off his goods unless he first binds the strong man. It is only then that he will ransack his house.

28 "I solemnly declare to y o u: all things will be forgiven to the sons of men, all their sins and whatever blasphemies they utter; 29 but whoever utters blasphemy against the Holy Spirit will never receive forgiveness, but is guilty of an everlasting sin." 30 (He said this) because they were saying, "He has an unclean spirit."

---

116 Or: those associated with him. See comments.
117 Literally, "He has Beelzebul."
118 Literally, but has an end. Meaning: he is doomed; his days are numbered.

3:20-30 Were Christ's Miracles Proof of Beelzebul's Dominion or of His Doom?
Cf. Matt. 12:22-32; Luke 11:14-23; 12:10

At this point, after the calling of The Twelve, we might have expected some phrases from the Sermon on the Mount. Cf. Luke 6:12-49. But Mark, being predominantly the Gospel of action—see pp. 18, 19—, does not specialize in discourse material. [119]

Abruptly Mark's account continues: **20. He came home; and again a crowd gathered, so that they were not even able to eat a meal.** There are no indications as to just when the incident (verses 20, 21) took place. It must have happened sometime during the Great Galilean Ministry, but there is no definite *chronological* link. Nevertheless, there may well be a *logical* connection between Mark 3:20-30 and what has gone before, in 2:1–3:19. Mark has shown that the hostility of the religious authorities had advanced to the point where they were plotting Jesus' destruction (3:6), and where he, in turn, by means of the calling of The Twelve was establishing the foundation of the church in its New Testament manifestation. Cf. Matt. 16:18, 19; Rev. 21:14. But now something is added to the burden of the Man of Sorrows. Not only his enemies, the Pharisees and scribes, but now also his "friends" begin to make matters difficult for him.

In the sense already explained (see on 2:1) Jesus was "at home" once more in Capernaum, his headquarters. And just as on a previous occasion the crowd had been so large that the entrance was blocked (2:4; cf. 1:33), so now also the throng was so enormous that it was impossible for Jesus and his disciples—note "they"—even to eat. [120]

Result: **21. Now when his friends heard (about this), they went out to take charge of him, for they said, He is out of his mind.** Who were those people who thought that Jesus was bereft of his senses, [121] and who therefore wanted to take him into protective custody? [122] The phrase used

---

119 It contains scattered phrases found also in the Sermon on the Mount:

Mark	cf.	Matthew	Mark	cf.	Matthew
1:22		7:28, 29	9:43-47		5:29, 30
4:21		5:15	10:4		5:31
4:24		7:2	10:21		6:20
7:22		6:23	11:24		7:7
9:38		7:22	11:25		6:14

120 Literally, "to eat bread." But "eating bread" had developed into the more general meaning: eating, eating a meal. See LXX on Gen. 37:25; II Sam. (= II Kingd.) 12:20; and for the New Testament Mark 7:2; Luke 14:1.

121 The aorist ἐξέστη may be regarded as timeless.

122 κρατῆσαι, aor. infin. of κρατέω. This verb is used also in connection with Herod's *arrest* of John the Baptist (Matt. 14:3; Mark 6:17); the attempt of the religious

in the original to describe them [123] is rather ambiguous. It means basically "those from his side." The theory according to which the reference is to Jesus' immediate family, that is, to his mother Mary and to his brothers, [124] is held, by those who favor it, to be supported by the following considerations:

a. "Family" (parents and other relatives) is the meaning of this phrase in Prov. 21:21 and in a passage of the apocryphal writing Susanna 33. See context, verse 30.

b. John 7:5 states, "Even his brothers did not believe in him [Jesus]."

c. Here in Mark the context, verses 31-35, mentions Jesus' "mother and his brothers."

d. The atmosphere of tension revealed in the chapter's closing paragraph is best explained by the supposition that Jesus' immediate family had originated—or at least given credence to— the opinion, "He is out of his mind."

On the basis of considerations such as these it is not surprising that the phrase "his family" occurs in several translations of Mark 3:21 (Beck, Good News for Modern Man, N.E.B., etc.). Others offer the not very different rendering "his relatives" (Phillips, Goodspeed, Berkeley, Norlie, Weymouth, Jerusalem Bible) or something similar. That the phrase used in the original does at times have this meaning has already been shown. See a. above.

Nevertheless, by no means all translators have adopted the rendering "his family," or even "his relatives." Several avoid it, in favor of "his friends" (A.V., A.R.V., R.S.V., Living N.T., R. Young). F. C. Grant [125] states, "*His friends* is probably the best translation."

Whatever one may think of the rendering "his family" or "his relatives," the further conclusion, namely, that the passage (3:21) must be interpreted

---

authorities to *lay hold on* Jesus (Matt. 21:46; 26:4; Mark 12:12; 14:1); the *actual arrest* of Jesus (Matt. 26:48, 50, 55, 57; Mark 14:44, 46, 51); the *seizure* of Paul (Acts 24:6) and of the dragon (Rev. 20:2). In a somewhat more general sense it can mean to *grasp* or *grab hold of* (a sheep for the purpose of rescuing it, Matt. 12:11; a debtor, with evil intent, 18:28; the feet of Jesus, 28:9). At times it means to *take by the hand* (in a context of healing, Matt. 9:25; Mark 1:31; 9:27; or restoring to life, Mark 5:41). Still more general uses are: to attain, hold fast, support, bear in mind, restrain, retain.

With such a wide variety of meanings the importance of the individual context becomes clear. In the present case the meaning is probably: by means of forceful persuasion to take Jesus into protective custody. It must be borne in mind that those who desired to do this were "friends," not enemies.

[123] οἱ παρ' αὐτοῦ.

[124] See Vincent Taylor, *op. cit.*, pp. 235-237; C. R. Erdman, *op. cit.*, p. 65; H. B. Swete, *op. cit.*, p. 63; M. H. Bolkestein, *Het Evangelie naar Marcus*, Nijkerk, 1966, pp. 88, 89; and many others.

[125] *The Gospel according to St. Mark* (*The Interpreter's Bible*) New York and Nashville, 1951, Vol. VII, p. 689.

to mean that Mary and Jesus' brothers were the ones who were calling Jesus insane is not nearly as unavoidable as it may seem to be. As for the arguments that have been used in its support (see a.-d. above), note the following:

As to a. True, but the word also has other meanings. In I Macc. 9:44; 11:73; 12:27; 13:52; 15:15 the meaning is probably "his men," "his envoys," "his company," "his adherants or followers." Josephus, *Antiquities* I.193 reflects Gen. 17:27, where many more are included than those who belonged to Abraham's immediate family. In the papyri, too, the expression used in the original has many different meanings, in accordance with the specific context in each individual case. See F. Field, *Notes on the Translation of the New Testament,* Cambridge, 1899, p. 25. It can mean neighbors, agents, friends, etc.

As to b. It is true that John 7:5 teaches that even Jesus' brothers "did not believe in him," but the context clearly shows that they did not consider him mentally unbalanced. Otherwise would they have said, ". . . show yourself to the world"? Whether or not these brothers were included in 3:21 is not known. John 7:5 does not prove that they were.

As to c. "The words . . . 'those with him' may mean 'his family,' though it is doubtful if Mark meant to anticipate vs. 31 in this way" (F. C. Grant). The theory according to which vss. 31-35 resume the story begun in verse 21 is questionable. To be sure, there is a relation between vss. 20-30, on the one hand, and vss. 31-35, on the other. But that relation is probably of a different character. See on vss. 31-35.

As to d. This point concerns both Jesus' brothers *and his mother.* For the brothers see above, under "As to b." With respect to Mary: even though it is true that she erred at times and that her criticisms and attempts at interference with Christ's program were always firmly reproved (see Luke 2:49; John 2:4; and so probably also Mark 3:31-35), yet we have no reason to doubt that the relation between Mary and Jesus was ever one of tenderness and respect, proceeding from both sides (Luke 2:51; John 2:5; 19:26, 27). There is no reason to believe that Mary's faith in God's revelation regarding her "firstborn son" (see below, on verses 33-35) was ever obliterated to the extent that she regarded Jesus as having lost his mind. The burden of proof rests entirely on those who think otherwise. [126]

Who, then, were those "friends" or "associates" of Jesus that were convinced that he had taken leave of his senses? We simply do not know! They may have been people with whom he had grown up in Nazareth,

---

[126] E. P. Groenewald, *op. cit.,* p. 79, though believing that Jesus' "brothers" were among those that regarded him to be mentally unbalanced, stops short of ascribing this same sentiment to Mary!

including possibly even relatives. Or, again, they may have been "persons well disposed toward Jesus, an outer circle of disciples." [127] That there was indeed such an outer circle, probably consisting of a great number of people, is clear from many passages (Matt. 11:12; Mark 12:34; 14:3, 12-16, 51, 52; 15:43; Luke 6:13, 17; 10:1; 23:50-56).

What may have been the reason(s) causing these "friends," "associates," or "followers" to consider Jesus to have become demented? Many possibilities suggest themselves. They may have thought: "At times the Master acts so strangely; for example, at an earlier occasion, when everybody in Capernaum wanted him to return to that town, he said, 'Let us go elsewhere, to the next towns (1:36-38).' Also, he is constantly opposing 'the establishment,' consisting of scribes and Pharisees. That is not what is generally done by those who aspire to leadership. He pronounces pardon as if he were God himself (2:7)! Yet, on the other hand, he is on close terms with . . . of all people, sinners and tax collectors (2:15, 16). Horrors! Moreover, his teaching, too, is unusual." As to the latter, see, for example, Mark 2:17, 19, 27, 28; to which later on would be added such baffling passages as those found in 8:34, 35; 9:43-50; 10:23, 24. Because of such and similar teaching—and this by a carpenter!—were not the people of Nazareth going to take offense at him? See 6:3.

All this and more should be borne in mind when we try to determine why friends of Jesus considered him bereft of reason. Nevertheless, the main consideration that led those who stood in some undefined relation to him to arrive at this judgment may well have to be found in the immediate context. That context indicates that it was especially Christ's willingness to move from one large crowd to another, teaching, healing, casting out demons (1:32-34; 2:2), and now his presence among a throng so large that he and his disciples did not even have an opportunity to eat (3:20), that led to the remark, "He is out of his mind." It was—at least seems to have been—what looked to his friends as his slighting of rest, recreation, and refreshment, that occasioned the exclamation. Add to this the fact that whenever Jesus granted sight to the blind, hearing to the deaf, healing to the sick, and liberty to the demon-possessed, *his heart was in it!* He sympathized as no one else invested with the human nature ever sympathized before or after him. "In all *their* afflictions he was afflicted" (Isa. 63:9). In him was fulfilled the prophecy, "Surely, he has borne our griefs and carried our sorrows" (Isa. 53:4). Is it not possible that all of this caused the friends to think, "He is altogether too hard on himself," and to say, "He is mentally unbalanced, is being consumed by religious frenzy"? Granted that this judgment, no matter

---

[127] See A. B. Bruce, *op. cit.*, p. 360.

how well intentioned, was untrue and unjust, is it not understandable? If even The Twelve, who benefited from close and constant fellowship with Jesus, were often confused (Luke 9:45; 18:34; John 12:16), we can well imagine that those friends of Jesus who were further removed from him might indeed have interpreted his behavior, so strange by human standards, to be that of a person who had lost his mind.

In later days Christ's followers, too, have often been charged with madness. This happened to Paul (Acts 26:24). Francis of Assisi, the man with the life and commandments of Jesus ever before his eyes, was called "the mad son of Bernadone." When Martin Luther defended the supremacy of the Word of God over the traditions of men he was regarded even by some of his former sympathizers as a fool and one possessed by the devil. And see I Cor. 1:18; 3:19.

The "friends," we may assume, meant well. The enemies did not: **22. And the scribes who had come down from Jerusalem said, He is possessed by Beelzebul and It is by the prince of the demons that he is casting out the demons.** Scribes had been sent to spy on Jesus. *Down* from Jerusalem—elevation about 2400 feet above sea level—they came to Galilee, the Sea of Galilee being about 600 feet *below* sea level. However, when these law experts, probably delegated by the Sanhedrin, descended toward Capernaum, they must have considered their descent ideological—Jerusalem being the citadel of Jewish orthodoxy—fully as much as merely physical.

They came down when Jesus had just healed a demon-possessed man who could neither see nor speak. As a result of this multiple miracle, "All the people were amazed and were saying, 'Surely this cannot be the Son of David?' " (Matt. 12:22, 23; cf. Luke 11:14). Mark, paralleling Matt. 12:24-32; Luke 11:15-23, continues the story from here on. In its main points the account is the same in all the Synoptics. [128]

The scribes are not going to allow the people to remain thoroughly amazed, even to the point of entertaining messianic notions with respect to

---

[128] Mark, however, adds a few touches not found—or not found in that exact form—in the other two: that the investigators were scribes (Matthew: Pharisees); that Jesus summoned them and spoke to them in parables; that he asked them, "How can Satan cast out Satan?"; and told them that whoever utters blasphemy against the Holy Spirit is guilty of an everlasting sin. Also, the explanatory note at the close of Mark's account (verse 30) is found only in that Gospel. On the other hand, Matthew and Luke add details not found in Mark. Both show that Jesus had read the thoughts of his critics; that he asked them, "By whom do y o u r sons cast out demons?" (followed by a "therefore" clause); and told them, "He who is not with me is against me . . ." and "But if it is by the Spirit"—Luke: by the finger—"of God that I cast out demons, then the kingdom of God has come upon y o u." In fact, throughout the story there are minor differences—see especially Luke 11:21, 22—, so that it is very clear that each Gospel writer has his own style.

Jesus. For his demon expulsions and other miracles they offer an entirely different, in fact a sharply conflicting, explanation: Jesus, being possessed by Beelzebul, is casting out demons by strength derived from that prince or ruler of the demons!

When these men mentioned Beelzebul, of whom were they thinking? Opinions differ. In the Old Testament we read about Baal-zebub = Beelzebub. But whatever may have caused the name Beelzebub to be changed to Beelzebul, [129] one fact is clear, Beelzebul is definitely the prince of the demons. Beelzebul is Satan. A comparison of verse 22a with 22b and with 23; of Matt. 9:34 with 12:24; and 12:26 with 12:27 proves this.

The charge leveled against Jesus by scribes and Pharisees was wicked. It was the result of envy. Cf. Matt. 27:18. They felt that they were beginning to lose their following, and this they were unable to endure. How completely different had been the attitude of John the Baptist (John 3:26, 30). The thoroughly shameful character of the charge becomes apparent also from the fact that it regards Beelzebul not as an evil spirit exerting his sinister influence upon Jesus from the outside; no, Beelzebul is regarded as being inside the soul of Jesus. The latter is said to *have*—that is, to be possessed by—this unclean spirit (Mark 3:22, 30; cf. John 8:48). The charge, then, amounts to this, that Jesus, indwelt by and in league with Satan, is by the power derived from that evil spirit driving out demons.

Christ's reply follows in verses 23-30, which may be divided as follows: *a.* refutation of the charge (verses 23-26); *b.* explanation of Christ's demon expulsions and other miracles (verse 27); *c.* exhortation (verses 28-30).

Refutation, verses 23-26. **So he called them to himself and spoke to them in parables: How can Satan cast out Satan? If a kingdom is divided against itself, that kingdom cannot stand. And if a house is divided against itself, that house will not be able to stand. And if Satan has risen up against himself and is divided, he cannot stand—he is finished.** In all three accounts the charge of the antagonists is given in the third person. What is in their minds is being expressed behind Christ's back. So now Jesus summons these slanderers into his presence. He gives them an opportunity to make their

---

[129] It was as Baal-zebub (II Kings 1:2, 3, 6; LXX IV Kingd. 1:2, 3, 6 Βααλ μυῖαν), that is, lord of the carrion-fly, and thus also protector against this nuisance, that Baal was worshiped at Ekron. King Ahazia, who sent messengers to inquire of Baal-zebub whether he would recover from the results of his fall, was told that because of this disloyalty to Jehovah he would die. The New Testament passages substitute Beel[=Baal]zebul for -zebub. Beelzebul means "lord of the dwelling." The reason for the change in spelling is not clear. It may have amounted to no more than an accident of popular pronunciation. Another explanation is that there is here a play on words, for *-zebul* resembles *zebel:* dung. Thus, those who despised the Baal of Ekron were able, by means of a slight change in pronunciation, to heap scorn upon him by conveying the thought that he was nothing but a "lord of dung."

charge before the very face of the One whom they deride, and to answer his refutation if they care to do so. Understandably they do not avail themselves of this opportunity: they cannot answer his refutation.

Jesus points out that the charge is ridiculous. If it were true, Satan would be casting out Satan. How can that be? Have the scribes pictured Satan as a prince or ruler of a domain? In their own terms, and making use of "parables"—here meaning "brief illustrative comparisons"—, Jesus answers them. If their charge were true, the ruler would be destroying his own realm; the prince, his own princedom. First, he would be sending out his envoys, the demons, to work havoc in the hearts and lives of men, destroying them body and soul, often little by little. Afterward, as it were in base ingratitude and suicidal folly, he would be supplying the very power needed for the shameful defeat and expulsion of his own obedient servants. No kingdom, thus divided against itself, can maintain itself. Under similar conditions any household, too, would go down to ruin. If this is actually what Beelzebul is doing, "He cannot stand, but has an end," says Jesus literally.

Explanation. Having refuted the Pharisees' contention, Jesus now presents the true explanation of his victories over the demons and their lord: **27. On the contrary, no one can enter the strong man's house and carry off his goods unless he first binds the strong man. It is only then that he will ransack his house.** The rhetorical question of Matt. 12:29 becomes a positive statement here. The idea conveyed is the same in both cases. In ordinary life the burglar does not receive willing help from the home owner. Instead, in order to get what he wants the intruder first ties up the owner. Then he burglarizes. Jesus by word and deed is depriving Satan of those values which the evil one regards as his own and over which he has been exercising his sinister control (Luke 13:16). The Lord is casting out Beelzebul's servants, the demons, and is restoring that which through their agency Satan has been doing to men's souls and bodies. Jesus is doing all this because by means of his incarnation, his victory over the devil in the desert of temptation, his words of authority addressed to the demons, his entire activity, he has begun to bind Beelzebul, a process of binding or curtailment of power that was going to be further strengthened by means of his victory over Satan on the cross (Col. 2:15) and in the resurrection, ascension, and coronation (Rev. 12:5, 9-12). He has done, is doing, and will do this through the power not of Beelzebul himself surely but of the Holy Spirit (see verses 28, 29). Yes, the devil is being, and is progressively going to be, deprived of his "goods," his "furniture," that is, of the souls and bodies of men, and this not only through healings and demon expulsions but also through a mighty missionary program, reaching first the Jews but later on also the nations in general (John 12:31, 32; Rom. 1:16). Is not this the key to the understanding of

Rev. 20:3? [130] Note how also in Luke 10:17, 18 the "fall of Satan as lightning from heaven" is recorded in connection with the return and report of the seventy missionaries.

It is clear, then, that Christ's miracles, far from being proof of Beelzebul's dominion, as if the evil one were the Great Enabler, are instead a prophecy of his certain doom. Already his realm is being broken down, and a glorious kingdom, which had existed for ages, is now arising in a marvelously new form. And Beelzebul, active and mighty though he be, can do nothing to prevent it, for he is bound. His power is being very seriously curtailed through the coming and work of Christ.

Exhortation. 28-30. **I solemnly declare to y o u: all things will be forgiven to the sons of men, all their sins and whatever blasphemies they utter; but whoever utters blasphemy against the Holy Spirit will never receive forgiveness, but is guilty of an everlasting sin.** Luke's parallel section (11:14-23) does not contain this earnest warning; but see Luke 12:10. The parallel in Matt. 12:31, 32 is very similar. [131]

With a deeply earnest "Amen I say to y o u" Jesus introduces this exhortation. As to this "Amen," which in Mark's Gospel occurs here for the first time, in Hebrew it refers, in general, to ideas of *truth* and *faithfulness*. It occurs in statements which affirm or confirm a solemn truth. In the Old Testament the single Amen is found in Deut. 27:15, 16-26; I Kings 1:36; I Chron. 16:36; Neh. 5:13; Ps. 106:48; and Jer. 28:6. The double Amen is found in Num. 5:22; Neh. 8:6; Ps. 41:13; 72:19; and 89:52. In the New Testament the word Amen, is an adverbial accusative, combines the ideas of truthfulness and solemnity. The rendering "verily"="in very truth" of the A.V. is certainly not bad, but today is considered somewhat archaic. Whether "truly" (R.S.V., N.A.S.) conveys that same fulness of meaning or whether, through association with such phrases as "yours truly," it has lost some of the strength or solemnity usually associated with "verily," is a matter with respect to which opinions differ. In every case—let the reader examine this for himself with the use of a Concordance—in which this word occurs in the New Testament it introduces a statement which not only expresses a truth or fact—as, for example, 2x2=4 would be a fact—but an *important*, a *solemn* fact, one that in many cases is at variance with popular

---

130 See my *More Than Conquerors, An Interpretation of the book of Revelation,* Grand Rapids, 1970, p. 223-229.

131 There are a few variations that do not touch the essence. Thus Mark has "the sons of men," where Matthew has "men," but "son of man" can have the meaning "man." See N.T.C. on Matt. 8:20. Mark has "all their sins and whatever blasphemies they utter," where Matthew has "every sin and blasphemy." Matthew spells out what is implied in Mark, namely, that among the sins that are forgiven are those committed against "the Son of man."

opinion or expectation or at least causes some surprise. It is for that reason that I have adopted the rendering "I solemnly declare." [132]

The words that follow the solemn introduction state that "all things," meaning all sins, and specifically in the present connection all blasphemies, will be forgiven to the children of men. The reference is, of course, to all sins of which men sincerely repent. That applies also to Matt. 12:31; Luke 12:10. To be sure, in none of these passages is the condition of repentance mentioned. That it was, however, implied is clear from Mark 1:15; 2:17; 6:12; cf. Matt. 4:17; 12:41; Luke 5:32; 13:3, 5; 15:7; 17:34. See also Ps. 32:1, 5; Prov. 28:13; James 5:16; I John 1:9. This rule holds also with respect to that very heinous sin, namely, blasphemy. In this connection we must be careful, however, to bear in mind that Scripture at times uses this word in a broader sense than we do. Among us "blasphemy" may be defined as "defiant irreverence." In this connection we think, for example, of such crimes as cursing God or the king who reigns by the grace of God, of willful degradation of things considered holy, pulling them down to the realm of the secular, or of claiming for the secular or purely human the honor that belongs to God alone. In Greek, however, a more general sense was also ascribed to the word "blasphemy," namely, the use of insolent language directed against either God *or man,* defamation, railing, reviling (Eph. 4:31; Col. 3:8; I Tim. 6:4). Accordingly, when Jesus assures us that "all things will be forgiven to the sons of men, all their sins and whatever blasphemies they utter" he is using the term "blasphemy" in the most general sense. However, when he makes an exception—"but whoever utters blasphemy against the Holy Spirit shall never receive forgiveness"—he is referring to a sin which even in our English language would be considered "blasphemy." Cf. Mark 2:7; Luke 5:21; John 10:30, 33; Rev. 13:1, 5, 6; 16:9, 11; 17:3.

Nevertheless, even for all but one kind of defiant irreverence there is forgiveness. If this were not true how could Peter's sin have been forgiven (Mark 14:71), and how could he have been reinstated (John 21:15-17)? How could Saul (=Paul) of Tarsus have been pardoned (I Tim. 1:12-17)? On the other hand, for "blasphemy against the Holy Spirit" there is *never* forgiveness. Such a person is guilty of "an everlasting sin"; that is, never will his sin be blotted out.

The question remains, "How is it to be understood that blasphemy against the Holy Spirit is unpardonable?" As to other sins, no matter how grievous or gruesome, there is pardon for them. There is forgiveness for David's sin of adultery, dishonesty, and murder (II Sam. 12:13; Ps. 51: cf. Ps. 32); for the "many" sins of the woman of Luke 7; for the prodigal son's "riotous living" (Luke 15:13, 21-24); for Simon Peter's triple denial accompanied by pro-

---

[132] Cf. Williams: "I solemnly say."

fanity (Matt. 26:74, 75; Luke 22:31, 32; John 18:15-18, 25-27; 21:15-17); and for Paul's pre-conversion merciless persecution of Christians (Acts 9:1; 22:4; 26:9-11; I Cor. 15:9; Eph. 3:8; Phil. 3:6). But for the man who "speaks against the Holy Spirit" there is no pardon.

Why not? Here, as always when the text itself is not immediately clear, the context must be our guide. From it we learn that the scribes are crediting Satan with that which the Holy Spirit, through Christ, was achieving. Moreover, they are doing this willfully, deliberately. In spite of all the evidences to the contrary they still affirm that Jesus is expelling demons by the power of Beelzebul. Not only this, but they are making progress in sin, as a comparison between 2:7; 3:6; and 3:22 clearly shows. Now to be forgiven implies that the sinner be truly penitent. Among the scribes here indicated such genuine sorrow for sin was totally lacking. For penitence they substituted hardening, for confession plotting. Thus, by means of their own criminal and completely inexcusable callousness, they were dooming themselves. Their sin is unpardonable because they were unwilling to tread the path that leads to pardon. For a thief, an adulterer, and a murderer there is hope. The message of the gospel may cause him to cry out, "O God be merciful to me, the sinner." But when a man has become hardened, so that he has made up his mind not to pay any attention to the promptings of the Spirit, not even to listen to his pleading and warning voice, he has placed himself on the road that leads to perdition. He has sinned the sin "unto death" (I John 5:16; see also Heb. 6:4-8).

For anyone who is truly penitent, no matter how shameful his transgressions may have been, there is no reason to despair (Ps. 103:12; Isa. 1:18; 44:22; 55:6, 7; Mic. 7:18-20; I John 1:9). On the other hand, there is no excuse for being indifferent, as if the subject of the unpardonable sin is of no concern to the average church member. The blasphemy against the Holy Spirit is the result of gradual progress in sin. Grieving the Spirit (Eph. 4:30), if unrepented of, leads to resisting the Spirit (Acts 7:51), which, if persisted in, develops into quenching the Spirit (I Thess. 5:19). The true solution is found in Ps. 95:7b, 8a, "*Today* O that y o u would listen to his voice. Harden not y o u r hearts!" Cf. Heb. 3:7, 8a.

Mark adds: **(He said this) because they were saying, He has an unclean spirit.** This is one of these explanatory statements found frequently in Mark's Gospel. Cf. 4:33, 34; 7:3, 4; 7:19b; 15:16. The word "they" refers to the scribes, calling attention to what these men were saying, as recorded in verse 22. The idea that the words of blasphemy, "He has an unclean spirit" would imply that these enemies of Jesus did not regard Beelzebul to be Satan but rather some other evil spirit is unacceptable. It no more means this than John 4:24 would mean that God is merely one among many spirits, as if they and he were on the same level. The identification Beelzebul=Satan

139

has already been established. And, of course, he too is "an unclean spirit," the worst of them all.

---

31 Then his mother and his brothers arrived. Standing outside they sent (someone) to him to call him.   32 A crowd was sitting about him, and they were saying to him, "Behold, your mother and your brothers outside are looking for you."   33 He answered and said to them, "Who is my mother and (who are) my brothers?"   34 And looking around at those who were sitting in a circle about him he said, "Here are my mother and my brothers!   35 For whoever does the will of God, he is my brother and sister and mother."

3:31-35 *The Mother and the Brothers of Jesus*
Cf. Matt. 12:46-50; Luke 8:19-21

31. Then his mother and his brothers arrived. Standing outside they sent (someone) to him to call him. Just why the mother and the brothers of Jesus had arrived at the scene and were trying to contact him has not been revealed. It is probable, however, that verses 21, 22 shed some light on this. If so, then the most charitable and probably also the most natural explanation would be that disturbing remarks about Jesus—for example, that his opponents regarded him as being demon-possessed and that even his friends thought that he was out of his mind—had induced Jesus' mother and his brothers, out of natural affection, to try to remove him from the public eye and to provide for him a haven of rest and refreshment. As has been pointed out, this interpretation does not warrant anyone to say, as some commentators do, that Mary and her other children shared the view of the "friends" (verse 21), and were actually of the opinion that the one dear to them was, or was becoming, mentally unbalanced.

As to the identity of these brothers of Jesus, the evidence favors the position that Jesus and these men had issued from the same womb, Mary's. Arguments in favor of this position:

a. Elsewhere, too, we are definitely told that Jesus had brothers and sisters, evidently together with him members of one family (Matt. 12:46, 47; Mark 6:3; Luke 8:19, 20; John 2:12; 7:3, 5, 10; Acts 1:14).

b. Luke 2:7 informs us that Jesus was Mary's "firstborn." Though in and by itself this second argument may not be sufficient to prove that Jesus had uterine brothers, in connection with argument a. the evidence becomes rather conclusive.

c. Also in view of Matt. 1:25 the burden of proof rests entirely on those who *deny* that after Christ's birth Joseph and Mary entered into all the relationships commonly associated with marriage, and had children who therefore were Jesus' brothers and sisters. [133] The names of the brothers are given in Mark 6:3; cf. Matt. 13:55.

Since because of the crowd (verse 20; cf. Luke 8:19) it was impossible for the new arrivals to get through to Jesus—the house was that full—, someone is sent to call him. 32. **A crowd was sitting about him, and they were saying to him, Behold, your mother and your brothers outside are looking for you.** The picture is very vivid. One can almost see and hear how the message is being passed from Jesus' mother and brothers to the special messenger, from him to the people sitting closest to the Master, and from them to Jesus himself. In a very natural, thoroughly human way Jesus has now received the information that his mother and brothers are looking for him and wish him to come out to them.

Jesus uses the interruption to good advantage. He always did exactly that with interruptions. Interrupted while he was praying (1:35), addressing a crowd (2:1 ff.), sleeping in a boat (4:37 ff.), conversing with his disciples (8:31 ff.), or traveling (10:46 ff.), he always knew how to turn an interruption into a springboard for the utterance of a great saying or for the performance of a marvelous deed.

So also here, as is shown in verses 33-35. **He answered and said to them, Who is my mother and (who are) my brothers? And looking around at those who were sitting in a circle about him he said, Here are my mother and my brothers.** Although the relation between Jesus and his mother was one of tender concern, as has been shown in connection with verse 21, he never permitted her to divert him from doing what he knew that his heavenly Father wanted him to do, as has also been indicated. See above, on verse 21, under "*As to d.*" Neither did he permit his brothers to sidetrack him. See John 7:2 ff. By saying, "Who is my mother and (who are) my brothers?" he teaches that what holds for himself holds for all: all must strive to do the will of God. Cf. Matt. 10:37; Luke 14:26. In this connection physical ties are not nearly as important as are spiritual.

Mark relates that when Jesus answered his own question he was looking around at those who were *sitting*—all were probably in a house—in a circle about him. Matthew adds that he was stretching out his hand toward and over his disciples. It was with this meaningful look and gesture that the Master remarked, "Here are my mother and my brothers." This "brothers" must not be interpreted as if Jesus recognized only males as members of his

---

[133] It is clear, therefore, that the doctrine of Mary's "perpetual virginity" has no warrant in the *New* Testament. As to Ezek. 44:2, "This gate shall remain shut," and Song of Sol. 4:12, "A garden locked is my sister, my bride," how such *Old* Testament passages can be used to support this doctrine is hard to understand!

spiritual family. He probably said, "my mother and my brothers" to correspond with "your mother and your brothers are looking for you." That people are not excluded from Christ's family because of sex is clear from the words that immediately follow, namely, **For whoever does the will of God, he is my brother and sister and mother.** In all probability the words and the gesture of gracious inclusion were directed first of all to The Twelve (though in a favorable sense they could hardly have applied to Judas Iscariot). In all likelihood they were sitting closest to Jesus. Having immediately responded to Christ's call, regardless of the sacrifice this implied (Matt. 19:27-29; Luke 5:28; 9:58; 14:26), they had shown that it was indeed their basic intention to carry out the will of God for their lives. It is not surprising, therefore, that Jesus points to them and publicly acknowledges that they are included in his spiritual family. And, since the word "whoever" is very broad, "disciples" other than The Twelve were certainly also included.

As to Mary, though her affectionate solicitude should be recognized, it must also be admitted that she erred. She was in a sense repeating that sinful interference manifested also on an earlier occasion (John 2:3). If, therefore, in connection with Mark 3:31-35 we are justified in speaking about an atmosphere of "tension," it was this effort of sinful interference—not Mary's and Jesus' brothers' alleged opinion that Jesus was out of his mind—that brought about this tension. But just as on that earlier occasion Mary quickly saw her mistake and was strengthened in her faith (see John 2:5) by the very word of tender and earnest reproof which Jesus addressed to her (John 2:4), may we not believe that also in the present instance the Savior's word (Mark 3:33-35) had the same wholesome effect on her? There is no reason to believe that Mary's faith, which comes to beautiful expression in Luke 1:38; 1:46-55; 2:19; and 2:51, did not, by God's grace, triumph over all temporary set-backs. That it was victorious is clear from Acts 1:14. Jesus' brothers shared in this victory (same passage).

The generous nature of Christ's declaration (Mark 3:33-35) is evident from the fact that those whom he thus honored had by no means reached the pinnacle of spiritual perfection. For example, The Twelve were, and remained for a long time, men of "little faith." See above, on verses 16-19. Yet he was not ashamed to acknowledge them as his "brothers" (Heb. 2:11).

Note the inclusiveness of this "whoever" (does the will of God). It means black and white, red, brown, and yellow; male and female; old and young; rich and poor; bond and free; educated and unlettered; Jew and Gentile. But note also the exclusiveness: those and those alone who do God's will are included. The substance of what God requires is readily learned by examining the following passages of Mark's Gospel: 4:9, 20, 21, 24; 5:19, 34; 6:31, 37; 8:34-38; 9:23, 35-37, 41; 10:9, 14, 29-31, 42-45; 11:22-26; 12:17,

29-31, 41-44; 13:5, 10, 11, 13, 23, 28, 29, 37; 14:6-9, 22-26, 38; 16:6, 7, 15.

It must be emphasized, however, that no one is able to "do the will of God" except by the power and sovereign grace of God. This is not only Pauline doctrine (Eph. 2:8; Phil. 2:12, 13). It is also definitely the teaching of Christ. According to that teaching, as reported by Mark, God—one can also say Jesus Christ—is the great Enabler (1:17). It is the power of God (10:27) and the substitutionary, atoning sacrifice of his Son Jesus Christ (10:45; 14:24) that saves. In the final analysis man is helpless in himself. He is completely dependent upon the mercy and compassion of the Lord (5:19; 6:34; 8:2). Is it not this fact that accounts for the emphasis, in the teaching of Christ as reflected by Mark, on the necessity of genuine faith and persevering prayer (1:35; 5:36; 9:23, 29; 11:22-24)?

Summary of Chapter 3

The chapter contains five sections that may be summarized as follows:

a. Sabbath controversies continued (verses 1-6). In this section the Son of man continues to assert his authority as Lord of the sabbath. From the grainfield the attention shifts to the synagogue. Jesus is taking a leading part in the sabbath service (Luke 6:6). Among the worshipers are some Pharisees, unfriendly to Jesus. Present also is a man with a withered hand. The Pharisees hope that Jesus will try to heal this man, their purpose being that they may be able to press charges against and destroy the Healer for unnecessarily practicing medicinal therapy on a day when, according to the rules of the rabbis, this was not permitted. To restore the hand was exactly what Jesus was going to do. The actual situation, then, was this: the Pharisees were trying *to do harm, to destroy.* Jesus was planning *to do good, to restore.* So, having requested the man to stand at a place where all could see him, Jesus, who had read his opponents' thoughts even before they expressed them, asked them, "On the sabbath what is permitted? To do good or to do harm, to save or to kill?" Continued sullen silence was their answer. In holy indignation Jesus looked at each of them in turn, until he had rounded the circle. He then ordered the man to stretch out his hand. He did not touch the man's hand, neither did he say, "Hand, be restored to health," or anything of the kind. Nevertheless, the hand was immediately and fully restored. So furious were the Pharisees that, having left the synagogue, they at once went into consultation with the Herodians, with a view to destroying Jesus.

b. Motley crowds at the shore (verses 7-12). On a former occasion, after the healing of *the paralyzed man,* Jesus had retired to the shore of the Sea of

Galilee (2:1-13). So he does now also, after the restoration of *the paralyzed hand.* The more he healed, the more the crowds increased. From all parts of Palestine, and even from the outside, people came streaming toward him, in many cases in order to be healed or to be delivered of the demons that were in control over them. So closely do the people press in upon Jesus that he tells his disciples that a little boat should be kept in readiness for him constantly, so that whenever needed it might be available . . . a lesson for all time. As to the demons, for reasons of his own Jesus forbids them to reveal his identity as "the Son of God."

c. The Twelve chosen (3:13-19). However, Jesus considered the crowds to be a blessing rather than merely a burden. Had he not come into the world to seek and to save the lost? He therefore now appoints The Twelve in order that, beginning even now but especially after his departure from the earth, these men might proclaim his message and perform his gracious deeds.

d. Jesus versus Beelzebul (3:20-30). Not only his enemies (verses 1-6, 22) but even his well-meaning "friends," that is, some of those who in one way or another were associated with him, begin to make matters difficult for him. When they notice that even while at home he, on account of the assembled crowd, did not permit himself or his disciples the opportunity to eat, they declare, "He has taken leave of his senses," probably meaning, "He is being consumed by religious frenzy." Though these well-meaning friends certainly erred, the judgment of the sworn enemies, the scribes, was far more wicked and cruel. They had taken note of the many healings and demon expulsions, notably also of the one reported in Matt. 12:22, 23; Luke 11:14, and had come down from Jerusalem, saying, "He is possessed by Beelzebul," and "It is by the prince of the demons that he is casting out the demons." They were filled with bitterness when they heard about the enthusiasm of the people, who were beginning to wonder whether Jesus might perhaps be the Messiah. He refutes their arguments ("How can Satan cast out Satan?"), supplies the true explanation of his miracles (he has bound the strong man Satan=Beelzebul, and is therefore able to deprive him of his goods: the souls and bodies of men), and earnestly warns them that for those who persevere to the end in their impenitence and hardened hearts there is no pardon.

e. The mother and the brothers of Jesus (3:31-35). It may have been disturbing remarks about Jesus—that his opponents regarded him to be demon-possessed, and that even some of his friends thought he was out of his mind—that caused his mother Mary and his brothers to make an attempt to contact him, with the intention, probably, to take him along with them, removing him from the public eye and providing for him a haven of rest and refreshment. But however well-intentioned this attempt, it amounted to sinful interference with Christ's own pre-designed program of activities. Mary and Jesus' brothers must be made to understand that his comings and goings cannot be determined by physical ties but only by the will of God. Hence, beautifully the chapter ends as follows, "And looking around at those who were sitting in a circle about him [The Twelve and perhaps some other followers], he said, 'Here are my mother and my brothers! For whoever does the will of God, he is my brother and sister and mother.' "

Outline of Chapter 4

Theme: *The Work Which Thou Gavest Him To Do*

4:1-9   Parables: Opening Words and The Parable of The Sower
4:10-12   The Purpose of the Parables
4:13-20   Explanation of the Parable of the Sower
4:21-25   Various Sayings of Jesus
4:26-29   The Parable of The Seed Growing in Secret
4:30-32   The Parable of The Mustard Seed
4:33, 34   Christ's Use of Parables
4:35-41   A Tempest Stilled

CHAPTER IV

4 1 Again he began to teach beside the sea. The crowd that gathered about him was so very large that he stepped into a boat and sat (in it) out on the sea, while all the people were on the land, facing the sea. 2 He was teaching them many things in parables, and in his teaching he said to them: 3 "Listen! Once upon a time [134] the sower went out to sow. 4 It so happened that, as he was sowing, some seed fell along the path. The birds came and gobbled it up. 5 Some fell on rocky ground, where it did not have much soil, and because it did not have depth of soil it sprang up immediately. 6 But when the sun came up it was scorched, and since it had no root it withered away. 7 Some fell among the thorns. The thorns shot up and choked it, and it did not yield any grain. 8 And some seeds fell into good soil. Coming up and growing they were bearing fruit, yielding: some thirty(fold), some sixty, and some a hundred." 9 And he said, "He who has ears to hear, let him hear."

4:1-9 *Parables: Opening Words and The Parable of the Sower*
Cf. Matt. 13:1-9; Luke 8:4-8

1. Again he began to teach beside the sea. The meaning is "Again, as he had done earlier (2:13; 3:7)." The reference is to the shore of the Sea of Galilee. Exactly when this renewed teaching beside the sea took place Mark does not report. But see Matt. 13:1. **The crowd that gathered about him was so very large that he stepped into a boat and sat (in it) out on the sea, while all the people were on land, facing the sea.** While on previous occasions the crowd had been "large" (3:7; cf. 1:34; 2:2, 15; 3:8, 10), the present multitude is described as "very large." [135] Result: This time *we know* (contrast 3:9) that Jesus actually stepped into a boat, which was then rowed out a little distance from the beach. From the land the huge throng was facing [136] the sea; hence, was also facing Jesus, who in turn was facing the people.

---

134 Or: either "Behold" or "Lo" or "Look" (instead of "Once" or "Once upon a time.").

135 Note πλεῖστος, superlative of πολύς. This superlative is here used in the elative sense.

136 Although πρὸς τὴν θάλασσαν can be rendered "by the seaside," yet "facing the sea" (cf. John 1:1) is also possible, and perhaps even preferable in view of Mark's characteristic vividness.

This time, therefore, the Lord used a boat as his pulpit. This point should not be quickly passed by. One of the astounding facts with respect to Christ's earthly ministry is the rich variety of methods he employed to reach his audiences. Many a time he must have preached and taught at the regular synagogue service (Mark 1:21, 39; 3:1; 6:2); and in Judea also in the temple (John 18:20). He believed in regularity of worship (Luke 4:16). This shows that the habit of some, who have begun to substitute their own group meetings for church attendance, would—except in special circumstances of stress or necessity—not meet with his approval. On the other hand, this regularity did not prevent him from availing himself of *additional* opportunities to spread the good news. He did not limit himself to temple and synagogue, but addressed the crowd anywhere. He spoke to the people from a mountain (Matt. 5:1 ff.), while with them in a house (Mark 2:1 ff.), by the seaside (4:1a), in the desert (8:1-4), while sitting in a boat (4:1b), or even when a group had gathered in a cemetery (John 11:38 ff.). There was no "stiffness" or rigidity about the Master. Without losing sight of principle—for he never sinned (John 8:46)—he was always adapting himself to circumstances, or circumstances to himself. Cf. I Cor. 9:19-22.

The same holds with respect to his flexibility in selecting an audience, or allowing an audience to select him as the Speaker. He spoke to anyone who was willing to listen: crowds, The Twelve, separate individuals; publicans and sinners; men but also women; Jews but also non-Jews; the poor as well as the rich. To all he proclaimed the good tidings.

Finally, as the present section indicates, in his preaching and teaching he made use of illustrations, parables, that is "earthly stories with heavenly meanings." In fact, a study of Christ's sayings and discourses reveals that his style ran the gamut of interest-arousing devices. Nevertheless, all his words were "from the heart to the heart." There were no artificial smiles, unnatural gestures, stilted phrases. Everything was genuine. "Never did a man speak as this man speaks" (John 7:46). It was thus he commanded, commissioned, admonished, exhorted, explained, questioned, consoled, refuted, and predicted.

The minister, therefore, whose spiritual (?) contact with the world of human beings destined for eternity consists of delivering—mostly reading?— to "his own" people one sermon a week, or even two, without stirring appeals, tender admonitions, illustrations, and/or a climax; and who then retires to his study for the next six days, may well ask himself whether anyone will ever say about him, "I recognize that he has been with Jesus." Cf. Acts 4:13. The so-called "layman" whose heart is never so filled with the warmth of Christ's love that he listens eagerly and that his mouth overflows with praise and witness-bearing, should ask himself the same question.

2. He was teaching them many things in parables. Mark presents only a very small selection of these parables (verses 2b-32); Matthew, a much wider selection (most of chapter 13). And even Matthew's group of seven kingdom parables need not be considered the full record of all the parables Jesus spoke at this time. Mark, after presenting the parable of The Sower, The Seed Growing in Secret, and The Mustard Seed, concludes his story on this theme by adding, "With many such parables he was speaking the word to them . . ." (verses 33, 34); then turns to another subject. After the words, **and in his teaching he said to them,** Mark records that Jesus began the first of this series of parables by saying, 3. **Listen! Once upon a time the sower went out to sow.** After the introductory word "Listen," in this connection found only in Mark, not in Matthew and Luke, and arousing the attention of the audience, the sentence continues literally, "Behold" or "Lo" or "Look." The word used in the original has about the same interest promoting effect as our "Once" or "Once upon a time." [137] In the present case the focus of attention is not the fact as such that the sower went out to sow, but the entire story.

Instead of "the sower" the rendering "a farmer" has been suggested. However, when this is followed up consistently, so that verse 14 then becomes "The farmer sows the word," the inadequacy of such a rendering becomes immediately apparent, for it is not a farmer who sows the word, but it is the Son of man who does this. [138] 4. **It so happened that, as he was sowing, some seed fell along the path.** It was customary for wheat or barley to be sown by hand. But it makes all the difference in the world how that seed is received. As this man is sowing, it was unavoidable that a portion of the seed fell along the footpath on which he was walking through the field. Since the place where it fell had not been reached by the plow, and/or many feet had walked here, the soil was too hard for anything to fall "into" it. So this seed remained on the surface, with the result: **The birds came and gobbled it up.** The feathered creatures acted very quickly and greedily. The seed was snatched *up;* then *down* it went into the alimentary tract; hence literally, "they (the birds) ate it *down.*" 5. **Some fell on rocky ground, where it did not have much soil, and because it did not have depth of soil it sprang up immediately.** It is typical of Palestine—now "Israel" and its surroundings—that a considerable portion of its tillable soil is found on top of layers of rock. In such a situation the seed, in the process of sprouting, has only one way to go, namely, up. So, instead of first becoming firmly rooted,

---

137 The first of these two alternatives ("Once") is the rendering proposed by Phillips and by Norlie; the second ("once upon a time"), the one suggested by J. A. Alexander, *The Gospel according to Matthew,* New York, 1867, p. 353.

138 Besides, the original uses two words—σπείρων and σπείραι—derived from the same stem, in reality two forms of the same word, the first being a noun derived from a present participle; the second, an aorist infinitive. Last but not least, the transition from the parable to the meaning is made much easier by means of the translation "sower . . . to sow" than by any other rendering.

the seed described in this part of the parable "sprang up immediately." **6. But when the sun came up it was scorched, and since it had no root it withered away.** Because this seed lacked depth of earth, it could not take root; hence, when the sun was risen it was scorched, thus Matthew and Mark. Luke 8:6 supplies the intermediate cause of withering: (for lack of roots) this seed "had no moisture." No wonder that it was scorched to death. **7. Some fell among the thorns. The thorns shot up and choked it.** . . . This soil was infested with the roots of thorns. Since generally nothing grows faster than that which is not wanted, and each patch of ground had adequate room for only a definitely restricted amount of healthy plant life, it is not surprising that the faster growing weeds were soon choking the very life out of the noble grain. Mark states the result as follows: **and it did not yield any grain. 8. And some seeds fell into good soil. Coming up and growing they were bearing fruit, yielding: some thirty(fold), some sixty, and some a hundred.** Note Mark's change from singular to plural, from collective seed to individual seeds. Could it be that in this case the evangelist (and before him Jesus) wishes to place special emphasis on the variety in the yield? Mark describes this yield in the ascending order: thirty(fold), sixty, hundred; contrast Matt. 13:8 (descending order). By the use of the imperfect (were bearing, yielding) he *pictures* the scene!

An earnest admonition concludes the parable: **9. And he said, He who has ears to hear, let him hear.** Ears must be used to hear, that is, to listen closely and take to heart. In all of Christ's teaching, both on earth and from heaven, it would be difficult to discover any exhortation that he repeated more often, in one form or another, than the one of verse 9 (see also verse 23; cf. 8:18 in both Mark and Luke; 13:9 in both Matt. and Rev.; further: Matt. 13:43; Luke 8:8; 14:35; Rev. 2:7, 11, 17, 29; 3:6, 13, 22). This repetition is not surprising. Is not lack of receptivity that which, if persisted in, leads directly to the unpardonable sin? The results of unwillingness to hear, or of hearing but not heeding, are set forth in Jesus' own explanation of the parable (verses 13-20).

---

10 When he was alone, those who were about him together with the twelve were asking him concerning the parables. 11 He said to them, "To y o u has been given the mystery of the kingdom of God, but for the outsiders everything comes in parables, 12 that:

> They may see and see but not perceive;
> And hear and hear but not understand;
> Lest they should turn again and be forgiven."

4:10-12 *The Purpose of the Parables*
Cf. Matt. 13:10-17, 36; Luke 8:9, 10

The admonition, "He who has ears to hear, let him hear," did not remain unheeded. **10. When he was alone, those who were about him together with** the twelve were asking him concerning the parables. Jesus was now *alone,* in the sense that he had dismissed the crowds and had gone home. Nevertheless, he was not entirely alone. With him were The Twelve. But note: "those who were about him together with the twelve." The meaning must be that in addition to twelve well-known disciples there were present also some who belonged to the wider circle of constant followers. Mark pictures this combined group in the act of asking Jesus about the parable*s.* The plural is significant. Though Mark, before describing Jesus as being now "alone" has related only one parable, that of The Sower, Matthew reports four parables—The Sower, The Tares, The Mustard Seed, and The Leaven—before telling the readers (13:36) that Jesus dismissed the crowds and went home (or "into the house"), where he was interrogated by his disciples. However, when we fix our attention on the *wording* of the incident recorded in Mark 4:10-12—the questioning done by the disciples and the answer given by Jesus—, we should turn again to Matthew 13, but this time to verses 10-17, especially verses 10, 11, 13-15. Luke's report (8:9, 10) looks like a very brief summary.

Those who surrounded Jesus wanted to know two things: *a.* why he used parables in addressing the crowds (cf. Matt. 13:10), and *b.* what was the meaning of a certain particular parable; for example, that of The Tares (Matt. 13:36), or (here in Mark 4:13) that of The Sower. 11. **He said to them, To y o u has been given the mystery of the kingdom of God, but for the outsiders everything comes in parables . . . .**

This word "mystery" is very interesting. Outside of Christendom, in the realm of paganism, it referred to a secret teaching, rite, or ceremony having something to do with religion but hidden from the masses, and known (or practiced) only by a group of initiates. In the LXX (Greek) translation of Daniel 2, where the word occurs no less than eight times (as a singular in verses 18, 19, 27, 30, and 47b; as a plural in verses 28, 29, and 47a), it refers to a "secret" that must be revealed, a riddle that must be interpreted. In the book of Revelation, where it occurs four times (1:20; 10:7; 17:5, 7), it is perhaps best explained as being "the symbolical meaning" of that which required explanation. The word occurs twenty-one times in Paul's epistles (Rom. 11:25; 16:25; I Cor. 2:1, 7; 4:1; 13:2; 14:2; 15:51; Eph. 1:9; 3:3, 4, 9; 5:32; 6:19, Col. 1:26, 27; 2:2; 4:3; II Thess. 2:7; I Tim. 3:9, 16). There it can be defined as *a person or a truth that would have remained unknown had not God revealed him or it, a revealed or open secret.* Thus, had it not been disclosed we would not have known that in every age a remnant of Jews (as well as of Gentiles) will be saved, until at last through faith in Jesus Christ "all Israel" will thus have been gathered; and that this process will continue until Christ's return, when the full number of Gentiles destined to be saved will also have been brought in (Rom. 11:25). Again, had it not been revealed we would not have known that "we shall not all sleep," etc. (I Cor.

15:51). A very similar "mystery" or revealed secret is Christ himself in all his glorious riches, actually dwelling through his Spirit in the hearts and lives of both Gentiles and Jews, united in one body, the church (Eph. 3:4-6; Col. 1:26, 27). And how, apart from divine disclosure, would we have been able to discover that one day the spirit of lawlessness will become incarnate in "the man of lawlessness"? (II Thess. 2:7).

This same general definition of "mystery," namely that it is a divinely disclosed secret, a person or thing which apart from revelation could not have been discovered, fits very well into the context of the present passage of Mark's Gospel (4:11) and its parallels (Matt. 13:11; Luke 8:10), the only Gospel instances of its use. Here *the mystery* is the powerful manifestation of the reign ("kingdom," "kingship") of God in human hearts and lives; which reign, in connection with Christ's coming, was attended by mighty works in both the physical and the spiritual realms. Jesus declares that this mystery—that it was indeed God who was doing all these things, not Satan— had been "given," that is, "graciously disclosed" to those who were with him at this time; in fact, to all who had accepted him by genuine faith. To outsiders (literally: "to those outside") "everything comes in parables"; that is, to them Christ's teaching had to be presented in parabolic form. From what follows it is clear that when Jesus here speaks about "outsiders" he is thinking especially of hardened Pharisees and their followers, men with impenitent hearts (cf. Matt. 13:13, 15), for he continues: 12. **that**

> **They may see and see but not perceive;**
> **And hear and hear but not understand;**
> **Lest they should turn again and be forgiven.**

In this way Mark summarizes the substance of Christ's quotation from Isa. 6:9, 10. Luke 8:10 is even shorter. A fuller statement is found in Matt. 13:13-15. [139]

---

[139] Mark's summary (cf. LXX rendering): "That they may see indeed . . . , and hear indeed . . . ," preserves the emphasis of the underlying Hebrew construction in Isa. 6:9, 10. The imperative plurals followed by infinitive absolutes in Hebrew are in Mark's Greek represented by present participles followed by subjunctives. In Hebrew the entire passage (verses 9 and 10) consists of a series of emphatic commands, introduced by, "And he said, Go and tell this people." There follows:

> "Hear and hear, but do not understand,
> And see and see, but do not perceive
> [Or: "Hear indeed, but understand not,
> And see indeed, but perceive not"],
> Make the heart of this people fat,
> And their ears heavy,
> And shut their eyes,
> Lest they see with their eyes,
> And hear with their ears,
> And understand with their heart,
> And turn again, and be healed."

Jesus, then, is saying, "For the outsiders everything comes in parables, that they may see and see but not perceive ... lest they should turn again and be forgiven." But how can that be? Isn't this shocking? Can it be true that the kind and merciful Savior, the very One who was constantly extending tender invitations, would take great pains to prevent people from perceiving and understanding the truth? That he would actually go out of his way to keep men from turning to God and being forgiven?

There have been various attempts to solve this problem. Among them are the following:

1. We misinterpret the little word "that" when we take it to mean "in order that" or "so that." [140] Or else, Mark himself misinterpreted the Aramaic word which Jesus probably used.

Answer. Mark represents Jesus as saying not only "that" but also "lest." This combination *that . . . lest* shows that the little word "that" can best be taken to indicate purpose.

2. The saying is an unauthentic and intolerable version of a genuine saying of Jesus. [141] It is sometimes added that in view of such passages as Matt. 11:28-30; Rev. 3:20 Jesus could never have spoken the words ascribed to him in Mark 4:11, 12.

Answer. For the theory that this saying is unauthentic and intolerable there is no proof. Also, is it fair to refer to Matt. 11:28-30, but to forget about verse 25; or, to Rev. 3:20, and to ignore verse 16? Besides, does not Mark's summary truly reflect Isa. 6:9, 10?

3. If Christ's words were those reported by Mark, they must have been spoken in jest. Jesus evidently wanted his words to be taken in a sense which was the exact opposite of their literal meaning. This is clear from the fact that Matthew diametrically changes the meaning of the statement, for he makes Jesus say *"because* [instead of *that*] seeing they do not see. . . ." [142]

Answer. If it be granted that when the Master uttered the words, "To y o u has been given the mystery of God" he was speaking in earnest, stating what he knew to be a fact, and not making a joke, the rest of the closely knit saying must also be considered a fact. And as to the alleged conflict between Matthew, on the one hand, and Mark and Luke, on the other, why cannot both be right?

It is clear that Mark abbreviates, leaving out any reference to "Make the heart of this people fat and their ears heavy. . . ." However, he retains, ". . . lest they should turn again and be forgiven," a legitimate restatement of ". . . lest they turn again and be healed."

[140] Cf. A. T. Robertson, *Word Pictures*, Vol. I, p. 286. He maintains that if ἵνα (here in Mark 4:12) is given the causative sense of ὅτι (in Matt. 13:13) the difficulty disappears.
[141] See Vincent Taylor, *op. cit.*, p. 257.
[142] See E. Trueblood, *The Humor of Christ*, New York, Evanston, London, 1964, pp. 91, 92.

The true explanation, as this author sees it, is as follows: Both *because* and *that* (whether "in order that"—my preference—, or "so that") are correct. It was *because* by their own choice these impenitent Pharisees and their followers had refused to see and hear, that, as a punishment for this refusal, they are now addressed in parables, "*that* they may see and see but not perceive, and hear and hear but not understand, lest they should turn again and be forgiven." They must "endure the blame of their own blindness and hardness" (Calvin on this passage). [143] God had given these people a wonderful opportunity. It is his sovereign will to remove what man is unwilling to improve, to darken the heart that refuses to hearken. He hardens those that have hardened themselves. If God even surrenders to the lusts of their hearts the unenlightened heathen when they hold back the truth in unrighteousness (Rom. 1:18, 26), will he not punish more severely the impenitents before whom the Light of the world is constantly confirming the truthfulness of his message? And if he blesses those who accept the mysterious, will he not curse those who reject the obvious? It is evident, therefore, that Matt. 13:13 is in harmony with Mark 4:12; in fact, the "because" of the former helps to explain the "that" or "in order that" of the latter. When, of their own accord and after repeated threats and promises, people reject the Lord and spurn his messages, then he hardens them, in order that those who were not willing to repent will not be able to repent and be forgiven. See also N.T.C. on Matt. 13:10-15; and on John 12:37-41.

---

13 And he said to them, "Do y o u not know what this parable means? How then are y o u going to understand all the parables? 14 The sower sows the word. [144] 15 The ones along the path where the word is sown are the kind of people in whose case, whenever they hear, Satan immediately comes and takes away the word that was sown in them. 16 And the ones sown on rocky ground are the kind of people who, whenever they hear the word, immediately accept it with joy. 17 However, they have no root in themselves and last but for a short while. Then, when affliction or persecution arises on account of the word, they immediately fall away. 18 And some, the ones sown among the thorns, are the kind of people who hear the word, 19 and then the cares of this present world, the deceitful glamor of riches, and the desires for other things enter in and choke the word, and it becomes unfruitful. 20 And those sown on the good soil are the kind of people who hear the word, accept it, and bear fruit, some of them (yielding) thirtyfold, some sixty, and some a hundred."

4:13-20 *Explanation of The Parable of The Sower*
Cf. Matt. 13:18-23; Luke 8:11-15

Mark has already told us that, having dismissed the crowds, Jesus was alone with The Twelve and some other constant followers, and that this

---

143 See also H. B. Swete, *op. cit.*, p. 76.
144 Or: the message; so throughout the parable.

combined group then asked him about the parables (4:10). Luke, more specifically, adds that these disciples asked Jesus what this particular parable, the one of The Sower, meant (8:9). This explains what we now read in Mark 4:13. **And he said to them, Do y o u not know what this parable means? How then are y o u going to understand all the parables?** If they have no insight into the parable of The Sower, how will they be able to sense the meaning of [145] any parable? This implies that the Master wants them to listen carefully, so they may be able to catch the meaning of other parables also. Jesus then proceeds to explain the parable: **14. The sower sows the word.** This is one of the key passages for the understanding of the story illustration. It should be borne in mind throughout. It fixes our attention upon two objects: the sower and the seed. *As to the first,* although in this parable he is nowhere identified—for the emphasis is on the kind of soil rather than on the sower—, in that of The Tares it is definitely stated that the sower is the Son of man (Matt. 13:37), that is, Jesus himself (Matt. 16:13-15). There is no good reason to believe that this identification does not also hold for the parable of The Sower. Jesus, therefore, points to himself as the sower. By a legitimate extension of the figure (see Matt. 10:40) we are justified in saying that the sower is not only Jesus but anyone—minister, missionary, evangelist, any genuine witness-bearer—who truly proclaims the Son of man's message. *As to the second,* we have already been told—and this is implied in the very term—that "the sower" sows *the seed* (Mark 4:3 ff.). So, when Jesus now states, "The sower sows *the word,*" the conclusion must be that the seed symbolizes the word, the message from God. See also Matt. 13:19; Luke 8:11.

To these two tenets *the third* can now be added: The "ground" or "soil" upon which the seed falls is clearly man's heart, or, if one prefers, man himself. This is definitely implied in Matt. 13:19a, "what was sown in his heart." In each of the four instances recorded in the parable the "ground" or "soil," that is, the "heart," hence the person, is different. One might speak of *the unresponsive heart* (Mark 4:15), *the impulsive heart* (verses 16, 17), *the preoccupied heart* (verses 18, 19), and *the good, responsive, or well-prepared heart* (verse 20). Substitute the word "person" for "heart" and the meaning remains essentially the same. The "heart" indicates the "person" or "hearer" as he is in his inner being. Correct is therefore the following: "What, then, is the lesson? The Savior has given us the answer in his own interpretation of the story. The seed is the word of God, or the word of the kingdom; and the soil is human hearts: so that, reduced to a general law, the

---

[145] The two verbs used in the original are οἶδα (here οἴδατε) and γινώσκω (here γνώσεσθε). The first indicates knowledge by intuition or insight; the second, by recognition, observation, experience, and/or acquaintance. See N.T.C. on John 1:10, 11, 31, 3:11; 8:28, 55; 16:30; 21:17.

teaching of the parable is, that the result of the hearing of the gospel always and everywhere depends on the condition of heart of those to whom it is addressed. The character of the hearer determines the effect of the word upon him." [146]

Unresponsive Hearts

Jesus continues: **15. The ones along the path where the word is sown are the kind of people in whose case, whenever they hear, Satan immediately comes and takes away the word that was sown in them.** Meaning: the people that are represented by seed sown along the path (see verse 4) are the kind that allow Satan, the great adversary (see above, on 1:13), to take away the message that had been sown in them. By no means does Jesus excuse these people, as if only Satan and not they themselves were responsible for what happened to the divine message that had been spoken to them. Verse 15 does not cancel verse 9! But here in verse 15 these frivolous hearers are being told that in treating the word of God so lightly they are co-operating with the prince of evil!

These people do nothing with the message. They do not use it to good advantage. "Immediately" after they have heard it any favorable effect it might have had on them is annihilated. What accounts for their negative reaction? Perhaps it is ill-will toward the messenger. Or perhaps hostility with respect to this particular message. Or they do not wish to be inconvenienced (Acts 24:25). The spirit of indifference may have crept into them, perhaps little by little until it was total, their hearts having become as hard as the path on which the seed of the parable was scattered.

The Lord, addressing Ezekiel, gave this description of the prophet's audience: "You are to them like a lovely song, sung with a beautiful voice, and played well on an instrument; for they hear your words, but refuse to practice them" (Ezek. 33:32). Cf. Matt. 7:26. The following lines may also be appropriate in this connection:

> "The Baptist found him far too deep,
>   The Deist sighed with saving sorrow,
> And the lean Levite went to sleep,
>   And dreamt of eating pork tomorrow."
>
> Praed—*The Vicar*

Impulsive Hearts

16, 17. And the ones sown on rocky ground are the kind of people who, whenever they hear the word, immediately accept it with joy. However, they

---

[146] W. M. Taylor, *The Parables of Our Savior, Expounded and Illustrated*, New York, 1886, p. 22.

have no root in themselves and last but for a short while. Then, when affliction or persecution arises on account of the word, they immediately fall away. The description of unresponsive hearts or hearers is followed by that of impulsive ones. Note how in this particular case both Mark and Matthew *twice* make use of the word "immediately." These people act "on the spur of the moment." *Immediately* they accept the word, with joy even! And then *immediately* they fall away. They get caught, are ensnared, by affliction and persecution. It is this that induces them to give up what at first they had so enthusiastically embraced. [147] Had they been genuine believers they would not have been *to the end* thus ensnared.

In the midst of *affliction,* that is, all kinds of pressure mostly from the outside in a non-Christian environment, and *persecution,* actual suffering deliberately brought about by the enemy, all of this on account of the message, *perseverance* is the mark of the true believer. This perseverance, which by implication is here commended, must however be genuine. It must take place for the sake not of self but of Christ. It must be a willingness to suffer out of love for the Lord, his word, his people, and his cause. When such love is absent, the endurance is futile (see I Cor. 13:3b). When it is present, it produces gladness of heart, assurance of salvation. See Matt. 5:11, 12; John 16:33; Acts 5:41; Rom. 8:18, 31-39; Phil. 1:27-30; I Peter 4:14; Rev. 2:9, 10.

But the people symbolized by the seed that had fallen on rocky soil (see on verses 5, 6) lacked such stick-to-itiveness. They never took to heart the examples of Ruth, Jonathan, Stephen, and Paul. The word "loyalty" was not in their vocabulary.

As to examples of such fair-weather "friends," is it not reasonable to suppose that among the many Hosanna shouters (Mark 11:9, 10 and parallels) there were also some who a few days later screamed, "Crucify, crucify"? It must be borne in mind that not only after Christ's resurrection (Acts 4:3; 5:18; 6:11, 12; 7:54-60; 8:1; etc.) but even earlier (as is definitely established by John 9:22, 34, and may well be implied also in Matt. 5:10-12; 10:23, 25, 28; Luke 6:22; 12:4) Christ's followers were being persecuted. Not everyone affected by such persecution stood the test. To some the words of I John 2:19 applied: "They went out from us, but they never actually belonged to us." As to genuine believers, see John 10:28, "My sheep listen to my voice, and I know them, and they follow me. I give them everlasting life, and they shall certainly never perish, and no one shall snatch them out of my hand."

---

[147] Note the verb σκανδαλίζονται, literally meaning: they are ensnared, lured into sin; hence, fall away. The σκάνδαλον is basically the bait-stick in a trap or snare. It is the crooked stick that springs the trap. Derived meanings: trap (Rom. 11:9); enticement, temptation (Matt. 18:7); cause of offense, stumbling-block (I Cor. 1:23).

The erstwhile outward adherants, never *genuine* followers at all, for their confessions did not spring from inner conviction (they had "*no root*"), failed to consider that true discipleship implies self-surrender, self-denial, sacrifice, service, and suffering. They ignored the fact that it is the way of the cross that leads home.

Preoccupied Hearts

18. 19. **And some, the ones sown among the thorns, are the kind of people who hear the word, and then the cares of this present world, and deceitful glamor of riches, and the desires for other things enter in and choke the words, and it becomes unfruitful.** This passage describes the case of people whose hearts resemble soil infested with roots and runners of thorns. Such "dirty" soil is a serious threat to the growth of any desirable plant. Similarly hearts filled with worry with respect to the workaday world, beclouded by dreams about riches, and (Mark adds) the desire for other things, thwart any influence for good that might otherwise proceed from the entrance of the kingdom message. Such hearts are preoccupied. They have no room for calm and earnest meditation on the word or message of the Lord. Should any such serious study and reflection nevertheless attempt to gain entrance, it would immediately be choked off.

Cares, that is, constant anxiety about worldly affairs—namely, about matters pertaining to the age in which they are living—fill such minds and hearts with dark foreboding. When these persons are poor they deceive themselves into thinking that if they were only rich they would be happy.

When they are rich they delude themselves into imagining that if they were only still richer they would be satisfied, as if material riches could under any circumstances guarantee contentment. In fact, the glamor that pertains to riches is *deceitful glamor*.

To the two thorns already mentioned Jesus, as reported by Mark, adds a third, namely, *the desires for other* [or: *for the remaining*] *things*. No doubt he includes all other wrong desires [148] under this heading. Such desires or cravings are wrong either *a.* because the object for which these people yearn is wrong; for example, a desire for dangerous drugs, or for intimate relations with another man's wife; or *b.* because, even though the thing which one desires to have or to do is perfectly legitimate, the desire itself may be inordinate; for example, to play baseball or chess *to the neglect of everything else*. That Jesus was especially thinking of sinful pleasures would seem to follow from Luke's brief summary: "cares and riches and pleasures of

---

148 For a word study of the term ἐπιθυμία (note the plural here: ἐπιθυμίαι) see N.T.C. on I and II Timothy and Titus, pp. 271, 272, footnote 147.

life" (8:14). So interpreted, we notice that Luke's enumeration runs parallel with that of Mark.

Doubtlessly when Jesus mentioned the thorns that choked the sprouting seed, he left out nothing that could be placed in this general category. Anything at all in the entire realm of Possessions, Power—or if one prefers Prestige—, and Pleasure, that destroys the effect of the good seed of the word is included. "For all that is in the world, the lust of the flesh and the lust of the eyes and the vainglory of life, is not of the Father, but is of the world" (I John 2:16 A.R.V.).

In the days of Amos outwardly religious men would ask, "When will the new moon be over, that we may sell grain? And the sabbath, that we may offer wheat for sale [or: that we may open the wheat market], making the bushelbasket small and the shekel large, and dealing deceitfully with false balances?" The deceptive glamor of riches was the thorn that choked to death whatever good the message from God might have done. Other examples, both from Scripture and daily life, abound.

The people here indicated cannot be richly blessed nor can they be a blessing. The word as it affects them cannot be fruitful. There is nothing wrong with the sower. Also, there is nothing wrong with the seed. With these people, however, everything is wrong. They should ask the Lord to deliver them from corroding cares and dream-world delusions, so that the kingdom message may begin to have free course in their hearts and lives. Then their minds, rescued from gnawing anxieties and delusory fantasies, will be able to reflect meaningfully on such precious passages as Prov. 30:7-9; Isa. 26:3; Matt. 6:19-34; 19:23, 24; Luke 12:6, 7, 13-34; I Tim. 6:6-10; and Heb. 13:5, 6.

Responsive Hearts

20. And those sown on the good soil are the kind of people who hear the word, accept it, and bear fruit, some of them (yielding) thirtyfold, some sixty, and some a hundred. With these people the message of the kingdom falls into good soil, the kind of soil that, negatively speaking, is neither hard nor shallow nor preoccupied; positively speaking, is receptive and fertile.

These people hear because they want to hear. They reflect on what they hear, for they have faith in the speaker. So they reach a measure of true understanding. They put the message into practice and bear fruit: conversion, faith, love, joy, peace, longsuffering, etc.

The importance of spiritual fruitbearing, as the mark of the true believer, is stressed even in the Old Testament (Ps. 1:1-3; 92:14; 104:13). This line of thought is continued in the Gospels (Matt. 3:10; 7:17-20; 12:33-35; Luke 3:8; John ch. 15) and in the rest of the New Testament (Acts 2:38; 16:31;

Rom. 7:4; Gal. 5:22; Eph. 5:9; Phil. 4:17; Col. 1:6; Heb. 12:11; 13:15; James 3:17, 18).

There is, however, a difference in the degree of fruitfulness. Not all are equally penitent, trustful, loyal, courageous, meek, etc., hence also not all are equally productive in bringing other lives to Christ. In the case of some believers the seed, the message, yields thirtyfold, that is, thirty times as much as was sown; in some sixty, and in some a hundred. Matthew has the opposite order (100, 60, 30). In faithfully reproducing Christ's message, each evangelist employs his own style. There is no essential difference.

Consider Timothy, Titus, and Paul: three eminent men of God, men in whom the seed of the gospel had sprouted and had brought forth fruit. After their conversion the three have in common unwavering loyalty to the cause of the gospel, willingness to perform difficult kingdom tasks, love for souls, a love that sprang from love for God, the very God who had first loved them. *Yet, there was a difference between the three.* Timothy—a wonderful Christian indeed! (Phil. 2:19-23)—needed a little prodding. He was the timid type. The Corinthians were told to see to it that when Timothy arrived, he would be with them "without fear" (I Cor. 16:10). And see also II Tim. 2:22a. Titus, on the other hand, is the man who is able not only to take orders but also to go ahead of his own accord (II Cor. 8:16, 17). He is resourceful, a man of initiative in a good cause. One finds in him something of the aggressiveness of Paul. Neither Timothy nor Titus, however, can compare with Paul. Anyone who reads II Cor. 11:23-28 should be convinced of that. Without exaggeration he was able to write the words of I Cor. 15:10, ascribing all the glory to God alone.

The comparison here made between Timothy, Titus, and Paul is not intended to convey the idea that Timothy produced only thirtyfold, Titus exactly sixty, and Paul a hundred. It is intended only as evidence for the basic truth, which this concluding part of the parable establishes, namely, that even among those whose lives are spiritually fruitful there are differences. Let everyone do his best to produce much fruit (John 15:5), always remembering however that even though the parable emphasizes that the result of the hearing of the gospel depends on the condition of the hearts of those to whom it is addressed, so that *human responsibility* is stressed, in the final analysis every good thought, disposition, word, deed, character has its source in God and his sovereign grace (Rom. 11:36; I Cor. 4:7). See also the explanation of the parable of The Seed Growing in Secret (Mark 4:26-29).

---

21 And he said to them, "The lamp is not brought in to be put under the peck-measure, is it, or under the bed? Is it not (brought in) to be put on the lampstand? 22 For there is nothing concealed except to be disclosed, nor is anything covered up except to come to light. 23 If anyone has ears to hear, let him hear." 24 And he said to them, "Be careful what y o u hear. In accordance with the measure whereby y o u mea-

sure it shall be measured back to y o u, and more besides shall be given to y o u.   25 For he who has, to him shall be given; and he who does not have, from him shall be taken away even what he has."

4:21-25 *Various Sayings of Jesus*
For verse 21 cf. Matt. 5:15; Luke 8:16; 11:33.
For verse 22 cf. Matt. 10:26; Luke 8:17; 12:2.
For verse 23 cf. Matt. 11:15; 13:9, 43; Mark 4:9; Luke 8:8, 18a; 14:35.
For verse 24a see above, on verse 23.
For verse 24b cf. Matt. 7:2; Luke 6:38.
For verse 25 cf. Matt. 13:12; 25:29; Luke 8:18b; 19:26.

In this paragraph are found several sayings of Jesus that, as shown above, are recorded also elsewhere. It is natural to believe that Jesus repeated some of his famous words.

The connection between verse 21 and the preceding is not clear. This holds also for the relation between the verses of the new paragraph (21-25). This does not mean that the sayings are here grouped artificially. But though an attempt will be made to show inner coherence—the thought connections between the several verses—, it must be admitted at the very outset that certainty in such matters is unobtainable.

21. And he said to them, The lamp is not brought in to be put under the peck-measure, is it, or under the bed? Is it not (brought in) to be put on the lampstand?

"And he said to *them*." To whom? Probably to the same group as in verse 10; hence, not to the general public. Contrast "And he said to them" of verses 21 and 24 with "And he said" of verses 26 and 30. In the latter case Mark returns to the time when from the boat the Master was addressing the crowds.

Jesus, in the parable of The Sower, had emphasized the necessity of fruitbearing, the result of seed falling upon good soil, that is, of the word entering well-prepared hearts. Fertile hearts resemble shining lamps. If this view of the connection is right, then by means of a different figure Jesus is stressing the same basic truth, namely, that hearts and lives should be fruitful, that they should shine so as to benefit others, to God's glory.

Nevertheless, in the light of the then prevailing conditions, as set forth in the Gospels, the conclusion would seem to be warranted that the basic thought is taking a slightly different turn here. What is it that causes hearts and lives to shine? Answer: the word of God asserting its influence within these hearts and lives. That word is symbolized by the seed (Matt. 13:19; Mark 4:14; Luke 8:11); also by the lamp (Ps. 119:105). It was that word and that lamp which the rabbis were hiding under an elaborate load of human traditions (Matt. 15:3; ch. 23) and hypocritical actions (Matt. 6:1-18;

161

23:15). That word must reveal its power once more. That lamp must shine forth again in all the pristine purity of its light, in order to be a blessing to men. See Matt. 5:15, 16; Luke 8:16b. This interpretation sheds light on what Jesus says about the absurdity of putting the lamp under the peck-measure or the bed, instead of on the lampstand.

Note the article ("the") before the name of each piece of furniture here mentioned. This is not strange, for: *a.* lamp, peck-measure, bed, and lamp-stand were familiar pieces in a typical Galilean home; *b.* in the homes of the poor there may have been only one lamp, only one peck-measure, etc.

As to the lamp, picture a terra cotta saucer-shaped object with handle on one end; on the other end a nozzle-shaped extension with hole for a wick. As to the two holes in the lamp's upper surface, one is for adding oil, the other for air. Of course, not all lamps were similar. For the different types consult encyclopaedias; better still, visit the museum.

The question Jesus asks is a double one. It is immediately evident not only from the Greek but from the translation as here proposed, [149] that the first part looks forward to the answer "No"; the second expects "Yes." Who would ever think of first lighting the lamp and then putting it under the peck-measure? [150] Or under the "bed," a kind of mattress which, when not in use was rolled up. Doing this with the lamp would be absurd. A lit lamp belongs on the lampstand! Such a lampstand was generally a very simple object. It might be a shelf extending from the pillar in the center of the room (the pillar that supported the large cross-beam of the flat roof), or a single stone projecting inward from the wall, or a piece of metal conspicuously placed and used similarly.

The point is, of course, that believers, too, should let their light shine. They should permit the word of God to be in full control over their own lives: their inner self, dispositions, thoughts, words, teachings, writings, deeds. And they should never hold back but should testify. See Ps. 66:16; 107:2; Matt. 5:16; II Tim. 4:2; I John 2:12-14. God intended that the mystery given to his children should be disclosed. It is hidden only from those who continue to harden themselves against its appeal. Thus, while the teaching of Mark 4:11, 12 is not refuted, the emphasis now is rather on that which must happen first of all: the sower must sow the seed; the lamp must be placed where it can shine; the mystery must be disclosed, not concealed.

But whether revealed or concealed, whatever is done with it will not go

---

[149] See also N.A.S., Williams, Beck, Lenski. All of these are excellent. Some of the others are not so exact or not so clear on this passage. They do not bring out as clearly as does the Greek that μή (here μήτι) expects the answer "No," and οὐ (here οὐχ) anticipates "Yes."

[150] Greek μόδιος, from Latin *modius*, a capacity measure = 16 sectarii, about 8.75 liters or almost exactly a peck.

unnoticed: 22. **For there is nothing concealed except to be disclosed, nor is anything covered up except to come to light.** Men may try to cover up things, but in this they will always be unsuccessful, for God brings everything out into the open. One day whatever is now concealed will be revealed. See Eccl. 12:14; Matt. 12:36; 13:43; 16:27; Luke 8:17; 12:2; Rom. 2:6; Col. 3:3, 4; Rev. 2:23; 20:12, 13.

Now this is a fact that is often ignored. Men think they can get away with their evil thoughts, plans, words, and actions. God, however, will expose all this. It is therefore not surprising that, as reported by Mark, Jesus continues: 23. **If anyone has ears to hear, let him hear.** Essentially verse 23 is the same as verse 9, though the form differs slightly (verse 9: "he who has"; verse 23: "if anyone has"). Therefore see on verse 9.

Another but closely connected thought is now added: 24. **And he said to them, Be careful what y o u hear.** With respect to men's—here in verses 21-25 especially Christ's followers'—duty and responsibility in the matter of hearing, three things are stressed in the Gospels:

a. *That* they should hear or listen (Mark 4:9, 23), the emphasis being on hearing over against refusing to hear;

b. *What* they should hear (verse 24), what to hear over against what not to hear; and

c. *How* they should hear (Luke 8:18), attentively, judiciously, over against how not to hear.

As to "Be careful," "Take heed," or "Be on y o u r guard," see also Mark 13:33; Luke 8:18. When a person is constantly listening to what he should not be hearing—for example, malicious gossip—, he will be inclined to judge rashly and condemn. He will be wrongly *measuring* people, condemning them. Let him then bear in mind: **In accordance with the measure whereby y o u measure it shall be measured back to y o u** . . . If the one who does the measuring is kind, he will judge favorably, will take delight in giving credit where credit is due, in bestowing favors (see Luke 6:38). On the other hand, if he is of the opposite disposition, he will easily fall into the habit of judging severely, unkindly (see Matt. 7:1-5; especially verse 2). Whatever it be, the measure he gives will be the measure he gets. If he gives generously he will receive even more generously: **and more besides shall be given to y o u.** This reminds one of Matt. 6:33, where the original uses the same verb, [151] and similarly in a favorable sense: "all these things shall be added to y o u," that is, "shall be granted to y o u as an extra gift."

God's gifts are always most generous. He is forever adding gift to gift, favor to favor, blessing to blessing. He gives not only "of" his riches—as a billionaire might do when he gives a dollar to charity—, but "according to"

---

[151] προστεθήσεται, third per. sing. fut. indic. pass. of προστίθημι.

163

his riches, the riches of his grace (Eph. 1:7). He imparts "grace upon grace" (John 1:16). He not only pardons but pardons *abundantly* (Isa. 55:7). He *delights* in lovingkindness (Mic. 7:18). "Before they call I will answer; and while they are still speaking I will hear" (Isa. 65:24; cf. Dan. 9:20-23). When he loves, he loves the world; and when he gives, he gives his only begotten Son (John 3:16). That Son, moreover, not only intercedes for his people but "ever lives to make intercession for them" (Heb. 7:25). Truly, "He giveth and giveth and giveth again."

"More besides shall be given to y o u." When Abraham's servant asks Rebekah for a drink, she not only quenches *his* thirst but *in addition* also that of the camels (Gen. 24:13, 14, 18-20, 42-46).

This is only a faint reflection of what God in Christ is doing constantly:

He not only grants Solomon's wish for wisdom, but *in addition* promises him riches and length of days (I Kings 3:9-15).

He not only accedes to the centurion's request to heal the latter's servant, but *in addition* pronounces a blessing upon the centurion (Matt. 8:5-13).

He not only answers the plea of Jairus, restoring to life his daughter, but *in addition* sees to it that the child gets something to eat (Mark 5:21-24, 43).

He, the resurrected Christ, not only fulfils his promise to meet the disciples in Galilee (Matt. 26:32; 28:7, 16-20), but *in addition* meets and blesses them even earlier, in Jerusalem (Luke 24:33-48).

He not only pardons the sinner—as a governor might grant pardon—but, *in addition,* adopts him and grants him peace, holiness, joy, assurance, freedom of access, super-invincibility (Rom. chapters 5–8).

This interpretation of the final clause of verse 24 is supported by what immediately follows in verse 25. **For he who has, to him shall be given, and he who does not have, from him shall be taken away even what he has.** In matters spiritual, standing still is impossible. A person either gains or loses; he either advances or declines. Whoever has, to him shall be given. The disciples (exception Judas Iscariot) had "accepted Jesus." With reference to them he was later on going to say to the Father, "They have kept thy word" (John 17:6) and "They are not of the world" (17:16). To be sure, this faith was accompanied by many a weakness, error, and flaw. But the beginning had been made. Therefore, according to heaven's rule, further progress was assured, an advance in knowledge, love, holiness, joy, etc., in all the blessings of the kingdom of heaven, for salvation is an ever deepening stream (Ezek. 47:1-5). Every blessing is a guarantee of further blessings to come (John 1:16). "He shall have abundantly." The theory according to which Jesus (or Mark) was referring only to an increase of knowledge or even insight is improbable. Such discernment is, to be sure, included, but there is nothing in the context that would limit so rigidly the blessing here promised.

On the other hand, whoever does not have, from him shall be taken away even that semblance of knowledge, that superficial acquaintance with matters spiritual, which he once had. Is there not an analogy of this in the realm of knowledge on a level below the strictly spiritual? Is it not true that the person who has learned enough music to play a few simple melodies, but not really enough to be able to say, "I have mastered this or that instrument," and then stops practicing altogether, will soon discover that the little skill which he had at one time has vanished? The man who refuses to make proper use of his one talent loses even that (Matt. 25:24-30).

---

26 And he said, "The kingdom of God is as if a man should scatter seed on the earth, 27 and should sleep and rise night and day, and the seed should sprout and grow—how he does not know. 28 By itself the earth produces crops: first the blade, then the ear, [152] then the full grain [153] in the ear. 29 But whenever the (condition of the) crop permits, at once he puts in the sickle, because the harvest has come. [154]

4:26-29 Parable of the Seed Growing in Secret

It would appear from verses 33, 34 (cf. Matt. 13:31, 34) that when Jesus spoke the pair of parables recorded in Mark 4:26-32 (as also the one in 4:3-9), he was speaking to the crowds. In other words, Mark returns here to the situation that prevailed when from a boat the Lord addressed the people (verse 1).

Between the parable of The Sower, to which such prominence is given in the Synoptics, and which Mark also reports first of all (verses 3-9), and the one about The Seed Growing in Secret, which is peculiar to Mark, [155] there is a close relationship. The first stresses *human responsibility:* the seed cannot sprout, grow, and bear fruit unless it falls into good soil. Meaning:

---

152 Or: the head.
153 Or: kernel.
154 Or: the time of the harvest has arrived.
155 The theory according to which the parable of The Seed Growing in Secret and that of The Tares had a common source and were originally *one* is based on the circumstance that several of the same words occur in both:

	Mark 4	Matt. 13
καθεύδω	verse 27	verse 25
βλαστάω,-άνω	verse 27	verse 26
πρῶτον	verse 28	verse 30
χόρτος	verse 28	verse 26
σῖτος	verse 28	verse 30
καρπός	verse 29	verse 26
θερισμός	verse 29	verse 30

But since both parables are based on that which happens or may happen when fields are being sown, a certain amount of verbal similarity seems natural. Besides, the stories themselves are different, and so were the reasons for telling them. The theory is therefore unacceptable.

the word or message of God, the gospel, bears fruit only when the heart responds favorably. This is an aspect of the truth that must never be neglected. Yet, this may happen at times. A preacher asks his audience, "What can man do in order to be saved?" and then creates suspense by remaining silent a few moments..., after which he continues, "Let me tell y o u: he can do exactly nothing! God does it all!" Should he not also tell the other side of the story? When the jailer asked, "Men, what must I do to be saved?" Paul and Silas did not say, "You can do nothing at all." What they said was, "Believe in the Lord Jesus and you shall be saved, you and your household" (Acts 16:30, 31).

It is true, nevertheless, that *of himself* man can do nothing. It is only by means of power imparted by God that man is able to turn to God in true faith. He cannot be converted unless he is first of all regenerated (John 3:3, 5). See also Jer. 31:18; I Cor. 4:7; Eph. 2:8; Phil. 2:12, 13; 4:13. On this aspect of the truth, namely, *God's sovereignty,* the present parable places the emphasis. It teaches that just as God alone, not the farmer, thoroughly understands and is in fact the Author of *physical* growth, so also God alone, not man, thoroughly understands and is the Author of *spiritual* growth, the establishment and progress of the reign of God in hearts, lives, and spheres. It is because of his will that the spiritual seed, the word or message of the gospel, asserts its increasingly powerful influence upon the hearts of men and thus also upon society generally. What a comfort this is, for now with patience we await the harvest that is certain to arrive. Victory is assured: God's plan must be and is going to be carried out.

Accordingly, the parable sets forth three thoughts. So closely are they linked that the three actually form a unit. They are as follows:

1. To man growth is a mystery (verses 26, 27).
2. The seed reveals its potency (verse 28).
3. The harvest-time spells victory (verse 29).

Thus it is in the realm of nature; thus also in that of grace, for the kingdom's growth is also a mystery. Its (the kingdom's) word (cf. Matt. 13:19; 24:14) reveals its potency, which is going to become very clear on the day of the harvest, the final judgment, certain to arrive at the appropriate moment.

1. *To man growth is a mystery*

26, 27. And he said, The kingdom of God is as if a man should scatter seed on the earth, and should sleep and rise night and day, and the seed should sprout and grow [156] **—how he does not know.**

---

156 In the original the supposed casting or scattering of seed is viewed as one act; hence, the aor. subjunctive is used. For the "sleeping" and "rising"; "sprouting" and "growing," present subjunctives occur, since these supposed actions are viewed as continuing processes.

Jesus is again describing "the kingdom of God." See on 1:15. He is saying that this reign of God over hearts and lives, with consequent influence in every sphere, is mysterious in its growth. It is with this kingdom or kingship as it is with a man who casts seed on the earth. Having entrusted the seed to the soil, evening arrives. For the Jews that meant the beginning of a new day. Soon afterward the man, tired out from a day of hard labor, goes to sleep, sleeping on and on until dawn. In the morning he arises. As to the seed he has been scattering the preceding day, he fully realizes that he can do nothing about it. He lacks all control over the processes of germination and growth. When night falls once more, he again goes to sleep. Again he rises in the morning. That routine of sleeping and rising, sleeping and rising, night and day, night and day, goes on and on and on.

Meanwhile the seed is sprouting and growing. Just how this growth takes place he, the farmer, does not know. Neither does the chemist or the most learned agricultural specialist. He has never been able to figure out exactly how the seed is able to transform a tiny bit of—shall we say "dead"?—soil into a living plant cell; no, not just into *a* cell, any cell, but into the kind of cell that is precisely similar to the cells that were in the plant from which the seed originated.

All the farmer can do is trust. To be sure, he can cover the seed, root up weeds, loosen the soil, add fertilizer, and perhaps even channel water to his plot. All these things are important. But he cannot cause the seed to sprout and grow. As to that, all he can do is sleep night upon night, and rise day after day. The rest he must leave entirely to the seed, ultimately to the One who created the seed, who knows it thoroughly, and activates it. The farmer must trust and pray. He must wait patiently.

In the spiritual realm this holds also. The admissions "I cannot" and "I know not" are just as true with respect to the establishment and growth of the reign of God as they are with respect to germination and development of physical seed. For "I cannot" see I Cor. 3:6, "I planted, Apollos watered, but God supplied the growth." For "I know not" see John 3:8, "The wind blows where it wills, and you hear the sound, but you do not know where it comes from and where it goes to. So is everyone who is born of the Spirit."

2. *The seed reveals its potency*

28. By itself the earth produces crops: first the blade, then the ear, then the full grain in the ear. "By itself" (literally "automatically") means "without visible cause," and "apart from any human help." Think of the city gate which opened to Peter "of its own accord" (Acts 12:10, the only other New Testament instance of the occurrence of this word).

The secret of growth has, as it were, been entrusted to the earth. However, this term "earth" by metonymy must here mean "the seed embedded in the

167

earth." To that seed God entrusted the secret, so that it now, as it were, "knows" exactly what it has to do, when to do it, and how.

As to man, if the day after sowing, or even the next day or the following one, he looks at the field, he sees no sign of life whatever. But some time later when he looks again, he stands amazed when he beholds ever so many little sprouts where before nothing had been visible. He exclaims, "What potency was concealed in things so small!"

So it is also with the kingdom, the reign of God. A faithful minister scatters the seed year upon year. He explains, pictures, invites, exhorts, comforts, warns, urges, makes pastoral calls. Nevertheless, to a considerable extent his efforts seem to have been futile. Then of a sudden the winds of God begin to blow upon the gardens (hearts) of his parishioners (cf. Song of Sol. 4:16). *The word shows its power.* It had been active before, but results had not been greatly in evidence. But now men and women, old and young, educated and unlettered, rich and poor, jubilantly confess their faith and show this in their lives. The Spirit is working mightily, always in connection with the word, the gospel. The people have peace within their hearts, the assurance of salvation. They look forward to the inheritance stored up for them in heaven.

But that is by no means all. These people are grateful. Therefore they realize that everything everywhere must be done to the glory of their wonderful God (Ps. 150; John 17:1-4; Rom. 11:36; I Cor. 6:20; 10:31; Jude 24, 25; Rev. 4:11; 5:12-14; 19:1-8). They also begin to put forth every effort not only to be the means in God's hand for the conversion of others, a worthy ideal indeed (Prov. 11:30; Dan. 12:3; Matt. 11:28-30; 23:37; I Cor. 9:22), but also to see to it that the will of God as revealed in his Word is recognized and obeyed in every sphere: the family, the church, government (on every level), education, art, science, literature, commerce, industry, etc., etc. Thus the kingdom or reign of God becomes established upon the earth.

Note the progress that is here indicated: from blade to ear to full grain in the ear. [157] In the plant world this transition from one stage to another is so

---

[157] In the original the three nouns are the accusatives of χόρτος, στάχυς, and σῖτος. The first, easy to associate with *grass*, in the New Testament frequently refers to the green grass of the field (Mark 6:39; cf. Matt. 14:19; John 6:10; see also Rev. 8:7; 9:4). It may, however, also refer to the wild flowers (Matt. 6:30; Luke 12:28; James 1:10, 11). The parallelism in I Peter 1:24 brings out this meaning strikingly. Here in Mark 4:28 (cf. Matt. 13:26) the term indicates grain in its early, grass-like, stage; hence, *early grain, blade.* We ourselves speak of the *grass* family as being the most important of all plant families and including such cereals as: rice, wheat, barley, corn, rye, millet, and oats.

The second of the three nouns refers to the *ear* or *head of grain*, that is, the grain-bearing spike of the cereal plant. Cf. Mark 2:23; also Matt. 12:1; Luke 6:1. Is the STACH stem a modification of STA (cf. ἵστημι), hence also related to English *stand*, depicting ears or heads of grain as standing, or standing out, being prominent? But this etymology is very uncertain. Certain is that Paul included Stachys of Rome among those believers to whom he sent a greeting (Rom. 16:9).

gradual that it can truly be called imperceptible. Try to indicate the precise moment when the blade develops into the ear, or the latter produces a row of full kernels. It cannot be done. Nevertheless, though imperceptible, development is also inevitable. Under normal conditions nothing can stop growth. Who has not seen places where a plant pushed its head through a sidewalk or a wall or at times even through a pipe?

Something very similar happens in the case of the kingdom of heaven. Though it may not be possible clearly to describe growth in holiness—hence, progress in the reign of God over one's life—from one day to another, nevertheless it remains true that "The path of the righteous resembles the light of dawn, that shines more and more brightly until the full-orbed day" (Prov. 4:18). This holds not only with respect to the life of the individual believer; it holds also with reference to the influence of the gospel as throughout the centuries, little by little, it travels from one nation to another, and increasingly causes its power to be felt in every sphere of life. See N.T.C. on Matt. 24:14. This clearly reveals the potency of the word (Isa. 40:6-8; I Peter 1:24, 25; Heb. 4:12).

3. The harvest-time spells victory

29. But whenever the (condition of the) crop permits, at once he puts in the sickle, because the harvest has come. Whenever the (condition of the) crop permits [158] means when the proper time arrives; then, but not until then.

The description of harvest or harvest-time—the word used in the original can mean either—is very dramatic. *At once,* without any delay, the man (of verse 26) [159] puts in the sickle, for the moment for which he has been waiting has finally arrived. Farmers who wait too long are going to suffer loss.

The third noun, *wheat,* and more in general *grain,* refers here to the (full) kernel in the ear or head. In other Greek literature it also indicates the food that is made from grain; hence, *bread. Sitology* is the science of dietetics and nutrition.

158 παραδοῖ, aor. subj. of παραδίδωμι. This verb does not here have its more usual meaning of hand over, or hand down, or even commit, commend; but in this case signifies *permits, allows.* Somewhat similar but not identical is the use of this verb in I Peter 2:23 ("yielded," "entrusted himself").

159 The theory according to which this "man" indicates Christ is rather general among commentators. Some of the arguments favoring it might be: *a.* According to Jesus' own explanation of the parable of The Tares (Matt. 13:37) the sower in that story-illustration is the Son of man. So why not in *this* parable? *b.* In Rev. 14:14-16 the one who swings the sickle is again none other than the Son of man. So why not here?

On the other hand, the following points should also be taken into consideration: *a.* Here (Mark 4:26) we do not read "the sower" but simply "a man." *b.* That Jesus Christ would describe himself as sleeping night after night and getting up morning upon morning sounds somewhat strange; and that he would actually say that he himself does not know how the seed sprouts and grows would, to say the least, appear to be the injection into this parable of an element that is foreign to its central idea.

Consequently, the best procedure, it would seem to this author, would be to refrain

Thus it is in nature. Thus also in the spiritual realm. The picture drawn is truly apocalyptic. See Joel 3 [Heb. 4]:13; Rev. 14:14-16. The lesson is: the victory is sure; harvest is approaching and will certainly arrive at the very moment decided in God's eternal plan. Then God's kingdom will be revealed in all its splendor (Rev. 11:15; 17:14).

"Be patient, therefore, brothers, until the arrival of the Lord. Look, the farmer waits for the precious produce of the soil, being patient over it until he receives the early and the late rain. Y o u also should continue to wait patiently. Strengthen y o u r hearts, for the arrival of the Lord is near" (James 5:7, 8).

---

30 And he said, "With what shall we compare the kingdom of God, or by what parable shall we present it? 31 It is like a mustard seed which, when sown on the ground, is the smallest of all the seeds on the ground; 32 yet, once sown, grows and becomes the biggest of all the garden herbs, and sends out branches so large that the birds of the air can lodge [160] under its shade."

4:30-32 *The Parable of the Mustard Seed*
Cf. Matt. 13:31, 32; Luke 13:18, 19

In our treatment of The Synoptic Problem (N.T.C. on Matthew, pp. 6-54) it was pointed out that one of the reasons why Matthew, Mark, and Luke resemble each other so closely may have been literary relationship, both Matthew and Luke having probably used Mark's Gospel; all three having utilized Matthew's earlier notes; Luke perhaps also Matthew's Gospel (p. 53). It was also shown that one of the reasons why the three are so different may have been that in the use of sources, whether oral or written, each evangelist exercised his Spirit-guided judgment, in accordance with his own character, education and general background, and with a view to the realization of his own distinct plan and purpose (p. 54). An illustration both of the variety and the unity is found in this parable of The Mustard Seed.

Matt. 13	Mark 4
verse 31	verse 30
He presented another parable to them, saying,	And he said, "With what shall we compare the kingdom of God, or by what parable shall we present it?

---

from saying that everything in this parable that is said about this "man" must be ascribed to Jesus Christ. This still leaves room for the belief that the Son of man described in Rev. 14:14-16 does indeed symbolize Christ the Judge and Conqueror. And the action described in that passage is the same as is indicated here in Mark 4:29.

160 Or: tent, roost, live.

<table>
<tr><td></td><td>verse 31</td></tr>
</table>

	verse 31
"The kingdom of heaven is like a mustard seed which a man took and sowed in his field.	It is like a mustard seed which, when sown on the ground,

verse 32	
It is the smallest of all the seeds;	is the smallest of all the seeds on the ground;

	verse 32
yet, when it is full-grown, it is the biggest of the garden herbs, and becomes a tree, so that the birds of the air come and lodge in its branches."	yet, once sown, grows and becomes the biggest of all the garden herbs, and sends out branches so large that the birds of the air can lodge under its shade."

What a variety of expression! Nevertheless, no discrepancy anywhere! And the similarity is as striking as is the variety.

Luke 13 also contains this parable, as follows:

verse 18

He said therefore, "What is the kingdom of God like, and to what shall I compare it?

verse 19

It is like a mustard seed, which a man took and cast into his garden; and it grew to be a tree, and the birds of the air lodged in its branches."

Here, too, there is no discrepancy, no conflict between Luke and the others. We note, moreover, the close resemblance between Luke's eighteenth verse and *Mark's* thirtieth. Matt. 13:31a is wholly different. Did Luke, though retaining his own style, have Mark before him as he wrote? There is also a close resemblance between Luke's nineteenth verse and *Matt.* 13:31b, 32. Luke resembles Matthew more closely than he does Mark. Was he making use of what Matthew had already written: the latter's notes, or perhaps even his Gospel? However that may be, the fact stands out that amid pleasing variety of presentation an equally delightful harmony is evident. In the selection of his sources, both oral and written, as well as in everything else pertaining to his writing, each Gospel writer, for his own purpose employing his own style, was being guided by the Holy Spirit.

In the parable of The Sower (verses 3-9, 13-20) the emphasis was on *human responsibility;* in that of The Seed Growing in Secret (verses 26-29),

171

on *divine sovereignty*. When these two co-operate—man working out his own salvation because God is working within him (Phil. 2:12, 13)—, *abundant growth* results, as shown in the parable of The Mustard Seed.

To be sure, this idea of growth, success, a good harvest, was already brought to the fore in the preceding parables (see verses 8, 20, 28, 29). But there are two differences. Here, in the parable of The Mustard Seed, *a.* this fact receives *all* the emphasis; and *b.* added stress is placed on the truth that *great* results develop from *small* beginnings. The central idea of the new parable, then, is this: the kingdom of God, no matter how small and insignificant it may appear at first, will continue to expand and to become increasingly a blessing to all who enter it. [161]

30. And he said, With what shall we compare the kingdom of God, or by what parable shall we present it? What we have here is an oratorical question [162] to arouse interest. Note the striking resemblance in form to the similarly double question found in Isa. 40:18 and to the one in Luke 7:31.

It was not a question rising from embarrassment, Jesus being at a loss as to what he should say next in illustration of the kingdom and its growth. It was a device—not unknown to the rabbis—to sharpen the attention of the audience. So very important did the Lord consider the amazingly marvelous theme of the kingdom and its growth that he wanted everyone to listen carefully. Hardened foes would remain hardened; rather, were to become even more hardened (verse 12), but though the lesson is lost on them, it would be revealed and savingly applied to the others.

Under the symbolical figure of a mustard seed, the parable first of all describes the smallness of the kingdom in the beginning of its new dispensation phase: **31. It is like a mustard seed which, when sown on the ground, is the smallest of all the seeds on the ground . . . .** Among seeds sown in the garden (Luke 13:19) the mustard seed was generally the smallest. Proverbially it therefore indicated anything that was very minute in its beginning (Matt. 17:20; Luke 17:6). Thus also the kingdom of God in the days of Christ's sojourn on earth was represented by a small band of genuine believers. Compared to the entire population of the Roman empire, or to all those who were at that time living in Palestine, or even to the large crowds that followed Jesus but for selfish reasons, Christ's real "kingdom"—see on 1:15—was indeed insignificant in human eyes. Moreover, its immediate

---

161 All extraneous notions, such as that the mustard kernel is Jesus himself—it is granted that Christ and Kingdom cannot be separated (Rom. 8:31-39; Rev. 17:14)—, that it was because of its pungent taste that he chose the mustard seed to illustrate the kingdom, that the field or garden in which the seed was planted represents Israel, should be dismissed as unwarranted and fanciful speculations that have little or nothing to do with the real meaning of the parable.

162 ὁμοιώσωμεν and θῶμεν are aorist deliberative subjunctives.

prestige was small. It resembled a small flock of defenseless sheep: "Fear not, little flock . . ." (Luke 12:32). Its shepherd was "despised and rejected by men" (Isa. 53:3). It was like a mere stone (Dan. 2:34). Cf. also Luke 17:17; John 6:66; Acts 28:22; I Cor. 1:26; Rev. 3:8.

But the "little flock" was to become the countless multitude (Rev. 7:9). The "stone" was predestined to become a mountain so huge that it would fill the entire earth (Dan. 2:35). **32. yet, [the seed] once sown, grows and becomes the biggest of all the garden herbs, and sends out branches so large that the birds of the air can lodge under its shade.** The sprout resulting from a mustard seed grows and grows until it becomes a shrub, which in turn grows until it is taller than any of the other plants that grow from seeds entrusted to the soil of the garden plot. Ultimately it looks like a tree, and, loosely speaking, may actually be called a tree. It sends out branches—thus Mark correctly interpreted Christ's words—so large that the birds of the air are able to lodge or tent in its shade. Even today mustard grows vigorously in Palestine. It reaches ten feet, sometimes even fifteen. In the fall of the year, when the branches have become rigid, birds of many species find here a shelter from the storm, rest from weariness, and shade from the heat of the sun. [163]

Similarly the kingdom of God, once established, expands and keeps on expanding. As to the birds finding shelter in the shade of the tree (cf. Ezek. 17:22-24; Dan. 4:10, 21), does this not indicate that the kingdom becomes a blessing for men of every clime, race, and nation? Truly,

"Around the throne of God in heaven
Thousands of children stand." [164]
Anne H. Shepherd

Within forty years of Christ's death the gospel had reached all the great cultural centers of the Roman world, and ever so many out-of-the-way places besides. Since that time it has been spreading, gaining men of every race, and influencing every sphere of life. It is doing this today. "From vict'ry unto vict'ry his army he shall lead."

Accordingly, to those who first heard it, this parable was saying, "Have patience, exercise faith, keep on praying, and keep on working. God's program cannot fail." It is saying the same thing to those who have come afterward. Only, it is saying it today with even greater force, because the story-illustration is really a prophecy, and this prophecy has already been

---

[163] They also find delicious food—the small black seeds—which they remove from the pods, but this feature is not included in the parable. For a most interesting description of the action of birds in connection with mustard see A. Parmelee, *All the Birds of the Bible*, New York, 1959, p. 250.

[164] A striking illustration is found in W. Barclay, *op. cit.*, pp. 108-110.

partly fulfilled! As to this matter of fulfilment see N.T.C. on Matt. 24:14 (pp. 854-856).

Great results have developed from small beginnings. See Ps. 118:22, 23; Isa. 1:8, 9; 11:1 ff.; 53:2, 3, 10-12; Ezek. 17:22-24; Zech. 4:10. Christ's rule of grace, no matter how despised it may be at first, and how insignificant in the eyes of men, is bound to go forward "conquering and to conquer" (Rev. 6:1, 2; 17:14). That kingdom will be established more and more widely and firmly. It will do this because it is *God's* kingdom!

What we have here, then, is a striking illustration of the lines:

> "Large streams from little fountains flow,
> Tall oaks from little acorns grow."
> David Everet—*Lines Written for a*
> *School Declamation*

Implied in all this is the important lesson: Blessed is the one who takes an active part in promoting the growth of the kingdom; always beginning at home (Mark 5:19), but never forgetting "the whole creation" (16:15).

---

33 With many such parables he was speaking the word to them, as far as they were able to hear (it). 34 And without (using) a parable he was not saying anything to them; but privately to his own disciples he was explaining everything.

4:33, 34 *Christ's Use of Parables*
Cf. Matt. 13:34, 35

33. With many such parables he was speaking the word to them, as far as they were able to hear (it). Mark is saying that these three parables were but samples of the many spoken by the Lord. By means of them he reached his audience to the extent in which these parables, even though uncomprehended, were able to arrest and hold the attention of the crowd. This reminds us of verses 11, 12, with which it is in complete harmony. **34. And without (using) a parable he was not saying anything to them;** . . . This probably means that whenever Jesus addressed the multitude he would in his discourse include a parable or even more than one. Continued: **but privately to his own disciples he was explaining everything.** What is said here is entirely in line with verse 10. See also Matt. 13:10, 36.

We are not surprised that this evangelist does not record nearly as many parables as do Matthew and Luke. As was pointed out earlier—see sections II and IV of the Introduction—, Mark was writing for Romans, people who were interested in action, power, conquest. To them he pictures Jesus as an active, energetic, swiftly moving, conquering King, a Victor over the destructive forces of nature, over disease, demons, death, and moral-spiritual darkness, the One and only Deliverer. So, having related these three parables, Mark now turns quickly to an awe-inspiring *action* account.

35 On that day, when evening had come, he said to them, "Let us cross over to the other side." 36 Leaving the crowd behind, they took him along in the boat, just as he was. Other boats were with him. 37 A heavy storm [165] came up, and the waves were dashing into the boat, so that the boat was already filling up. 38 But he was in the stern, on the headrest, sleeping. And they were waking him up and saying to him, "Master, don't you care that we're perishing?" 39 He got up, rebuked the wind, and said to the sea, "Hush! Be still!" Then the wind fell, and there was a deep calm. 40 And he said to them, "Why are y o u afraid? Have y o u still no faith?" 41 They were awestruck, and were saying [166] to each other, "Who then is this, that even the wind and sea obey him?"

4:35-41 *A Tempest Stilled*
Cf. Matt. 8:18, 23-27; Luke 8:22-25

By combining the three accounts we obtain the following collation, in which whatever is peculiar to Mark is in italics. These italicized vivid touches, the ones not found in Matthew and Luke, confirm the theory that Mark had heard an eye-witness, Peter, tell the story:

In the evening (of a day filled with activity, Mar, 4:1 ff.) Jesus bade his disciples go with him to the opposite (eastern) side of the Sea of Galilee. So, leaving the crowd behind, *they took him along in the boat just as he was. Other boats were with him.* As they sailed he fell asleep (Luke 8:23a).

A violent storm came up, so that the boat was being swamped by the waves, and the men were in danger. *But he was in the stern, on the headrest,* sleeping.

They were waking him up and saying to him, "Master, *don't you care that we're perishing?"* [167]

He said to them, "Why are y o u frightened, O men of little faith?" (Matt. 8:26).

Jesus got up and rebuked the wind and the sea (the raging waves). *He said to the sea, "Hush! Be still!"* Then the wind fell and the raging waves ceased. There was a deep calm.

He asked his disciples, "Why are y o u afraid? *Have y o u still no faith?"* Where is y o u r faith?" (Luke 8:25).

The men were awestruck, and were saying to each other, "Who—or: What kind of person—is this, that even the wind and the sea obey him?" . . . "that he commands even the winds and the water, and they obey him?"

* * *

When we omit Matt. 8:26, and confine ourselves to Mark's account, we have six paragraphs, as follows: Theme: *A Tempest Stilled.* Points or head-

---

165 Or: fearful squall, violent gust, furious tempest.
166 Or: began to say.
167 ἀπολλύμεθα. The hysterical cry, "We're perishing" is reported by all three evangelists. In Mark, however, the expression occurs in a context of reproach.

ings: *a.* an evening embarkation, *b.* a furious tempest, *c.* a frantic outcry, *d.* an astounding miracle, *e.* a loving reproach, *f.* a profound effect.

1. *An evening embarkation*

35, 36. On that day, when evening had come, [168] **he said to them, Let us cross over** [169] **to the other side. Leaving the crowd behind, they took him along in the boat, just as he was. Other boats were with him.** It had been a busy day for Jesus. From a boat offshore he had been speaking to the multitudes in parables. Afterward, "at home" (or: in a house) he had given private instruction to the disciples. It is not surprising that when the evening arrived, he was tired and exhausted.

So back to the shore he went, and said to the disciples, "Let us cross over to the other side." He wanted to cross over from the busy western or Capernaum side to the eastern or "country of the Gerasenes" side. See Mark 5:1. Since he was not only thoroughly divine but also thoroughly human, he was in need of rest. He needed to get away from all those people: not only did they crowd the shore; they even surrounded him in boats!

Mark states that the disciples took Jesus along (with them) in the boat. It was he who took the initiative by issuing the order, "Let us cross over ..." But *they* were the boatsmen, the navigators. [170] So they took Jesus along "just as he was" (cf. II Kings 7:7), tired, exhausted, in need of rest and sleep. See verse 38, and cf. Luke 8:23a.

2. *A furious tempest*

37, 38a. A heavy storm came up, and the waves were dashing into the boat, so that the boat was already filling up. But he was in the stern, on the headrest, sleeping. To describe this atmospheric disturbance Mark and Luke in the original speak of a *lailaps,* that is, a whirlwind (cf. Job 38:1; Jonah 1:4) or a storm that breaks forth in furious gusts, a fearful squall. Matthew calls it "a great shaking" or "sea-quake." It must have been a very violent upheaval, a howling tempest. Suddenly this *lailaps* came down upon the *lake.* [171]

The Sea of Galilee is located in the north of the valley of the Jordan. It is about thirteen miles in length and seven and one-half miles in width. It lies approximately six hundred eighty feet below the level of the Mediterranean.

---

168 ὀψίας γενομένης, genitive absolute.

169 The verb διέλθωμεν is first per. pl. hortative aor. subj. of διέρχομαι.

170 Swete's opinion (*op. cit.,* p. 88) that Matt. 8:23 and Luke 8:22 "overlook" the fact that Jesus was already on board (Mark 4:1) can be maintained only by overlooking the fact that according to Matt. 13:36 (cf. Mark 4:34b) Jesus had left the boat and entered a house before reboarding.

171 Note alliteration in Luke 8:23: λαῖλαψ ... λίμνην. Even more important note κατέβη, came down, fell.

Its bed is a depression surrounded by hills, especially on the east side with its precipitous cliffs. It is understandable that when the cool currents rush down from Mt. Hermon (9,200 feet) or from elsewhere and through narrow passages between the steep hills collide with the heated air above the lake basin, this downrush is impetuous. The violent winds whip the sea into a fury, causing high waves that splash over bow, side rails, etc., of any vessel that happens to be plying the water surface. In the present instance the small fishing craft, swamped by towering billows, was becoming water-logged, the toy of the raging elements.

Howling winds, raging billows . . . "but he [Jesus] was in the stern, on the headrest, sleeping." Thus reads the original, with the word "sleeping" at the very end of the sentence, creating a dramatic effect, a most striking contrast. The present participle "(was) . . . sleeping" pictures Jesus slumbering peacefully. Luke 8:23 creates the impression that Jesus had fallen asleep as soon as (or almost as soon as) the boat had left the shore. Soon he was sound asleep, showing how very tired he must have been; also showing that his trust in the heavenly Father—*his own* Father—was unfaltering. Neither the roaring of the wind nor the dashing and splashing of the billows nor even the rolling and pitching of the rapidly filling boat was able to awaken him.

This sleeping, moreover, must not be pictured as if the head of Jesus was necessarily resting on a very soft pillow. Note: "on *the* headrest," not "on *a* headrest." It may have been a "cushion" that belonged to the boat, the only one on board. It may have been a headrest of leather; perhaps even of wood (part of the boat), in which case "headrest" would be a better rendering than "cushion." According to its derivation, all the word used in the original really means is that it was something "for the head" to rest on; hence, a headrest.

3. A frantic outcry

38b. And they were waking him up and saying to him, Master, don't you care that we're perishing? Amid unity, to which reference has been made, there is variety in the reports concerning the cries of the fear-stricken men. Matthew has, "So they came to him and woke him up, saying, 'Lord, save (us), we're perishing' "; Luke, "Master, master, we're perishing"; Mark, "Master, [172] don't you care that we're perishing?" It is reasonable to

---

172 Thus Διδάσκαλε is also rendered by A.V., N.E.B., Phillips, Jerusalem Bible, etc. Cf. German "Meister," Dutch "Meester." Others prefer "Teacher." Neither can be called incorrect. In the present instance the attitude of the disciples may well have been a mixture of terror, reverence, and reproach. That reverence was not entirely lacking appears from Matthew's use of the word κύριε and Luke's Ἐπιστάτα in reporting the manner in which the disciples addressed Jesus. Therefore in a search for the best English equivalent of Mark's Διδάσκαλε the rendering "Master" must not be quickly dismissed.

suppose that in a situation of terrified distress this disciple would cry one thing, another something else.

It is difficult to ascribe any other meaning to the outcry, "Master, don't you care that we're perishing" than that it was adverse criticism addressed to Jesus, as if whatever happened to his disciples did not concern him. In all honesty, such a stinging remark cannot even be justly called "mild" reproach. There was nothing mild about it. It meant, "Do we mean so little to you? With death staring us in the face, how can you sleep? Don't you care whether we're all swallowed up by the angry deep?"

Nevertheless, before we judge these men too harshly, the following facts must be borne in mind: a. They were thoroughly frightened: in such a situation even normally loyal and courageous people will at times say things which they later regret; and b. their bitterness is not unmixed with a measure of trust. If that were not true, they—some of them being experienced sailors—would not now have turned to a "carpenter" for help. To be sure, their faith was far from perfect, but even "little faith" is faith, and holds out hope for purification and enlargement.

According to Matthew it was at this time that Jesus, awakened by his disciples' agonizing appeal, said to them, "Why are y o u frightened, O men of little faith?" [173] Not frightened was *he*. On the contrary, he was in full control of this storm even when the winds were still roaring and the waters seething. See N.T.C. on Matthew, p. 411.

4. *An astounding miracle*

39. He got up, rebuked the wind, and said to the sea, Hush! Be still [or: silent, quiet] ! Then the wind fell, and there was a deep calm. According to Matt. 8:26 Jesus stood up and "*rebuked* the winds and the sea." According to Luke 8:24 he "*rebuked* the wind and the raging of the water." And according to Mark 4:39 he "*rebuked* the wind," and told the sea to be quiet. The verb "rebuked" [174] is the same in all three cases. There are those who maintain that this verb implies an animate object. They say that this inference is strengthened by Mark 4:39, which is then translated, "Peace! Be

---

[173] I can see no reason to say, with some, that Mark and Luke have given us the true order of events, but Matthew has not. Neither Mark nor Luke were present during this storm, but Matthew was. Besides, is it not natural to assume that the lack of sufficient faith was by Jesus considered a subject so important that he would refer to it both before and after performing the miracle? And is it not also true that the disciples were twice filled with fear; first because of the tempest, secondly, because of the presence of him who stilled the tempest? See Luke 8:24, 25.

[174] ἐπετίμησεν, third person sing. aor. indic. of ἐπιτιμάω. It has the sense *rebuke* in such passages as Matt. 8:26; 16:22; 17:18; 19:13; Mark 4:39; Luke 4:39; 9:42, 55; 19:39; 23:40; but at times means *warn*, tell (men) *not* to do something, forbid (them) (Matt. 12:16; 16:20; Mark 3:12; Luke 9:21).

muzzled!" But, to begin with the latter, a word does not always retain its basic or primary connotation. "Hush! [or: Peace!] Be still!" is the more usual and better rendering of Mark 4:39. As to the expression, "He rebuked," it should be borne in mind that Mark does not say, "Jesus rebuked the devil," or "the demons," or "the evil spirits that were in the wind." He simply says, "He rebuked the wind." It would seem, therefore, that this is simply a figurative or poetic manner of speaking (cf. Ps. 19:5; 98:8; Isa. 55:12; etc.). So also in Luke 4:39, where we are told that Jesus "rebuked" the fever by which Peter's mother-in-law was being afflicted. The really important fact conveyed by the expression "He rebuked the wind" (and parallels in the other Gospels) is that in a very effective manner Jesus asserted his authority over the elements of nature, so that there was a deep (literally "great") calm.

Here in Mark the progressive parallelism is very impressive: Jesus separately addresses the wind and the sea. He rebukes the wind; to the sea he says, "Hush! Be still!" The result is also indicated separately: the wind fell; the sea became calm.

What is very striking is that not only the winds immediately quiet down, but so do even the waves. Generally, as is well-known, after the winds have perceptibly diminished, the billows will continue to roll for a while, surging and subsiding as if unwilling to follow the example of the now subdued air currents above them. But in *this* instance winds and waves synchronize in the sublime symphony of a solemn silence. Something comparable to an evening stillness of the starry heavens settles upon the waters. Suddenly the surface of the sea had become smooth as a mirror.

5. A loving reproach

40. And he said to them, Why are y o u afraid? Have y o u still no faith?

Before proceeding with the explanation of this verse it may be well to point out that there are times when a comment should be made not only about what Scripture says but also about what it omits. The disciples, by implication, had accused the Master of indifference or hard-heartedness, of not being concerned about them (verse 38). Is it not really marvelous and very comforting to take note of the fact that Jesus never rebuked them for the grim, thoughtless words, "Don't you care that we're perishing?" This is the same Savior who was going to give an answer to Simon's base denials accompanied by curses. His answer, however, would not be a sharp rebuke but a look full of pain, yet also full of love; and subsequently (after the resurrection) a penetrating, soul-searching yet loving interrogation: "Simon, Son of John, do you love me more than these? . . . Do you love me? . . . Do you have affection for me?"

Luke 8:25 makes it very clear that not only before but also *after* the miracle the disciples were afraid. They had been frightened by the storm. *Now* they were filled with fear because of the presence of the One who had so suddenly, completely, and dramatically stilled the storm. For similar instances of awe induced by the consciousness of being in the presence of Majesty see Isa. 6:5; Luke 5:8. So Jesus asks them, "Why *are*—not Why *were*—y o u afraid?" As if to say, has not the stilling of the storm and the soothing of the waves, in answer to y o u r hysterical outcry, taught y o u that this Master of y o u r s is not only very powerful but also very loving? Therefore, should not y o u r response be that of complete, childlike trust?

What Jesus actually said was, "Have y o u *still* no faith?" See also Mark 8:17-21; 9:19. They were "men of little faith," that is, men who were too *timid* sufficiently to rely upon the comfort and confidence which they should have derived from the presence, promises, power, and love of their Master (Matt. 6:30; 8:26; 14:31; 16:8; Luke 12:28); too hesitant to realize that the Father's loving care was bestowed upon them through the Son.

Still no faith; that is, no faith in spite of all that y o u have seen, heard, experienced? This little word "still" must not escape us. By using it Jesus is teaching that the experiences of life are sent to men with a purpose. They must be used to good advantage, for furtherance in sanctification. Joseph understood this (Gen. 50:19-21). So did David (II Sam. 23:5; Ps. 116); the man born blind (John 9:25, 30-33); Paul (I Cor. 15:9, 10; Phil. 2:7-14; 4:11-13). Laban, too, learned something by experience, but applied his knowledge selfishly (Gen. 30:27b).

6. *A profound effect*

41. They were awestruck. . . . Because of all that Jesus had revealed with reference to himself, but probably mostly because of the power he had manifested, these men "feared (with) great fear," thus literally. [175] The "awe" here indicated was a combination of fear and reverence. Matt. 8:27 says that the men "were amazed (or: astonished)." Luke 8:25 reports both the fear and the amazement. The disciples began to realize: Jesus is greater by far than we had previously imagined. He exercises control not only over audiences, sicknesses, and demons, but even over winds and waves: **and were saying—or: and began to say** [176] **—to each other, Who then is this, that even the wind and the sea obey him?**

Much that is wrong on earth can be corrected. There are mothers who dry

---

175 Though Mark is writing for the Romans, he is himself a Jew, and shows it in expressing himself in this typically Semitic fashion. Cf. I Macc. 10:8; Jonah 1:10. Or else, he is reporting what he had derived from a Jewish source, faithfully preserving the very phraseology—translated, however, into Greek—in which this item of the story had been conveyed to him. Cf. Luke 2:9.

176 Note the meaningful change from the aor. ἀφοβήθησαν to the imperf. ἔλεγον.

tears, repairmen who fix machines, surgeons who remove diseased tissues, counselors who solve family problems, etc. As to correcting the weather? People talk about it, to be sure. But it takes deity to change the weather. It is Jesus who commands the elements of the weather, with the result that even the wind obeys him, and so does even the sea. [177]

We receive the impression that for the moment at least the disciples were deeply impressed with the power, majesty, and glory of their Master. "Who then is this?" (Mark 4:41; Luke 8:25) they asked. The meaning must have been, in the phraseology of Matt. 8:27, "What kind of person is this?"

Their answer to this question is not given. See also Jonah 4:1; Mark 12:37 (cf. Matt. 22:45). Very appropriately the narrative ends by fixing the attention upon the person of Jesus Christ, so that everyone who reads it may give his own answer, may profess his own faith, and add his own doxology.

Summary of Chapter 4

The eight sections of this chapter may be summarized as follows:

a. The parable of The Sower (verses 1-9). It had happened before that Jesus had left a crowded building, whether house or synagogue, for the shore (2:2, 13; 3:1, 7). So also here (3:20; 4:1; cf. Matt. 13:1). On the present occasion the throng that had gathered about Jesus was so large that he stepped into a boat and sat in it out on the sea, thus face to face with his audience. In his teaching from the sea the Master made generous use of parables. In fact, the book-division here summarized can be called *Mark's parable chapter,* since six of its eight sections record, or at least refer to, parables.

First of all Jesus tells the parable of The Sower. "Listen," says the Master, and he continues, "Once (upon a time) the sower went out to sow." The seed fell on various types of soil: hard, rocky, thorn-infested, and good. Only the last of the four produced a harvest, the seed yielding thirty, sixty, and a hundredfold.

b. Purpose of the parables (verses 10-12). In a house Jesus afterward, at the request of a group of disciples wider than The Twelve, explains why he was speaking in parables; namely, to reveal the truth to those who accepted it, and to conceal it from those who obstinately opposed it, that the latter might "endure the blame of their own blindness and hardness" (Calvin).

c. Explanation of the parable of The Sower (verses 13-20). Jesus shows that the four types of soil indicate, respectively, unresponsive, impulsive, pre-occupied, and responsive hearts. It is the latter kind of heart alone that is

---

[177] Note the sing. ὑπακούει: wind and sea are here regarded separately, as they were also in verse 39.

fruitful. Man's duty to respond properly to the word or message of the kingdom is therefore the real "point" of the parable. The stress is definitely on *human responsibility*. See 4:9, 23, 24; 8:18.

d. Various sayings of Jesus (verses 21-25). Fertile hearts resemble shining lamps. The word of the kingdom and the life in harmony with it must not be concealed but brought out into the open, in imitation of God who one day is going to reveal whatever men have tried to conceal. Then (and in a sense even before then) the measure which a person has given will be the measure he is going to receive; with this qualification, however, that the work of salvation is a matter of pure grace: God is ever adding gift to gift. On the contrary, from him who, because of his own unwillingness to listen and to take to heart, does not possess the greatest treasure, shall be taken away even that semblance of knowledge, that superficial acquaintance with matters spiritual, which he once had.

e. The parable of The Seed Growing in Secret (verses 26-29). This parable stresses *God's sovereignty* as displayed in the matter of man's salvation and its effect in every sphere of life. Jesus shows that to man growth is a mystery: "the seed sprouts and grows, how he does not know"; that the seed, nevertheless, reveals its potency: "by itself the earth produces crops"; and that the harvest (or: harvest-time) spells victory: "whenever the (condition of the) crop permits, at once he—the sower, now also reaper—puts in the sickle, because the harvest has come." Since it is true, therefore, that the power to sprout and grow has *by God* been embedded in the seed, and man can do nothing about this—after scattering the seed, all he can do is sleep and rise, sleep and rise—, the harvest is assured. Christ's kingdom, his royal reign, shall expand and shall one day reveal itself in all its splendor.

f. The parable of The Mustard Seed (verses 30-32). When man works out his own salvation because God is working within him—see the two preceding parables—, growth abounds. Great results develop from small beginnings. Just as mustard, at first a very small seed, attains at last to such a height that it sends out branches so large that the birds of the air can lodge under its shade, so also the reign of God in Christ, acknowledged by a very small group at first, is going to expand and keep on expanding, becoming a blessing to men of every race, and influencing every sphere of life, to God's glory.

g. Christ's use of parables (verses 33, 34). By means of parables and parabolic expressions, by Jesus included in all his public discourses, he reached his audiences to the extent in which these story-illustrations and figures of speech were able to arrest and hold their attention. When at home (or: in a house), alone with his disciples, he was in the habit of explaining everything to them.

h. A tempest stilled (verses 35-41). First Mark pictures an evening embarkation. After a busy day Jesus, at his own request, is taken aboard by the disciples. The group is headed for the opposite (eastern) shore. A furious tempest arises, the winds howling, the waves crashing against and splashing into the boat, which is becoming water-logged. All the while Jesus is in the stern, his head on a headrest, fast asleep. There is a frantic cry, "Master, don't you care that we're perishing?" An astounding miracle follows: Jesus gets up, rebukes the wind, and says to the sea, "Hush! Be still!" The wind subsides. There is a deep calm. At this point Mark records Christ's tenderly loving reproach (Matthew does so even earlier), "Why are y o u afraid? Have y o u still no faith?" "Still," that is, even after all the miracles y o u have seen me perform, the words y o u have heard from my lips, and the life I have lived in y o u r presence? Has all this experience taught y o u nothing?

The Master does not even sharply rebuke his disciples for having addressed him so censoriously. The profound effect of the miracle is by Mark recorded in these words, "They were awestruck and were saying [or: began to say] to each other, 'Who then is this that even the wind and the sea obey him?'"

Outline of Chapter 5

Theme: *The Work Which Thou Gavest Him To Do*

5:1-20   In the Land of the Gerasenes: Helpfulness over against
          Heartlessness
5:21-43   The Restoration to Life of Jairus' Daughter
                              and
          The Healing of the Woman Who Touched Christ's Garment

CHAPTER V

5 1 And they came to the opposite side of the sea, to the country of the Gerasenes. 2 Just as he was getting out of the boat, there met him out of the tombs a man with an unclean spirit. 3 This man had his living quarters among the tombs, and not even with a chain was anyone any longer able to bind him. 4 Indeed, he had often been bound with shackles and chains; but the chains had been torn apart by him, the shackles broken in pieces, and no one was strong enough to subdue him. 5 Always, night and day, in the tombs and in the hills, he kept on screaming and gashing himself with stones.

6 When he saw Jesus from a distance he ran, fell on his knees in front of him, 7 and at the top of his voice yelled, "Why do you bother me, Jesus, Son of the Most High God? Swear to God that you won't torture me." 8 For he [Jesus] had been saying to him, "Come out of the man, you unclean spirit!" 9 Then he asked him, "What is your name?" He replied, "My name is Legion, for we are many." 10 And he begged him [Jesus] again and again not to send them out of the area.

11 Now a large herd of pigs was feeding there on the hillside; 12 and they [the unclean spirits] begged him, "Allow us to go into the pigs, so that we may enter them." 13 So he gave them permission. And the unclean spirits came out and went into the pigs, and the herd of about two thousand rushed headlong down the cliff into the sea and were drowning in the sea.

14 And those in charge of them fled and spread the news in the city and countryside. And the people came to see what it was that had happened. 15 They came to Jesus and saw the demon-possessed man, sitting there, clothed and in his right mind, the very man who had had the legion; and they became frightened. 16 Those who had seen it told them how it went with the demoniac, and about the pigs. 17 And they began to beg him to leave their district.

18 And as he [Jesus] was getting into the boat, the man who had been demon-possessed begged to go with him. 19 But he refused and said to him, "Go home to your people, and tell them what great things the Lord has done for you and how he had mercy on you." 20 So he went away and began to proclaim in the Decapolis [178] what great things Jesus had done for him; and everybody was amazed.

5:1-20: *In the Land of the Gerasenes:*
Helpfulness over against Heartlessness
Cf. Matt. 8:28—9:1; Luke 8:26-39

The connection between the preceding story (Mark 4:35-41) and the present narrative (5:1-20) is easy to remember. From a description of the

---

[178] the Ten Cities.

wild sea (4:37) the Gospel writer moves on to that of a *wild* man (5:3-5). Humanly speaking *both were untamable,* but Jesus subdued both.

It was evening when the Lord and his disciples crossed the sea. They landed on the eastern shore, hence "opposite Galilee" (Luke 8:26). Is it not reasonable to assume that at verse 14 or 15 of Mark's account the evangelist reports what happened on the following day?

The three accounts vary greatly in length and fulness of detail. By far the most detailed is Mark. He is followed by Luke. Matthew's coverage is very brief. Common to all three is this summary:

When, accompanied by The Twelve, Jesus arrives on the eastern shore, he is met by a demon-possessed man (or: by two such men, according to Matthew). On seeing Jesus, the demoniac addresses (or: the demoniacs address) him as follows, "Why do you bother me (or: us), Jesus, thou Son of God (or: " . . . of the Most High God," according to Matthew and Luke)?" The demons are afraid that Jesus has come to torment them. In the vicinity a herd of pigs is feeding. The unclean spirits, just before relinquishing their stranglehold on the man (or: the men), beg permission to enter the pigs. Permission is granted, with the result that the entire herd, now demon-possessed, rushes down the cliff into the sea, and is drowned. Those in charge of the animals return to the city and relate what has happened. The people come out to see Jesus. They beg him to leave their region.

In each of the three Gospels certain details are added: Matthew, in addition to mentioning two men instead of one, states that they were so violent that travel on their road had become unsafe; that they expressed fear that Jesus had come to torture them "before the appointed time"; and that the herd was feeding "at some distance away" from the point where the confrontation between Jesus and the demoniacs took place.

Luke adds that the demon-possessed man was "from the city"—had apparently lived there—; that for a long time he had been running around naked; that the demons caused their presence to be felt by spurts ("seized him many a time"); and that the man had been kept under guard, and driven into the deserts by the demons. He also reports that the demons begged Jesus not to send them "into the abyss," and that the liberated man was sitting "at the feet of Jesus" and subsequently proclaimed "throughout the whole city" what the Lord had done for him.

Mark vividly describes how all previous attempts to keep the demoniac under control and to subdue him had failed; that he was screaming night and day and cutting himself with stones; that the spokesman of the demons wanted Jesus to swear that he would not torment him; that the herd consisted of about two thousand pigs; and that everybody was amazed about the cured man's report concerning the great things God had done for him.

Finally, the question of Jesus, "What is your name," and the answer to that question; as well as the request of the cured and grateful man to be allowed to accompany Jesus on the latter's further travels, and his reply, are reported only by Mark and Luke.

Returning now to Mark 5:1-20, we notice that the section under study can be conveniently divided into five short paragraphs; see above, the translation. These five focus the attention respectively on: the man; the demons; the pigs; the swineherds; and Jesus.

Or, more fully stated:

The wretched man meeting Jesus. Description of the man (verses 1-5).

The demons in control of this man. Their confrontation with Jesus. The demons identified and ordered out (verses 6-10).

The pigs, by the demons plunged down the cliff and into the sea, where they perish (verses 11-13).

The swineherds and the people to whom they report. The people's request that Jesus leave the district (verses 14-17).

The cured man's request and Jesus' reply. Implication of that reply (verses 18-20).

Furthermore, the first paragraph describes a man in need of help. The first, second, and fourth show that this man received no help from any source other than Jesus. *Heartlessness* characterized demons, swineherds, and people in general. Over against this attitude stands the *helpfulness* of Jesus, as is described in the second, third (yes, also third!), and fifth paragraphs.

1. *The wretched man meeting Jesus. Description of the man.*

1. And they came to the opposite side of the sea, to the country of the Gerasenes. The original as represented by Grk. N.T. (A-B-M-W) has *Gadarenes* in Matt. 8:28; *Gerasenes* here in Mark 5:1; and *Gergesenes* in Luke 8:26. In each case variant readings are recognized in the footnotes. In order to locate the place where Jesus landed, a description as given in the Gospels (Matt. 8:28, 32; Mark 5:2, 13; and Luke 8:27, 33) is helpful. We learn that it was a region of caves used as tombs, and that a steep hill descended sharply to the very edge of the water. This description does not fit Gerasa, a town situated at least thirty miles to the south-southeast of the Sea of Galilee. See map on p. 199. It does, however, suit *Khersa,* which could very well be indicated as the town inhabited by the Gerasenes or Gergesenes. If it be assumed that the larger city of Gadara (also on the sketch), mainly located a few miles southeast of the sea but extending all the way to the shore, was, as it were, the capital of the entire district to which Khersa belonged, the various geographical designations begin to make sense. Moreover, at Khersa, situated on the eastern shore, about six miles diagonally (oversea) southeast of

Capernaum, there is indeed a hill descending sharply to the edge of the water. There are also many caves—evident even today—suitable for tombs. [179]

2. **Just as he was getting out of the boat, there met him out of the tombs a man with an unclean spirit.** The confrontation between Jesus and this man takes place right near the shore, the very moment when the Master stepped out of the boat. The expression "a man with an unclean spirit" means "a demon-possessed man," as is clear from the entire description—see especially verses 8-12—, and is definitely stated in the parallel accounts (Matt. 8:28; Luke 8:27). "Unclean" means "evil" (cf. Luke 7:21; 8:2 with 4:33, 36). The unclean spirits are morally filthy. They are evil in themselves and a source of harm and evil for those over whom they exercise control. For more about demon-possession see on 1:23 and N.T.C. on Matthew, pp. 436, 437.

Why Matthew mentions *two* demoniacs, while Mark and Luke tell the story of *one* [180] is not known, but such a variation in reporting is not uncommon even today. It has been suggested that the demoniac to whom Mark and Luke refer was the leader and spokesman, but this opinion is merely a guess. It should be noted, however, that these other evangelists do not say that *only* one demoniac met Jesus that day. No one, therefore, has a right to speak about a Matthew versus Mark-Luke "contradiction."

This demoniac, then, "met" Jesus "just as" he was disembarking; that is, "immediately," "at once." Add to this the fact that in verses 3b-5 Mark describes this man as being a very violent person (cf. Matt. 8:28), and the inference is warranted that already in the impetuous manner in which he rushed toward Jesus this fierceness was displayed. It would seem that out of the tombs he streaked downhill to meet the new arrivals. A "streaker" indeed was he! See Luke 8:27.

The tombs which were this man's "home" are mentioned again in verses 3 and 5. In fact, as the original shows, verses 3-5 belong together, and furnish a very vivid description of the "wild" man:

3-5. **This man had his living quarters among the tombs, and not even with a chain was anyone any longer able to bind him. Indeed, he had often been bound with shackles and chains; but the chains had been torn apart by him, the shackles broken in pieces, and no one was strong enough to subdue him. Always, night and day, in the tombs and in the hills, he kept on screaming and gashing himself with stones.**

We are definitely dealing here with a demoniac, not merely with a maniac. The picture Mark draws is filled with terror. It describes a man who is the

---

[179] See A. M. Ross, art. *Gadara, Gadarenes*, Zondervan Pictorial Bible Dictionary, Grand Rapids. 1963, p. 293; and J. L. Hurlbut and J. H. Vincent, *A Bible Atlas*, New York, etc., 1940 ed., p. 101.

[180] Cf. also Matt. 20:29 ("two blind men") with Mark 10:46 and Luke 18:35.

victim of demonic malevolence coupled with human indifference and impotence. But in the end divine omnipotence and benevolence come to the rescue and triumph. The helpfulness of Jesus is strikingly contrasted with the heartlessness of demons and men.

The man here pictured used to live in the city, as has been indicated. But now, demon-possessed, his dwelling is among "the tombs." This term probably refers to abandoned burial chambers hewn into the side of the cliffs. Habitually, at intervals during the night and day, this man's ear-splitting screams are echoing eerily from cavern to cavern near the rocky shore, striking terror into the hearts of any traveler who might dare to come within hearing distance. Most people simply bypassed this neighborhood (Matt. 8:28b). Moreover, in the midst of his hideous screaming the demoniac was making things worse for himself by gashing the flesh of his naked body with the sharp edges of broken stones.

As to the attitude of his neighbors toward him? It would seem that all they ever thought of was their own safety and protection. With that in mind they were in the habit of binding the man hand and foot. But no matter how frequently they resorted to this means of safeguarding themselves, they were never successful, for the handcuffs were torn apart by him and the leg irons were broken in pieces. In fact, no one, but no one, had the strength to tame him down. [181]

---

[181] These three verses contain several items of vocabulary and grammar that deserve mention:

κατοίκησις (verse 3, acc.—ιν) is in the New Testament found only here. It is the place where one "settles down," a person's home or habitation. With the base of the Greek word cf. English *wick*, *vic*inity, paro*ch*ial.

εἶχεν, ἐδύνατο, ἴσχυεν (verses 3, 4). These imperfects show that Mark is picturing the scene. He is describing things in a leisurely manner, and conceives of them as actually occurring. In this connection note also the periphrastic ἦν κράζων καὶ κατακόπτων (verse 5).

οὐδὲ . . . οὐδείς: popular style double negative; really *triple*, for Mark even adds οὐκέτι (verse 3). Altogether, this is a very strong negation of the supposition that anyone at all was able any longer to bind this demoniac effectively.

ἄλυσις, chain, handcuff (cf. Luke 8:29; Acts 12:6, 7; 21:33; 28:20); the form used is first of all the dative of means (sing. in verse 3; pl. in verse 4); then in verse 4 also the acc. pl. Also in verse 4 πέδη occurs first of all as a dat. pl. of means; then as acc. pl. With this word cf. πούς; "foot," "pedal." We may perhaps think of a pair of metal rings around the ankles, the fasteners being tied together by means of a chain. "Leg irons" of any kind may have been in mind. But see Robertson, *Word Pictures* I, p. 295.

διά with acc. at beginning of verse 4 ("indeed" or "because") introduces the evidence for the preceding statement: the past explains the present. Binding the man hand and foot had often been tried but always failed.

Also in verse 4 δεδέσθαι (from δέω; cf. Mark 3:27 and many other New Testament passages; cf. also "diadem"); διεσπάσθαι (from διασπάω; cf. Acts 23:10; also "span"); and συντετρίφθαι (from συντρίβω; cf. Mark 14:3; also Matt. 12:20; Luke 9:39; John 19:36; note "tribulation") are perfect infinitives. They indicate what had been done in the past, plus result: the man had been bound, leaving him in a bound condition. Similarly,

2. *The demons in control of this man. Their confrontation with Jesus. The demons identified and ordered out*

6, 7. When he saw Jesus from a distance he ran, fell on his knees in front of him, and at the top of his voice yelled, Why do you bother me, Jesus, son of the Most High God?

It is sometimes argued that verse 6 contradicts verse 2. According to verse 2 when Jesus steps out of the boat the demoniac is right there, while according to verse 6 he is still a considerable distance away. [182] But surely this argumentation amounts to creating a conflict where there need not be one at all. A legitimate interpretation of Mark's account is that before the boat even reaches the shore the demoniac, "from a distance" spying its approach, comes running, and that he actually meets Jesus as the latter steps ashore. [183]

Perhaps somewhat more difficult to understand is the behavior of the demoniac. On the surface it seems to be very inconsistent: one moment we see him rushing down with hostile intent; the next moment he has thrown himself at Jesus' feet and is worshipping him; only to change once more to the immediately following sinister outcry. To say that, after all, irrational behavior is exactly what one can expect from a demoniac is probably only half the solution. In addition it should be pointed out that when this man started to run toward the company, he did not as yet recognize its Leader. When he—really the demons inside him, represented by their leader—in a manner that surpasses human understanding did recognize him, the first reaction, because of the majesty of Christ, was that of awe, resulting in prostration. [184] But when the demon's spokesman reflected on the fact that Jesus was, after all, his great Opponent, the One who had arrived on earth with the very purpose of "destroying the works of the devil" (I John 3:8), he, making use of the poor man's vocal organs, gave vent to his feeling of anger, frustration, and despair, in the outburst, "Why do you bother me, Jesus, son of the Most High God?"

---

the chains had been torn apart, the shackles broken, with the result that the broken pieces of chains and shackles, for all to see, pointed to the impossibility of keeping the demoniac permanently subdued.
In verse 5 διὰ παντός indicates "at intervals during the night and the day."

[182] See Vincent Taylor, *op. cit.*, p. 280.

[183] Another objection that is sometimes voiced is this: the expression "from a distance" (or: "from afar") is rather meaningless, for Mark uses it again and again (see also 8:3; 11:13; 14:54; 15:40). Answer: This by no means implies that we are dealing here with a mere stock phrase. Not only do Matthew (26:58; 27:55) and Luke (16:23; 18:13; 22:54; 23:49) also use the phrase, but wherever it occurs in any of the Gospels (and elsewhere; see Rev. 18:10, 15, 17) it fits the situation that is being described. Its occurrence can never be called unnatural.

[184] In the present instance it is unnecessary to interpret the word used in the original in the full sense of rendering sincere, humble worship (as in Matt. 2:2, 11).

The behavior of this demoniac is very similar to the one described in 1:23, 24. In both cases note the loud, angry outcry, the confession of Christ's deity, and the fear that even now Jesus might have in mind to torture his hellish adversaries. Therefore, see on 1:23, 24.

Though men will at times do their utmost to deny Jesus' deity, the demons do not; note the exalted title given to the Master by the spokesman of the unclean spirits that inhabited this man. He calls Jesus "Son of the Most High God," nothing less! And Jesus was and is exactly that. Cf. Gen. 14:18, 19; Isa. 6:3 (in the light of John 12:41); Luke 1:32, 35, 76; 6:35; 8:28; Heb. 7:1.

It would seem that immediately after this outcry Jesus said, probably more than once, to the demon who acted as spokesman for all, "Come out of the man, you unclean spirit" (see on verse 8). Instead of immediately obeying, the demon answered, **Swear to God that you won't torture me.** Or, more literally, "I adjure you by God . . ." [185] The substance of this insolent remark is reflected more mildly in Luke's passage, "I implore you, do not torture me." This meant: Do not order us to depart "into the abyss" (8:28, 31).

The demon's request that Jesus bind himself by means of an oath was passed by in silence, in keeping with Matt. 5:33-37; see N.T.C. on that passage. The demonic scream is by Matthew interpreted to mean, "Did you come here to torture us before the appointed time?" The demonic world realizes that on the day of the final judgment its relative freedom to roam about on earth and in the sky above it (see N.T.C. on Eph. 2:2; 6:12) must cease forever, and that its final and most terrible punishment is destined to begin at that time. Its representative who is now speaking to Jesus knows that right now he is face to face with the One to whom the final judgment has been committed, and he is afraid that even now—"before the appointed time"—Jesus might hurl him and his partners into "the abyss" or "dungeon," that is, into hell, the place where Satan is kept. That fear on the part of this unclean spirit was engendered and intensified by Christ's repeated command that the demon depart from the horribly frustrated man, as is clearly stated in verse 8. **For he [Jesus] had been saying to him, Come out of the man, you unclean spirit.**

The story continues: 9. **Then he asked him, What is your name?** Just why was it that Jesus, ignoring the demon's demand (verse 7b), asked this question? Among commentators:

a. Several completely omit any attempt to solve this difficult puzzle.

b. Others [186] are of the opinion that Jesus, in common with other exorcists, believed that knowledge of the demon's name carried with it the

---

[185] The verb is followed by two accusatives both here and in Acts 19:13.
[186] See W. Barclay, *op. cit.*, p. 118; Vincent Taylor, *op. cit.*, p. 282.

ability to cast out the demon. The moment a demon's name was known, his power was broken.

Objection. This certainly looks like an attempt to reduce the power of Jesus to that of any exorcist. Moreover, if the theory were true, we would expect that also in other cases of demon-expulsion recorded in the Gospels there would be a reference to asking the name of the demon.

c. Still another [187] confidently affirms that Jesus questions about the name in order that—supposedly by means of the answer to this question—his disciples, etc. would know that he was dealing not just with one demon but with ever so many of them.

d. What may well be the best answer—though we cannot be sure—is the one suggested in one form or another by several other commentators. [188] It amounts to this: Jesus wishes to reveal to the demoniac the seriousness of his condition. In order to deliver him from this condition he wishes to calm him down and to strengthen his consciousness of his real self. He desires to tear him loose from his close association—almost identification—with the demon, or demons, that had for so long a time dominated him.

He replied, My name is Legion, for we are many. The reply indicates the depth of the demoniac's misery. He is under the control not of just one demon, the spokesman, but of an entire host, a Legion! [189] The word must not be taken literally, as if it meant that a force of at least 6000 demons were in control of the poor man. The meaning here is undoubtedly figurative: a very large number. It is also possible that the term "Legion" conjured up the vision of an army of occupation, cruelty, and destruction. We are not dealing here with a legion of protecting angels (cf. Matt. 26:53: "more than twelve legions of angels"). We are confronted here with Satan's army of terror and death. That more than one demon would at times occupy and enslave a person is clear also from other Scripture passages. See Matt. 12:45 (cf. Luke 11:26); Mark 16:9 (cf. Luke 8:2).

10. And he begged him [Jesus] again and again [190] not to send [191] them out of the area. See on verse 7. However, at this point another item may have to be added. Not only do the demons feverishly desire to stay away from the abyss, but they prefer to remain in *this* particular area, because it is the terrain of tombs, skeletons, desertion, death, and destruction. They feel

---

[187] R. C. H. Lenski, *op. cit.*, p. 132.

[188] See R. A. Cole, *The Gospel according to St. Mark*, Grand Rapids, 1961, p. 98; A. B. Bruce, *op. cit.*, p. 372; C. R. Erdman, *op. cit.*, p. 82; N. Geldenhuys, *Commentary on the Gospel of Luke*, Grand Rapids, 1951, p. 255.

[189] The Latin term *legio* had been absorbed by Hellenistic Greek and even by Aramaic.

[190] πολλά used adverbially: *fervently, often;* here used in connection with a verb in the imperfect tense; hence, *begged him again and again;* or perhaps even: *fervently kept on begging him.*

[191] ἵνα μή ... ἀποστείλη (aor. active subjunctive); literally, "that he would not send."

"at home" here. If we are accustomed to associate the good angels with places in which order, beauty, and fulness of life prevail, does it not seem natural, in harmony with Scripture (Matt. 12:43) to link evil angels with regions where disorder, desolation, desertion, and death dominate?

3. *The pigs, by the demons plunged down the cliff and into the sea, where they perish*

At this point the story takes a new turn: a new element is added. **11, 12. Now a large herd of pigs was feeding there on the hillside; and they [the unclean spirits] begged him, Allow us to go into the pigs, so that we may enter them.** The demons realize that they cannot successfully resist Christ's command that they take their departure from the demoniac. They must leave him, and they are going to do exactly that. But they present a final request in connection with pigs that were feeding on the hillside.

Note "there on the hillside." This must mean "in that general vicinity." If we place this herd of pigs too close to the scene of Christ's confrontation with the demoniac we create a conflict between Mark 5:11 and Matt. 8:30. Actually there is no conflict, for "there on the hillside" leaves room for the idea that the herd was "at some distance away" from Jesus and the demon-possessed man (or: "men," according to Matthew).

What was the reason for the request of the demons that they be allowed to enter the pigs? Was it simply a yearning to destroy? Was it perhaps a sinister hope that the owners of the herd, seeing their property destroyed, would be filled with antagonism toward Jesus? The answer has not been revealed. It is, however, worthy of special attention that the demons are fully aware of the fact that without Christ's permission they will not be able to enter the pigs.

Continued: **13. So he gave them permission. And the unclean spirits came out and went into the pigs, and the herd of about two thousand rushed headlong down the cliff into the sea and were drowning in the sea.** Finally, then, the unclean spirits actually obeyed Christ's command and released their vise-like grip. In answer to their request (verse 12) Jesus *gave* them permission. So they *came out of* the man and *went into* the pigs. Result: the herd—two thousand strong; Mark likes to mention numbers; see Introduction IV, footnote 5 c—*rushed* pell-mell *down* the cliff, and . . . Here Mark suddenly changes the tense of the verb. So far he has very briefly stated four incidents, four summary facts: *gave, came out of, went into, rushed down.* It is as if he, in very rapid succession, showed us four snapshots. Then we are shown a slow-motion movie: one by one we see the (approximately) two thousand pigs choking to death in the sea, until all have drowned. [192]

---

[192] Note in the original the four aorists and the final imperfect.

Two questions demand consideration. First, *"What ethical justification was there for Jesus to allow this to happen to these animals?"* Shall we say that one of these days those pigs would have had to die anyway; so they might as well die now? Shall we add that quick death by suffocation or asphyxiation through drowning may even have been more merciful than slower death by fire, or by animal attack, starvation, slaughter at the hands of a clumsy butcher, etc.? But is not Rom. 9:20, "Nay but, O man, who art thou that repliest against God?" (to use the A.V.) the real answer? Cf. Dan. 4:35.

In this commentary the *love* of God in Christ and his *power* have been mentioned again and again. We believe rightly so, for Scripture itself mentions these qualities repeatedly. But no less important, surely, are God's *holiness* and his sovereignty. God is sinless. Rather, he is holy, and the source of holiness for all who place their trust in him. Cf. Isa. 6:1-5. Moreover, he owes us no explanation of his deeds. We should live *by faith!* (Hab. 2:4; Rom. 1:17; Gal. 3:11). See also Job 21:5; 40:4. Says H. Bavinck: "Round about us we observe so many facts which seem to be unreasonable, so much undeserved suffering, so many unaccountable calamities, such an uneven and inexplicable distribution of destiny, and such an enormous contrast between the extremes of joy and sorrow, that any one reflecting on these things is forced to choose between viewing this universe as if it were governed by the blind will of an unbenign deity, as is done by pessimism, or, upon the basis of Scripture and by faith, to rest in the absolute and sovereign, yet—however incomprehensible—wise and holy will of him who one day is going to cause the full light of heaven to dawn upon these mysteries of life. . . . In the midst of terrible reality Calvinism does not come forth with a solution, but it offers this comfort: that, in whatsoever happens, it recognizes the will and the governing hand of an omnipotent God, who is at the same time a merciful Father. Calvinism does not offer a solution, but it causes man to rest in him who dwells in light unapproachable, whose judgments are unsearchable and whose ways are past tracing out." [193]

That same answer will do also for *the second question*, namely, *"Was it right for Jesus to permit the demons to destroy so much property, that is, to deprive the owners of so large a proportion of their material possessions?"* In addition, however, to the appeal to God's sovereignty, which, after all, is basic, it should also be pointed out that, rightly considered, by permitting this loss Jesus was actually *helping* these owners; that is, he was helping them if only they were willing to take the lesson to heart. These owners—and in general the people of this community—were selfish. In their scale of values

---

[193] *The Doctrine of God*, Grand Rapids, 1955, (my translation from the Dutch), pp. 396, 397.

the acquisition, retention, and multiplication of material possessions ranked higher by far than the liberation and restoration of a man unfree, unhappy, unloved, and uncared for; yes, enslaved, wretched, hated, and abandoned. For proof see on verse 17. Hence they needed this lesson. [194]

4. *The swineherds and the people to whom they report. The people's request that Jesus leave the district.*

14-17. **And those in charge of them fled and spread the news in the city and countryside. And the people came to see what it was that had happened. They came to Jesus and saw the demon-possessed** [195] **man sitting there, clothed and in his right mind,** [196] **the very man who had had the legion; and they became frightened. Those who had seen it told them how it went with the demoniac, and about the pigs.**

The men who had been tending the pigs must have witnessed the meeting between Jesus and the demoniac. They had also observed that the wildness of this man had left him and had, as it were, been transferred to the pigs, with the result that the entire herd had perished in the water. The swineherds drew the correct conclusion that it was Jesus who had ordered and allowed all this to happen. He had ordered the demons to leave, and had allowed them to enter the pigs. The loss of the pigs was therefore not the fault of those who had been tending them. The herdsmen, accordingly, ran back to where the people were living. They wanted the owners and everybody else, in town and countryside, in the little city and on the farms, to know who was and who was not to blame.

Mark pictures the people coming to see what it was that had happened. This was probably the morning after the miracle had occurred. What do the people see? They see Jesus. They also carefully observe the man who had been a demoniac. There was no doubt about it. It was the very man. Now, however, he was no longer rushing down the hill but sitting down, and right at the feet of Jesus. No longer was he naked (Luke 8:27) but clothed. And no longer was he acting like a madman, screaming night and day and gashing

---

194 An entirely different line of reasoning is followed by Lenski, *op. cit.*, pp. 133, 134. As he saw it, the owners of the hogs were Jews. Jesus confined himself to his own people. He caused the animals to be destroyed because it was illegal for these Jewish owners to possess them.

Answer. This line of reasoning injects into this story an element that is entirely foreign to it. Besides, not even such passages as Matt. 10:5; 15:24, 26 can be correctly interpreted to mean that non-Jews were *absolutely* excluded from the realm of Christ's sympathies and activities. See Matt. 4:24; 8:5-13; Mark 7:24-30; 15:21-28; Luke 4:25-27; 6:17-19; 7:1-10; John 1:29; 3:16, 17; 4:42; 6:51; 8:12; 9:5; 10:16; 11:52; 12:32.

195 For explanation of the present participle see on verse 18.

196 ἱματισμένον καὶ σωφρονοῦΝτα: a perfect passive participle (he had become—hence, still was—clothed) followed by a present participle "in his right mind."

himself with the sharp edges of stones, but in his right mind (cf. II Cor. 5:13).

The power and majesty of Jesus who had brought all this about caused these people to become frightened, a reaction that was not lessened when right here, on the spot where it had all happened, the details of the story—"how it went with the demoniac, and about the pigs"—were rehearsed by the eye-witnesses: herdsmen and disciples.

What should have been the result? Initial sadness because of the loss of the pigs would have been natural. But should not the owners and all who were in any way affected by this loss have spoken somewhat as follows: "We see now that the loss of our property was a small price to pay for the lesson we have learned. These pigs, that property, meant everything to us. We were selfish. We never felt concerned about the needs of our fellow-citizen, this poor, wretched man. Now we see things differently. We now understand that human values surpass material values by far"? Should they not have congratulated the man who was sitting there at Jesus' feet? Should they not have brought their sick and handicapped to Jesus to be healed? Surely, the people of this general region could not have been entirely ignorant about this great Benefactor! See Matt. 4:25. Should they not have tried to prevail upon Jesus to stay a while longer in their midst, in order to impart blessings for body and soul? Cf. John 4:40.

Their real reaction was quite different. It was in fact the very opposite. Jesus must leave, the sooner the better: **And they began to beg him to leave their district.** This is reported by all three evangelists. It is essential to the understanding of the lesson here conveyed.

These men were scared of Jesus. Besides, they resented him. Had he not deprived them of their property? Was he not a disturber of their familiar mode of life?

How often, even in our own day and age, has not this incident been repeated? People are eager to listen to the story of Jesus and his love . . . just so the gospel's implications for daily life and conduct (Matt. 18:23-35; 25:31-46; John 13:14, 15; II Cor. 8:7-9; Eph. 4:32–5:2) are not emphasized, for that would be upsetting!

5. *The cured man's request and Jesus' reply. Implications of that reply.*

18. And as he [Jesus] was getting into the boat, the man who had been demon-possessed [197] **begged to go with him.** It was a very natural request. The man wishes to be in the company of his Benefactor, to whom he has

---

[197] Note *aor.* participle δαιμονισθείς now. Cf. this with *present* participle δαιμο νιζόμενον in verse 15. When the people went out to see this man, the picture of one actually demon-possessed was still very vividly *present* to them. Nevertheless even then

become so heavily indebted. He wishes to render to him every service he may require. **19. But he refused and said to him, Go home to your people, and tell them what great things the Lord has done for you and how he had mercy on you.** Several points should be noted:

a. Is it not striking that the One who had granted the request of the demons, permitting them to enter the pigs, and of the people, that he leave their district, *refuses* to grant the request of a man who has become his own ardent follower? We learn from this that when God allows his people to get whatever it is they wish to have, this is not always an unmixed blessing. And when he refuses to say "Yes" in answer to their earnest petition, this is not necessarily a sign of his disfavor.

b. True missionary activity begins at home . . . but does not end there. It does indeed begin at home (Acts 1:8; cf. Matt. 10:5, 6). Does this not also imply that a true church member is at least as concerned about providing a thorough Christian education for his own children as he is about sending missionaries to the heathen? The latter task is indeed very important and necessary, but the former should have the priority.

c. The man is ordered to tell his people what great things "the Lord" has done for him. As verse 20 indicates, he understands this word "the Lord" to refer to Jesus. In Luke 8:39a the word "God" is substituted for "the Lord." The man again interprets "God" to refer to Jesus (8:39b). This shows that, as the evangelists and the cured demoniac saw it, Jesus is the Lord. He is God.

d. What may well be considered the main lesson is this: by ordering the man to go to his own "folks"—the term not to be taken too narrowly (see verse 20), and with the implied idea that neighbor will tell neighbor—, Jesus is showing a great kindness, and this not only to the former demoniac but also to the entire community that had so shamefully rejected him. *They* had asked him to leave, but he, in his great love, cannot completely separate himself from them. So he sends them a missionary, in fact the best kind of missionary, one who can speak from experience. See Ps. 34:6; 66:16; 116; John 9:25; I Cor. 15:9, 10; Gal. 1:15, 16; Phil. 3:7-14; I Tim. 1:15-17; II Peter 1:16; I John 1:1-4.

The man obeyed. **20. So he went away and began to proclaim in the Decapolis what great things Jesus had done for him; and everybody was amazed.** The healed man did exactly what the Lord wanted him to do. He went home and there related what great things Jesus had done for him. But

---

Mark, by using the perfect participle ἐσχηκότα, points out that a change has taken place. When verse 18 is reached the story has reached a new stage. Everybody now knows that the man is no longer a demoniac. Hence, the aorist participle is very proper here. For a somewhat different explanation of this point of grammar see Gram. N.T., p. 1117.

he did not stop then and there. So filled was he with joy and gratitude that he soon included the entire city where he was living in the sphere of his missionary activity (Luke 8:39). Even this did not satisfy his eagerness to ascribe the glory to God. Soon he was bearing testimony to God's goodness in the Decapolis as a whole, as Mark states.

This "Decapolis" was a league of ten Hellenic cities: Scythopolis (located west of the Jordan River); east of the Jordan: Philadelphia, Gerasa, Pella, Damascus, Kanata, Dion, Abila, Gadara, and Hippos. See the sketch. These ten cities, at one time deprived of their freedom by the Maccabees, had by the Romans been delivered from their yoke and had even been given a considerable measure of home rule. Though required to render tribute and military service to Rome, they had been allowed to form an association for commercial progress and for mutual defense against any encroachment from the side of either Jews or Arabs. They had their own army, courts, and coinage. Throughout this region there was a scattering of Jews, but by and large this was definitely Gentile territory; a fact to which, for example, many Greek amphitheatres bore witness. [198]

Everybody was amazed. The people who heard this man testify probably continued for some time [199] to be filled with wonder and praise. No doubt some did more than merely marvel. In Decapolis, too, there must have been a "remnant" of people in whose hearts and lives the word of God was effective unto salvation, to his glory. See Isa. 55:11; Matt. 4:24, 25; Mark 7:31-37.

---

21 Now when Jesus had again crossed over[200] to the other side, a large crowd gathered about him; and he was beside the sea.   22 Then came one of the rulers of the synagogue, Jairus by name; and seeing him, fell at his feet   23 and pleaded earnestly with him, saying, "My little daughter is at the point of death; please come and put your hands on her, that she may get well and live."   24 So he [Jesus] went with him. A large crowd was following him and pressing upon him.

25 And a woman who had been subject to hemorrhages for a period of twelve years, 26 and who had suffered much from many physicians, and had spent all she had and instead of getting better had grown worse,   27 after hearing about Jesus came from behind in the crowd and touched his garment.   28 For she said, "If I touch just his clothes I shall get well."

29 And at once her bleeding stopped and she felt in her body that she had been healed of her illness.

30 Now Jesus, being well aware in himself that power which issued from him had gone out of him, immediately turned around in the crowd and asked, "Who touched my clothes?"   31 "You see the crowd pressing on you," said his disciples, "and you ask,

---

198 For source material on the Ten Cities see especially Josephus, *Jewish War* I. 155-158; II. 466-468; III. 446; V. 341, 342, 410; *Antiquities* XIV.74.

199 Note imperfect ἐθαύμαζον, were in a state of amazement, were marveling.

200 There is considerable textual support for (crossed over) "by boat."

THE TEN CITIES

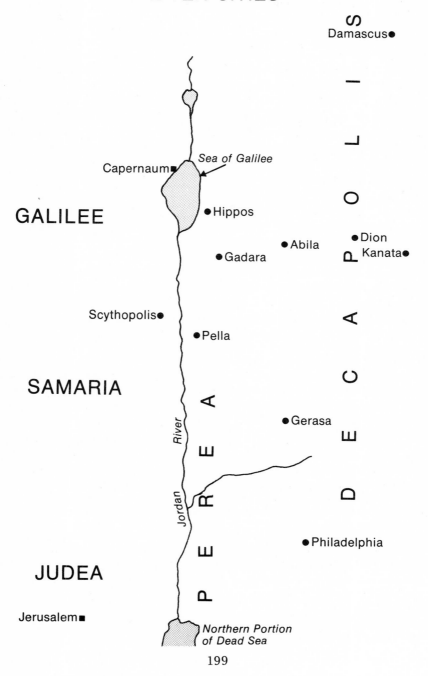

Damascus●

Sea of Galilee

Capernaum■

GALILEE

●Hippos

●Abila ●Dion
Kanata●

●Gadara

Scythopolis●

●Pella

SAMARIA

●Gerasa

JUDEA

●Philadelphia

Jerusalem■

Northern Portion
of Dead Sea

DECAPOLIS

PEREA

Jordan River

'Who touched me?' " 32 But he [Jesus] continued to look around to see who had done it. 33 Then the woman, trembling with fear since she knew what had happened to her, came and fell down before him and told him the whole truth. 34 He said to her, "Daughter, your faith has made you well; go in peace, and be healed of your illness."

35 While he [Jesus] was still speaking, some men came from the synagogue ruler's (house). "Your daughter is dead," they said. "Why bother the Teacher any further?" 36 Ignoring [201] what was being spoken, Jesus said to the ruler of the synagogue, "Fear not, only believe."

37 And he allowed no one to accompany him except Peter and James and John the brother of James. 38 They came to the house of the synagogue ruler; and he noticed the hubbub, with people loudly weeping and wailing. 39 And having entered he said to them, "Why do y o u make a hubbub and weep? The child is not dead but asleep." 40 But they were laughing in his face.

But he turned them all out, and taking with him (only) the child's father and mother and his own companions entered (the room) where the child was. 41 And having grasped the child's hand he said to her, "Talitha koum" [202] ; which means "Little girl, I say to you, get up." 42 At once the little girl stood up and started to walk around, for she was twelve years old. And at once they were utterly astonished.

43 He strictly charged them that no one should know this, and he ordered that she be given (something) to eat.

5:21-43 *Two Miracles*
The Restoration to Life of Jairus' Daughter
and
The Healing of the Woman Who Touched Christ's Garment
Cf. Matt. 9:18-26; Luke 8:40-56

The transition from the preceding section (verses 1-20) to this one (verses 21-43) is well-nigh unforgettable. From the request amounting to "Please go away," the story advances to the earnest and moving petition "Please come" (contrast verse 17 with verse 23). When Jesus was asked to leave, he left; that is, he recrossed the sea and landed at the Capernaum side, where a ruler of the Capernaum synagogue was in sore need of help, for his little daughter was at the point of death. So, from the story of the miraculous blessing bestowed on a man who had his dwelling in a locality associated with death (verse 3) we advance to that of triumph over death itself (verses 41, 42). From being *amazed* (verse 20) we are led to being *utterly astonished* (verse 42).

It would seem that when Jesus landed, the disciples of John the Baptist were waiting for him, with their question about fasting. See N.T.C. on Matt. 9:18. It was while he was still speaking with them that Jairus made his request.

---

[201] Or: Disregarding, Paying no attention to, Not heeding. Also possible is: Overhearing.

[202] Or, based upon another reading, "Talitha koumi (or: cumi)."

The synagogue was ruled by a board of elders. One of its responsibilities was to maintain good order at the synagogue meetings. The man who came to Jesus and whom Matthew does not mention by name but whom Mark and Luke call Jairus was a member of such a board. Since he was probably living in Capernaum we may assume that he had heard about, and perhaps even witnessed, some of the miracles performed by Jesus.

Matthew's report of the double miracle is very brief, nine verses; Luke's covers seventeen verses; Mark's twenty-three. For more information on the synagogue see above on 1:39.

Matthew omits the ruler's request (see Mark and Luke) that Jesus heal the very *sick* child. In fact, Matthew in his very brief summary leaves out several items mentioned by one or both of the other synoptists. However, it is he alone who relates that the ruler asks Jesus to lay his hand upon the dead girl, adding "and she will live" (9:18). Also, he alone mentions the flute-players in the house of mourning (9:23).

Mark alone, in his very lengthy account, represents Jairus as using the term of endearment "my little daughter" (verse 23), pictures a vast crowd "thronging" or "pressing upon" Jesus (verse 24), relates that Jesus paid no attention to the message delivered to Jairus, "Your daughter is dead . . ." (verses 35, 36), *emphasizes* the weeping and wailing that was going on among the mourners (verses 38, 39), reports the Aramaic words spoken by Jesus to the child (verse 41), and adds that the girl, brought back from the dead, walked (verse 42).

Several items are common to Mark and Luke, though not found in Matthew. Thus we are told that the name of the ruler was Jairus (Mark 5:22; Luke 8:41), that Jairus made his first request before the child had died (Mark 5:23; Luke 8:42), that she was about twelve years of age (Mark 5:42; Luke 8:42), that Peter, James, and John, and also the child's parents were with Jesus when he performed the miracle (Mark 5:37, 40; Luke 8:51), and that Jesus did not want the news of this miracle to spread (Mark 5:43; Luke 8:56).

It is Luke alone who reports that the daughter was an only child (8:42), and that Jesus did indeed hear the remark to which he paid no attention (8:50).

In all the three accounts the story of the bringing back to life of the daughter of Jairus is interrupted by that of the healing of the woman who touched Christ's garment.

The material as here presented permits the following outline. Under the general theme that has already been indicated (The Two Miracles, etc.) we arrive at these subdivisions or "points":

201

	Verses
The first miracle introduced	21-24
The first miracle interrupted	
by	
the second miracle	
faith concealed	25-28
faith rewarded	29
faith revealed	30-34
The first miracle performed	
a word of encouragement	35, 36
a word of revelation	37-40a
a word of love and power	40b-42
a word of tender concern	43

* * *

1. *The first miracle introduced*

21-23. Now when Jesus had again crossed over to the other side, a large crowd gathered about him; and he was beside the sea. Then came one of the rulers of the synagogue, Jairus by name; and seeing him, fell at his feet and pleaded earnestly with him, saying, My little daughter is at the point of death; please come and put your hands on her, that she may get well and live.

As often previously (1:16; 2:13; 3:7; 4:1), Jesus was again to be found "beside the sea," near Capernaum; with a large crowd assembled about him, as usual. It was then that Jairus fell prostrate at his feet. This very action was a manifestation of high respect for Jesus. The ruler's earnest entreaty, "My little daughter is at the point of death—literally: has reached the final stage—; please come and put your hands on her, that she may get well and live," was an expression of *tender affection, intense anxiety,* and a *considerable measure of faith.*

Tender affection! Jairus says, "my little daughter." At the age of twelve many children resent being considered "little." But to this father the child is still "little"; with emphasis, however, not so much on her tender years as on her loveliness in his eyes. [203]

Intense anxiety! "Please come. . . ." Fearful apprehension is coupled with strong desire.

A considerable measure of faith! The man believes in the effectiveness—even now with death so close—of the touch of Jesus' hands. For this touch

---

[203] As often, the diminutive is here predominantly a term of endearment. See Introduction IV, footnote 5 h; also on 3:9, footnote 108.

see on 1:41. Note: "... that she may get well and live." [204] This ruler must have seen and heard Jesus many a time, right here in Capernaum, where the Master had his headquarters and where, whenever possible, he attended the synagogue. Jairus may well have witnessed previous miracles. It is remarkable, nevertheless, that with his darling daughter, his only child, so near to death, the man still has hope, still manifests a considerable degree of faith.

It is no surprise to read: **24. So he [Jesus] went with him.** Is he not the Savior, and this not only for the soul but for the entire person, soul and body?

However, a statement follows which is both closely connected with that which precedes and also introduces what follows in verses 25-34. The statement is: **A large crowd was following him and pressing upon him.** This was not unusual; see 3:9; 4:1. What adds significance to it in the present situation is *a*. The very size of the crowd, together with the fact that the people were pressing upon or thronging Jesus, made progress toward the house of Jairus difficult. *b*. The presence of this crowd explains the action of the woman whose story follows. She thought that because of the enormous crowd she would be able to do what she wanted to do, and escape undetected (cf. Luke 8:47).

2. *The first miracle interrupted* by *the second miracle*
a. faith concealed

It has already been shown that the swirling crowd, delaying the performance of the first miracle and to a certain extent explaining what happened in connection with the second, connects the two stories. Two consecutive verses in Luke's Gospel (8:42, 43) also supply a connection: the daughter of Jairus was *twelve* years of age; the woman had been suffering for a period of *twelve* years. But the two narratives can also be viewed as one, namely, the narrative of an interrupted and therefore all the more glorious miracle (Mark 5:21-43 and parallels).

In telling the story of Jesus and the woman, Matthew is again very brief. Note his three verses (9:20-22). Luke has nine (8:40-48). Mark, the action Gospel, spreads the various vivid details over ten verses (5:25-34).

It is true here, as well as everywhere else in the Gospels, that none of the accounts is mere repetition. Each evangelist contributes something not

---

204 As to the first ἵνα in verse 23 (ἵνα ἐλθὼν ἐπιθῇς), opinions differ. Perhaps it can best be considered an elliptical manner of expressing a polite imperative; hence here, "Please come ...." The second ἵνα in the same verse introduces purpose: "that" or "in order that" she may be saved and live. Here "be saved" (thus literally) means "be restored to health," hence "get well."

The verbs ἐπιθῇς (second per.); σωθῇ and ζήσῃ (both third person) are all aor. subjunctives after the first or second ἵνα.

reported by the others. Thus we would not want to miss Matthew's reference to the woman talking "to herself" (9:21), or his report of Jesus turning to the woman and saying to her, "Take heart" (or: "Take courage," "Be of good cheer"). Neither would we want to do without the clever manner in which *Dr.* Luke (8:43b), without contradicting Mark, yet prevents a possible misunderstanding of what Mark says about the physicians of that day (Mark 5:26, "a woman . . . who had suffered much from many physicians"). Luke is also the only one who brings Peter into the story (8:45). And as for Mark, neither Matthew nor even Luke presents the details of this story as vividly as he does. See especially 5:29-33. On the other hand, Mark does not even mention the tassel, only the garment (5:27, 28). Contrast Matt. 9:20; Luke 8:44.

25-27. **And a woman who had been subject to hemorrhages for a period of twelve years, and who had suffered much from many physicians, and had spent all she had and instead of getting better had grown worse, after hearing about Jesus came from behind in the crowd and touched his garment.**

While Jesus is on his way to the home of Jairus suddenly there is an interruption. Again and again during his earthly ministry Jesus was interrupted; namely, in his speaking to a crowd (Mark 2:1 ff.), conversing with his disciples (Mark 8:31 ff.; 14:27 ff.; Luke 12:12 ff.), traveling (Mark 10:46 ff.), sleeping (Mark 4:38, 39), and praying (Mark 1:35 ff.). The fact that none of these intrusions floor him, so that for the moment he would be at a loss what to do or what to say, shows that we are dealing here with the Son of man who is also the Son of God! What *we* would call an "interruption" is for him a springboard or take-off point for the utterance of a great saying or, as here, for the performance of a marvelous deed, revealing his power, wisdom, and love. What for us would have been a painful exigency is to him a golden opportunity.

This time the interrupter is a woman. For twelve years she had been subject to hemorrhages; literally she had been "in (a condition of) flow of blood." There are those who believe that the drain was constant. Another view would be that throughout the twelve years an excessive loss of blood, occurring periodically, had made it impossible for her ever to feel strong and healthy, and that at this particular moment she was again suffering as a result of loss of blood.

She had suffered much at the hands of many physicians. For the form of the expression cf. Matt. 16:21. An apocryphal book (Tobit 2:10) states, "I went to the physicians, but they did not help me." On the other hand read the statement from another apocryphal writing (Ecclus. 38:1), "Honor a physician according to your need of him, with the honors due to him; for, indeed, the Lord has created him." Verse 3 of the same chapter speaks of "the skill of the physician" and states, "In the sight of great men he shall be admired." Though it is true that even today doctors sometimes err, as do also men of other professions, it would be difficult to over-estimate the value of a capable and devoted doctor. In the case here reported the results of medical treatment had been anything but favorable. The poor woman's condition had gradually deteriorated, and this partly because of the very care (?) the doctors had bestowed on her.

This should not be interpreted to mean that the art of healing in Israel, in comparison with that practiced in the surrounding nations at that time, was very, very poor. It is true that medical science in the technical sense was still in its infancy. Nevertheless, the Jews, at least in some important respects, were ahead of all others. They believed in the efficacy of prayer to the one and only God, Ruler of heaven and earth, hence also of soul and body, and over life and death, health and sickness (II Kings 1; Ps. 116; Isa. 36). To them had been given the Ten Commandments, which have been called "the greatest mental hygiene code." The ordinance of circumcision also deserves consideration in this connection. Add to this the many hygienic regulations found in the Pentateuch, the emphasis on the influence of the mind on the health of the body (Prov. 17:22), exhortations against unlovely emotions (e.g., Exod. 23:4, 5; Prov. 15:17) with their sinister effect upon physical well-being, the repeated commandment to trust in God and not to worry (Ps. 91; 125; Isa. 26:3, 4; 43:2); and it will be seen that with respect to the care of the body, as well as with respect to many other things, Israel was far ahead of all other peoples. See also Exod. 15:26.

Nevertheless in this particular case the doctors had been unsuccessful. Why? Can it be that the very fact, clearly implied in the text, that this woman had been running to "many physicians" had something to do with this? Even today the custom of some people to run from one doctor to another, and still another, and another, cannot be unreservedly recommended, though there may indeed be certain cases where this is necessary. It would seem, however, that the best answer to the question why this woman was not healed is given by the man who himself was a doctor, namely, Luke, who plainly states that her illness was humanly speaking, and in the light of the therapeutics of that day, incurable (Luke 8:43). [205]

By the time this woman finally decided to cast her lot with Jesus she had spent all her—shall we say "little"?—money. She had lost her health, her

---

205 For more on the general subject of the history of the healing art, especially in Israel, see W. H. Ogilvie, "Medicine and Surgery, History of," article in Enc. Brit., Chicago, London, etc., 1969 ed., Vol. 15, pp. 93-106; S. I. McMillen, *None of These Diseases*, Westwood, N. J., 1963; L. Finkelstein, *The Jews, Their History, Culture, and Religion*, New York, 1949, Vol. II, pp. 1013-1021; I. Benzinger, "Diseases and the Healing Art," article in S.H.E.R.K., Vol. III, pp. 445-448; and E. S. Turner, *The Astonishing History of the Medical Profession*, New York, 1961.

wealth, and because of the nature of her illness, also her standing in society, particularly in the religious community. Her condition was such that it would make her ceremonially "unclean" (Lev. 15:19 ff.).

There was this last reason for hope: Jesus! What is so striking in this connection is that not only prominent people, such as Jairus, turned to Jesus in their distress, but so did also proletarians, like this poor woman. They seemed to have sensed that his power and his pity would respond to the needs of people from every social class.

It is not surprising, however, that because of her condition she is afraid to come out into the open. She is not going to come into physical contact with Jesus himself. She will merely touch his garment, and even then (see Matthew and Luke), only one of the four wool tassels which every Israelite was ordered to wear on the corners of his square, outer robe (Num. 15:38; cf. Deut. 22:12) to remind him of the law of God. See also N.T.C. on Matt. 23:5. [206] Naturally the quickest and easiest way to bring oneself into physical contact with a garment without being noticed was to come from behind and touch the tuft swinging freely from the back of the robe. The wearer, so this woman thought, would never even notice what was happening. So, having heard the wonderful reports about Jesus, she came from behind and touched the tassel, [207] or as Mark has it, "his garment."

The reason for touching Christ's garment is given in verse 28. **For she said, If I touch just his clothes I shall get well.** The greatness of this woman's faith consisted in this, that she believed that the power of Christ to heal was so amazing that even the mere touch of his clothes would result in an instant and complete cure. [208]

That this faith was nevertheless by no means perfect appears from the fact that she thought that such an actual touch was necessary and that Jesus

---

[206] Cf. S.BK. IV, p. 277.

[207] In these three verses (25-27) Mark uses no less than seven participles, the first five being in the attributive position and modifying "a woman," the last two being predicative and modifying "touched." The seven are:

οὖσα	*being*, present p. of εἰμί. Cf. *is, essence, parousia.*
παθοῦσα	*having suffered,* aor., of πάσχω. Cf. *pathology, passion.*
δαπανήσασα	*having spent,* aor., of δαπανάω.
(μηδὲν)ὠφεληθεῖσα	*(not at all) having benefited, (not at all) having been helped,* aor. passive of ὠφελέω. Cf. the *anopheles* mosquitoes. They are not helpful.
ἐλθοῦσα	*having come,* aor., of ἔρχομαι. Cf. *origin, proselyte.*
ἀκούσασα	*having heard,* aor., of ἀκούω. Cf. *acoustics.*
ἐλθοῦσα	*having come* (used both in verse 26 and 27, first attributively, then predicatively).

[208] If the imperfect tense of the Greek verb (λέγω, here ἔλεγεν) must be stressed— which is not always the case—, she repeated this saying again and again. For the verb σῴζω (here σωθήσομαι) see above, footnote 204.

would never notice it. But he did notice it, rewarded her faith by restoring her to health (verse 29), and then gave her an opportunity to change "faith concealed" (Matt. 9:21) to "faith revealed" (Mark 5:33), which resulted in further encouragement (5:34).

b. faith rewarded

29. **And at once her bleeding stopped and she felt in her body that she had been healed of her illness.** Literally, "And at once dried up was the fountain of her blood." The recovery was instant. In one brief moment the hemorrhage stopped completely. Health and vigor were surging through every part of her body. The "scourge" or "illness" by which she had been afflicted was gone. For the word which basically means "scourge" or "whip" and here refers to the woman's torturing illness see on 3:10. [209] Not only was her trouble gone; she felt and knew that it was gone.

What is striking in this connection is the fact that although this woman's faith, as has been shown, was far from perfect, nevertheless the Lord graciously rewards it. The reward, moreover, affected not only her body but also her soul; or, to state it differently, not only was her faith rewarded, it was also improved, brought to a higher stage of development, so that faith concealed became:

c. faith revealed

30. **Now Jesus, being well aware in himself that power which issued from him had gone out of him, immediately turned around in the crowd and asked, Who touched my clothes?** Jesus was not ignorant of the fact that someone had touched him, and this not accidentally but purposely, and not just with a finger but with faith. He knew that it was to that faith that the power within him and proceeding from him had responded.

What Jesus wants is that whoever it was that has thus meaningfully touched him shall now complete the circle. What circle? The one indicated in many passages of Scripture, including, for example, Ps. 50:15:

Call upon me in the day of trouble;
I will deliver you,
And you shall glorify me.

When blessings descend from heaven, they must in the form of thanksgiving be returned to heaven by those who received them. Thus the circle is completed. See also N.T.C. on Eph. 1:3. This woman, in her own way, had called upon Jesus. He had rescued her, but she had not as yet glorified him. Up to this point she was like the nine cleansed lepers of Luke 17:17, 18:

---

209 In Acts 22:24 the word μάστιξ is used in the more literal sense of scourging by means of a whip. For a moment it looked as if Paul was going to be scourged to discover what crime he supposedly had committed; but see Acts 22:25, 26, 29. For the literal sense see also Heb. 11:36.

"Then Jesus said, 'Were not ten cleansed? Where are the nine? Was no one found to return and give thanks to God except this foreigner?' " To be sure, she had "believed with her heart." But she had not as yet "confessed with her mouth" (Rom. 10:9). It was in order to bring about this favorable change that Jesus immediately turned around in the crowd and asked, "Who touched my clothes?" Or, as Luke phrases it, "Who was it that touched me?" (8:45), meaning "touched me meaningfully?"

31. **You see the crowd pressing on you, said his disciples, and you ask, Who touched me?** The disciples commit the oft repeated error of interpreting Christ's words in the most starkly literal sense, as if Jesus were thinking of a merely physical touch. These men, and others too, were in the habit of applying the literal interpretation rule to the words of Jesus, the very rule which by certain segments of Christendom is even today recommended so very highly. The following passages are among those that show why this rule, unless it be very substantially modified, is anything but safe: Mark 8:15, 16; John 2:19-22; 3:3-5; 4:10-15; 6:52; 8:56-58; 11:11-13. To be sure, Jesus was not denying the literal touch, but he meant something far more than this, namely, the touch *in faith,* the very effective touch, so that in response to that touch power had gone forth from him.

The response of the disciples—led by Peter (Luke 8:45)—, "You see the crowd pressing on you, and you ask . . ." revealed not only lack of insight but even lack of the proper respect, the subdued reverence which these men should have shown to their Master. Briefly, the critical remark was thoughtless and tasteless, crude and rude. It reminds one of Matt. 16:22.

The Master showed his greatness by not answering it. 32. **But he [Jesus] continued to look around to see who had done it.** It was a long and scrutinizing gaze. [210] Those commentators who have commented on it differ rather widely. There are three main interpretations. According to *the first,* Jesus already knew who this person was. He was looking around and suddenly his eyes rested on the woman. [211]

Now the fact that according to his divine nature Jesus was omniscient cannot be denied. Also, it cannot be denied that this divine nature at times imparted to the human nature information which that human nature apart from such impartation would probably not have received. See Matt. 17:27; John 1:47, 48. Yet, this does not mean that Christ's human nature was also in itself omniscient. See Matt. 24:36; Mark 11:13. Is not Mark 5:32 in the

---

[210] See above, footnote 105.

[211] Lenski, *op. cit.,* p. 142. He derives this information from the use of the imperfect tense ("he was looking around") followed by the aorist ἰδεῖν. While agreeing with much of what this interpreter says, I cannot follow him here. Grammatically περιεβλέπετο ἰδεῖν is *one* expression: "he continued to look—or: was looking—(in order) to see." It cannot be split up into two time periods.

same class? The expression, "He continued to look around—or: was looking around—to see," certainly seems to support the view that the *first* explanation, namely, that Jesus already knew who the person was that had touched him, is unacceptable. For more on Christ's two natures in the teaching of Mark see *Introduction*, III.

On the basis of the use of the feminine participle in the original, [212] so that the rendering, "But he was looking around to see her who had done this," is acceptable, it has been argued *secondly* that Jesus at least knew that the person who had touched him was a woman. [213]

But is it not more reasonable to view that feminine participle in the light of what Mark, the Gospel writer, subsequently knew to be the case?

All things considered, the most natural interpretation would seem to be *the third one*, namely, that Jesus, with the tender Savior's heart, wished to bestow an additional favor upon *whoever it was* that had touched him. "He kept looking around to find out" (thus A. T. Robertson [214]) who that person was.

33. Then the woman, trembling with fear since she knew what had happened to her, came and fell down before him and told him the whole truth.

The woman had heard Jesus ask, "Who touched my clothes?" Also, she had noticed his searching eyes. She knew "what had happened to her" in answer to her touch of faith. She had probably also heard the disciples' wholly inadequate reply. Her conscience must have told her that the true answer to Christ's question must be given, and given by *her!*

Nevertheless, it was not easy for her to do what she felt she had to do. At that time and in that country for a woman to speak in public was generally considered improper. This all the more on a subject such as this, the particular physical scourge by which she had been afflicted. And would not even the fact that she, in that condition, deliberately had touched the Master add to the impropriety in the eyes of the bystanders? Yes, and even, perhaps, in the eyes of Jesus himself? Would he scold her perhaps?

We can understand, therefore, both why she confessed and why she did this "fearing and trembling" (thus literally; cf. II Cor. 7:15; Eph. 6:5; Phil. 2:12). She was scared and shaking all over.—But she came, and told the whole truth, probably referring to all the facts stated in verses 25-29.

The result was not a reprimand, but the very opposite, as is evident from the very first word Jesus uttered and also from what followed. **34. He said**

---

[212] τὴν . . . ποιήσασαν.

[213] A. B. Bruce, *op. cit.*, p. 375, offers this as a possibility.

[214] *Word Pictures*, Vol. I, p. 300. Along this line also Taylor, *op. cit.*, p. 292; Schmid, *op. cit.*, p. 115; and Bolkestein, *op. cit.*, p. 125. On the other hand, A. B. Bruce, *op. cit.*, p. 375, and Swete, *op. cit.*, p. 105, leave room for either of the last two interpretations.

to her, Daughter, your faith has made you well; go in peace, and be healed of your illness. Lovingly Jesus calls her "Daughter," even though she may not have been any younger than he was. But he speaks as a father to his child. Moreover, he praises her for her faith, even though that faith, as has been indicated, was by no means perfect; and even though, as verse 27 indicates, it was he himself who, through his earlier marvelous words and deeds, had brought about that faith. Her faith, though not the basic cause of her cure, had been the channel through which the cure had been accomplished. It had been the instrument used by Christ's power and love, to effect her recovery. Cf. Eph. 2:8. Is it not marvelous that Jesus, in speaking to this woman, says nothing about his own power and love, the root-cause of her present state of well-being, but makes special mention of that which apart from him she would neither have possessed nor have been able to exercise? Moreover, by saying, "Your faith has made you well," was he not also stressing the fact that it was his *personal response* to her *personal faith* in him that cured her, thereby removing from her mind any remnant, however small, of superstition, as if his clothes had contributed in any way to the cure?

By means of these cheering words Jesus also opened the way for the woman's complete reinstatement in the social and religious life and fellowship of her people. Now she can go and continue to travel the rest of her life "in peace," that is, with the smile of God upon her and the joyful inner knowledge of this smile. Cf. Isa. 26:3; 43:1, 2; Rom. 5:1.

Probably even more is included in this encouraging command, "Go in peace." In view of the immediately following words, namely, "Be—meaning *Be and remain*—healed of your illness (literally: your scourge)," and in view of the fact that in all probability Jesus spoke these words in the then current language of the Jews (Aramaic), have we not a right to conclude that nothing less than the full measure of the Hebrew *Shalom,* well-being for both soul and body, is here implied?

Although none of the evangelists report the woman's reaction to these gracious words of the Savior, is it unrealistic to affirm that her soul was flooded not only with relief but also with boundless gratitude, the kind of emotion experienced by the inspired composer of Ps. 116 (see especially verses 12-19)? Jesus had healed her. He had imparted to her a double blessing: restoring her body and causing her soul to testify, so that faith concealed had become faith revealed. Now she was able to be, and undoubtedly had become, a blessing to others, to the glory of God.

A few days after a certain minister preached on this section of Scripture (Mark 5:25-34 and parallels), he received the following poem from a lady who had composed it after hearing the sermon:

"Who touched me?"

'Twas the voice of the Master,
And the woman's heart beat faster and faster.

Trembling she came and bowed her head.
"I touched thee, Lord," was what she said.
But the Master answered, "Go thy way,
Thy faith has made thee whole this day."

"Have you touched me?"
I heard it. 'Twas the voice of the Master,
And O my heart beat faster and faster.
"You came with the throng to God's house today,
But I felt not your touch as you went your way."
   I was ashamed and bowed my head.
"Reach out a bit farther next time," he said.

3. *The first miracle performed*
a. a word of encouragement

35. **While he [Jesus] was still speaking, some men came from the syna-gogue ruler's (house). Your daughter is dead, they said. Why bother the Teacher any further?** The messengers may have been relatives of Jairus, or they may have been friends. At any rate, they were not very diplomatic about conveying the alarming news. Rather bluntly they said, "Your daughter is dead."[215] They add, "Why bother[216] the Teacher any further?" As these relatives and/or friends saw it, there was not even the remotest possibility that Jesus would be able to restore a dead person. For a while there had been hope, namely, when the child was sick; very sick, to be sure, but Jesus was on the way. But then there had been that tragic interruption (verses 25-34). And now the blossoms of hope had withered away. "For the living there is hope, for the dead there is none" (Theocritus–*Idyl* IV. 42). However, note what happens:

36. **Ignoring[217] what was being spoken, Jesus said to the ruler of the synagogue, Fear not, only believe.** Though Jesus hears the words of the messengers (Luke 8:50), he pays no attention to them. With majestic calmness he refuses completely to lend an ear to the heralds of doom, the messengers of despair. He wants Jairus to do the same.

Jairus is afraid. Now it is not easy to drive out fear. There is only one way

---

215 ἀπέθανεν. This aor. form of ἀποθνῄσκω is generally and correctly thus translated, though instead of "is dead" the rendering "died" (Beck) or "has died" (N.A.S.) is also possible.

216 σκύλλεις. The original meaning of σκύλλω is *skin, flay*. The modified and weaker connotation, as here intended, is *bother, trouble.* See also N.T.C. on Matt. 9:36.

217 Though "overhearing" is also possible, yet the meaning "ignoring," "not heeding," "refusing to heed," "paying no attention to," is probably intended; for:
  a. This is the meaning of the word παρακούω in the LXX.
  b. Also in Matt. 18:17, the only other New Testament passage in which it occurs.

to do it, namely, by firmly believing in the presence, promises, pity, and power of God in Christ. It takes the positive to drive out the negative (Rom. 12:21).

Throughout the history of redemption it has ever been thus. When it seemed that all was lost, believers placed their trust in God and were delivered (Ps. 22:4; Isa. 26:3, 4; 43:2). This was true with respect to Abraham (Gen. 22:2; James 2:22), Moses (Exod. 14:10 f.; 32:10, 30-32), David (I Sam. 17:44-47; Ps. 27), and Jehoshaphat (II Chron. 20:1, 2, 12), to mention but a few. When the need was highest help was nighest.

This was true also in the case of Jairus. *The word of encouragement* was not in vain. He took it to heart (Matt. 9:18) and was heard.

b. a word of revelation

37. And he allowed no one to accompany him except Peter and James and John the brother of James. As Jesus resumes his journey to the house of Jairus, the crowd must have wondered what he was going to do, now that the situation—as the people must have viewed it—was utterly hopeless. With authority the Master dismisses the entire multitude, including even the disciples . . . with the exception of Peter, James, and John.

Most of the events pertaining to Jesus' sojourn on earth could be safely witnessed by all the twelve disciples. There were others, however, that took place in the presence of only three of these men. Exactly why this was we can only guess. Did Jesus allow only three disciples to enter the room where the resurrection of the daughter of Jairus took place, because the presence of the entire group would not have been in accord with proper decorum and might have disturbed the child when she reopened her eyes? Was the Master's Gethsemane agony too sacred to be witnessed by more than three of the disciples (Matt. 26:37; Mark 14:33), and was it for this reason that even then it was "witnessed" by these three to only a very limited extent? And is it possible that the transfiguration could have only three disciples as eye-witnesses (Matt. 17:1; Mark 9:2; Luke 9:28), because otherwise the injunction mentioned in Matt. 17:9 would have been more difficult to enforce? Such may have been the reasons, but we do not know.

That Peter was among the three does not surprise us, in view of Matt. 16:16-19. It is entirely possible that John's spiritual affinity with his Master—he was "the disciple whom Jesus loved" (John 13:23; 19:26; 20:2; 21:7, 10)—accounted for his inclusion in this innermost circle. But what about James, John's brother? Was it not considerate of the Lord to grant to him, who was going to be the first of The Twelve to seal his testimony with his blood (Acts 12:2), the privilege of being included among the three most intimate witnesses?

These are considerations that may well be taken into account in attempting to answer the question, "Why these three?" Nevertheless, it must be frankly admitted that the answer to this question has not been revealed. It is easier to understand why there had to be witnesses at all, namely, so that, when the proper time arrived, they could testify to the church concerning the things they had seen and heard. Besides, see Deut. 19:15; Matt. 18:16; John 8:17; II Cor. 13:1; I Tim. 5:19.

38. They came to the house of the synagogue ruler; and he noticed the hubbub, with people loudly weeping and wailing. A scene of confusion greeted Jesus and the three disciples as they entered the home of the synagogue ruler. Matt. 9:23 mentions the noisy (or: noise-making) crowd; Mark, the noise or tumult or hubbub. It was a thoroughly disorderly mob.

As, according to custom, burial followed soon after death, this was the crowd's only opportunity, and everybody, especially the professional mourners (cf. Jer. 9:17, 18), made the most of it, perhaps all the more because a ruler of the synagogue was a very important man! Here then was weeping and wailing, moaning and groaning, at its loudest. There was howling without any attempt at restraint. And every once in a while, above the confused noises issuing from the throats of the mourners, could be heard the shrill notes of the flute-players (Matt. 9:23).

39. And having entered he said to them, Why do y o u make a hubbub and weep? The child is not dead but asleep. What the mourners were doing was completely out of place, and this for two reasons: *a.* they—at least many of them—were insincere, as verse 40 shows; and *b.* there was cause here not for lamentation but for jubilation, not for bewailing a death but for celebrating a near at hand triumph over death.

Of course, we cannot very well blame these people for not knowing that life was about to triumph over death. What was wrong, though, was *a.* their insincerity, and *b.* their unwillingness to accept the fact that what Jesus was saying about the child not being dead but sleeping was a *word of revelation,* deserving of solemn reflection, not scorn.

That Jesus cannot have meant that the child had merely fallen into a coma is clear from the following:

a. Luke 8:53 declares that the people knew that she was dead.

b. Luke 8:55 states that at the command of Jesus "her spirit returned." It is clear, therefore, that there had been a separation between spirit and body.

c. In John 11:11 we have something similar. Jesus tells his disciples, "Our friend Lazarus has fallen asleep." But in verse 14 he affirms, "Lazarus died."

In both instances the meaning is that death will not have the final say. Not death but life is going to triumph in the end. Also, just as natural sleep is followed by awakening, so this child is going to become awake, that is, is going to live again.

40a. But they were laughing in his face. This identical statement is found also in Matt. 9:24 and in Luke 8:53. The reference is probably to repeated bursts of derisive laughter aimed at humiliating Jesus. It seems that these mourners were endowed with the dubious gift of shifting in one sudden moment from dismal moaning to uproarious mirth. Does not this very laughter also confirm the belief that the child had really died? Does it not therefore also bear witness to the genuine nature of the child's restoration from death?

c. a word of love and power

40b-41. But he turned them all out, and taking with him (only) the child's father and mother and his own companions entered (the room) where the child was. And having grasped the child's hand he said to her, Talitha koum; which means, Little girl, I say to you, get up.

Jesus expels the scornful noise-makers. Left with him in the room where the dead child lay were only the child's parents and Peter, James, and John (see verse 37). The ruler had asked the Master to place his hands upon the child (verse 23). However, he does even better, for with authority, power, and tenderness he grasps the child by the hand. As he does this he addresses her in her own native tongue (cf. N.T.C. on John 20:16), using the very words by means of which her mother had probably often awakened her in the morning, namely, "Talitha koum." For the sake of his non-Jewish readers Mark freely renders this, "Little girl, I say to you, Get up." [218]

42. At once the little girl stood up and started to walk around, for she was twelve years old. Immediately the spirit of the child returns and she gets up. Apparently without any assistance she starts to walk. Now that she is alive again it was natural for her to walk, for though she was her parents' "little girl" (verse 23, and see also verse 41), the only child (Luke 8:42), she had been able to walk for several years, being not less than twelve years of age. Mark probably adds this in order to prevent the reader from misinterpreting the term of endearment "little girl."

It is hardly surprising to read: **And at once they were utterly astonished;** more literally, "astonished with great astonishment." A moment ago she was a corpse, pale and lifeless. Now she is walking around, filled with life, health, and vigor. Therefore the astonishment of the overjoyed parents and of the three disciples as well knows no bounds. And in this astonishment all others who saw her afterward must have joined.

d. a word of tender concern

43. He strictly charged [219] **them that no one should know** [220] **this. For**

---

[218] "Little girl . . . get up" is translation; "I say to you" is interpretation.

[219] διεστείλατο mid. aor. from διαστέλλω. Basically the verb means *to divide* or *to distinguish*. However, in the middle, as here, it developed the sense: *to issue an order;* and with a negative particle either expressed or implied: *to forbid, to charge not to do this or that, to beware of.* See also 7:36; 8:15; 9:9; cf. Matt. 16:20; Acts 15:24; Heb. 12:20.

[220] γνοῖ, aor. subj. active of γινώσκω after ἵνα. For similar forms see 4:29; 8:37; and 14:10, 11.

the probable reason or reasons why such an injunction was issued see on 1:44. It may seem to be in conflict with verse 19, where Jesus orders the very thing to be done that he here (verse 43) forbids. But, after all, Decapolis, with its strongly Gentile atmosphere, was not Galilee. The latter, although far more under the influence of the Gentiles than Judea (see Matt. 4:15), was at the same time far more Jewish than Decapolis. Galilee was full of Pharisees, scribes, spies, etc. To be sure, Jesus came on earth to die, but he wishes to die at his own predestined hour, not earlier.

The *word of tender concern* is: **and he ordered that she be given (some-thing) to eat.** Cf. Luke 8:55. The prohibition in the first part of the verse is followed by a command or exhortation in the second part. [221] Jesus realizes that the little girl, who because of her fatal illness had probably not been able to eat for some time, was in need of food; and that the parents, in the ecstasy of their joy, might overlook this need. Hence, the command. [222]

This is a very important point. It should not be lightly passed by. Cf. Isa. 57:15. One moment Jesus triumphs over death; the next moment he appeases hunger; rather, in all probability, prevents it from becoming a reality. His power cannot be fathomed; nor his compassion measured.

This is the same Savior who went out of his way to enhance the reputation of one doubter (Matt. 11:1-19) and to accept the presumptuous terms of another (John 20:24-29), who defended widows (Luke 18:1-8; 21:1-4), helping them in their needs (Luke 7:11-17), took little children into his arms and blessed them (Mark 10:16), wept over Jerusalem's recalcitrant inhabitants (Matt. 23:37-39), and showed kindness to the woman who was a public sinner (Luke 7:36-50). In his own most bitter agony he provided a home for his mother (John 19:26, 27), entrance into paradise for a robber (Luke 23:43), and forgiveness for his torturers (Luke 23:34). Even after his resurrection he is the same tender-hearted Savior, witness his treatment of the man who had but recently disowned him (Mark 16:7; John 21:15-17). This is the context in which that very precious passage, Mark 5:43b, should be read.

---

221 Why is it that several commentaries say nothing at all about this very revealing command? Others merely mention the point of grammar, namely, that what we have here is an impersonal construction: Jesus does not say that *the parents* should give the child something to eat—why should he; may we not assume that this is implied?—but simply, by the use of the aor. pass. infinitive δοθῆναι, that something should be given her. Others add that the very fact that the child was ready to take some food proves that she was not only alive but in good health, or proves that her resurrection was real. On the favorable side, some commentators—for example, Lenski, Robertson and Taylor—do far better, and clearly state that the evangelist adds this detail in order to reveal the marvelous care of Jesus, as the Great Physician, his tender thoughtfulness and compassion. That is exactly the point!

222 One of the meanings of εἶπεν (used as 2nd aor. of λέγω) is *commanded, ordered*.

He is, moreover, *the Hope of the hopeless.* He showed this to the man who could not be tamed (Mark 5:1-20); to the woman who could not be cured (verses 25-34; Luke 8:43); and to the father who was told that he could no longer be helped (verses 21-24; 35-43).

Summary of Chapter 5

The chapter consists of two main sections: verses 1-20 describe the healing of the Gerasene demoniac; verses 21-43, a double miracle: *a.* restoration to life of Jairus' daughter; and *b.* the healing of the woman who touched Christ's garment For the subdivisions under *a.* see pp. 202, 211-216; and for those under *b.* see pp. 202, 204-211.

From the story about the taming of the wild waves (4:35-41) Mark proceeds to the account of the taming—rather, the complete and marvelous restoration—of a wild man, a maniac to be sure, but first of all and most of all a demoniac.

The chapter describes Jesus as the Hope of the hopeless. In doing so it moves to a gradual and exciting climax. [223] It describes a demoniac who was hopelessly wild, a woman who was hopelessly ill, and a father who became hopelessly bereaved; *hopelessly* in each case "by human standards." But now notice the climax: *the people in general* (see verses 3, 4) had reached the point where they were totally unable effectively to bind the demoniac; even *the experts,* that is the doctors (see verse 25; cf. Luke 8:43) were unable to cure the woman; and, of course, *no power in the universe* was able to raise a child from the dead! Not even the Teacher? No, not even the Teacher . . . so everybody thought. Note the statement: "While he [Jesus] was still speaking, some men came from the synagogue ruler's (house). 'Your daughter is dead,' they said. 'Why bother the Teacher any further?' "

Yet Christ, in his majesty, power, and compassion, triumphed over this hopelessness in all three cases: he dispelled the demons and transformed the demoniac into a missionary; he healed the woman and perfected her faith, changing it from faith concealed to faith revealed; and he not only, to the amazement of everybody, brought the child back to life, but even in his tenderness took care that she got something to eat!

What is especially important is the fact that in the entire chapter not only the power but also the pity of Christ is revealed. His compassionate heart is laid bare. The chief lesson, therefore, is this: "Give your heart to the wonderful Savior." A second lesson is this:

---

[223] Although the three miracles of chapter 5 are *introduced* in the order: demoniac (verse 1), Jairus (22), woman (25), they are *concluded* in the order: demoniac (verse 20), woman (34), Jairus (41-43).

I have given y o u an example, in order that just as I did to y o u so also y o u should do (John 13:15).

Be therefore imitators of God, as beloved children, and walk in love, just as Christ loved y o u and gave himself up for us, an offering and a sacrifice to God, for a fragrant odor (Eph. 5:1, 2).

Outline of Chapter 6

Theme: *The Work Which Thou Gavest Him To Do*

6:1-6a   The Rejection of Jesus at Nazareth
6:6b-13   The Charge to The Twelve
6:14-29   Herod's Wicked Birthday Party
                       and
          John the Baptist's Gruesome Death
6:30-44   The Feeding of the Five Thousand
6:45-52   Walking on the Water
6:53-56   Healings in Gennesaret

CHAPTER VI

6   1 He left that place and came to his hometown; and his disciples followed [224] him.   2 And when the sabbath came he began to teach in the synagogue. Many listeners were astonished and said, "Where did this man get these things, and what sort of wisdom is it that has been given to him, so that even miracles [225] are done by his hands?   3 Isn't this the carpenter, the son of Mary, and brother of James and Joses and Jude and Simon? And aren't his sisters here with us?" And they took offense at him.   4 So Jesus said to them, "A prophet is not without honor except in his hometown, among his relatives, and in his own family."   5 And he was unable to do any miracle there, except that he laid his hands on a few sick people.   6 And he was amazed because of their unbelief.

6:1-6a *The Rejection of Jesus at Nazareth*
Cf. Matt. 13:53-58; Luke 4:16-30 [226]

With the exception of the incidents reported in 5:17 and 5:40, all through chapter 5 faith triumphed; namely, in the case of the cured demoniac, who testified (verse 19, 20), the woman who touched Christ's garment (28, 34), and Jairus, who took to heart Christ's admonition, "Fear not, only believe" (36; cf. Matt. 9:18).

But if chapter 5 can be called *The Faith Chapter,* chapter 6 deserves the title *The No Faith Chapter.* Nazareth lacks faith. So does Herod, many mission objects, and even to a certain extent The Twelve. See verses 6, 11, 16, 52. Nevertheless faith triumphs in the end (verses 53-56).

The mourners (5:40) had "laughed down" (the Greek idiom), and the people of Nazareth look down on Jesus (6:3). Undaunted, he intensifies his efforts in the interest of the good news. Not only does he himself go around among the villages teaching, but he even sends his disciples on a tour of their own. Result? The "king" hears about Jesus. Did Nazareth *criticize?* Herod *cringes,* believing that Jesus is John the Baptist come back to life. It was he,

---

224 Or: accompanied
225 Or: works of power; so also in verse 5 (there sing.: work of power, miracle).
226 With the exception of section 2, devoted to *The Charge to The Twelve* (Mark 6:6b-13; cf. Matt. 10:1, 5, 9-14), Mark 6 is paralleled, *with retention of the same sequence,* in Matt. 13:53—14:36. Sections 2, 3, and 4 of Mark 6 are similarly paralleled in Luke 4:16-30. Sections 5 and 6—Walking on the Water, Healings in Gennesaret—are not found in Luke.

this very Herod Antipas, who had ordered John's execution. The gruesome story of this decapitation is told in 6:14-29.

The Twelve return and excitedly report to their Master. He lovingly bids them, "Come away by yourselves to a lonely place and rest a while" (6:30). For the results and further happenings see 6:32-56.

That Matthew should devote an entire chapter to *The Charge to The Twelve* (ch. 10), summarized in Mark 6:6b-13 and Luke 9:1-6, was to be expected, for Matthew specializes in Christ's discourses. There is no agreement on the question why Luke departs from what was probably the historical sequence, and in his Gospel places the account of the rejection at Nazareth in the forefront of his coverage of the Great Galilean Ministry, while Matthew and Mark give a much later place to it. Some have suggested two rejections at Nazareth. [227] For the rest, see commentaries on Luke.

Reasons for accepting the theory that in all three cases the reference is to the same incident:

a. The general outline of the story is the same in all three: On a sabbath Jesus enters his hometown. He teaches in the synagogue. Result: astonishment, adverse criticism, rejection.

b. Essentially the same dominical saying occurs in all three accounts (Matt. 13:57; Mark 6:4; Luke 4:24).

c. The historical background creates no difficulty, since even according to Luke's account (see 4:23) Christ's rejection at Nazareth did not occur at the beginning of Christ's Galilean Ministry but much later.

The identification is made easier by the fact that, aside from what is implied in 4:23, there are no time references attached to Luke's account. It is clear from Matt. 13:53, 54 that the visit to Nazareth occurred sometime after Jesus spoke his kingdom parables, although how long afterward is nowhere indicated. Did this visit and rejection take place late A.D. 28? This possibility must be granted.

As to Mark 6:1-6a and its parallels in Matthew and Luke, details recorded by Mark but not by Matthew and Luke are: *a.* Jesus' disciples accompany him to Nazareth; *b.* Jesus was amazed because of the people's unbelief; and *c.* because of this lack of faith in him he *could not* perform any miracle there; exception: he placed his hands on and healed a few sick people.

As to Matthew, except for the already indicated details, his account just about coincides with that of Mark.

Luke, in his far richer coverage—15 verses compared to 6 for Matthew and 5½ for Mark—, supplies the text and gist of Christ's sermon. In addition to telling us how it was received Luke gives us a much fuller account (than do

---

227 Robertson, *Word Pictures* I, p. 305; contrary: A B. Bruce, *op. cit.*, p. 377.

Matthew and Mark) of the manner in which Jesus answered his critics and of their resulting hostile reaction.

6:1. **He left that place and came to his hometown; and his disciples followed him.** Sometime—we do not know how long—after leaving Capernaum Jesus entered his "hometown," that is, the place where he had been brought up. Basically the word used in the original and here translated "hometown" means "fatherland," but here the definition "the place where he had been brought up" is clearly correct, as Luke 4:16 proves. See also Mark 6:4; Matt. 13:54, 57; Luke 4:23, 24; John 4:44. Cf. Heb. 11:14.

Even though Jesus was born in Bethlehem (Matt. 2:5, 6; Luke 2:4, 15; John 1:45; 7:42; cf. Mic. 5:2), and during a large part of his public ministry had his headquarters in Capernaum (Matt. 4:13), he was and remained "Jesus of Nazareth" (Matt. 2:23; 21:11; 26:71; Mark 1:24; 10:47; 14:67; 16:6; Luke 18:37, etc.).

It may be of some importance to note that The Twelve are with their Master again; contrast 5:37. There are those who interpret this to mean that the visit to Nazareth was not of a private nature. They could be right.

However that may be, Mark continues: 2. **And when the sabbath came he began to teach in the synagogue. Many listeners were astonished and said, Where did this man get these things, and what sort of wisdom is it that has been given to him, so that even miracles are done by his hands?** See what has been said about the synagogue in connection with 1:39, the special section on this subject. See also on 1:21 ff.; and on 3:1. From Luke 4:17 f. we learn that by the synagogue's "attendant" the scroll of Isaiah had been handed to Jesus. As his text he selected Isa. 61:1, 2a; or else this portion of Isaiah was the "haphtarah" (lesson from the Prophets) for that particular sabbath. As Luke relates, Isaiah predicts that in the age to come the Spirit would rest upon God's Anointed One, who would proclaim good tidings to the poor, release to the captives, recovery of sight to the blind, liberty to the oppressed, "the acceptable year of the Lord."

At this point, so that evangelist continues, Jesus rolled up the scroll, gave it back to the attendant, and while all eyes were fixed on him, said, "Today, in y o u r very hearing, this passage of Scripture has been fulfilled." He was affirming that by means of himself and his ministry Isaiah's bright promise was being realized.

As Mark agrees, the first reaction on the part of the audience was favorable. Jesus had spoken with such inner conviction, freshness, authority, and graciousness that his old acquaintances were struck with astonishment.

However, this favorable reaction did not last. Enthusiasm began to be replaced by adverse criticism. Surely, the words were wonderful, but coming from him . . . from *him?* How was that possible? Where did this man . . . one might even translate *"this fellow"* . . . get *"these* things?" The man and the

221

things—the speaker and the things he spoke—seemed to them to be utterly incongruous, to clash. Surely an ordinary, unschooled individual, such as they "knew"(?) Jesus to be, had no business revealing "this kind of" [228] wisdom!

Then also, what about the miracles or "works of power" reportedly performed "by his hands," that is, through him as the agent? The people of Nazareth could not very well deny the facts. The distance between Nazareth and Capernaum was only about twenty miles, and this audience knew that in and around that city many *works of power*—for that is what the word here used for "miracles" means—had been performed by their townsman Jesus. See Mark 1:21-34, 40-45; 2:1-12; 3:1-6; 5:21-43. But what was the source of all this? Cf. Matt. 11:28. That the source of both the words and the works might be God did not seem to occur to them.

Besides, if in Capernaum he did all this—and they did not reject the reports—, then why does he not do something similar here in Nazareth? Let him start his performance! See Luke 4:23. Did he not owe this to *his own hometown?* The evangelist Mark places special stress on *a.* the source of Jesus' teaching, and *b.* the nature of the wisdom that even enables him to perform miracles.

The derogatory reaction continues in verse 3. **Isn't this the carpenter, the son of Mary, and brother of James and Joses and Jude and Simon? And aren't his sisters here with us?** Jesus, the carpenter! Writing sometime between A.D. 155 and 161, Justin Martyr, in his *Dialogue with Trypho* LXXXVIII, speaking about Jesus says, "He was in the habit of working as a carpenter when among men, making plows and yokes." The word for "carpenter," used in the original is *tektōn,* related to English "technician." The cognate verb means *to bear, give birth to, bring forth.* The tektōn, accordingly, is basically any skilled workman, anyone who "brings forth," "makes" or "creates" an object. One might say, any "craftsman" or "builder," whether the materials he uses consist of wood, stone, metal, or anything else. In the present case we shall assume that "worker in wood," "carpenter" (see the quotation from Justin Martyr) is correct. It is worthy of note that here in Mark, Jesus himself is called "the carpenter," whereas in Matt. 13:55 he is called "the son of the carpenter." This cannot rightfully be called a discrepancy, since he may well have been called both. In times ancient and even comparatively recent a son would often, as to chosen occupation, follow in the footsteps of his father.

What the detractors wanted to say was on this order: "What does a mere carpenter know about oratory and particularly about prophetic interpreta-

---

228 Greek τίς = ποῖος.

tion and fulfilment?" Is he not "the son of Mary?" Joseph is not even mentioned, probably because by this time he had died.

The brothers of Jesus are also mentioned. There was first of all James (cf. Matt. 13:55), a man who after his conversion was to become prominent in the early church, especially in Jerusalem (Acts 12:17; 15:13-29; 21:18; I Cor. 15:7; Gal. 1:19; 2:9, 12: James 1:1; Jude 1). About Joses, mentioned next (called Joseph in Matt. 13:55), not to be confused with the Joses of Mark 15:40, 47, nothing further is known. Then there was Jude (cf. Matt. 13:55; Jude 1); last of all Simon (cf. Matt. 13:55), as unknown to us as is Joses. These were the uterine brothers of Jesus; see above, on 3:31. As to the sisters, they are never mentioned by name. Presumably they were married and still living with their husbands in Nazareth.

"Familiarity brought contempt," that is, the very fact that the people of Nazareth were so well acquainted with Jesus' family, having known them for so long a time, caused them to look down upon him. Who did this carpenter think he was anyway? **And they took offense at him,** that is, they allowed themselves to become ensnared [229] into the sin of being repelled by him. **4. So Jesus said to them, A prophet is not without honor except in his hometown, among his relatives, and in his own family.** See N.T.C. on John 4:44, where substantially the same proverbial saying is found, with this exception that in that passage, according to its context, the word used in the original, namely *patris*, refers to the home*land* or "fatherland," i.e., Galilee, whereas here in Mark 6:4 (and its parallel Matt. 13:57) it refers to the home*town*, as is clear from its setting and from Luke 4:16.

Other translations, such as that a prophet is always honored except, etc., or never fails to be honored except, etc., or is without honor *only* in, etc., are not precise. Jesus did not say that a prophet is respected everywhere except in his hometown, among his relatives, and in his family. What he did say was to the effect that wherever it might be that a prophet would be honored, certainly not in his hometown, etc.

As to this reference to his family, it should be interpreted in the light of such other passages as John 7:5 and Acts 1:14. It will then be seen that in the case of Christ's brothers unbelief was by God's grace subsequently changed to faith.

Before leaving this passage it should be pointed out that Jesus here definitely implies that he is indeed a prophet, with the right to be honored as such (cf. Deut. 18:15, 18; Matt. 21:11; Luke 24:19; John 9:17; Acts 3:22; 7:37).

The result of the rejection at Nazareth was: **5. And he was unable to do**

---

[229] For the word here used in the original see on 4:17, footnote 147.

any miracle there, except that he laid his hands on a few sick people. Because the people of Nazareth rejected Jesus—and were in that respect even worse than the Gerasenes (5:17), for the Nazarenes had received more light, greater privileges—they did not flock to him to be healed or to bring their sick. So these many grossly rebellious unbelievers were not healed. For them Jesus did not perform any miracle. He did, however, lay his hands on a few sick people. For the expression "sick people" see on verse 13. These presumably came up to him, or with their consent were brought to him. It is implied that these few were healed.

Now even these few may have been moved by considerations below the level of genuine faith, sometimes called "saving faith," perhaps better described as "faith which, by the grace of God, leads to salvation," the *genuine* faith to which reference is made in John 3:16; Rom. 5:1; Eph. 2:8, etc. On the basis of Scripture, theologians speak of historical faith, temporal faith, miraculous faith, as well as of genuine faith that leads to salvation. [230] In the present case it may well have been merely faith in Jesus as a miracle worker, hence miraculous faith, that caused the few to come to Jesus to be healed. Even then Jesus was not in the habit of refusing to heal. See Luke 17:17b. On the other hand, *if* these few were *true* believers—a possibility that must not be entirely ruled out—, then the situation in Nazareth would remind one of that which at a later time existed in the church of Sardis. See Rev. 3:4. Cf. Isa. 1:9; Jer. 31:7; Joel 2:32; Luke 12:32; Rom. 9:27; 11:5. The "remnant" doctrine runs as a golden thread through Scripture. But whatever the situation may have been with respect to these few, the Nazareth audience as a whole turned its back upon Jesus. By and large the sick remained unhealed, the sinners unpardoned.

However, the form of expression in Mark differs somewhat from that in Matthew. Matt. 13:58 reads, "And because of their unbelief he *did not do* many miracles there." Mark has, "He *was unable to do* any miracle there." Probable solution: he could not perform these miracles because, under these circumstances of unbelief and opposition, he did not want to do them. Instead of asserting his almighty power to suppress the people's rebellious stand, he respected their own responsibility for their attitudes and actions. Cf. Matt. 24:37. See also Luke 22:22; Acts 2:23.

In the soul of Jesus the hostile attitude of the people, an attitude that led to hostile action (Luke 4:28, 29) and was rooted in lack of faith, gave rise to the condition described in verse 6a. **And he was amazed** [231] **because of their unbelief**. Although in the original the verb *to be amazed* or *to marvel* occurs

---

230 See L. Berkhof, *Systematic Theology*, Grand Rapids, 1949, p. 501 ff.
231 Or: "was marvelling," imperfect tense. For the verb see on 5:20, footnote 199.

thirty times in the four Gospels, in only three instances—Matt. 8:10 (cf. Luke 7:9); Mark 6:6—, representing two separate events, is it used with reference to Jesus. In the one instance he is amazed or astonished at the remarkable faith of a centurion of Gentile origin. In that man's case faith could hardly have been expected, for he was far less privileged than were the Jews. Here in Nazareth, on the contrary, Jesus is amazed about the people's lack of faith. Here faith could have been expected, for Nazareth was a town in Galilee, the very Galilee which had become so highly privileged because of the ministry of Jesus.

But rather than dwell in detail on the psychology of Jesus' human soul, a subject that is too difficult for the human mind to grasp, the attention should be centered on the fact that the passage under study clearly reveals man's responsibility for his attitudes and actions, a responsibility that is his *according to the light he has received* (Matt. 11:20-24; Luke 12:47, 48; Rom. 2:12).

And he was going around among the villages, teaching. 7 He called to himself the twelve, began to send them out two by two, and was giving them authority over the unclean spirits. 8 He instructed them to take nothing for the road [232] except a staff, no bread, no traveler's bag, no money in their belt; 9 but to wear sandals, and not to put on two tunics. 10 And he said to them, "Wherever y o u enter a house, remain there until y o u leave [that town]. 11 And if any place will not welcome y o u or listen to y o u, when y o u leave shake the dust from the soles of y o u r feet, as a testimony to them.

12 So they went out and preached that men should be converted; 13 and they were casting out many demons and were anointing with oil many sick people and healing them.

6:6b-13 *The Charge to The Twelve*
Cf. Matt. 10:1, 5, 9-14; Luke 9:1-6

6b, 7. And he was going around among the villages, teaching. He called to himself the twelve, began to send them out two by two, and was giving them authority over the unclean spirits. Jesus appointed The Twelve after finishing a teaching tour among the Galilean villages. Teaching tour and appointment of these twelve men are combined also in Matt. 9:35—10:4. The appointment as such probably occurred just previous to the preaching of the Sermon on the Mount. See Luke 6:12, 13, 17, 20. And *now* (perhaps somewhat later during the same summer, namely of the year A.D. 28?) the Master sends out these men on a mission assignment.

Note, "He began to send them out." One interpretation of this *began* is that this assignment is of a preliminary nature, the mission to Israel, to be

---

232 Or: for the journey.

followed by the charge to preach the gospel to the whole world. Matt. 10:5, 6, contrasted with 18:19 (cf. Mark 16:16; Luke 24:47) might lend some support to this view. [233]

However that may be, one fact is clear: these men were to be Christ's official ambassadors or "apostles," men clothed with authority to represent their Sender. That exactly twelve men, no more and no less, receive this assignment must mean that the Lord designated them to be the nucleus of the new Israel, for the Israel of the old dispensation had been represented by the twelve patriarchs. Cf. Rev. 21:12, 14.

Mark—he alone—relates that the men were sent out "two by two." [234] This two by two arrangement may well be what Matthew has in mind in 10:2-4. See N.T.C. on that passage. When the question is asked, "Why two by two?" practical considerations such as *a.* to help and encourage each other (cf. Eccles. 4:9) and *b.* to be valid witnesses (Num. 35:30; Deut. 19:15; Matt. 18:16; John 8:17; II Cor. 13:1; I Tim. 5:19; Heb. 10:28) occur to the mind immediately. At a later time we notice that Peter and John bring their united testimony (Acts 3:1, 4:1, 13, 19); that Barnabas and Saul are sent out together on their missionary journey (Acts 13:1-3); and that afterward Paul and Silas are together "commended by the brothers to the grace of God" (15:40). And let us not forget Barnabas and Mark! (15:39).

To The Twelve was given authority over the unclean spirits; that is, Jesus imparted to them the right and the power to expel these demons from the hearts and lives of men. Cf. verse 13a; Matt. 10:1. For more on demon possession and expulsion see above, on 1:23; also N.T.C. on Matthew, pp. 436, 437.

Although in the summarized charge recorded in Mark 6:7 nothing is said about preaching nor about healing the sick, these two functions must have been included in the charge. The order to preach is implied in verse 11 ("or listen to y o u") and verse 30 ("and reported to him all that they had done *and taught*"); the mandate to heal the sick is implied in verse 13b. Just why these two other matters—preaching and healing—are not specifically mentioned in the charge we simply do not know. Some answer this question by affirming that the greater gift (authority to expel demons) implies the lesser

---

[233] We cannot be sure of this, however. This could be an instance of the pleonastic use of ἄρχω. See L.N.T. (A. and G.), p. 113. Also Vincent Taylor, *op. cit.*, p. 48, and above, on 1:45.

[234] Though the construction δύο δύο has been considered a Hebraism, not only does it also occur in Aeschylus and Sophocles, but the modern *Greek New Testament*, London, 1943, has retained it. This repetition of the cardinal number may therefore be considered an illustration of a coincidence between the vernacular phraseology of different languages. On this point see A. Deissmann, *Light from the Ancient East*, English translation New York, 1927, pp. 122, 123.

(preaching and healing the sick), an answer that impresses me as being, for more than one reason, less than satisfactory. See on verses 12, 13. For the phrase "unclean spirits" see on 5:2.

8, 9. He instructed them to take nothing for the road except a staff, no bread, no traveler's bag, no money in their belt; but to wear sandals, and not to put on two tunics. [235] Only that which is absolutely necessary must be taken along on the trip. Why? Because God will provide. The disciples, and now also apostles, must place their trust entirely in him. No doubt that is the basic answer. See Matt. 6:19-34; Mark 8:19-21; Luke 22:35. To this may be added Matt. 10:10b, "The worker is entitled to his support," meaning: upon those who *hear* the gospel rests the obligation to provide for those who *bring* it. This also is in line with the teaching of the Old Testament and the New: Deut. 25:4; I Cor. 9:7, 14; and see N.T.C. on I Thess. 2:9 and on I Tim. 5:18.

The list of things to be taken along, or (mostly) *not* to be taken along, consists of the following items, in the order as mentioned here in verses 8 and 9:

Staff. [236] In non-biblical Greek it refers at times to a *magic wand.* Other meanings are: *fishing rod, rodlike streak of light* from the sun, etc. In Ps. 23:4 (LXX 22:4) the word refers to *the shepherd's rod.* Cf. Mic. 7:14. In the New Testament the rod is at times an *instrument of punishment* (I Cor. 4:21), a meaning which easily connects with "the rod of iron" of Rev. 2:27; 12:5; 19:15. Then there is also *the ruler's scepter* (Heb. 1:8); *the rod that gives support* so that one can lean on it (Heb. 11:21); and *Aaron's rod* that budded (Heb. 9:4). But here in Mark 6:8 and its parallels it is *the traveler's staff* that is meant.

Bread. Here and in Luke 9:3 the word is used generically.

Traveler's bag. This was a kind of knapsack, a bag "for the road" or "for traveling." It is a bag that, before leaving, a person would fill with supplies which he thinks he might need while traveling. Because of the context, which seems to form a kind of climax: "Do not take along any bread, nor even a bag to carry it in, in fact not even money to purchase it," the idea

---

235 As to the grammatical construction of verses 8, 9, note that the non-final ἵνα of verse 8 ("He instructed them *that* they should take nothing"; hence, "He instructed them to take nothing") is in verse 9 (according to the best text) changed to the accusative construction, with πορεύεσθαι implied: ἀλλὰ (πορεύεσθαι) ὑποδεδεμένους σανδάλια = "but (to travel) shod with sandals," which can be simplified to "but to wear sandals." See Gram. N.T., p. 441. This feature should not be considered strange, since heterogeneous grammatical construction of this and similar character can be found in many languages other than the Greek of the New Testament. Daily conversation supplies many examples.

236 The six words used in the original are: ῥάβδος, ἄρτος, πήρα, χαλκός, σανδάλιον, χιτών.

that the reference is to "a beggar's collecting bag" (A. Deissmann, *op. cit.*, p. 109) lacks probability. Besides, as Matt. 10:10b clearly indicates, Jesus does not look upon the apostles as being beggars!

Money. The word used in the original has the basic meaning *copper, brass, bronze.* In the second place it may refer to anything made from any of these metals. See I Cor. 13:1. Accordingly it may also refer to *coins, small change;* thus probably here in Mark 6:8; cf. 12:41. Note the expression "no money in their belt." By winding or wrapping a belt, of whatever material, around the body a few times its folds would serve admirably as "pockets" for money or other valuables. Even today those who go abroad will often carry money or traveler's checks, etc., in a belt for security reasons.

Sandal; here plural *sandals.* In Matt. 10:10 a synonym, with little if any difference in meaning, is used. See also Matt. 3:11; Mark 1:7; Luke 3:16; 10:4; 15:22; 22:35; Acts 13:25. Sandals consisted of flat soles, made sometimes of wood, often of leather, or even of matted grass. By means of straps the sandal was kept from falling off the foot.

Tunic; here plural *two tunics.* This was an undershirt worn next to the skin. It reached almost to the feet and was equipped with arm-holes (Cf. Matt. 5:40; 10:10, Luke 3:11, 6:29; 9:3). In Mark 14:63 the plural refers to *clothes* in general.

So far we experience no great difficulty. But, as the following summary indicates, there seems to be a discrepancy or conflict with respect to two items: the staff and the sandals.

Must the following be taken along on the journey?

Item	Matt. 10:9, 10	Mark 6:8, 9	Luke 9:3
staff	No	Yes	No
bread		No	No
traveler's bag	No	No	No
money	No	No	No
sandals	No	Yes	
two tunics	No	No	No

It would seem then as if according to Mark, Jesus wanted the disciples to take along a staff; according to Matthew and Luke he told them not to take it along. According to Mark, the Master wanted them to wear sandals, but according to Matthew (cf. Luke 10:4 in the Mission of the Seventy or Seventy-two), he prohibited this.

No universally satisfying solution has been offered.

Those writers who frequently refer to variant and at times conflicting sources from which, as they see it, the Gospel writers have derived their material, accept discrepancies or contradictions. [237]

Others—and there are several—conveniently skip the entire problem.

Calvin's solution in connection with the staff is that Matthew and Luke refer to a "rod" that could become burdensome; hence, must be left home; while Mark, though using the same word, is thinking of a "walking stick" to support and relieve the traveler. The reformer does not show, however, why in two parallel accounts the identical word would have these two different meanings.

The solution as this interpreter sees it, is probably found in Matt. 10:9, 10: "Don't supply yourselves with gold or silver or copper (money) to put into y o u r belts, nor with a traveler's bag, two tunics or sandals or a staff." What Matthew probably means is, "Do not take along an *extra* pair of sandals." This seems all the more probable in view of the fact that in his Gospel the reference to sandals follows immediately upon the injunction against taking along *two* tunics. Therefore the warning against taking along *extras* probably carries over to the next item *sandals,* and to the next *a staff.* If this is correct, what Jesus is saying also here in Mark is: an *extra* tunic, *extra* pair of sandals, and an *extra* staff must not be taken along. [238] The staff y o u have in y o u r hand must be the only staff y o u take along; the sandals y o u wear must be the only ones y o u have with y o u.

10. **And he said to them, Wherever y o u enter a house, remain there until y o u leave [that town].** How the disciples must decide in which home

---

[237] Thus, for example, M. H. Bolkesteyn, Vincent Taylor, F. C. Grant, H. A. W. Meyer (emphatically), in their respective comments on Mark 6:8, 9. See Bibliography for titles of books.

[238] Along this line also S. Greijdanus, *Het Heilig Evangelie naar de Beschrijving van Lucas (Kommentaar op het Nieuwe Testament)*, Amsterdam, 1940, p. 403; Lenski, *op. cit.*, p. 152.

Those who scoff at this attempt at a solution, and constantly refer to conflicting source-material—some of these "sources" await discovery!—, as if this were a cure-all for the solution of New Testament problems, fail to realize that they are confronted with difficulties of their own. For example, if, as some maintain, Matthew has the original saying, and if, as they contend, this means that Jesus instructed the disciples to travel barefooted, but Mark, writing for westerners, allowed sandals, to suit his readers, then the following puzzles remain:

a. Shaking the dust off one's feet (Matt. 10:14; Mark 6:11; Luke 9:5, with slight variation in the wording) would have to mean one thing in Matthew and Luke, another in Mark.

b. Why, according to Matthew, as interpreted by them, Jesus would have sent the disciples on their way barefooted, adding to the difficulty of their task, is not explained.

c. Not explained either is how it was that the early church allowed the (supposed) discrepancy to remain.

d. Besides, in Scripture barefootedness is associated with totally different ideas (Exod. 3:5; II Sam. 15:30; Isa. 20:2; Ezek. 24:17).

to stay is answered in Matt. 10:11. It was the duty of the hearers to extend hospitality. All the more so when the travelers enrich the people with the pearl of great price. And the visitors themselves must show a co-operative spirit. They must not be so fastidious that whenever some small detail is not to their liking in one home, they immediately leave and enter another where the facilities seem to be more desirable and the food more palatable. The spread of the gospel has the priority over personal likes and dislikes. Hence the missionaries—not only traveling but probably also lodging two by two?— must remain in the home that was kind enough to extend hospitality to them. A very practical lesson!

11. **And if any place will not welcome y o u or listen to y o u, when y o u leave shake the dust from** [239] **the soles of y o u r feet,** [240] **as a testimony to them.**

After traveling through heathen territory Jews had the custom of shaking the dust off their sandals and clothes before re-entering the Holy Land. [241] They were afraid that otherwise in their own country levitically clean objects might be rendered unclean. What Jesus is here saying, therefore, is that *any* place whatever, be it a house, village, city, hamlet, that refuses to accept the gospel must be considered unclean, as if it were pagan soil. Therefore such a center of unbelief must be treated similarly. Paul and Barnabas did exactly that when a persecution was organized against them in the Jewish district of Antioch in Pisidia (Acts 13:50, 51). A colossal responsibility, a heavy load of guilt, rests on such a place. See Matt. 10:15.

In the wording of Christ's instruction there are a few variations. These suffice to show that even though the Gospel-writers in all probability used written as well as oral sources, they remained authors or composers, were never merely copyists. Thus in the original Matthew (10:14) and Luke (9:5) use one word for dust, Mark (6:11) another, [242] but in either case "dust" is the proper English translation. So also Matthew mentions "that house or that city," Mark "any place," Luke "that city," but there is no basic difference. Matthew in this connection says nothing about a *testimony*, but see 10:15. Mark has "(shake the dust from the soles of y o u r feet) as a testimony *to* them"; Luke: "as a testimony *against* them." But properly interpreted, the meaning is the same. In either case the symbolical action, in

---

[239] Literally Matthew and Mark speak of "shaking out," Luke, of "shaking off." The difference is minor.

[240] Literally: "from below y o u r feet."

[241] S.BK. I, p. 571.

[242] Respectively κονιορτός (from κόνις and ὄρνυμι; hence, that which is stirred up from the ground; e.g., by storming cavalry, cf. Luke 10:11; Acts 13:51; 22:23); and χοῦς the top soil that sticks to the soles; in Rev. 18:19 the dust which grief-stricken individuals throw on their heads.

obedience to the command of Christ, is a public declaration of the divine displeasure that rests on a place that has refused the gospel. The testimony addressed "to" them is therefore also a testimony "against" them . . . that they might repent. Cf. Rev. 16:9.

It is a revelation of God's marked disapproval, for the spreaders of the good tidings are *his* ambassadors. They are bringing *his* word. So, by rejecting them, these wicked people are rejecting God; or, if one prefers, Christ.

12, 13. So they went out and preached that men should be converted; and they were casting out many demons and were anointing with oil many sick people and healing them. Note the following:

a. They went out and *preached.* They *heralded.* Preaching, if it is true to the original meaning of the term, is the earnest proclamation of news initiated by God. It is not the abstract speculation on views excogitated by man. See also 1:4, 7, 14, 38, 45; and N.T.C. on II Tim. 4:2.

b. They preached "that men should be *converted.*" For the meaning of the important verb used in the original see on 1:15. Repentance, to be sure, is indicated, but the word has a far richer meaning.

c. For "they preached" the original uses one tense; for "they were casting out" and "were anointing" another. [243] This may well indicate that the main task of these disciples was preaching. But from time to time, in connection with the preaching and as a divinely approved and ordered (see verse 7) confirmation of the truthfulness of their message and the genuine character of their calling, these men performed miracles of healing. [244]

d. They were casting out *many* demons. One might say that they were very successful in this activity. That the disciples were not always successful in expelling these unclean spirits is clear from 9:18. Apart from power granted to them by God they were powerless. That also shows why prayer was of primary significance, a lesson which these men needed to learn. See on verse 7 for demon-possession and expulsion.

e. "They were anointing with oil. . . ."

In Biblical times oil of one kind or another (often olive oil) was used for many different purposes: as a cosmetic (Exod. 25:6; Ruth 3:3; Luke 7:46); as food, instead of butter (Num. 11:8; Deut. 7:13; Prov. 21:17); as an illuminent (Exod. 25:6; 27:20; Matt. 25:3, 4, 8); as a symbol of divine grace and power in consecrating a person for office (Lev. 2:1 ff.; Num. 4:9 ff.; Ps. 89:20); in connection with offerings (Ezek. 45:14, 24; 46:4-7, 11, 14, 15); and in connection with burial (Mark 14:3-8; John 12:3-8).

That oil was also used as a physical remedy appears from Luke 10:34: the

---

[243] Note the aor. ἐκήρυξαν, and cf. with the imperfects ἐξέβαλλον and ἤλειφον.
[244] Cf. H. B. Swete, *op. cit.*, p. 119.

231

good Samaritan poured oil and wine on the wounds of the man who had fallen into the hands of bandits.[245]   It is a fact that in the ancient world oil was used extensively as a remedy. Did not Galen, the great Greek doctor, say, "Oil is the best of all remedies for healing diseased bodies"?

The question, then, is, "As mentioned here in Mark 6:13, did the disciples use oil as a medicine?" The answer, as this interpreter sees it, is *probably not*. It was in all probability a symbol of the presence, grace, and power of the Holy Spirit.

That oil did at times serve as a symbol of the invigorating presence and power of the Spirit is very clear from Zech. 4:1-6. Matt. 25:2-4 also deserves consideration in this connection. In the light of Exod. 25:37 and Zech. 4:1-6 examine also Isa. 11:2; Rev. 1:4, 12. Now if that is true, then anointing the sick with oil meant, "Look to *God* for healing, not to us." It meant, "His Spirit is able to heal both body and soul."

Other commentators have shed valuable light on this use of oil, as follows:

"Oil is a biblical symbol of the Holy Spirit's presence, and thus the very anointing is an 'acted parable' of divine healing."[246]

"Oil must here be viewed as a visible sign of spiritual energies and grace imparted to them [the apostles]."[247]

"The healings were always miraculous and instantaneous—olive oil never works in that way."[248]

"Anointing was a frequent specific . . . in ordinary medical treatment, and this would suggest its use in the symbolism of supernatural healing."[249]

"Jesus en sy dissipels het siekes genees deur die aanraking en die krag van die Woord en nie deur die aanwending van olie nie" ("Jesus and his disciples healed the sick through the touch and the power of the Word, and not through the application of oil."[250]

The very fact that *a.* in the public mind *oil* was already connected with healing, and *b.* as has been shown, was a symbol of the presence and power of the Holy Spirit, made its use understandable, especially during the very early period of gospel proclamation. Hence, we find it mentioned here in what was probably the earliest Gospel, and in James 5:14 (for whatever reason) in what may well have been the earliest of the canonical epistles. As time went on, and spiritual knowledge increased, oil is no longer mentioned. It was apparently no longer deemed necessary for instruction. —The Roman

---

245 For James 5:14 see commentaries on that book.
246 R. A. Cole, *op. cit.*, p. 109
247 J. A. C. Van Leeuwen, *op. cit.*, p. 75.
248 R. C. H. Lenski, *op. cit.*, p. 155.
249 E. P. Gould, *The Gospel according to St. Mark* (*The International Critical Commentary*), New York 1970, p. 108.
250 E. P. Groenewald, *op. cit.*, p. 140.

Catholic sacrament of extreme unction is not even suggested here, for that rite is administered in the expectation of impending *death,* whereas the anointing mentioned here in Mark 6:13 occurs in a context of giving a person a new lease on *life.*

Many *sick* people were healed. The word used in the original is found also in Matt. 14:14; Mark 6:5; 16:18; and I Cor. 11:30. It looks at sick people from the aspect of their powerlessness. They are weak, feeble, but Jesus, through his Spirit, can make them strong.

---

14 Now King Herod heard (about this), for his [Jesus'] name had become well-known; and some people[251] were saying, "John the Baptist is risen from the dead; that's why these miraculous powers are at work in him." 15 But others were saying, "He is Elijah," and still others, "He is a prophet, like one of the prophets (of long ago)." 16 But when Herod heard (this) he said, "The man whom I beheaded, namely John, he is risen."

17 For, by order of Herod, John had been arrested, bound, and put in prison, on account of Herodias, his brother Philip's wife, because he [Herod Antipas] had married her. 18 For John kept telling Herod, "It isn't right for you to have your brother's wife." 19 So Herodias had it in for[252] him and wanted to kill him but could not; 20 for Herod was afraid of John, knowing him to be a righteous and holy man, and he kept him safe. And when he listened to him he was greatly perplexed;[253] still, he used to enjoy listening to him.

21 But an opportunity arrived when Herod on his birthday gave a dinner for his high civil officials and military commanders and the chief men of Galilee. 22 And when the daughter of Herodias herself came in and danced, she fascinated Herod and his dinner guests. So the king said to the girl, "Ask me for anything you wish, and I'll give it to you." 23 He promised her on oath, "Whatever you ask I'll give you, up to half of my kingdom." 24 And she went out and said to her mother, "What shall I ask for?" She answered, "The head of John the Baptist." 25 She rushed right back to the king and made this request, "I want you to give me right now on a platter the head of John the Baptist." 26 And although the king was deeply grieved, yet because of his oaths and his dinner guests he did not want to refuse her. 27 So at once the king ordered an executioner to bring his [John's] head. He went and beheaded John in the prison, 28 brought his head on a platter, and gave it to the girl; and the girl gave it to her mother. 29 Now when his [John's] disciples heard about it they came and took away his body and laid it in a tomb.

6:14-29 *Herod's Wicked Birthday Party*
and
John the Baptist's Gruesome Death
Cf. Matt. 14:1-12; Luke 9:7-9

14, 15. Now King Herod heard (about this), for his [Jesus'] name had become well-known; and some people were saying, John the Baptist is risen

---

251 There is considerable textual support for the reading "he [Herod] was saying."
252 Or: bore a grudge against.
253 According to another reading: he did many things.

from the dead; that's why these miraculous powers are at work in him. But others were saying, He is Elijah, and still others, He is a prophet, like one of the prophets (of long ago).

Without any temporal reference this story is introduced; that is, we are not informed as to just how long after the events previously related news concerning the miraculous powers at work in Jesus reached Herod. Nevertheless, we can infer from the words "John the Baptist is risen from the dead" that we have now reached a time that extends beyond John's execution, which, in turn, probably occurred months after the beginning of his imprisonment. It is not improbable that the murder of Christ's herald took place in or near the beginning of the year A.D. 29. [254]

The "Herod" to which reference is made here, and everywhere in the Gospels except in Matt. 2:1-19 and Luke 1:5, where his father "Herod the Great" (or "Herod I") is meant, had at the latter's death been appointed *tetrarch* over Galilee and Perea. He continued in that position from A.D. 4 to 39. He was a son of Herod the Great by Malthace the Samaritan. Though in the Gospels (and in Acts 4:27; 13:1) he is simply called "Herod," elsewhere (see, for example, Josephus, *Jewish War* I. 562) his name is frequently given as "Antipas." He may therefore be called "Herod Antipas."

Mark writes, "Now King Herod heard. . . ." The title "King" is here used in a loose, very general or popular sense, for technically this man was not a king and was never going to become one. See on verse 28.

What was it that Herod heard? We are tempted to answer: "He heard about Christ's charge to The Twelve and the manner in which they carried it out, for that was the theme of the immediately preceding section." Nevertheless, as the context indicates, the reference is broader and centers in Jesus himself, as is clear from the fact that Mark continues "for his [Jesus'] name had become well-known."

It is not strange that when at Christ's word even hopelessly sick people were suddenly and completely healed, even lepers cleansed, storms hushed, demons expelled, and a dead child brought back to life, as the preceding sections of Mark's Gospel have indicated, the name and fame of the One who accomplished all this had become well-known. What *is* somewhat strange is that it took so long for the news to reach the ears of Herod. A possible explanation would be that the palace where he was now staying—probably Machaerus, on the eastern shore of the Dead Sea—was too far removed from Capernaum for the news to have reached him earlier.

---

[254] For a discussion of the tentative dates during which the various events of Christ's ministry occurred see N.T.C. on the Gospel according to John, Vol. I, pp. 36, 188, 189; also the author's *Bible Survey*, pp. 59-62.

The king heard about "the miraculous powers"[255] of Jesus. The reports that reached him were threefold:

a. Some people[256] were convinced that Jesus was John the Baptist restored to life. This may seem somewhat odd, since Scripture nowhere ascribes any miracles to the Baptist. But it is probable that by this group John was held in such high esteem that the ability to perform miracles was attributed to him.

b. Another group said, "He is Elijah." Had not Elijah's return, as Messiah's forerunner, been predicted by Malachi (4:5)? Cf. Isa. 40:3; and see above, on Mark 1:1-3.

c. The third group, not wishing to be very definite, was convinced nevertheless that Jesus was one of the great Old Testament prophets.

See also on 8:28.

The "king"—perhaps after some hesitation, to which Luke 9:7-9 may refer—accepted the first of these three opinions, as is clear from the words of verse 16. **But when Herod heard (this) he said, The man whom I beheaded, namely John, he is risen.** That was the answer of his morbid, feverish imagination, influenced by a guilty conscience. As Matthew shows, it was what he told his servants.

Mark realizes that this statement made by Herod—namely, "The man whom I beheaded . . . he is risen," requires explanation and amplification. He therefore at this point proceeds to tell the story of the Baptist's imprisonment and execution: **17, 18. For, by order of Herod, John had been arrested, bound, and put in prison, on account of Herodias, his brother Philip's wife, because he [Herod Antipas] had married her. For John kept telling Herod, It isn't right for you to have your brother's wife.**

Before entering into the details of this narrative a preliminary remark with reference to Mark's contribution may well be in order. We admire Luke's brevity and Matthew's reserve. In fact, Luke (9:7-9) presents what may have been a stage in the historical setting. Briefly he touches upon the ruler's admission ("John I beheaded"), mental confusion ("But who is this about whom I hear such things?"), and aspiration ("And he wanted to see Jesus"). Matthew (14:3-12) furnishes what may be called a rather complete summary—with emphasis, over against Luke, on the word *complete;* and over

---

[255] Here the pl. of δύναμις (cf. *dynamite*) has a slightly different meaning than the word has in verses 2 and 5. There the reference is to the miracle (or: miracles) itself (themselves); here in verse 14 the meaning is "miraculous powers" or "the power to perform miracles."

[256] Though the reading "He [Herod] was saying" has considerable support, the continuation "but others . . ." . . . "and still others . . ." favors the plural text (ἔλεγον instead of ἔλεγεν) for verse 14 as well as (twice) for verse 15.

against Mark, on the word *summary*—of the events leading up to the Baptist's death. For the more detailed story we must turn to Mark (6:17-29). Here alone is plainly stated what in Matthew is only implied, that Herod had married Herodias, his brother Philip's wife. Here alone the wrath of Herodias against the Baptist, who denounced this incestuous and adulterous relationship in courageous, unmistakable terms, is reported ("Herodias had it in for him and wanted to kill him"). In the entire New Testament is there even one other passage that portrays more vividly the storm raging in a ruler's conscience? See verses 19b, 20. And as to the denouement of the narrative, compare Mark's *five* direct quotations (in verses 22b-25) with Matthew's *one* (14:8). To be sure, each Gospel has a beauty of its own. All are fully inspired. It would be rash to praise one Gospel above another. Matthew's reserve is as consonant with that evangelist's aim as is Mark's love for vivid detail, reflecting undoubtedly the preaching of an eye-witness, effervescent Peter. But God be praised for having given to the church, in his wisdom, not only Matthew, Luke, and John, but also the man who as a story-teller is unsurpassed among the four, namely, John Mark!

"For, by orders of Herod, John had been arrested. . . ." One might also say, "For, Herod had ordered—or caused—John to be arrested,[257] bound, and put in prison."

All this happened "on account of Herodias." Who was this Herodias? She was the daughter of Aristobulus, who was a son of Herod the Great by Mariamne I. She had married her half-uncle (her father's half-brother) Herod Philip, son of Herod the Great by Mariamne II. To this Herod Philip she bore a daughter, who in 6:22 is referred to simply as "the daughter of Herodias," but who by Josephus is called Salome (*Antiquities* XVIII.136).

Now Herod Antipas, on a visit to Herod Philip, became infatuated with Herodias. The two illicit lovers agreed to separate from their present marriage partners—Herodias from Herod Philip; Herod Antipas from the daughter of Aretas, king of the Nabatean Arabs—and to marry each other. This was done. When John the Baptist heard about this he rebuked Herod Antipas. He kept telling Herod, "It isn't right for you to have your brother's wife." There

---

[257] It is not necessary, with most translations, to retain the word "sent"; for example, "For Herod having sent arrested John. . . ." Or: "For this very Herod having sent forth and arrested John. . . ."

First, αὐτός here may probably be considered pleonastic, merely resumptive (see verse 16), used in Greek where we frequently would not use it. And as to "sent," in the original, verbs of *sending*, when used in connection with other verbs, often indicate that by direction of one person an act is performed by another. Cf. Matt. 2:16, "Herod, having sent killed the boy-babies" = "Herod had the boy-babies killed." Matt. 14:10, "Having sent he beheaded John" = "He had John beheaded." See also L.N.T. (A. and G.), p. 98.

was good reason for the rebuke, for such a marriage was incestuous (Lev. 18:16; 20:21). Was it not also adulterous (Rom. 7:2, 3)?

Of course, Herodias knew very well that whenever John rebuked the tetrarch he was also, by implication, denouncing her. So to satisfy her, Herod had John arrested, bound, and put in prison.

But Herodias was not satisfied with John's *imprisonment*. She craved nothing less than John's *assassination*. Even in his imprisonment the Baptist could be—and was probably—summoned to appear before her "husband" again and again. She probably feared that Herod might come under John's spell, and who knows what might happen if those words, "It isn't right for you to have your brother's wife" continued to be dinned into the adulterer's ear!

Her yearning to get her spouse to do away with John did not meet with immediate success however: **19, 20. So Herodias had it in for** [258] **him and wanted to kill him but could not; for Herod was afraid of John, knowing him to be a righteous and holy man, and he kept him safe. And when he listened to him he was greatly perplexed;** [259] **still he used to enjoy listening to him.**

Various elements enter into the mental state of Herod, as here described:

a. *Desire* to keep peace with Herodias. It was for her sake that he had put John in chains and had shut him up in a terrible, deep, and hot dungeon that formed part of the castle-palace at Machaerus.

b. *Awe* in the presence of John. Herod knew that John was not just "innocent" of any crime but an outstandingly excellent person, being "righteous," that is, an object of God's approval, and "holy," that is, a man of upright conduct, separated and consecrated to God and his service.

c. *Gladness* whenever he listened to John. One might say, "The ruler admired his accuser." Was this admiration due, perhaps, to the very fact that, in sharp contrast with the flatterers usually found in the company of rulers, here was one man who dared to speak his real mind? Was it John's manly eloquence that caused the tetrarch to hear him gladly? Was that why he kept John safe, [260] so that Herodias could not harm him?

d. *Sense of guilt.* Herod knew very well that he had sinned by putting

---

258 The Greek idiom ἐνεῖχεν αὐτῷ resembles the English "had it in for him."

259 Though both πολλὰ ἐποίει ("he did many things") and πολλὰ ἠπόρει ("he was greatly perplexed") have wide textual support, I favor ἠπόρει, which is more closely in line with the context. The king was clearly in a quandary: his conscience pulling him one way; his wife the other way. The psychology of the situation would therefore favor ἠπόρει over ἐποίει. See Vincent Taylor, *op. cit.*, pp. 313, 314.

260 Note the word συνετήρει. It is the perfective of τηρέω, *to keep*. The compound form can mean *to preserve*, as in Matt. 9:17: "both are preserved." In Luke 2:19 the meaning is *"to treasure up"* in the memory (literally "in her heart").

away his own wife, by stealing his brother's wife and marrying her, by keeping her as his wife, and by causing the accuser, John the Baptist, to be arrested, bound, and imprisoned. To summarize, the man knew that he was repressing the voice of his conscience. The result of all this:

e. *Perplexity*. He was "greatly perplexed," "terribly disturbed." In his very interesting and instructive book, *Souls in the Making*, New York, 1930, p. 114, the author, John G. Mackenzie, states, "The worst forms of functional mental disorder arise from a repressed conscience."

David, also perplexed and having similarly committed gross sins including adultery, not only relates his experience while in this state of horrible guilt feelings, but also shows the true solution:

> While I kept guilty silence
> My strength was spent with grief,
> Thy hand was heavy on me,
> My soul found no relief;
> But when I owned my trespass,
> My sin hid not from thee,
> When I confessed transgression,
> Then thou forgavest me.
> > From Psalm 32, Stanza 2, No. 55 in the
> > *Psalter Hymnal* (Centennial Edition)
> > of the Christian Reformed Church,
> > Grand Rapids, 1959.

But Herod Antipas refused to follow David's example of humble confession. Instead he became hardened, with the result that he did not prosper (Prov. 28:13). The very fact that even after he, the murderer, heard about Jesus, he did not repent, shows how far he had wandered away from the path of righteousness and truth. In fact, he never chose to walk on that path. Dark forebodings clouded his mind when, with respect to the rumors concerning Jesus he exclaimed, "The man whom I beheaded, namely John, he is risen." When at last Herod's desire to see Jesus (Luke 9:9b) was fulfilled, he mocked the Silent Sufferer (23:8-12). For what happened to Herod afterward see on verse 28.

So far—that is, as pictured in verses 17-20—Herodias had failed to persuade Herod to destroy the Baptist. But at last what she must have considered her "lucky day" arrived: 21-23. **But an opportunity arrived when Herod on his birthday gave a dinner for his high civil officials and military commanders and the chief men of Galilee. And when the daughter of Herodias herself came in and danced, she fascinated Herod and his dinner guests. So the king said to the girl, Ask me for anything you wish, and I'll** give it to you. He promised her on oath, Whatever you ask I'll give you, up to half of my kingdom. [261]

Herod's birthday was "opportune" or "suitable" because it was exactly right for the purpose Herodias had in mind, namely, to settle her score with John the Baptist and to make sure that she would not be cast off. This was her "golden opportunity."

The "dinner" served on this day of celebration was, of course, of a festive nature; hence, one might call it a "banquet." According to Mark, three kinds of guests were invited: *a.* the "high civil officials," more literally *grandees* or *magnates; b.* the "chiliarchs," thus literally; according to the basic meaning each was a commander of a thousand men, but the more general sense of "military tribunes or commanders" must probably be accepted; and *c.* "the chief men of Galilee," probably those socially prominent friends of Herod who did not hold any civil or military position.

If what happened at this banquet was similar to what is described in Esther 1:10, 11, Salome entered and danced "when the king was merry with wine," therefore toward the end of the banquet.

We can well imagine the erotic and suggestive manner in which the probably half-naked girl danced. And her step-father was a typical Herod, as his very marriage—if it can be called that—with Herodias proves. The guests whom he had invited must have been men of the same class. It is not surprising that both "king" and guests were enchanted. They looked on with voluptuous delight.

The dance over, on impulse Herod tells the girl, "Ask for anything you wish, and I'll give it to you." When she hesitates, he quickly repeats his promise, this time under oath, "Whatever you ask I'll give you, up to half of my kingdom."

It is probably not advisable to interpret this "up to half of my kingdom"

---

261 Note the following:

a. The original has two gen. absolutes: the first temporal: γενομένης ἡμέρας εὐκαίρου, "an opportune day having arrived"; the second circumstantial: εἰσελθούσης τῆς θυγατρὸς αὐτῆς τῆς Ἡρωδιάδος καὶ ὀρχησαμένης, "the daughter of Herodias herself having come in and danced."

b. The plural τοῖς γενεσίοις αὐτοῦ means "on the day of his birthday festivities"; hence, "on his birthday." The idiomatic plural may be due to the many items on the program of such a day. Cf. N.T.C. on Matt. 22:2.

c. As to αὐτοῦ or αὐτῆς in verse 22, if without qualification one accepts the rule that of two readings, both of which have substantial support, the hardest one must be accepted, αὐτοῦ must be adopted. The girl, according to this, is the daughter of Herod Antipas. Her name is Herodias. But, as many commentaries have pointed out, this is contrary to the context. With most translators and commentators I therefore—contrary to Grk. N.T. (A-B-M-W)—adopt the αὐτῆς text.

too literally. It is true that the tetrarch was not really a king at all, hence had no kingdom which he could give away. But the phrase—cf. Esther 5:3; 7:2—must probably be understood proverbially. It was a kind of hyperbole, so that what Herod really meant was something like, "I'll give you whatever you ask, no matter how much it costs me."

24, 25. And she went out and said to her mother, What shall I ask for? She answered, The head of John the Baptist. She rushed right back to the king and made this request, I want you to give me right now on a platter the head of John the Baptist.

The plot unfolds as if Herodias herself had not only planned every detail but was even pulling all the wires. Her fondest hopes as to what just might happen if her daughter would dance were fully realized.

Of course, the girl's mother did not dine with men. But she quickly hears what had transpired. Salome's report to her mother ends with the question, "What shall I ask for?" [262] Bluntly her mother replies, "The head of John the Baptist."

Without a moment's hesitation the daughter with animated step returns to the generous, profligate promiser, and surpasses even her mother in unabashed and imaginative impudence. She blurts out, "I want you to give me right now [263] on a platter [264] the head of John the Baptist." She wants it *right here* (Matt. 14:8) and *right now* (Mark 6:25). That is the daughter's wish. It is also the mother's wish. Mother and daughter are a perfect match . . . in cruelty! Right here and now the murder must be committed, because there must be no chance for John to escape, no chance either for the "king" to escape from the snare in which he has entangled himself.

26-28. And although the king was deeply grieved, yet because of his oaths and his dinner guests he did not want to refuse her. So at once the king ordered an executioner to bring his [John's] head. He went and beheaded John in the prison, brought his head on a platter, and gave it to the girl; and the girl gave it to her mother.

---

[262] There are those—for example, Lenski, *op. cit.*, p. 162—who press the distinction between *a.* the "king's" encouraging command: aor. *active* imper. αἴτησον in verse 22; note also the aor. *active* subjunctive in verse 23: αἰτήσῃς; and *b.* the girl's question: aor. *middle* subjunctive τί αἰτήσωμαι in verse 24, which is then rendered, "What shall I ask *for myself?*" Though this distinction may be valid, this is by no means certain; see James 4:2, 3 where the same verb is used in both voices, but with little if any difference in meaning. ᾐτήσατο here and in 15:43 is third per. s. aor. middle indic. of this verb αἰτέω.

[263] ἐξαυτῆς = ἐξαυτῆς τ. ὥρας, in this selfsame hour (or: moment), that is, as quickly as possible.

[264] "on a platter" also in Matt. 14:8. The noun πίναξ can also be translated "plate" or "dish"; cf. "pine-board." In modern Greek πίναξ means a board or table. The rendering of Mark 6:25b found in the A.V.—"I will that thou give me by and by in a charger the head of John the Baptist"—was undoubtedly excellent in its day, but fails to convey any clear meaning today.

The king was "distressed," says Matthew (14:9); "sorely distressed" or "deeply grieved" says Mark. In answer to the question, "What were the reasons for his emotional pangs?" the following items deserve consideration:

a. He had always admired John, and felt uneasy about killing him. Conscience (see verse 20) told him that murdering John, who was not only innocent but righteous and holy, was terribly wrong. [265]

b. He was aware of the fact that the people in general held John to be a prophet. Therefore he must have asked himself, "What will the people think of me if I grant Salome's ardent wish?" See Matt. 14:5.

c. He must also have realized that his wife had tricked him into this difficult situation and that she, after all, was now getting her way.

It can be argued that the way out of his predicament would have been for him to say to Salome, "I promised to favor you with a *gift;* I did not promise to commit a *crime.*" Or else, "I promised *you,* not your mother, a gift." Best of all would have been the way of escape pointed out in Lev. 5:4-6.

But Herod's stubborn pride, his dread of losing face before his cronies, the dinner guests who had heard his promise backed up by oaths, kept him from saying. "How can I do this great wickedness, and sin against God" (Gen. 39:9). False pride won the victory over all other considerations, including even the voice of conscience. So he ordered one of his guards, an executioner, [266] to bring in John's head. Since the prison in which John was kept was in all probability part of the palace at Machaerus (so also Josephus, *Antiquities* XVIII.119), the executioner did not have far to go. He beheaded John and, as requested, on a plate delivered John's head to the girl, who handed it to her mother.

---

265 Calvin addresses himself to the problem of the apparent contradiction between Matt. 14:5, "And although he wanted to kill him, he was afraid of the people . . ." and Mark 6:19, 20, "So Herodias had it in for him and wanted to kill him but could not; for Herod was afraid of John, knowing him to be a righteous and holy man, and kept him safe."

He states the problem as follows: "The former passage says that Herod was desirous to commit this shocking murder, but was restrained by his fear of the people; while the latter charges Herodias alone with this cruelty." His solution: Although from the very start Herodias wanted John murdered, Herod was prevented by conscience—that is, by "his religious scruples"—"from practicing such atrocious cruelty against a prophet of God." Afterward, however, he "shook off this fear of God, as a result of the incessant urging by Herodias." But still later "he was withheld by a new restraint, because he dreaded on his own account a popular commotion." See J. Calvin, *Commentary on a Harmony of the Evangelists, Matthew, Mark, and Luke* (tr. of *Commentarius in Harmoniam Evangelicam, Opera Omnia*), Grand Rapids, 1949 ff., Vol. II, pp. 222, 223. From here on this commentary will be referred to as Calvin, *Harmony.*

266 The original uses a Latin loanword: "speculator," (cf. *speculor: to look out, spy*), basically a *spy* or *scout,* but sometimes— see Seneca, *On Benefits* III. 25—an *executioner.* As to ἀποστείλας (verse 27) see on verse 17, footnote 257.

As to the results of Herod's wicked deeds here recorded (rejecting his own wife, marrying Herodias, and murdering John), note the following:

a. *The increased displeasure of many of the Jews.*

b. *The wrath of Aretas,* the father of Herod's rejected wife.

Aretas bitterly resented what Herod had done to his daughter. He therefore waged war against him and "in the ensuing battle the entire army of Herod was destroyed" (Josephus, *Antiquities* XVIII. 114, 116, 119, for points a and b).

c. *Banishment.*

Herod Antipas later allowed himself to be persuaded by Herodias to go to Rome in order to be elevated to the rank of king, the same rank that had been granted to her brother Herod Agrippa I. However, when the latter informed Emperor Caligula about the aspirant's plotting against the very ruler whose special favor he was now seeking, the result for the conspirator was perpetual exile to Lyons in Gaul.

The story of John the Baptist is concluded as follows:

29. Now when his [John's] disciples heard about it they came and took away his body and laid it in a tomb. For John's disciples see on 2:18; also N.T.C. on Matt. 11:1-3, and on John 3:25, 26.

From Matt. 11:2 ff. we learn that these men had been allowed to visit their teacher in prison. It is not surprising, therefore, that they were also allowed to provide an honorable burial for his decapitated body.

What happened to the disciples of John? From John 1:35, 40 it is clear that previously some of Christ's earliest disciples had been disciples of John. Many other disciples of the Baptist must have followed their example. They, too, had become followers of Jesus, which was exactly what John, while still alive, wanted them to do (John 3:22-30). From Matt. 14:12 ("And they went and reported it to Jesus") the conclusion can be drawn that now also, in connection with John's death and burial, his disciples were on friendly terms with Jesus; in fact, believed in him. Though it is true that more than twenty years later, in Ephesus—hence, far away from Palestine—, there were certain followers of Jesus, including even Apollos, who "knew only the baptism of John" (Acts 18:24, 25; 19:1-5), and had not heard about the outpouring of the Holy Spirit, it is also a fact that when these men received further instruction they were immediately ready to receive Christian baptism.

There can be no doubt about the fact, therefore, that John was, as had been predicted concerning him, a true way-preparer for Christ (Matt. 11:11-13; 17:10-13; Mark 1:1-3, 7, 8; 9:11-13; John 1:29-34). Even Paul, in Acts 19:4, implies as much.

For John the Baptist and the Qumran movement see N.T.C. on Matthew, p. 506.

30 And the apostles gathered around Jesus and reported to him all that they had done and taught. 31 He said to them, "Come away by yourselves to a lonely place and rest a while." For they did not even have a chance to eat, so many people were coming and going. 32 So by themselves they went away in the boat [267] to a lonely place.

33 Now many saw them leaving and recognized them. They ran there on foot from all the towns and outwent them. [268]   34 And, having come out, he [Jesus] saw a great multitude, and his heart went out to them, [269] because they were like sheep without a shepherd; and he began to teach them many things.   35 And since the day was already drawing to a close, [270] his disciples came up to him and said, "This is a lonely place, and since the day is already drawing to a close,   36 send the people away that they may go to the farms and villages round about [271] and buy themselves something to eat."   37 But he answered, "*Y o u* give them to eat." They said to him, "Shall we go and buy bread for two hundred denarii, and give it to them to eat?"   38 Then he asked them, "How many bread-cakes do *y o u* have? Go and see." When they knew they said, "Five, and two fishes."   39 Then he ordered them all to sit down company by company upon the green grass.   40 They reclined group by group, in hundreds and in fifties.   41 He took the five bread-cakes and the two fishes, and looking up to heaven gave thanks and broke the bread-cakes and kept giving them to his disciples to set before the people, and he divided the two fishes among them all.   42 They all ate and were filled.   43 And they picked up twelve baskets full of broken pieces and of the fishes.   44 And there were five thousand men who ate the bread-cakes.

6:30-44 *The Feeding of the Five Thousand*
Cf. Matt. 14:13-21; Luke 9:10-17; John 6:1-14

All four evangelists report this event. The similarities and differences are summarized in the chart on pages 244-246.

1. *Setting indicated*

30. And the apostles gathered around Jesus and reported to him all that they had done and taught.

Having accomplished their mission tour (verses 7-13), The Twelve are gathered around Jesus. Here and probably also in 3:14 Mark calls these men "apostles." They must be regarded as men through whom Jesus Christ himself is accomplishing his work on earth. They are his official ambassadors, having been commissioned by him to carry out certain specific tasks: preaching, healing, and casting out demons. He who rejects them rejects Christ himself (Matt. 10:40; Luke 10:16; John 13:20). It is in their capacity as "apostles" that they have been at work on the tour that is now ended. Therefore the term "apostles," also in 3:14, is very appropriate.

---

267 Or: by boat.
268 Or: outstripped them, outran them; or: got ahead of them.
269 Or: and he had compassion on them.
270 Or: since it was already late in the day. So also in 35b.
271 Or: to the surrounding countryside and villages.

The Feeding of the Five Thousand

	Matthew 14:13-21	Mark 6:30-44	Luke 9:10-17	John 6:1-14
1. Setting indicated	Jesus hears the report of John's death.	Jesus hears the report of The Twelve, returned from their mission tour.	Similar to Mark	"After these things."
2. Rest needed	He withdraws [implied: with his disciples] to a lonely place.	He invites The Twelve to accompany him to a lonely place, for rest. They are seen, leaving by boat.	Jesus takes his disciples to Bethsaida.	Jesus [implied: with his disciples] goes to the other side of the Sea of Tiberias.
3. Rest curtailed	Crowds follow on foot from the towns.	Crowds rush around the "top" of the lake in order to be with Jesus.	Similar to Matthew	Jesus, already arrived, from a hill sees the crowd approaching. Passover is near.
4. Compassion shown	Jesus, already arrived, comes out of his seclusion, is moved with compassion, and heals the sick.	He, the tender Shepherd, having come out, takes pity on the people, the sheep, and teaches them.	Jesus welcomes the people, speaks to them about the kingdom of God, and heals their sick.	Not in John

5. Hunger anticipated	Day drawing to a close, the people need nourishment. The disciples want Jesus to dismiss the people, so that they may buy food.	Similar to Matthew	Similar to Matthew and Mark	Jesus engages in conversation with Philip and Andrew about feeding the people. The lad with five barley-cakes and two fishes.
6. Orders issued: **a. to the disciples:** **b. to the people**	Jesus to disciples: "*Y o u* give them to eat." They: "All we have here is five bread-cakes and two fishes." Jesus to disciples: "Bring them here to me." He then orders the people to sit down on the grass.	Similar to Matthew. Main additions: *a.* Question of the disciples, "Shall we buy bread-cakes for two hundred denarii?" *b.* Jesus orders the people to sit down "company by company." *c.* They recline, group by group, in hundreds and in fifties.	Similar to Matthew and Mark. Slight variations: *a.* Disciples to Jesus, "We have no more than five bread-cakes and two fishes, unless we are to go and buy food for all these people." Luke adds: For there were about five thousand men. *b.* Jesus to disciples, "Make them sit down in companies about fifty each."	Jesus said, "Make the people sit down." Now there was plenty grass in that place. So the men sat down, in number about five thousand.

continued:

The Feeding of the Five Thousand (continued)

	Matthew 14:13-21	Mark 6:30-44	Luke 9:10-17	John 6:1-14
7. Miracle performed	Jesus takes the five bread-cakes and the two fishes, gives thanks, breaks the bread-cakes, and gives them to the disciples, who distribute them among the people. All eat and are filled.	Similar to Matthew. Mark adds, "and he divided the two fishes among them all."	Similar to Matthew.	Similar to Matthew and Mark, except for the fact that the disciples are not mentioned as the distributers.
8. Leftovers collected	Twelve baskets of broken pieces are collected. There were five thousand men, not counting women and children.	Similar to Matthew. Exceptions: *a.* In addition to the pieces of bread, Mark also mentions the (pieces of) fish that were collected. *b.* He omits any mention of women and children.	Luke is brief: And they pick up what was left over, twelve baskets of broken pieces.	Jesus orders his disciples to pick up the broken pieces that were left, so that nothing be wasted. Result: twelve baskets full. People's reaction: *a.* "This is really the prophet who is to come into the world." *b.* They want to take Jesus by force to make him king. He retires to the hill.

The report which these men brought back to Jesus must have been exciting: "they reported to him everything, whatever they had done and whatever they had taught," thus literally.

Much had been happening during the last few months: John had been cruelly murdered. His decapitated body had been buried. Jesus had been informed about this. Herod had become greatly disturbed when he heard about Christ's miracles. All kinds of rumors had been doing the rounds as to the identity of Jesus. The "king" had accepted one of them as his own belief, causing him to say, "The man whom I beheaded, namely John, he is risen." The disciples-apostles had been sent on their mission tour and had now returned.

All of this had taken time. It is not strange, therefore, that the miracle of the feeding of the five thousand, described here in 6:30-44—especially in verses 35-44—took place when Passover, probably April of the year A.D. 29, was already approaching, as is clear from John 6:4. The Great Galilean Ministry, probably extending from about December of A.D. 27 to about April of A.D. 29, was drawing to its close.

2. *Rest needed*

31, 32. He said to them, Come away by yourselves to a lonely place and rest a while. For they did not even have a chance to eat, so many people were coming and going. So by themselves they went away in the boat to a lonely place.

Working without resting, being busy without ever taking a vacation, performing all the often arduous duties pertaining to ministerial or missionary activity and not making a retreat for relaxation, calm discussion, prayer and meditation, will never do. Even Jesus, because of his human nature and the great burden which he had taken upon himself, needed periods of withdrawal (1:35). And because he was also thoroughly acquainted with the needs of his disciples he invited them to come away with him to a lonely place, a secluded spot, where they would be able to "rest up." [272]

What made the need even more urgent was the fact that a boisterous and demanding crowd, with people constantly coming and going, was making even eating impossible. Result: "By themselves," that is, Jesus, The Twelve, *but no one else,* they take off for a quiet place in the vicinity of Bethsaida Julias. See Luke 9:10 and N.T.C. on John, Vol. I, pp. 216, 217. They cross over to the northeast side of the sea "in a boat." Was this the boat mentioned in 3:9; 4:1; 5:2? Or is this a case where the Greek article should

---

272 ἀναπαύσασθε sec. per. pl., aor. middle imperative of ἀναπαύω. Cf. somewhat similar meaning of this verb in Matt. 11:28; 26:45; Mark 14:41; Luke 12:19; I Cor. 16:18; II Cor. 7:13; and Philem. 7.

not be translated, so that "by boat," instead of "in the boat" would be the proper rendering? The parallel passage Matt. 14:13 would seem to favor the latter view. But either view is possible, and excellent translations can be quoted on either side.

3. *Rest curtailed*

33. Now many saw them leaving and recognized them. They ran there on foot from all the towns and outwent them. Many people from the Capernaum region not only saw the boat but also recognized the occupants. They draw the correct conclusion that Jesus was leaving them. That was not at all what they wanted. What to do in this situation? Follow him in other boats, those that are mentioned in 4:36; cf. John 6:23, 24? For some reason at this particular moment those other boats were not immediately available. So, rather than wait until they were available, these people, in their anxiety to be with Jesus, started to run around the northern shore of the lake. For them the entire distance averaged about ten miles. The straight distance by boat was in the neighborhood of four miles. Who first reached the landing place just southeast of the point where the Jordan River, coming from the north, flows into the Sea of Galilee? The little company (Jesus and The Twelve) or the crowd?

According to most translations the crowd was the first to arrive. With slight variations as to wording, verse 33b is rendered as follows: "They ran on foot from all the towns *and got there ahead of them* [i.e., ahead of Jesus and The Twelve]."

By no means all translators and commentators are satisfied with this translation. Facts deserving consideration are the following:

a. Though the reading on which most translators base their rendering [273] is probably correct, there is some degree of doubt.

b. Even when this reading is accepted, as it should probably be, Mark 6:33 would be the only New Testament passage in which the verb in question means "arrived first (or: earlier)." Other passages in which the same verb occurs but with variant meanings are Matt. 26:39; Mark 14:35; Luke 1:17; 22:47; Acts 12:10, 13; 20:5, 13; II Cor. 9:5.

c. With starting-point and landing area the same for both, and that which connects the two being a straight line of approximately four miles for the boat, but an arc of about ten miles for the pedestrians, the boat would ordinarily land first. This holds especially in the present case because of certain additional handicaps for those who traveled by foot: (1) they had to cross the Jordan and the difficult adjacent terrain; and (2) there were also women and children (Matt. 14:21). Of course, the boatsmen may have had

---

273 καὶ προῆλθον αὐτούς.

to cope with unfavorable weather conditions, but the text does not say this.

d. If Mark had intended to say that the crowd *arrived first,* would he not have used clearer language to express this thought? See, for example, John 20:4, "But that other disciple started to run ahead, faster than Peter, *and arrived . . . first."*

e. If the translation "and got there ahead of them" or "and arrived first" is adopted, it is hard to see how the conclusion can be avoided that Mark 6:33 contradicts Matt. 14:13, 14; Luke 9:11; and John 6:3, 5. Matthew, Luke, and John all picture Jesus as disembarking before the arrival of the great multitude. *They* follow. *He* gets there first, goes up the hill, is in seclusion with his disciples for a little while, and then sees a crowd gathering on the shore and goes out to meet them.

It is therefore not surprising that other translations have been suggested: "and (the pedestrians) outwent them" (A.R.V.), "got ahead of them" (Goodspeed). So rendered there is no problem. What Mark is saying must receive full justice. It is also very understandable. Because of their eagerness to be with Jesus, the people start to run toward their destination [274] so fast that for a while they are actually surpassing the boat in speed, may even have gotten ahead of the boat. But this does not necessarily mean that the crowd *got there ahead of* Jesus and The Twelve.

The fact that deserves special attention is this: the rest and relaxation which the Master and his disciples were seeking is to a large extent denied them. Not entirely, for Jesus and The Twelve seem to have been together for a little while, but this breathing-spell is considerably curtailed.

How does Jesus react to this interruption of his rest? The answer is found in:

4. *Compassion shown*

34. And having come out, he [Jesus] saw a great multitude, and his heart went out to them, because they were like sheep without a shepherd; and he began to teach them many things. Those who in verse 33 have adopted the rendering "and got there ahead of them" must be given credit for consistency when they now translate verse 34 thus, "And disembarking," or "And getting out of the boat." The participle used in the original [275] is derived from a verb which basically means "to go out" or "to come forth." It is used in a wide variety of contexts: going out of a house (Matt. 9:31 f.; cf. John 11:31), synagogue (12:14), king's presence (18:28), highpriests's palace (26:75), person (Mark 5:8), tomb (John 11:44), to mention only a few. In Mark 5:2 and 6:54 it is used in connection with *stepping out of a boat,*

---

274 ἐκεῖ = "thither," i.e., "there" in the sense of "to (or: toward) that place." The word modifies συνέδραμον; not προῆλθον, as in several translations.
275 ἐξελθών nom. sing. masc. aor. participle of ἐξέρχομαι.

disembarking. However, in those passages the boat is distinctly mentioned in the same clause. The present situation is different: neither in all of verse 34 nor even in the preceding verse is there mention of a boat. Reference to a boat is found, however, in verse 32. This may give some support to those who in verse 34 favor the rendering "And getting out of the boat."

A safer method to arrive at the right interpretation of "having come out" as here used would be to discover what *the same verb* means in the parallel passage, Matt. 14:14. There, as the immediate context shows, it means that Jesus *came forth* from his place of seclusion on the slope of a hill. [276] Another passage that sheds light is John 6:3-5, "Jesus went up into the hill and there he was sitting with his disciples. . . . So when he lifted up his eyes and observed that a vast crowd was coming toward him, he. . . ."

It is clear, therefore, that it was from this quiet retreat that Jesus *came forth* when he saw that the large multitude that had arrived on the shore was starting to move toward him. He came forth to do what? To scold these people? To say to them, "We came here for rest, relaxation, and refreshment; so please go home, for we are tired; see us some other time"? On the contrary, he went forth to welcome them, for *his heart went out to them.* See what is said about this expression in 1:41. [277]

In his mind he probes their sorrows. He understands them. On his heart he takes their burdens. He loves them. With his will he removes their affliction. He heals them. With him sympathy is not just a feeling. It is a tender feeling transformed into helpful action. It is, as far as possible, an identification. It is not just an emotion but a deed; better still; a whole series of deeds. He teaches them, heals them, feeds them.

He sees these people as sheep without a shepherd. To understand what this means one should first read I Kings 22:17; then Ps. 23; then Matt. 9:36; then John 10. See also N.T.C. on Matthew, pp. 439, 440; and on John, Vol. II, pp. 97-132.

No animal is as dependent as is a sheep. Without someone to guide it, it wanders, is lost, becomes food for wolves, etc. Without someone to graze it, it starves. Jesus knows that the people are like that: their leaders fail to give them reliable guidance. They do not supply their souls with nourishing food. The minds of the would-be guides are too occupied with legalistic niceties about sabbath restrictions, fasts, phylacteries, tassels, etc., to be concerned about souls.

So Jesus began to teach them many things. Words of life and beauty

---

276 So also F. J. A. Hort and B. F. Westcott, *The New Testament in the Original Greek*, Cambridge and London, 1882, p. 99; cf. Lenski, *op. cit.*, p. 166.

277 Here, in 6:34, the form is ἐσπλαγχνίσθη, third per. sing. aor. indic. pass. of σπλαγχνίζομαι. See also N.T.C. on Philippians, p. 58, footnote 39.

issued from his lips, as he told them about the marvelous kingdom of God (Luke 9:11), a kingdom in which childlike trust in God's sovereign care brings peace (Matt. 6:24-34), love is law (6:43-48), and truth is on the throne (John 14:6; 18:37).

5. *Hunger anticipated*

35, 36. And since the day was already drawing to a close, his disciples came up to him and said, This is a lonely place, and since the day is already drawing to a close, send the people away that they may go to the farms and villages round about and buy themselves something to eat.

Jesus not only healed the sick (Matt. 14:14) but also spent some time in teaching the people. All this activity must have taken a considerable amount of time. Almost at once after Jesus from the place where he was had stepped out toward the people, he had asked Philip, testing him, "How are we to buy bread-cakes that these people may eat?" Philip had answered, "Bread-cakes for two hundred denarii would not be sufficient for them so that each might get a little something." So Philip had struggled with this problem, Andrew also. All the time Jesus knew exactly what he was going to do (John 6:5-9). But the disciples were at a loss what to do, and this in spite of all the miracles they had already witnessed. And now, though the sun had not yet set, it was already late in the day; that is, the day was already drawing to a close. [278] By means of his miracles and teachings the Lord so captivated the vast crowds that even now they were not leaving. If they were to depart they must be sent away. So the disciples remind their Teacher of the loneliness of the place and the lateness of the hour.

"This is a lonely place," they say. In other words, this is not a city, containing all kinds of places within easy reach where food may be bought; it is a desolate region. To go to any of the surrounding villages in search of food will take time. Besides, "The day is already drawing to a close." Accordingly, they advise Jesus to send the people away right now in order that they may still try to go to the surrounding farms and villages to buy food for themselves.

6. *Orders issued*

Christ's answer was striking: **37a. But he answered, Y o u give them to eat.**

What did Jesus mean by saying, "Y o u give them to eat"? It may be impossible to give a fully satisfactory answer to this question. A few things can be pointed out however:

---

[278] Literally (gen. absolute) "much day-time already gone." The words are repeated in verse 35b.

a. Jesus means that these men must not be so quick to shake off responsibility. They were often ready to do this very thing, and to say, "Send the people away" (here in verse 36); "Send her [the Syrophoenician woman] away" (Matt. 15:23). They even "rebuked" those who brought little children to Jesus that he might touch them (Mark 10:13). See also Luke 9:49, 50. "Don't bother the Master and don't bother us," was too often their slogan. In the light of this evidence it is safe to say that Jesus wants to remind these men of the fact that simply trying to get rid of people in need is not the solution. It is certainly not God's way of doing things (Matt. 5:43-48; 11:25-30; Luke 6:27-38; John 3:16).

b. He wants them to ask, seek, and knock (Matt. 7:7, 8); in other words, to claim God's promise for themselves, and to go to him who is able to supply every need. He who, when there was a shortage, supplied wine (John 2:1-11), can he not also supply bread?

c. In view of the fact that "bread," as the term is used in this account (see verses 38, 41), while referring to be sure to that which supplies a physical need, is also symbolical of Jesus as the Bread of Life (John 6:35, 48), is he not also telling these "fishers of men" that they must be the means in God's hand to supply the *spiritual* needs of the people?

Continued: **37b. They said to him, Shall we go and buy bread for two hundred denarii, and give it to them to eat?** According to John 6:7 it was Philip, one of The Twelve, to whom this idea first occurred. However, having considered it and having even mentioned it to his fellow-disciples, he also immediately dismissed it from his mind as being impracticable. This is clear from the fact that he said to Jesus, "Bread-cakes for two hundred denarii would not be sufficient for them so that each might get a little something." As a group, however, the men do not wish to drop the idea altogether. So they ask Jesus, "Shall we go and buy bread for two hundred denarii . . . ?"

The silver *denarius* was, perhaps, the most used Roman coin in New Testament times. Literally the name *denarius* means *containing ten*. It was called thus in relation to the *as,* a bronze coin having the value of 1/10 denarius. However, when it is said, as is done in many commentaries, that the denarius is equal to 16 or 17 or even 20 American cents, and that the disciples, in mentioning two hundred denarii, were therefore thinking of a total amount of $32, $34, or $40, this is misleading. The value of the dollar and of the humble penny is constantly fluctuating. It is therefore better to point out, on the basis of Scripture (Matt. 20:2, 9, 13), that a denarius represented the wages paid to a laborer for one day's work; hence two hundred denarii means the amount of remuneration which one man receives for two hundred days work. The disciples then are asking[279] Jesus whether

---

279 Note ἀγωράσωμεν a deliberative aor. active subjunctive: "Shall we buy?" Also the subjunctive δώσωμεν would be more usual than a change to the indicative future

they should so late in the day go out and try to buy the huge quantity of bread that would be necessary for this vast multitude. Granted even that they would be able to obtain it and to lug it with them to feed all these hungry mouths, did they even have in their possession that large sum of money? But how else can they satisfy the Master's order. "*Y o u* give them to eat"?

Jesus does not at this moment chide them for their lack of faith, nor does he answer their specific question. **38. Then he asked them, How many bread-cakes do y o u have? Go and see. When they knew they said, Five, and two fishes.** The disciples' answer was one not of faith but of near-despair. This appears especially from the phrasing of the reply in Matthew's Gospel, "We do not have (anything) here except five bread-cakes [or: rolls] and two fishes." Clearly these men had not caught the meaning of the exhortation, "*Y o u* give them to eat."

John 6:8, 9 supplies further details: "One of the disciples, Andrew, the brother of Simon Peter, said to Jesus, 'There is a young lad here who has five barley-cakes and two fishes, but what are these for so many?' "

The Lord is going to strengthen their faith by means of an unforgettable miracle. In preparation for this he now addresses the multitude: **39, 40. Then he ordered them all to sit down company by company upon the green grass. They reclined group by group, in hundreds and in fifties.** Jesus ordered all the people to recline against the grass-covered hillside "company by company"; literally, "symposium symposium." [280] A "symposium," as the very word implies, was originally a "drinking together," or "drinking party." Cf. *potion*. The word developed into a secondary meaning: *party* of any kind. Often, but not necessarily, such a party was characterized by eating and drinking together, music, and song. We still have our "symposiums" at which speakers express their views on various aspects of a subject agreed on beforehand. The anthology of such views may itself also be called a "symposium." However, in Mark 6:39 the meaning is simply party, company; hence here "company by company."

The command was easy to obey, since about this time of the year the slopes of the hill must have been covered with grass. Mark states that the people reclined "group by group," or possibly even "garden-bed by garden-bed," *if* the basic meaning of the phrase used in the original [281] still shines through, which is by no means certain.

δώσομεν, although the external evidence is rather evenly divided, and there is a close affinity between the subjunctive and the future indicative. Note also δηναρίων διακο-σίων, genitive of price.

280 This kind of construction (distribution expressed by repetition), though not necessarily a Semitism, corresponds to Semitic usage. See also on verse 7 above: "two by two."

281 πρασιαὶ πρασιαί.

However that may be, there was this strikingly colorful arrangement of people dressed in their bright garments, reclining under the blue vault of heaven, upon the green grass, with the Sea of Galilee nearby.

Does "group by group in hundreds and in fifties"—or: "in groups of a hundred and of fifty"—mean *in a hundred rows of fifty each?* If so, this would be in harmony with verse 44—"And there were five thousand men"—in both cases (verses 40 and 44) "women and children" (Matt. 14:21) being left uncounted. Or is the meaning that some groups consisted of a hundred people, some of fifty? Either way the grouping was very practical. It made distribution of bread and fish, and also counting, easier.

7. *Miracle performed*

41, 42. He took the five bread-cakes and the two fishes, and looking up to heaven gave thanks and broke the bread-cakes and kept giving them to his disciples to set before the people, and he divided the two fishes among them all. Jesus took the five bread-cakes and the two fishes. He looked up to heaven. For this lifting heavenward of the eyes in prayer see also Ps. 25:15; 121:1; 123:1, 2; 141:8; 145:15; John 11:41; 17:1; I Tim. 2:8. [282]

Looking up to heaven Jesus "blessed," thus literally. The same verb is also found in the Synoptic parallels (Matt. 14:19; Luke 9:16). John, on the other hand, has "having given thanks" (6:11). Solution: "blessed" in this instance means "gave thanks," and can be thus translated. When a person blesses or praises God is he not giving thanks to him? [283] It was the custom of the Jews to thank God before starting a meal. However, since it is abundantly clear from the Gospels that our Lord never spoke as the scribes, that is, that his words were always characterized by freshness and originality (cf. Matt. 7:29), we may well believe that this was true also on the present occasion.

Then from the bread-cakes Jesus began to break off fragments of edible size. He kept giving [284] these to his disciples who carried them (in baskets collected here and there from the crowd?) to the people. With the fishes the procedure was somewhat similar. Mark says, "He . . . *divided* the two fishes among them all."

The striking beauty of the account is heightened by the fact that only a few simple words are used to relate the miracle of the multiplication of the fragments. One might even say that the miracle is implied rather than expressed. **They all ate and were filled.** Exactly when was the bread and the fish multiplied? "Under his hands"? Probably, but even this is not stated. All

---

282 The subject *Prayer Postures* is treated in some detail in N.T.C. on I and II Timothy and Titus, pp. 103, 104.

283 In the present tense, first per. sing. indic. the two verbs are εὐλογέω and εὐχαριστέω.

284 Imperfect tense ἐδίδου here and also in Luke 9:16. Contrast Matt. 14:19 "gave."

we really know is that there was plenty of bread and fish—in fact, plenty and to spare—for everybody. At some point of time between the breaking or dividing and the reception of the fragments by the people the miracle must have occurred. All ate and "were filled," that is, "had all they wanted," "were fully satisfied." [285]

8. *Leftovers collected*

43, 44. And they picked up twelve baskets full of broken pieces and of the fishes. And there were five thousand men who ate the bread-cakes. Pollution is irresponsible: what cannot be eaten must not be scattered about. Littering is sinful; wastefulness condemnable. What cannot be eaten must be collected. According to Mark this applies not only to bread but also to fish.

So great was the miracle that Mark's statement to the effect that the five rolls and two fishes were more than sufficient for five thousand men is putting it mildly, for he does not even mention "women and children" (Matt. 14:21); yet these also enjoyed the bounties which Jesus had so miraculously and abundantly provided.

Here as elsewhere Jesus reveals himself as the perfect Savior, the One who provides for both body and soul (cf. Mark 8:19-21; John 6:35, 48). He is the One foreshadowed in the Old Testament (I Kings 17:16; II Kings 4:43, 44; see also John 6:14; cf. Deut. 18:15-18; and John 6:32). The tragedy was that the masses had accepted an earthly, erroneous, materialistic view of the Deliverer, as is clear from John 6:15.

A detailed study of the crowds often surrounding Jesus and of his attitude toward them sheds light on the depth of his love and tender mercy. See Mark 6:34; 8:2; cf. Matt. 9:36; etc. But though it can be granted that the Lord experienced periods of "popularity," and that in the Gospels it is not the hostility of the *multitudes* but that of the *leaders* which is emphasized, nevertheless it must not be supposed that the relation between Jesus and his audiences was always smooth and friendly. At times people would ask him to depart (Mark 5:17) or were offended in him (6:3). At times they deserted him (John 6:66). Moved by selfish considerations (John 6:26), they generally misunderstood him and his true mission (John 6:15). At last they allowed themselves to be persuaded by their leaders to demand his death by crucifixion (Mark 15:11-14).

---

[285] ἐχορτάσθησαν third per. pl. aor. passive of χορτάζω. Though this verb was used at first with respect to the feeding and fattening of animals (of which meaning there is an echo in the clause: "all the birds gorged themselves with their flesh," Rev. 19:21), and was applied to men chiefly by the Comic poets, it gradually lost its deprecatory sense and is here used simply as a synonym for *to have plenty, to be (come) fully satisfied.* Cf. Matt. 14:20; 15:33, 37; Mark 7:27; 8:4, 8; Luke 6:21; 9:17; 15:16; 16:21; John 6:26; Phil. 4:12; James 2:16.

Over against all this stands the fact that Jesus never employed his miracle-working power to destroy or even to hurt the people but always to help them. He fed the hungry, healed the sick, had compassion on and taught the misled, and sought the lost. In fact, even when he felt constrained to pronounce Jerusalem's fall, he did so with a heavy heart (Matt. 23:37-39).

It should be no surprise, therefore, that for those who permit such spontaneous, deep, unselfish love to go unrequited punishment is in store. In speaking about Christ's deep and tender love this "other side," for which the Gospels supply abundant evidence—Mark 7:1-13; 8:15, 31; 9:19, 31; 10:33, 34; 11:12-18, 20, 21; 12:1-12; 13:2; cf. Matt. 7:24-27; 11:20-24; 21:12-16; 21:23—22:14; 23; 25:41-46; etc.—must not be overlooked. For those who turn their backs upon the love of the Shepherd there is "the wrath of the Lamb" (Rev. 6:16)!

---

45 Then immediately he made his disciples get into the boat and go ahead (of him) to the other side, to Bethsaida, while he was dismissing the crowd. 46 And after taking leave of them he departed into the hill to pray. 47 When evening fell, the boat was in the middle of the sea, and he alone on land. 48 And seeing them straining at the oars, for the wind was against them, about the fourth watch of the night he came to them, walking on the sea. He was about to pass them by. 49 Now when they saw him walking on the sea, they thought that he was a ghost, and they screamed; 50 for they all saw him and were terrified. But at once he spoke with them and said to them, "Take courage, it is I; do not be afraid." 51 Then he climbed into the boat to them; the wind fell, and they were greatly astonished, 52 for they had not grasped the significance of (the incident of) the bread-cakes. In fact, their hearts were hardened.

6:45-52 *Walking on the Water*
Cf. Matt. 14:22-33; John 6:15-21

When we compare Mark's account with that of Matthew (14:22-33), what at once strikes us is how much the two overlap. In both accounts Jesus orders his disciples to get into the boat and cross over to the other side. Alone he goes up into the hill to pray. On the sea the progress of the rowers is being curtailed by a ferocious head-wind. In the fourth watch of the night Jesus comes toward them. He is walking the waves. Failing to recognize him and taking him to be a ghost, the terrified men scream aloud. At once Jesus addresses them in the comforting words: "Take courage, it is I; do not be afraid." He climbs into the boat and the wind ceases. The disciples are filled with a feeling of astonishment (Mark) and worship (Matthew).

The story is not found in Luke but occurs also in John (6:15-21). Though that evangelist tells it in his own way, in all essential details the three accounts (Matthew, Mark, John) coincide. Nevertheless, each, without ever coming into conflict with the others, makes his own contribution.

Matthew most vividly pictures the storm. He is also the only one who narrates the story of Peter's venture upon the waters. He states that at the conclusion of the entire incident the disciples confessed Jesus to be "God's Son" (14:33).

John mentions the reason—or one of the reasons—why Jesus withdrew into the hill. That reason was the attempt by the people to take him by force and make him king (6:15). He states that the disciples were heading for Capernaum (6:17). Broadly interpreted this is not in conflict with Mark 6:45, 53. It is also John who tells us that it was after having proceeded "twenty-five or thirty stadia" that someone who later on revealed himself to be Jesus appeared to the rowers. When they knew who he was they were willing to receive him into the boat, which then immediately landed. How it must be explained that neither Mark nor John duplicate Matthew's story with reference to Peter (14:28-31) cannot be determined, though there have been many conjectures.

Mark makes his own contribution. It was to Bethsaida and Gennesaret that Jesus sent his disciples. The boat was "in the midst of the sea" when the storm struck. Jesus saw the disciples "straining at the oars," and "was about to walk by them." He spoke "with" them. The miracle left the disciples "greatly astonished." Reason: their hearts being hardened, they had not grasped the full significance of the miracle of the multiplication of the rolls.

1. *The disciples without Jesus*
45. Then immediately he made his disciples get into the boat and go ahead (of him) to the other side, to Bethsaida, while he was dismissing the crowd.

Jesus dismissed the crowd. While [286] he is doing this he orders his disciples by boat to go ahead of him to the western side of the sea.

Why did Jesus dismiss the crowd? The answer may be as follows—at least the following items deserve careful consideration—:

a. It was getting late, and many of the people were far from home.

b. The people were not eager to leave Jesus of their own accord.

c. They "wanted to take Jesus by force to make him king" (John 6:15), which was exactly what he did not want (see John 18:36).

d. Jesus desired to have time for private communion with his Father in heaven.

As to the question why Jesus dismissed his disciples, the need for private communion (point d) would also explain this. Besides, in connection with point c., Jesus knew that even his own disciples were not free from errone-

---

[286] Note ἕως followed by *present* indic. = "while" (w. aor. subj. = "until"). See E. D. Burton, *Syntax of the Moods and Tenses in New Testament Greek*, Chicago, 1900, pp. 126-128, especially paragraphs 321, 325, and 328. But this rule is flexible, see footnote 723.

ous Messianic expectations (cf. Acts 1:6). We may assume that he was therefore also aware of the fact that it was best for them not to be influenced by the clamor of the multitude.

The Bethsaida to which Mark here refers was clearly on the western side of the sea, as was the plain of Gennesaret south of Capernaum (cf. Mark 6:53; John 6:17). For more on the two Bethsaidas see N.T.C. on John, Vol. I, pp. 216, 217, 225.

46. **And after taking leave of them he departed into the hill to pray.**

A very delightful and instructive book is that by R. E. Speer, *The Principles of Jesus Applied to Some Questions of Today,* New York, Chicago, Toronto, 1902. In this volume the writer points out that the purpose of Christ's coming to earth was, in part, "to displace legalism by the spirit of a true life, to supplant prescription by principle" (p. 10). Now prayer belongs to the very essence of this "true life." So in a passage that certainly also elucidates Mark 6:46 Speer points out that prayer was Christ's very breath, namely, "unselfish prayer (Luke 22:32), forgiving prayer (Luke 23:34), earnest prayer (Luke 22:44), submissive prayer (Matt. 11:26; 26:39, 54)" (p. 20).

The picture of Jesus on the hill praying, as was his custom (cf. John 17) for himself and also for others, including his disciples, must not be separated from that of the disciples on the stormy sea:

47. **When evening fell, the boat was in the middle of the sea, and he alone on land.**

"In the middle of the sea!" John's Gospel informs us that the boat had proceeded twenty-five to thirty stadia, hence about three or four miles, a stadium being about 1/8 of a mile. Now if the distance between Bethsaida Julias (Luke 9:10), the point from which the disciples began their return voyage, to Bethsaida of Galilee (Mark 6:45; cf. John 12:21), where they landed, was about five miles, as seems probable, then these men were now indeed "in the middle of the sea."

Then, evening having arrived, a storm arose. John states, "And the sea was getting rough, as a strong wind was blowing." Matthew adds, "The boat was ... battered by the waves, for the wind was from the opposite direction." Mark in verse 48 presupposes rather than describes the storm. But he, as well as the others, stresses the time of the day—evening, hence darkness—, the place—the middle of the sea—, and the absence of Jesus: "he alone on land"; however, on land *engaged in prayer* (verse 46).

Put together these two scenes: *a.* Christ's prayer including intercession, and *b.* the disciples' dangerous (humanly speaking) position! Result: their situation was actually not dangerous at all, for on yonder hill Christ's prayer must have included the petition that their lives might be spared so that they would be able to fulfil their mission. Does not this combined picture have many comforting applications for every time of trouble and distress; yes, for every "crisis"? And has there ever been a period in the history of the church when there was no crisis?

2. *The disciples with the unknown Jesus*

48. And seeing them straining at the oars, for the wind was against them, about the fourth watch of the night he came to them, walking on the sea.

Matt. 14:24 states that *the boat* was being "tortured" or "battered" or "harassed" by the waves. Mark here uses the same participle in connection with *the disciples*. Jesus saw them as they were being "harassed" in rowing, were straining at the oars. Both Mark (6:48) and John (6:19) refer to this rowing activity. [287]

It was then that Jesus, in fulfilment of his promise (implied in verse 45) came to them. The time was "about the fourth watch of the night" (cf. 13:35). That watch covered the period from 3 to 6 o'clock A.M. Note the word "about." It may have been 3 o'clock, a little earlier or even somewhat later.

In spite of the fact that it is dark, Jesus sees his disciples laboring with great difficulty to drive their vessel forward. In spite of the fact that water is—at least is considered to be—by its very nature unfit to be walked on, he walks on it. In spite of tempestuous billows and buffeting head-winds he, without deviation, continues step by step to walk toward this boat. No, not all the way up to the boat but rather toward a place near or alongside of it; for Mark writes, **He was about to pass them by.** Some have interpreted this to mean that it was the Master's intention to meet his disciples not now but a little later, after they had landed. But in view of the words "He came *to them*" a different interpretation is probably preferable; namely, he arrived to a place near the boat and then was about to continue onward past the boat, so as graciously to afford them an opportunity to invite him to come aboard. Without that glad welcome on their part he would have passed them by.

This is an important point. Divine disposition of events by no means rules out human action. Election is not inconsistent with exertion. See Phil. 2:12, 13; II Thess. 2:13. Besides, does not this interpretation of the thought of Jesus—"I shall give them an opportunity to welcome me aboard; and if they do not do this I shall pass them by"—find support in John 6:21? For a somewhat similar action on the part of Jesus see Luke 24:28.

The amazing manner in which the attributes of our Lord are here displayed merits special study. There is first *his knowledge*. The preceding context—see verses 46, 47—leaves the impression that it was while Jesus was still "on land" that he through—or in spite of—the darkness *saw* these

---

[287] Contrast Lenski, *op. cit.*, p. 172.

disciples! For more about the close connection between Christ's human and his divine nature, between his knowledge and his omniscience, see above, on Mark 5:32; also *Introduction* III. And study such passages as Matt. 17:27; 21:19; 24:36; Mark 2:8; 5:30; 11:13; John 1:47, 48; 2:23-25.

Next, consider his *power.* Mark has already related several events in connection with which this power was displayed in a most remarkable manner (1:25-27, 31-34, 39-42; 2:8-12; 3:5, 10, 11; 4:39; 5:9-13, 34, 41, 42). Now here in 6:48 the One who was able to still the waves (4:39) shows that he is even able to make them a path for his feet. See Job 9:8.

Attempts have been made to escape this conclusion and to change "walking on the sea" to "walking *by* (or *along*) the sea." In the present context, however, this will not do. If the exactly similar expression in the preceding verse (6:47) means that Jesus alone was "on land," verse 48 must mean that he actually walked "on the sea."

It would not be correct, in taking note of the Master's *knowledge* and of his *power,* to forget his *love,* as here revealed. That these men in distress were by no means perfect is shown in verses 49 (they were superstitious) and 52 (in a sense their hearts were hardened). Nevertheless, so tender is his compassion, so paternal his affection, that no darkness, tempest, or billows can keep him away from those who are very, very dear to his heart. When they need him he wants to be with them. [288]

49, 50a. Now when they saw him walking on the sea, they thought that he was a ghost, and they screamed; for they all saw him and were terrified.

With the boat heading southwest, the rowers must have been facing northeast. By the little light there was—coming perhaps from the pre-Passover moon intermittently peeping from between the dark clouds—they

---

[288] The word βασανιζομένους (cf. 5:7; Luke 8:28) is present passive participle acc. pl. (after ἰδών) of βασανίζω. See the related form in Matt. 14:24 (present passive participle nom. sing.). Matthew also uses this verb with reference to the centurion's "boy" who was "fearfully tortured" (8:6); and cf. "Do you come to torture us before the appointed time?" (8:29). Similarly the word is used in connection with Lot, who was "distressed" or "vexed" by the lawless deeds of his wicked neighbors (II Peter 2:8); to which can be added the instances of its use in Rev. 9:5; 11:10; 12:2; 14:10; 20:10. Jesus came to heal those that were distressed by "torments" (Matt. 4:24; cf. Luke 16:23, 28). The noun βάσανος (cf. our English word "basanite") indicates *a.* basically, a *touchstone* to test gold and other metals; *b. the instrument of torture* by which slaves were tested, i.e., forced to reveal the truth; and *c. torment* or *acute pain.*

Jesus saw the disciples "straining at the oars," literally: tortured ἐν τῷ ἐλαύνειν. The pres. act. infinitive is here used as a verbal noun: "in the (act of) rowing." The verb ἐλαύνω reminds one of the related English term *elastic.* An elastic has driving force: it springs back. By the elastic force of the bent bow the string when released expels or drives away the arrow. Thus rowers by means of plying the oars *drive* a boat; they row (Mark 6:48; John 6:19). The wind *drives* ships (James 3:4) or clouds (II Peter 2:17). Demons *drove* a demoniac into the wilderness (Luke 8:29).

see, probably not far away from them, what looked like a man coming toward them from the direction of Bethsaida Julias. Of course, the mysterious form could not really be a man, for human beings cannot walk on water! Of this the boat's occupants are sure. They do not realize how wrong they are. So, thoroughly frightened, they thought that what they saw was a ghost. [289]

By no means is it true that Herod Antipas was the only superstitious person mentioned in the New Testament (Mark 6:14). The disciples, too, were still being influenced by deeply rooted irrational beliefs. Cf. Acts 13:15.

Even today there are people, including church members, who consult media in order to find out what the stock market is going to do; and who, on Friday the thirteenth, when a black cat has just crossed their path, would shrink back in horror from walking under a ladder on their way to room No. 13—assuming that there is even such a room!—, and there spill a generous amount of salt! They refuse all the more emphatically to do this if their horoscope marks the day as being "unlucky" for them.

How small was the faith of The Twelve! They were looking at their Lord and Savior but thought that what they saw was an infernal, haunting specter, a "phantasm" or "ghost." Let everyone make his own application!

So they screamed (literally "cried up"). All were "scared to death," to use a colloquial expression. Mark reports that they *all* saw him and "were shaken," "were terrified." Among the entire group there was not one disciple, no not even Peter, who being himself courageous was able to impart courage to his companions. See also the parallel passage Matt. 14:26.

The verb used in the original to indicate this condition of panic and alarm [290] is very descriptive. In Matt. 2:3 it is used to describe Herod the Great's horror when he heard about the birth of a "king of the Jews." In the active voice it means *to shake, stir up, trouble, agitate,* as when Egypt's king is said to resemble a monster that *troubles* the waters with his feet, polluting them (LXX Ezek. 32:2). Figuratively it refers, in the active, to *upsetting* heart and mind *throwing them into confusion and alarm;* in the passive to *being thus terrified or frightened.* [291] Here in Mark 6:50a and Matt. 14:26 the picture is one of violently shaken men who during the darkness and the

---

[289] Note that here, by way of exception, it is Matthew who uses direct discourse, "It's a ghost," while Mark expresses himself in indirect discourse. See *Introduction* IV, footnote 5 g.

[290] ἐταράχθησαν third per. pl. aor. indic. passive of ταράσσω.

[291] In Mark the verb occurs in this passage only. In addition to Matt. 2:3; 14:26 it is also found in Luke 1:12; 24:38; several times in John (11:33; 12:27; 13:21; 14:1, 27); in Acts 15:24; 17:8, 13; Gal. 1:7; 5:10; and in I Peter 3:14.

storm utter a loud and frantic cry because of their fear that a malevolent specter is catching up with them, intent on doing them harm.

What should be done about such fears? Somewhat later, during the memorable night of the institution of the Supper, Jesus, addressing his disciples in the Upper Room, gave the answer. Using the same verb—"be troubled"—he said in lines that have a rhythmic flow, a soothing and consoling tenderness:

> "Let not y o u r hearts any longer be troubled.
> Continue to trust in God, also in me continue to trust"
>   (John 14:1).

3. *The disciples with Jesus, whom they now recognize because he speaks with them*

50b. But at once he spoke with them and said to them, Take courage, it is I; do not be afraid [or: stop being afraid]. The response of Jesus is immediate. In a friendly and affectionate manner he begins to speak "with" them. He says exactly what was needed to abolish their alarm borne of superstition. As far as the record shows, in the New Testament, with a single exception, the only one who says "Take courage" or "Be of good cheer" (A.V.) is Jesus. In addition to Mark 6:50 see also 10:49 (the one exception)[292] ; Matt. 9:2, 22; 14:27; John 16:33; and Acts 23:11. "It is I," says Jesus; hence, it is the very Master who has chosen y o u to be his disciples, has been guiding y o u step by step, and has already given y o u so many proofs of his power and love. Jesus therefore adds, "Do not be afraid." The disciples must stop being alarmed; rather, they should take courage and be filled with joy.

When Jesus spoke the words, "Take courage, it is I; do not be afraid," he must have momentarily shocked his disciples. But the immediate shock became a tremendously glad surprise. For other glad surprises see Gen. 13:14-18; 15:1 ff.; 17:1-21; 18:1-8; 22:10b-19; 26:23-25; 28:10-22; 45: 1 ff.; Exod. 3:1-12; 14:15; 33:14; 34:6, 7; 40:34, 35; Josh. 5:13 ff.; 10:12-14; I Kings 18:38-40; Isa. 37:36; Jer. 39:16-18 (cf. 38:7-13); Matt. 28:1-10; Mark 16:1-8; Luke 24:30-32; John 20; 21; Acts 2:1; 4:31; 12:7 ff. And see especially I Cor. 2:9 (cf. I Kings 10:6, 7).

51. Then he climbed into the boat to them; the wind fell, and they were greatly astonished. The Peter episode (Matt. 14:28-31) probably took place

---

292 And even this does not necessarily have to be viewed as an exception, for it is the friends' reaction to Christ's command that the blind man be called. It is almost as if Jesus by the mouth of these friends were saying to the blind man, "Be of good cheer." Paul's words in Acts 27:22, 25 approach those repeatedly spoken by the Lord; but *a.* in the original the apostle uses a different verb; and *b.* he echoes, though wholeheartedly, the words of heaven spoken by an angel.

about this time. As Jesus now climbed into the boat to be with his disciples his cheering presence banished the last remnant of their earlier superstitious panic. And when the storm in their hearts abated, so did the literal storm: "the wind fell," as had happened also on a previous occasion (4:39).

Result: the disciples were greatly astonished. What had been the reason for their hysterical alarm a moment ago, and what was the reason for their bewildered amazement now? Answer: **52. for they had not grasped the significance of (the incident of) the bread-cakes.** If they had fully understood the significance of the miraculous feeding (6:35-44), they would have known that it implied Christ's power to bend the material universe—including not only the product of the soil (bread) but also the billows of the sea and the currents of the air—to his wishes. The trouble was with their hearts: **In fact, their hearts were hardened.**

In Scripture the heart is the fulcrum of feeling and faith as well as the mainspring of words and actions (Matt. 12:34; 15:19; 22:37; John 14:1; Rom. 10:10; Eph. 1:18). It is the root of man's intellectual, emotional, and volitional life, the core and center of man's being, his inmost self. "Out of it are the issues of life" (Prov. 4:23). "Man looks on the outward appearance, but Jehovah looks on the heart" (I Sam. 16:7). When Mark says that the hearts of these disciples were "hardened," this probably means that the obtuseness of The Twelve, their inability to draw the necessary conclusions from the miracles of Jesus, was the result of sinful neglect to ponder and meditate on these marvelous works and on the nature of the One who performed them. Amazement, so that in their exhilaration these disciples would even ascribe deity to their Master, as happened even at the present occasion (Matt. 14:33), did not prevent them from falling into a kind of spiritual torpor or sluggishness; that is, they failed to ask themselves what could be expected of such a divine Being. Again and again they needed to be aroused out of their spiritual drowsiness. On the other hand, this hardness of heart must not be confused with the callousness and imperviousness of the scribes and Pharisees. That attitude was the result of unbelief and hatred. The disciples, on the contrary (Judas excepted), were men of faith . . . *little* faith.

The fact that faith should be sufficiently wide awake to derive legitimate conclusions from firmly established premises is the lesson which Scripture teaches (Matt. 6:26-30; Luke 11:13. Rom. 8:31, 32), but which is not always taken to heart.

---

53 Having crossed over they landed at Gennesaret and anchored (there). 54 And as soon as they got out of the boat the people recognized him [Jesus], 55 ran about the entire region, and on their pallets began to bring those that were ill to any place where they would hear that he was. 56 And wherever he would enter, into villages, towns or

countryside, they would lay the sick in the market-places and would beg him to allow them to touch merely the tassel [293] of his garment; and as many as touched him [294] were healed.

6:53-56 *Healings in Gennesaret*
Cf. Matt. 14:34-36

53. Having crossed over they landed at Gennesaret and anchored (there). On the basis of John 6:17 some interpreters believe that the wind had prevented the vessel from landing at Capernaum or even at Bethsaida (Mark 6:45) and compelled it to find anchorage a little farther to the south. This, however, is not certain. "Gennesaret" is the name of a densely populated and fertile plain south of Capernaum. It measures about 3 miles in length along the Sea of Galilee (also called the Lake of Gennesaret, Luke 5:1), and 1½ miles in width away from the shore. According to Josephus (*Jewish War* III. 516-521) its natural beauty and fertility were most remarkable. Says he, "There is not a plant that is rejected by its fertile soil," that is, which that soil refuses to produce. According to that author the plain produced walnuts, palms, figs, olives, and grapes. Such a high reputation did the fruits of Gennesaret have among the rabbis that they were not allowed in Jerusalem during the festivals lest a person might be tempted to come merely for their enjoyment. It was here that the little company decided to cast anchor. [295]

From that landing place Jesus is going to proceed to nearby Capernaum (John 6:17, 24, 25), but not before he has blessed the people of this region by his gracious presence, as shown in the following verses: **54, 55. And as soon as they got out of the boat the people recognized him [Jesus], ran about the entire region, and on their pallets began to bring those that were ill to any place where they would hear that he was.** It is clear that in verses 54-56 Mark is far more vivid and detailed than Matthew in 14:35, 36. When Jesus steps ashore he is immediately recognized. By this time he has become widely known as the Healer. There had been very striking individual healings (1:23-31, 40-45; 2:1-12; 3:1-5; ch. 5) and also mass healings (1:32-34; 3:7-12). It is not surprising therefore that the news of his arrival quickly spread. People *ran* to spread the good tidings. Result: from everywhere in the surroundings the sick were brought to Jesus.

They were brought on pallets, probably thin straw-filled mattresses (see on 2:4). To whatever place he was reported to be, the sick of every

---

293 Or: fringe.
294 Or: it.
295 Note προσωρμίσθησαν third per. pl. aor. indic. passive of προσορμίζω; ὅρμος = *anchorage* or *roadstead*. It was a place where sea and land met; cf. "horizon" where sky and sea—or land—appear to meet.

description were carried. [296] They were carried from wherever they were to wherever he happened to be.

56. **And wherever he would enter, into villages, towns or countryside, they would lay the sick in the market-place and would beg him to allow them to touch merely the tassel of his garment; and as many as touched him were healed.** [297]

What a rich ministry this was! There may have been teaching, but if so, nothing is said about it. Healing is emphasized. It took place in villages, towns, and countryside (cf. 5:14; 6:6). Often those who had dear ones that were ill would lay them in market-places, expecting these to be the spots to which Jesus would come. The word *market-place* may, however, also refer to a square or open space in a village that was too small to have a real market-place.

Such faith did these people have in the healing power and sympathy of the Savior that—as in the case of the woman described in 5:27-30, but see especially Matt. 9:20, 21—they were convinced that if the sick would be permitted to touch merely the tassel (fringe or edge) of the Master's robe, healing would immediately result. Mark does not even take the trouble to inform us whether such permission was given. In the case of Jesus he very correctly takes this for granted! As many as touched him (or: "it," but the meaning remains the same) were instantly and completely healed. The Gospels teach us that Jesus healed people by touching them, or by allowing them to touch him. More on this above, in connection with Mark 1:41.

In hymnology this work of our Lord in the plain of Gennesaret has not been passed by unnoticed. See the lines in E. H. Plumptre's beautiful hymn "Thine Arm, O Lord, in Days of Old":

---

[296] Note τοὺς κακῶς ἔχοντας: "those who had it bad" = those that were ill; cf. 1:32, 34; 2:17; ὅπου ἤκουον, iterative imperfect: "where they would hear"; ὅτι ἐστίν: "that he is," where we would say "that he was." After secondary tenses the Greek *generally* retains the tense of the direct discourse. See Gram. N.T., p. 1029.

[297] Note the following mostly grammatical items:

a. ὅπου ἂν εἰσεπορεύετο: in the New Testament in such clauses the optative is replaced by the indicative with ἄν. See E. D. Burton, *op. cit.*, pp. 124, 125, par. 315.

b. The verbs indicating *entering, laying, begging,* and *being healed* are all in the imperfect, iterative. The rendering might be: "*would enter... would lay* (or: *would place*) *...would beg...would be healed.*" However, it is not always necessary or advisable to render each expression in this manner. E.g., "would be healed" might then be erroneously interpreted to mean "were going to be healed." The intention of the author is that they were definitely healed on the spot. Hence in this instance the translation "as many as touched him were healed" is probably best, especially since though ὅπου ἂν εἰσεπορεύετο is indefinite, ὅσοι ἂν ἥψαντο(aor.) is definite. In each particular case the momentary touch was followed by healing, and these healings happened again and again.

c. κἄν means "if only" or "merely."

d. Verbs of touching take the gen.; hence κρασπέδου.

And now, O Lord, be near to bless,
Almighty as of yore,
In crowded streets, by restless couch,
As by Gennesaret's shore.

Summary of Chapter 6

On a sabbath Jesus teaches in the synagogue of his hometown Nazareth. The audience is astonished about his wisdom. After further reflection, however, the people cannot understand how these words of wisdom can proceed from the lips of one who grew up among themselves as "the carpenter." They know his brothers intimately, can even mention them by name. His sisters are still living among them. What, then, is the source of these words? Also, how is it possible for him to perform the miracles that have been ascribed to him, and some of which people in the audience may even have witnessed? A Nazareth carpenter speaking words of wisdom and performing miracles? Impossible! They are offended in him. Says Jesus, "A prophet is not without honor except in his hometown, among his relatives, and in his family." In such a hostile environment only a few people can be healed (1-6a).

Among ordinary mortals it frequently happens that those who are rejected concede defeat and give up their endeavor. Not so Jesus. On the contrary, he intensifies his evangelical efforts. He carries on a personal campaign, "going around the villages teaching," and sends his disciples on a mission tour. In addition to teaching, many miracles—healings, demon-expulsions—are performed (6b-13). The result is twofold.

First, the ruler, Herod Antipas, hears about Jesus. His conscience is aroused. He says, "The man whom I beheaded, namely John, he is risen." In this connection Mark tells the story of Herod's wicked birthday party and the Baptist's gruesome death (14-29).

Secondly, the disciples, returned from their mission tour, are in need of rest. Perhaps John's murder has also had a disquieting effect on them. Jesus himself feels the need of communion with his Father. So he addresses his disciples as follows, "Come away by yourselves to a lonely—or *quiet*—place and rest a while." By boat they start out for Bethsaida Julias. When the Galileans see their departure they hurry on foot around the upper part of the lake in order to be with Jesus. When he surveys this great multitude his heart goes out to them because they are like sheep without a shepherd. So, from his place of seclusion he goes forth to meet them and begins to teach them many things. When evening arrives, instead of dismissing the hungry crowd, he performs the miracle of making five bread-cakes and two fishes do for five thousand men. Twelve baskets full of left-overs are collected after everyone

266

has had plenty to eat. Should not this have convinced The Twelve that he who exercises control over the ingredients from which bread is made is also able to cause the ingredients of a storm—air currents and billows—to obey his will (30-44)?

Yet, what happens? Having for good reasons dismissed the multitude, and having ordered the disciples to go back to the opposite side of the sea, Jesus, still ashore, departs into the hill to pray. When from the land he sees The Twelve straining at the oars while facing a strong head-wind, he walks toward them on the sea. Imagining that they are looking at a ghost they start to scream. He quiets them by saying, "Take courage, it is I; do not be afraid (or: stop being afraid)." He would have passed them by but they welcome him aboard. When he climbs into the boat the wind ceases. Profound astonishment takes possession of The Twelve. If their hearts had been more fully inclined to ponder the implications of the miraculous multiplication of the bread-cakes, they would not have been: first, so terrified; and later, so surprised and astonished (45-52).

When Jesus and The Twelve land in the fertile plain of Gennesaret, those who recognize the Master begin to spread the news all around. So the sick are brought to him wherever he happens to be. All who touch, be it merely the tassel or the fringe of his garment, are completely and immediately restored to health (53-56).

Chapter 7:1-23

Theme: *The Work Which Thou Gavest Him To Do*

Ceremonial versus Real Defilement

CHAPTER VII: 1-23

7   1 And there gathered together to him the Pharisees and some of the scribes who had come from Jerusalem, 2 and they saw that some of his disciples were eating their food with defiled, that is with unrinsed, hands. 3 —Now the Pharisees, in fact all the Jews, unless they rinse their hands thoroughly, [298] do not eat, thus clinging to the tradition of the elders. 4 And (when they come) from the marketplace, unless they ceremonially wash themselves [299] they do not eat. And there are many other things which they have received in order to cling to, such as ceremonial washings [300] of cups, pitchers, and kettles. [301] —5 So the Pharisees and the scribes were asking him, "Why don't your disciples live in accordance with the tradition of the elders but eat with defiled hands?"

     6 He said to them, "Isaiah was right when he prophesied about y o u hypocrites, as it is written:

         'This people honor me with their lips
         But their heart is far from me.
     7 But in vain do they worship me,
         Teaching (as their) doctrines precepts of men.'

8 Y o u let go the commandment of God in order to cling to the tradition of men."

     9 And he said to them, "How beautifully y o u are setting aside God's command in order to establish [302] y o u r own tradition! 10 For Moses said, 'Honor your father and your mother,' and 'He who curses father or mother must certainly be put to death.' 11 But y o u say, 'If anyone says to his father or to his mother, (It's) corbān, that is, a gift (set apart for God), whatever it be by which I might benefit you'—12 then y o u no longer permit him to do anything for his father or mother. 13 Thus y o u nullify the word of God by y o u r tradition which y o u have handed down. And many such things y o u do."

     14 And he called the people to him again and said to them, "Hear me, all of y o u, and understand: 15 There is nothing outside a man which by going into him is able to defile him; no, it is the things that come out of a man that defile a man." [303]

     17 And after he had left the people and had gone home, [304] his disciples were asking him (the meaning of) this parable. 18 He said to them, "Are y o u also so

---

298 "thoroughly" is uncertain: the Greek is obscure.
299 Literally: unless they baptize themselves.
300 Literally: baptisms.
301 Another reading adds "couches."
302 According to another reading, with considerable support: in order to observe [or: to keep, guard, preserve, retain].
303 The insertion of verse 16, "If anyone has ears to hear, let him hear," does not rest upon sufficient textual evidence.
304 Or: had gone indoors.

lacking in understanding? Do y o u not know that nothing that enters a man from the outside can defile him,   19 since it does not enter his heart but his stomach and goes out into the latrine?"—Thus he pronounced all foods clean—.   20 He continued, "What comes out of a man, it is that which defiles a man.   21 For it is from inside, from men's hearts that the evil schemes arise: sexual sins, thefts, murders,   22 adulteries, covetings, malicious acts, deceit, lewdness, envy, [305] abusive speech, arrogance, folly.   23 All these evil things proceed from inside and defile a man."

7:1-23 *Ceremonial versus Real Defilement*
Cf. Matt. 15:1-20

The ending of Mark 6 and of Matt. 14 pictured Jesus in the plain of Gennesaret, busily engaged in healing the sick. It is probable that from here he with The Twelve proceeded to Capernaum (John 6:17, 24, 25, 59), where he delivered the discourse on The Bread of Life. It may have been about the same time and place that the event described in Mark 7:1-23 took place. See also on verse 17.

It is clear (see especially verses 1, 5, 6 ff.) that what is here described is another bitter confrontation between Jesus and the religious leaders of the Jews.

Among the many sharp clashes of this character there are several, as the present may well be, where Christ's hostile critics seem to be impatiently waiting for him on the western side of the Sea of Galilee or of the Jordan, ready for the attack. In addition to Mark 7:1-23 see also 5:21, 22 (in connection with Matt. 9:18); 8:10, 11; 9:2, 14. Later, after the final crossing of the Jordan from east to west there would occur the series of attacks that finally issued in Christ's crucifixion just outside Jerusalem's gate (Heb. 13:12).

Both the episode in connection with ceremonial versus real defilement and Jesus' discourse recorded in John 6 resulted in rejection (Matt. 15:12; John 6:66). The crucifixion is in sight. It is going to take place about a year from this point in the narrative. The Great Galilean Ministry, the record of which began at Mark 1:14, may be conceived as ending at 7:23.

Taking Mark 7 as a unit we notice that this S eventh Chapter is not duplicated in Luke (just as Luke 7 is not paralleled in Mark). Mark 7 treats three subjects:

S cribes and Pharisees question Jesus regarding defilement. The

S yrophoenician woman's faith is rewarded.

S peech and hearing are fully restored to a handicapped man.

7:1, 2. And there gathered together to him the Pharisees and some of the scribes who had come from Jerusalem, and they saw that some of his

---

[305] Literally: a wicked eye.

disciples were eating their food with defiled,[306] that is, with unrinsed, hands.

The beginning of the sentence can mean either: *a.* Both the Pharisees and some scribes had come from Jerusalem; or *b.* The Pharisees were local people, Galileans, but the scribes were Jerusalemites.[307] But Matt. 15:1, the parallel passage, would seem to settle the argument in favor of *a.*

It is proper to speak of the *profession* of the scribes, and the *sect* of the Pharisees. The *scribes* were the law specialists. They studied, interpreted, and taught the law, that is, the Old Testament. More exactly, they transmitted to their own generation the traditions which from generation to generation had been handed down with respect to the interpretation and application of the law, traditions that had their origin in the teaching of the venerable rabbis of long ago. The *Pharisees* were those Israelites who tried to make everybody believe that they, these *Separatists,* were living, or at least were trying very hard to live, in accordance with scribal teaching. Naturally many scribes were also Pharisees. See also N.T.C. on Matthew, pp. 201-203; and see above, on 1:22; 2:6, 16; and 3:22.

Most Pharisees and scribes hated Jesus, because: *a.* he claimed divine prerogatives; *b.* he did not honor their traditions with respect to the sabbath, fasts, ablutions, etc.; *c.* he associated with publicans and sinners; *d.* he exerted what they considered a baneful influence upon the people; and *e.* he was their opposite.

This last point is in need of emphasis. In their heart of hearts Christ's enemies must have realized that Jesus was infinitely better than they were. His humility (Luke 22:27) contrasted sharply with their pomposity (Matt. 23:5-7); his sincerity (John 8:46), with their hypocrisy (Mark 7:6); his sympathy (Mark 6:34), with their cruelty (Matt. 23:14). To a considerable extent their "religion" was activity in the interest of self (Matt. 6:2, 5, 16); his ministry was a sacrifice in the interest of others (Mark 10:45) and to the glory of the Father (John 17:1, 4). Did some of these enemies sense that he knew their real character, that he "had their number"?

However that may have been, here they are, having traveled all the way down from Jerusalem, the headquarters of Jewish "orthodoxy." Undoubtedly they had come here at the behest of the Sanhedrin. Their aim must have been to discover a ground for pressing charges against Jesus, that they might destroy him. See Mark 3:6; 11:18. Does the reference to "some scribes" indicate that these particular scribes had been selected because they were considered experts in matters that might come up in controversies with Jesus? This is possible, not certain.

---

306 Or: ceremonially unclean.
307 Alternative *b.* is adopted by Vincent Taylor, *op. cit.,* p. 334.

The committee's spying was soon rewarded. The men saw that some—only *some,* not even all—of The Twelve were eating [308] with "defiled" hands, that is, with hands that had not been subjected to ceremonial rinsing, and therefore were not "ceremonially clean.": Is it possible that if the spies had waited a moment longer they would have noticed that not only some but all of The Twelve had this habit, and in fact Jesus himself also? See Luke 11:38. [309]

The explanatory note "that is, with unrinsed (hands)" must have been inserted for the benefit of the non-Jewish readers for whom first of all this Gospel was intended. That is true also with respect to the parenthetical passage: verses 3, 4. **Now the Pharisees, in fact all the Jews, unless they rinse their hands thoroughly, do not eat, thus clinging to the tradition of the elders. And (when they come) from the market-place, unless they ceremonially wash themselves they do not eat. And there are many other things which they have received in order to cling to,** [310] **such as ceremonial washings of cups, pitchers, and kettles.**

The following points should be noted:

a. "The Pharisees, in fact all the Jews." Here "all," as often in Scripture and even today in daily conversation, is used loosely; see on 1:5 ("And there were going out to him *all* the land of Judea and *all* the people of Jerusalem"). The meaning is "very many," "the people in general."

b. ". . . unless they rinse their hands *thoroughly.*" The readings vary between "with the fist"; "often"; and absence of any adverb. [311] Even if the first of these should be correct, which many regard as probable, the interpretation is not entirely certain. Does this mean "with the fist twisting and turning in the palm of the other hand"? A quotation from a Talmudic tractate [312] may be helpful: "Hands become unclean and are made clean as

---

[308] See above, on 3:20, footnote 120.

[309] R. C. Trench, *op. cit.,* par. xlv, has shown that while πλύνω refers to the washing of inanimate things—nets (Luke 5:2), garments (Rev. 7:14)—, and λούω to bathing the entire body (Acts 9:27; II Peter 2:22; Rev. 1:5), νίπτω—a derivative of which is used here in Mark 7:2 (dat. pl. adj. ἀνίπτοις), and a form in verse 3 (third per. pl. middle aor. subjunctive νίψωνται)—generally has reference to the cleansing of part of the body: hands (Mark 7:3), feet (John 13:5), face (Matt. 6:17), eyes (John 9:7). He points to Lev. 15:11, Septuagint, as giving us all three words, all in their exact propriety of meaning.

I agree; yet, we find in examining the Hebrew that shātaph, as in Lev. 15:11, is by Brown-Driver-Briggs rendered *"rinse or wash off,"* and by A.V., A.R.V., R.S.V., Berkeley, Leeser, etc. *rinse.* A.V. translates as follows: "And whomsoever he toucheth that hath the issue, and hath not *rinsed* his hands in water, he shall wash his clothes, and bathe himself in water, and be unclean until the even." Such "rinsing" or "ceremonial washing," and not the washing of hands in a basin is undoubtedly also the meaning here in Mark 7:2. For further remarks on this see N.T.C. on Matt. 15:1, 2.

[310] Not merely, "There are many other traditions which they observe."

[311] Some have πυγμῇ; some πυγνά; some omit both.

[312] *The Babylonian Talmud:* Seder Tohoroth, London, 1948, p. 552.

far as the wrist. How so? If he poured the water over the hands as far as the wrist and poured the second water over the hands beyond the wrist and the latter flowed back to the hands, the hands nevertheless become clean." In any case the conclusion that a thorough ceremonial affusion or rinsing is indicated seems justified.

c. "... clinging to—or: holding fast [313] —the tradition of the elders." The scribes and their many followers continued to advocate strict compliance with the rules laid down by the prominent rabbis of long ago. These rules had been "handed down"—the very word "tradition" means "what was handed down"—from one generation to another, and were now again being handed down by the scribes to the then present generation. In fact, ever so many minute ceremonial stipulations regarding hundreds of matters were being handed down as if salvation itself depended on all-out obedience. Thus also the strict Jews refused to eat unless they had first of all subjected their hands to the already indicated thorough ritual cleansing.

d. "... and (when they come) from the market-place. ..." The market-place, a gathering center for many people, was naturally looked upon as being especially defiling. A Jew might brush against a Gentile! Therefore, coming from such a place, these Jews did not dare to eat unless they had first of all complied with whatever it was that tradition demanded regarding hand rinsing.

e. "... unless they ceremonially wash themselves," or simply: "unless they ceremonially wash." Here, as in b. above, there is variety in readings. Was the authentic text "unless they ceremonially wash themselves" or "unless they ceremonially sprinkle themselves"? [314] In all probability the first—"unless they ... wash"; literally "unless they baptize themselves" or simply "unless they baptize" is probably correct. Merely sprinkling the hands would probably not have satisfied the rabbis. Nothing less than a thorough rinsing or ceremonial washing seems to have been required. [315]

That this "baptizing" to which the passage refers must not be interpreted as an immersion of the entire body is clear from Luke 11:38, where a form of the same verb, *baptize,* is used: "But the Pharisee was astonished (to see) that he [Jesus] did not first wash [lit. baptize] before dinner." It is hardly reasonable to imagine that the Pharisee was expecting that Jesus would first take a complete bath, a bath in which he would have totally immersed himself! The reference is, of course, to the ritualistic cleansing of *the hands* before a meal. So also here in Mark 7:4. The preceding context supplies the

---

313 For the verb used in the original see above, on 3:21, footnote 122.

314 The Greek verbs (third per. pl. aor. subjunctive middle) are respectively βαπτίσων-ται and ῥαντίσωνται.

315 For the opposite opinion see Vincent Taylor, *op. cit.,* p. 336.

key to the interpretation: the ceremonial baptizing or washing of verse 4 refers to the hand rinsing of verse 3.

f. Mark adds that the Jews had been taught to observe many other traditions; such as "baptisms" or ceremonial washings of cups, pitchers, [316] and kettles (or: vessels of bronze).

5. So the Pharisees and the scribes were asking him, Why don't your disciples live in accordance with the tradition of the elders but eat with defiled hands?

In a formal manner both the Pharisees and the scribes are asking this question. As in 2:23, 24 they hold Jesus responsible for what his disciples are doing. After all, their purpose is to destroy *him*.

The trouble with these men is that they are constantly stressing man-made rules. Worse even, they are doing this at the expense of the honor they should have bestowed on the divine law. They are devotees of hollow ritualism, as if that could save them!

6, 7. He said to them, Isaiah was right when he prophesied about y o u hypocrites, as it is written:

> **This people honor me with their lips**
> **But their heart is far from me.**
> **But in vain do they worship me,**
> **Teaching (as their) doctrines precepts of men.** [317]

In his answer Jesus refers mainly to two Old Testament passages: *a.* Isa. 29:13, and *b.* Exod. 20:12 (and similar texts). Matthew (15:4-9) has Exod. 20:12 first, followed by a reference to the Isaiah passage. Mark reverses this order. The advantage of this variety in presentation is that thus equal prominence is given to both passages; one might say: to the law and to the prophets, to the prophets and to the law. In substance the reply is the same in both Gospels.

Now Mark—really Jesus himself as quoted by Mark—did not necessarily mean that Isaiah [318] was thinking of the Pharisees and scribes of Jesus' day.

---

[316] The word ξέστης is by many regarded as a loanword from the Latin, a corruption of *sextarius.* The sextarius is basically a liquid vessel containing about one pint (=½ liter); secondarily, a pitcher of any size whatever.

[317] The manner in which this passage supports the position that Greek Matthew was not merely a translation of an Aramaic original is explained in N.T.C. on Matthew, pp. 89, 90.

[318] The quotation as found in Matthew and Mark resembles the Septuagint rendering of Isa. 29:13 much more closely than it does the Hebrew original. The Hebrew original has: "Forasmuch as this people draw near with their mouth, and with their lips honor me, but have removed their heart from me, and their fear toward me (is but) acquired precept of men, therefore . . . ." The Septuagint has: "This people draw near to me (and) with their lips honor me, but their heart is far from me. But in vain do they worship me, teaching precepts of men and (their) doctrines." The main idea, however, is the same in both.

He probably meant that what the prophet wrote concerning the people of his own day was still very relevant, for both then and now those condemned were honoring God with their lips, while their hearts were far removed from him. History was repeating itself.

Jesus calls these men "hypocrites." In Mark this term occurs only in this one passage—see, however, also 12:15—, but it is found three times in Luke and frequently in Matthew, especially in two of Christ's discourses: The Sermon on the Mount and The Seven Woes (respectively chapters 5—7 and ch. 23). Though the word does not occur in the Old Testament—the A.V. passages from the Old Testament which have it are erroneous renderings—, the *idea* as such is found there also (Ps. 10:7; Prov. 26:24, 26).

The hypocrite is the man who hides or tries to hide his real intentions under (*hypo*) a mask of simulated virtue. As the passage now under study presents it: he honors God with his lips but his *heart* (see on 6:52) is far from God. Also (note last two lines), while pretending to teach doctrines that are divine in origin he is actually teaching "precepts of men," fussy ("persnickety") rules and regulations laid down by hair-splitting, legalistic ancient rabbis—mere *men!*—and passed on from one generation to the next. See Matt. 6:2, 5, 16; 23:23-28.

So also at this occasion, these "pious" (?) critics pretended to be very concerned about that which they presented as an infraction of a divine (?) statute that had been handed down to them. Their real intention was the destruction of the very Son of God. A hypocrite, then, is a fraud, deceiver, phony, snake in the grass, wolf in sheep's clothing. He pretends to be what he is not.

Of course, his "worship" of God is vain, utterly futile; and this for two reasons: *a.* because the attitude of his heart is wrong, and *b.* because his emphasis is wrong, as Jesus now indicates by saying: **8. Y o u let go the commandment of God in order to cling to the tradition of men.** Pharisees and scribes were guilty of placing mere human tradition above divine revelation, a man-made rule above a God-given command. The rabbis had divided the Mosaic law or Torah into ·613 separate decrees, 365 of these being considered prohibitions and 248 positive directives. Then, in connection with each decree, by drawing arbitrary distinctions between what they considered "permitted" and "not permitted," they had attempted to regulate every detail of the conduct of the Jews: their sabbaths, travel, meals, fasts, ablutions, trade, relation toward outsiders, etc., etc. One finds an example of their hair-splitting, casuistic reasoning in Matt. 23:16-18. For many other interesting illustrations see A. T. Robertson, *The Pharisees and Jesus,* especially pp. 44, 45, 93 ff. Thus, having an eye only for the multiplicity of the decrees and of their myriad applications to concrete life situations, they had piled up precept upon precept (cf. Isa. 28:10, 13) until at last, by most of these scribes and Pharisees, the unity and purpose of God's holy law—see Deut. 6:4; then Lev. 19:18; Mic. 6:8; cf. Mark 12:28-34—had suffered a total eclipse.

Jesus, accordingly, accuses his opponents of having relinquished the commandment of God in order to cling to the tradition of men. If anyone but Jesus had voiced this withering criticism against the religious leaders of the day, we might feel inclined to regard it as being possibly a bit extreme. What? Did these Pharisees and scribes actually set their oral law above the written law of the Old Testament? Was not this too harsh a judgment? The answer is: not at all. In fact, there is some evidence in support of the proposition that the rabbis themselves defended that position. They said, "To be opposed to the word of the scribes is worthy of greater punishment than to be opposed to the word of the Bible." See Robertson's work to which reference was made in the preceding paragraph, p. 130. They probably reasoned as follows: historically the oral law preceded the law in written form; therefore the oral law has precedence. It is clear, therefore, that the opponents were not in a position to maintain that what Jesus was saying was untrue.

How must it be explained that Jesus disagreed with the position of subordinating God's written commandment to oral tradition? The answer is, apart from the obvious fact that, other things being equal, the spoken word is less durable, more subject to change from one generation to another, than the written document, the commandment came from the Holy God, and is therefore infallible, but the tradition, a tradition of *interpretation,* originated with sinful men, and is therefore fallible. In the present case, as has been shown, it was frequently wretched, misleading, corrupt.

It would be entirely wrong to draw the conclusion that Jesus was opposed to tradition, that he wanted to overthrow whatever was old and was in that sense a revolutionist. Passages such as Matt. 5:17, 18; 23:1-3; Mark 10:5-9 prove that he was not. What he opposed was any man-made teaching or rule that was in conflict with the divine law. He was "old-fashioned" in the best sense of the term, for he went back all the way until beyond faulty and misleading tradition he found his Father's original revelation and commandment.

In the present passage Jesus refers to *the commandment* of God, using the singular. If he was even now thinking of the precept which he was about to quote (verse 10) we can see the reason for this singular. However, it may be generic, the *one* command representing the entire class. [319]

---

[319] In the Synoptics an ἐντολή refers at times to a command of the Decalog. See Mark 7:9, 10; cf. Matt. 15:3, 4. But in Luke 23:56 the word may have a wider reference. See not only Exod. 20:10 but also 12:16. Cf. Matt. 19:17; Mark 10:19; Luke 18:20. In Mark

9. **And he said to them, How beautifully y o u are setting aside God's command in order to establish y o u r own tradition!** In a sense Jesus repeats verse 8. However, the sting is even more fiery, the exposure more startling. How beautifully! This is irony. It amounts to: "Y o u have a fine way of setting aside. . . ." Note also "*y o u r* tradition," and cf. verse 8. These men are trying to make gods of themselves. They are setting aside God in order to establish themselves. They are nullifying an infallible command in order to confirm their own weak and miserable tradition. [320] How wicked!

Yes, how wicked! But also how foolish! Think of a man who in the midst of a violent storm has found a place of shelter on top of a high rock (cf. Ps. 18:2; 27:5; 92:15; 119:114, 117, 165), where he is entirely safe, but who then jumps off in order, for the sake of protection, to grab hold of a drifting straw. What utter folly. Cf. Jer. 2:13.

In order to illustrate what he has in mind and to prove his point Jesus continues: 10. **For Moses said, Honor your father and your mother, and He who curses father or mother must certainly be put to death.** "Moses said." As is clear from verse 13 Jesus regards what Moses said as being the very word of God. Accordingly there is no real difference between Matt. 15:4, "For God said," and Mark 7:10, "For Moses said."

As to the positive commandment to bestow honor on father and mother see Exod. 20:12; Deut. 5:16; Prov. 1:8; 6:20-22; cf. Mal. 1:6; Matt. 19:19; Mark 7:10-13; 10:19; Eph. 6:1; Col. 3:20. *To honor* father and mother means more than *to obey* them, especially if this obedience is interpreted in a merely outward sense. It is the inner attitude of the child toward his parents that comes to the fore in the requirement that he *honor* them. All selfish obedience or reluctant obedience or obedience under terror is immediately ruled out. To honor implies to love, to regard highly, to show the spirit of respect and consideration. This honor is to be shown to *both* of the parents, for as far as the child is concerned they are equal in authority.

In Exod. 21:17; Lev. 20:9 the death penalty is pronounced on those who curse father and mother, but see also Exod. 21:15; Deut. 21:18-21 and Prov. 30:17.

What did these Pharisees and scribes do with this clear and definite

---

10:5 the term used in the original refers to the bill of divorce. In the present context (Mark 7:10) the fifth commandment is immediately followed by a related Mosaic provision that is not part of the Ten Commandments. And in 12:28-31 the word ἐντολή used by the scribe may initially refer to any command of the entire Mosaic law. As Jesus, in his answer, employs the term in that passage, the summary of each table is called an ἐντολή. For the use of the term ἐντολή in John's Gospel see N.T.C. on John, Vol. II, pp. 252, 253. For an excellent article on this word and related ones see G. Schrenk, Th.D.N.T., Vol. II, pp. 544-556.

320 Even if τηρήσητε is substituted for στήσητε, the result is about the same: they reject the one in order to *observe* the other.

teaching of the Word of God? The answer is given in verses 11, 12. **But y o u say, If anyone says to his father or to his mother, (It's) corbān, that is, a gift (set apart for God), whatever it be by which I might benefit you—then y o u no longer permit him to do anything for his father or mother.** [321]

Christ's critics, though highly esteemed by the people in general, were guilty of deliberate and detestable chicanery. They were playing ducks and drakes with God's holy law. The commandment with respect to children's duty toward their parents was very clear. But the Pharisees and scribes were telling the children that there was a way to get around the heavy burden of having to bestow honor upon their parents by supporting them. If a son had something that was needed by the parent, all that was necessary was for the son to say, "(It's) *corbān!*" For his non-Jewish readers Mark adds the Greek equivalent *dōron,* gift or offering; that is, a *sacred* gift or offering, one set apart for God, i.e., for sacred uses. By making this assertion or exclamation and giving it a very wide application—"whatever it be by which I might benefit you"—this son, according to Pharisaic teaching based on tradition, [322] had released himself from the obligation of honoring his parents. In fact, as Mark puts it, *permission* to help one's parents was then withdrawn.

It is even possible that a broader interpretation may be correct. If so, the son would be saying, "Whatever it is by which I might benefit you, whether now or in the future, I here and now declare that it is to be considered an offering." The conclusion, as reported by Mark, "then y o u no longer permit him to do *anything* for his father or mother" might support this interpretation.

Interpreted either way, it was an example of irresponsible Pharisaic sophistry, a wicked device to deprive parents of the honor and the support

---

[321] The difference between the two reports of this dominical saying, Matthew's and Mark's, is slight. Note the following:

Matt. 15:5, 6a	Mark 7:11, 12
Anyone who says (It's) a gift . . . surely does not have to honor his father.	If anyone says (It's) corbān, that is, a gift . . . then y o u no longer permit him to do anything for his father or mother.

Mark's sentence ("But y o u say . . . then y o u no longer") is an obvious example of anacoluthon. A.V., R.S.V., and several other translations do justice to this. Others avoid it by changing the given text (for example, they change "then y o u no longer permit" to "he is no longer permitted" or "he need not"). I cannot follow Lenski's reasoning here (*op. cit.,* pp. 183-185). Does not even his own rendering, p. 183, prove a change in grammatical construction? One way to account for this anacoluthon is to bear in mind that it is in line with Mark's popular style. Besides, it is possible that Mark did not fully report what Jesus said. Truthful reporting does not necessarily always imply total reporting. Cf. Matt. 15:19 with Mark 7:21, 22. See John 21:25.

[322] See S.BK, Vol. I, p. 71 f.

due to them. Moreover, what was thus unjustly withdrawn from the parents was not necessarily offered to God at all. The one who shouted, "(It's) corbān!" could simply keep it for himself.

It is not surprising that Jesus, in a sense repeating, but now even strengthening what he had spoken previously (cf. verses 8, 9), adds: **13. Thus y o u nullify the word of God by y o u r tradition which** [323] **y o u have handed down.** Not only were these "hypocrites" (verse 6) ignoring, they were actually invalidating the word of God. They were depriving the fifth commandment of its binding authority, as the original implies. [324] On the other hand, they were handing down the wicked tradition! Moreover, that was true not only in the present case, as if the Pharisees and scribes were nullifying only this *one* commandment. No, Jesus immediately adds: **And many such things y o u do.** Merely by way of illustration had he referred to the Pharisaic manner of dealing with the fifth commandment. It was but a sample of what was constantly going on. Tradition was regularly being enthroned; God's Word dethroned!

A very practical subject indeed, capable of application in any age. Is not the objective principle of Protestantism *"The Bible is the only infallible rule of faith and practice"*? This, in opposition to the Roman Catholic co-ordination of Scripture and ecclesiastical *tradition,* as the joint rules of faith? Does not the latter position often degenerate into placing tradition above Scripture? And even today should not care be exercised lest subjective decisions and interpretations begin to interfere with unbiased exegesis of the Word of God?

There is a striking similarity between Mark 7:14-23 and its parallel Matt. 15:10-20. The main differences are as follows:

a. Matt. 15:12-14: the question of the disciples ("Do you know that the Pharisees were offended when they heard what you said?") and Jesus' answer are not found in Mark.

b. According to Matt. 15:15 it was Peter who asked Jesus to explain "the parable." Mark simply says, "the disciples." Mark, however, states—and Matthew omits—that it was after Jesus had left the people and had entered a house that the question was asked.

c. Mark's statement (7:19b), "Thus he pronounced all foods clean" is not found in Matthew.

d. Matthew's list of evil things that proceed from within and defile a man

---

323 Note ᾗ "by means of" or perhaps even "for the sake of." What would have been an accusative is attracted to the dative because of the antecedent τῇ παραδόσει.

324 ἀκυροῦντες mas. nom. pl. pres. participle of ἀκυρόω, to deprive of *authority,* render void, nullify, annul; in the New Testament used only in Mark 7:13 (parallel Matt. 15:6); and Gal. 3:17 ("the law does not annul"). Cf. κύριος, one in *authority,* lord, master, owner; κυρόω, to impart *authority* to, to make valid.

(15:19) consists (after an introductory term) of 6 items; Mark (7:21, 22) has 12. If Mark's "deceit" is tantamount to Matthew's "false testimonies," then all of Matthew's 6 items occur, with slight verbal changes, also in Mark's list. These are items 5, 6, 8, 9, 11, and 12 on Mark's list, occurring therefore from about the middle to the end of that evangelist's enumeration. See chart, pp. 284, 285. Accordingly, the inference that Matthew, with Mark's list before him, was abbreviating, would not seem to be unreasonable.

14, 15. **And he called the people to him again and said to them, Hear me, all of y o u, and understand: There is nothing outside a man which by going into him is able to defile him; no, it is the things that come out of a man that defile a man.** It would seem that just before the arrival of the committee consisting of Pharisees and scribes Jesus had been addressing the people. Then, probably out of respect for the delegation that had come to question Jesus, the people had withdrawn a certain distance. But now, the critics having left or having been dismissed, the Lord invites the people to draw close to him again. By means of the words, "Hear me, all of y o u, and understand"—who does not detect the solemn Old Testament (cf. Ps. 49:1; 50:7; 81:8) ring?—Jesus at the very beginning of his resumed message emphasizes the fact that what he is about to say is very important. Again and again the Gospels picture him as the compassionate Savior, the One who feels deeply hurt because the common people are being misled by their leaders. See Matt. 9:36; 11:28-30; Mark 6:34.

What Jesus wishes to impress upon the multitude has to do with the contemptuous question of the Pharisees and scribes (see verse 5), "Why don't your disciples live in accordance with the tradition of the elders but eat with defiled hands?" The assumption of these critics was: unrinsed hands defile the food and therefore the eater. The defilement, as they saw it, worked its way from the outside to the inside. Jesus shows that the very opposite is true. Not what goes into but what comes out of the man is able to defile him. Note Mark's use of the plural. According to his report Jesus speaks about "the things that come out of the man" as being those that render him "unclean." Now it is true that in Greek such a plural can often be correctly rendered by the use of a singular in English. Nevertheless, in the present case, in view of the lengthy list of things that defile (see verses 21, 22), it is probably better to retain the plural even in the translation. What Jesus is saying, therefore, is that the real defilement is not physical but moral and spiritual. Defilement, in other words, issues from the heart. In our own day, in which so much is said and something is even being, done about various types of physical pollution, that is, pollution that works its way from the outside inward, Christ's warning against defilement *from within* is certainly needed.

17. **And after he had left the people and had gone home, his disciples were asking him (the meaning of) this parable.** Finally Jesus is alone with his disciples. He has entered his home. It is true that instead of "and had gone home" another rendering, namely, "and had entered a house," or "had gone indoors" is also possible. Complete certainty about the meaning of the phrase in the original is impossible. Nevertheless, as has been shown, the references in 2:1 and 3:20 are probably to Jesus' home in Capernaum. See on these passages. We shall assume, therefore, that the happenings related in Mark 7:1-23 took place somewhere in or near Capernaum, where Jesus during his Great Galilean Ministry had his headquarters.

Here, then, in Jesus' home in Capernaum his disciples, with (as Matthew informs us) Peter as their spokesman, ask their Master for an explanation of "this parable." It is clear that the term "parable" is here used in the sense of a pithy saying, mashal, the aphorism of verse 15.

18, 19a. He said to them, Are y o u also so lacking in understanding? Do y o u not know that nothing that enters a man from the outside can defile him, since it does not enter his heart but his stomach and goes out into the latrine? Jesus seems to be saying, "That others—for example, the Pharisees and scribes, the people in general—do not grasp my teaching is not strange, but that y o u, who have associated with me for so long a period and so closely, are also so dense, that is inexcusable." Cf. John 14:9. Do The Twelve fail to realize that whatever enters a man from the outside is finally eliminated from the body? And since during its journey through the body it enters man's stomach but never his heart, the very core and center of his entire being (see on 6:52), how then can it render the man unclean, polluted, or defiled?

19b. Mark adds his own observation to the words of Jesus. It is the inspired evangelist's interpretation of the significance of Jesus' saying regarding ceremonial versus real defilement: **Thus he pronounced all foods clean.**

Actually the original says no more than: "declaring—or: making, pronouncing—clean all the foods." [325] The question is, Who or what is it that makes or pronounces the foods "clean"? As some see it, it is the latrine or "privy" that does this. [326] Reasons for accepting the view of most commentators, namely, that what Mark means is that it was Jesus who, by the principle which he laid down in verse 15, made all foods clean, are the following:

---

[325] With βρώματα cf. *ambrosia:* the imagined food of the Greek and Roman gods; also *ambrosial:* delicious.

[326] See Lenski *op. cit.,* pp. 188, 189. But Swete, *op. cit.,* p. 152, correctly remarks that such a view scarcely calls for consideration.

a. How a privy can make or declare all foods clean is very, very difficult to understand.

b. The last time Mark mentioned Jesus by name was in 6:30, but by means of a pronoun, either independent or implied in a verbal form, he made reference to Jesus again and again afterward (6:31, 34, 35, 37, etc., and so again in ch. 7:1, 5, 6, 9, 14, 17, 18). Is it not natural to assume that the reference also in 19b is to Jesus?

c. If the widely held opinion that Mark was "Peter's interpreter" (see *Introduction,* I) is correct, then we may assume that Peter's own experience recorded in Acts 10:9-16 and 11:1-18 (the vision of the great sheet holding all kinds of unclean creatures) was included in his preaching and was by him brought into relation with Jesus' saying as recorded in Mark 7:15. Peter's conclusion, we may well believe, was the one which Mark remembered, accepted as his own belief, and reported in Mark 7:19b. Do we not find an echo of "Thus he [Jesus] pronounced all foods clean" in Acts 10:15 (cf. 11:9), "What God has cleansed you must not call common [or: unclean]"?

d. If the One who pronounced all foods clean is Jesus, then the logic is clear, for in Mark 7:15 it is he who declares that whatever enters a man from the outside is undefiling. Hence, all foods, also meat from ceremonially "unclean" animals, is in principle undefiling. Interpreters may differ on the question exactly when, according to God's will, the abolition of the ceremonial laws regarding clean and unclean went into effect. Did it take place right now, at the very moment when Jesus spoke these words? Did it occur when Jesus was crucified? See Col. 2:14. On the day of Pentecost? Whatever be the answer, it remains true that *in principle* all foods were pronounced clean here and now.

Having made clear what is *not* defiling, Jesus again (cf. verse 15b above) stated what actually defiles a person. Only, this time he combines all the separate defiling items of verses 15b, 21-23 into one contaminating lump, as **20. He continued, What comes out of a man, it is that which defiles a man.** He enlarges on this by adding: **21, 22. For it is from inside, from men's hearts that the evil schemes arise: sexual sins, thefts, murders, adulteries, covetings, malicious acts, deceit, lewdness, envy, abusive speech, arrogance, folly.**

After what has been said about *the heart* in connection with 6:52, it is not strange that Jesus describes it here as the source of men's feelings, aspirations, thoughts, and actions; in the present connection, of all his real moral and spiritual defilements.

In the New Testament the terms [327] which, according to Mark, were at

---

327 By means of English cognates the meaning of most of the Greek originals can be immediately approximated. However, diligent exegesis—including in each case study of

this time used by Jesus, in describing man's defiling vices, are distributed as shown in the chart on pp. 284, 285.

A detailed item-by-item grouping is impossible to detect. In this respect the parallel passage Matt. 15:19 is different. There after the introductory designation "wicked schemes," and thus beginning with "murders," the arrangement more or less follows the sequence of the second table of the Decalog. But here (Mark 7:21, 22) all we can safely say is that, after what may be regarded as the caption—"the evil schemes," "designs," or "devisings" [329] —the first 6 of the 12 items are in the plural, the second 6 retain the singular. The first 6 describe wicked actions; the second 6 the evil drives and words that are related to such and similar actions.

Other lists of vices may be found in Rom. 1:18-32; 13:13; I Cor. 5:9-11; 6:9, 10; II Cor. 12:20; Gal. 5:19-21; Eph. 4:19; 5:3-5; Col. 3:5-9; I Thess. 2:3; 4:3-7; I Tim. 1:9, 10; 6:4, 5; II Tim. 3:2-5; Titus 3:3, 9, 10; I Peter 4:3; Rev. 21:8, 22:15.

To say that Mark's list is Pauline because 8 of the 12 items are also found in Paul's epistles (see chart) is going too far. Would it not be rather surprising if in Paul's more than a dozen lists of vices most of the items mentioned here in Mark 7:21, 22 were not included? Besides lists of vices were popular in those days and even earlier. An apocryphal book *The Wisdom of Solomon* 14:25 f. includes items 2, 3, 4, 7, and 8 of the list found in Mark 7:21, 22. The Dead Sea Scrolls also have such lists. [330] And the list of 12 items ascribed to Christ does not bear close resemblance to any single list found in Paul's (or Peter's, etc.) writings. It must have been Christ's own list, reproduced by Mark and abbreviated by Matthew.

---

context and of parallel passages—is needed to discover the exact connotation of each term. Study of cognates and of word derivations is useful. It is, however, not the most important. For example, $\beta\lambda\alpha\sigma\phi\eta\mu\iota\alpha$ suggests *blasphemy;* nevertheless, there are many cases in which "blasphemy" would be the wrong translation of the Greek word. With that warning in mind note the following:

$\delta\iota\alpha\lambda\sigma\gamma\iota\sigma\mu\delta\varsigma$	dialogue
$\kappa\alpha\kappa\delta\varsigma$	cacophony (bad, harsh sound)
$\pi\sigma\rho\nu\epsilon\iota\alpha$	pornography (pictures arousing sexual desire)
$\kappa\lambda\sigma\pi\dot{\eta}$	kleptomaniac (persistent thief)
$\phi\delta\nu\sigma\varsigma$	baneful (deadly, murderous)
$\pi\sigma\nu\eta\rho\iota\alpha$	actions that reveal moral-spiritual penury
$\delta\phi\theta\alpha\lambda\mu\delta\varsigma$	ophthalmologist (eye-doctor)
$\beta\lambda\alpha\sigma\phi\eta\mu\iota\alpha$	blasphemy
$\dot{\alpha}\phi\rho\sigma\sigma\dot{\nu}\nu\eta$	without the organs near the dia*phragm*; hence, without heart (and mind), foolish.

Other words, too, are easy to analyze; e.g., $\pi\lambda\epsilon\sigma\nu\epsilon\xi\iota\alpha$ the sinful desire always *to have more and still more;* $\dot{\nu}\pi\epsilon\rho\eta\phi\alpha\nu\iota\alpha$ *fancying* oneself *above* ($\dot{\nu}\pi\epsilon\rho$) others.

329 $\sigma\iota\ \delta\iota\alpha\lambda\sigma\gamma\iota\sigma\mu\sigma\iota\ \sigma\iota\ \kappa\alpha\kappa\sigma\iota$ = "the (or: those) schemes, the evil (or: bad) ones."
330 See M. Burrows, *The Dead Sea Scrolls*, New York, 1956, pp. 375, 386, 387.

N. T. Terms Used in Mark 7:21, 22

TERM	Mark	Matt.	Luke	John	Acts	Rom.	I Cor.	II Cor.	G
οἱ διαλογισμοί οἱ κακοί	7:21	cf. 15:19							
1. πορνεῖαι	7:21	5:32; 15:19; 19:9		8:41	15:20, 29; 21:25		5:1(2) 6:13, 18; 7:2	12:21	5
2. κλοπαί	7:21	15:19							
3. φόνοι	7:21; 15:7	15:19	23:19, 25		9:1	1:29			
4. μοιχεῖαι	7:22	15:19		8:3[328]					
5. πλεονεξίαι	7:22		12:15			1:29		9:5	
6. πονηρίαι	7:22	22:18	11:39		3:26	1:29	5:8		
7. δόλος	7:22; 14:1	26:4		1:47	13:10	1:29		12:16	
8. ἀσέλγεια	7:22					13:13		12:21	5
9. ὀφθαλμὸς πονηρός	7:22	cf. 20:15							
10. βλασφημία	3:28; 7:22; 14:64	12:31(2) 15:19; 26:65	5:21	10:33					
11. ὑπερηφανία	7:22								
12. ἀφροσύνη	7:22							11:1, 17, 21	

[328] On John 8:3 (μοιχεία) see N.T.C. on John, Vol. II, pp. 33-36.

Eph.	Col.	I Thess.	I Tim.	Heb.	I Peter	II Peter	Jude	Rev.	TERM
									the evil schemes or wicked designs
5:3	3:5	4:3						2:21;9:21; 14:8;17:2, 4; 18:3; 19:2	1. sexual sins or immoral acts
								cf. 9:21	2. thefts
				11:37				9:21	3. murders
									4. adulteries
4:19; 5:3	3:5	2:5				2:3, 14			5. covetings
6:12									6. malicious acts
		2:3		2:1, 22; 3:10					7. deceit
4:19					4:3	2:2, 7, 18	4		8. lewdness
									9. envy; literally: a sinister eye
4:31	3:8		6:4				9	2:9; 13:1, 5, 17:3	10. abusive speech or slander
									11. arrogance
									12. folly

As to the separate items note the following:

The introductory term "the evil schemes," "designs," or "devisings" is literally "those bad dialogizings." In his own mind a person frequently carries on a dialogue. See Ps. 14:1; 39:1; 116:11; Dan. 5:29, 30; Obad. 3; Mark 2:6, 7; 5:28; Luke 12:17 f.; 15:17-19; 16:3, 4; Rev. 18:7. In three of these instances of talking to oneself—namely, Ps. 39:1; Mark 5:28; Luke 15:17-19, such a "dialogue" or "deliberation" can be described as being good. One—Luke 16:3, 4—is half good, half bad, as the context shows. All the rest are wicked. This holds also in such cases where the very word "dialogue" or "dialogizing" is used. In nearly every instance—Luke 2:35 is a possible exception—the deliberations, inner reasonings, or devisings are of a definitely sinful nature. In addition to Matt. 15:19; Mark 7:2, see Luke 5:22; 6:8; 9:46, 47; 24:38; Rom. 1:21; 14:1; I Cor. 3:20; Phil. 2:14; I Tim. 2:8; James 2:4. Nevertheless what a person says within his heart is tremendously important, probably often even more important than what he says audibly (Prov. 23:7).

One of the reasons why such dialogizings are so important is that they give rise to actions and stimulate inner drives. They also reveal themselves in spoken words. These several items are now enumerated by means of examples: 6 plurals are followed by 6 singulars; 6 kinds of actions are followed by 6 items that represent drives (or states) of the heart (see Nos. 7, 8, 9, 11, 12 on the chart) and speech (No. 10). In the present context, which pictures Jesus in the act of describing what it is that defiles or pollutes a person, all the twelve items are naturally of an evil nature.

The first six are as follows:

Sexual sins or immoral acts. In its widest sense the term here used indicates sexual sin in general, illicit sexual behavior of any description, whether within or outside of the marriage bond, often but not always the latter. In Matt. 5:32; 19:9 the reference is to marital infidelity. In John 8:41 unlawful sexual intercourse is indicated. In Acts 15:20, 29; 21:25 there may be a special reference to marriage within the forbidden degrees of affinity or consanguinity. See Lev. 18:6 f. Paul uses the word frequently (see the chart). It covers a wide range of sinful sexual actions.

Today, too, attention should be called to this broad belt of misbehavior. We need only mention such things as rape, the showing and/or reading of pornographic literature, pre-marital sexual intercourse, telling or eagerly listening to off-color jokes, etc.

Theft. Though, as the chart shows, in the New Testament this term occurs but seldom, the sin itself is referred to rather frequently. See N.T.C. on Eph. 4:28; Titus 2:9, 10; Philem. 18-20. Many slaves were in the habit of stealing. Even after their conversion they had to be warned against falling back into their evil ways.

Today should not warnings be issued against shoplifting? Against loafing on the job? Squandering what God has given us? Intentional withholding from Caesar the things that are Caesar's? And when a government or one of its agencies plays fast and loose with the tax-payer's money, is that not also a form of stealing? And what about withholding from God the things that are God's?

Murders. Just why it is that murders are mentioned here in connection with the two preceding items we do not know. There may be a reason for this. Are not murders often committed at the very scene where the immoral act or the theft is occurring?

We are horrified by Herod's murder of Bethlehem's infants. Does not the present-day wholesale murder of infants that are still inside the womb (abortion) cry to heaven for vengeance? Can this in any way be harmonized with Scripture? Read Exod. 20:13; Lev. 18:21; 20:2 f.; II Kings 23:10; Jer. 32:35; Ezek. 16:21; Amos 1:13; Matt. 7:12; Eph. 4:32; 5:1, 2.

Adulteries. This is the violation of the marriage bond: a married man's voluntary sexual intercourse with someone other than his wife; or a married woman's voluntary sexual intercourse with someone other than her husband.

It should be made clear, however, that Jesus sharpened the edge of every commandment. He taught that hatred is murder (Matt. 5:21, 22), and that a married man's lustful look at another woman is adultery (Matt. 5:28).

It has been said that one of the reasons for the downfall of the Roman Empire was that women married in order to get divorced, and got divorced in order to get married. What of conditions today?

Covetings. Though we do not know the reason for the sequence adulteries . . . covetings, yet if there was intended to be a connection we might think first of all of the ravenous self-assertion in matters of sex, at the expense of others: "You shall not covet your neighbor's . . . wife." But Exod. 20:17 and Mark 7:22 are broad enough to include *every form* of avarice. Cf. Luke 12:15.

When the elders of Israel sinfully asked for a king, they were told that this king would take . . . take . . . take . . . take . . . take . . . take (I Sam. 8:11-17). God, in Christ, gives and gives and gives again, without end (John 1:16; 3:16; 5:26; 17:22; Rom. 8:32; Gal. 1:4; 2:20; Eph. 1:22, 5:25; I Tim. 2:6; Titus 2:14; I John 5:10; etc.). His true followers are not avaricious or greedy. See II Cor. 8:8, 9.

Malicious acts. This could well be a summing up of all manifestations of wickedness, both those already mentioned and all others besides.

The remaining six are:

Deceit. This is the first of the sinful qualities or drives that are here mentioned. With such wicked propensities of the human nature the deeds that have already been enumerated are closely connected.

287

Where Mark says *deceit,* Matthew mentions *false testimonies.* It was by deceit that the leaders of the Jews planned to bring about Christ's death (Mark 14:1). According to II Cor. 12:16 Paul's enemies accused the apostle of deceit. Did they insinuate that the apostle was going to take for himself some of the money that had been donated for the poor in Jerusalem? Of course, this was the farthest from Paul's thoughts. Cf. I Thess. 2:3. That deceit is very common is clear from John 1:47. A beautiful passage is I Peter 3:10.

Lewdness. Other ways of designating the same sinful drive: lasciviousness, licentiousness. By means of the chart note the many references to this sinful propensity of the human nature. The term stresses the lack of self-control that characterizes the person who gives free play to his perverse impulses. It has been remarked that it was not lava but lewdness that buried Herculaneum. And the frescoes found amid the ruins of nearby Pompeii show that this city was not much better.

Envy. The true parallel is not Matt. 6:23 but Matt. 20:15: "Is your eye evil . . . ?" means "Are you envious because I am generous?" Whenever jealousy and envy can be distinguished, jealousy is the fear of losing what one has, envy is the displeasure of seeing someone else have something.

One of the most soul-destroying vices is envy. Is it not "the eldest born of hell"? "Rottenness of the bones"? (Prov. 14:30). Our English word *envy* comes from the Latin *in-video,* meaning "to look against," that is, to look with ill-will at another person because of what he is or has. It is interesting to note that the Greek original which is found here in Mark 7:22 expresses this idea literally, for its basic meaning is "a sinister eye," an eye that views another person with fierce and grudging displeasure.

It was envy that caused the murder of Abel, threw Joseph into a pit, caused Korah, Dathan, and Abiram to rebel against Moses and Aaron, made Saul pursue David, gave rise to the bitter words which the "elder brother" (in the parable of The Prodigal Son) addressed to his father, and crucified Christ. *Love* never envies.

From a sinful drive or quality the text now turns to the wicked work of the tongue:

Abusive Speech or Slander. The word used in the original is *blasphemy.* But see above, on 3:28. In the present connection, since the term occurs here in Mark 7:22 between "envy" and "arrogance," it probably has reference to defamation of character, railing, slander, scornful and insolent language directed against another person, whether it be addressed to him directly or spoken behind his back.

> Sometimes life is filled with troubles
> Oft its burdens are severe,

Do not make it any harder
By a careless word or sneer.
Button up your lips securely,
'Gainst the words that bring a tear,
But be swift with words of comfort,
Words of praise and words of cheer. Effie Wells Loucks

Arrogance. The evil tendency of fancying oneself better, abler, or greater than someone else is a universal trait of the human heart as it is by nature. The rulers of the Gentiles in any age make themselves guilty of this sin (Matt. 20:25; Luke 22:25). Note the arrogant language of one of them, as reproduced in Isa. 14:13, 14. Read also Isa. 37:8-13. But the scribes and Pharisees were bitten by the same bug (Matt. 23:5-12; Mark 12:38, 39; and read especially Luke 18:11, 12). And even the disciples had to fight this sin (Matt. 18:1-6; 20:20-27; Mark 10:35-44; Luke 9:46-48.) Over against all this, note the words of Jesus (Matt. 20:28; Mark 10:45; Luke 22:27; John 13:14, 15).

Folly is the term that probably sums up the preceding five drives and words, just as "malicious acts" summed up the deeds. Cf. Matt. 25:2.

Jesus closes this section by saying, **23. All these evil things proceed from inside and defile a man.** In view of the biblical conception of the term *heart* (see above, on 6:52), it is easy to see that if the vices mentioned in Mark 7:21, 22 proceed from man's heart, they will indeed pollute his entire intellectual, emotional, and volitional life. What people should do, therefore, is pray for a new, *a transformed heart,* and not pay so much attention to *unrinsed hands.* Real defilement is moral and spiritual, not physical.

David phrased it beautifully:

Create for me a clean heart, O God;
And a firm spirit renew thou within me.

Summary of Chapter 7:1-23

See also N.T.C. on Matthew, p. 619. So far Mark has described five confrontations between Jesus and the leaders. The latter have accused him of assuming divine prerogatives (2:7), closely associating with "bad" people (2:16), allowing his disciples to desecrate the sabbath (2:24), not keeping the sabbath himself (3:2, 6), and casting out demons by the prince of the demons (3:22).

The present (sixth) confrontation centers around the basic question, "Human tradition or Word of God, by which should doctrine and life be regulated?"

The occasion was the arrival—probably in Galilee (Capernaum?)—of Jerusalemites: Pharisees and scribes. They had come to spy on Jesus. They asked him, "Why don't your disciples live in accordance with the tradition of the elders but eat with defiled hands?" He answered, "Y o u let go the commandment of God in order to cling to the tradition of men." He proved this by showing how they discouraged obedience to the fifth commandment. To the people in general and afterward to his disciples he explained that real defilement does not arise from the outside but from inside men's hearts.

Outline of Chapter 7:24-37

Theme: *The Work Which Thou Gavest Him To Do*

B. The Retirement Plus Perean Ministries

7:24-30 The Faith of a Syrophoenician Woman Rewarded
7:31-37 A Deaf and Dumb Man Healed

CHAPTER VII: 24-37

24 From there he arose and went [331] to the region of Tyre. He entered a house and did not want anyone to know it, but could not escape notice.   25 In fact, as soon as she heard about him, a woman whose little daughter was possessed by an unclean spirit came and fell at his feet.   26 Now the woman was a Greek, a Syrophoenician by nationality. And she kept asking him to cast the demon out of her daughter.   27 He said to her, "First let the children eat all they want, for it is not proper to take the children's bread and toss it to the house dogs."   28 Answering she said to him "Lord, [332] even the house dogs under the table eat some of the children's scraps." 29 Then he said to her, "Because of this statement of yours, go your way; the demon has left your daughter."   30 And she went home, and found the child lying in bed and the demon gone.

7:24-30 *The Faith of a Syrophoenician Woman Rewarded*
Cf. Matt. 15:21-28

The theme of the Synoptics, including Mark, we may conceive to be *The Work Which Thou Gavest Him To Do.* The first division under this theme is *Its Beginning or Inauguration* (Mark 1:1-13). The second is *Its Progress or Continuation* (1:14—10:52). The first subdivision of this second part, namely, *The Great Galilean Ministry* (1:14–7:23), has now been completed. The second subdivision, *The Retirement plus Perean Ministries,* begins at this point (7:24) and continues through 10:52. Reasons for this kind of outline, as also a brief description of the main contents of each division and subdivision, can be found on pp. 8-10 of N.T.C. on Matthew. *Tentative* dates (certainty is impossible) are as follows: Retirement Ministry A.D. 29, April to October; Perean Ministry A.D. 29, December, to A.D. 30, April. For the intervening Later Judean Ministry, October to December, see especially the Gospel according to John (7:2—10:39).

Mark 7:24 to the end of the ninth chapter covers events that occurred during *The Retirement Ministry.* The shift to this ministry from the one that preceded it is not abrupt and radical but rather a matter of emphasis. For

---

331 Or: He left that place and went, etc.
332 According to another reading: "Right, Lord" or "Yes, Lord." Cf. Matt. 15:27.

example, during the lengthy period which to a large extent Jesus spent in Capernaum and vicinity (Mark 1:14–7:23) he was often surrounded by crowds. Now too (7:24–9:50) he does not escape those multitudes (8:1; 9:14). At times he even invites the throngs to come to him (8:34). But there is a difference in emphasis: generally he is now seen in the presence not of crowds but of his disciples. He is *teaching* them (8:1, 14-21, 27-33; 9:28, 29, 31-50). He fully realizes that the cross cannot be far away. Accordingly, he is expounding to The Twelve the lessons of the cross (8:31; 9:31). This continues even into the Perean Ministry (10:33, 34). In order to be able to impart this important information effectively Jesus is seeking places of seclusion, apart from the busy centers. A considerable amount of time is spent in predominantly Gentile territory.

If allowance is made for areas of relative uncertainty, the map (p. 295) showing Christ's Retirement Ministry (Mark 7:24—9:50) may be helpful. There may, however, have been trips not reported in the Gospels. Cf. John 20:30, 31; 21:25. Fourteen Marcan sections cover events that occurred during this period, in the following places:

1. The region of Tyre (7:24-30).
2, 3. Decapolis (respectively 7:31-37; 8:1-10).
4. Dalmanutha (8:11-13).
5. Sea of Galilee between Dalmanutha and Bethsaida (8:14-21).
6. Bethsaida (8:22-26).
7, 8. Caesarea Philippi (respectively 8:27-30; 8:31—9:1).
9, 10. Mt. of Transfiguration and vicinity (respectively 9:2-13; 9:14-29).
11. Road toward Capernaum (9:30-32).
12, 13, 14. Capernaum (respectively 9:33-37; 9:38-41; 9:42-50).

Mark 7:24-30 and Matt. 15:21-28 tell essentially the same story. Also, the space devoted to it is about the same, Mark's account being shorter by only a few words. In both accounts Jesus has left the place where he had been staying—presumably Capernaum—and has reached the vicinity of Tyre. Here a non-Jewish woman of that district appeals to him for help because her daughter is demon-possessed. The child's mother is very persistent in her pleas. Jesus does not immediately grant her wish. He tells her, "It is not proper to take the children's bread and toss it to the house dogs." She answers, "But even the house dogs eat some of the children's scraps." Jesus praises her faith and grants her wish.

To this story each of these two evangelists makes his own specific contribution. Nowhere is there any conflict. Each uses his own style and reports the happening so as to suit the needs of his own readers. Matthew

THE RETIREMENT MINISTRY
Begin at Capernaum and follow the arrows

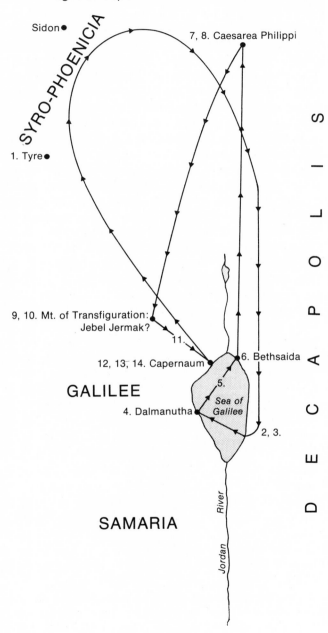

calls the woman a Canaanite. The Jews who read Matthew's Gospel had heard much about these wicked people (Gen. 12:6; 13:7; 38:2; and see especially Josh. 9:1 f.; 11:3 f.). They had caused a great deal of trouble in the days of Joshua and even later. What? Was there salvation also for *them?* Matthew's account is somewhat more dramatic than that of Mark. The woman addresses Jesus as "Lord, Son of David," and asks him to "take pity" on her. Though from the very beginning she identifies her sorrow with that of her daughter—"Take pity on *me, my daughter . . .*"—that process of identification increases in intensity, reaching its climax when the mother drops all mention of her daughter, and simply blurts out, "Help *me.*" According to Matthew, the woman addresses Jesus three separate times, and also in each case that evangelist reproduces her very words by means of direct discourse. Mark reproduces only two of her lines, and only once by means of direct discourse. Matthew introduces the disciples. Characteristically they ask Jesus to get rid of the woman. Mark in his account never mentions the disciples. Matthew states that at first Jesus did not answer the petitioner and that afterward he said to her, "Only to the lost sheep of the house of Israel was I sent." In view of the people to whom Mark is writing it does not surprise us that Mark does not contain that item.

Mark makes his own very valuable contribution. Though he was not himself an apostle, he had probably heard Peter tell the story. To show how "famous" Jesus had become by now, Mark reports that although, having arrived in the region of Tyre, the Master entered a house and sought seclusion, "he could not escape notice." Mark also reports that the woman was a Greek, that is, a born Gentile, a person with a pagan background, and a Syrophoenician by race or nationality. These little touches must have been appreciated by the Gentile readers for whom Mark wrote his Gospel. This evangelist also shows even more clearly than does Matthew that when Jesus compared the woman's situation with that of house dogs, he was not completely shutting the door of hope. He was definitely leaving it ajar (see on verse 27a). Mark, differing also in this respect from Matthew, even relates what happened after the mother returned to her home: she found the child resting calmly in bed, the demon having left.

24. **From there he arose and went to the region of Tyre.** Also possible is, "He left that place and went to [or: into] the region of Tyre." [333] The difference is minor.

---

[333] Justification for this alternative is the fact that ἀναστάς may in this case be a redundant participle. See Vincent Taylor, *op. cit.*, pp. 183, 348. As he sees it, 1:35 and 2:14 belong to the same class. This is debatable, for in these two cases the person indicated by the participle had been lying down (1:35) or sitting (2:14), so that it would be natural for him to arise. In 7:24 this may also be true. Jesus may have been sitting down teaching, a possibility which, in view of verse 17 is not remote, especially if there

This is the Tyre whose kings in bygone days had formed an alliance with David and Solomon. It furnished timber and skilled artisans for Israel, while the latter shipped to Hiram and later rulers the grain needed by Tyre's people (I Kings 5; Acts 12:20). It was the Tyre that had introduced Baal worship into Israel. It was an island stronghold just off the Mediterranean coast. See Isa. 23: Ezek. 26-28. It was situated south of Sidon and north of Carmel. Alexander the Great took it by building a stronghold to it.

It had been predicted that the people of Tyre and vicinity would one day share the blessings of the Messianic age (Ps. 87:4). That prophecy was beginning to be fulfilled when people of these surroundings traveled to Galilee to hear Jesus and to be healed of their illnesses (Matt. 4:24, 25; Luke 6:17). This time it is Jesus who is coming to them.

He entered a house and did not want anyone to know it, but could not escape notice. Did Jesus' coming have a missionary purpose? Commentators have arrived at different conclusions:

a. Mission work at this place and time was farthest from his mind. Herod Antipas was ill-disposed toward Jesus (Mark 6:14, 16; cf. Luke 13:31). The Jewish leaders were plotting his death. Many people had left him. The Twelve were in need of instruction. Rest and relaxation is what he needs. So he enters a house. Of a friend? No, more likely, of a stranger in the hope of getting some uninterrupted leisure for confidential intercourse with The Twelve. [334]

b. Jesus went in a northwestern direction into the borders of Phoenicia because he was looking for "a more fruitful field of labor." [335]

c. It is useless to speculate. [336]

d. Jesus endeavored to remain concealed *for a time*. [337]

There may well be some truth in all of these answers. As to a., it has already been shown that the purpose—at least one of the purposes—of the Retirement Ministry was indeed to teach The Twelve, to prepare them for what was coming: his death by crucifixion, his resurrection. As to b., it is hard for us to conceive of the compassionate Christ traveling all the way to Phoenicia without any plan to be a blessing to its population. As to c., it is indeed true that a full and definite answer has not been given. And as to d., Calvin may well have a point. It is probable that Jesus' desire to be alone

---

was a close chronological connection between the preceding paragraph and 7:24 f. But since this point cannot be established, it is probably best here to allow for either translation.

[334] See A. B. Bruce, *op. cit.*, p. 390.

[335] J. W. Russel, ed. *Teacher's New Testament with Notes and Helps*, Grand Rapids, 1959, p. 102.

[336] M. H. Bolkestein, *op. cit.*, p. 158.

[337] John Calvin, *Harmony*, Vol. II, p. 262.

with his disciples was only "for the time being," to be followed—cf. b.—by missionary activity (see verses 34-38).

"But he could not be hid" (A.V.). Many sermons have been preached on this passage. It has been pointed out, for example, that when Jesus has once entered a man's heart, this fact will soon reveal itself in the man's words, actions, and attitudes. Or: every attempt to relegate Christ to the background is bound to fail. One generation may forget all about him, but the next will rediscover him, etc.

Though, to be sure, there is some value in all this, such thoughts have very little to do with the passage in its present context. For the present all that is necessary is to point out that due to the fact that some—perhaps many—of the Phoenicians had already had contact with Jesus and/or had heard about him, it was impossible for him to remain concealed for any great length of time. Hence, this period of rest and concealment soon came to an end. He himself, because of his great love for sinners, allowed the "discovery" to take place. There was a repetition here of 6:34.

25, 26. In fact, as soon as she heard about him, a woman whose little daughter was possessed by an unclean spirit came and fell at his feet. Now the woman was a Greek, a Syrophoenician by nationality. And she kept asking him to cast the demon out of her daughter.

A woman appears upon the scene. Not a word is said about a husband. Was this woman a widow perhaps, and does the scene remind us of a miracle performed centuries earlier, in this same general territory, a miracle that gladdened the heart of another widow (I Kings 17)? However that may be, fact is that one of the qualities that comes to the fore again and again in the Gospels is Christ's kindness toward women, certainly also including widows (Mark 12:4-44; cf. Luke 21:1-4; see also Luke 7:11-18; cf. Ps. 146:9; Prov. 15:25; Isa. 1:17).

Now this woman was oppressed with a very deep sorrow. She had a daughter [338] —Mark tenderly says "a little daughter" [339] —who was very, very dear to her. But this child was demon-possessed. Demon possession has been discussed earlier: see on 1:23; also N.T.C. on Matthew, pp. 436-438.

Was there hope for *this* woman and for *her* child? Was not the door of hope closed for this mother because of her race? She was a Greek, that is a born Gentile, a woman with a pagan background, a Syrophoenician, that is, a native of Phoenicia with its main cities of Tyre and Sidon, called Syrophoenicia because it belonged to the province of Syria, and to distinguish it from the Libyan Phoenicia on the coast of North Africa.

She came—came *at once*—and fell at his feet. This act of prostration was a

---

338 Note ἧς . . . αὐτῆς, perfectly natural in vivid, conversational style, *Mark's* style.
339 On diminutives see Introduction IV, footnote 5h; see also on 3:9, footnote 108.

revelation of her humility, reverence, submissiveness, and anxiety. Cf. 5:22. She asked, yes asked again and again, pleading with Jesus to rid her dear child of the demon, the unclean spirit.

27. He said to her, First let the children eat all they want, for it is not proper to take the children's bread and toss it to the house dogs. In the plan of God it had been decided that the blessings centering in Christ were to be offered first to "the children," that is, to the Jews. The opportunity to be fully satisfied with this food [340] would first be extended to them, later to the Gentiles. Cf. Matt. 22:1-10; Acts 13:44-48; 18:6; Rom. 1:17. That was *the rule.* Any wholesale departure from this rule would amount to taking the children's bread and tossing it to the house dogs. Surely, dogs—even pet dogs—cannot expect to be treated like children. The woman needs to know this, in order that she may understand that if her wish is going to be granted, it will be by way of exception, and thus a very great privilege indeed.

Was this rule rigid, no exceptions being allowed, or was it flexible? That was the question. If rigid, and to be literally enforced with respect to all those who did not owe their physical descent to Abraham, then "out—out are the lights—out all" (with apologies to E. A. Poe), and this woman might as well go home. Tossing the children's bread to the doggies would in that case not only be highly improper, unbecoming, it would be impossible.

Note, however, that Jesus is already slightly opening the door. By saying "*First* let the children eat all they want," he is at least telling this sorrow-filled woman that God did not completely lose sight of the Gentiles. She might well begin to reason: "If blessings are in store for the Gentiles *tomorrow,* why not already *today* . . . even if it be by way of exception?"

Her God-given faith was strong enough to realize that Jesus was not turning her away. Overpowered by his love and tenderness, a compassionate attitude which even his apparent sternness was unable to hide, **28. Answering she said to him, Lord, even the house dogs under the table eat some of the children's scraps.** Jesus by referring to house dogs had given this woman a finger. She took the whole hand. She turned the word of seeming reproach, house dogs, [341] into a reason for optimism, thereby transforming an impending defeat into a brilliant victory. She is saying, as it were, "Am I being compared with a house dog? I accept what is implied in this comparison. I not only accept it, I rejoice because of it, for certainly under the table these dogs eat some of the children's scraps."

---

340 On the verb $\chi o\rho\tau\acute{a}\zeta\omega$ (here aor. infin. passive $\chi o\rho\tau a\sigma\theta\tilde{\eta}\nu a\iota$) see 6:42, footnote 285.

341 $\tau\grave{a}$ $\kappa\upsilon\nu\acute{a}\rho\iota a$. The view that *in the New Testament* a $\kappa\acute{\upsilon}\omega\nu$ is the same as a $\kappa\upsilon\nu\acute{a}\rho\iota o\nu$ must be rejected. Note the contexts in which consistently the word $\kappa\acute{\upsilon}\omega\nu$ is used (Matt. 7:6; Luke 16:21; Phil. 3:2; II Peter 2:22; Rev. 22:15). Contrast Matt. 15:26, 27; Mark 7:27, 28.

The position of some, namely, that Jesus' mission while on earth was limited *entirely and without any exception* to the Jewish nation, is not supported by the evidence. True is what Calvin says, "At no time, certainly, did God shut up his grace among the Jews in such a manner as not to bestow a small taste of it on the Gentiles." [342]

If the principle announced by Jesus in Matt. 15:24, 26; Mark 7:27 did not allow for any exceptions, if that rule were not flexible, then how would it have been possible for Jesus to say to the non-Jewish centurion, "Go home; as you believed, so let it be done for you," and to the people who were present at that occasion, "Many, I tell y o u, shall come from east and west and recline at table with Abraham, Isaac, and Jacob, in the kingdom of heaven, but the sons of the kingdom shall be cast out into the most distant darkness"? (Matt. 8:10-12). Again, how could he have said, "I tell y o u in truth, there were many widows in the days of Elijah, when the sky was shut up for three years and six months . . . yet Elijah was sent to none of them, but only to Zarephath, in the region of Sidon, to a widow. And there were many lepers in Israel in the time of Elisha the prophet, yet none of them was cleansed but only Naaman the Syrian"? (Luke 4:25-27). How, a little later, would it have been possible for him to say, "I also have other sheep which do not belong to this fold; them also I must lead, and they will listen to my voice, and become one flock, one shepherd"? (John 10:16). Again, how could Jesus have granted the request of this Syrophoenician woman? And finally, how could he, after his departure from Tyre, have brought healing to multitudes, many of whom were Gentiles, as Matt. 15:31 implies?

Not even during the old dispensation were God's special blessings ever *absolutely* limited to the Jews. To a large extent, yes. This must be fully maintained. See Ps. 147:20; Isa. 5:4; Amos 3:2. But in a totally unrestricted sense? Definitely not (Luke 4:25-27).

That, on an increasing scale, with the coming of Christ the blessings granted to Israel were destined to reach the Gentiles was certainly known to Jesus. For the prophecies and, in certain cases, their explicit fulfilments, see Gen. 17:5 (cf. Rom. 4:17); 22:18; 26:4; 28:14; Ps. 72:8-10; Isa. 11:10 (cf. Rom. 15:12); 28:16 (cf. Rom. 10:11); 54:1-3 (cf. Gal. 4:27); 60:1-3; 65:1; and Hos. 2:23 (for both cf. Rom. 9:24, 25); Joel 2:32 (cf. Rom. 10:12, 13); Amos 9:11, 12 (cf. Acts 15:15-18); Mic. 4:1-3; Mal. 1:11.

We usually refer to Pentecost as the day when, in connection with the outpouring of the Spirit upon all flesh, the church became international. That is correct. Nevertheless, that great event was foreshadowed already during the old dispensation and certainly on a somewhat more expanded scale during Jesus' ministry upon earth, including even the period before the

---

[342] *Harmony*, Vol. II, p. 268.

crucifixion. There must have been several blessed exceptions to the rule of Matt. 15:24, 26; Mark 7:27.

Now we can also understand that Jesus fully approved of the woman's perseverance in the three Christian graces of faith, hope, and love: faith in him as the One whose "love is broader than the measure of man's mind," hope in him as the One who was not about to disappoint her, and love for him who by the very fact of his refusal to turn her away had already indicated that though she loved him, he had first loved her.

29. Then he said to her, Because of this statement [or: word] of yours, go your way; the demon has left your daughter. When Jesus said, "Because of this statement of yours," he meant far more than "Because what you just said (verse 28) showed how clever, how quick witted you are." Basically he was praising her for her *faith,* the basic virtue that had expressed itself most gloriously in her hope, steadfast and firmly anchored, and in her love, pure and warm.

It is true that according to Matthew, Jesus said, "O woman, great is your *faith*," whereas in Mark he is represented as praising her for her *statement,* her *word.* However, since by means of this *word* she revealed her *faith* there is no essential difference.

She revealed her faith in still another way, namely, by going home. Had it not been for the fact that she believed that Jesus had healed her daughter— yes, healed her without ever seeing her, from a distance bringing about a complete recovery; cf. Matt. 8:5-13 (Luke 7:1-10); John 4:46-54—, she would not have hurried home.

Nor was she disappointed: **30. And she went home, and found the child lying in bed and the demon gone.** Calmly the little one is resting now. There is peace on her brow and in her heart, for all is well. The demon is gone. It has been completely vanquished and will never return. [343] The mother must have been overjoyed: she had "found" a healthy child . . . and a marvelous Savior!

Two practical lessons must not escape us:

a. If today's parents loved their Lord and their children as she did, what a vast amount of harm would be prevented, and what a mountain of blessings would result!

b. If a woman born a Gentile put her little knowledge of the Lord to such good advantage, what is required of those who have received far greater privileges?

---

31 Starting out once more, he left the region of Tyre, and by way of Sidon went toward the Sea of Galilee, crossing the region of Decapolis. 32 They brought to him a man who was deaf and spoke with difficulty, and they begged him [Jesus] to place his

---

343 Note βεβλημένον and ἐξεληλυθός perfect participles.

hand on the man. 33 He took him aside by himself, away from the crowd, put his fingers into the man's ears, and after spitting touched the man's tongue. 34 Having looked up to heaven he sighed and said to him, "Ephphatha!" that is, "Be opened." 35 At once the man's ears were opened, his tongue was released, [344] and he started to speak distinctly. 36 He [Jesus] charged them to tell no one. However, the more he kept on charging them, the more widely they kept on publishing it. 37 The people were astonished beyond all measure, and were saying, "How excellently he has done all things! Why, he even causes the deaf to hear and the speechless to speak!"

7:31-37 *A Deaf and Dumb Man Healed*
Cf. Matt. 15:29-31

31. Starting out once more, he left the region of Tyre, and by way of Sidon went toward the Sea of Galilee, crossing the region of Decapolis. How long Jesus remained in the vicinity of Tyre is not stated. Even the place to which he now wended his way is not exactly indicated. Nevertheless, the situation is not nearly as hopeless as some would have us believe. We know the following:

a. Jesus traveled via Sidon.

b. He went right through the heart of Decapolis.

c. He probably reached the Sea of Galilee or that general neighborhood. Cf. 7:31 with 8:10.

See the map on p. 295 for his possible route; also the map on p. 199 for a more detailed view of The Ten Cities.

32. They brought to him a man who was deaf and spoke with difficulty, and they begged him [Jesus] to place his hand on the man. It is clear from verses 32, 36, 37 that Jesus is surrounded by a crowd. Matt. 15:29-31 describes the many miracles he performed among these people. From all of them Mark selects just this one, which he, *he alone*, describes.

"They" brought him a man. This "they" is an impersonal plural. [345] The clause means, "A man was brought to him." Cf. "They shall drive you from men," meaning, "You shall be driven from men" (Dan. 4:32).

The man that was brought to Jesus suffered from a double handicap. First, he was deaf. [346] Secondly, he spoke with difficulty; at best, he stammered. So the people who brought him asked Jesus to lay his hand on

---

[344] Or, with A.V., "The string of his tongue was loosed."

[345] Like German *man*, Dutch *men*, French *on*, and Spanish *se*.

[346] κωφός can relate either to speech; hence *dumb* (Matt. 9:32, 33; 12:22; 15:30, 31; Luke 1:22; 11:14); or to hearing; hence *deaf* (Matt. 11:5; Mark 9:25; Luke 7:22). Since this man's speech defect is indicated by another adjective, it is clear that in the present case (Mark 7:32, 37) the meaning must be *deaf*. The reason for the ambiguity in meaning is probably due to the basic sense of the word. It is related to κόπτω. One of the meanings of that verb is *to cut off*. Cf. English chop, syncope, apocope, etc. This cutting off, blunting, or dulling, can affect either the sense of speech or of hearing.

302

the man. It is probable that in other cases of healing they had seen Jesus do this. Cf. 6:5. And that was not the last time the Master would do it. Cf. 8:23. Now placing his hand on people was fine, indeed. Did it not mean that something from him was being transferred, or at least applied, to them? See I Tim. 4:14; 5:22; II Tim. 1:6; and for a decidedly different transference see Lev. 16:21.

But these people were to discover that the Master has his own way of doing things. Thus, for example, Jairus, who made a similar request (Mark 5:23), saw the Great Physician do something else, something probably even more expressive of tender, personal love (5:41). And so it was going to be also in the present case. In dealing with people the Lord chooses his own methods. Naaman had to learn this lesson (II Kings 5:10-14). So did Jacob, much earlier (Gen. 42:36; 45:25-28). So did also Joseph and his brothers (Gen. 50:15-21). And so, later, did Paul (II Cor. 12:7-10). We should never try to tell God what methods he should use in answering our petitions . . . just where he should place his hand! His own way is always best. He loves people not only in the mass, but also individually. His heart goes out not only to a multitude (Mark 6:34) but also to a man, this particular man, whom he treats differently than he would have treated anyone else.

33, 34. He took him aside by himself, away from the crowd, put his fingers into the man's ears, and after spitting touched the man's tongue. Having looked up to heaven he sighed and said to him, Ephphatha!, that is, Be opened!

Note the six actions:

a. He took him aside by himself, away from the crowd. He probably did this so that the deaf stammerer would feel more at ease (cf. Mark 5:37; Luke 8:51) and would be able to concentrate all his attention on his Benefactor.

b. He put his fingers into the man's ears. Unless the man was a lip reader he would have been unable to hear any preliminary questions Jesus might have asked him (cf. Mark 10:51; cf. Matt. 9:28). So Jesus accords him the special treatment he, this deaf-mute, needs. What Jesus did meant, "Something will be done for your ears . . . and I will do it."

c. He spat, probably on his own finger, and with that wet finger touched the man's tongue. [347] The meaning was, "Something will be done for your tongue . . . and I will do it." In support of this interpretation see the analogous passage John 9:6 (in connection with restoration of sight). And cf. Mark 8:23.

d. He looked up to heaven, indicating that his help came from above; in other words, that in prayer he was "taking hold of" his heavenly Father. Cf. Isa. 64:7. In this connection see also Ps. 25:15; 121:1; 123:1, 2; 141:8;

---

347 See Lenski for a different view; *op. cit.*, p. 196.

145:15; John 11:41; 17:1; Acts 7:55. For different prayer postures mentioned in Scripture consult N.T.C. on I Tim. 2:8.

e. He sighed. See also on 8:12. With him, that is, with the Sympathizing Jesus, this was entirely natural. It showed that he was taking the man's condition to heart. So also Calvin on this passage. The sorrows of this man were his sorrows. Jesus never healed anyone half-heartedly. He always put everything he had into his work of mercy. See Matt. 8:17; 9:36; 14:14; 15:32; 18:27; 20:34; Mark 1:41; 6:34; Luke 7:13; 8:46; John 11:33; Heb. 4:14-16. Each of these passages should be carefully pondered.

f. He said, "Ephphatha!" This, too, was natural for him, for Aramaic was the Master's mother tongue. [348] For his non-Jewish readers Mark translates the term, informing them that this means, "Be opened." [349] It probably applied to the entire man: both ears and tongue, both reception and response.

35. **At once the man's ears were opened, his tongue was released, and he started to speak distinctly.** His ears were opened completely. This happened *at once*. He probably heard the very word *Ephphatha* as it was being spoken by the Lord. [350]

His ears were opened. [351] His tongue was released. More literally, "the bond" [352] —that is, whatever it was that hindered the tongue from functioning properly—all at once came loose, so that suddenly the former mumbler

---

[348] That the word "Ephphatha" is in fact Aramaic has of late been disputed. But for the evidence in support of the Aramaic theory see S. Morag, *"Ephphatha (Mark 7:34): Certainly Hebrew, not Aramaic?" JSS* 17 (2, 1972), pp. 198-202).

[349] διανοίχθητι sec. per. sing. aor. imperative passive of διανοίγω.

[350] Does the fact that Jesus spoke this word in Aramaic conclusively prove that this man must have been a Jew? Of course, he may have been, for even in this predominantly Gentile region there were many Jews. On the other hand, the Jews were not the only bilingual people, and non-Jews were not absolutely excluded from Christ's sympathies and activities. See above, on 5:13, footnote 194, and on 7:27, 28. That many of those healed at this time were Gentiles is clear from Matt. 15:31. See N.T.C. on that passage. But whether this particular man was Jew or Gentile is not the point of the story.

[351] ἠνοίγησαν third per. pl. aor. passive of ἀνοίγω (alternate form of ἀνοίγνυμι). In Mark the present is the only occurrence of this verb. In the rest of the New Testament it is found most often in Matthew, John, Acts, and Revelation. A few examples: opening treasures (Matt. 2:11), the heavens (3:16), the mouth (5:2; 13:35; 17:27), a door (7:7, 8; cf. 25:11; Acts 5:19; 12:10; 16:26 f.; Rev. 4:1), the eyes (Matt. 9:30; 20:33), tombs (27:52), a seal (Rev. 6:1). Note also metaphorical usage in I Cor. 16:9; II Cor. 2:12; Col. 4:3.

[352] ὁ δεσμός; cf. δέω, to bind, to tie on; cf. diadem. In the epistles the plural of this noun refers to "bonds" (A.V., A.R.V.,). That English term has about the same flexibility of meaning as does the word used in the original. It may refer to literal *shackles, chains, or fetters* (Luke 13:16; Acts 16:26; 23:29), but also to all the hardships of *imprisonment* (Acts 20:23; 23:29; 26:31; Phil. 1:7, 13, 14, 17; Col. 4:18; Philem. 10, 13). *Fetters* and *imprisonment* are so closely related that it is not always easy to decide on the best rendering. But "bonds" will do for either concept.

or stammerer was speaking distinctly, clearly. The recounting of these various vivid details shows that the story of an eye-witness (probably Peter) is being transmitted here by Mark.

36. He [Jesus] charged them to tell no one. At first this prohibition seems rather strange, and this for two reasons: *a*. Jesus is not in Judea with its bitter enemies who are determined to kill him; in fact, he is not even on the western side of the Sea of Galilee; and *b*. that being the case, would we not rather expect that the Master would have ordered the man to proclaim throughout Decapolis what great things the Lord had done for him? Was that not exactly what had happened previously in the case of another person belonging to this general region, a man sorely in need of help and then graciously and fully restored? See 5:19, 20.

To reach a fully satisfactory solution is perhaps impossible. There are, nevertheless, two considerations that may be of some help. First, after the event related in Mark 5:1-20 much time has elapsed. Not many days are left, and the enemies are now more determined than ever to bring about Jesus' death. Nevertheless, the Father's program for the Son must be carried out in full. The day of the crucifixion must not be hastened. Also, as that day draws nearer, Jesus is going to place more emphasis on the spiritual, the redemptive, import of his mission. See 10:45; 14:24. He did not come into this world to be the Thaumaturgist (Miracle Worker) but the Savior. It is that which requires emphasis, *now* more than ever.

The charge was not heeded: **However, the more he kept on charging them, the more widely they kept on publishing it.** [353] The intensity and frequency of the disobedience was keeping pace with the intensity and frequency of the charge: the two remained side by side. [354] How emphatically the obstinacy and perversity of sinful human nature is here revealed. It reminds one of the mother who knew that the only way she could get Johnnie to run an errand was to say to him, "Don't you dare go to the store to get me five pounds of sugar!" Boys pass an apple orchard a hundred times without attempting to pick one from the tree's overhanging branches. But let a sign be put up, "Those who steal apples will be prosecuted," and see if the pockets of these boys do not begin to bulge with apples. Did not Mark Twain mention "swimming pools which were forbidden us and therefore much frequented"? However, these people who resolutely disobeyed Christ's

---

[353] For the verb διαστέλλω see above, on 5:43, footnote 219, to forbid, charge not to. Note how here in 7:36 first the aorist form is used, then the imperfect. Note the two corresponding imperfects: he kept on charging . . . they kept on publishing (or: proclaiming).

[354] μᾶλλον περισσότερον double comparative for the sake of added emphasis. Cf. Phil. 1:23.

command were no boys. For the most part they must have been grown-ups.
For their defiant and persistent disobedience to his specific and repeated
order there was no excuse whatever. Even their *admiration* for what Jesus
had done was no atonement for their recalcitrant behavior.

They did, however, show admiration: **37. The people were astonished
beyond all measure, and were saying, How excellently he has done all things!
Why, he even causes the deaf to hear and the speechless to speak.**

Verses 36, 37 show that it takes more than admiration and enthusiasm to
be a true follower of Christ. Many Christ-admirers are lost. The true mark of
discipleship is revealed in John 15:14, "Y o u are my friends if y o u do
what I bid y o u." Cf. John 8:31, 32. These people were doing just the
opposite.

Yet, so marvelous were the deeds of Jesus that even these disobedient
people were astonished, knocked out of their senses (cf. 1:22; 6:2), and this
"beyond all measure," so that they had to exclaim, "How excellently has he
done all things!" They pointed especially to the fact that those who had
previously been deaf were now hearing, and those previously speechless were
now speaking. [355] This also shows that Mark was conscious of the fact that
the incident he has just recorded was only one out of many, a fact stated
definitely by Matthew in his parallel passage.

Above all, it must not be overlooked that by means of the event here
described (Mark 7:31 f.) and by those similar to it prophecy was being
fulfilled. See Isa. 35:5, 6.

"How excellently he has done all things." R. A. Cole, in his commentary [356] very appropriately calls attention to the fact that *all* God's creative
works are perfect. Not only *God* saw that they were good (Gen. 1:4, 10, 12,
18, 21, 25, 31), but so also, on this occasion (Mark 7:37), does *man*.

Summary of Chapter 7:24-37

This section consists of two paragraphs: *a.* verses 24-30; and *b.* verses
31-37.

As to the first, here begins the Retirement Ministry. Jesus and The Twelve
wend their way toward the region of Tyre. He enters a house, seeking
seclusion. But, as happened before (6:34), when Jesus is confronted with
human need he goes into action. A woman from the Gentile world falls at his
feet and keeps urging him to deliver her daughter from an unclean spirit. He
tells her, "First let the children eat all they want, for it is not proper to take
the children's bread and toss it to the house dogs," meaning, "The Messianic

---

[355] Note play on words: ἀλάλους . . . λαλεῖν.
[356] *op. cit.*, p. 125.

blessing must be bestowed first on the Jews, then on the Gentiles." Her answer, "Lord, even the house dogs under the table eat some of the children's scraps," results in the rewarding reply, "Because of this statement of yours, go your way; the demon has left your daughter." Arriving home the woman finds her little daughter lying quietly in bed, the demon gone.

From Sidon Jesus travels to Decapolis, to a place somewhere near the eastern shore of the Lake of Galilee. Thus, from a woman urging him to rescue her child he turns to a handicapped man, one afflicted with deafness and a speech impediment. From healing at a distance he makes the transition to healing at close quarters. Those who bring the man to Jesus ask him to lay his hand on him. But Jesus has his own way of dealing with each individual case. He removes the man from the crowd, puts his fingers into the man's ears, and then a wet (with saliva) finger on the man's tongue. Then, lifting up his eyes in prayer, Jesus heaves a deep sigh of genuine, tender compassion. Finally he utters the word "Ephphatha," which, as Mark explains, means "Be opened." Immediately the man's speech and hearing are completely restored. Jesus strictly forbids the crowd to give any publicity to the miracle, a command which is as thoroughly and repeatedly disregarded as it is issued. Nevertheless, the miracle elicits from the astonished multitude the exclamation, "How excellently he has done all things! Why, he even causes the deaf to hear and the speechless to speak."

Matthew (15:29-31) in a roughly parallel passage shows that in this same place and at this same time Jesus healed many other handicapped individuals. Those who saw what was happening "glorified *the God of Israel*," a statement which is most naturally interpreted to mean that they ascribed honor to the God who originally was not their God. Accordingly, if we combine Matthew's account with that of Mark we reach the conclusion that the two events—the one near Sidon and the other in Decapolis—herald the wide-opening of the kingdom's door to the Gentiles. Thus the Lord who according to Mark 7:1-23 (see especially verse 19) was erasing the line of demarcation between clean and unclean *foods,* soon afterward started to remove the barricade between unclean and (supposedly) clean *people.* That these two are closely related was made very clear to Peter. See Acts 10:1—11:18.

Outline of Chapter 8:1-9:1

Theme: *The Work Which Thou Gavest Him To Do*

8:1-10   The Feeding of The Four Thousand
8:11-13   The Craving for Signs Rebuked
8:14-21   The Yeast of the Pharisees and of Herod
8:22-26   The Healing of a Blind Man at Bethsaida
8:27-30   Peter's Confession and Christ's Strict Order
8:31−9:1   The First Prediction of the Passion and the Resurrection

CHAPTER VIII:1—IX:1

8 1 In those days when again a huge crowd had gathered, and they had nothing to eat, he [Jesus] called his disciples to him [357] and said to them, 2 "My heart goes out to the multitude, [358] because already for three days they have remained with me and have nothing to eat; 3 and if I send them away hungry to their homes they will collapse on the way, for some of them have come a long distance." 4 And his disciples answered him "Where in this uninhabited [359] region can anyone get bread enough to feed them?" 5 He asked them, "How many bread-cakes do y o u have?" They said, "Seven." 6 So he ordered the people to take their places on the ground. Then he took the seven bread-cakes, and having given thanks he broke them and kept giving them to his disciples to set before the people, and this they did. 7 They also had a few small fishes, and after he had given thanks for them he ordered them as well to be set before them. 8 They ate and were filled. [360] And they [the disciples] picked up what was left over of the pieces, seven hampers. 9 About four thousand men were present. And he dismissed them. 10 Then immediately he got into the boat with his disciples and went to the region of Dalmanutha.

8:1-10 *The Feeding of the Four Thousand*
Cf. Matt. 15:32-39

There is a striking, almost word for word, resemblance between the two accounts of this event (Matt. 15:32-39; Mark 8:1-10). [361] The most reasonable explanation would seem to be that there was a literary relationship: one fully inspired Gospel writer having before him the account of the other, equally inspired. See N.T.C. on Matthew, The Synoptic Problem, pp. 6-54.

1-3. In those days when again a huge crowd had gathered, and they had nothing to eat, he [Jesus] called his disciples to him and said to them, My heart goes out to the multitude, because already for three days they have remained with me and have nothing to eat; and if I send them away hungry to their homes they will collapse on the way, for some of them have come a long distance.

---

357 Or: summoned his disciples.
358 Or: I am moved with compassion for the multitude.
359 Or: desolate.
360 Or: They ate as much as they wanted.
361 Thus, if from Mark's report as found in 8:1-3 we subtract the introductory words, "In those days when again a huge crowd had gathered and they had nothing to eat," and

There is no mention of any traveling that took place between the preceding event (7:31-37) and this one (8:1-10), though there may have been. But since the "uninhabited region" mentioned in 8:4 can easily have been Decapolis near the eastern shore of the Sea of Galilee (7:31), the conclusion that Jesus is still, or is again, in or near the same place where he healed the man who was deaf and who spoke with difficulty is reasonable.

Again "a huge crowd." This "again" may refer to 7:33 (cf. Matt. 15:30, 31) or to 6:31-34, 44, 55, 56. It could even refer to the entire series of multitudes already mentioned by Mark (1:33, 45; 2:2-4, 13; 3:7-10, 20, 32; 4:1, 36; 5:21, 27, 31, etc.), as if to say, "again," as so often previously.

They had nothing to eat.[362] So magnetic was the presence of Jesus, so marvelous was he in word and deed, that those who surrounded him regarded it to be almost impossible to leave.

In this situation the Master addresses his disciples. Even though during this Retirement Ministry the Lord by no means completely withdrew from the crowds, yet *teaching the disciples* was now one of his main objectives. Yet, his interest in the multitude is evident from the very words he speaks to The Twelve:

---

the final clause, "for some of them have come a long distance," what remains is almost exactly identical:

Matthew	Mark
Jesus called his disciples to him and said to them, "My heart goes out to [or: I am moved with compassion for] the multitude, because already for three days they have remained with me and have nothing to eat. I do not want to send them away hungry, lest they collapse on the way."	He [Jesus] called his disciples to him and said to them, "My heart goes out to [or: I am moved with compassion for] the multitude, because already for three days they have remained with me and have nothing to eat; and if I send them away hungry to their homes, they will collapse on the way."

The disciples' answer of near-despair is also almost identical. Except for the transposition of two words in the original, the immediately following question of Jesus, "How many bread-cakes do y o u have?" is again identical. In Matthew the answer is, "Seven, and a few fishes." Mark introduces the little fishes somewhat later (8:7), as an item in his own report and not indirectly as information supplied by The Twelve. Both evangelists in almost identical language report that Jesus ordered the people to take their places on the ground. The rest of the story is also very similar in Matthew and Mark. Matthew *stresses* the fact that the four thousand were males, and after mentioning the four thousand adds "not counting women and children." Finally, the concluding item in both states that Jesus dismissed the crowd and stepped into the boat. Here, however, Mark adds "with his disciples," and calls the place of arrival Dalmanutha; Matthew calls it Magadan.

[362] Note the genitive absolute extending to μὴ ἐχόντων. The participle ἐχόντων is pl. because ὄχλος,-ου is a collective noun. As to φάγωσιν (cf. *esophagus*), third per. pl. aor. subjunctive of ἐσθίω, this can best be construed as a deliberative subjunctive that is retained in the indirect question.

"My heart goes out to the multitude." Another equally valid rendering is "I am moved with compassion for the multitude." Had he not himself experienced the pangs of hunger? See Matt. 4:2; cf. Heb. 4:15, 16. Note what was said previously (1:41) about the tender, moving, deep, and earnest sympathy of Jesus, a sympathy that expressed itself not only in words but also in deeds. In the present case the occasion for the feeling and outpouring of compassion was that these many people had been with Jesus for three days and that whatever food they may have had with them upon arrival was now completely used up. If under these circumstances they should simply be dismissed, they would not even be able to reach home but would collapse [363] on the way. This all the more because some, as Mark reports, had come "from afar."

What is so strikingly evident is that Jesus is not only himself the Great Sympathizer but also wants the disciples to share this compassion. The reason why he now turns to them is not that he himself is at a loss what to do. Is he not the One who has previously taken care of a similar situation? See Mark 6:30-44. Besides, does not John 6:6—"He himself knew what he was about to do"—apply also in the present case? The Master addresses his disciples in order to awaken them to their responsibility. So thoroughly must the disciples take to heart the problem faced by the hungry multitude that they, these twelve men, will say, "It is *our own* problem. *We* must do something about it." Without compassion can a person be a true follower of Christ? The least these men could and should have done was to beg the Master to repeat what he had done before, and then to inform the crowd that help was on the way. That they failed is clear from verse 4. **And his disciples answered him, Where in this uninhabited region can anyone get bread enough to feed them?** This region to the east or southeast of the Sea of Galilee was a desolate place, a veritable wilderness. The scene of the feeding of the *five* thousand was somewhat more favorable, for in that case food could be purchased from the surrounding farms and in the nearby villages (6:36), but that was not the case here. Apart from Jesus and his power to perform miracles, the present terrain was worthless as a source of needed food supply. And—strange but true—the disciples had failed to take to heart the lesson they should have learned. That is why they said what they did, namely, that in this desolate region it would be entirely impossible for anybody to find bread, particularly to get enough of it to satisfy the needs of so huge a crowd.

---

363 ἐκλυθήσονται, third per. pl., fut. indic. passive of ἐκλύω. In the passive this means *to have one's strength loosened or relaxed;* hence, *to be weakened to the point of complete exhaustion; to collapse.*

It strikes us that Jesus does not even rebuke them. Instead, 5. **He asked them, How many bread-cakes do y o u have? They said, Seven.** He wants them to fix this number firmly in their minds, so they will never forget it. The accurate knowledge of the (humanly speaking) totally inadequate supply will cause the miracle to stand out all the more strikingly. A little later (see 8:19, 20) Jesus is going to remind them again of the numbers that figure in this pair of miracles: 5, 5,000, 12; and 7, 4,000, 7.

6, 7. So he ordered the people to take their places on the ground. Then he took the seven bread-cakes, and having given thanks he broke them and kept giving them to his disciples to set before the people, and this they did. They also had a few small fishes, and after he had given thanks for them he ordered them as well to be set before them. Note the following:

a. Jesus ordered the people to sit on the ground, not on the green grass, as in 6:39. It is later in the season now.

b. "seven bread-cakes." Not "loaves" as we think of them, but flat cakes or sheets, such as could easily be broken into pieces of edible size.

c. Jesus "gave thanks." See the explanation of 6:41, 42. The same interchangeable use of two Greek verbs occurs in the present narrative: Matthew uses "having given thanks" (thus literally, 15:36); Mark in verse 6 "having given thanks," in verse 7 "having blessed." Both can be translated "having given thanks" or "after he had given thanks."

d. Mark leaves the distinct impression that Jesus gave thanks twice: first for the bread and then for the fishes. Although Matthew does not say this, there is nothing in his narrative that is in conflict with it.

e. Note the very graphic manner in which what Jesus does with the bread-cakes is described (here both in Matthew and in Mark); "he broke them and kept giving them. . . ."

f. Literally Mark states that Jesus kept giving the broken pieces to his disciples "to set (them) before, and they set them before the people [or: the crowd, the multitude]." Matthew states the same fact thus, ". . . and the disciples (kept giving them) to the people." Exactly when did the miracle occur? "Under his hands," that is, while he was breaking off edible pieces and handing them to the disciples? That is probably what happened, though not stated in so many words.

g. Mark points out that what occurred in the case of the bread took place also with respect to the *few*—more than two; contrast 6:38—small fishes. "Prepared fish" was a regular side dish with bread in a region where fish abounded.

The detailed, item by item, description of what occurred shows that underlying these accounts there was the observation of an eyewitness. Matthew was there and reported in his Gospel what he had himself observed. This by no means excludes the possibility—probability even—that before depositing his thoughts in writing he had read Mark's report. Mark had heard the story from the lips of another eye-witness, namely, Peter.

8. They ate and were filled. See on 6:42. **And they [the disciples] picked up what was left over of the pieces, seven hampers.**

Note the twelve *baskets* of broken pieces that were picked up in connection with the feeding of the five thousand, as compared with the seven *hampers* filled with such pieces that were collected now. The distinction between the two words used in the original is maintained consistently in the New Testament; that is, in connection with the leftovers from the feeding of the five thousand the New Testament always uses one word (Matt. 14:20; 16:9; Mark 6:43; 8:19; Luke 9:17; John 6:13); in connection with the leftovers from the feeding of the four thousand, it always uses the other (Matt. 15:37; 16:10; Mark 8:8, 20). [364] That the basket used in connection with the feeding of the four thousand was probably larger would seem to follow from the fact that a similar basket or hamper was large enough to hold Paul and to lower him from the wall (Acts 9:25).

9. About four thousand men were present. And he dismissed them. As Matthew reports, in addition to these four thousand there were women and children. Having provided for the needs of these people—probably both for their spiritual needs (he had been with them three days!) and their physical—, Jesus sends them away, and he himself also departs: **10. Then immediately he got into the boat [365] with his disciples and went to the region of Dalmanutha.** There is some evidence to support the belief that Dalmanutha was located south of the Plain of Gennesaret, on the southwestern side of the Sea of Galilee. In this vicinity a cave was found bearing the name "Talmanutha." Whether Matthew's "Magadan" was simply another name for the same place or the name of a nearby place is not known.

Is the account of the feeding of the four thousand a near-repetition of the earlier miracle, so that had it been omitted entirely we would not have been any poorer? Definitely not. Two additional points are now made clear: *a.* Jesus is able not only *to perform* but also *to repeat* his mighty works; and *b.* his sympathy is shown not only to the people of the covenant but even to those outside of it. As to the latter—that this was predominantly Gentile territory—see N.T.C. on Matt. 15:31.

---

11 Now the Pharisees came out and started to argue with him, seeking from him a sign from heaven, tempting him.   12 And sighing deeply in his spirit he said, "Why does this

---

364 The two words are κόφινος, a wicker-basket, and σπυρίς, a larger wicker-basket or a hamper.

365 This may well have been the same boat which earlier (6:32) had brought Jesus and The Twelve to the eastern side of the sea. However, that boat had returned to the western

generation seek a sign? I solemnly declare to y o u, no sign shall be given to this generation." 13 Taking leave of them he again embarked and went away to the other side.

8:11-13 *The Craving for Signs Rebuked*
Cf. Matt. 16:1-4
See also Matt. 12:38-42; Luke 11:29-32; 12:54-56

11. Now the Pharisees came out and started to argue with him, seeking from him a sign from heaven, tempting him. Jews demand "signs," that is, proofs that Jesus is all he claims to be. [366] See John 2:18; 4:48; I Cor. 1:22. Here again we meet those bitter enemies, the Pharisees! We have met them and the scribes before. See on 1:22; 2:6, 16; 3:22; 7:1, 2. Matthew informs us that in connection with the present confrontation the Pharisees were accompanied by the Sadducees. How it was possible for these two opposing sects to combine against Jesus is explained in N.T.C. on Matthew, pp. 201-204, 636.

The Pharisees came out! Now that Jesus has arrived once more on the western, more Jewish (though still ethnically "mixed") side of the Sea of Galilee, another encounter with the Pharisees is not surprising. It is they who take the initiative, not Jesus. They start to [367] argue [368] with Jesus. Had they become informed about the miracles he had performed on the eastern side of the sea, including that of the multiplication of the bread-cakes? Was it this that had nourished afresh their ever-present envy? They try to convince themselves that what happened in Decapolis was not a true sign of greatness on the part of Jesus. After all, what he had provided was *earthly* bread, not "bread from heaven," as Moses had done. Let him then produce "a sign from *heaven.*" Yes, let him do what Moses had done (Exod. 16; cf. John 6:32). Or, like Joshua, let him cause the sun and the moon to stand still (Josh. 10:12-14). Let him repeat what Samuel had done (I Sam. 7:10),

---

side (6:54). Did a follower of Jesus subsequently bring it back to the eastern side for his use? Or was there at least one crossing not reported by Mark? Cf. John 20:30, 31; 21:25. Another possibility would be that in 8:10 we should simply translate "by boat." See also on 6:32. In 8:10 certain textual witnesses even omit τό before πλοῖον. Allowance must be made for all these possibilities.

366 For the meaning of σημεῖον see also N.T.C. on John, Vol. I, p. 117. K. Kohler, *Jewish Encyclopedia,* New York and London, 1916, Vol. VIII, p. 606, furnishes no proof for his rejection of Paul's saying recorded in I Cor. 1:22.

367 For ἤρξαντο see on 1:45; 6:7, footnote 233. In the present case the auxiliary may be no more "redundant" or "pleonastic" than similar language would be today; e.g., "He started to argue with me," probably meaning that after a pause the argument began.

368 Though συζητέω at times has a milder meaning—to talk (to each other), to discuss (1:27); to question (9:10)–, the present context shows that here the meaning is *to argue, to dispute;* thus also in 9:14, 16.

or Elijah (I Kings 18:30-40; cf. James 5:17, 18). As if, had he done any of these things, or anything of similar sensational nature, they would not have ascribed also such a sign to Beelzebul as its source! See Luke 16:31.

Their purpose was *to tempt* Jesus, to get him to attempt to produce such a sign. They hoped that he would try and fail, so that he might be publicly discredited.

12. And sighing deeply in his spirit he said, Why does this generation seek a sign? I solemnly declare to y o u, no sign shall be given to this generation.
Note the following:

a. *sighing deeply.* Jesus had filled the land with "infallible proofs" (cf. Acts 1:3) of the fact that he was indeed the One who had been sent by the Father, as predicted by the prophets. These signs had been of various kinds: restoration of the handicapped, healing of the sick, cleansing of the lepers, stilling of the waves, feeding of the hungry, and even raising of the dead. Asking for still another sign was clearly an insult. It implied that the miracles already performed were insufficient as credentials. So it was no wonder that Jesus greeted the request for a sign by sighing deeply [369] in his spirit. Deeply, because the hardness of heart revealed by this request wounded him sorely.

b. *in his spirit.* The anguish which Jesus experienced came from deep down inside him. Here the word "spirit" is used in a sense not much different from "heart" or "inner being." [370] So also in 2:8; cf. 14:38.

---

[369] The original has ἀναστενάξας, aor. participle of ἀναστενάζω, in the New Testament found only here. For the simple form στενάζω see above, on 7:34. The form used here in 8:12 is perfective in meaning: sighed *deeply*. With the verb στενάζω cf. *stentorian, thunder;* German *stöhnen,* Dutch *steunen.*

[370] In an unpublished study which the author made of the concepts ψυχή and πνεῦμα, the following conclusions were established after examining each word in the light of the context wherever it occurs in the New Testament:
In the New Testament as a whole ψυχή occurs about 100 times, πνεῦμα more than 370 times. It is entirely impossible to draw a sharp distinction—as is often done—between these two words, as if in the New Testament ψυχή always has one meaning, πνεῦμα another. It is true that when *the apostle Paul* was thinking of man's invisible being in its relation to God, he generally used the word πνεῦμα. However, in the New Testament as a whole there is considerable overlapping of meanings. One should never say, "In the New Testament ψυχή is man's invisible part considered as that which animates his body; πνεῦμα is that same immaterial entity viewed in its relation to God." The subject is far more complicated than this generalization indicates. For example, the Greek equivalent for *breath* can be either ψυχή (Acts 20:10) or πνεῦμα (II Thess. 2:8). Similarly, the concept *life,* with emphasis on the physical, can be expressed either by πνεῦμα (Luke 8:55) or by ψυχή (Matt. 2:20). Not only is it possible for the πνεῦμα to be provoked (Acts 17:16), the ψυχή, too, can be stirred up (Acts 14:2). The πνεῦμα rejoices in God, to be sure (Luke 1:47), but the ψυχή, too, is said to magnify the Lord (Luke 1:46). An incorporeal being may be a πνεῦμα (Heb. 12:23), but may also be a ψυχή (Rev. 6:9). On the other hand, when the reference is to the Holy Spirit the word used is always πνεῦμα,

c. *this generation.* Jesus is perplexed and perturbed because these Phari-sees and their many followers, a very large percentage of his contemporaries, are demanding a sign. The term "generation" in such passages as Mark 8:12, 38; 9:19 refers to the people among whom one is living. By and large those people, especially here on the western side of the Sea of Galilee, were Jews, though this point is not stressed here. It is not surprising that when this national or racial characteristic is emphasized, the word "generation" can attain the meaning "the Jewish nation or people," as in 13:30; cf. Matt. 24:35.

d. *I solemnly declare.* See on 3:28. Here in 8:12, also, the solemn introduction leads to a statement that deserves very careful consideration.

e. *no sign shall be given.* [371] In the light of the parallel passage in Matthew (16:4) the meaning is, "No sign such as y o u are demanding shall at all be given." See N.T.C. on Matt. 16:4. The triumphant resurrection of Jesus from the dead, foreshadowed in the experience of Jonah (Jonah 1:17; 2:10), would mark the doom of all sin-hardened Pharisees. As for the sign these men are now requesting, Jesus solemnly assures them that they will receive nothing of the kind. [372]

13. Taking leave of them he again embarked and went away to the other

---

with or without modifier (Mark 1:8-12; 3:29, 12:36; 13:11; Luke 1:5, etc.). An *unclean spirit* is πνεῦμα ἀκάθαρτον (Mark 1:23, 26, etc.). At times a synonym is used (Mark 9:17, 25). The word πνεῦμα can even indicate a disposition (I Cor. 4:21, "a spirit of gentle-ness"). On the other hand, when the reference is to the entire *self* or *person,* so that in a parallel passage a personal pronoun is used, or so that such a pronoun might have been substituted, this *self* is always ψυχή (Mark 10:45; cf. I Tim. 2:6). This meaning of ψυχή is probably influenced by Hebrew usage. The *self* so understood may be viewed from a twofold aspect. See on Mark 8:35-38.

Since there are these distinctions but also many areas of overlapping, it is impossible to lay down rigid rules. One can perhaps say that in general πνεῦμα stresses mental activity, ψυχή emotional. It is the πνεῦμα that perceives (Mark 2:8), plans (Acts 19:21), and knows (I Cor. 2:11). It is the ψυχή that is sorrowful (Matt. 26:38). The πνεῦμα prays (I Cor. 14:14), the ψυχή loves (Mark 12:30). Also ψυχή is often broader in scope, indicating the sum-total of life that rises above the physical; while πνεῦμα is more restricted. Often, *but by no means always,* πνεῦμα indicates the human spirit in its relation to God, man's self-consciousness or personality viewed as the subject in acts of worship or in acts related to worship, such as praying, bearing witness, etc. But again, no hard and fast rule can be laid down. Every occurrence of either word will have to be interpreted in the light of the origin of the particular passage in which it occurs, and in the light of its specific context and of parallel passages.

371 δοθήσεται third per. sing. fut. indic. passive of δίδωμι.

372 Literally the original reads, "I solemnly declare to y o u, *if* there shall be given to this generation a sign . . ." The conclusion or apodosis remains unexpressed. This reminds one of the underlying Hebrew idiom illustrated in II Sam. 11:11, "As you live, and as your soul lives, *if* (Heb. *'im*) I do this thing . . ." In that particular instance the unexpressed apodosis was probably "then may I die," or something similar. It is easy to see that such an *if* with unexpressed conclusion is a very strong negation.

side. They are abandoned to the destiny which they, by their hardness of heart, have chosen for themselves.

---

14 Now they [the disciples] had forgotten to take along bread, and had only one bread-cake with them in the boat. 15 And he [Jesus] was warning them, "Look out! Be on y o u r guard against the yeast of the Pharisees and the yeast of Herod." 16 And they began to reason among themselves, "(It's) because we have no bread." 17 Now when he noticed this he said to them, "Why are y o u reasoning among yourselves about the fact that y o u have no bread? Do y o u still lack understanding? Do y o u still fail to grasp? Are y o u r hearts hardened? 18 Having eyes, do y o u not remember? 19 When I broke the five bread-cakes for the five thousand, how many baskets full of pieces did y o u pick up?" They answered, "Twelve." 20 "When (I broke) the seven bread-cakes for the four thousand, how many hampers full of pieces did y o u pick up?" "Seven," they replied. 21 He said to them, "Do y o u still fail to grasp?"

8:14-21 *The Yeast of the Pharisees and of Herod*
Cf. Matt. 16:5-12

The incident here reported probably took place on the Sea of Galilee, during the trip from Dalmanutha to Bethsaida. See the map on p. 295.

14. Now they [the disciples] had forgotten [373] to take along bread, and had only one break-cake with them in the boat. From a purely human standpoint—i.e., when the power of Jesus is discounted—, this oversight was bad, for it was easier to obtain bread on the populous western side of the sea than on the eastern, though, as indicated previously, around Bethsaida it was less difficult to obtain provisions than farther south. One bread-cake would never do for thirteen men!

15. And he [Jesus] was warning [374] them, Look out! Be on y o u r guard against the yeast of the Pharisees and the yeast of Herod. Jesus was undoubtedly still thinking about the hardened unbelief of the Pharisees who had requested a sign from heaven, as if no sign of any significance had been furnished. See 8:11-13. But what had brought about that insulting request? Answer: the contrast between Jesus' teaching and that of the Pharisees: *his* emphasis on the law of God, hence on genuine worship of God, over against *theirs* on tradition.

According to Matt. 16:1, in this wicked attempt to discredit Jesus, the Pharisees had been joined by the Sadducees. Matthew does not mention Herod in this connection. Mark, on the other hand, here omits any reference to the Sadducees but links "the yeast (or "leaven") of the Pharisees" with "the yeast of Herod." Since there was a close connection between the Herodians and the Sadducees, there is no contradiction between the two

---

373 ἐπελάθοντο third per. pl. aor. indic. of ἐπιλανθάνομαι. Cf. *Lethe, lethargy, latent.*
374 For the Greek verb see above, on 7:36b; also on 5:43, footnote 219.

accounts. The Sadducees were the sacerdotal party, the party to which the highpriests, etc. generally belonged. The priestly oligarchy was for its very existence and continuity dependent upon the favor of the Herods. See N.T.C. on Matthew, pp. 159, 162. But there was an even closer connection. The Sadducees, though ostensibly clinging to the law of God, were not at all opposed to the spread of Hellenism. Since they rejected both the resurrection of the body and the immortality of the soul, their interests were absorbed in the here and now. They were "worldly," and in this respect resembled Herod and his friends.

The characteristic "yeast" or "teaching," whether by precept, example, or both, that is indicated in the Gospels with respect to the three groups is as follows:

The Pharisees, *traditionalism* (Mark 7:4, 8).

Herod and his followers, the Herodians, *secularism* (Mark 6:17 ff.).

The Sadducees, *skepticism* (Mark 12:18; cf. Acts 23:8).

There was, of course, considerable overlapping. In a sense secularism marked all three. See N.T.C. on Matt. 16:6.

Both imperatives—"Look out!" and "Be on y o u r guard against" are durative in character. Therefore the meaning is: "Keep on looking out (or being on the alert)"; "Always be on y o u r guard against."

The Twelve needed this warning. In spite of their daily association with Jesus, they were constantly in danger of paying too much attention to the views of those whose teachings were opposed to his. See Matt. 15:12; 19:3-10; Mark 7:1, 17-23; 10:2-12, 35-45; Acts 1:6.

16. And they began to reason among themselves, (It's) because we have no bread. These men began to carry on—or "were carrying on"—a dialogue with each other. [375] Jesus had mentioned *yeast*. He meant *teaching*. See Matt. 16:11, 12. In view of what is recorded in Mark 8:11-13 and in earlier accounts of confrontations between Jesus and his opponents, this meaning should have been clear to the disciples. Also, these men had heard the parable of The Leaven (Matt. 13:33). This too, should have taught them that the word *yeast* or *leaven* must not always be taken literally. Yeast and teaching resemble each other in several respects: *a.* both operate invisibly, *b.* are very potent, and *c.* have a tendency gradually to augment their sphere of influence. For the figurative use of the term "yeast" see also I Cor. 5:6 ff.; Gal. 5:9. Just now (Mark 8:15) Jesus used this word in an unfavorable sense: evil teaching, considered as a very powerful, increasingly corrupting influence.

The disciples, however, failed to consider carefully and to ponder seriously the meaning of Christ's warning to be on their guard against the yeast

---

[375] In 2:6 and 7:21 the dialogue takes place within their own hearts.

of the Pharisees and the yeast of Herod. They quickly ascribed a literal meaning to "yeast," and probably concluded that the Master was forbidding them to accept bread from Pharisees and from people associated with Herod. What we have here, then, is another instance of erroneous literal interpretation of dominical sayings. Cf. John 2:19, 20; 3:3, 4; 4:13-15; 6:51, 52; 11:11, 12.

These men were guilty of still another error, as is clear from Christ's reaction as recorded in verses 17-21. They thought that Jesus was very displeased with them because they had forgotten to take along bread and they were worried about this lack of bread-cakes. Their basic error, then, was lack of sufficient faith. This is exactly what, according to Matt. 16:8, Jesus on this occasion told them when he called them "men of little faith." With Jesus in their midst, the very One who had given proof of his power in the two miraculous feedings, should they not have been optimists? But no, they were pessimists. We can say, therefore, that the section Mark 8:14-21, in combination with its parallel Matt. 16:5-12, warns against four errors: the *traditionalism* of the Pharisees, the *secularism* of the Herodians, the *skepticism* of the Sadducees, and the *pessimism* of the disciples.

The back and forth worried whispering of the disciples was met by the Master's frank and open reply. It was a reply that consisted of several closely knit questions, reproachful to be sure but also helpful, their purpose being to rouse The Twelve out of their inexcusable pessimism and to revive in their hearts the spirit of trust and optimism:

17-21. **Now when he noticed this he said to them,**

a. **Why are y o u reasoning among yourselves about the fact that y o u have no bread?**

b. **Do y o u still lack understanding; do y o u still fail to grasp?**

c. **Are y o u r hearts hardened?**

d. **Having eyes, do y o u not see; and having ears, do y o u not hear?**

e. **And do y o u not remember?**

f. **When I broke the five bread-cakes for the five thousand, how many baskets full of pieces did y o u pick up? They answered, Twelve. When (I broke) the seven bread-cakes for the four thousand, how many hampers full of pieces did y o u pick up? Seven, they replied.**

g. **He said to them, do y o u still fail to grasp?**

In Matt. 16:8-10 this touching paragraph occurs in considerably reduced form, retaining only a, b (in part), e, and f of Mark's report. Matt. 16:11, 12 reflects on the disciples' literal interpretation of Christ's warning. It reports that the words of Jesus had the favorable result of ridding the disciples of their misinterpretation, a result that is not recorded by Mark.

A few remarks on each element in the series a-g:

a. Concern about the lack of bread is unnecessary.

319

b. The disciples should have used their heads (cf. 7:18; 13:14). They should have put two and two together (cf. 4:12; 6:52; 7:14). Failure to take to heart the lessons which Jesus had taught them earlier by word and deed was inexcusable.

c. For the meaning of the word "heart" and the latter's central significance see on 6:52. "Hardened" is here used not in the sense of the obstinacy and resulting imperviousness that marked the Pharisees, but of spiritual sluggishness. Again see on 6:52.

d. This reference to eyes that do not see and ears that do not hear (cf. Jer. 5:21; Ezek. 12:2; Mark 4:12) is very closely related to the immediately preceding item. The hardened heart had brought about this condition.

e. This item may be considered transitional. It can be linked either with the immediately preceding, *inability to recall* in the present instance also being considered an indication and result of hardness of heart (A.V., A.R.V., R.S.V.); or with the immediately following ("And do y o u not remember, when I broke . . ."; N.A.S., cf. Williams). The disciples should have paid more attention to these miracles, should have taken time to ponder their meaning in relation to the greatness of Christ.

Memory can indeed be aided by spiritual reflection, meditation, and where possible translation into action. It is reported that an Oriental convert to Christianity confessed that committing to memory the Sermon on the Mount had caused him great difficulty until by the grace of God, he had begun to put its principles into daily practice!

It should be added that Jesus did more than reproach the disciples for their lack of memory. See John 14:25, 26.

f. Note the distinction which, as in every instance, is made in the Gospels between the two kinds of baskets. See above, on 8:8. The argument is basically as follows: if five bread-cakes more than sufficed for five thousand people, and seven bread-cakes more than sufficed for four thousand—facts which the disciples here and now reaffirm—, then would not Jesus be able to feed himself and The Twelve with *one* (8:14) bread-cake? In fact, would he not be able, even without any bread-cake, to provide all that was necessary?

g. There is no good reason to interpret this final "Do y o u still fail to grasp?" in any other sense than as asked previously (see b.). Christ's question was sufficiently important to justify repetition. The words and works of Jesus must be pondered and taken to heart. They must not be quickly forgotten. Dwelling on them prayerfully will increase faith and abolish pessimism.

---

22 They came to Bethsaida, and some people brought a blind man to him, and begged him to touch him. 23 He took the blind man by the hand, led him outside the village, and after spitting on his eyes and laying his hands on him, asked him, "Do you see

anything?" 24 He looked up and said, "I can make out the people, for I see them as trees, walking around." 25 Then he [Jesus] again laid his hands on the man's eyes, and he opened them wide, was fully restored, and was seeing everything clearly. 26 And with the warning, "Do not go into the village" he [Jesus] sent him to his home.

8:22-26 *The Healing of a Blind Man at Bethsaida*

The present section is found only in Mark's Gospel. **22. They came to Bethsaida, and some people brought a blind man to him, and begged him to touch him.** The boat landed on the northeastern side of the sea, near the entrance of the Jordan. See map on p. 295. The place of arrival was Bethsaida Julias, where the miracle of the feeding of the five thousand had occurred (Luke 9:10). Mark calls it a "village" (verse 23). Luke, in the passage to which reference has just been made, states that it was a "city." There is nothing unusual or disturbing about this seeming discrepancy. For a long time Bethsaida had been a mere village. Then Philip the tetrarch (Luke 3:1) enlarged and beautified it. It now became a city, and in honor of Julia, the daughter of Emperor Augustus, was named Bethsaida Julias. However, having been a "village" for so long a time, it is not surprising that the designation "village" continued for some time to be applied to it. The same thing happens even today. When "West St." changes to "Westnedge Avenue" it continues for several years to be called "West St." Similarly what today is "Marne" (Mich., U.S.A.) continued for a while to be called "Berlin," and one still occasionally hears, "He lives in The Brickyard," when the real brickyard is today but a faint memory. As to the two Bethsaidas see N.T.C. on John, Vol. I, pp. 216, 217, 225.

At Bethsaida a blind man was brought to Jesus. His guides begged Jesus to touch [376] him. As to the significance of this touch see on 1:41.

23. He took the blind man by the hand, led him outside the village, and after spitting on his eyes and laying his hands on him, asked him, Do you see anything?

It is a striking fact that among those healings of blind men which in the Gospels are described in some detail not two are alike. This shows that in his love and wisdom the Master dealt with each case individually. His heart went out to the needy ones not just in general but to each one in particular, so that his treatment of a case was never a mere duplication of what had been done before. Anyone can see this for himself by studying and comparing the following passages: Matt. 9:27-31; Mark 8:22-26; 10:46-52 (and parallels); John 9. See also on Mark 7:33, 34.

First, Jesus took this man by the hand. Not as if the handicapped

---

376 ἅψηται, third per. sing. aor. subjunctive middle of ἅπτω.

individual did not have any guides. He did, and these guides had brought him to Jesus. But the latter wishes to impart his own very personal attention and love to this man. Therefore he himself now becomes the Guide.

Secondly, Jesus led him out of the village. For "village" see on verse 22. Commentaries are divided on the question why this man had to be led away from the village. Was it because Jesus did not wish to see a large crowd running up to him for cures? Or was it in the interest of the blind man himself, to make him feel more at ease and able to concentrate all his attention on his Benefactor? Both are possible, or either is. In harmony with what was said in connection with 7:33, the second reason seems best.

Thirdly, Jesus spat on the man's eyes. Here, too, compare the cure of the deaf-mute (7:31-37). In that case Jesus applied saliva to the man's tongue; in the present, since this man's trouble was in the eyes, he spat on his eyes. Cf. John 9:6. The meaning again was clear: "Something will be done for your eyes . . . and I will do it."

Fourthly, reassuringly the Master laid his hands on the man, an action that often preceded healing, and was therefore a hopeful sign to the blind person.

Fifthly, Jesus asked him, "Do you see anything?" [377] It is clear that the Lord wants this individual to become "involved" in his own cure, step by step.

24. He looked up and said, I can make out the people, for I see them as trees, walking around. Three different words are used in the original of this verse, all having to do with vision. [378] The man *looked up*, involuntarily he raised his eyes. He said, "I *can make out* the people." This refers here to outward, rather vague, discernment. He added, "for I see them as trees, walking around." He *perceives* that certain objects which to him resemble trees differ from trees in one important respect: they are walking around, and must therefore be people. He may well have been looking at the disciples of Jesus. His outward vision was still blurred, but his perception or mental observation was correct: those moving objects were indeed people. What made him all the more certain of this was the fact—high probability at least—that he had not been *born* blind. Accordingly, he knew how people looked.

Nevertheless, when men resemble trees—except for the fact that men move, trees do not—, something is still wrong. Since Jesus always completes

---

[377] Is the Greek form εἴ τι βλέπεις an abbreviation of "I would like to know whether you see anything"? This would not be at all surprising, for language, *any* language, then and now, is full of abbreviated expressions. See N.T.C. on John, Vol. I, p. 206. But even if so, the form, through frequency of use, had probably become the equivalent of a direct question, and can be thus rendered. See Gram. N.T., p. 916.

[378] The three are ἀναβλέψας (aor. participle of ἀναβλέπω); βλέπω; and ὁρῶ (the latter two being first per. sing. pres. indicatives).

his work (cf. John 17:4; Phil. 1:6), there follows: **25. Then he [Jesus] again laid his hands on the man's eyes, and he opened them wide, was fully restored, and was seeing everything clearly.** [379] This time when the man focused his eyes intently, opening them wide, people no longer looked like trees. Vision had been fully restored. He saw and continued to see distant objects as if they were nearby.

It should be emphasized that this act of healing is by no means in line with slow present-day healings that require several visits to the "healer." In the case here recorded the entire healing process was accomplished within a few moments, with the result: a change from complete blindness to perfect vision.

Exactly why it was that in this particular case the healing process occurred in two stages has not been revealed to us. Was it, perhaps, because especially *this* person was in need of understanding the inestimable nature of the blessing that was being bestowed upon him? The reason cannot have been initial lack of power on the part of Jesus. Surely, he who was able instantly to raise the dead was also able to impart instant recovery to this blind man. For a reason known to the Healer the present restoration occurred in two stages.

26. And with the warning, Do not go into the village he [Jesus] sent him to his home. Why this warning? Perhaps for the same reason as mentioned in connection with earlier miracles. See on 1:44; 7:36. It was not the purpose of Christ's coming to create excitement and encourage false expectations of approaching political deliverance. It is possible, however, that in sending this man directly to his home Jesus also had in mind the interest of this man, namely, that he might calmly meditate on the great blessing he had received, and that he would have an opportunity without interference to talk about it to those nearest and dearest to himself, so that together they might glorify God. Cf. 5:19.

---

27 Jesus along with his disciples went away to the villages around Caesarea Philippi. And on the way he was asking his disciples, "Who do the people say I am?" 28 They answered him, "John the Baptist; and others (say) Elijah; and still others, one of the prophets." 29 Then he was asking them, "But y o u, who do y o u say I am?" Peter answered him, "Thou art the Christ." 30 And he [Jesus] warned them to tell no one about him.

---

379 Here are two more verbs having to do with vision. They are διέβλεψε (looked sharply, opened his eyes wide), aor. indic. of διαβλέπω; and ἐνέβλεπεν τηλαυγῶς; i.e., τῆλε afar (cf. *television*) and αὐγῶς radiantly; but note the imperfect, contrasted with the two aorists διέβλεψε and ἀπεκατέστη; hence, "was seeing (or: continued to see) . . . clearly," so that even distant objects were now radiantly clear to him. Note also the double compound verb ἀπεκατέστη aor. indic. of ἀποκαθίστημι (was fully restored).

8:27-30 *Peter's Confession and Christ's Strict Order*
Cf. Matt. 16:13-20; Luke 9:18-21

The *resemblance* between Mark's account of this happening and the
reports, respectively, of Matthew and Luke, is striking, as is also the *contrast*.
First, the *resemblance;* note the following parallels:

Mark	Matthew	Luke
8:27	16:13	9:18
8:28	16:14	9:19
8:29a	16:15	9:20a
8:29b	16:16	9:20b
8:30	16:20	9:21

Except for Matt. 16:17-19, in all three the sequence is the same, and even
the phraseology is to a considerable extent almost identical. Literary relationship between the three accounts would seem to be the most logical
explanation. Nevertheless, there is enough variation to show that the evangelists were not mere copyists. Each Gospel writer tells the story as the Spirit
guides him, which implies that each employs his own style. The variations,
however, except for Matt. 16:17-19, are minor.

27. **Jesus along with his disciples.** . . . The fact that these men were with
their Master is also definitely stated by Luke and implied by Matthew ("He
asked his disciples"). Continued: **went away to the villages around Caesarea
Philippi.** See the map on p. 295. Here Matthew has "in the district of
Caesarea Philippi," and Luke "as he was praying." Obviously there is no
conflict. **And on the way he was asking his disciples, Who do the people say I
am?** So also Luke, except that he substitutes "the multitudes" for "the
people," or "men." Instead of "I am" Matthew reads "the Son of man is,"
with no difference in meaning. 28. **They answered him, John the Baptist;
and others (say) Elijah; and still others, one of the prophets.** Matthew's "and
others (say) Jeremiah" is not found in Mark and Luke. It may be regarded as
included in "one of the prophets." It is clear from this answer that in general
the crowds believed that Jesus was a very prominent messenger from God,
that he was someone who had died and in the person of Jesus had arisen
from the dead. Luke makes special mention of this fact when he states, "and
others that one of the old prophets had risen." 29. **Then he was asking
them, But y o u, who do y o u say I am?** The phrasing is exactly the same
in all three. With tremendous emphasis Jesus places this "But *y o u,* who
do *y o u* say . . . ?" over against "Who do *the people* say . . . ?" **Peter
answered him, Thou art the Christ.** Peter's answer, representing the conviction of The Twelve, is by Matthew reproduced in fuller form, "Thou art the
Christ, the Son of the Living God"; by Luke more concisely, "The Christ of
God." And the warning, 30. **And he [Jesus] warned them to tell no one**

about him, is expressed in language that is essentially the same for all three, yet varies slightly.

If the reader will bear in mind these generally slight variations, he will find the explanation of the contents of Mark 8:27-30 in N.T.C. on the parallel passage, Matt. 16:13-16, 20, pp. 641-643, 652 of that volume.

The three columns of parallel passages—see above p. 324—, also clearly indicate a *contrast*—no contradiction—between Matthew, on the one hand, and Mark and Luke, on the other. The noticeable contrast consists in this, that verses 17-19 of Matthew's sixteenth chapter are absent from Mark and Luke. These verses are: "Jesus answered and said to him, 'Blessed are you, Simon Bar-Jonah, for it is not flesh and blood but my Father who is in heaven who has revealed this to you. And I say to you, you are Peter, and upon this rock I will build my church, and the gates of Hades shall not overpower it. I will give you the keys of the kingdom of heaven, and whatever you shall bind on earth shall be bound in heaven, and whatever you shall loose on earth shall be loosed in heaven." *For the possible reason of this omission from Mark and Luke, as well as for the explanation of this exclusively Matthean passage, see N.T.C. on Matthew, pp. 644-652.*

Before leaving this subject, special attention should be called to the fact that the words of Jesus, "But y o u, who do y o u say I am?" convey a very important lesson, namely, that a true believer is one who is willing, whenever necessary, to fly in the face of popular opinion and openly to express a conviction that is contrary to that of the masses. In the best sense of the term, the believer is willing to come forth *boldly* in the interest of the truth. The kingdom is for "vigorous people" (Matt. 11:12); for strong and sturdy men like Joseph (Gen. 39:9); Moses (Exod. 32:31, 32); Joshua and Caleb (Num. 13:30; 14:6-10); Samuel (I Sam. 7:5); David (I Sam. 17:41-49; Ps. 27); Nathan (II Sam. 12:7); Elijah (I Kings 18:21); Jehoshaphat (II Chron. 20:5-12); Daniel and his three friends (Dan. 1:11-13; 3:16-18; 6:10, 21-23); Mordecai (Esther 3:4); Peter (Acts 4:20); Stephen (Acts 6:8; 7:51); Paul (Phil. 3:13, 14); Epaphroditus (Phil. 2:15-30; 4:18); Onesiphorus (II Tim. 1:15-18); and the apostle John (Rev. 1:9). It is for such valiant women as Ruth (Ruth 1:16-18); Deborah (Judg. 4:9); Abigail (I Sam. 25:14 ff.); Esther (Esther 4:16); and Lydia (Acts 16:15, 40).

Conformity with the world, compromise on basic issues, the unwillingness to be distinctive, is strongly condemned in Scripture (Rom. 12:2; II Cor. 6:14; I John 2:15-17). When "the sons of God" marry "the daughters of men" (Gen. 6:1, 2), the result is the deluge. When Israel worships a golden calf, three thousand Israelites lose their lives (Exod. 32:28). When Israel, with the purpose of being like other nations, demands a king, the final result is shameful defeat in a battle in which that king commits suicide (I Sam. 31:4). When the compromiser Jeroboam institutes calf-worship at Bethel and

Dan, he is leading the people into a path that finally results in shameful deportation into a pagan country (I Kings 12:26-30; 14:16, 19, 26, 31; II Kings 3:3; 10:29, 31, etc.).

Not being "of the world" (John 17:16), believers are shining lights in the midst of the world (Matt. 5:14; Phil. 2:15). They are spiritually different from the world, in order to be a blessing to the world. So also here in Mark 8:28, 29, while everybody else is saying that Jesus is but a man—whether John the Baptist, Elijah, or one of the (other) prophets, it makes no essential difference, for all these were but men—, the true follower of Jesus answers, "Thou art the Christ" (thus Mark), "the Son of the Living God" (adds Matthew).

---

31 And he [Jesus] began to teach them that the Son of man must suffer many things and be rejected by the elders and the chief priests and the scribes, and be killed, and after three days rise again. 32 He was telling them this fact without any reservation. And Peter took him aside and began to rebuke him. 33 But turning around and seeing his disciples, he rebuked Peter and said, "Get out of my sight, Satan, for you are looking at things not from God's point of view but from men's." 34 And having called the people to him along with his disciples, he said to them, "If anyone wishes to come behind me, let him deny himself, take up his cross, and follow me. 35 For whoever would save his life shall lose it, but whoever loses his life for my sake and the gospel's shall save it. 36 For what good does it do a man to gain the whole world and forfeit his life? 37 For what shall a man give in exchange for his life? 38 For whoever is ashamed of me and my words in this adulterous and sinful generation, of him also shall the Son of man be ashamed when he comes in the Glory of his Father with his holy angels."

9:1 And he was saying to them, "I solemnly declare to y o u that there are some of those who are standing here who shall not taste death until they see the kingdom of God come with power."

8:31—9:1 *The First Prediction of the Passion*
and the Resurrection
Cf. Matt. 16:21-28; Luke 9:22-27

The resemblance between Mark and its parallels is again rather striking. As to the relation between Mark and Matthew, the main differences are as follows: Matt. 16:21 substitutes "he" for Mark's "the Son of man," and adds "must go away to Jerusalem." Matthew's verse 22 reports the very words used by Peter in rebuking Jesus; verse 23 adds that Jesus told Peter, "You are a trap to me"; verse 24 mentions only Jesus and his disciples, not also the people; verse 25 omits Mark's "and the gospel's sake." After minor grammatical variations in verse 26 (=Mark 8:36, 37), Matt. 16:27, differing rather strikingly from Mark 8:38, reads, "For the Son of man shall come in the glory of his Father, with his angels, and then shall he render to each according to his deeds." Finally, Matthew's verse 28 ends with the phrase "until they see the Son of man coming in his kingdom" or "in his royal dignity"; Mark's 9:1 with the essentially similar "until they see the kingdom of God come with power."

Luke's parallel (9:22-27) is clearly an abbreviation. Sometimes it resembles Mark more closely, sometimes Matthew. Thus in verse 22 Luke speaks of Jesus as saying that "the Son of man" [thus also Mark] must be raised up "on the third day" [thus also Matthew]; Mark has "after three days." In verse 23 Luke adds the word "daily" ["let him take up his cross daily"]. In verse 24 Luke, like Matthew, omits Mark's "and the gospel's sake." In verse 25 Luke has "lose or forfeit." Luke's verse 26 resembles Mark 8:38 more closely than it does Matt. 16:27. Finally, Luke 9:27 continues this close resemblance to Mark (9:1), though Luke abbreviates.

Obviously there are no essential differences, no contradictions.

Turning now to Mark's own account, the reader is referred to its parallel in Matthew. See N.T.C. on that Gospel, pp. 653-660, bearing in mind the (on the whole) slight differences that have been pointed out between the two reports (Mark's and Matthew's).

Here in N.T.C. on Mark observations for the most part not found in N.T.C. on Matthew will be added.

31, 32a. And he [Jesus] began to teach them that the Son of man must suffer many things and be rejected by the elders and the chief priests and the scribes, and be killed, and after three days rise again. He was telling them this fact without any reservation.

The prediction here given has the following characteristics:

a. It was *necessary*. When the disciples, by the mouth of Peter, had said, "Thou art the Christ" (verse 29), Jesus by not contradicting this had obviously assented to it. Therefore, in view of the fact that messiahship was by many interpreted in an earthly and political sense, it was necessary that the disciples be taught what it meant to be the Christ.

b. It was *startling*. "The Son of man"—see on 2:10; N.T.C. on Matthew, pp. 403-407—that is, Jesus himself, the Messiah . . . about to suffer and to die! Actually *to be killed!* And not only was this going to happen; it *must* happen. He *must* be subjected to suffering and *must* be killed, because of the Father's will (John 3:16; Rom. 8:32), his own promise (Ps. 40:7), prophecy (Isa. 53), and basically the demands of the law (Gen. 2:17; Rom. 5:12-21; II Cor. 5:21). He *must* do what he himself also wanted to do (John 10:11; II Cor. 8:9; Gal. 2:20). However, note also: after three days—meaning "on the third day"—he *must* rise again. See Isa. 53:10; Luke 24:26, 27. But in view of Mark 9:32; cf. Luke 18:34 it is very doubtful whether this optimistic climax was even fully appreciated by those who heard it.

c. It was *revealing*. Elders, chief priests, and scribes, the men who were supposed to be watchmen for the people, those from whose circles the Sanhedrin was chosen, are going to kill Israel's own Messiah!

d. It was *kind and wise*. In order to spare the feelings of the men who are so very dear to him, Jesus does not at this time tell them the details of his gruesome approaching passion. Cf. John 16:12; Ps. 103:12.

e. It was *clear*. Before this time Jesus had spoken in a veiled manner about his coming suffering and resulting victory (Mark 2:20; cf. Matt. 12:39, 40; 16:4). Now he speaks *plainly*. [380]

32b. There follows Peter's rebuke (32b) and Christ's reaction to that rebuke (33). **And Peter took him aside and began to rebuke him.** For Peter the very idea of messiahship excluded suffering and execution. This disciple, as also the others, had been walking behind Jesus. Now he pulls the Master aside and begins to rebuke him. What the others may have thought he uttered. He was the man of words and action. What they may have wanted to do he did. According to Matthew, Peter said, "Mercy on thee, Lord, this shall never happen to thee." Of course, Peter should have known better. Had he never read Isa. 53? Did he not remember that John the Baptist had described Jesus as "the Lamb of God who is taking away the sin of the world"? What Peter did was therefore inexcusable. But if that be true, what shall we say about those critics today who are constantly pointing to Jesus as the Example to follow but reject the fact that he cannot be our Example unless first of all and most of all he is our Lord and Savior, who by his voluntary, sacrificial, substitutionary death saves his people from their sin and brings them to glory?

Christ's reaction was prompt, decisive, and forceful. He fully realized that back of Peter stood Satan, who was attempting once more, as he had done previously (Matt. 4:8, 9), to turn the attention of Jesus away from the cross. Not for a moment does the Savior dilly-dally. He puts into practice the advice he gave to others (9:43; cf. Matt. 5:29, 30): 33. **But turning around and seeing his disciples, he rebuked Peter and said, Get out of my sight, Satan, for you are looking at things not from God's point of view but from men's.** In speaking to Peter, Jesus is actually addressing Satan; or, if one prefers, is addressing whatever in Peter has been perversely influenced by the prince of evil. With speed and finality he rejects the implied temptation. True, from the human point of view being subjected to suffering and being killed is unacceptable. From God's point of view, however, this course was absolutely necessary, as has already been shown (see on verse 31). Divinely ordained also was the subsequent reward, the glorious resurrection. "Be gone, Satan," or "Get out of my sight, Satan," says Jesus, using language which the devil had heard before from the same lips (Matt. 4:10).

To man as he is by nature the cross is indeed offensive. He is unwilling to

---

[380] Though the etymology of παρρησία is "telling all," the derived meaning "plainly" obviously applies here.

accept the fact that "without the shedding of blood there is no remission" (Heb. 9:22). Christ crucified is to the Jews a stumblingblock, and to the Gentiles foolishness. Yet, in this very cross is revealed the power of God and the wisdom of God, a fact which those alone are able to appreciate who are saved, whether Jews or Gentiles (I Cor. 1:18, 24).

Jesus now shows an enlarged audience that what was true for himself holds also for everyone else, namely, that it is the way of the cross that leads to glory. This statement must not be misinterpreted. Christ's humiliation and his people's differ by a whole heaven. *His* death is unique, for it has atoning value (Mark 10:45; cf. Matt. 20:28). Ours does not (Ps. 49:7). Nevertheless, the principle as such, that the cross leads to the crown, holds not only for Christ (Heb. 12:2) but also for his people (Acts 14:22; II Cor. 4:17; II Tim. 3:12). In fact, between Christ's afflictions and his people's there is a close connection, so that the believer is "a partaker of Christ's suffering." He is hated because he serves a Master who is also hated (Matt. 10:24, 25; John 16:33; Col. 1:24; Heb. 13:13; I Peter 4:13; Rev. 12:4, 13).

This introduces verses 34-38. The brief but beautiful little paragraph begins with: **34a. And having called the people to him along with his disciples, he said to them. . . .** Jesus at this point called the multitudes to himself, to be *with* his disciples. The earnest exhortation which follows has significance for all; in fact, is for all a matter of life or death, everlasting life versus everlasting death. Hence, *all*—not only The Twelve—must hear it. The essence of the exhortation is that everyone should become a disciple of Jesus, who points out what one must do in order to be a disciple, that is, a follower, a true believer: **34b. If anyone wishes to come behind me, let him deny himself, take up his cross, and follow me.** To "come behind" Jesus means to attach oneself to him as his disciple. The figure is based on the fact that Christ's "followers"—not only The Twelve but also many others—often accompanied the Master, frequently literally *came on behind* him.

What, then, must a person do in order to be considered a true disciple? Well, if he wishes to come behind me, says Jesus, then *first,* he must deny himself; that is, he must once and for all say farewell to the old self, the self as it is apart from regenerating grace. A person who denies himself gives up all reliance on whatever he is by nature, and depends for salvation on God alone. He turns away in dismay not only from whatever thoughts and habits are patently sinful but even from reliance on "religious"—for example Pharisaic—thought patterns that cannot be harmonized with trust in Christ. See II Cor. 10:5. He must be willing to say with Paul, "Such things that once were gains to me these have I counted loss for Christ. . . ." See Phil. 3:7-11.

Secondly, he must take up his cross. The underlying figure is that of a condemned man who is forced to take up and carry his own cross to the place of execution. However, what the convict does under duress, the disciple of Christ does willingly. He voluntarily and decisively accepts the pain, shame, and persecution that is going to be *his* particular—note: *his,* not someone else's—lot because of his loyalty to Christ and his cause.

Finally, he must begin to follow and must keep on following Jesus. Here following the Master means trusting him (John 3:16), walking in his footsteps (I Peter 2:21), and obeying his commands (John 15:14) out of gratitude for salvation in him (Eph. 4:32–5:2). [381]

We must be careful, however, not to conceive of this self-denial, etc., in a chronological fashion, as if the Lord were exhorting his hearers to practice self-denial for a while, then after a lapse of time to take up and carry the cross, and, once having shouldered that burden for another time-period, to follow Jesus. The order is not chronological but logical. Together the three indicate *true conversion,* followed by life-long *sanctification.*

A second error to be guarded against is the notion that a person would be able *in his own power* to deny himself, take up his cross, and follow the Savior. Conversion (as well as the process of sanctification that follows it), though certainly a human responsibility, is impossible without regeneration (John 3:3, 5), which is the work of the Holy Spirit in man's heart. Moreover, that Spirit does not leave man to his own resources once the latter has been reborn, but remains with him forever, enabling him to do what otherwise he would not be able to do. It is, nevertheless, human responsibility and activity upon which the emphasis falls here in verse 34 ff.

In the next four verses (35-38) the obligation to be converted, etc., and the reward that results are brought into sharp contrast with the loss experienced by those who refuse to deny themselves, to take up their cross, and to follow Jesus. Each of the four verses begins with "For." [382] These "For" sentences or verses may therefore be considered as presenting, in a way, the basis for the urgent command of verse 34. What we have here is a phenomenon often occurring in Scripture and also in daily conversation, namely, *abbreviated expression.* [383] Fully expressed, the meaning of verses 35-38

---

[381] Note the following points of grammar: "wishes" or "desires" or "wants" adequately translates θέλει; 34b is a conditional sentence of the first class, the condition being one of reality, with εἴ τις having about the same meaning as ὅστις. See Gram. N.T., pp. 727, 1007, 1008. Note ἀπαρνησάσθω, third per. sing. aor. imper. middle of ἀπαρ-νέομαι, *to say No, deny, renounce, abnegate, disown;* and ἀράτω, third per. sing. aor. imper. active of αἴρω, *to take up.* Both of these imperatives are ingressive. Finally, note ἀκολουθείτω third per. sing. *present* imper. of ἀκολουθέω, *to follow.* This indicates an action which, once begun, continues.

[382] In the original γάρ is never found at the very beginning of a sentence. In the present case, as often, it is in each instance the second word. In English, however, γάρ is properly represented by the first word in the sentence. So also A.R.V., N.A.S., R.S.V., and Williams.

[383] See N.T.C. on John, Vol. I, p. 206; and on γάρ, as represented in Mark 8:35; Luke 9:24, see L.N.T. (A. and G.), p. 151.

would be somewhat as follows, with implied words in parentheses: 35 (Let him not refuse) For whoever would save his life shall lose it, but whoever loses his life for my sake and the gospel's shall save it. 36(Let him not follow the wrong course) For what good does it do a man to gain the whole world and forfeit his life? 37 For (once that life is lost) what shall a man give in exchange for—i.e., to buy back—his life? 38 (Let him not refuse, therefore) For whoever is ashamed of me and my words in this adulterous and sinful generation, of him also shall the Son of man be ashamed when he comes in the glory of his Father with his holy angels.

Accordingly, with an implied "Let him not refuse," there follows in verse **35. For whoever would save his life shall lose it, but whoever loses his life for my sake and the gospel's shall save it.** Meaning: the individual who would—or "should wish to" [384] —save his life shall lose it. Exactly what is it that he wishes to save? Answer: his life, that is, himself. [385] Here, however, we must make a distinction. In the present case the "life," "soul" or "self" which this person presumably wishes to save is his own immaterial and invisible being considered apart from regenerating grace. This man clings to that sinful life of his, holding on to it tenaciously. He reminds us of the rich fool described in Luke 12:16-21. See also Luke 16:19-31. He piles up material goods, thinking all the while of self, never of others. He imagines that material possessions, or else pleasure, prestige, fame, can bring him the inner peace and satisfaction he is looking for. But this selfish narrowing of his horizon makes his soul narrower and narrower. He loses it; that is, he loses whatever remnant of the higher, nobler life was left in him at the beginning.

On the other hand, whoever loses [386] his life "for my sake and the gospel's"—note "the gospel's sake," a reference to the good tidings, so characteristic of Mark (1:1, 15; 10:29)—shall save it. One "loses" his life in the present sense by devoting oneself completely to Christ, to the service of those in need, to the gospel. Note that Christ lays claim to such absolute devotion. This proves that he regards himself as Lord of all, and that the evangelist was fully aware of this! The person who offers this devotion saves his life, that is, his soul, or as we can also say, *himself.* The *self* here indicated is the inner being as influenced by divine grace. It is only by losing oneself—looking away from self in order to serve the Master and his "little ones" (cf. Matt. 25:40)—that one can ever be saved. The soul with wide horizons expands, becomes wonderfully enlarged. It overflows with peace, assurance, joy, etc. In helping others, it helps itself. In loving, it experiences

---

384 Note here ἐάν with third per. sing. pres. subjunctive θέλῃ, after the indefinite (here) relative ὅς. Such a subjunctive is futuristic in meaning. See Gram. N.T., p. 957.

385 See above, footnote 370 on p. 315f.

386 Or *shall lose.*

love, that of others, especially that of God. Consequently, Jesus urges upon every person in his audience not to follow the wrong course, the course of turning inward upon oneself, in an attempt to hang on to all one's earthly "treasures." To do so would amount to stupendous and, if persisted in, incurable folly. **36. For what good does it do a man to gain the whole world and forfeit his life?** Imagine for a moment that a person should gain the whole world—all its hidden gems and resources, whatever good things grow on it, the cattle upon a thousand hills, all the world's splendor, prestige, pleasures and treasures—, but in the process of doing this should forfeit, i.e., lose the right to possess, his own (higher) life or self, what good will this do him? Implied answer: no good whatever, only evil. This becomes even clearer when attention is focused on the fact that merely earthly goods lack permanence. When the person dies, he cannot take any of them along with him. But the soul, the self, exists on and on and on . . . in all its wretchedness and horror. All the selfish person's treasures are gone now. But even if he still had them, they would not be able to be exchanged for peace of heart and mind. Nothing, no absolutely nothing, will ever be accepted in exchange for the life, the *real* life, he so badly needs: **37. For what shall a man give in exchange for his life?** The loss he has suffered is simply irreparable. Nothing will compensate for it.

Here, and throughout, the underlying implication is that of yearning, wooing love: "O that each person in the audience might deny himself, take up his cross, and follow me!" The urgent appeal of verse 34 is never lost sight of.

Let no one therefore reject this appeal. Let no one disobey the command or refuse the implied invitation, **38. For whoever is ashamed of me and my words in this adulterous and sinful generation, of him also shall the Son of man be ashamed when he comes in the glory of his Father with his holy angels.** To be ashamed of Jesus means to be so proud that one wants to have nothing to do with him. Thus, for example, Heb. 2:11 states, "He is not ashamed (i.e., not too proud) to call them brothers." Jesus knew that not only his sworn enemies, the scribes and Pharisees, but also their many followers were in that sense ashamed of him and of his teachings; hence, he speaks of "this sinful and adulterous generation." Christ's Jewish contemporaries were adulterous, unfaithful to Jehovah, Israel's rightful Husband (Isa. 50:1 ff.; Jer. 3:8; 13:27; 31:32; Ezek. 16:32, 35 ff.; Hos. 2:1 ff.). Cf. Matt. 12:39; 16:4. They were definitely sinful, having completely missed the goal of serving and glorifying God.

Having been ashamed of Jesus, the latter is going to be ashamed of them. Cf. Matt. 7:23; Luke 13:27. At his return he will reject and condemn them. Cf. Matt. 25:41-46a. Note Christ's self-designation, "the Son of man," derived from Dan. 7:13, 14 (cf. Mark 14:62). See above, on verse 31; also on

2:10; and N.T.C. on Matthew, pp. 403-407. The Son of man is the One who, coming from above and therefore intrinsically glorious throughout, here on earth suffers. But through his vicarious suffering he attains to a glory that is not only inward but also outward. He shall come "in the glory of his Father with his holy angels." Meaning: at his second coming the Father will impart his own glory to him, and will give to him his own angels, to function as his brilliant retinue. Cf. Matt. 25:31.

9:1. And he was saying to them, I solemnly declare to y o u that there are some of those who are standing here who shall not taste death until they see the kingdom of God come with power. For "I solemnly declare" see on 3:28. To "taste death" means to experience it, that is, to die. Here in 8:38; 9:1 Jesus regards the entire state of exaltation, from his resurrection to his second coming, as a unit. In 8:38 he refers to its final consummation; here in 9:1 to its beginning. He is saying that some of those whom he is addressing are going to be witnesses of this beginning. They are going to see the kingdom or kingship or reign of God come "with power." The reference is in all probability to Christ's glorious resurrection, his return *in the Spirit* on the day of Pentecost, and in close connection with that event his position, with great power and influence, at the Father's right hand. Changes so vast would then begin to take place on earth that, as outsiders were going to remark, the world would be "turned upside down" (Acts 17:6). Momentous events would occur: the becoming "of age" of the church, its extension among the Gentiles, the conversion of people by the thousands, the presence and exercise of many charismatic gifts, etc. Jesus predicts that all this will begin to take place during the lifetime of some of those whom he is now addressing. That, too, was literally fulfilled. For more on this see N.T.C. on Matthew, pp. 659, 660.

The coming of Christ's royal reign "with power" is foreshadowed in the transfiguration, recorded in the next paragraph, Mark 9:2-8. There are those who believe that this event was included in Christ's prediction recorded in 9:1. Certainty on this point is probably unobtainable.

Summary of Chapter 8:1—9:1

The six sections may be summarized as follows:

a. Verses 1-10 record the miraculous feeding of the four thousand. Jesus and his disciples are still in a desolate region east of the Sea of Galilee. A huge crowd has been with him three days. There is no more food. So, the Master tells the disciples, "My heart goes out to the multitude. . . ." The disciples merely answer, "Where in this uninhabited region can anyone get bread enough?" They had only seven bread-cakes. For these hungry people Jesus then performs a miracle that is largely similar to that of the previous feeding (6:30-44). Seven hampers full of broken pieces are left after everybody has had plenty to eat. The fact that Jesus was able to repeat his miracles shows his greatness. Also, the present miracle reveals wide-embracing divine love.

b. According to verses 11-13, after arriving on the western shore Christ's miracle-working power was challenged by the Pharisees, who demanded "a sign from heaven," as if all the previous miracles amounted to zero. Sighing deeply because of their stubborn unbelief, Jesus refused.

c. The incident reported in verses 14-21 took place on the sea from Dalmanutha to Bethsaida Julias. The disciples had forgotten to take along bread, only one bread-cake remaining. Jesus warned them against "the yeast of the Pharisees and the yeast of Herod." The Twelve thought that he was referring to literal bread and was finding fault with them for not having provided it. By means of a series of questions Jesus exhorts them to trust in him.

d. Only Mark records the miracle found in verses 22-26. It took place at Bethsaida Julias. A blind man was brought to Jesus, with the request that he be healed. After Jesus for the first time laid his hands on him the handicapped individual saw "men as trees, walking." After he again laid his hands on the man's eyes, his sight was fully restored.

Among the detailed restoration of sight narratives not two are alike, showing that divine love touches people individually, not only in the mass.

e. According to verses 27-30, near Caesarea Philippi, Jesus asked his disciples, "Who do the people say I am?" They answered, "John the Baptist . . . Elijah . . . one of the prophets." There followed, "But *y o u,* who do *y o u* say I am?" Peter answered, "Thou art the Christ." Jesus warned the disciples not to reveal this fact to anyone. He knew that popular misconceptions concerning messiahship could have brought his public ministry to an untimely end. For the full story see N.T.C. on Matthew, pp. 641-652.

f. Jesus now makes his first *clear* prediction of the approaching passion and resurrection (verses 31—9:1). He says, "The Son of man must suffer many things and be rejected by the elders and the chief priests and the scribes, and be killed, and after three days rise again."

Jesus the Messiah? Yes, but the *Suffering* Messiah. Peter's attempt at rebuking the Master for this interpretation—an attempt in which Jesus discerns a temptation by Satan—received a decisive rebuff. To an audience consisting of The Twelve plus many others Jesus explains that his true disciples are partakers of his suffering: "If anyone wishes to come behind me, let him deny himself, take up his cross and follow me." For fuller explanation of 9:1 see N.T.C. on Matthew, pp. 659, 660.

Outline of Chapter 9:2-50

Theme: *The Work Which Thou Gavest Him To Do*

9:2-13   The Transfiguration of Jesus on a High Mountain
9:14-29   The Healing of an Epileptic Boy
9:30-32   The Second Prediction of the Passion and the Resurrection
9:33-37   Who Is the Greatest?
9:38-41   He Who Is Not against Us Is for Us
9:42-50   Guard the Little Ones and Do Not Yield to Temptation

CHAPTER IX: 2-50

9 2 Six days later Jesus took with him Peter and James and John, and led them up a high mountain by themselves; and he was transfigured before them. 3 His clothes became dazzling white, whiter than any bleacher on earth could bleach them. 4 And there appeared to them Elijah and Moses, who were engaged in conversation with Jesus. 5 Then Peter spoke up and said to Jesus, "Rabbi, how good it is for us to be here! Let us make three shelters, one for you, one for Moses, and one for Elijah." 6 For he did not really know what to say, so frightened were they. 7 Then there came a cloud that covered them; and out of the cloud there came a voice: "This is my Son, my Beloved; listen to him." 8 And suddenly, when they looked around, they no longer saw anyone with them, except Jesus.

9 And when they were coming down from the mountain, he charged them not to tell anyone what they had seen, until after the Son of man had risen from the dead. 10 They scrupulously kept the charge, meanwhile questioning among themselves what "rising from the dead" meant.

11 And they asked him, saying, "Why do the scribes say that first Elijah has to come?" 12 And he said to them, "Elijah does come first, and restores everything; and yet, how is it (that it is) written about the Son of man that he must suffer many things and be treated with contempt? 13 But I say to y o u that Elijah has indeed come, and they treated him as they pleased, just as it is written about him."

9:2-13 *The Transfiguration of Jesus on a High Mountain*
Cf. Matt. 17:1-13; Luke 9:28-36

Touchingly beautiful is the connection between chapters 8 and 9. In the closing paragraph of chapter 8 (really the paragraph embracing 8:31–9:1) Jesus was pictured as the One who withstood Satan's temptation to avoid the cross. He said, "Get out of my sight, Satan." By means of this reaction to the devil's sinister attack he reasserted his decision to be "the Lamb of God who is taking away the sin of the world." Speaking in human terms, this deeply touched the heart of the Father (see 9:7b), who therefore now, on the Mount of Transfiguration (9:2-13) responds by imparting to his Son "glory and honor." He did this, as Mark states, by

a. *enveloping* his body, including even his clothes, with heavenly brilliance (verses 2, 3);

b. *sending* him two heavenly messengers, Elijah and Moses, who conversed with him (verse 4), about his coming passion and (probably also) subsequent reward (Luke 9:31b); and

c. *proclaiming,* in the hearing of Peter, James, and John, "This is my Son, my Beloved; listen to him."

Once we grasp this connection between the two chapters, not only will the transition from chapter 8 to chapter 9 be easier to remember, but also—and this is more important—we shall have a better insight into the real meaning of the transfiguration, as indicated in II Peter 1:16, 17.

From the manner in which this story is treated in the Synoptics it is clear that although even here written as well as oral source material is probable at least for the later Gospels, no evangelist is slavishly dependent upon any other: each of these parallels contributes items not found in the others. Note the following individual contributions:

Matthew alone reports that the face of Jesus "shone like the sun." Luke merely says that the appearance of his countenance was changed. Mark omits this item entirely. It is also Matthew alone who states that when a voice spoke from the cloud "the disciples fell on their faces," that Jesus came and touched these frightened men, and that he told them not to be afraid. Note also Matthew's vivid and dramatic touches in 17:5: "while he was still talking, *lo,* a *bright* cloud. . . ."

It is *Luke* who reports that the transfiguration occurred when Jesus was praying, and when Peter and those with him were heavy with sleep. The theme of the conversation between Jesus and the heavenly messengers is also reported only by Luke.

Note also the slight difference among the three in the wording of the Father's address in commending his Son to the disciples:

Matthew: "This is my Son, my Beloved, with whom I am well pleased; listen to him!"

Mark: "This is my Son, my Beloved; listen to him."

Luke: "This is my Son, my Chosen One; listen to him."

As to *Mark,* after a brief explanation of 9:2-8, together with reference to N.T.C. on Matthew for fuller exegesis, certain points of special interest will be discussed. The same treatment will subsequently be given to verses 9-13.

2-8. Six days later—i.e., six days after Peter's confession and Christ's first prediction of the passion and the resurrection—**Jesus took with him Peter and James and John**—so that after the great event of Easter they might bear witness of what they had seen—**, and led them up a high mountain**—Jebel Jermak in Upper Galilee?—**by themselves**—the other nine disciples stayed behind; cf. verse 14—**; and he was transfigured**—his outward appearance was changed—**before them. His clothes became dazzling white, whiter than any bleacher**—"fuller" or "launderer"—**on earth could bleach them. And there appeared to them Elijah and Moses**—probably representing respectively the prophets and the law, both of which Christ had come to fulfill—**, who were engaged in conversation with Jesus.** They talked with him about his fast approaching "departure" in Jerusalem (Luke 9:31). **Then Peter spoke up and said to Jesus, Rabbi, how good it is for us to be here! Let us make three shelters, one for you, one for Moses, and one for Elijah**—as if heavenly visitors needed earthly shelters—. **For he did not really know what to say, so frightened were they.** Besides, they were, at least had been, "heavy with sleep" (Luke 9:32). **Then there came a cloud that covered them**—often in Scripture the presence of God is indicated by means of a luminous cloud; see Exod. 16:10—; **and out of the cloud there came a voice: This is my Son, my Beloved; listen to him.** For voices of encouragement and approval spoken by God the Father to his Son, the Mediator, see also Matt. 3:17; Mark 1:11; Luke 9:35; John 12:28. The Father, by calling his Son "my Beloved," and by telling the trio to listen and keep on listening to him, is honoring his Chosen One (Luke 9:35) before them. **And suddenly, when they looked around, they no longer saw anyone with them, except Jesus.** What an act of divine kindness toward the three men, that the dazzling brilliance did not last very long, so that presently they were again with Jesus, alone with him.

See N.T.C. on Matthew, pp. 663-669 (the explanation of 17:1-8).

Attention should be called to points of special interest:

verse 3

While all three accounts report the effect of the transfiguration on the clothes Jesus was wearing, each does this in his own way. According to Matthew "his clothes became white as light." Luke says that Christ's apparel "flashed like lightning." Mark uses a term found nowhere else in the New Testament. [387] In the Septuagint it indicates the radiance of the stars. A good translation here in Mark 9:3 is, "His clothes became dazzling white." Moreover, Mark is the only evangelist who reports that no "fuller" on earth would have been able to make these garments as white. A fuller is one who cards and cleans woolen clothes. In the present instance of its use the emphasis falls on cleaning, making white; hence, a bleacher. Another rendering that deserves consideration would be, ". . . as white as no laundryman on earth could make them."

verse 4

The word "appeared" [388] (in "there appeared to them Elijah and Moses") does not indicate mere subjective or mental appearance. It has reference to an objective manifestation. It is used in connection with the coming into view of angels (Luke 1:11; 22:43; Acts 7:30, 35), the risen Christ (Luke 24:34; Acts 9:17; I Cor. 15:5-8); etc. It was with their physical eyes that Peter and his companions saw these visitors from heaven. Note also: (Elijah

---

387 στίλβοντα nom. pl. neut. pres. participle of στίλβω, to shine, sparkle, glisten.
388 ὤφθη, third per. sing. aor. indic. passive of ὁράω.

and Moses) "were talking with" or "were engaged in conversation with." [389]
We receive the distinct impression that for Elijah and Moses this speaking
with an exalted being like Jesus Christ was not something unusual. These
two messengers from heaven were filled with reverence, of course, as they
stood there on the Mount of Transfiguration, "talking with" Jesus. But it
was a reverence which excluded any earthly fear and alarm. Does not the
description offered to us here in Mark 9:4 and parallel passages shed some
light on the character of heavenly fellowship?

verse 5

Literally this verse begins as follows, "And Peter answering said to Jesus."
However, no question had been asked; so how could Peter be answering? The
solution is that the word used in the original for "answering" has a very
broad meaning. Here—as often—it simply means that Peter *reacted* or *responded* to a situation, namely, that of (what he conceived to be) the need
of Jesus and of the two men who had suddenly arrived from heaven. See also
N.T.C. on Matthew, p. 84, footnote 89.

According to Mark 9:5 Peter addresses Jesus as "Rabbi"; according to the
parallel passage in Matthew (17:4), as "Lord"; and according to Luke (9:33),
as "Master." Clearly, in the present passages these three terms must be
considered synonyms: all aim to do justice to the exalted character of the
Savior. Each evangelist offers his own translation of the Aramaic word which
Peter must have used.

Compare "let us make" with "I will make" of Matt. 17:4. [390] Solution:
Peter's idea was that under his own direction all three disciples would
construct these tents.

verse 6

Peter's suggestion was ill-considered: his *condition* was that of a man who
makes a hasty remark. He "was not really knowing," did not really
know, [391] what to say. Under such circumstances it is generally best not to
say anything. This, however, would hardly have been in character for
loquacious Simon, especially for a Simon just awakened out of sleep, and,
like James and John, filled with fear. But before we begin to criticize this

---

[389] Note the periphrastic ἦσαν συλλαλοῦντες; cf. Acts 25:12, where Festus *is confer-
ring* with his advisers.

[390] In Matt. 17:4 it is natural after εἰ θέλεις to interpret ποιήσω as a future *indicative*
(not as aor. subjunctive); but Mark 9:5 (ποιήσωμεν has the aor. *subjunctive* (hortatory);
also, the former is first per. *sing.*; the latter first per. *plural*.

[391] ἤδει, third per. sing. pluperf. (with sense of imperfect) of οἶδα. Note τί ἀποκριθῇ:
the deliberative subjunctive of the direct question is retained in indirect discourse. Here,
as in verse 5 and often, the verb ἀποκρίνομαι has a wide meaning, so that τί ἀποκριθῇ
means "what he should say," or simply "what to say."

apostle too severely, would it not be in order to take to heart the warning of James 1:19? [392]

Matthew connects the fear of the three disciples with the voice that came out of the cloud (17:6); Luke (9:34) with the experience of entering the cloud; but Mark (verses 2b-6) with the entire scene. Conclusion: the reaction of the disciples was that of increasing awe, to which every item contributed its quota. The real *lesson* of the transfiguration, a lesson indicated earlier, must have dawned upon them gradually, after subsequent reflection.

Even though it is generally Mark's Gospel that is the most dramatic, at times Matthew's excels in this respect. So also here: cf. Mark's and Luke's "there came a cloud" with Matthew's "*lo*—or: *suddenly*—a *bright* cloud."

verse 7

Note: "listen to him," an exhortation occurring in all three. Here the Father joins the Son—see above, on 4:9—in emphasizing the importance of hearing and taking to heart; only now it is specifically the Son who is indicated as the One to whom men should give heed.

The exhortation was certainly necessary. In general, how had the words or messages of Jesus been received? It is only fair to emphasize that tremendous interest had been shown (3:7-9, 20; 4:1; 6:4; cf. Matt. 7:28, 29). Christ's teaching answered a need. Moreover, it was penetrating, refreshing, and original, not like that of the scribes. But though, by God's grace, many hearts had been changed and lives transformed, often the reaction had been that of disobedience (1:44, 45), unbelief (6:2-6), and even ridicule (5:39, 40). From the side of his sworn enemies, Jesus had met with contradiction (2:5, 6) and hot resentment (3:4-6). Even the disciples had at times expressed disbelief (5:30, 31), had revealed misunderstanding (8:15, 16), and once, in the case of Peter, had even descended to the level of flat, breath-taking contradiction (8:32b). The parable of The Sower was being constantly re-enacted in the reaction of individuals and audiences: many heard, few heeded. Nevertheless, faith is induced by hearing, is awakened by the message (Rom. 10:17); and without faith it is impossible to please God and to be saved. We can therefore appreciate the voice from heaven, "Listen to him." And is it not true that this earnest exhortation proves the fact that God the Father—as well as God the Son, and God the Holy Spirit—takes delight in men's salvation? See Ezek. 18:23; 33:11; John 3:16. The Three are One.

9. **And when they were coming down from the mountain, he charged them not to tell anyone what they had seen, until after the Son of man had risen from the dead.** This verse is almost literally the same as its parallel

---

[392] Read L. A. Flynn's very interesting book, *Did I Say That?*, Nashville, 1959.

Matt. 17:9. The latter, however, uses direct discourse in recording Christ's charge, while Mark has indirect discourse. Jesus knew that the time for public disclosure of his glory—as about to be revealed in his death and resurrection, and as even now foreshadowed in his transfiguration—had not yet arrived. When the first open announcement to his people, as represented by their leaders, must be made, he himself will make it (Mark 14:61, 62: note "Son of man" in that passage as also here in Mark 9:9, 12; and see on 2:10). After his resurrection the disciples would be free and duty-bound to relate far and wide whatever they had seen and heard on the Mount of Transfiguration. The very fact of Christ's death followed by his resurrection would illumine the account, setting it in its proper perspective.

Note "what they had seen." It is clear that neither Jesus himself nor his reporter, John Mark, viewed what had happened on the mount as being a merely subjective vision or—worse even—a figment of the imagination. And the three disciples, too, were thoroughly convinced that they had been "eye-witnesses of his majesty" (II Peter 1:16).

10. They scrupulously kept the charge, meanwhile questioning among themselves [393] what "rising from the dead" meant. These men sedulously observed the order—literally, *the word*—Jesus had given them. They as it were fastened on to it, clung to it. [394] Luke 9:36 is in full agreement: "They kept silence and told no one in those days anything of what they had seen." As to the words of Jesus . . . "until after the Son of man had risen from the dead," they asked each other questions about that. They were utterly baffled. As if the very idea of the Messiah being tormented and even put to death were not sufficiently exasperating, their minds had now been burdened by this added conundrum: that same Messiah rising again! Perhaps their questions were somewhat along this line: "Peter, what do you think he meant by this?" "John, do you think he was referring to the resurrection at the last day?" "James, why is the Master going to die at all if he is going to rise again?" Another question may have been, "Was he referring to a physical resurrection?" But these are merely guesses.

11, 12a. And they asked him, saying, Why do the scribes say that [395] **first Elijah has to come? And he said to them, Elijah does come first, and restores everything.** . . . An almost exact parallel to these words is found in Matt. 17:10, 11. Therefore see N.T.C. on that passage, p. 669 ff. Meaning in brief: Jesus just now had predicted his resurrection from the dead, implying his imminent death. What bothers the disciples is that such a death would seem

---

[393] For the verb see on 8:11, footnote 368. I combine πρὸς ἑαυτούς with συζητοῦντες.

[394] Note the verb ἐκράτησαν, third per. pl. aor. indic. of κρατέω, to take (something) into one's possession and/or hold on to (it).

[395] After "And they asked him saying," note ὅτι . . . . . . ὅτι. The first ὅτι must mean *why?* See on 2:16, footnote 75; the second *that*.

to leave Messianic prophecies unfulfilled. Are not the scribes constantly saying that Messiah's coming would be preceded by that of Elijah? See Mal. 4:5, 6. But even though on the one hand the Tishbite obviously has not as yet reappeared upon the scene of history, restoring everything, yet on the other hand Jesus, the Messiah, not only has already arrived but even declares that he is about to die. How is this possible? In his answer Jesus first of all declares that the scribes were right in maintaining that Elijah's coming would precede that of Messiah. In verse 13 Jesus adds that Elijah did actually come. See further on verse 13.

This, however, creates another problem in the minds of the disciples, as Mark now points out. Granted that this was true, namely, that the scribes were right about Messiah's arrival being preceded by that of Elijah, who restores everything, then where does the idea of *a suffering and dying Christ* fit in? Jesus now points out that this, too, had been predicted. He therefore continues: 12b. **and yet, how is it (that it is) written about the Son of man that he must suffer many things and be treated with contempt?** This, says Jesus as it were, is a very important prediction, one that must not be ignored. He does not quote any particular prophecy, but may it not be safely concluded that he was thinking of such passages as Ps. 22:1-18; 69:8, 9, 11, 20, 21; 118:22a; and especially of Isa. 53:3? Yes, the predictions had been clear enough, but they had been by-passed!

Jesus concludes his answer as follows: 13. **But I say to y o u that Elijah has indeed come, and they treated him as they pleased, just as it is written about him.** It is Matthew's Gospel that supplies the commentary: " 'But I say to y o u that Elijah already came. But they failed to recognize him, and treated him as they pleased. Similarly the Son of man is about to suffer at their hands.' Then the disciples understood that he had spoken to them about John the Baptist." See N.T.C. on Matt. 17:12, 13, pp. 671, 672. By and large the people had not taken to heart the preaching of John the Baptist. They had failed to recognize him as the fulfilment of prophecy (Matt. 11:16-18). The religious leaders of the Jews had turned against him (21:25). At the instigation of wicked Herodias, Herod Antipas had killed John (14:3, 10). Instead of asking, "How does *God* want us to treat John the Baptist?" they had done to him whatever *they* pleased. And the same combination was about to kill Jesus. The Tishbite . . . John the Baptist . . . Jesus, by and large none were accepted; all were treated with contempt. Note "as it is written about him." That writing begins already at I Kings 19:2, 10b. All were able to say, "They seek my life, to take it away."

This very fact—that it was written, hence divinely planned—is filled with comfort. It shows that without in any way erasing human responsibility and guilt, these murderous intentions and (in the case of the Baptist and Jesus) deeds happened in accordance with the divine decree. In the end, therefore,

343

God always triumphs. His truth is victorious. Cf. Luke 22:22; Acts 2:23, 24. See also Isa. 53:4-6.

---

14 And when they came to the (other) disciples, they saw a large crowd around them, and scribes arguing with them. 15 Now as soon as all the people saw him [Jesus], they were greatly amazed and were running forward to welcome him. 16 He asked them, "What are y o u arguing about with them?" 17 And one of the crowd answered him, "Teacher, I brought my son to you, for he is possessed by a spirit that has deprived him of the ability to speak. [396] 18 Moreover, whenever it seizes him, it dashes him to the ground, and he foams at the mouth, grinds his teeth, and becomes rigid. I asked your disciples to cast it out, but they could not." 19 He answered and said to them, "O faithless generation, how long shall I be with y o u? How long shall I put up with y o u? Bring him to me." 20 So they brought the boy to him. And when the spirit saw him [Jesus], it immediately threw the boy into a convulsion. He fell to the ground and was rolling around, foaming at the mouth. 21 And he [Jesus] asked the boy's father, "How long has this been happening to him?" He answered, "From childhood. 22 Again and again it has thrown him into fire or into water in order to kill him; but if you can do anything, take pity on us and help us." 23 Jesus said to him, "As to that 'if you can,' all things are possible for him who believes." 24 Immediately the boy's father cried out, "I do believe, help my unbelief." [397] 25 Now when Jesus saw that a crowd came running together, he rebuked the unclean spirit, saying to it, "You deaf and dumb spirit, I command you, come out of him and don't you ever enter him again." 26 Shrieking and throwing the boy into terrible convulsions, it came out. To such an extent did the boy resemble a corpse that most people were saying, "He is dead." 27 But Jesus grasped his hand and lifted him to his feet, and he stood up. 28 And after he [Jesus] had gone indoors, his disciples asked him privately, "Why couldn't we cast it out?" 29 He told them, "This kind can come out only by prayer."

9:14-29 *The Healing of an Epileptic Boy*
Cf. Matt. 17:14-20; Luke 9:37-43a

When we compare Mark's account of this miracle with that of Matthew, it is the difference rather than the resemblance that stands out. Of Mark's 16 verses devoted to this event only 18b, 19, 28—plus a trace here and there in the remaining part—clearly suggest literary relationship. When Mark's account is laid alongside of Luke's the result is about the same. With one exception, namely, Mark 9:29; cf. Matt. 17:20, Mark's account is by far the most detailed of the three. Contrast Mark's 16 verses with Matthew's 7 and with Luke's 6½. It cannot be denied that the shorter accounts contain important items not found in Mark. Thus Matthew records that the father of the grievously afflicted boy "approached Jesus and kneeling before him said . . ."; and also that the Master pointed to lack of sufficient *faith* as the cause of the disciples' failure to heal this boy (17:14, 20). And Luke *a.* indicates the time when the miracle occurred—"on the next day," that is,

---

[396] Literally: . . . "who has a dumb spirit." Cf. verse 25.
[397] Or: help me in my unbelief.

the day after the transfiguration—*b*. reproduces a significant item of the father's moving appeal—"he is my only child"—; and *c*. closes his account by stating, "All were astonished at the majesty of God" (9:37, 38, 43). For the rest, it is to Mark that we turn for the most detailed and vivid report.

14. And when they came to the (other) disciples, they saw a large crowd around them, and scribes arguing with them. Having completed their descent from the mountain, Jesus and the three, on the day after the Master's transfiguration, were approaching the place where they had left the other nine disciples. They saw a large crowd surrounding the nine, and soon were close enough to notice some scribes in argument [398] with the nine.

If the Mount of Transfiguration was *Jebel Jermak* in Upper Galilee, not far from Capernaum, which was reached soon afterward (9:33; cf. Matt. 17:24), the presence of this crowd and of these scribes is understandable. Nor is it surprising that these scribes were filled with chortling, malicious glee [399] because of the inability of the nine to cure an epileptic boy. So, to use a slang expression, "they were rubbing it in." The nine were having a difficult time in defending themselves before all these people.

15. Now as soon as all the people saw him [Jesus], they were greatly amazed [400] **and were running forward to welcome him.** As far as the crowd and the disciples were concerned, Jesus' sudden appearance was most welcome. They had not yet expected him; hence, were greatly amazed. They ran to receive him into their midst. The scribes could not very well stay behind; neither did they want to.

For the theory of some, that the transfiguration brightness was still visible on the face of Jesus, and that it was this that gave rise to the crowd's amazement, there is no proof whatever. Moses and Jesus, Mount Sinai and the Mount of Transfiguration, how different they were in this respect! See Exod. 34:29 f.; II Cor. 3:7.

Jesus rushes to the defense of his disciples. He does this by turning his attention to the scribes: **16. He asked them, What are y o u arguing about with them?** He was fully aware of the weaknesses of his disciples (see verses 28, 29; also N.T.C. on Matthew, pp. 246, 247, 455). Yet . . . he loved them, and came to their rescue!

For the scribes the "fun" they were having suddenly ends. So embarrassed are they that they do not know what to say. So the arguing and jeering suddenly stops. Not even one of the law-experts was anxious to answer Christ's question. Nevertheless, the silence does not last very long; for out of

---

[398] συζητοῦντας, as in verse 10, but now accusative. Besides, the meaning is slightly different.

[399] The Germans would say *Schadenfreude;* the Dutch, *leedvermaak.*

[400] ἐξεθαμβήθησαν, third per. pl. aor. indic. passive of ἐκθαμβέω; with ἐκ, probably intensive.

the crowd one man steps forward, as is clear from verses 17, 18. And one of the crowd answered him, Teacher I brought my son to you, for he is possessed by a spirit that has deprived him of the ability to speak. Moreover, whenever it seizes him, it dashes him to the ground, and he foams at the mouth, grinds his teeth, and becomes rigid. Thus spoke the father of a grievously afflicted *only* child (Luke 9:38). Compare this with the "only son" of the widow at Nain (Luke 7:12), and with the "only daughter" of Jairus (Luke 8:42). The heart of God's only Son went out to these only children, to their parents, and to many, many others besides!

Respectfully the father addresses Jesus as "Teacher" (thus also in Luke), as "Lord" (thus in Matthew). In the course of his speech the man may well have used both titles, or else each evangelist is giving his own translation of an Aramaic form of address.

"I brought to you my son" should be compared with "I asked your disciples" (verse 18). Evidently the man's original intention had been to bring his grievously stricken son to Jesus to be healed. But when he noticed that Jesus was not in the company of the disciples, he had asked the latter to heal the afflicted one. And why not? Did not casting out demons and healing the sick belong to the task that had been assigned to the disciples? See 6:7; cf. Matt. 10:1. And is it not true that to a certain extent these men had been successful in fulfilling this mandate? See Mark 6:13, 30; Luke 9:6-10. But in the present case—for a reason mentioned later (verse 29)—the disciples had failed: **I asked your disciples to cast it out, but they could not.**

When we carefully review the various symptoms of the affliction endured by this boy, we are forced to conclude that we are dealing here with a case of epilepsy. Verses 18, 20, 26 make mention of the very conditions commonly associated with this disease: seizures, convulsions, falling to the ground, foaming at the mouth, teeth grinding, rigidity. However, we hasten to add, "This was not an *ordinary* case of epilepsy. It was far worse." This boy, in addition to being plagued with the convulsive disorder called *grand mal,* was also a deaf-mute. "He has a dumb spirit," says the father, making use of abbreviated discourse; hence, really meaning, "He is possessed by a spirit that has deprived him of the ability to speak" (and to hear, as Jesus adds in verse 25). The boy was therefore an epileptic, a deaf-mute, and worst of all, a demoniac, his grievous physical condition having been brought about by an unclean spirit. This was therefore not a case of simple epilepsy; no, it was a very complicated condition, in which the boy did not merely *fall* to the ground but was actually again and again *knocked down* by the evil spirit. [401] For more about demon-possession see above, on 1:23.

---

401 Note the following words in verse 18:

ὅπου ἐάν   can mean *whenever* as well as *wherever*.
καταλάβη   (cf. *catalepsy*), third per. sing. aor. active subjunctive of κατα-

Deeply moved—note "O"—: 19. **He answered and said to them, O faithless generation, how long shall I be with y o u? How long shall I put up with y o u?** By means of this exclamation Jesus expressed his pain and indignation. The fact that he directed his complaint to the "generation" shows that he cannot have been thinking only of the nine disciples who had failed in this emergency. He was evidently deeply dissatisfied with his contemporaries: with the father, who lacked sufficient faith in Christ's healing power (9:22-24); with the scribes, who, instead of showing any pity, were in all probability gloating over the disciples' impotence (9:14); with the crowd in general, which is pictured in the Gospels as being generally far more concerned about itself than about others (John 6:26); and, last but not least, with the nine disciples, because of their failure to exercise their faith by putting their whole heart into persevering prayer (9:29).

To a greater or lesser extent all were faithless, lacking in the exercise of true, warm, enduring faith, a faith operating effectively. When Jesus adds, "How long shall I be with y o u; how long shall I put up with y o u?" he shows that in view of his own trust in the heavenly Father, a confidence that was faultless, and in view of his own love which was infinite and tender, it was painful for him to "put up with" (the exact meaning of the original) those who lacked these qualities or who failed to exercise these virtues in a sufficient degree. His ministry had lasted almost three years by now. He was longing for the end.

By means of the heart-warming and positive command, **Bring him to me,** Jesus gave the perfect example of proper behavior during annoying and distressing circumstances. In what he was about to do he revealed not only his power but also, as always, his love.

The story continues as follows: 20. **So they brought the boy to him. And when the spirit saw him [Jesus], it immediately threw the boy into a**

	λαμβάνω, to lay hold of, grasp, take possession of; here: seizes (cf. seizure).
ῥήσσει	(cf. break, wreck, fracture), third per. sing. pres. active indicative of ῥήσσω, an alternative form of ῥήγνυμι, here: dashes to the ground. Third per. sing. pres. *active* indicatives are also:
ἀφρίζει	(cf. froth), foams.
τρίζει	(cf. *strident*), grinds, an onomatopoeia occurring only here in the New Testament. See, however, βρύχω (Acts 7:54), and the noun βρυγμός (Matt. 8:12; 13:42, etc.) *Passive* indic. is:
ξηραίνεται	, becomes rigid (cf. *xerosis,* abnormal dryness). This verb is used also in connection with a *withered* hand (Mark 3:1), plant (4:6), fig tree (11:20, 21); and a *dried up* fountain (of blood, 5:29). See also John 15:6; James 1:11; I Peter 1:24; Rev. 14:15; 16:2.
ἐκβάλωσι	, third per. pl. aor. act. subjunctive of ἐκβάλλω; here: that they might cast—or: to cast—(it) out.
(οὐκ) ἴσχυσαν	, third per. pl. aor. indic. of ἰσχύω; they were (not) able; did (not) have the strength (cf. ἰσχύς).

convulsion. **He fell to the ground and was rolling around, foaming at the mouth.** The remark made earlier, namely, that this was *not an ordinary* case of epilepsy but one brought about and aggravated by a demon, is clear from these facts: *a.* the convulsion occurs at the very moment when the demon sees Jesus; and *b.* it was not a cerebral disorder operating by itself that produced the muscle spasms, etc.; no, it was the demon that convulsed[402] the lad, so that presently he was rolling[403] on the ground, foaming at the mouth.

21, 22. And he [Jesus] asked the boy's father, How long has this been happening to him? He answered, From childhood. Again and again it has thrown him into fire or into water in order to kill him; but if you can do anything, take pity on us and help us. Like a sympathetic physician Jesus asks the father how long the boy has been in this condition. Not that Jesus needs this information in order to bring about recovery, but the father needs to reflect on the lengthy period of time during which his son has been in this condition, in order that he may be all the more thankful for the miracle that is about to take place. Such a reflection will also have a wholesome effect on those standing around.

The father's state of mind and heart is revealed by the fact that he not only answers Christ's question but also supplies further details, beyond those already reported in verses 17, 18. Clearly, the father's soul is wrapped up in that of his son: tender and intense was his love for this boy. And note here again—see also verse 20—it is not the *falling* into fire or water that is stressed but the *being thrown* into these potential killers, with the sinister purpose, on the part of the evil spirit, *to destroy* him.

But though the situation was very grievous, it was not entirely hopeless, not even to the mind of this father. An inkling—perhaps not more—of hope was left. He is convinced that Jesus *wants* to help him. The question is, "Can he?" Contrast this father's implied "If you can,[404] you will" with the leper's "If you will, you can" (1:40). The demoniac's father grants the possibility that Jesus might be able to help, but he is not sure: he lacks sufficient faith in the power of the Savior.

---

402 συνεσπάραξεν, third per. sing. aor. indic. of συσπαράσσω; cf. (threw him into) paroxysms (fits). A. T. Robertson (*Word Pictures*, Vol. I, p. 341) states that the prefix still retains its perfective force; hence, *grievously*. This may well be correct (see verse 26), but cannot be proved.

403 ἐκυλίετο, third per. sing. middle imperfect indic. of κυλίω; cf. *cylinder* (basically *roller*).

404 εἰ τι δύνῃ (contracted form of δύνασαι), first class condition; second per. sing. pres. indicative of δύναμαι. The word δύναμαι can mean *to be able to do* as well as simply *to be able*. Therefore the usual translation "If you can do" is correct. In other words ποιεῖν does not have to be expressed; it can be understood. See L.N.T. (A. and G.), p. 206, under 3. Contrary Lenski, *op. cit.*, p. 240.

Note "Take pity [405] on us." It is the pity or active sympathy of Jesus that stands out in the Gospels. See above, on 1:41, including footnote 57. ". . . and help us." The word "help" is very meaningful and touching. In the original it consists of two smaller words: *a cry* and *run*. [406] In any context in which this word is used it is an earnest and moving request that the Lord, or whoever the potential helper happens to be, may rush toward the person who is in need, and may help him. A detailed study of the various specific contexts in which this verb is used is rewarding. Besides Mark 9:22, 24 see also Matt. 15:25; Acts 16:9; 21:28; II Cor. 6:2; Heb. 2:18; Rev. 12:16.

How thoroughly this loving father identifies himself with his only son! He says, "Take pity on *us* . . . help *us*." In heart and mind he is as close to his son as is the Syrophoenician woman to her daughter. See Matt. 15:22, 25. If the suppliant's wife was still alive, this "us" would also embrace her. It would then mean, "Take pity on and help our distressed little family."

23. Jesus said to him, As to that *if you can,* **all things are possible for him who believes.** It is interesting to notice how quickly and dramatically Jesus turns the tables on this man. "The question is not whether *I* am able but whether *you* believe," the Lord is, as it were, saying. Though it is not true that Jesus never healed anyone unless that person manifested genuine faith, it is true that he placed great emphasis on faith. See 1:15; 5:36; 6:5, 6; 11:23; cf. Matt. 17:20.

24. Immediately the boy's father cried out, I do believe, help my unbelief. Very striking is this answer in which the tempest-tossed father pours out his very heart. He was certain of two things: *a.* that he did indeed have the kind of faith Jesus demanded; and *b.* that this faith was imperfect, beset by fears and doubts. Only five words (in the original), but these five comprised *a.* a sincere profession of faith: "I do believe," and *b.* an earnest, moving petition, "Help my unbelief," meaning, "Continue moment by moment and day by day to come to my aid, [407] so that I may overcome my unbelief."

25. Now when Jesus saw that a crowd came running together, he rebuked the unclean spirit, saying to it, You deaf and dumb spirit, I command you, come out of him and don't you ever enter him again. A crowd was again gathering and running toward the scene. [408] There had been a crowd of considerable size, a multitude of spectators, curiously watching the quarrel between the scribes and nine disciples of Jesus (verse 14). On seeing Jesus approach, these same people had rushed forward to welcome him (verse 15).

---

405 σπλαγχνισθείς, aor. participle of σπλαγχνίζομαι.
406 βοή and θέω. The form βοήθησον is the second per. sing. (ingressive) aor. act. imperative of βοηθέω.
407 Note *present* (continuative or durative) imperative here. βοήθει, as contrasted with the aor. imperative in verse 22.
408 Note another hapax legomenon: ἐπισυντρέχει. Cf. with προστρέχοντες in verse 15.

Is it not reasonable to suppose that out of *respect*—in the case of some even *reverence*—for Jesus and out of consideration for the distressed father and his pathetic son, the crowd had at first stepped back a little (see on 7:14), but that now that a miracle seemed to be in sight everybody drew nearer, so as not to miss out on what was about to happen? On the other hand, Jesus never encourages such vain curiosity, nor does he wish to be viewed as being first and most of all a miracle-worker; so he now very quickly brings this incident to a conclusion. So he rebuked [409] *the unclean spirit.* Mark uses this designation more often than either Matthew or Luke. For explanation see on 3:11; and for more on demon-possession see on 1:23. In expelling this demon, Jesus addresses it as "You deaf and dumb spirit." What he meant was that the demon had caused the possessed person to be in that condition.

As always, so also here, the depth of Christ's tender sympathy for the boy and for his father is evident from the peremptory nature of the expulsion order, "Come out of him and don't you ever enter him again." [410]

26, 27. Shrieking and throwing the boy into terrible convulsions, it came out. To such an extent did the boy resemble a corpse that most people were saying, He is dead.

The scene of 1:26 is virtually repeated here. Exceptions: in 1:26 the demon's *shriek* is emphasized ("a loud shriek"); here in 9:26 the *convulsions* are: in leaving, the unclean spirit convulsed the boy "terribly." [411]

What a vivid description of the manner in which the boy was cured! Mark alone has all the details. He must have listened very carefully as Peter (and/or others) told the story. There was the shriek uttered by the demon who made use of the boy's vocal organs. Along with it there were those ghastly, horrible muscle spasms. And then there was rigidity.

---

409 ἐπετίμησε third per. sing. aor. indic. of ἐπιτιμάω. See above, on 3:12, including footnote 111.

410 Note sec. per. sing. aor. *imperative* for the *positive* command; hence, ἔξελθε; but the sec. per. sing. aor. *subjunctive* for the *negative* command (or prohibition); hence, μηκέτι εἰσέλθῃς. See Gram. N.T., p. 925.

411 This is another example of Mark's frequent use of πολλά in the adverbial sense. He does not always use it in that sense; for instance in 6:34 the word probably means "many things." By several translators and interpreters that meaning is also assigned to the word in 15:3, which is then rendered ". . . accused him of many things." That is probably correct, though others prefer the rendering "harshly." See on 15:3. It is clear that in every case the connotation of adverbial πολλά depends on the verb which it modifies and the general context. The following meanings deserve consideration:

1:45 widely	5:38 loudly
3:12 and 5:43 strictly	6:20 greatly
5:10 again and again, or	10:48 πολλῷ μᾶλλον, all
fervently	the more
9:23 earnestly	12:27 badly
	15:3 harshly (?)

Deathly still is the body, stiff and still. Even respiration seems to have stopped. All this, coupled with the body's ashen pallor, convinces the majority—literally "the many"—of the people that the lad has died. "He is dead," they are saying.

But Jesus grasped his hand and lifted him to his feet. The Master was always doing things of this nature, it mattered not whether the one in need was Peter (Matt. 14:31), Peter's mother-in-law (Mark 1:31), Jairus' daughter (5:41), or whoever it might be. Is he not, in a *very glorious* sense, doing the same even today? See C. H. Gabriel's inspiring hymn *He Lifted Me*.

It was not a lifeless body that Jesus was lifting. On the contrary, the boy was now vibrant with life and energy: **and he stood up.** [412] By means of the strength that Jesus imparted to him when he lifted him up, the boy himself was now also able to "get up" and to stand erect, for from the very moment when the demon left, this lad was completely cured (Matt. 17:18).

28, 29. And after he [Jesus] had gone indoors, his disciples asked him privately, Why couldn't we cast it out? He told them, This kind can come out only by prayer.

After he had performed the great miracle of rescuing this demon-possessed boy from the clutches of an unclean spirit, and restoring to him the ability to hear and to speak, Jesus went "indoors." [413] In the present case this translation is probably the best, especially since the Lord had not as yet reached Capernaum (see verse 33). Did he, as presumably often during his travels, receive lodging at the home of one of his followers? However that may be, it was at this time that his disciples—think of the nine—came to him with the question, "Why [414] couldn't we cast it out?" It was a reasonable question, for though these men had successfully handled many a case of demon-possession, in the present case they had failed. [415]

According to Matthew, Jesus answers this question by saying, "Because of y o u r little faith. . . ." Essentially Mark's report of Christ's answer amounts to "Because of y o u r little (slack, slapdash) prayer." Of course, these two go together. Where there is little faith, there is little prayer.

---

412 ἀνέστη, third per sing. aor. indicative of ἀνίστημι. Though it is true that this boy had never been dead—the crowd had been deceived by appearances—, yet this same verb is used with respect to those who from death return to life: the daughter of Jairus (Mark 5:42; Luke 8:55); the *dead* in Christ (I Thess. 4:16); Jesus (Matt. 17:9; 20:19; Mark 8:31; 9:9, 10, 31; 10:34; 16:9). It also has more general uses; e.g., to rise up against, fight or rebel against (Mark 3:26); stand up (e.g., to read, Luke 4:16), etc.

413 See also on 2:1; 3:20; 7:17.

414 There is no good reason to interpret this ὅτι in any sense other than "Why?". See on 2:16, footnote 75; cf. 9:11. ἠδυνήθημεν first per. pl. aor. indic. of δύναμαι.

415 Luke omits this question of the disciples from his account; hence also Christ's answer. But cf. Matt. 17:20 with Luke 17:6.

351

Conversely, where there is an abundance of genuine, persevering faith, there is also fervent, unrelenting prayer:

> "My *faith* looks up to thee,
> Thou Lamb of Calvary,
> Savior divine!
> Now hear me while I *pray*. . . ." Lowell Mason

"This kind" says Jesus, "can come out only by prayer." He is saying, therefore, that in the world of the demons there are differences: some are more powerful and more malignant than others. The disciples, therefore, should not have allowed their faith to flag, their prayers to take a holiday. Not only does Jesus urge his followers to pray; he also encourages them to persevere in prayer (Matt. 7:7; Luke 18:1-8; 21:36). [416] So does Paul (Col. 1:9; I Thess. 5:17; II Thess. 1:11).

Beautifully Luke adds, "And he [Jesus] gave him back to his father." In the Savior's works of pity and love nothing is lacking. Not only does he love, he loves *to the uttermost* (John 13:1).

---

30 After they had left that place they were making a trip through Galilee, and he did not want anybody to know it; 31 for he was teaching his disciples, and telling them, "The Son of man is about to be betrayed [417] into the hands of men, and they shall kill him. But three days after he has been killed he shall rise again." 32 But they did not know what to make of this statement and were afraid to ask him about it.

9:30-32 *The Second Prediction of the Passion and the Resurrection*
Cf. Matt. 17:22, 23; Luke 9:43b-45

30a. After they had left that place they were making a trip through Galilee. . . . See the map on p. 295 for the possible route Jesus and The Twelve may have traveled from the high mountain (9:2) to Capernaum (9:33). The route as there indicated has in its favor that it represents the little company as indeed "making a trip through Galilee," yet not through the most thickly populated part of Galilee. This, too, is in harmony with what follows, namely, 30b, 31. **and he did not want anybody to know it; for he was teaching his disciples, and telling them, The Son of man is about to be betrayed into the hands of men, and they shall kill him.** Clearly, the Retirement Ministry is still continuing, though it is hastening to its close. It has already been pointed out (p. 294) that this was the period during which Jesus was in a very special way devoting himself to the task of training The Twelve. That was why he did not want the general public to know his whereabouts. He needed privacy, so as to have the time and the opportunity

---

416 Some manuscripts add: and fasting.
417 Or: is being betrayed (or: delivered).

for teaching The Twelve, so that they in turn, especially after his resurrection, would be able to convey the truths concerning Jesus and his kingdom to others. Specifically, he was teaching them the lessons of the cross.

In the main these lessons were delivered on three separate occasions. To be sure, this instruction may well have been given right along, for by no means everything that took place has been recorded. Cf. John 20:30; 21:25. But the record as found in all three Synoptics calls attention to three consecutive lessons. They are found in Mark 8:31; 9:31; 10:33, 34; and their parallels in Matthew and Luke.

Of these three the present is the second. It bears a close resemblance to the first. In both Jesus calls himself the Son of man (see on 2:10; also N.T.C. on Matt. 8:20), predicts that he is going to be killed, and that three days later he is going to rise again. Yet, there is a difference. In this second prediction it is not so much the necessity as the certainty of this impending death that is stressed. Also, this time Jesus states that he is about to be betrayed—handed over, delivered—into the hands of men. Though the name of Judas, the betrayer, is not mentioned, yet in the light of 14:18, 20, 21 the finger of accusation is beginning to point at him. The glorious Son of man is being delivered—probably meaning "is about to be delivered" (Matt. 17:22; Luke 9:44)—into the hands of men, wicked men, those described in the first lesson: the elders and the chief priests and the scribes, the Sanhedrin. The very men who should have been leaders in honoring the long-awaiting Messiah were about to kill him.

But three days after he has been killed he shall rise again. How these three days must be counted has been discussed in N.T.C. on Matthew, p. 534. In fulfilment of this prophecy the body of Jesus actually rested in the grave during three day-and-night periods: part of Friday, all of Saturday, and part of Sunday.

Mark represents Jesus as predicting that he shall "rise again"; Matthew, "be raised up." [418] These are not in conflict. Both are true. What Mark reports Jesus as saying is that he is going to rise again *by his own power*. This is in harmony not only with Christ's own teaching as found elsewhere but also with other passages of Scripture. John 10:17, 18 is very clear on this point: "I lay down my life in order that I may take it again. . . . I have the right to lay it down and I have the right to take it again." Cf. John 10:11, 14. Thus also John 2:19, ". . . in three days I will raise it up." Is not he himself "the resurrection and the life" (John 11:25); And does he not hold "the keys of Death and Hades" (Rev. 1:18)?

On the other hand, what Matthew represents Jesus to have said is just as

---

418 Mark's ἀναστήσεται is the third per. sing. fut. *middle* indic. of ἀνίστημι; Matthew's ἐγερθήσεται is the third per. sing. fut. *passive* indic. of ἐγείρω.

factual. The Father was indeed going to raise the Son from the dead (Acts 2:32; 3:26; 10:40; 13:34; 17:31; Rom. 4:24, 25; 6:4; etc.).

And the Holy Spirit also had a part in this great event. Was it not especially by means of Christ's resurrection from the dead that the Spirit fully vindicated the claim of Jesus that he was the Son of God (I Tim. 3:16)? Moreover, the Spirit imparts life. See Gen. 1:2; Ps. 104:30; Rom. 8:11. The outgoing works of God must be ascribed to all Three: Father, Son, and Holy Spirit. These Three are One.

The disciples' reaction to this prediction is reported in verse 32. **But they did not know what to make of this statement and were afraid to ask him about it.** The mental condition of these men, as they again heard Jesus speaking about his approaching rejection, was one of sorrow, bewilderment, and fear. Matthew registers the sorrow: "And they were deeply distressed" (17:23). [419] Luke reports the bewilderment and fear, and does this in a most impressive fashion: "But they did not understand this statement, and it was concealed from them, so that they might not grasp it; and they were afraid to ask him about this statement" (9:45). In thus expressing himself, Luke may well have had a copy of Mark's Gospel before him. It is clear at least that Mark, too, describes the men's befuddlement and apprehension. [420]

There may well be merit in the suggestion of Robertson (*Word Pictures* I, p. 344) that the fear of the disciples, so that they did not dare to ask Jesus any questions about this prediction of impending suffering and death, was "with a bitter memory of the term 'Satan' hurled at Peter when he protested the other time when Jesus spoke of his death (Mark 8:33 = Matt. 16:23)."

---

33 They came to Capernaum. And when he was in the house, [421] he was asking them, "What were y o u discussing on the road?" 34 But they kept still, because on the road they had been disputing with each other who was the greatest. 35 So he sat down, called the twelve to him, and said, "If anyone would be first, he must be last of all and servant of all." 36 And he took a little child and had him stand in the midst of them. And taking him in his arms he said to them, 37 "Whoever in my name welcomes one of such little children welcomes me; and whoever welcomes me does not welcome me but him who sent me."

9:33-37 *Who Is the Greatest?*
Cf. Matt. 18:1-5; Luke 9:46-48

33, 34. They came to Capernaum. And when he was in the house, he was asking them, What were y o u discussing on the road? But they kept still,

---

419 By the use of the aor. indic. passive he reports a fact.
420 Luke's two imperfects coupled by a past perfect passive, and Mark's two imperfects—"did not know what to make of" [or: "did not understand"] —, and "were afraid to ask," present a vivid picture of a continuing situation.
421 Or: at home.

because on the road they had been disputing with each other who was the greatest.

With respect to this incident the accounts of the three Gospel writers resemble each other to a considerable degree both in phraseology and with respect to the sequence in which the various items follow each other. All three stories tell how among the disciples an argument developed anent the question, "Who is the greatest?" To set them straight Jesus takes a child so that by means of its humble trustfulness these men may learn the lesson of true greatness. The Master concludes by saying, according to Matt. 18:5, "The person who in my name welcomes one such little child as this, welcomes me." See also Matt. 10:40. With slight verbal variations and augmentations this conclusion is also found in Mark 9:37 and in Luke 9:48. Particularly close is the resemblance between Mark 9:36, 37 and Luke 9:47b, 48a.

It is, however, on what some consider *discrepancies* that the attention is often focused. These discrepancies are said to be so formidable that the attempt to read Mark 9:33-37 as a consistent, in every respect historical, account is given up. It is assumed that what we now have is a jumbled narrative, drawn from various discordant sources. [422]

The assumed items of conflict are:

a. Matthew and Luke omit any reference to Capernaum, while Mark places the event in Capernaum and thus in a Galilean context.

b. According to Matthew the disciples take the initiative. It is they who ask Jesus, "Who then is greatest in the kingdom of heaven?" In Mark, however, it is Jesus who takes the initiative. It is he who asks them, "What were y o u discussing on the road?"

c. According to Mark 9:33 Jesus is present with his disciples. They are together in a house. Nevertheless, according to verse 35 these men seem not to have been with him, for he has to *call* them.

The following answers certainly deserve consideration:

As to a. While it is true that Luke, as so often, does not locate the event, Matthew has just mentioned Jesus' arrival in Capernaum. Note: "And when they had come to Capernaum" (17:24). The story of the payment of the temple tax follows. And then we read, "At that moment—or: in that hour—the disciples came to Jesus asking, 'Who then is greatest . . . ?' " (18:1).

As to b. The very fact that Matthew phrases the disciples' question thus, "Who then—note this *then*—is greatest . . . ?" may well indicate that some-

---

422 The reader should see for himself the treatment that is given to this paragraph of Mark's Gospel, by an author who otherwise presents much that is excellent, namely, Vincent Taylor, *op. cit.*, p. 404.

thing has preceded the asking of this question. The sequence of events may have been as follows:

On the way to the house an argument concerning rank develops among the disciples (Luke 9:46). Indoors Jesus asks them, "What were y o u discussing on the road?" But they kept quiet, etc. (Mark 9:33, 34). Jesus, however, knows (Luke 9:47). When they become aware of this, they ask him, "Who then *is* greatest in the kingdom of heaven?" (Matt. 18:1). —In any event the assumption of a discrepancy is unwarranted.

As to c. Was it not natural for men oppressed by a sense of guilt to remain at some distance from their Master? And was it not just as natural for him, when he was about to impart needed instruction to them, to *sit down* as their *Teacher* (cf. Matt. 5:1; 13:1; Luke 5:3; John 8:2) and to summon them into his immediate presence?

Jesus is back in Capernaum again, the very city which for so long a time had been his headquarters. He was "in the house," or "at home," as in Matt. 8:6; see also on the synonymous phrase in Mark 2:1. His disciples have by this time also entered this house. Jesus was questioning—or: began to question [423] —them, "What were y o u discussing on the road?" Evidently he knew that a subdued conversation had been carried on among these men as they were walking behind him. Did he know more than this? The very topic and nature of the conversation?

It is useless for us to try to comprehend the exact manner of Christ's acquisition of knowledge. Three considerations must be borne in mind, however: *a.* His human nature was not in and by itself omniscient (Mark 13:32; cf. Matt. 24:36); *b.* his divine nature would at times impart information to his human nature which the latter apart from that impartation would not have received (Matt. 17:25, 27; John 1:47, 48; 2:25; 21:17); and *c.* at times Jesus received information in a thoroughly human way, by asking questions or by search (Mark 5:32; 6:38; 11:13). In the present instance (Mark 9:33), as already indicated, we must probably think of *b.* See also 2:8. He already knew before they told him, but he asked the question so that they might begin to reflect on what they had done, and might feel thoroughly ashamed.

---

[423] In this passage (verses 33, 34) note the following: ἐπηρώτα, third per. sing. imperf. act. indic. of ἐπερωτάω. On διελογίζεσθε, sec. per. pl. imperf. indic. of διαλογίζομαι; and on διελέχθησαν, third per. pl. aor. indic. of διαλέγομαι see G. Schrenk's art. in Th.D.N.T., Vol. II, pp. 93-98. The word ἐσιώπων is the third per. pl. imperf. indic. of σιωπάω; and the adjective μείζων, though literally "greater," clearly has the sense of a superlative, as in I Cor. 13:13: "greatest of these is love." The last example also shows that this comparative form does not always need to be preceded by the definite article to be equal in force to a superlative. On the substitution of a comparative form for a superlative, in Koine Greek, see Gram. N.T., pp. 281 and 667.

In answer to Christ's question deathly silence prevailed. It was a silence that was not immediately broken. Clearly, the disciples were embarrassed.

It seems strange that one of the first recorded results of Christ's second prediction (9:30-32) of his rapidly approaching agony should have been the disciples' debate about *rank!* How quickly their sorrow (Matt. 17:23b) caused by this prediction had given way to craving for exaltation! Yet such men as these Jesus had chosen to be his disciples! For such as these he was going to lay down his life. Thus the sovereign character of God's electing love is made to stand out. Cf. Ps. 103:14; 115:1; Ezek. 16:1-14; Dan. 9:7, 8; I John 4:19; and see N.T.C. on Eph. 1:4.

There may well have been a connection, however, between Christ's prediction and the dispute among the disciples. Though Jesus had spoken about his passion, in the same breath he had also mentioned his resurrection. Moreover, shortly before this he had promised that some of the disciples were going to see "the kingdom of God come with power" (9:1). So, since earthbound thoughts had not as yet been completely erased from the minds of these men—not even for a long time afterward; see Acts 1:6—, the very predictions which Jesus had made may have caused them to start thinking and arguing about the relative degree of eminence which each disciple would enjoy in that kingdom. Besides, especially of late Peter had been in the limelight. Was the highest rank reserved for him? See N.T.C. on Matthew, pp. 684, 685.

The solemn moment has now arrived for Jesus to show his disciples what should be the true attitude of *any* kingdom citizen. **35. So he sat down, called the twelve to him, and said, If anyone would be first, he must be [424] last of all and servant of all.**

Having summoned the men into his immediate presence, Jesus, by means of the gesture of sitting down, as already explained, indicates that as their Teacher, he is about to give them a very important lesson. That lesson is this: their idea of what it means to be "great" must be changed; in fact, radically reversed. True greatness does not consist in this, that from a towering height a person, in a self-congratulatory manner, has the right now to look down upon all others (Luke 18:9-12); but in this, that he immerses himself in the needs of others, sympathizes with them and helps them in every way possible. So, if any person—whether he be one of The Twelve or anyone else—wishes to be *first,* he *must* be *last;* that is, servant [425] of all.

---

424 Though ἔσται is the third per. sing. fut. *indic.* of εἰμί, the tense as employed in the present context does not indicate mere futurity, what is going to happen, but what a person must want to happen; hence, "shall be" or "must be"; in other words, ἔσται has imperative force. See Gram. N.T., pp. 874, 943.

425 διάκονος. See on 10:43, 44.

Jesus must have repeated this lesson many a time throughout his ministry, probably at various places and in slightly varying ways. See also Matt. 20:26, 27; 23:11; Mark 10:43, 44; Luke 9:48b; 14:11; 18:14. In fact, is not this a lesson that is stressed throughout Scripture? See Job 22:29; Prov. 29:23; Isa. 57:15; James 4:6; I Peter 5:5.

As to self-centered ambition and vanity, "Before downfall goes pride; and before stumbling, a haughty spirit" (Prov. 16:18). Was not this the experience of Sennacherib (II Chron. 32:14, 21), of Nebuchadnezzar (Dan. 4:30-33), and of Herod Agrippa I (Acts 12:21-23)? On the other hand, note what is said about the commended centurion (Matt. 8:8, 10, 13), the humble Syrophoenician woman (Mark 7:29; cf. Matt. 15:27, 28), and the penitent tax-collector (Luke 18:13, 14).

One reason why the lesson taught by Jesus is unforgettable is that he himself was constantly exemplifying it in his own life (Mark 10:44, 45; Luke 22:27; John 13:1-15; Phil. 2:5-8).

Another reason why this lesson of being humble and trustful instead of inordinately ambitious has become very familiar is the fact that by means of a most delightful and impressive living illustration Jesus stamped it indelibly upon the minds and hearts of his followers: **36a. And he took a little child and had him stand in the midst of them.** What Jesus *did* at this occasion revealed not only his thorough understanding of the nature of the kingdom and of the way of entering it, but also his tenderness toward the little ones. What he *said* deserved all the praise that has ever been ascribed to it, and far more than that. But was not the amazing glory of the Mediator's soul revealed also in his restraint, that is, in what he did not do and did not say? He did not even scold his disciples for their callousness, their insensibility with respect to this approaching agony, the non-lasting character of their grief, their quickness in turning the mind away from him to themselves, their selfishness. All this he passed by, and addressed himself directly to their question.

It is pleasing to note the frequency with which the presence of children around Jesus and/or his love for them is mentioned in the Gospels. See Matt. 14:21; 15:38; 18:3; 19:13, 14 (cf. Mark 10:13, 14; Luke 18:15, 16); 21:15, 16; 23:37 (cf. Luke 13:34). Undoubtedly children felt attracted to Jesus, wanted to be with him. Whenever he wanted a child there was always one present, ready to do his bidding, to come when he called him. So also here. To speculate who this child was is useless. The point is that this was indeed a child, endowed with all the favorable and amiable qualities generally associated with childhood in any clime and at any time.

The Lord calls this little one to his side, and places him "in the midst of" all these "big" men, perhaps in such a position that the child faced them while they were arranged in a crescent before him. The child was not afraid, for it stood by the Lord's very side (Luke 9:47).

Mark now adds a precious touch not found in the other Gospels: **36b. And taking him in his arms** [426] **he said to them.** . . . In these arms the little one would feel perfectly at ease and would be able trustfully to look into the face of Jesus. Continued: **37. Whoever in my name welcomes one of such little children welcomes me; and whoever welcomes me does not welcome me but him who sent me.** This dominical saying fits into the present context, just as it is also suitable to the context of Matt. 10:40; see N.T.C. on that passage.

Here in Mark 9:37 the logic is somewhat as follows: Jesus is telling his disciples to forget all about rank, pre-eminence, prominence. Instead, they should concentrate their attention on the needs of one, *any* one, even just *one,* of such little ones; for example, the child which Jesus is now holding in his arms, or any similar one. They should welcome such a child "in Christ's name." The name of Christ is Christ himself viewed in his glorious self-revelation. Therefore, to welcome such a little child "in Christ's name" means to treat it with all the love and consideration which he, Christ, in accordance with the manner in which he has revealed himself in word and deed, has a right to expect of his followers. In doing this, they will be welcoming the child—or anyone who in his weakness, need, and humble dependence, resembles a child—"for Christ's sake" (cf. 10:29). Now if this is done with all the sincerity, warmth, and enthusiasm that can be put into it, it will certainly tend to benefit the one on whom this affection is bestowed. And that is what Jesus wants, for he loves the little ones.

But it will do more than this. It will also benefit those who bestow such care. In the process of identifying themselves with these children will they not themselves also become childlike?

Moreover, obedience to Christ's command glorifies Christ; for, as Jesus continues to point out, since the relation between himself and one such child is very close, therefore whoever in his name welcomes one of these little children welcomes their Redeemer, that is, Jesus Christ.

Finally, since the relation between Jesus and his Sender, the Father (Mark 12:6; cf. Matt. 15:24; Luke 10:16; John 3:16, 17; etc.), is infinitely close (John 17:10, 21, 24-26), it follows that whoever welcomes Jesus does not welcome him—that is, *only* him—but *also* his Sender.

---

426 ἐναγκαλισάμενος, nom. masc. sing. aor. participle of ἐναγκαλίζομαι. In the New Testament this verb occurs only here and in 10:16. See, however, also Luke 2:28: "Simeon . . . took him [the child Jesus] in his arms." In that passage the noun ἀγκάλας (acc. pl. of ἀγκάλη) indicates arms that are *bent* in order to receive something or someone. Cf. *angle.*

To summarize: instead of asking, "Who among us is the greatest?" the followers of Jesus should learn to focus their loving attention on Christ's little ones, that is, on the lambs of the flock and on all those who in their condition of need and trustful dependence resemble these lambs. Such is the essence of true greatness, the greatness that reflects the same quality which in an infinite degree resides in God (Isa. 57:15).

The objection might be raised, "But was not this question, namely, 'Who among us is the greatest?' so ridiculously puerile as to be of no practical significance for later times?" This conclusion would be utterly wrong. The yearning to be great dwells in every human heart as it is by nature. Witness the "So Big" gesture which fond parents teach their little ones; the "my dad can lick your dad" of the first grader; the widely advertised books that aim to teach a person "how to gain control over everybody"; and last but not least, the raucous raving by means of which Hitler sought to bolster up his restless ego, resulting finally in what has been called "the most terrible nightmare mankind has ever endured." And even believers in the Lord Jesus Christ, as long as they are on this earth, have not completely overcome the urge to display at least an inkling of Lucifer's arrogance. Also, in many cases they have failed to make use of opportunities to render service to Christ's little ones: the young, the weak, those who have gone astray, etc. Hence, such passages as the present (Mark 9:33-37); Rom. 15:1-3; Gal. 6:1, 2; Phil. 2:3 f.; James 4:6; I Peter 5:5; etc., never outlive their usefulness on this side of heaven.

---

38 John said to him, "Teacher, we saw someone casting out demons in your name, and we tried to stop him because he was not following us." 39 But Jesus said, "Do not stop him, for there is no one who shall do a mighty work in my name and be able soon afterward to speak ill of me; 40 for he who is not against us is for us. 41 For I solemnly declare that he who, because y o u belong to Christ, gives y o u a cup of water to drink, shall certainly not lose his reward."

9:38-41 *He Who Is Not against Us Is for Us*
Cf. Luke 9:49, 50

38. John said to him, Teacher, we saw someone casting out demons in your name. . . .

On the surface it might seem that between the preceding paragraph (verses 33-37) and this one (verses 38-41) there is no thought connection of any kind. It has been suggested that the apostle John, embarrassed by the implied reprimand which he and the rest of The Twelve had received, brought up this incident concerning an exorcist merely to change the subject. Others are of the opinion that the insertion of the present little paragraph, not found in Matthew but only in Mark and (abbreviated) in

360

Luke, was suggested by the phrase "in my—or your—name" which occurs both in verse 37 and again in verses 38, 39. However, another possibility must not be ignored. John's conscience may have been aroused by Christ's remarks of implied disapproval (verses 35-37), so that he now wondered whether he, John, and others had behaved properly toward a certain exorcist. Whether there is any truth in any of these guesses as to the nature of the connection or lack of connection cannot be ascertained.

The title "Teacher" or "Master," [427] used by John in addressing Jesus, was always very appropriate (John 13:13), and might seem all the more appropriate if Christ's teaching on humility has just now been completed.

What bothered John was that he and others—note "we"—had seen someone cast out demons in Christ's name, though that exorcist did not belong to The Twelve and perhaps not even to the broader circle of constant followers (Luke 6:13; 10:1).

What kind of man was John talking about? Not a would-be exorcist, like the seven sons of Sceva (Acts 19:13-16), for these were frauds. Nor was he an exorcist in the sense of those condemned in Matt. 7:22. No, this man was in all probability a true believer in Jesus. He may have been someone who, having listened to the Master and having given his heart to him, had not as yet established close relationships with the Master's other followers. All that we know for certain is that he had been casting out demons in Christ's name, and that John and others—perhaps other apostles—had strongly disapproved of his actions: **and we tried to stop** [428] **him because he was not following us.** Apparently the attempt had not succeeded. The man must have been fully convinced of the fact that what he was doing was right and proper. He had been doing it "in Christ's name," that is, as explained previously, in full accordance, as he saw it, with the mind and words of Jesus. With this man the phrase "in Christ's name" was not a magical formula; it was reality.

The reason given by John for the attempt to stop him was "because he was not following [429] us." It is entirely possible that John had taken a leading part in the attempt to stop this man from doing what he was doing. If this seems strange, could the reason have been that it took some time before this "son of thunder" (Mark 3:17; cf. Luke 9:54) was changed into "the disciple whom Jesus loved"? See John 13:23; 19:26; 20:2; 21:7, 20. But is it not more likely that it was exactly love for his Master—misguided love—that caused John and others to try to stop that exorcist, who had not joined Christ and his steady followers?

---

427 See on 4:38b, footnote 172.

428 ἐκωλύομεν first per. pl. imperf. active of κωλύω, hinder, prevent, stop; here conative imperfect: tried to stop.

429 ἠκολούθει, another imperfect; here probably progressive. Cf. acolyte, anacoluthon.

39. But Jesus said, Do not stop him [430] . . . . The reason given is: **for there is no one who shall do a mighty work in my name and be able soon afterward to speak ill of me.** [431] The reason is so obvious, the language so clear, that very little need be said by way of explanation. When in the name of Jesus—in harmony with his revealed will—a person performs a mighty work, he will, of course, speak well—not ill—of the One whom he acknowledges as the real Author of this miracle.

40. The reason that he cannot *speak* ill of Jesus is that he does not *think* ill of him, is not opposed to him. Hence, with another "for" Jesus continues, **for he who is not against us is for us.** Lovingly the Master associates his followers with himself by saying "us" instead of "me."

Since it is a fact that once a person has been confronted with Christ neutrality is forever impossible, it stands to reason that whoever is not *against*—down on—him is *for*—in favor of—him. The same truth can also be expressed by means of the words found in Matt. 12:30: "He who is not with me is against me."

41. With a final "for" clause—meaning: this reasoning is true as appears from the fact that, etc.—Jesus completes his answer, as follows: **For I solemnly declare that he who, because** [432] **y o u belong to Christ, gives y o u a cup of water to drink, shall certainly not lose his reward.** [433]

For "I solemnly declare" see on 3:28. With "a cup of water" compare "even as much as a cup of cold water" (Matt. 10:42). What makes this cup of water so precious is that it is given to a person *because he belongs to Christ.* Jesus therefore regards such a gift as one that is given to himself. Cf. Matt. 25:40, "And the King shall answer them, 'I solemnly assure y o u, whatever y o u did for one of these brothers of mine, (even) for one of the least, y o u did it for me.'" On the precious truth that believers are not their own but belong to Christ see also Rom. 8:9; 14:8; I Cor. 3:23; 6:19,

---

430 Because of μή followed by the sec. per. *pres.* imperat. active, Robertson translates "Stop hindering him" (*Word Pictures,* Vol. I, p. 346). But since John and his partners were obviously not hindering the exorcist at this particular time, the more usual rendering "Do not stop him," "Forbid him not," "Do not forbid—or hinder—him" is probably preferable.

431 ποιήσει and δυνήσεται are third per. sing. fut. indicatives.

432 The preferred reading ἐν ὀνόματι ὅτι has resulted in difficulty, which probably accounts for the many textual variants. The translation preferred by some, namely, "in my name because" is too labored, tautological, and besides inserts a "my" where there probably was none. Better, it would seem to me, is L.N.T. (A. and G.), p. 577, "in your capacity as," or simply "because" (V. Taylor, *op. cit.,* p. 407).

433 Both ποτίσῃ and ἀπολέσῃ are aor. subjunctives. But instead of "shall give y o u" one may substitute "gives y o u," as I have done, since the two mean about the same thing. As to "shall certainly not lose," this is what Burton calls "solemnly predictive" and "emphatically negative" (*op. cit.,* pp. 34, 35). See also Gram. N.T., p. 930, where this construction is called a "futuristic subjunctive."

20; II Cor. 10:7; Eph. 1:14b; I Peter 2:9. And see Heidelberg Catechism, Question and Answer 1.

What reward do such givers receive? Think of peace of mind now (Matt. 10:13), public acknowledgment by Christ at his return (Matt. 25:34 ff.), and ever afterward "the inheritance of the saints in the light."

What kind of attitude is it against which Jesus warns in this little paragraph? Answer: that of intolerance, narrow exclusivism. It is the kind of mental state that was present already during the old dispensation. Eldad and Medad, who are very definitely children of God and true witnesses, for some reason or other have remained in the camp instead of going to the tent or tabernacle where they may have been expected. Perhaps they had not heard the call. But in the camp, among the people, they are prophesying. Excitedly a young tattletale rushes to the authorities with the news. "Eldad and Medad are prophesying in the camp!" Even Joshua thinks that this is appalling. "My lord Moses, make them stop!" he exclaims. But Moses answers, "Are you jealous for my sake? Would that all Jehovah's people were prophets, that Jehovah would put his Spirit upon them!" (Num. 11:26-29).

Even today that spirit of narrow exclusivism is at times mistaken for loyalty to one's church or denomination. We hear people say, "*Our* denomination is the purest manifestation of the body of Christ on earth." As long as we are on this sinful earth, a terrain where hypocrisy in high places frequently corrupts not only political but even ecclesiastical life, would it not be better to leave such judgments to God? Let us not be more restrictive than was Moses. Let us not be less broadminded than was Paul (Phil. 1:14-18). Let us follow the teaching of Jesus and, while maintaining what we ourselves regard as purity of doctrine, let us reach out the hand of brotherhood to all those who love the Lord Jesus Christ and build upon the firm foundation of his infallible Word. Doing this, let us pray that we may be instrumental in leading others to the way of salvation, to the glory of God (I Cor. 9:19, 22; 10:31, 33).

---

42 And whoever causes one of these little ones who believe in me [434] to sin, it is better for him that a heavy millstone be hung around his neck and he be thrown into the sea. 43 And if your hand lures you into sin, cut it off. It is better for you to enter life maimed than with two hands to go to hell, [435] to the unquenchable fire. [436] 45 And if your foot lures you into sin, cut it off. It is better for you to enter life lame [437] than with two feet to be thrown into hell. 47 And if your eye lures you into sin, pluck it out. It is

---

434 There is considerable doubt in connection with the reading ". . . in me." But see also Matt. 18:6.
435 Or Gehenna; thus also in verses 45 and 47.
436 There is insufficient textual support for verses 44 and 46, which are the same as verse 48.
437 Or crippled.

better for you to enter the kingdom of God with one eye than with two eyes to be thrown into hell,   48 where their worm does not die and the fire is not quenched. 49 For all shall be salted with fire.   50 Salt is good; but if salt loses its saltiness, how will y o u   restore its flavor? Always have salt within yourselves, and be at peace with each other.

9:42-50 *Guard the Little Ones and Do Not Yield to Temptation*

Compare with

Verse				
42		Matt. 18:6	Luke 17:1, 2	
43		Matt. 5:30; 18:8		
45		Matt. 18:8		
47		Matt. 5:29; 18:9		
48	Isa. 66:24			
50a		Matt. 5:13	Luke 14:34, 35	
50b				Col. 4:6
50c				Rom. 12:18; II Cor. 13:11; I Thess. 5:13

42. And whoever causes one of these little ones who believe in me to sin, it is better for him that a heavy millstone be hung around his neck and he be thrown into the sea.

Here begins a series of dominical sayings for the most part found also elsewhere in Scripture, as indicated above, under the heading. Several of them occur also in Matt. 5 and/or 18. It is entirely possible that such sayings were repeated by our Lord and therefore are in the Gospels reproduced in different contexts.

The first one (verse 42) may be considered the negative side of verse 37. There are always those who would lead Christ's "little ones" of any age astray. [438] Jesus is saying that even if such a sin is planned against *only one* of those precious in his sight, [439] physical death for such a seducer, death of

---

[438] σκανδαλίσῃ, third per. sing. aor. subj. active of σκανδαλίζω. The σκάνδαλον is the bait-stick in a trap or snare. It is the crooked stick that springs the trap; hence, snare, temptation to sin, enticement (Matt. 18:7; Luke 17:1); also: object of revulsion, the stumbling-block of the cross (I Cor. 1:23; Gal. 5:11). Similarly the *verb* basically means: to ensnare, lure into sin, lead astray.

[439] Note "little ones who believe" or "believe in me." Even without the addition "in me," about which there is some doubt, it is clear that the Lord is speaking about believers. It would be wrong, therefore, to insist that the Lord is speaking exclusively about babies. The term "little ones" is one of endearment for those of any age. They are weak and in that sense little, but he loves them. Cf. I John 2:1, 28; 3:7, 18; 5:21.

the most gruesome kind, would be preferable. He is saying that it would be better that a heavy (literally *donkey-drawn*) millstone be hung about his neck and he be cast into the sea.

The millstone of which Jesus speaks is the top-stone of the two between which the grain is crushed. The reference is not to the handmill but to the much heavier stone drawn by a donkey. In the middle of the top-stone, whether of a handmill or of a donkey-drawn mill, there is a hole through which grain can be fed so as to be crushed between the two stones. The presence of this hole explains the phrase "that a heavy millstone *be hung around his neck.*" With this millstone around his neck he will surely drown.

43, 45, 47. And if your hand lures you into sin, cut it off. It is better for you to enter life maimed than with two hands to go to hell, to the unquenchable fire. And if your foot lures you into sin, cut it off. It is better for you to enter life lame than with two feet to be thrown into hell. And if your eye lures you into sin, pluck it out. It is better for you to enter the kingdom of God with one eye than with two eyes to be thrown into hell. . . .

Hand, foot, and eye, how we value them! Nevertheless, Jesus says that it is better to get rid of any one of them than with two hands, two feet, or two eyes to perish everlastingly. Hence, if any of these lures a person into sin he should immediately dispose of that organ. If it is a hand or a foot it must be cut off; if an eye, plucked out.

As is true so often with respect to the sayings of Jesus, so also here: these words must not be taken literally. The lesson is this: sin, being a very destructive force, must not be pampered. It must be "put to death" (Col. 3:5). Temptation should be flung aside *immediately* and *decisively*. [440] Dillydallying is deadly. Halfway measures work havoc. *The surgery must be radical.* Right at this very moment and without any vacillation the obscene book should be burned, the scandalous picture destroyed, the soul-destroying film condemned, the sinister yet very intimate social tie broken, and the baneful habit discarded. In the struggle against sin the believer must fight hard. Shadow-boxing will never do (I Cor. 9:27).

Of course, these destructive, and in the sense negative, actions will never succeed apart from the powerful sanctifying and transforming operation of God's Spirit in heart and life.

Note triple occurrence of the term *Gehenna*. See also Matt. 5:22, 29, 30; 10:28; 18:9; 23:15, 33; Mark 9:43, 45, 47; Luke 12:5; James 3:6. Gehenna derived its name from Gē-Hinnom (Josh. 15:8; 18:6), abbreviated from Gē ben-Hinnom (Josh. 15:8), meaning: the Valley of the son—or in the pl. the sons (II Kings 23:10)—of Hinnom. It was located south of Jerusalem. It became known as a place of fire, for it was here that in the days of Ahaz and

---

[440] Note the crisp aor. imper. actives: ἀπόκοψον, ἔκβαλε.

Manasseh children were roasted to death as sacrifices to Moloch (II Kings 16:3; 21:6; II Chron. 28:3; 33:6). The God-fearing King Josiah accordingly declared the place to be unclean (II Kings 23:10), and by his friend Jeremiah terrible threats were pronounced over it (Jer. 7:32; 19:6). Also, it became the place where the city's garbage was burned. For these reasons the term Gē-Hinnom or Gehenna became at last the designation whereby hell was indicated.

Here in verse 43 Gehenna is defined as "the unquenchable [441] fire." The meaning is that the punishment for those who enter there is never-ending, everlasting. See Matt. 25:46.

What is the difference between Hades and Gehenna? It is this: *a.* Hades *may,* but does not necessarily have to, mean hell. It always has that meaning in the *Gospels:* Matt. 11:23 (=Luke 10:15); 16:18; Luke 16:23. Gehenna, however, always means hell. *b.* Hades, whenever it means hell, receives the wicked during the intermediate state (between death and resurrection); Gehenna receives both body and soul of the wicked after the final judgment. [442]

There is one more concept that is mentioned in these verses. It is *life.* It is clear, then, that Christ's views on *life* or *life everlasting* are not confined to the Gospel according to John (1:4; 3:16; 17:3, etc.). From the parallelism of the present lines—note "better for you to enter life" . . . "better for you to enter the kingdom of God"—it is clear that *entering life* means *entering God's kingdom.* Here the term "kingdom of God" must be taken in its eschatological sense: the new heaven and earth with all the glory pertaining to it. See above, on 1:15 (meaning d.). And what is "life" as it shall unfold itself in its final, yet evermore progressive, stage? Is it not the much fuller enjoyment of the reign of God in the heart? Is it not, therefore, also the far more intense experience of "the peace of God that passes all understanding" (Phil. 4:7), "the joy unspeakable and full of glory" (I Peter 1:8), "the light of the knowledge of the glory of God in the face of Christ" (II Cor. 4:6), and "the love of God shed abroad in—or: poured into—our hearts through the Holy Spirit" (Rom. 5:5)? All of that the seducer is going to forfeit, as he descends into Gehenna!

As a further description of hell note verse 48. **where their worm does not**

---

441 τὸ πῦρ τὸ ἄσβεστον, which literally means "fire that cannot be extinguished." Cf. asbestos, with a somewhat different meaning, however: that which does not burn and is a nonconductor of electricity.

442 For more details, including refutation or contrary opinions, see my book *The Bible on the Life Hereafter,* Grand Rapids 1959 (fourth printing 1971), pp. 83-87; 195-199. The book is also published in Spanish: *La Biblia Y La Vida Venidera* (T.E.L.L., 941 Wealthy St., S.E., Grand Rapids, Mich. 49506, U.S.A.), pp. 113-119; 281-287. See also Joachim Jeremias, art. γέεννα, in Th.D.N.T., Vol. I, pp. 657, 658.

die and the fire is not quenched, a passage quoted from Isaiah's final verse. The torment, accordingly, will be both external, the fire; and internal, the worm. Moreover, it will never end. This teaching of Jesus should not be weakened by the philosophical notion that in the universe on the other side of death or of the final judgment there will be no time. [443] Nowhere, not in Isa. 66:24, nor in Rev. 10:6, correctly translated, is there any ground for this assumption. [444]

When Scripture speaks of unquenchable fire, the point is not merely that there will always be a fire burning in Gehenna, but that the wicked will have to endure that torment forever. They will always be the objects of God's wrath, never of his love. Thus also their worm never dies, and their shame is everlasting (Dan. 12:2). So are their bonds (Jude 6, 7). "They will be tormented with fire and brimstone . . . and the smoke of their torment ascends forever and ever, so that they have no rest day or night" (Rev. 14:9-11; 19:3; 20:10).

One hears the objection, "But does not Scripture teach *the destruction* of the wicked"? Yes, indeed, but this destruction is not an instantaneous annihilation, so that there would be nothing left of the wicked; so that, in other words, they would cease to exist. The *destruction* of which Scripture speaks is an *everlasting destruction* (II Thess. 1:9). Their hopes, their joys, their opportunities, their riches, etc., have perished, and they themselves are tormented by this, and that forevermore. When Jeremiah speaks about shepherds who destroyed the sheep, did he mean that those sheep *ceased to exist?* When Hosea exclaims, "O Israel, you have destroyed yourself," was he trying to say that the people had been *annihilated?* Did Paul (Rom. 14:15) mean to imply that by eating meat you can *annihilate* your brother? Or that he himself had at one time *annihilated* the faith? (Gal. 1:23).

What is perhaps the most telling argument against the notion that the wicked are simply annihilated but that the righteous continue to live forevermore is the fact that in Matt. 25:46 the same word describes the duration of both the punishment of the former and the blessedness of the latter: the wicked go away into *everlasting* punishment, but the righteous into *everlasting* life.

Another objection might be, "But is not God also merciful, and does not Scripture speak of degrees of punishment (Luke 12:47, 48)? The answer must be, "Yes, indeed, and it is doubtful whether we have always done justice to that significant passage." Nothing can detract, however, from the fact that for those who stubbornly and hatefully reject and continue to

---

443 So, for example, Lenski, *op. cit.*, p. 258.
444 Permit me once again to refer for fuller treatment to my book *The Bible on the Life Hereafter,* this time pp. 72-74; Spanish edition pp. 97, 98.

reject the message of God's love and grace in Christ, hardening themselves to the point where they even begin to lead astray Christ's "little ones," and never repenting, the full force of Mark 9:48 and similar passages must be maintained.

Jesus closes his remarks with a trilogy of "salt" passages:

The first salt passage is: **49. For all shall be salted with fire.** Instead of wearying the reader with a summary of various interpretations that have been given to this passage, I shall at once present the one that appears to me to be the most reasonable. It is an explanation that aims to do justice to the preceding context, the historical background, and other biblical passages that mention "salt" and "fire."

As to the context: Jesus has been warning his disciples against becoming a snare to others and/or becoming themselves ensnared. To this he now adds a saying beginning with "for," as if to say, "Being on the alert is always necessary but especially in the period that lies immediately ahead, for *all*—here with special reference to The Twelve?—shall be salted with fire." Does this not immediately remind us of that other *all*—basically the same word in the original—of Mark 14:27 (=Matt. 26:31): "*All* of y o u shall become ensnared because of—or: shall become untrue to—me"?

"All shall be salted with fire" probably means, therefore, *a fiery trial* will come upon everybody, for the purpose of purification. Not only is it going to separate good people from bad people, believers from unbelievers, but even within the hearts and lives of believers it will destroy what is bad and bring out what is good, causing them to be *a preservative force,* a salting salt, in the midst of their environment. See the following passages: Job 42:5, 8; Ps. 119:67; Mal. 3:2; Matt. 5:13; John 16:33; II Cor. 4:17; II Tim. 3:12; I Peter 4:12, 13. Scripture even applies the idea of a testing and separating fire to the final judgment (I Cor. 3:13), though when that occurs the idea of thereby becoming a preservative force must be dropped.

The second salt passage is: **50a. Salt is good; but if salt loses its saltiness, how will y o u restore its flavor?** As to the underlying figure, it is easy to understand that salt is good. It is good because it preserves (combats deterioration) and imparts flavor. However, salt may lose its flavor and become tasteless. The salt from the marshes and lagoons or from the rocks in the neighborhood of the Dead Sea easily acquires a stale or alkaline taste, because of its mixture with gypsum, etc. It is then literally "good for nothing" but to be thrown away and trampled underfoot (cf. Ezek. 47:11). Jesus, as he walked on earth, saw many Pharisees and scribes, people who advocated a formal, legalistic religion in the place of the true religion proclaimed by the ancient prophets in the name of the Lord. Thus by and large the salt had lost its flavor in the religious life of Israel. Many "sons of the kingdom" would be cast out (Matt. 8:12).

The implication is clear. Just as salt having lost its saltiness cannot be restored, so also those who were trained in the knowledge of the truth but who then resolutely set themselves against the exhortations of the Holy Spirit and become hardened in their opposition are not renewed unto repentance (Matt. 12:32; Heb. 6:4-6). Therefore, let that which is named salt be salt indeed! Ever so many people who never read the Bible are constantly reading us! If in our conduct we are untrue to our calling our *words* will avail very little.

The final salt passage is: **50b. Always have salt within yourselves. . . .** It is useless for a man to try to exert an influence for good upon others unless, by the grace of God, he has goodness within; that is, unless the Word of God as applied by the Holy Spirit, has transformed him into a true disciple of Christ. To have salt within oneself means, therefore, to have within oneself those qualities that promote truth, kindness, peace, joy, etc. within the brotherhood, and in the world at large a willingness to listen to the good tidings of salvation in Christ. To express it differently: to have salt within oneself means to *be* the salt of the world (Matt. 5:13), and therefore also to see to it that one's speech is always "seasoned with salt." See N.T.C. on that passage.

Very logical, therefore, is the continuation: **and be at peace with each other.** If within the brotherhood there is nothing but carping and quarrelling, how can those who call themselves Christians expect to win others to Christ? It is therefore not surprising that an echo of this exhortation is found also in the epistles of Paul (Rom. 12:18; II Cor. 13:11; I Thess. 5:13). The reward for being a man of peace and therefore a peacemaker is stated in Matt. 5:9, "Blessed the peacemakers, for they shall be called sons of God." Add Gal. 5:22; James 3:18.

Summary of Chapter 9:2-50

Like the preceding chapter (8) and the following (10), so also this chapter (9) consists of six paragraphs. The first one (verses 2-13) tells the story of Christ's transfiguration on a high mountain which he climbed in the company of Peter, James, and John. It was here that the Father imparted glory and honor to the Son (II Peter 1:16, 17), who had just previously resisted the temptation to avoid the cross (8:31-33). The Father did this by enveloping the Son's body, including even his clothes, with *heavenly brilliance,* by sending two *heavenly messengers* to talk with him about his approaching passion (and resurrection?), and by causing the Son, as well as the others, to hear the *heavenly voice* say, "This is my Son, my Beloved, listen to him." Jesus ignored Peter's suggestion that by building three shelters—one each for Jesus, Moses, and Elijah—the glory scene might be prolonged. While descending, the Master told his disciples that until after his resurrection they should keep to themselves what they had seen. They kept this charge. He also cleared up the prophecy of Malachi regarding the coming of Elijah before the arrival of the Messiah.

What a contrast between the glory on top of the mount and the misery, shame, and confusion below (verses 14-29). Here Jesus and the three saw a distraught father and his demon-possessed, deaf-and-dumb, epileptic, only son. The nine disciples, who had been left behind when Jesus and the three had ascended the mount, had been unable to cure this lad. Scribes, gloating over their failure, were arguing with them. Curiosity seekers, many in number, were looking on. Jesus cried out, "O faithless generation, how long shall I be with y o u? How long shall I put up with y o u? Bring him to me." When the boy was brought—and also later— the demon threw him into a convulsion. Questioned by Jesus, the father related how cruelly the lad, ever since his childhood, had been treated by the demon. "If you can do anything, take pity on us and help us," the father added. Jesus answered, "As to that 'if you can,' all things are possible for him who believes." After the father's outcry, "I do believe; help my unbelief," Jesus ordered the unclean spirit to leave the boy and never to enter him again. Shrieking, the demon came out. By Jesus the now seemingly dead boy was lifted to his feet. Afterward, when the disciples, now indoors with Jesus, asked him why they had been unable to expel the demon, he answered, "This kind can come out only by prayer."

The agonizing words of Jesus, "How long shall I be with y o u?" showed that he was thinking about his fast approaching passion. Hence, he now uttered his second prediction with reference to this subject (verses 30-32). The new element in this announcement was that he would be betrayed into the hands of men. However, he again declared that three days after he was killed he would rise again. The disciples did not know what to make of these words and were afraid to ask questions.

In fact, the reaction of these men was the very opposite of the proper one. On the way to the house they had been asking, "Who—meaning: who among us—is greatest?" While their Master was thinking of giving his life *for others,* they were thinking of rank, priority, high position, *for themselves* (verses 33-37). Jesus told them, "If anyone would be first, he must be last of all and servant of all." Having taken a little child into his arms, he added, "Whoever in my name welcomes one of such little children welcomes me; and whoever welcomes me does not welcome (only) me but (also) him who sent me."

Though the connection between what precedes and the following paragraph (verses 38-41) cannot be proved, it is possible that the exhortation "He must be servant of all" had pricked the conscience of the apostle John. Recently he and others with him had treated a certain exorcist in a rather unfriendly manner. They had tried to stop him from casting out demons. They had done this because he had not, or not as yet, joined the ranks of steady followers of Jesus. "Do not stop him," said Jesus, "for he who is not against us is for us. . . . He who, because y o u belong to Christ, shall give y o u a cup of water to drink, shall certainly not lose his reward." Thus the Savior placed his own bigheartedness over against the spirit of petty exclusiveness.

Jesus had said, "Whoever in my name welcomes one of such little children welcomes me" (verse 37). Now (verses 42-50) he restates this same truth in negative terms, "Whoever causes one of these little ones who believe in me to sin, it is better for him that a heavy millstone be hung around his neck and he be thrown into the sea." He tells his disciples that they must be on their guard lest they cause either other people or themselves to go astray. If any bodily organ—hand, foot, eye, or whatever—threatens to become a trap to them, they must immediately take drastic action with reference to this source of enticement. Those who refuse are headed for hell. Finally, returning now to the positive, in three salt passages the Master predicts that all are going to endure a fiery trial. The remedy? They should always have salt in themselves, that is, those qualities that would make them a blessing to themselves and to others. To be most effective in this respect they must maintain peace among themselves.

Outline of Chapter 10

Theme: *The Work Which Thou Gavest Him To Do*

10:1-12   Teaching about Divorce
10:13-16   Jesus and the Children
10:17-31   The Peril of Riches and the Reward of Sacrifice
10:32-34   The Third Prediction of the Passion and the Resurrection
10:35-45   The Request of the Sons of Zebedee
10:46-52   The Healing of Blind Bartimaeus at Jericho

CHAPTER X

10   1 He departed from that place and came into the region of Judea [and] [445] beyond the Jordan. Again crowds were flocking toward him, and again, as his custom was, he began to teach them.

    2 Then some Pharisees came up to him, and tempted him by asking, [446] "Is it lawful for a man to divorce (his) wife?" 3 He answered, "What did Moses command y o u?" 4 They said, "Moses allowed (a man) to write a certificate of divorce and send (her) away." 5 But Jesus replied, "It was because of y o u r hardness of heart that Moses wrote y o u this commandment, 6 but from the beginning of creation he [God] made them male and female. 7 'For this reason a man shall leave his father and mother and shall cleave to his wife, [447] 8 and the two shall be one flesh.' It follows that they are no longer two but one flesh. 9 What therefore God has joined together, let not man separate."

    10 And in the house the disciples were again asking him about this. 11 He said to them, "Whoever divorces his wife and marries another woman is committing adultery [448] against her; 12 and if she herself divorces her husband and marries another man, she is committing adultery."

10:1-12 *Teaching about Divorce*
Cf. Matt. 5:31, 32; 19:1-12

Mark 10 is a lengthy chapter. Only chapters 6 and 14 surpass it in length. Its material that is paralleled in Matthew is there distributed over two chapters: 19 and 20. Moreover, with two Matthean exceptions, namely, 19:10-12 (about eunuchs) and 20:1-16 (The Laborers in the Vineyard), Mark 10 and Matt. 19, 20 not only contain substantially the same material but even present this material in the same sequence. Paragraphs 1, 2, and 3 of Mark 10 are paralleled in Matt. 19; paragraphs 4, 5, and 6 in Matt. 20.

As to Luke, because of the rule 10+8=18—see N.T.C. on Matthew, pp. 13, 15—we expect to find Mark 10's parallel in Luke 18; and we do actually discover that more than half of Mark 10 is paralleled there. Luke lacks the

---

445 Whether "and" belongs to the text is not at all certain.

446 Or: and in an attempt to put him on the spot asked him . . . .

447 Though "and shall cleave to his wife" is omitted in some manuscripts, it may well be authentic, as it certainly is in Matt. 19:5.

448 Or: involving himself [in verse 12: herself] in adultery. . . .

paragraph on divorce and the one on the request of the sons of Zebedee. As if to make up for this, Luke 18 begins with two beautiful little parables, peculiar to that Gospel. One is about The Widow and the Judge, the other about the Pharisee and the Publican. For minor differences between Mark's material and its parallels see the treatment of the separate paragraphs.

The Retirement Ministry has ended. Mark 10 contains that evangelist's account of the Perean Ministry. It will be recalled that The Great Galilean Ministry and The Retirement and Perean Ministries together make up that large division of the Synoptics to which we have given the name "The Work Which Thou Gavest Him To Do, Its Progress or Continuation." See the Outline, pp. v, 26.

In all probability, however, the Perean Ministry did not immediately follow that of The Retirement. Intervening was the Later Judean Ministry, lasting from the final October to December of Christ's life on earth. See John 7:2; 10:22. Consequently the Perean Ministry probably fell within the period December of the year 29 to April of the year 30.

Mark is rather vague with respect to the time when the event indicated in 10:1-12 took place. He writes: 1. **He departed from that place.** ... The *place* from which Jesus (and The Twelve) departed is clearly indicated. It must have been Galilee (9:30); better still, Capernaum (9:33).

As to the *time?* The text does not say that from Capernaum Jesus *immediately* started his ministry in Perea. All we can safely affirm is *a.* that rather soon after the events recorded in chapter 9 Jesus entered the region east of Jordan; and *b.* that the events selected for narration by Mark lead from there, by way of Jericho, to Jerusalem; and from Jerusalem's temple, via the various stations of The Passion Week (Mt. of Olives, Bethany, large upper room, Gethsemane, house of the highpriest, Judgment Hall, Pilate's Praetorium, Golgotha), to the tomb, from which the Lord arose gloriously. See 10:1, 32, 33, 46; 11:1, 11, 12, 27; 13:1, 3; 14:3, 15, 32, 53; 15:1, 2, 16, 22, 46; 16:1 ff. For any mention of a return to Galilee after the resurrection we must turn to the Gospel according to Matthew (28:16).

Continued: **and came into the region of Judea [and] beyond the Jordan.** Another possible translation is: "and came to the boundaries of Judea, beyond the Jordan." Whether, with some, one thinks of Judea as extending politically somewhat beyond (that is, to the east of) the Jordan; or, with others, one interprets the evangelist as meaning that Jesus went to the Perean or trans-Jordanic region, "bounded by Judea," in either case we find the Lord, together with his disciples (verse 10), traveling south through Perea— hence Perean Ministry—, east of the Jordan, which he subsequently recrosses, arriving in Jericho (10:46).

Mark continues: **Again crowds were flocking toward him, and again, as his custom was, he began to teach them.** It deserves attention that in its general

374

chracter this *Perean Ministry* (chapter 10)[449] in certain respects resembles *The Great Galilean Ministry* more closely than it resembles *The Retirement Ministry*. No longer does Jesus generally withdraw himself from the multitudes. In fact, as is evident from the present passage (10:1) and also from 10:46; cf. Matt. 19:2, 13; 20:29, 31; Luke 18:15, 36, 43, great multitudes assemble to hear him. He heals their sick, just as he had done previously in and around Galilee. Always he is ready to heal, and his love overleaps every boundary.

However, here in Mark 10:1 it is not, as in Matt. 19:2, the healing that is mentioned but the teaching. We see, therefore, that during this ministry, as often, healing and teaching go hand in hand. Whenever a crowd gathered around Jesus it was his custom [450] to teach them. It must not be overlooked, however, that though the present passage refers to teaching *the multitudes,* nevertheless even the intensive teaching and training of *The Twelve,* which was a characteristic of The Retirement Ministry, continues during The Perean Ministry. See verses 10-12, 14, 15, 23-27, 29-31, 32-34, 38-45.

2. Then some Pharisees came up to him, and tempted him by asking, Is it lawful for a man to divorce (his) wife? We have met the Pharisees before and have become acquainted with their hostility toward Jesus (2:16, 24; 3:6, 22; 7:1-5; 8:11). Their present intention is to catch him in their trap, to put him on the spot, and thus to discredit him in the eyes of the public, so that the crowds would turn away from him. They were convinced that their question, answered either way, would create a serious difficulty for Jesus. To understand this, the following facts should be taken into consideration:

Among the Jews there was a difference of opinion as to what Moses had taught with respect to the problem of divorce. He had written, "When a man takes a wife and marries her, if then she finds no favor in his eyes because he has found *'erwath dābhār* in her, and he writes her a bill of divorce . . ." (Deut. 24:1). But what is meant by *'erwath dābhār?* Does it mean "a scandalous thing"? Other guesses are "some indecency," "something improper," "improper behavior," "something offensive," "a shameful thing" (LXX), etc. According to Shammai and his followers the reference was to unchastity or adultery.

According to Hillel and his disciples the meaning was far broader. They emphasized the words, "If then she finds no favor in his eyes," and accordingly would allow divorce for the flimsiest reasons, so that the husband could reject his wife if she accidentally served him food that had

---

449 If one wishes to be precise 10:46-52 would have to be excluded from this ministry, since Jericho was west of Jordan. However, for practical reasons this exclusion is not necessary.

450 εἰώθει third per. sing. pluperf. of εἴωθα; from obsolete ἔθω. Cf. ethos, ethics. The pluperfect has the sense of the imperfect. See Gram. N.T., p. 904.

been slightly burned, or if at home she talked so loud that the neighbors could hear her. If Jesus endorsed the more strict interpretation, favored by Shammai, he would be displeasing the followers of Hillel. Moreover, there seem to have been very many—perhaps even these Pharisees (cf. Matt. 19:7)—who agreed with Hillel's "liberal" opinion. Even the disciples may have shared this view; see Matt. 19:10. Besides, if the Lord sided with Shammai the Pharisees might have accused him, though not justly, of being inconsistent when he nevertheless consorted with sinners and ate with them.

On the other hand, if Jesus endorsed the lax—"anything will do as ground for divorce"—interpretation, what would the disciples of Shammai think of him? Would not the more serious and conscientious people charge him with tolerating moral looseness? And what would the female part of the population think of him?

Jesus shows that the underlying emphasis of the question is wrong. Why all this talk about the possibility of divorce, as if to say, "If this marriage does not work out I can always divorce my wife"? Why not go back beyond Deut. 24 to God's marriage ordinance recorded in such passages as Gen. 1:27 and 2:24?

3, 4. He answered, What did Moses command y o u? They said, Moses allowed (a man) to write a certificate of divorce and send (her) away. At first glance there might seem to be a conflict between Matthew and Mark. The true situation, however, is as follows: In both Gospels it is the Pharisees who raise the question about divorce (cf. Matt. 19:3 with Mark 10:2). In Mark Jesus replies by asking them a question, namely, "What did Moses command y o u?" They answer, "Moses allowed. . . ." Jesus then concludes the conversation by answering, "It was because of y o u r hardness of heart that Moses wrote y o u this commandment, but from the beginning of creation he [God] made them male and female. . . . What therefore God has joined together, let not man separate." Matthew abbreviates. He omits Christ's question, "What did Moses command y o u?" This omission is not at all serious, because the position of the Pharisees, "Moses allowed (a man) to write a certificate of divorce . . ." is recognized in both accounts (cf. Matt. 19:7 with Mark 10:4), though it is only Mark who makes clear that it was in answer to Christ's question that this position was first put into words. There was nothing to prevent these Pharisees from restating that position in the form of a question, "Why then did Moses command . . . ?" (Matt. 19:7). Also, while *Matthew,* as he does frequently, tells the story in one breath, as a connected whole, *Mark* shows that the dictum, "Whoever divorces his wife, . . ." (verse 11) was pronounced by Jesus while he was in a house and in answer to a question by *his disciples* (verses 10, 11). *Matthew* (19:9) also includes this authoritative pronouncement in his report, but as spoken to *the*

Pharisees. However, Jesus may have spoken these words twice; first to the Pharisees; later to the disciples. For "commanded" see on Mark 13:34.

The Pharisees answered Jesus' question by saying, "Moses allowed (a man) to write a certificate of divorce and send (her) away." This Mosaic regulation (Deut. 24:1 ff.) was by many—probably including several of these Pharisees— interpreted as meaning, "If you wish to divorce your wife for any reason whatever, go right ahead, but be sure to hand her a divorce certificate." The real meaning of the passage, however, is this, "Husband, you better think twice before you reject your wife. Remember that once you have put her away and she has become the wife of another you cannot afterward take her back; not even if that other husband should also have rejected her or should have died." Moses had mentioned the "bill of divorce" only in passing, but the scribes and Pharisees placed all the emphasis on it. While *they* were always stressing the Mosaic *concession,* Jesus constantly emphasized the *principle,* namely, that husband and wife are and must remain *one.*

This becomes clear from what follows in verses 5-8. **But Jesus replied, It was because of y o u r hardness of heart that Moses wrote y o u this commandment, but from the beginning he [God] made them male and female. For this reason a man shall leave his father and mother and shall cleave to his wife, and the two shall be one flesh.** Moses had done everything in his power to discourage divorce. It was only because of[451] the hardness or stubbornness of heart,[452] the coarseness and harshness of the people, that Moses had made a concession. It was a merciful concession made for the sake of the wife, for without this regulation a harsh man might be inclined to dismiss his wife even without giving her any written evidence that she was now no longer married.

Now in this *concession* of Deut. 24 the Pharisees are far more interested than in the creation and marriage *institution* of Gen. 1:27 (cf. 5:2); 2:24. Jesus points back to the original ordinance, that is, to the way things had been "from the beginning of creation." It was then that God, even though he created Adam before Eve, at once created him as a male; hence, with a view to intimate union with Eve, who was created later on from the very body of Adam, and as a female. Each, accordingly, was made for the other, with the definite purpose of joining together *one* man to *one* woman. Those who are

---

[451] πρός in the sense of "having regard to," "because of." Cf. somewhat similar meaning ("with respect to") in Acts 24:16; Rom. 10:21a; Heb. 1:7 f.

[452] Note σκληροκαρδία, both here and in Matt. 19:8. This combines σκληρός, hard, and καρδία, heart. As to σκληρός (cf. *arteriosclerosis*), see also Matt. 25:24, a hard—i.e. harsh, stern, unrelenting—man; John 6:60, a hard (to accept) message; Acts 26:14, "It is hard for you to kick against the goads"; James 3:4, driven by hard—i.e., strong—winds; and Jude 15, hard—i.e., harsh—words.

eager for divorce ignore this fact. Moreover, God ordains that for this very reason—that is, because the union between the two was intended to be so intimate and they were designed for each other (see both Gen. 1:27 and 2:23)—a man shall leave his father and his mother, and shall do this with a view to a more intimate and more lasting attachment, namely, "and shall cleave to his wife, and the two shall be one flesh"; yes, "no longer two but one flesh," says Jesus.

It is clear that Jesus viewed Gen. 2:24 (in combination with Gen. 1:27) as a divine ordinance, and not as a mere description of what generally takes place on earth. And since one is not doing injustice to the Hebrew original of Gen. 2:24 by bringing out this divine institution idea in the translation—hence "a man shall leave . . . and shall cleave," not merely "a man leaves and cleaves"—what good reason can there be for not expressing it? On this passage (Gen. 2:24), therefore, the translation adopted by A.V. and A.R.V. is to be preferred to some of the more modern versions.

That Jesus did indeed so regard marriage, namely, as an indissoluble union, changing what used to be "two" into what has now become "one"— note: **It follows that they are no longer two but one flesh**—, a union until death parts the two, a definitely divine institution that must not be tampered with, is clear from the following: *a.* Otherwise his argument would lose its force; *b.* the audience hardly needed to be told that it is customary for men to get married; and *c.* this is in line with the words immediately following, namely, 9. **What therefore God has joined together, let not man separate.**

This does not mean that a man is committing a sin by not getting married. Rather, it means that those who decide to marry must view marriage as a divine institution, a state in which they must so conduct themselves that true union—sexual, to be sure; note "shall cleave to his wife," but also intellectual, moral, and spiritual—is not only established but more and more firmly cemented.

It was God who made this union possible (Gen. 1:27); God also who issued the command, "Be fruitful . . ." (Gen. 1:28). It was he, again, who said, "It is not good that man should be alone; I will make him a help fit for him" (Gen. 2:18). It was also God who brought Eve to Adam, to be the latter's wife (Gen. 2:22). Indeed, from every angle, it was God who established marriage as a divine institution (Gen. 2:24; Matt. 19:5, 6). Marriage is therefore indeed "an honorable estate." Therefore, let not man separate what God has joined together! [453]

---

[453] See also W. A. Maier, *For Better Not for Worse*, St. Louis, 1935, pp. 80, 81; and N.T.C. on Eph. 5:22-23.

The indissolubility of marriage is stated by Jesus in a very forceful manner. The word "Therefore" or "For this reason" shows that he is summarizing the divine revelation concerning the marriage bond. Note "joined together." [454] According to Christ's teaching, then, husband and wife form a *team*. They work, plan, pray, play, pull, etc. together. For a man to separate that which God has yoked or joined together means arrogantly to defy an act of God!

In a world where one divorce follows another in rapid succession, so that it is difficult at times to count the number of times a person has been divorced, the teaching of Jesus deserves to be repeated and emphasized.

10-12. And in the house the disciples were again asking him about this. He said to them, Whoever divorces his wife and marries another woman is committing adultery against her; and if she herself divorces her husband and marries another man, she is committing adultery. [455]

Between verses 2-9, on the one hand, and 10-12, on the other, there are these differences: *a*. In the former passage Jesus is addressing Pharisees, in the latter his disciples; *b*. in the former he is outside, in the latter inside a house; and *c*. in the former he is discussing divorce, in the latter divorce followed by marriage to someone else.

---

[454] συνέζευξε third per. sing. aor. indic. of συξεύγνυμι; literally, to yoke together. A ζεῦγος (cf. ζυγός) is a *yoke* (of oxen, horses, etc.); or a *pair* (of turtle doves, Luke 2:24).

[455] With respect to grammar and vocabulary note the following: First of all, as to verse 10, in the New Testament as elsewhere the preposition εἰς has several other meanings in addition to *into* and *toward*. It occurs at times where ἐν is expected. In such cases, as here, it simply means *in*. But see also N.T.C. on Matthew, pp. 1000, 1001.

In verse 11 ἀπολύσῃ is third per. sing. aor. subjunctive active of ἀπολύω, which in this case means *send away, divorce*. Note both here and in verse 12 γαμήσῃ, same construction as ἀπολύσῃ; also in both verses μοιχᾶται, third per. sing. pres. middle indic. of μοιχάω, involves himself (verse 11), herself (verse 12) in—or makes himself, herself guilty of, hence *commits*—adultery. The New Testament uses only the middle-passive forms, but also has μοιχεύω.

Wherever a distinction between μοιχεία and πορνεία is possible, the former has reference to *adultery*, that is, basically, the sinner's sexual intercourse with someone other than his or her marriage partner. The term πορνεία is much broader in meaning and refers basically to *all* sexual immorality. Thus voluntary sexual immorality exclusively involving unmarried persons would be πορνεία, not μοιχεία. However, the exact connotation of each of these words depends in any particular case on the context. There are several derived meanings. Thus μοιχεία may indicate unchastity in thought, look, or gesture; note the verb ἐμοίχευσε in Matt. 5:28. As to πορνεία, πορνεύω, see N.T.C. on Matthew, pp. 716, 717, footnote 684. On the meaning of μοιχάω = μοιχεύω (Matt. 5:32), see N.T.C. on Matt. 5:32; also L.N.T.(Th), p. 417; Liddell and Scott, *A Greek English Lexicon*, London, etc., Vol. II, p. 1141; and F. Hauck, Th.D.N.T., Vol. IV, pp. 729-735, especially top of page 730. For a somewhat different view see L.N.T. (A. and G.), p. 528.

In verse 12 note ἀπολύσασα, nom. sing. fem. aor. act. participle of ἀπολύω. Verse 12 is a third class (future more vivid) conditional sentence.

Matt. 19:10 may indicate that Christ's disciples were inclined to favor the lax marriage-and-divorce position of Hillel. So, *again* the Master is questioned about this matter, this time not by the Pharisees but by his own disciples. As shown previously, he gives them essentially the same answer as he had given the Pharisees (cf. Matt. 19:9 with Mark 10:11). This time, however, he omits the exception found in Matt. 5:32; 19:9. See N.T.C. on these passages. The exception does not change the basic fact, taught in both Gospels, that in the eyes of God, hence ideally considered, marriage is indissoluble.

What Jesus is saying here in verse 11 is that a husband who rudely divorces his wife, thereby separating what God has joined, is committing a grievous sin, and that he aggravates this sin by marrying someone else. Such a husband is sinning against *God* not only but also against *his wife:* he is involving himself in adultery *against her;* or, "is exposing her to adultery," as the same thought is recorded in Matt. 5:32.

At this point Mark adds something that is not found in Matthew. Mark points out that in the house Jesus applied the same rule also to the wife who without regard to the divine ordinance divorces her husband.

Why this difference between Matthew and Mark? Answer: Matthew was writing primarily for Jews, among whom rejection of a husband by a wife was so rare that the law had not made any provision for this possibility. Nevertheless, among the Jews, or those who stood in close relation to them, such dismissals of husbands by their wives were not entirely unknown. For example, with reference to Salome, the wicked sister of Herod the Great (see N.T.C. on Matthew, p. 165), Josephus writes: "Sometime later Salome had occasion to quarrel with [her husband] Costobarus, and soon sent him a document dissolving their marriage, which action was not in accordance with Jewish law. For it is (only) the husband who is permitted by us to do this" (*Jewish Antiquities* XV. 259).

Salome, in turn, had a grandniece named Herodias. See N.T.C. on Matthew, p. 189, the chart. It has already been pointed out (Mark 6:17, 18) that she had rejected her husband Herod Philip and had married Herod Antipas. Herodias was partly Jewish.

But what was exceptional among Jews was very common among Greeks and Romans (cf. I Cor. 7:10, 13) ... and is common today also. The principle which Jesus here enunciates is that such violations of the sacred institution of marriage, whether committed by the husband or by the wife, is *adultery,* an abomination in the eyes of the One who issued the creation and marriage ordinance (Gen. 1:27; 2:24; 5:2).

Thus, by means of a few simple words, Jesus discourages divorce, refutes the rabbinical misinterpretation of the law, reaffirms the law's true meaning, censures the guilty party, defends the innocent, and throughout it all upholds the sacredness and inviolability of the marriage bond as ordained by God.

A few additional remarks are in order:

a. In verses 11, 12 the rights of the husband and the wife are equally balanced. Before God they are the same in worth. Is the husband "an heir to the grace of life"? The wife is "a fellow-heir" (I Peter 3:7). She is not her husband's property. She is his partner. To be sure, the husband remains "the head of the wife" (Eph. 5:22, 23), but before the Lord both are equally precious. A wife who has by sovereign grace accepted Jesus as her Lord and Savior does not feel any need to join the so-called Women's Liberation Movement. The Bible offers her something far better.

b. On the one hand Jesus regards the break-up of a marriage to be a most serious matter, an abomination. Yet, on the other hand that same uncompromising Lord is also the merciful Savior, who comforts the heart of the penitent sinner by saying, "Go, and from now on sin no more" (John 8:10, 11). [456]

c. Is there any thought connection between the end of Mark 9—"And be at peace with each other"—and the opening paragraph (verses 1-12) of Mark 10? Probably not. Nevertheless, is not Christian marriage the divine institution in which peace and love, harmony and devotion, are most marvelously displayed . . . as every supremely happy Christian couple can testify?

---

13 And they were bringing little children to him, for him to touch. But the disciples rebuked (those who brought) them. 14 Now when Jesus saw this he became indignant, and said to them, "Let the little children come to me, and stop hindering them, for to such belongs the kingdom of God. 15 I solemnly declare to y o u, whoever shall not receive the kingdom of God as a little child shall never enter it." 16 And having taken them in his arms he tenderly blessed them one by one, laying his hands upon them.

10:13-16 *Jesus and the Children*
Cf. Matt. 19:13-15; Luke 18:15-17

So closely do the three accounts resemble each other that literary relationship is probable. Yet, so distinct is each, in comparison with the other two, that it is once again apparent that, under the guidance of the Holy Spirit, each evangelist selected his material as he saw fit.

As to Mark 10:13, where Mark and Luke have "touch" ("for him to touch"), Matthew provides a fuller explanation by expanding this into "lay his hands (on them) and pray." Mark's statement (verse 14) that when Jesus saw his disciples' rude behavior he "became indignant" is not paralleled in Matthew and Luke. Neither is Luke's remark, "But Jesus called them [the infants with those who brought them] to him" duplicated in Matthew and Mark. Our Lord's gracious invitation, "Let the little children come to me,

---

[456] With respect to the authenticity of John 7:53—8:11 see N.T.C. on John, Vol. II, pp. 33-35.

..." is reproduced almost identically in all three Gospels. Mark 10:15 = Luke 18:17, not found in Matthew, but cf. Matt. 18:3. At this point Luke's report of this incident ends. Matt. 19:15 adds, "And he laid his hands on them and went away from there." Mark alone has retained the unforgettably beautiful touch, "And having taken them in his arms he tenderly blessed them one by one, laying his hands upon them" (verse 16). Whatever one may think about the possibility of a connection between the last clause of 9:50 and the opening paragraph of chapter 10, the appropriateness of the sequence *marriage* (10:1-12), *children* (verses 13-16), and *property* (verses 17-31) is readily apparent.

13. And they were bringing little children to him, for him to touch. Note complete absence of time or place indications. On the basis of 10:1, 32, a reasonable assumption is that the incident here reported took place in a house in Perea while Jesus and The Twelve were traveling south toward Jerusalem. Was it perhaps the house mentioned in 10:10, and did the two incidents (verses 1-12; 13-16) happen in close succession?

Luke 18:15 makes clear that the "little children" that were brought[457] to Jesus were actually infants.

These little ones were brought to Jesus, presumably by their parents or other close relatives, "that he might touch them," or "for him to touch," meaning, as has been indicated, for him to place his hands on them while asking the Father to bless them.

There was nothing magical about Christ's touch. It was mainly by means of his further action, his word of prayer, that these infants were blessed. All the same, the touch must have been a very tender one. It was far more than a *mere* touch, as verse 16 clearly indicates. It may therefore be considered part of the blessing the children received. See also on 1:41.

But the disciples rebuked[458] (those who brought) them. They rebuked not the children, of course, but their parents and in general all who brought them. Were these disciples standing at the doorway of a house (cf. 10:10) and were they with angry gestures shooing away those who approached with children in their arms? The reaction of these disciples was rather characteristic of them: they did not want to be bothered; also, they did not want their Master to be bothered by such unimportant (?) creatures as infants! See above, on 6:37a.

---

457 Mark's impersonal "they—or people—were bringing little children" sounds more Semitic (cf. Dan. 4:25, 32) than Matthew's "little children were brought to him," but the meaning is the same.

458 ἐπετίμησαν, third per. pl. aor. indic. active of ἐπιτιμάω. Basically the word means to award a τιμή (penalty) ἐπί (upon). In the sense of *rebuked* this word also occurs in 1:25; 4:39; 8:32, 33; 9:25. The meaning *warned* must be ascribed to this verb in 3:12; 8:30; 10:48.

14. **Now when Jesus saw this he became indignant.** . . . . Jesus took note of this reaction on the part of The Twelve, and did not like it at all. In fact, he "became indignant." [459] Cf. 3:5, where a synonym is used. See also what is said about Christ's sighing (8:12) and cf. 14:33 f. Of course, this indignation of our Lord was a concomitant of his love. He was angry with his disciples because he loved so deeply and tenderly the little ones and the ones who brought them.

Continued: **and said to them, Let the little children come to me, and stop hindering them, for to such belongs the kingdom of God.** "Let [460] the little children come to me." The reason Jesus gives for ordering the disciples to allow the little children to come to him and to stop hindering them is "for to *such*—that is, to them and to all those who in humble trustfulness are like them—belongs the kingdom of God." For the meaning of "the kingdom of God" see on 1:15. In the present case the verse means that *in principle* all the blessings of salvation belong even now to these little ones, a fact that was to be realized progressively here on earth and perfectly in the hereafter.

15. **I solemnly declare to y o u, whoever shall not receive the kingdom of God as a little child shall never enter it.** For the introductory formula see on 3:28. Receiving the kingdom of God as a little child means to accept it with genuine trustful simplicity, with unassuming humility.

The gold pieces were piled up on the outside windowsill. "Take One," said the sign. All day long people passed by thinking, "This fellow can't fool me." Evening fell, and the owner was about to remove the pile. But just before he did, a child came by, read the sign, and calmly, without the least hesitancy, took one!

There has been some dispute about the exact meaning of the words as they occur in the original. Grammatically, the saying could be read to mean, "Whoever shall not receive the kingdom of God as one receives a little child shall never enter it." But the very context and also such near-parallels as Matt. 11:25; 18:3 (cf. John 3:3, 5) clearly show that Jesus is talking about the simple, humble, unquestioning, trustful manner in which a child accepts what is offered to him.

Another attractive interpretation that is probably also wrong is this, "Whoever does not *receive* the *present* kingdom as a gift shall never *enter* the

---

459 ἠγανάκτησε, third per. sing. aor. indic. of ἀγανακτέω. See also 10:41; 14:4; cf. Matt. 20:24; 21:15; 26:8; Luke 13:14. The verb is derived from ἄγαν, *much* (cf. the motto urging moderation in all things: μηδὲν ἄγαν, "nothing too much"), and ἄχομαι, to grieve (cf. anguish).

460 Ἄφετε, sec. per. pl. aor. imper. active of ἀφίημι. There is a slight difference between the wording of Mark 10:14; Luke 18:16, on the one hand, and Matt. 19:14, on the other. Matt. 19:14 literally reads, "Leave the children alone and stop hindering them . . . ." The difference is not essential.

future kingdom." This division of the kingdom idea into two phases, within a short sentence, is rather unnatural. Far more simple is the meaning: *the only possible way to enter the kingdom is by accepting it readily and trustfully, as a child accepts it.*

The kingdom is the rule of God in heart and life, together with all the blessings that result from this rule. The parallelism of Mark 9:45; 9:47—see on those passages—has made clear that "entering the kingdom" means "entering life," that is, everlasting life. And a comparison between Matt. 19:24 and 19:25 shows that "entering the kingdom of God" amounts to "being saved." According to John 17:3 "This is everlasting life, that they should know thee, the only true God, and Jesus Christ whom thou didst send." Such knowledge of or fellowship with God implies having freedom of access to his throne of grace (Rom. 5:2; Heb. 4:16), experiencing the love of God that is poured out into our hearts through the Holy Spirit (Rom. 5:5), being transformed into the image of Christ (II Cor. 3:18), being illumined by the light of the knowledge of the glory of God in the face of Christ (II Cor. 4:6), possessing the peace of God that passes all understanding (Phil. 4:7) and the joy unspeakable and full of glory (I Peter 1:8). At Christ's return a transformed body and a new heaven and earth for both body and soul are added (Rom. 8:23; Eph. 1:14; Phil. 3:21; II Peter 3:13; Rev. 21:1 f.).

16. **And having taken them in his arms he tenderly blessed them one by one, laying his hands upon them.** By means of a careful use of tenses [461] Mark draws a delightful picture, as will become clear.

Not only has Jesus rebuked the disciples for their attempt to prevent the little ones from being brought to him, but he has also actually called to himself these infants together with those who wanted to bring them to him (Luke 18:16). And now each mother or father, etc., carries his little child into the very presence of Jesus; that is, each does this in turn. The Master takes the first child in his arm and places the hand of his other arm upon its head. Then he tenderly—or fervently—blesses it, by means of uttering a brief but earnest prayer to the Father, that his blessing may be bestowed on it (probably implied in Matt. 19:13). While he does this, his heart, filled with love and compassion, goes out to this little one. Finished, he returns the child to the one who had brought it. He then treats the next little one in the same manner, and the next, until all have been blessed. It must have been a most impressive, comforting, and memorable scene.

The fact that the Lord regarded these little children that were brought to him as being already "in" the kingdom, as being even now members of his

---

461 ἐναγκαλισάμενος, aor, participle; see on 9:36, footnote 426. κατευλόγει is an intensive expansion of the verb εὐλογέω. Mark uses the imperfect tense, and because of the context this imperfect is probably iterative; τιθείς, pres. active participle of τίθημι.

church, must not escape our attention. He definitely did not view them as "little heathen," who were living outside of the realm of salvation until by an act of their own they would "join the church." He regarded them as "holy seed" (see I Cor. 7:14). How wonderful that in later years believing parents would be able to say to such a child, now arrived at the age of understanding, "Think of it, when you, my child, were just a suckling, Jesus took you in his arms and blessed you. Then already you were the object of God's tender love. And he has been with you ever since. What, then, is your response?"

On the basis of such a passage as Mark 10:13, 14—to which should be added Gen. 17:7, 12; Ps. 103:17; 105:6-10; Isa. 59:21; Acts 2:38, 39; 16:15, 33; I Cor. 1:16; Col. 2:11, 12—the belief that since the little children of believers belong to God's church and to his covenant, baptism, the sign and seal of such belonging, should not be withheld from them, must be regarded as well-founded. In later years, through parental, etc. instruction applied to the heart by the Holy Spirit, the divine blessing received earlier becomes a mighty incentive to wholehearted personal surrender to Christ.

What Jesus Did for the Family

1. He honored the marriage bond, declaring its indissolubility as a divine institution (Mark 10:5-9).

2. To husband and wife he accorded equal standing before God (Mark 10:11, 12).

3. He assumed that parents would be kind to their children, and would provide them with whatever was best for them (Matt. 7:9-11).

4. Over against Pharisees and scribes he re-emphasized the divine rule that children should honor their parents (Mark 7:6-13).

5. He reinforced this rule by his own example, being obedient to his parents, and even on the cross tenderly providing for his mother (Luke 2:51; John 19:26, 27).

6. He loved the little ones, took them into his arms, and tenderly blessed them (Mark 10:13-16).

7. When children shouted Hosannas in his honor, he defended them over against the chief priests and the scribes (Matt. 21:15, 16).

8. He insisted, however, that the ties that pertain to earthly family life are superseded by those that knit together the members of the spiritual family (Mark 3:31-35; cf. Matt. 7:11; 10:37; and see N.T.C. on Eph. 3:14, 15). Consequently, he regarded the earthly family as a training school for the heavenly.

---

17 And as he [Jesus] started out on the road a man ran up to him, fell on his knees before him, and was asking him, "Good Teacher, what shall I do that I may inherit

everlasting life?" 18 Jesus said to him, "Why do you call me good? No one is good except One—God. 19 You know the commandments: You shall not kill, you shall not commit adultery, you shall not steal, you shall not bear false witness, you shall not defraud, honor your father and your mother." 20 "Teacher," he said to him, "All these things have I observed ever since I was a child." 21 Jesus looked at him and loved him. "One thing you lack," he said to him, "Go, sell whatever you have and give (the proceeds) to the poor, and you will have a treasure in heaven; and come, follow me." 22 But he, crestfallen because of these words, went away sorrowful, [462] for he possessed much property.

23 Looking around, Jesus said to his disciples, "How hard it will be for those who possess wealth to enter the kingdom of God!" 24 The disciples were startled at these words. But Jesus continued and said to them, "Children, how hard it is to enter the kingdom of God! 25 It is easier for a camel to go through the eye of a needle than for a rich man to enter the kingdom of God." 26 Shocked even more they said to each other, "Then who can be saved?" 27 Fastening his eyes on them Jesus said, "With men (this is) impossible but not with God, for with God all things are possible."

28 Peter began to say [463] to him, "Look, we have given up everything, and followed thee." 29 Jesus replied, "I solemnly declare to y o u, there is no one who has given up house or brothers or sisters or mother or father or children or fields for my sake and for the gospel's sake, 30 who shall not receive a hundredfold; now in this time: houses and brothers and sisters and mothers and children and fields, along with persecutions; and in the age to come everlasting life. 31 But many that are first shall be last, and (many) last first."

10:17-31 *The Peril of Riches and the Reward of Sacrifice*
Cf. Matt. 19:16-30; Luke 18:18-30

With reference to Mark's account of this event, as compared with Matthew's, a controversy has been raging for many years. It is therefore important that even before entering into the exegesis of the individual passages certain statistics be disclosed.

A comparative study at once reveals that Mark's account is by far the longest and most detailed of the three. According to Grk.N.T. (A-B-M-W) Mark uses 270 words, Matthew 234 (when unparalleled Matt. 19:28 is subtracted from the total), and Luke 201. It is immediately apparent, therefore, that both Matthew and Luke may be considered abbreviated reports. This process of abbreviation concerns not just one item—for example, Matt. 19:16, 17a; cf. Mark 10:17b, 18—but the entire report, from beginning to end. As to the passage just mentioned, see below, on Mark 10:17, 18.

Continuing with Matt. 19, we notice that in verses 18, 19 the former publican omits "you shall not defraud" (Mark 10:19), but adds the summary of the second table of the decalog, "You shall love your neighbor as

---

462 Or: 22 But at these words his countenance fell, and he went away sorrowful.
463 Or: said.

yourself." In verse 20 Matthew again abbreviates, leaving out Mark's "ever since I was a child," but adding, "(The young man said) . . . what do I still lack?" Or, more accurately, according to Matt. 19:20 this "lack" is *first of all* a matter about which the young man makes enquiry. Christ's command follows in verse 21. According to Mark 10:21 it is simply a matter in connection with which Jesus issues a command.

Verses 21, 22, and 23 in both Gospels (Matt. 19; Mark 10) are almost the same in substance, though each evangelist employs his own phraseology. In verse 21, however, Matthew represents Jesus as having prefaced the command to the young man with the words, "If you wish to be perfect." Cf. Matt. 5:48. Mark, on the other hand, makes the verse begin with the unforgettable words, "Jesus looked at him and loved him." This is followed by, "One thing you lack . . . Go, sell. . . ." The young man's sorrowful departure is described in verse 22, the meaning being identical in both Gospels. Mark's language, however, as often, is more descriptive and striking: the young man departs *crestfallen*. Similarly, in verse 23, which according to both of these Gospels records the saying of Jesus that it will be hard for "a rich man" (thus Matthew), or for "those who possess wealth" (thus Mark), to enter the kingdom of "heaven" (Matthew), or of "God" (Mark), it is again Mark who most vividly portrays the scene by writing, "*Looking around,* Jesus said. . . ."

The saying "How hard" or "it will be hard . . ." is by Matthew reported once (19:23), but by Mark twice, though with variation (10:23, 24). Similarly, the startled reaction of the disciples is by Matthew reported once (19:25), by Mark twice (10:24, 26). Christ's saying, "It is easier for a camel to go through the eye of a needle than for a rich man to enter the kingdom of God" (verse 24 in Matthew) is almost identical with the one found in Mark (verse 25). The disciples' exclamation "Then who can be saved?" is found both in Matthew (verse 25) and Mark (verse 26). According to Mark (verse 27) Jesus replies, "With men (this is) impossible but not with God, for with God all things are possible," a reply found also in Matthew, but again in abbreviated form (verse 26).

Finally, though it is true that Matthew, in verse 27, adds, "What then shall we have?" (only four words in Greek), a question not found in Mark, nevertheless when Matthew's 29th verse is compared with its parallel, verses 29 and 30 in Mark, it will become apparent that after "shall receive a hundredfold," Matthew has "and in the age to come everlasting life," while Mark has no less than 26 words (in the original): "now in this present age: houses and brothers. . . ." Compare also verse 29 of both Gospels (Matt. 19:29; Mark 10:29): Mark's "for my sake and for the gospel's sake" is in Matthew shortened to "for my name's sake."

When we now turn to Luke's account (18:18-30), what strikes us immediately is that no less than three-fourths of that evangelist's words are those that occur also in Mark's report. The theory according to which Luke, in composing his book, actually had Mark's Gospel in front of him, and under the guidance of the Holy Spirit adapted it to his own use, seems altogether probable.

As to the differences between Mark's account and Luke's, in the main they are as follows: When Mark 10:17 is compared with Luke 18:18, it becomes clear that "the beloved physician" omitted the graphic description by means of which Mark introduced the rich young man. Yet, it is to Luke that we owe the information that this rich man was "a ruler." In verse 20 Luke mentions the command "You shall not commit adultery" before "You shall not kill." He omits Mark's "You shall not defraud." In verse 22 Luke omits Mark's interesting statement, "Jesus looked at him and loved him." In verse 23 Luke pictures the disappointed ruler as being "very sad" but does not repeat Mark's graphic touch, "His countenance fell." Luke has nothing that corresponds to Mark's (10:23) *"Looking around* he [Jesus] said. . . ." The remark of Jesus, "How hard it is . . ." is mentioned only once by Luke, not twice (with variations) as in Mark 10:23, 24. Mark mentions the disciples' startled reaction twice (10:24, 26), Matthew once (19:25), Luke (see 18:24-26) not at all. The latter uses a different word (in the original) for "needle" (see the original of verse 25 in both Mark and Luke). Verse 27 in both Mark and Luke illustrates the manner in which Luke abbreviates: Mark has, "Fastening his eyes on them Jesus said, 'With men (this is) impossible but not with God, for with God all things are possible.' " Luke writes, "What is impossible with men is possible with God." In verse 29 of both Gospels Luke reduces Mark's list of seven items to five, omitting any reference to sisters and to fields, and also leaving out "with persecutions." Also, Luke does not repeat the list of promised goods, as Mark virtually does in 10:30. And instead of Mark's longer expression "for my sake and for the gospel's sake" Luke writes the shorter "for the kingdom of God's sake." Finally, in verse 30 Luke substitutes "many times as much" for Mark's "a hundred times as much" or "hundredfold."

It has become clear, therefore, that both in Matthew and in Luke the event described in Mark 10:17-31 appears *in greatly reduced form.* Luke's account is the shortest of all three, but even Matthew omits much of that which is found in Mark.

Here, however, we should be careful. The remark is often made that these Matthean and Lucan omissions were made because Mark's additional material was considered "superfluous," "merely repetitious," and therefore altogether "unnecessary." In so judging, are we not in danger of belittling Mark and along with this, in rejecting divine inspiration? Read Mark's account again, including, for example, the supposedly "repetitious" passage 10:23-27. Does this passage not immediately strike the unbiased reader as being a very true and natural report of what actually happened? Why should it be difficult to believe that Jesus, having first said, "How hard it will be for those who possess wealth to enter the kingdom of God!," and having taken note of the startled expression in the eyes of The Twelve, then continued by saying, "Children, how hard it is to enter the kingdom of God!"? Similarly, it certainly is not at all unnatural for the disciples to have been "startled" when the Master pointed out how difficult it was for the rich to enter the kingdom, and a little later to have been "shocked even more" when Jesus added, "It is easier for a camel. . . ." Similarly, it should not at all be hard to believe that the statement regarding things given up (Mark 10:29) was repeated and gloriously expanded (note: "and in the age to come everlasting life") in the next verse.

What Mark writes must therefore be considered vivid, beautiful, historical, fully inspired. The fact that Matthew and Luke did not deem it necessary to repeat all this material was not because they considered it superfluous or unworthy, but because in their respective Gospels they wanted to save space for other material; for example, Matthew, for Christ's discourses; Luke, for many unforgettable parables. They therefore reproduced only the main outline of the story. The Holy Spirit guided all three.

17. And as he [Jesus] started out on the road a man ran up to him, fell on his knees before him, and was asking him, Good Teacher, what shall I do that I may inherit everlasting life?

It may well have been from the very house mentioned in 10:10 that Jesus and The Twelve (see verse 23) now proceed on their way. Mark's Gospel leaves the impression that the event recorded in verses 17-31 took place immediately, or almost immediately, after the bestowal of a blessing upon the little children. If so, then the sequence *marriage, children,* and *material possessions,* a very natural chain, becomes even more unforgettable.

As the little group was leaving, someone [464] *ran*—or *rushed*—up to Jesus. Less dramatically Matthew says *came up to* him. The stranger who did this is by Matthew called *a young man* (19:20), by Luke *a ruler* (18:18), and is by all three described as *a very rich person,* one who owned much property (Matt. 19:22; Mark 10:22; Luke 18:23). Therefore the composite title "rich young ruler" is generally applied to him. He was probably one of the officials in charge of the local synagogue.

Mark's description of this ruler's action is the most vivid of the three accounts. As he tells it, not only did this young man run up to Jesus, he also dropped to his knees in front of him, just as the leper had done (1:40). As he did this he "was asking" [465] him a question. In view of this ruler's highly

---

464 Indefinite εἷς.

465 While Matthew and Luke use the aorist (respectively εἶπε and ἐπηρώτησε), Mark is still *picturing* what was happening: he uses the imperfect ἐπηρώτα.

emotional state, shown by his running and dropping to his knees, he may well have been gasping out the question that was disturbing his heart and mind. He addresses Jesus as "Good Teacher," by Matthew abbreviated to "Teacher." Since his manner of addressing Jesus is intimately linked with the latter's reply (verse 18), I shall for the moment reserve any further comments on it. The young man continues, " . . . what shall I do that I may inherit everlasting life—or, according to the order of the words in the original, life everlasting—?"

The present passage and verse 30 (cf. Matt. 19:16, 29; Luke 18:18, 30, but see also, in a different context, Luke 10:25) are the only ones in which Mark makes use of the full term "life everlasting." It is the very term which the apostle John uses again and again (John 3:15, 16, 36, etc.). However, the simple term "life" occurs in Mark 9:43, 45, probably in about the same sense as "life everlasting." Hence, for the meaning of this term in the teaching of Jesus see above on these (Mark 9) passages.

It would be erroneous, however, to assume that the term "life everlasting," as used by the rich young ruler, had the same fulness of meaning as it has in Christ's teaching. Exactly what the anxious enquirer meant by it we do not know. In order to discover what it may have meant to him it should be borne in mind that he had undoubtedly been instructed by the Pharisaic scribes. The best informed among them knew that the concept "life everlasting" had its origin in what we now call the Old Testament. Dan. 12:2 mentions it in connection with the resurrection of God's faithful children: "And many that shall sleep in the dust of the earth shall awaken, some to everlasting life, and some to shame and everlasting contempt." And, to give but one example from apocryphal literature, II Macc. 7:9 states, "The King of the world shall raise us up . . . unto an everlasting renewal of life." It may be taken for granted, therefore, that by those who were well acquainted with Jewish religious literature the term "life everlasting" was associated with the resurrection. The rich young ruler's question can therefore perhaps be paraphrased as follows, "What must I do in order to become a partaker of salvation at the close of the age?" Coupled with this was undoubtedly the yearning to gain assurance in the here and now that he was indeed headed in the right direction toward that ultimate destiny. For the moment at least he *seemed* to be willing to do most anything that was necessary to reach this goal. He wanted peace of mind for the present and never-ending blessedness for the future. [466]

---

[466] Since Matt. 19:16 has ". . . that I may possess," it is clear that the synonym *inherit* here in Mark 10:17 does not have the fulness of meaning that it has at times. In the present instance, as also in several other places, it simply means *have, come into possession of, become a partaker of.*

It is time now to return to the manner in which this rich young ruler opens the conversation. It has been mentioned that he addresses Jesus as "Good Teacher." The designation "Teacher" or "Master" (cf. 4:38; 5:35; 9:17, 38; 10:20, 35; 12:14, 19, 32; 13:1; 14:14) was entirely proper. See above, on 4:38b, including footnote 172. Jesus was—and is—indeed The Teacher (Matt. 26:55; Mark 14:49; Luke 11:1; John 3:2; 7:35; Acts 1:1). To a certain extent this fact was even acknowledged by his opponents (Matt. 22:16). He was indeed The Prophet sent from God. See also N.T.C. on Matthew, pp. 82, 83.

According to Mark's report, however, the enthusiastic enquirer attaches an adjective to the noun: he addresses Jesus as "*Good* Teacher." Of course, this too was true, but evidently not in the sense meant by the young man. At least, as will now be shown, Jesus is not at all satisfied with the manner in which the man addressed him.

18. Jesus said to him, Why do you call me good? No one is good except One—God. Does Jesus by means of this statement disclaim goodness and deity? Does he mean, "You should not have called me *good,* for God alone is good. I am not God; therefore I am not good"? Many have so interpreted Christ's answer. They have concluded—with variations in minor details—that Jesus is here drawing "a tacit contrast between the absolute goodness of God and his own goodness as subject to growth and trial in the circumstances of the incarnation." [467] It will be recalled that the opening statement of Matthew's report is different. The converted publican writes as follows: "And look, a man came up to him and asked, 'Teacher, what good thing shall I do that I may possess everlasting life?' He answered him, 'Why are you asking me concerning that which is good? One there is who is good, and if you wish to enter into life, keep the commandments' " (19:16, 17).

In the opinion of many [468] this means that for doctrinal reasons Matthew toned down Mark's statement.

By no means is there agreement on this point, however. My own view agrees with that of those who say:

"Jesus says in effect, you are not conceiving of goodness in an adequate way when you so lightly address me as Good Teacher. If you wish to contemplate goodness, you should think of God who alone is good and of the keeping of his commandments."

---

467 Vincent Taylor, *op. cit.,* p. 427. Taylor's commentary contains much that is excellent. On the present point, too, we owe it to this author to read his own argument, so that full justice may be done to his view. This holds too for the other interpreters with whose somewhat similar views I also disagree.

468 See B. H. Streeter, *The Four Gospels,* London, 1930, p. 151 f.; J. C. Hawkins, *op. cit.,* pp. 117-125; H. R. Mackintosh, *The Doctrine of the Person of Christ,* New York, 1931, p. 37.

"Jesus' concern is not to glorify himself but God: it is not to give any instruction concerning his own person whatever, but to indicate the published will of God as the sole and perfect prescription for the pleasing of God."

"Christ wants the questioner to realize: Do not lightly—that is, without knowing to whom you are speaking—ascribe to me that which pertains alone to God."

"Jesus intimates that the thoughtless use of the word 'good' in addressing one whom he regards as a human teacher, is an index of his [the ruler's] superficial view of goodness." [469]

Jesus knew that the rich young ruler, in addressing him as "Good Teacher," was being very superficial. If this young man had really believed with all his heart that Jesus was good in the highest sense of the term, he would have obeyed the command the Lord was about to give him (see verses 21, 22). That same shallowness is evident also from the praise he bestows on himself (verse 20). The Master knew very well that if this enquirer was going to be saved, he must be confronted with the absolute standard of goodness, namely, the *perfect* law enacted by *The Perfect One,* God. That explains Christ's answer.

Reasons why I accept this view and not the other:

a. Matthew's omission of Christ's reflection on the ruler's manner of addressing him is in line with the fact that this Gospel writer, as has been shown, is constantly abbreviating. Matthew knew that this particular point, though important, was not of the highest importance. So he omits it.

b. If it were true that Matthew was trying to correct Mark, and this for doctrinal reasons, how is it to be explained that Luke, who was probably the last of the three to write a Gospel, retained Mark's passage? He omitted even more than Matthew, but he took care that in substance his 18:19 was identical with Mark 10:18.

c. If it were true that Mark had a lower estimate of Jesus' goodness and of his deity than did Matthew, this would be evident also elsewhere in Mark's Gospel. But everywhere in that Gospel not only the spotless morality but also the divinity (in the highest sense) of Jesus is taught. See above, under Introduction III; also on 1:1; and N.T.C. on Matthew, pp. 57-60. In fact, even in the present account Mark's Christology is very high indeed: Jesus is the One to whom men must render unquestioning obedience, and for whose sake they must be willing to give up everything (verses 21, 29).

---

[469] The four quotations are respectively those of N. B. Stonehouse, *Origins of the Synoptic Gospels,* p. 139; B. B. Warfield, *Christology and Criticism,* New York, Oxford, 1929, p. 139; J. A. C. Van Leeuwen, *op. cit.,* p. 125; and C. R. Erdman, *op. cit.,* p. 144. See also H. B. Swete, *op. cit.,* p. 223; and W. Manson, *Jesus the Messiah,* Philadelphia, 1946, p. 135: "Christology is not really here in question."

In answer to the ruler's question, " . . . what shall I do that I may inherit everlasting life?" Jesus now continues as follows: **19. You know the commandments: You shall not kill, you shall not commit adultery, you shall not steal, you shall not bear false witness, you shall not defraud, honor your father and your mother.** [470] Just why it was that in all three accounts "Honor your father and your mother" is made the last of the regular Decalog commandments we do not know. Was there a special reason why in this particular case Jesus placed this commandment at the very close (except for the summary in Matthew)? Neither do we know why Jesus mentioned only the commandments of the second table. To the many guesses I wish to add one more: It was not necessary for Jesus to include the commandments relating to man's duty with respect to God; for, failure to observe the second table implies failure to observe the first: "He who does not love his brother whom he has seen cannot love God whom he has not seen" (I John 4:20).

According to Mark, in his recitation of these commandments Jesus also included "You shall not defraud." Reasonable is the suggestion that this directive, not taken from the decalog but probably derived from such passages as Lev. 19:13; Deut. 24:14, 15; cf. James 5:4, represents the commandment "You shall not covet." [471] When a person covets the goods belonging to another, does he not in heart and mind defraud the neighbor of that which belongs to him? This interpretation, though reasonable, is not entirely certain, however. The indicated passages (Lev. 19:13, etc.) refer to the evil of *withholding* from the laborer that which is due to him; that is, they refer to the sin of not paying (or underpaying) him. Considered in this light, "You shall not defraud" might be viewed as a modification of "You shall not steal." [472] However, in that case the reason why this command follows "You shall not bear false witness" instead of "You shall not steal" is not clear.

Still another suggestion is that "You shall not defraud" is Mark's method of reproducing Christ's summary of the entire second table of the law. Cf. "You shall love your neighbor as yourself" (Matt. 19:19). [473] Thus interpreted, the meaning would be, "*Do not withhold from* your neighbor the love you owe him."

Interpreted in any of these various ways, the basic idea remains that the rich young ruler is reminded that both in heart and by deed he must give the neighbor whatever is due to him. In view of the fact that the enquirer was a

---

470 Note the five instances of μή followed by the aorist subjunctive, which is regular for these negative commandments, as is also the durative present imperative for the positive commandment "Honor—that is, keep on honoring—your father and your mother."

471 Cf. Lenski, *op. cit.*, p. 274.

472 Cf. Vincent Taylor, *op. cit.*, p. 428.

473 Cf. H. B. Swete, *op. cit.*, p. 224; A. B. Bruce, *op. cit.*, p. 410.

very rich man, one who probably employed many people, and was besides, as will become clear, a person who clung tenaciously to all his possessions, the appropriateness of this command becomes clear.

The order has wide application in every age. Not only should we refrain from stealing another person's possessions; we must also see to it that *we do not withhold* from the neighbor whatever should be his; whether that be his reputation, wages, knowledge of the gospel, assurance that he is being loved, help in time of need, etc., a big order indeed!

It is understandable that in answering the young man's question Jesus starts out by referring him to the law of God, for "through the law comes the knowledge of sin" (Rom. 3:20; cf. Gal. 3:24). However, not only does the law make us conscious of our sinful state, it also is a rule or norm of life—or "of gratitude"—for believers, constantly reminding them of their duties and serving as their guide while they gratefully tread salvation's path. [474]

However, the law does not make us conscious of our sins if we fail to discern its real meaning, its depth, as set forth by Jesus in Matt. 5:21-48. That the young man's attitude toward the law was of a superficial nature is clear from his reaction: **20. Teacher, he said to him, all these things have I observed ever since I was a child.** Here superficial smugness is struggling with deep discontent, the latter made very clear by Matthew's addition, "what do I still lack?" This young man tries to make himself believe that all is well; yet on the inside he is pathetically perturbed. Has he really loved his neighbor as himself, and not defrauded the neighbor by keeping from him that which was rightfully his? Why then this lack of peace of mind and heart that made him rush up to Jesus with a question borne of anxiety? He seems to be saying, "What additional good deed must I be doing over and above all those very many that I have already done, and this from my youth?"

The rich young ruler's attitude toward the law reminds one of those who today are saying, "Inasmuch as I am now a saved person I have nothing whatever to do with the law." Now it is indeed true that a genuinely regenerated and converted individual is free from *the curse of* the law (Gal. 3:13), and in that sense is able to sing,

"Free from the law, O happy condition,
Jesus hath bled and there is remission. . . ."

P. P. Bliss

Nevertheless, day by day is it not the duty even of the man who has already been saved by grace to go back to the law, so that over and over

---

[474] See L. Berkhof, *Systematic Theology*, pp. 614, 615. That author enumerates the threefold use of the law, as follows: *a.* usus politicus or civilis, *b.* usus elenchticus or pedagogicus, and *c.* usus didacticus or normativus (also called tertius usus legis). We are concerned here with *b.* and *c.*

again it may remind him of his sinfulness and drive him back to Christ for added strength and assurance? Is not that the lesson of Rom. 7:7-25? Should not his daily confession be:

> "Wretched man that I am! Who shall deliver
> me from this body of death? But thanks be
> to God through Jesus Christ our Lord"?

And can the rule "Love God above all, and your neighbor as yourself" ever become outdated? An inspiring song indeed, this "Free from the law ...." But it should be sung in conjunction with "O how love I thy law. It is my meditation all the day" (Ps. 19:7, 14, according to the versification of James McGranahan). If anyone thinks that Mark 12:30, 31; Luke 10:27; Rom. 13:8-10 are no longer applicable to believers, is he not just as superficial as was the rich young ruler? The latter thought that he had already observed the entire law and that he now needed to do something that went beyond it.

Continued: **21a. Jesus looked at him and loved him.** Just what can this mean in the present connection? There are two ideas which require a word of comment:

a. Because Mark used a particular Greek verb and not another, the love here indicated is of the highest kind, "far beyond mere affection."[475] But see footnote.

b. The meaning is: Jesus fell in love with this young man.[476] The Lord here and now *began* to love him. This possibility cannot be denied, but we must be careful. Otherwise a strange situation results, as if immediately after this man revealed his very superficial attitude toward God's holy law, Jesus fell in love with him!

Is not the following explanation to be preferred? As the Savior allowed his gaze to rest on the rich young ruler, he loved him; that is, *a.* he admired him for not having fallen into gross outward sins and for having gone to the best possible source to obtain a solution to his problem; and *b.* he deeply,

---

475 Cf. Lenski, *op. cit.*, p. 275. He very sharply distinguishes between ἀγαπᾶν and φιλεῖν, and states that ἀγαπᾶν is "far beyond" φιλεῖν. On the contrary, a careful study and tabulation of all the instances in the Gospels where either ἀγαπάω or φιλέω is used (see N.T.C. on John, Vol. II, pp. 497-501) indicates that in the New Testament the verb ἀγαπάω is gradually pushing out the verb φιλέω, and that, while in certain contexts—for example, where both verbs are used with evident purpose to draw a distinction—the two must still be distinguished, in many areas there is overlapping, so that one can say that in such cases the two verbs are used interchangeably.

476 Thus A. T. Robertson, *Word Pictures*, Vol. I, p. 351; and Gram. N.T., p. 834. There is, of course, no difference of opinion with reference to the fact that ἐμβλέψας (having looked at, having fastened his eyes on, as in verse 27) is the aor. participle of ἐμβλέπω; and that ἠγάπησε is the third per. sing. aor. indic. active of ἀγαπάω. The question is only whether ἠγάπησε is *ingressive*. It may be, but can also be viewed as a *normal* ("historical," "constative") aorist.

sorrowfully, ruefully pitied him, and decided to recommend to him a course of action which, if followed through, would solve his problem, and would give him the rest of soul he needed.

After saying, "Teacher, all these things I have observed ever since I was a child," the young man had added, "what do I still lack?" (Matt. 19:20). Jesus is now about to answer that question. However, while linking his answer to the young man's phraseology, the Master is not at all agreeing with that enquirer's philosophy of life. To the young man, supplying this lack was a matter of *addition*. He wanted to know which meritorious deed he had to add to all the other fine deeds he had already performed. But to Jesus, taking care of this lack was a matter of *substitution*. Cf. Gal. 2:19-21; Phil. 3:7 f. It is in that sense that Mark now writes: 21b. **One thing you lack,** [477] **he said to him. Go, sell** [478] **whatever you have and give (the proceeds) to the poor, and you will have a treasure in heaven** [479] . . .

The question may be asked, "But by thus instructing the young man was not Jesus endorsing the 'salvation by good works' doctrine?" Should he not rather have told him, "Trust in me"? The answer is that "Trust completely in me" was exactly what the Lord was telling him, for certainly without complete confidence in and self-surrender to the One who was issuing the order, the rich young ruler could not be expected to sell all he had and give the proceeds to the poor. This was the test. If he sustains it he will have "treasure in heaven." The reference is to all those blessings that are heavenly in character, are in full measure reserved for God's child in heaven, and of which we experience a foretaste even now. For more about this concept see N.T.C. on Matt. 6:19, 20. It is important to note that Jesus added, **and come, follow me.** Such "following," to be accompanied by and to prepare for active witness-bearing, would imply that the young man must learn to

---

[477] Here ἕν is the subject (cf. Dutch version: Eén ding ontbreekt u); the verb ὑστερεῖ is the third per. sing. pres. indic. of ὑστερέω, and is transitive; σε is the direct object of the verb. English either changes the direct into the indirect object, resulting in the wordier, "One thing is lacking to you," or interchanges subject and object, yielding, "You lack one thing" (with proper emphasis: "One thing you lack"). In the sense of *to fall short of*, ὑστερέω takes the genitive, "For all have sinned, and fall short of the glory of God" (Rom. 3:23).

II Cor. 11:5, "I do not think I am in the least inferior," reminds us of the fact that the Greek verb is derived from ὕστερος, inferior, lower, latter, behind. Cf. *uterus, hysterical, hysteron proteron.*

[478] πώλησον sec. per. sing. imperat. active of πωλέω, to sell (11:15; Luke 12:33, 18:22; 22:36; John 2:14, 16; etc.). Cf. *monopoly.*

[479] Cf. θησαυρός in heaven (Matt. 6:20; Luke 12:33); tr. on earth (Matt. 6:19); tr. hidden in the field (Matt. 13:44); "where your treasure is" (Matt. 6:21); tr. in earthen vessels (II Cor. 4:7); tr. of wisdom and knowledge (Col. 2:3); treasure chest (Matt. 2:11) storehouse or storeroom (Matt. 13:52). Cf. *thesaurus.*

"deny himself and take up his cross," and would therefore no longer be able to devote himself to the service of Mammon.

The young man's response was tragic. It showed that Christ's command had been the arrow that wounded his Achilles' heel, his most vulnerable spot, love of earthly possessions: 22. **But he, crestfallen because of these words, went away sorrowful, for he possessed much property.** Because of Christ's command and the young man's ingrained materialism, his countenance fell. It resembled a lowering cloud (cf. Matt. 16:3). As enthusiastic as he had been at first, so sad and sullen [480] he was now, so that he departed sorrowful and aggrieved, probably thinking, "This requirement is not fair. None of the other rabbis would have demanded this much of me."

The demand which Jesus had made on this bewildered man was suited to his particular circumstances and state of mind. The Lord does not ask every rich person—for example Abraham (Gen. 13:2), or Joseph of Arimathea (Matt. 27:57)—to do exactly this same thing. There are those opulent individuals who, speaking by and large, are living for themselves. What they contribute to the cause of others is wholly out of proportion to what they keep for themselves. There are other wealthy persons, however, who are willing to go all out in helping others, including even the ungenerous (Gen. 13:7-11; 14:14); and who, motivated by gratitude, are constantly building altars and bringing offerings to God (Gen. 12:8; 13:18; 15:10-12; 22:13). The young man "had much property." He had it; it had him, holding him tightly in its grasp. It is clear that this young man needed exactly the treatment Jesus gave him.

Did the rich young ruler persist forever in his deplorable refusal? The answer has not been revealed. Some reason as follows: Scripture tells us that Jesus loved him (Mark 10:21). God loves the elect, no one else. Conclusion: this young man must have become converted.

But this amounts to superimposing an erroneous theological idea upon the text. If those who cling to it would be satisfied with the proposition that God loves *in a peculiar way* all those who place their trust in him (Ps. 103:13; I John 3:1), their teaching would be on firm ground. But when they go beyond this and deny that there is a love of God which extends beyond the sum-total of the elect, we must part company with them. See Ps. 145:9, 17; Matt. 5:45; Luke 6:35, 36. And since this is true, there is no basis whatever for believing that the rich young ruler must have become a believer before he died. Instead of speculating about what may or may not have happened, the lesson of Luke 13:23, 24 should be taken to heart. It is in that vein that Mark's account now continues:

---

480 Note στυγνάσας, aor. participle of στυγνάζω, to have a gloomy appearance. Cf. *Styx, stygian.*

23. Looking around, Jesus said to his disciples, How hard it will be for those who possess wealth to enter the kingdom of God.

Jesus looked around. This is a vivid touch, such as we would expect from Mark, Peter's interpreter. [481] Picture the scene: the rich young ruler has left, so that Jesus and The Twelve are alone once more. So, in connection with what has just happened the Master wishes to impress deeply upon the minds of his disciples: *a.* the significance of the young man's sorrowful departure, and particularly *b.* the difficulty of entering the kingdom of God. As is clear from a comparison of verses 17, 23, and 26, entering that kingdom means obtaining a share in life everlasting. It means becoming saved, probably with emphasis on future salvation: becoming a partaker of ultimate bliss in the restored universe, and enjoying a foretaste of this even here and now. See also on 9:45, 47; 10:15. With what difficulty [482] those who possess an abundance of earthly wealth and continue to cling [483] to it will enter that kingdom. *Difficult* indeed (verses 23, 24); *impossible* even (verses 25, 27).

24. The disciples were startled at these words. Viewed from the aspect of erroneous ideas regarding prosperity (wealth, health) that were current in those days, the fact that these men were amazed and perplexed is not surprising. Had not Israel received the promise that if it would hearken diligently to the voice of the Lord it would receive an abundance of material (as well as spiritual) blessings? See Deut. 28:1-14. Did not riches and honor come from God (I Chron. 29:12)? However, many people drew the wrong conclusion that individual prosperity was a sign of God's favor and of virtue, and individual adversity a sign of God's disfavor and of perversity. The friends of Job were of that opinion: "The wicked man will not be rich" (Job 15:29). "Whoever perished being innocent?" (4:7). See also Job 4:8; 5:2; 8:6, 7; 11:6; 15:20. That Christ's contemporaries had imbibed some of this philosophy is clear from Luke 13:1-5; that it had even infected the thinking of The Twelve appears from John 9:1-3. If these people had made a more thorough study of the Old Testament they would have known better. See Ps. 73:12, 18; Jer. 9:23, 24. In line with this is Christ's teaching recorded elsewhere; for example, his parable of The Rich Fool (Luke 12:16-21) and that of The Rich Man and Lazarus (Luke 16:19-31).

It is in the light of the disciples' erroneous philosophy that we can understand why they were amazed to hear Jesus declare that it would be hard for a rich man to enter the kingdom of God.

---

[481] See on 3:5, footnote 105.

[482] δυσκόλως adv., with difficulty. Cf. adj. δύσκολος,-ον, where δυς has a meaning opposite to εὖ; and κόλον (cf. *colon, colic*) means food. Original meaning: hard to please with food; then, in general, hard to please, difficult.

[483] Note present participle ἔχοντες, probably durative.

But Jesus continued and said to them, Children, how hard it is [484] to enter the kingdom of God. Note this tender introduction "Children." The Master's eyes were filled with tender affection. The Twelve were very dear to him; yet he knows how weak, how prone to error, they are. Cf. Ps. 103:13, 14; Mark 2:5; Luke 15:31; 16:25; John 13:33; Gal. 4:19, I John 2:1, 12, etc.

When Jesus continues, "How hard it is . . ." he is sharpening the edge of his previous saying. He is now telling the disciples that what holds for the rich is true with respect to all, namely, that it is very hard to enter the kingdom of God.

If they had listened carefully they would have realized that what Jesus was now saying did not differ essentially from what he said before, namely, in The Sermon on the Mount: "Enter by the narrow gate; for wide (is) the gate and broad the way that leads to destruction, and many are those that enter by it. For narrow (is) the gate and constricted the way that leads to life, and few are those who find it" (Matt. 7:13, 14).

Is it difficult to enter the kingdom of heaven? Yes, so difficult that for a rich man it will in a sense (see on verse 27) even be impossible; for Jesus continues: 25. **It is easier for a camel to go through the eye of a needle than for a rich man to enter the kingdom of God.** It is, of course, entirely impossible for a camel to pass through the eye of a needle. [485] Yet, even this, says Jesus, impossible as it is, would be easier than for a rich man to enter the kingdom of God. To explain what Jesus means it is useless and unwarranted to try to change "camel" into "cable"—see Matt. 23:24, where a real camel must have been meant—or to define the "needle's eye" as the narrow gate in a city wall, a gate, so the reasoning goes, through which a camel can pass only on its knees and after its burden has been removed. Such "explanations" (?), aside from being objectionable from a linguistic point of view, strive to make possible what Jesus specifically declared to be impossible. The Lord clearly means that for a rich man in his own power to try to

---

484 Here some manuscripts add "for those who trust in riches." See Lenski's defense of these words; *op. cit.*, p. 278. He presents a strong argument for their authenticity. He may be right; yet, all in all, I believe the arguments in favor of leaving out these words is stronger. Not only does the textual evidence favor their omission, but also it is not nearly as easy to believe that, if these words were in the autograph, they would have been dropped, than to believe that an erring scribe added them, with an appeal, perhaps, to Prov. 11:28.

485 With τρυμαλία ῥαφίδος cf. τρῆμα ῥαφίδος (Matt. 19:24); and τρῆμα βελόνης (Luke 18:25). τρυμαλία, meaning hole, eye, is related to τρύω, to wear away; τρῆμα, to τιτράω, to bore.

With ῥαφίς, needle cf. ῥάπτω, to sew, to stitch, a "rhapsodist" being basically one who stitches songs together. βελόνη, needle, is related to βέλος, a sharply pointed dart or missile that is thrown; cf. βάλλω, to throw. "Dr." Luke's "needle" was the surgical kind.

work or worm his way into the kingdom of God is impossible. So powerful is the hold which wealth has on the heart of the natural man! He is held fast by its bewitching charm, and is thereby prevented from obtaining the attitude of heart and mind necessary for entrance into God's kingdom. See Matt. 6:24; cf. I Tim. 6:10. It should be noted that Jesus purposely speaks in absolute terms. A moment ago we used the phrase "in his own power." Though in view of verse 27 this qualification does not need to be retracted, yet it should be pointed out that here in verse 25 Jesus does not thus qualify his assertion. He speaks in absolute terms in order all the more to impress upon the minds of the disciples that salvation, from start to finish, is not a human "achievement." The fact that "man's extremity is God's opportunity" is reserved for later (see verse 27).

26. **Shocked** [486] **even more they said to each other, Then who can be saved?** The disciples' amazement, already present after Christ's declaration of verse 23, increases to the point where these men are sorely perplexed, "knocked out of their senses." The astonishment probably lasted for a little while. The Twelve drew the conclusion that if what Jesus had said was true, then no one could be saved. To reach that conclusion they probably reasoned: *a.* what Jesus said about rich men (verse 23) he had said about all men (verse 24); and *b.* though not all men are rich, even the poor yearn to become rich.

Christ's beautiful and reassuring answer is found in verse 27. **Fastening his eyes on** [487] **them Jesus said, With men (this is) impossible but not with God, for with God all things are possible.**

In this dramatic moment the eyes of Jesus, as he fixed them on his disciples, must have been filled with deep earnestness and tender love. When he now tells them, "With men this is impossible," he means exactly that. At every point, beginning, middle, end, man is completely dependent on God for salvation. Of himself man can do nothing. If he is to be saved at all he must be born again or "from above" (John 3:3, 5). Even when by faith— God-given faith! (Eph. 2:8)—he reaches out to God, yet in order to do this he must be enabled and supported every day, hour, minute, and second by God's omnipotent grace. For the religion of the rich young ruler (see verses 17, 20), which was the religion current among the Jews of that day and age, there is no room here. Whatever detracts from the sovereignty of God in the salvation of men stands condemned.

Glory be to God, however: there is a way out. What is impossible with men is possible with God, with whom all things are possible. It is he who,

---

[486] ἐξεπλήσσοντο, third per. pl. imperf. passive of ἐκπλήσσω. See on 1:22. Cf. also 6:2; 7:37; 11:18. The word is found also in Matthew, Luke, and Acts.
[487] For ἐκβλέψας see above, on verse 21a., footnote 475.

through Christ, is able to save to the uttermost (Heb. 7:25). His grace extends even to the determined and relentless persecutor Saul of Tarsus (Acts 9:1; 26:9-11; I Cor. 15:8-10; Gal. 1:15, 16; I Tim. 1:15). Just how, through the Mediator, this salvation is brought about, Jesus has already begun to reveal (Mark 8:31; 9:31). He will continue to do so with increasing clarity (see 10:32-34; especially 10:45; 14:22-24).

Peter is still thinking about the words which the Master had addressed to the rich young ruler (see verse 21). Jesus had asked him to sell all he had and give the proceeds to the poor, promising that if he did this he would have treasure in heaven.

So the story continues: **28. Peter began to say to him, Look, we have given up everything, and followed thee.** According to Matt. 19:27 Peter added, "What then shall we have?" Had the Twelve not done exactly what Jesus had asked the young man to do? Had they not "left everything" and followed Jesus? The answer, then, would seem to be obvious, namely, that The Twelve would have treasure in heaven. Nevertheless, Peter seems not to have been entirely certain about this, for the Master had also declared that with men it is impossible to be saved, and that it is God, he alone, who imparts salvation (verses 23-25, 27).

Peter and the other disciples receive a very comforting answer. It is in the nature of a reassurance (verses 29, 30), followed by a warning (verse 31):

29, 30. Jesus replied, I solemnly declare to y o u, there is no one who has given up house or brothers or sisters or mother or father or children or fields for my sake and for the gospel's sake, who shall not receive a hundredfold; now in this time: houses and brothers and sisters and mothers and children and fields, along with persecutions; and in the age to come everlasting life. [488]

It is clear that this promise is for all true followers of the Lord (cf. Matt. 19:29). It is not (like Matt. 19:28) a promise for The Twelve alone. It is for all who have chosen Christ above all else, even above their dearest relatives and most cherished possessions. They have made a sacrifice, says Jesus, "for my sake and for the gospel's sake," meaning: they were motivated by love for me and for my message of salvation.

These loyal followers of the Lord are promised "a hundredfold," that is, they will be reimbursed "many times over" (Luke 18:30). For "hundred-fold" see also Gen. 26:12 and Matt. 13:8. Even in the present day (cf. Luke

---

488 Ἀμὴν λέγω ὑμῖν, see on 3:28. ἀφῆκεν, third per. sing. aor. indic. active of ἀφίημι, leave, forsake, give up.

ἐὰν μὴ λάβῃ, except he shall take.

μετὰ διωγμῶν, along with—or: accompanied by—persecutions.

ἐν τῷ καιρῷ τούτῳ ... ἐν τῷ αἰῶνι τῷ ἐρχομένῳ, in this time (or: season) ... in the age to come.

401

18:30), that is, before the great day of judgment, and for each believer before his death, these loyal followers receive the blessings indicated in such passages as Prov. 15:16; 16:8; Matt. 7:7; John 17:3; Rom. 8:26-39; Phil. 4:7; I Tim. 6:6; Heb. 6:19, 20; 10:34; I Peter 1:8. In spite of the persecutions which they will have to endure, they will even be able to enjoy their material possessions (houses . . . fields) far more than the ungodly enjoy theirs. Reason? See Isa. 26:3; contrast 48:22. For the sake of Christ and his gospel has it become necessary to forsake close relatives? New "relatives" will now be theirs (Matt. 12:46-50; Mark 3:31-35; John 19:27; Rom. 16:13; I Cor. 4:15; Gal. 4:19; I Tim. 1:2; 5:2; II Tim. 2:1; Philem. 10: I Peter 5:13), relatives that belong to "the household of the faith" (Gal. 6:10), "the Father's Family" (Eph. 2:19; 3:15).

In the age to come believers are going to receive life everlasting. See on verse 17 and on 9:43, 45. In principle they have it here and now, but in a far more abundant and ever increasing measure they will have it in the hereafter. It should be borne in mind that the concept "life everlasting" is both quantitative and qualitative, with emphasis on the latter. It is the holiness, knowledge, fellowship, peace, joy, etc. pertaining to the life of all those who are in Christ, and as such a life that will last on and on and on forever and ever.

31. But many that are first shall be last, and (many) last first.

When Peter said, "Look, we have left everything and followed thee; what then shall we have?" (Mark 10:28; cf. Matt. 19:27), was his question the product of holy curiosity, or, in whatever slight degree, of a mercantile spirit? The division of opinion among commentators in their attempt to answer this question is most interesting. Some, in their zeal to defend Peter against every charge, go so far as to say that those who distrust Peter's motives are judging others by their own ethical standards. Others go to the opposite extreme and regard Christ's saying here in Mark 10:31, and also the parable in Matt. 20:1-16, to be inexplicable unless Peter's worldly motivation be taken into account. May not the best procedure be the following: A man is innocent unless his guilt can be established beyond any reasonable doubt? Accordingly, we have no right to charge Peter with anything wrong. On the other hand, it is also true that his question, though purely motivated, may have occasioned the warning that is found in the verse we are about to consider. Jesus may well have meant something on this order: "Peter, your question, 'What then shall we have?' is right and proper. Nevertheless, since it is so easy to fall into the error of expecting a reward based on supposed merit, I must warn you, so that you may not be caught unawares." Besides, is it not possible that the undoubtedly mercantile attitude of the rich young ruler (verse 17) may have caused Jesus to issue a needed warning?

402

As to the saying itself, we are reminded of the words of Jehovah addressed to Samuel, "Jehovah does not see as man sees; man looks on the outward appearance, but Jehovah looks on the heart" (I Sam. 16:7). The "first" are those who because of their wealth, education, position, prestige, talents, etc., are highly regarded by men in general, sometimes even by God's children. But since God sees and knows the heart many of these very people are by him assigned to a position behind the others; in fact, some may even be altogether excluded from the halls of glory. Cf. Matt. 7:21-23.

There does not seem to be any good reason for saying that Jesus meant that *all* of those who "shall be last" are going to be lost or outside the kingdom. Fact is: not only are there degrees of suffering in hell (Luke 12:47, 48), there are also degrees of glory in the restored universe (I Cor. 15:41, 42). There will be surprises however. Not only will many of those who are now regarded as the very pillars of the church be last, but also many who never made the headlines—think of the poor widow who contributed "two mites" (Mark 12:42), and Mary of Bethany whose act of loving lavishness was roundly criticized by the disciples (Matt. 26:8)—shall be first on the day of judgment (Mark 12:43, 44; cf. Matt. 26:10-13). The disciples, who were constantly quarreling about rank (Mark 9:33 f.; Matt. 18:1 f.; 20:20; Luke 22:24) better take note!

---

32 They were on the road going up to Jerusalem. Jesus was taking the lead; the disciples were amazed, and those who followed were afraid. Again he took the twelve aside and began to tell [489] them what was going to happen to him: 33 "Listen, we are going up to Jerusalem, and the Son of man shall be handed over to the chief priests and the scribes. They shall condemn him to death and hand him over to the Gentiles, 34 who shall mock him and spit upon him and scourge him and kill him; and three days later he shall rise again."

10:32-34 *The Third Prediction of the Passion*
and the Resurrection
Cf. Matt. 20:17-19; Luke 18:31-34

32. They were on the road going up to Jerusalem. Jesus was taking the lead; the disciples were amazed, and those who followed were afraid.

Though the time and place indication is indefinite, Passover seems to be drawing near. Was it perhaps sometime in March?

Here again Mark's description is more graphic and detailed than either Matthew's or Luke's. He is describing the trip from Perea via Jericho to Jerusalem. "Going up to Jerusalem" (John 2:13; 5:1; 11:55; Acts 11:2;

---

489 Or: and told.

25:1, 9; Gal. 2:1) must be understood as having reference not only to physical ascent, Jerusalem being situated on higher ground, so that from whatever side one approaches it, that approach is always an ascent; it is far more than that. It must be interpreted as a matter not just pertaining to the feet (Ps. 122:2), but also—in fact especially—to the heart (Ps. 84:5). In Jerusalem was God's temple! When in connection with the great feasts pilgrims wended their way to Jerusalem, they were going there to worship, which included the bringing of an offering. Jesus, too, is now "going up to Jerusalem," to bring *himself* as an offering for "the sin of the world." See Isa. 53:10; John 1:29.

He, as the Good Shepherd, is taking the lead. He is heading the procession (John 10:4). He walks with resolute steps. Stedfastly he sets his face to go to Jerusalem (cf. Luke 9:51). There, in Jerusalem, he is . . . shall we say "going to die"? Yes, but even better: he is going to *lay down his life* (John 10:11, 15).

Matters are becoming very serious now. The atmosphere is tense. The Twelve are *amazed*. Amazed about what? Undoubtedly about the unwavering advance of their Leader. There must have been something about the bearing of Jesus—the look in his eyes, the manner of his walk—that explains this amazement. Those who belonged to the wider circle of his followers (see Luke 6:13; 10:1) are *afraid*. In view of John 9:22; 11:8, 57 their consternation and alarm is understandable. Going to Jerusalem in the company of Jesus is risky![490]

Continued: **Again he took the twelve aside and began to tell them what was going to happen to him.**[491] Since the Lord knows that it would not be wise to make the announcement of his suffering and death to all the followers (8:30), he takes The Twelve aside, so that in private (cf. Matt. 20:17) he may give them detailed information regarding his approaching agony. Note "again," for this was not the only time that Jesus made a temporary separation between groups of followers, or even within a group. See Mark 3:13 (cf. Luke 6:13); 4:35, 36; 5:37, 40; 6:31, 45; 7:17, 33; 9:2; 14:32, 33; and see also 9:30. Specifically, "again," for the two previous lessons about the cross had also been given privately, to The Twelve.

What Jesus told The Twelve was: 33, 34. **Listen,**[492] we are going up to

---

[490] The two periphrastic imperfects, followed by two regular imperfects ἐθαμβοῦντο and ἐφοβοῦντο, indicate that Mark is as it were picturing, item by item, just what was happening. He wants us to linger a while and consider the seriousness of the situation, the determined manner in which Jesus is walking toward the place of his execution.

[491] συμβαίνειν, pres. infinitive of συμβαίνω (to step together), to happen. Hence, the meaning of the entire expression is: "the things that were about to happen to him."

[492] For Ἰδού see on 2:24, footnote 91; and N.T.C. on Matt. 1:20, p. 131, footnote 133.

Jerusalem, and the Son of man shall be handed over to the chief priests and the scribes. They shall condemn him to death and hand him over to the Gentiles, who shall mock him and spit upon him and scourge him and kill him; and three days later he shall rise again.

It will be recalled that somewhere in the vicinity of Caesarea Philippi, immediately after Peter's confession, "Thou art the Christ," Jesus had made his first prediction with respect to his coming passion and resurrection. That prediction (Mark 8:31) emphasized the *necessity* of these events. A little later, after Christ's transfiguration and the healing of the epileptic boy, and while Jesus was traveling through Galilee, he had made his second prediction, stressing the *certainty* of his approaching death and resurrection (9:31), and adding a new element, namely, that he, the Son of man, was about to be betrayed into the hands of men.

The present passage (10:33, 34) contains the third prediction. It is by far the most detailed. Of its seven distinguishable items the first prediction mentioned only Nos. 2, 6, 7; the second only Nos. 1, 6, 7. The seven items, as Mark has recorded them, together with a reference to their fulfilment, are as follows:

Mark

10:33 1. The Son of man shall be handed over or betrayed into the hands of the chief priests and the scribes. Fulfilment Mark 14:53.

10:33 2. They shall condemn him to death. Fulfilment 14:55-64.

10:33 3. And shall hand him over to the Gentiles. Fulfilment 15:1.

10:34 4. They shall mock him and spit upon him. Fulfilment 15:16-20. Cf. 14:65; 15:29-32.

10:34 5. And shall scourge him. Fulfilment 15:15.

10:34 6. And kill ("crucify," Matt. 20:19) him. Fulfilment 15:24, 37.

10:34 7. Three days later he shall rise again. Fulfilment 16:1 ff.

A few remarks about each of these:

For "the Son of man" see on 2:10 and on Matt. 8:20. The expression "the chief priests and scribes" replaces the fuller designation of the first prediction: "the elders and the chief priests and the scribes." In both cases the reference is to the Sanhedrin, the Supreme Court of the Jews. Here, in the third prediction, the elders are omitted, perhaps because they were the least important of the three, or perhaps in order to stress the fact that Jesus was going to be handed over[493] to the *spiritual* leaders of the people: the chief priests and the scribes. *They* surely should have known better!

The prediction that the members of this Supreme Court would condemn

---

493 παραδοθήσεται, third per. sing. fut. pass. indic. of παραδίδωμι, to hand over, deliver up, betray.

Jesus to death indicates that there was going to be a trial, and that at this trial the death penalty would be pronounced upon Jesus.

Since the Romans did not allow the Jews to carry out the death sentence, the Jewish authorities were in turn going to hand Jesus over [494] to the Gentiles, that is, in the present case to Pilate and those who carried out his commands.

Jesus also predicted that these Gentiles would mock him and spit upon him. In the fulfilment passages these two—being mocked and being spit upon—are mentioned together, and not in immediate connection with the scourging. Cf. 15:16-20 with 15:15. And cf. Matt. 27:27-31 with 27:26. For the mockery by Herod see Luke 23:11.

The *scourging* of which Jesus speaks was a prelude to the *crucifixion*. See Mark 15:15; cf. Matt. 27:26. Items 5 and 6 can therefore also be combined, yielding 6 instead of 7 items.

This prediction, as well as the previous ones (Mark 8:31; 9:31), ends on a note of triumph: he shall rise again. [495]

The question now arises, "How must we conceive of this very detailed passion announcement?" Was it really a prediction? Or was it rather, at least to a certain extent, a *vaticinium ex eventu,* that is, "a prophecy arising out of—and therefore made after—the event" to which it refers? That it was the latter is the opinion of many. [496] In one way or another, the suggestion is offered that although Jesus in a very general way did indeed predict his suffering, death, and resurrection, he did not predict it in this detailed form.

The question arises, "Why not?" He who knew beforehand exactly where a certain fish would be swimming at a definite moment of time and what it would have in its mouth (Matt. 17:27), how often a strange woman whom he had never met before had been married (John 4:17, 18), where a colt would be and what its owners would say to those who tried to untie it (Mark 11:1-7), and what kind of pitcher-bearer two disciples would meet as they entered the city of Jerusalem (Mark 14:12-16); he who was able to forecast the very manner of Jerusalem's fall (Matt. 21:40-43; 22:7; 23:37, 38; 24:1, 2, 15; Mark 13:1, 2; Luke 19:41-44), and the victorious march of the gospel along the path of the centuries (Matt. 24:14), would he not have been able to predict the details of his own imminent passion, not even after two messengers from heaven had discussed these matters with him (Luke 9:31)? I take it that what is here presented as prediction was exactly that. "A prophecy that grows out of an event" is no prophecy at all!

---

494 παραδώσουσι, third per. pl. fut. act. indic. of the same verb as in the preceding footnote.
495 ἀναστήσεται, third per. sing. middle indic. of ἀνίστημι, with active meaning.
496 See E. P. Gould, *op. cit.,* p. 198; F. C. Grant, *op. cit.,* pp. 809, 810; M. H. Bolkestein, *op. cit.,* p. 237; Vincent Taylor, *op. cit.,* pp. 437, 438.

It would be inexcusable to close the treatment of this precious passage (10:32-34) without showing what it implies with respect to the majesty of Christ's love. The prediction, as has been shown, is far more detailed than the previous ones. The *gradual* revelation of the approaching events had a pedagogical purpose, as has been indicated. See on 8:31, 32a. But the possibility must also be granted that even in the human consciousness of our Lord the "feel" of the approaching horror was little by little becoming more real. There was nothing static about the mind of Jesus. See Luke 2:52; Heb. 5:8. Even this third prediction, though indeed very comprehensive and detailed, does not necessarily prove that in the mind of Jesus the image of impending distress was already as vivid as it would be in Gethsemane.

Nevertheless, even now the horror must have been very real and very terrifying. See Luke 12:50. The man of sorrows sees it coming toward him. He already senses something of the perfidy, the hypocrisy, the calumny, the mockery, the pain, and the shame which like an avalanche threatens to overwhelm him. Yet, he does not retreat or even stand still. With unflinching determination he walks right into it, for he knows that this is necessary in order that his people may be saved. "Having loved his own . . . he loved them to the uttermost" (John 13:1).

---

35 Then James and John, the sons of Zebedee, approached him, saying, "Teacher, we want you to do for us whatever we ask." 36 He said to them, "What do y o u want me to do for y o u?" 37 They told him, "Grant us to sit, one at your right and one at your left in your glory." 38 But Jesus said to them, "Y o u do not know what y o u are asking for yourselves. Are y o u able to drink the cup that I drink, or to be baptized with the baptism with which I am baptized?" 39 They answered, "We are able." Then Jesus told them, "The cup which I drink y o u shall drink, and with the baptism with which I am baptized, y o u shall be baptized; 40 but to sit at my right and at my left is not for me to grant, but is for those for whom it has been prepared."

41 Now when the ten heard (what had happened) they were angry at James and John. 42 So Jesus called them (all) to him and said to them, "Y o u know that the so-called [497] rulers of the Gentiles lord it over them, and their great men keep them under their despotic power. 43 Not like that is it among y o u; rather, whoever wishes to become great among y o u let him be y o u r servant, 44 and whoever wishes to be first among y o u let him be the humble attendant of all. 45 For even the Son of man did not come to be served but to serve, and to give his life as ransom in the place of many."

10:35-45 *The Request of the Sons of Zebedee*
Cf. Matt. 20:20-28

By and large this story is not found in Luke, only in Matthew and Mark. See, however, Luke 22:25, 26; cf. Mark 10:42-44. In both Matthew and Mark what is presented to us is the report of a request for the two positions

---

497 Or: recognized.

of highest prominence in Christ's "kingdom" (thus Matthew) or "glory" (thus Mark). The main difference between the two accounts is that in Matthew the request is made by "the mother of the sons of Zebedee," in Mark by "James and John, the sons of Zebedee." This "main difference" is not a contradiction, for even Matthew reports that the mother came "with her sons," and that Jesus, in answering the request, spoke to more than one person. Clearly, the request of the mother was also that of the sons. For the rest, the differences between the two accounts are very minor. There are no conflicts or disagreements.

The question "[Are y o u able] to be baptized with the baptism with which I am baptized?" (Mark 10:38, and note the echo in verse 39) is not found in Matthew, but the synonymous phrase "to drink the cup . . ." occurs in both Gospels. To Mark's "but [this distinction] is for those for whom it has been prepared" Matthew adds "by my Father" (cf. Mark 10:40 with Matt. 20:23). In 10:41 Mark again (as in 10:35) refers to the two brothers by name. Nowhere in his account (20:20-28) does Matthew mention their names. He simply says "the sons of Zebedee" (20:20), "the two brothers" (verse 24). This, too, creates no difficulty, for twice previously in his Gospel this evangelist has written "James the son of Zebedee and John his brother" (4:21; 10:2; and cf. 17:1). In 10:42 Mark has "so-called rulers"; Matthew (20:25) omits "so-called."

All in all, the resemblance between the two accounts not only in the thoughts conveyed but even in the very wording is most striking. Is not literary relationship the most reasonable way to account for this?

There is a remarkable similarity between *a.* the second passion announcement and its sequel, and *b.* the third announcement and its sequel. In both cases Christ's prediction of his approaching voluntary *humiliation* in the interest of sinners is followed immediately by a report of his disciples' yearning for *exaltation.* Note:

second announcement and sequel:
"The Son of man is about to be betrayed into the hands of men, and they shall kill him . . ." (9:31).—"Who [of us] is the greatest?" (9:34).

third announcement and sequel:
"The Son of man shall be handed over to the chief priests and the scribes . . ." (10:33).—"Grant us to sit, one at your right and one at your left in your glory" (10:37).

And the sequel to the first announcement, though different, was not any better (8:31, 32). The conclusion seems warranted that, at the time when they were made, the meaning of none of these predictions struck home. The disciples had confessed Jesus to be the Christ (8:29, 30), and he had acknowledged the correctness of this confession (Matt. 16:17). But he had also repeatedly told The Twelve that he was going to be put to death. The combination of these two ideas—The Messiah . . . put to death—made no sense to them. And at the moment the added prediction "Three days later he shall rise again" did not make matters any easier for them.

In connection with the third prediction Luke 18:34 states, "The disciples did not understand any of these things." They did not understand them until much later, and, worse even, as the present account again proves, they failed to take to heart the lesson their Master was teaching them; the very lesson which in later years Paul, by the inspiration of the Holy Spirit, was going to express in words that for our present purpose can be summarized as follows: "Do nothing from selfish ambition or from vain conceit, but in humility let each person consider the other to be better than himself, each looking not only to his own interests but also the interests of others, so that y o u r attitude may be the same as that of Christ Jesus, who . . . humbled himself and became obedient even to the extent of death; yes, death by a cross." For the full text see Phil. 2:3-8.

The failure of these men—of two of them (verses 35-37); of the other ten (verse 41)—to apply this lesson to their own hearts and lives will now be shown.

35. Then James and John, the sons of Zebedee, approached him, saying, Teacher, we want you to do for us whatever we ask.

There is nothing precise about the time or the place. The word "then" does not always mean "at that very moment" or "immediately afterward." It can also signify "about that time." It should be borne in mind, however, that the third passion prediction has just been recorded. The present story concludes with another very pointed reference to the cross (verse 45). It would seem therefore that the request of the sons of Zebedee was made soon after this third prediction and very shortly previous to the week of the passion. And as to the place, from a comparison of verse 33 and 46 we may conclude with a fair amount of probability that the present incident occurred on the way to Jerusalem via Jericho, but before Jericho had been reached.

What is remarkable with respect to The Twelve is that in spite of their failure to make sense out of their Master's predictions, they did not desert him but—with the exception of Judas a little later—remained loyal to him. Not only that, but they even believed that somehow the establishment of the kingdom about which Jesus had spoken again and again (Mark 1:15; 4:11, 26, 30; 9:47; 10:14, 15; and see especially 9:1), and in which they had even been promised prominent places (Matt. 19:28) was very close at hand; in fact, would now immediately appear (Luke 19:11).

In view of this, two of Christ's disciples, namely James and John, the sons of Zebedee (cf. Mark 1:19, 20) decided that now was the favorable moment to see to it that they would get their share of the honor. They wanted to strike while the iron was hot. They therefore approached Jesus with the amazing request, "Teacher (see on 4:38b; 10:17), we want you to do for us whatever we ask."

It was like asking their Master to hand over a blank check, for them to fill in. It reminds one of little children who will at times, with a naughty gleam in their eyes, approach mother with a similar request. This demand is generally made when the little ones are not too sure that they have a right to receive what they are about to ask. The foolish promise of Herod, "Ask for anything you wish, and I'll give it to you" (6:22) probably occurs to the mind. There is, to be sure, a similarity. But there is also a contrast. That king was putting himself on the spot, but these disciples were trying to commit Jesus beforehand, that is, before even telling him what they wanted, an unethical procedure, to say the least. [498]

36. He said to them, what do y o u want me to do for you? Jesus refuses to commit himself. Making blind promises is wrong. Think again of Herod's promise to Salome! So the Master demands that James and John be specific.

37. They told him, Grant us to sit, one at your right and one at your left in your glory. These men pictured Jesus as sitting upon his royal throne, surrounded by his servants, and among all these high officials, they—even James and John—occupying the places of the highest honor, namely, at his right and at his left. [499] Was not this the way of kings and their attendants, and also of other dignitaries and those who waited on them? See Exod. 17:12; II Sam. 16:6; I Kings 22:19 (II Chron. 18:18); Neh. 8:4.

Their request was evidence of faith. They believed that according to his promise Jesus would be seated on the throne of his glory, and that each of The Twelve would also be seated on thrones. They were convinced of this in spite of the fact that at this moment there was little to show that events were moving in that direction. That much can be said in their favor.

---

498 For the sake of vividness Mark, as often, uses the dramatic present. Here, after a verb of wishing, non-final ἵνα introduces the object clause: literally, that whatever we ask you, you do for us. αἰτήσωμεν first per. pl. aor. act. subjunctive of αἰτέω; ποιήσῃς second per. sing. aor. act. subjunctive of ποιέω.

499 *Right* and *left* are plurals in the original; hence, literally, "from the right parts of your body and from the left parts." With δεξιός (here δεξιῶν) cf. *ambidextrous*. With ἀριστερός (here ἀριστερῶν) cf. *sinister*. Etymological connection? Probably not. A euphemistic synonym for ἐξ ἀριστερῶν is ἐξ εὐωνύμων (Mark 10:40; 15:27; cf. Matt. 20:21, 23; 25:33, 41; 27:38). We say "euphemistic," for actually *bad* things were thought of as coming from the left. For the Jew, facing east, the left was the north, where evil often originated (Jer. 1:14; 4:6: think of invasions). For the Greek, facing north, the left was the west, regarded by him as similarly unfavorable.

This note is appended only to explain the origin of these Greek words. It is perhaps unnecessary to add that divine revelation does not ascribe any validity to superstitious notions, omens, etc. All things are under God's control, and even that which is—or appears to be—bad, is by him overruled for good (Ps. 33:11; Prov. 16:4; 19:21; Isa. 14:24-27; 46:10; Dan. 4:24; Rom. 8:28; Eph. 1:11.)

On the other hand, it is clear that sinful ambition was playing a role here. They desired that the two most honorable places should be assigned not to Philip and Bartholomew, Matthew and Thomas, or even to Peter and Andrew, but to themselves, James and John, to nobody else!

What may have kindled this ambition?

a. Their mother wanted this. She was behind it all, as Matt. 20:20, 21 clearly shows. But there may have been other considerations, *though we cannot be certain that any of them played a role:*

b. Jesus had included them in the innermost circle of disciples, the trio Peter, James, and John (Mark 5:37; 9:2; cf. 14:33).

c. At the outset these men had belonged to a materially more privileged class than some of the other disciples. Did not their father have hired servants? See 1:20.

d. They may have been relatives of Jesus, cousins perhaps. Their mother Salome (not to be confused with the Salome mentioned above, in the explanation of verse 36) seems to have been a sister of Mary, the mother of Jesus. Cf. Matt. 27:56; Mark 15:40; John 19:25.

Nevertheless, what they were doing in making this request was definitely wrong. They were guilty of giving vent to their sinful, selfish, earthly ambitions. They were being anything but Christlike in seeking the highest positions (below Christ's own) for themselves.

38. But Jesus said to them, Y o u do not know what y o u are asking for yourselves. Are y o u able to drink the cup that I drink. . . .

Jesus here reminds them of something they were forgetting, namely, that a request for glory is a request for suffering; in other words, that it is the way of the cross, that alone, that leads home. So he asks them whether they are able to drink the cup that he is about to drink. In the idiom of the Old Testament and of those conversant with its literature "drinking a cup," i.e., its contents, means fully undergoing this or that experience, whether favorable (Ps. 16:5, 23:5; 116:13; Jer. 16:7) or unfavorable (Ps. 11:6; 75:8; Isa. 51:17, 22; Jer. 25:15; Lam. 4:21; Ezek. 23:32; Hab. 2:16). Jesus, too, spoke of his cup of bitter suffering (Matt. 26:39, 42; Mark 14:36; Luke 22:42). And for the New Testament see also Rev. 14:10; 16:19; 17:4; 18:6. Are these disciples, then, willing to become partakers of his suffering, that is, of the suffering for his name and his cause (Matt. 10:16, 17, 38; 16:24; II Cor. 1:5; 4:10; Gal. 6:17; Phil. 3:10; Col. 1:24; I Peter 4:13; Rev. 12:4, 13, 17)?

Mark records the synonymous expression which Jesus also used at that time: **or to be baptized with the baptism with which I am baptized?** If there is any real difference in the meaning of the two halves of Christ's question, it might well be that *drinking* the cup points rather to Christ's active; *being baptized,* to his passive obedience. Jesus rendered both. One might even say that the two are inseparable: each views Christ's obedience from its own aspect: he *chose* to die, and he *submitted to* the blows that descended upon

411

him. The word "to be baptized" is probably used here in the figurative sense of "to be overwhelmed," (here) by agony. Cf. Luke 12:50. Jesus must be plunged into the flood of horrible distress. [500] Note a somewhat similar use of the verb in Isa. 21:4 (LXX) and in Josephus, *Jewish War* IV.137. See also Ps. 42:7: "All thy waves and thy billows have gone over me"; and Ps. 124:4: "Then would the waters have overwhelmed us; the torrent would have passed over our soul."

It should be borne in mind, of course, that there is and remains a basic difference between Christ's own suffering and that of his followers: the first is vicarious (Mark 10:45; cf. Matt. 20:28); the second never can be (Ps. 49:7). But there is, nevertheless, also a close relationship: the Christian suffers "for Christ's sake," that is, because of loyalty to his anointed Lord and Savior. It is for that reason that Paul was able to write, "The afflictions of Christ overflow toward us" (II Cor. 1:5); and Peter, "But rejoice that y o u participate in Christ's suffering" (I Peter 4:13). See also Matt. 10:25; Mark 13:13; John 15:18-21; Acts 9:4, 5; II Cor. 4:10; Gal. 6:17; Phil. 3:10; Col. 1:24; and Rev. 12:13. It is in that sense, then, that Jesus is asking James and John, "Are y o u able to drink the cup that I drink and to be baptized with the baptism with which I am baptized?" [501]

39a. They answered, we are able. On the favorable side we can at least credit them with a considerable measure of loyalty toward their Master. Nevertheless, the future would prove that they were at this moment too self-confident. See 14:27, 50. Their answer was not nearly as commendable as the statement of Paul (Phil. 4:13).

Christ's reaction to their somewhat extravagant assertion, as also his final answer to their request, are recorded in verses **39b, 40. Then Jesus told them, The cup which I drink y o u shall drink, and with the baptism with which I am baptized, y o u shall be baptized; but to sit at my right and at my left is not for me to grant, but is for those for whom it has been prepared.** Indirectly, both the martyrdom of James (Acts 12:2) and the banishment of John to the island of Patmos (Rev. 1:9) are here foretold. These two future events were part of the suffering for Christ's sake that would be experienced by these disciples. With respect to James and John see also above, on 3:17; and see N.T.C. on John, Vol. I, pp. 28-31. As to the request itself, Jesus points out that the degrees and positions of eminence in his glorious kingdom have already been determined, that is, they were decreed in God's eternal counsel (cf. Matt. 20:23: "prepared by my

---

[500] This, however, does not mean that the verb βαπτίζω, as used in Scripture, always has the meaning *to immerse*. In such passages as Mark 7:4; Luke 11:38; I Cor. 10:1, 2 (cf. Exod. 14:16, 22, 29); Heb. 9:10 (cf. verses 13, 19, 21) it cannot very well have that meaning. See above, on Mark 7:4.

[501] For remarks on the Greek see the next footnote.

Father"). They cannot now be altered by the Mediator. See Matt. 24:36; 25:34; Luke 12:32; Acts 1:7; Eph. 1:4, 11. [502]

41. Now when the ten heard (what had happened) they were [503] angry at James and John. The report of the occurrence filled the remaining disciples with indignation. They probably felt that James and John, by asking for these positions of pre-eminence, had been plotting against *them*. It seems that they, too, had not yet taken to heart the lesson of 9:35-37. They probably wanted these highest posts for themselves. This indicates that the spiritual attitude of the ten was not any better than that of the two. How easy it is to condemn in others what we excuse in ourselves. It takes a Nathan to make this clear to us (II Sam. 12:1 ff.). Cf. Rom. 2:1.

It should not escape our attention that even though the attitude of all those twelve men must have caused the Lord much sorrow of heart, since it showed that even now, in spite of all his messages, they had not yet put into practice this part of his teaching, he reacts very gently. Is he not the tender Shepherd who loves his sheep? So, first he calls The Twelve to himself. Then calmly and earnestly he reproves and admonishes them: **42. So Jesus called them (all) to him and said to them, Y o u know that the so-called rulers of the Gentiles lord it over them, and their great men keep them under their despotic power.** That, says Jesus as it were, is the way of worldly people. They spend all their energies to get to the top; and, once having reached that peak, they cause all others to feel the weight of their authority.

According to Mark, Jesus described these monarchs as *"so-called* rulers." Another possible translation would be *"recognized* rulers." But in harmony with Gal. 2:2, 6, 9, the rendering *"so-called"* or *"those who are reputed to be"* or *"are supposed to be"* is probably correct. It is very well possible, therefore, that the Master's words are here tinged with irony. [504] If only those who are clothed with high authority would rule wisely, all would be well. But no, once they have arrived at the top, they think only of themselves. So they cause their subjects to quail under the crushing weight of their power. They "lord it over"—actually "lord it down on"—their

---

502 In verse 38 πιεῖν is the aor. act. infin., and in verse 39 πίεσθε is the sec. per. pl. fut. act. indic. of πίνω. In verse 38 βαπτισθῆναι is the aor. pass. infin., and in verse 39 βαπτισθήσεσθε is the sec. per. pl. fut. pass. indic. of βαπτίζω. With the passive forms, βάπτισμα is the cognate accusative. In verse 40 note the art. aor. infin. καθίσαι of καθίζω; ἡτοίμασται, third per. sing. perf. indic. pass. of ἑτοιμάζω; and ἐμόν, the neuter possessive adj. used predicatively as a nominative noun after ἔστι, and followed by δοῦναι, aor. inf. of δίδωμι. For ἐκ δεξιῶν–ἐξ εὐωνύμων see on verse 37, footnote 499.

503 Literally, "they began to be" or "they became." But in this case ἤρξαντο may well be a redundant auxiliary. For this pleonastic use of ἄρχω see on 1:45 and on 6:7.

504 The original has οἱ δοκοῦντες ἄρχειν. I agree, therefore, with the view of Vincent Taylor, *op. cit.*, p. 443, on this point. This presence of a touch of irony is also recognized by the following translations: R.S.V., Moffatt, Williams, Phillips. Good on this passage is also E. Trueblood, *op. cit.*, pp. 87, 88, 127.

subjects. But while they do this, they want those under their authority to believe that they have nothing but the interests of the subjects at heart.

The "touch of irony" interpretation is also supported by the—in a sense—parallel passage Luke 22:25, "Those who exercise authority over them are styled 'Benefactors.' "

The words of Jesus were true when he spoke them. They have been true ever since and are relevant to every age. Abundant evidence of this can be found on coins and monuments and in history books; witness, for example, the following titles ascribed to earthly tyrants and eagerly adopted by them: Savior, Benefactor, Protector, Leader, Liberator.

Jesus continues: **43, 44. Not like that is it among y o u; rather, whoever wishes to become great among y o u let him be y o u r servant, and whoever wishes to be first among y o u let him be [505] the humble attendant of all.**

Essentially this is the teaching of 9:35-57. Cf. 8:34, 35. See also Matt. 10:39; 16:24, 25; 18:1 ff.; Luke 9:23, 24. The form given to it is new and refreshing. It is an unforgettable paradox. Jesus is saying that in the kingdom over which he reigns greatness is obtained by pursuing a course of action which is the exact opposite of that which is followed in the unbelieving world. Greatness consists in self-giving, in the outpouring of the self in service to others, for the glory of God. To be great means to love. See John 13:34; I Cor. 13; Col. 3:14; I John 3:14; 4:8; I Peter 4:8.

It is the inverted pyramid, the believer being at the bottom—being the *servant,* the *humble attendant* [506] *"of all"* (peculiar to Mark)—that symbolizes the position of the Christian as, with simple trust in God and love for all men, he continues on his way to the mansions of glory. In doing this is he not following in the footsteps of his Lord and Savior? See Luke 22:27; John 13:34, 35.

In fact, that is the very thought which Jesus stresses, as he continues: **45. For even the Son of man did not come to be served but to serve, and to**

---

[505] In both verses (43 and 44) ἔσται has imperative force: "he shall be," "must be"; hence, "let him be." See Gram. N.T., p. 943.

[506] It is clear that in verses 43, 44 the two words διάκονος and δοῦλος are synonyms. The temptation is, with many others, to translate them "servant" and "slave." However, in the course of history the ideas of lack of freedom, unwilling service, cruel treatment, etc., have become so closely attached to "slave" that, together with other translators, I too find it impossible to accept this translation as truly representing what Jesus had in mind *in the present context.* Far better, it would seem to the present author, is therefore the rendering (for the pair): "minister . . . servant." My only reason for suggesting still another English equivalent is that today the term "minister" is very often understood in the technical sense of *clergyman.* For διάκονος see also N.T.C. on the Gospel according to John, Vol. I, p. 119; and N.T.C. on I and II Timothy and Titus, footnote 67 on p. 135; and for δοῦλος, N.T.C. on Philippians, p. 44.

give his life as a ransom in the place of many. Cf. Matt. 20:28. This has always rightly been regarded as one of the most precious of Christ's sayings. Note "For even the Son of man," clearly indicating that Christ's humiliation in the place of, and for the benefit of, his people, must be both their example and their motivation. He is "the Son of man," the fulfilment of the prophecy of Dan. 7:14. For a detailed study of the concept "Son of man" see on 2:10; and on Matt. 8:20. In himself and from all eternity he is the all-glorious One. Yet he humbles himself. He becomes incarnate, and this not with the purpose of being served but of serving. See also on 2:17. Study II Cor. 8:9; Phil. 2:5-8; and see N.T.C. on I Tim. 1:15.

The service which it was the Son of man's purpose to render is described in the words: "to give his life as a ransom in the place of many." "In the place of" or "in exchange for" must be considered the right translation here. [507] The passage is a clear proof of Christ's substitutionary atonement. A *ransom* was originally the price paid for the release of a slave. Jesus, then, is saying that he came into this world to give his life—that is, himself (see I Tim. 2:6)—in exchange for many. The conception of Christ's death on the cross as the price that was paid, a price far more precious than silver or gold, is found also in I Peter 1:18, 19. With this compare Exod. 30:12; Lev. 1:4; 16:15, 16, 20-22; Num. 3:40-51; Ps. 49:7, 8; I Cor. 6:20; 7:23; Gal. 3:13; 4:5; I Tim. 2:5, 6; II Peter 2:1; Rev. 5:6, 12; 13:8; 14:3, 4.

The phrase "a ransom for many" is in all probability an echo of Isa. 53:11, as the entire surrounding phraseology would seem to indicate. Now in Isa. 53 the idea of substitution predominates: see verses 4, 5, 6, 8, and 12. See also Matt. 26:28. It is, of course, perfectly true that this ransom "in the place of" and "in exchange for" many immediately implies that benefit accrues to the many. The two ideas "in the place of" and "for the benefit of" blend into one. How can we even for a moment entertain the idea that a ransom "in the place of" many would not be for their benefit? Besides, the very context states in so many words that by means of this ransom the Son of man *serves* the many. He rescues them from the greatest possible bane, namely, the curse of God upon sin; and he bestows upon them the greatest possible boon, namely, the blessings of God for soul and body throughout all eternity. See Isa. 53:10; Rom. 4:25; II Cor. 5:20, 21; Titus 2:14; I Peter 1:18, 19.

This "in the place of many" is very important. Not in the place of all but of many. Who these many are is clear from such passages as Isa. 53:8; Matt. 1:21; John 10:11, 15; 17:9; Eph. 5:25; Acts 20:28; Rom. 8:32-35. However also: not in the place of a few but of many, without any distinction as to

---

[507] See the author's doctoral dissertation, *The Meaning of the Preposition ἀντί in the New Testament*, Princeton Seminary, 1948.

race, nationality, class, age, sex, etc. (Rom. 10:12, 13; I Cor. 7:19; Gal. 3:9, 29; Eph. 2:14, 18; Col. 3:11). The glad tidings of salvation through the ransom paid by Christ for all who believe in him (Mark 10:45; John 3:16; II Cor. 5:20, 21) must be proclaimed to all. It must be made clear to all that God derives no pleasure from the death of the wicked but rejoices when the wicked turn from their wicked ways and truly live (Lam. 3:33; Ezek. 18:23, 32; 33:11; Hos. 11:8).

A point that must be stressed is that the very wording of our passage (Mark 10:45), namely, "to give his life as a ransom," indicates that Christ's death for his own must be considered *a voluntary self-sacrifice*. It was not forced upon the Mediator. He laid down his life of his own accord. See, again, John 10:11, 15. That fact gives to this death its atoning value.

Finally, the ransom price was paid not (as Origen maintained) to Satan, but to the Father (Rom. 3:23-25), who also himself, together with the Son and the Holy Spirit, had made arrangements for the salvation of his people (John 3:16; II Cor. 5:20, 21).

The context must not be overlooked. Here in Mark 10:45 Jesus is teaching that his own willingness to humble himself to the point of giving his life as a ransom for many must be reflected in The Twelve and in all his followers. In his own small degree and manner every follower of Christ must, by God's grace, show Christ's love to others.

---

46 They came to Jericho. And as he [Jesus] with his disciples and a large crowd was going out of Jericho, a blind man, Bartimaeus, the son of Timaeus, was sitting by the roadside begging. [508]   47 Now when he heard that it was Jesus of Nazareth he began to cry out, saying, "Jesus, son of David, take pity on me." 48 Many people were warning him to be quiet, but he cried out all the more, "Son of David, take pity on me." 49 Jesus stopped and said, "Call him." So they called the blind man and said to him, "Take courage! Get up! He's calling you." 50 Throwing aside his robe he jumped to his feet and came to Jesus. 51 In response Jesus said to him, "What do you want me to do for you?" The blind man told him, "Rabboni, I want to regain my sight." 52 "Go," Jesus said to him, "your faith has made you well." Immediately he regained his sight and began to follow him on the road.

10:46-52 *The Healing of Blind Bartimaeus at Jericho*
Cf. Matt. 20:29-34; Luke 18:35-43

The Jericho of Jesus' day and its present-day ruins lie somewhat to the south of Old Testament Jericho. The city which Mark mentions here in 10:46 was located about fifteen miles northeast of Jerusalem. Since Jerusalem was about 3,300 feet higher in altitude than Jericho, this fact sheds

---

508 Another reading, with considerable support, has, "Bartimaeus . . . a blind beggar, was sitting by the roadside." The difference in meaning is minimal.

light on Luke 10:30: "a certain man was *going down* from Jerusalem to Jericho." Herod the Great—and later also Archelaus, his son—had strengthened and beautified this city, giving it a theater, amphitheater, villas, and baths. Even before the reign of Herod I it was already "a little paradise," with its palm trees, rose gardens, etc. Its winter climate was delightful, making it a winter residence fit for a king. Had not Mark Antony given it to Cleopatra, the Egyptian queen, as a token of his affection?

However, it was not with the beauty and splendor of Jericho that Jesus was chiefly concerned, as he travels now, with his little company, from Perea southwestward, across the Jordan; and thus via Jericho to Jerusalem—and the cross. Though an indescribably heavy burden is resting upon his own heart (Matt. 20:17-19; cf. Luke 12:50), he has not lost his sympathy with the needs of others.

Before entering upon the exegesis of verses 46-52 it is, however, necessary to say a word about the little paragraph as a whole. It has proved to be a feast for *a.* on the one hand, *harmonizers;* and *b.,* on the other, *detractors.* The trouble is that Matthew speaks of *two* blind men, while Mark and Luke make mention of *one,* whom Mark calls Bartimaeus. Also, according to Matthew and Mark the miracle occurred as Jesus and his disciples were leaving Jericho; but according to Luke, as he drew near to Jericho.

As to the first difficulty, is it possible that Mark, who was Peter's interpreter, had heard only the story of Bartimaeus? Of course, this is not really a solution; it simply pushes the problem back a little, from Mark (and Luke, who presumably had read Mark) to Peter. On the other hand, the problem is not at all serious. There is no real contradiction, for neither Mark nor Luke tells us that Jesus restored sight to the eyes of *only* one blind man. For the rest, it must be admitted that we do not have the answer: we do not know why Mark wrote—and Peter, let us suppose, had spoken—about Bartimaeus and not also about the other blind man.

As to the second problem, among the solutions that have been offered are the following: *a.* There were two Jerichos: Jesus therefore could have performed the miracle while he was leaving the one and entering the other; *b.* One blind man was healed as Jesus entered Jericho, another as he left; *c.* Jesus entered the city, had passed through it, and was now leaving it. While he was *going out* of the city he saw Zacchaeus up in the tree, and told that little publican to come down. So, with Zacchaeus he *re-entered* the city to lodge at the tax-collector's home for the night. According to the proposed solution it was during this re-entry of the city that the miracle took place. Hence, Matthew and Mark can say that it was performed while he was leaving the city; Luke, as he drew near to it.

All three solutions are open to objections, however. As to solution *a:* in an account which presents so much resemblance—compare, for example, Mark's

417

account with that of Luke—it would be very strange, indeed, if the name "Jericho" meant two different things. As to *b,* this does not solve anything, for Mark and Luke are clearly speaking about the same blind man, "Bartimaeus, the son of Timaeus." Nevertheless, according to Mark this man had his eyesight restored "as Jesus was leaving Jericho"; according to Luke, as he "drew near to Jericho." And as to *c,* it does not explain why, as this view presupposes, the word "entered" would have the meaning "re-entered from the other side."—Other solutions are not any better: for example, that the blind man was sitting by the roadside begging, as Jesus entered the city from the east; that he then kept on following Jesus all the way through the city until finally, while Jesus was leaving the city, he cured him. The best answer is, There is, indeed a solution, for this "Scripture," too, is inspired. However, *we do not have that solution!*

There are other differences between the three Gospel accounts, but most of them are minor. None implies any contradiction or conflict between the accounts.

The most important difference is that here, as well as so often elsewhere, Mark is again the most detailed and vivid. It is he alone who tells us that the name of the blind man was Bartimaeus. He also informs us that Bartimaeus was a beggar (verse 46; cf. Luke 18:35). He goes into great detail in verses 49, 50: Jesus first addresses himself to the crowd, a detail that is completely omitted in Matthew's story, and is only implied in Luke's. Mark, however, dwells on it, describing exactly what Jesus said to the people, what they in turn said to Bartimaeus, and in what an excited manner he came to Jesus.

Luke, too, makes his contribution. He records that when the blind man heard a crowd passing by, he inquired what this meant. Unforgettable and often quoted in sermons was the reply, "Jesus of Nazareth is passing by" (18:36, 37). For "of Nazareth" see on Mark 6:1.

Though all three evangelists report the cure and the decision on the part of the cured to follow Jesus, each makes his own distinct contribution. Matthew adds that it was "in pity" (or: "moved with compassion") that the Healer "touched the eyes" and effected the cure. Mark reports that Jesus said, "Go, your faith has made you well." And Luke devotes two entire verses to the conclusion, repeating some of what the others have recorded and adding certain details: Jesus said to the blind man, "Receive your sight"; the cured man "glorified God"; and "all the people, when they saw it, gave praise to God." (18:42, 43).

We turn now to the story as Mark tells it. This means that we are not going to speak about the two blind men but only about Bartimaeus. The theme, accordingly, is The Healing of Blind Bartimaeus at Jericho. The division of the material covered by this theme is similar to what it would be for Matthew's account except for the change from the plural to the singular:

1. his wretched condition (verses 46, 47); 2. his added difficulty (verse 48a); 3. his commendable persistence (verse 48b); and 4. the marvelous blessing which Jesus bestowed on him (verses 49-52).

1. *His Wretched Condition*

46, 47. They came to Jericho. And as he [Jesus] with his disciples and a large crowd was going out of Jericho, a blind man, Bartimaeus, the son of Timaeus, was sitting by the roadside begging. Now when he heard that it was Jesus of Nazareth he began to cry out, saying, Jesus, son of David, take pity on me.

Jesus and The Twelve have recrossed the Jordan, from east to west, having followed one of the usual routes to Jerusalem. As Passover was approaching we are not surprised that a large [509] crowd, probably from Galilee and from Perea, was following Jesus. There may also have been some people who had their home in Jericho and were returning to that city.

The procession, then, consists of Jesus, The Twelve, and a large crowd. [510] The group reaches the city. Next, Jesus, The Twelve, and at least those other followers who were bound for Jerusalem, pass through it, so that presently they are "going out" of it. It is at this point of time and place that a blind man enters the picture. He is sitting by the roadside, begging. In that part of the world, as in many other regions even today, there was nothing unfamiliar about this sight. The name of the man was Bartimaeus, which, as Mark explains, means that he was the son of Timaeus.

Although Bartimaeus cannot see Jesus, he can hear the bustle of the crowd. Upon inquiry he learns that Jesus of Nazareth was passing by. He must have heard about Jesus before, for upon receiving the news, he immediately cries out, "Jesus, son of David, take pity on me." As far as is known, in pre-Christian literature the designation "Son of David" as a title for the Messiah occurs only in the pseudepigraphical Psalms of Solomon 17:21. [511] Though there are those who deny that Bartimaeus is using the term in the Messianic sense, the probability is that he did so intend it, for on the basis of Mark 11:9, 10; 12:35-37 (see on those verses) it is clear that during Christ's ministry on earth "Son of David" and "Messiah" had become synonyms. Otherwise how can one satisfactorily explain the indignation of the chief priests and the scribes when the children were honoring Jesus with the title "Son of David" (Matt. 21:15, 16)? Now the fact that Bartimaeus

---

509 ἱκανός,-οῦ. Mark uses this word three times, each time in a different sense. Here in 10:46 it has about the same meaning as πολύς; hence, *large*. In 1:7 (see above, on that passage) the sense is *able, fit*. In combination with ποιεῖν it acquires the meaning *to satisfy* in 15:15.

510 Note the gen. absolute: a present participle with its triple subject.

511 S.BK. I, p. 525.

addressed Jesus as "Son of David" does not mean that he fully appreciated the spiritual character of Jesus' messiahship. It does, however, indicate that he was among the few who were able to give a better answer to the question, "Who do the people say that the Son of man is?" than was given by the people in general (Mark 8:28).

Bartimaeus, then, is imploring Jesus to take pity on—that is, to show mercy to—him. [512] His situation was indeed deplorable. Not only was he blind but he was also a beggar, two circumstances that often went hand in hand. For his sustenance he had to depend on the generosity of the people.

2. *His Added Difficulty*

48a. **Many people were warning** [513] **him to be quiet. . . .** Just why the crowd did this we do not know. Possible answers: *a.* The people were in a hurry to get to Jerusalem and did not want Jesus to be stopped by this blind beggar; *b.* they deemed this yelling to be out of harmony with the dignity of the person addressed; *c.* they were not ready to hear Jesus publicly proclaimed as "the Son of David"; and *d.* they knew that their religious leaders would not appreciate this.

3. *His Commendable Persistence*

48b. **but he cried out all the more,** [514] **Son of David, take pity on me.** That was to his credit. He realized that if help was going to come from any source, it would have to come from the Son of David.

4. *The Marvelous Blessing Which Jesus Bestowed on Him*

49. **Jesus stopped and said, Call him. So they called the blind man and said to him, Take courage! Get up! He's calling you.** Jesus reveals himself throughout the Gospels as being not only very powerful but also very merciful. See above, on 1:41. So he stands still and orders the people to call the man away from the roadside where he was sitting. Eagerly they deliver the message to the beggar. They tell him, "Take courage." It was the command, so full of cheer and hope, which while he was on earth Jesus was heard to issue again and again. Moreover, he is "the same yesterday and today and forever," as shown by the fact that after his ascension to heaven the Lord was still uttering this same bracing exhortation. For the details and list of passages see above, on 6:50b. The people around him also tell the man to rise to his feet, adding, by way of further encouragement, "He's calling you."

Not many weeks earlier that same word, "He's calling you" had been

---

512 ἐλέησον, sec. per. sing. aor. imper. active of ἐλέω. Cf. *alms, eleemosynary.*

513 ἐπετίμων, imperfect tense. See also on 3:12, footnote 111; and on 4:39, footnote 174.

514 πολλῷ μᾶλλον, see on 9:26, footnote 411.

spoken to Mary. The one who addressed her was Martha, her sister. There is certainly a similarity in the two accounts. Both of these people whom Jesus was calling were in deep trouble: Bartimaeus, because he was poor and blind; Mary—Martha too, of course—because she had lost a dear brother. Even today, in such circumstances of life, yes and always, Jesus is calling us to his side, for he is a wonderful Savior. He calls in order to comfort, to cheer, and, as in this case, to heal, to restore.

50. Not everyone is ready to respond to the call. But this man was. Here was the opportunity of a lifetime. His heart leaps with joy: **Throwing aside his robe he jumped to his feet and came to Jesus.** As we read this story today we can almost hear lively Peter tell it, with all the fiery and picturesque eloquence at his command. He must have told it in such a way that Mark was unable to forget it. We see Bartimaeus as, without a moment's hesitancy, he jumps to his feet, throws aside his loose, foot-catching outer robe, lest it retard his speed, and rushes off to Jesus. **51. In response** [515] **Jesus said to him, What do you want me to do** [516] **for you?** Very tenderly Jesus asks this question. Is it alms this beggar wants? Let him concentrate for a moment on that which he wants most of all, so that the satisfaction of his desire will be appreciated all the more. To be sure, Jesus already knew what Bartimaeus wanted, but he wants him to ask for it. So also it is true in general that even though the heavenly Father is well acquainted with the needs of his children, he nevertheless tells them to "open their mouth wide" (Ps. 81:10), so he may fill it. What Jesus wants is not only to cure this man but *to enter into personal fellowship* with him, so that, as a result, his "faith" (verse 52) may be more than merely "miraculous" (the conviction that Jesus is able to perform miracles), and so that Bartimaeus may "glorify God," as was actually going to happen (Luke 18:43).

The blind man told him, Rabboni, I want to regain my sight. Literally, "Rabboni, that I may recover my sight." "I want to" is clearly understood, since Jesus had asked, "What do you want me to do for you?" Mark's "Rabboni" must not be downgraded. It probably is to be interpreted as a title which, in such cases, is equivalent to Matthew's and Luke's "Lord" (Matt. 20:33; Luke 18:41).

52. Go, Jesus said to him, your faith has made you well. [517] Thus also in

---

515 Note ἀποκριθείς, the aor. participle of ἀποκρίνομαι. Jesus is not directly answering a question, but is *responding* to an action or situation. The Greek word frequently has this meaning. Hence, in addition to *answered, replied*, it can also be rendered *responded, spoke up* (a good alternative here in 10:50), *continued*.

516 Note the aor. subjunctive ποιήσω, without a preceding ἵνα as in verse 35. This practice of asyndeton (leaving out a word when that word is clearly implied) is frequent not only in Greek (Gram. N.T., p. 430) but in language generally.

517 σέσωκε, third per. sing. perf. act. indic. of σώζω.

Luke 18:42. In view of the fact that faith is itself God's gift (see N.T.C. on Eph. 2:8), it is nothing less than astounding that Jesus in several instances praises the recipient of the gift for exercising it! This proves the generous character of his love. Undoubtedly Eph. 2:8 refers to what is often called "saving faith." However, even in the present case it may well be doubted that the faith of which Jesus speaks is merely miraculous. In view of what this man is about to do (see the last clause of this verse; cf. Luke 18:43), it would appear that when Jesus made him well by promptly restoring to him his vision, he blessed him not only physically but also spiritually. A. T. Robertson, *Word Pictures* I, p. 356, may therefore indeed be correct when he states that the expression "made thee whole" may well have the meaning here: *saved* thee. And is not more than physical restoration implied also in the other cases where the identical expression is used in the Gospels—the woman who suffered hemorrhages (Matt. 9:22; Mark 5:34; Luke 8:48); the great sinner (Luke 7:50); and the *one* cured leper who praised God and returned to thank Jesus (Luke 17:19)?

Conclusion: **Immediately he regained his sight.** . . . One moment total blindness . . . the next unimpaired vision. How tremendously astounding! Continued: **and began to follow** [518] **him on the road.** The man now wishes to be in the immediate company of Jesus. He did more than this: he glorified God. The people followed his example (Again Luke 18:43).

What a beautiful illustration of the way of salvation: "Call upon me in the day of trouble; and I will deliver you, and you shall glorify me" (Ps. 50:15; cf. I Cor. 10:31).

Summary of Chapter 10

In Mark's Gospel Christ's Perean Ministry begins here and continues to the end of the chapter. It immediately precedes The Week of the Passion, followed by The Resurrection.

Chapter 10 may be conveniently divided into two main parts: verses 1-31 and verses 32-52. The first part is paralleled in Matt. 19, the second in Matt. 20:17-34. Each main part has three paragraphs, so that, in all, Mark 10 has six paragraphs.

In the first paragraph (verses 1-12) Mark reports that while Jesus was teaching, some Pharisees came up to him, and with sinister intent asked him, "Is it lawful for a man to divorce his wife?" In his answer Jesus reminds his opponents of the divine creation-marriage institution (Gen. 1:27; 2:24), and concludes by saying, "What therefore God has joined together, let not man separate." When, away from the crowd and in a house, the disciples again ask

---

518 ἠκολούθει, imperfect, probably ingressive. So also in Luke 18:43.

Jesus about this subject, he, as Mark tells the story, ascribes equal standing and responsibility to husband and wife by saying, "Whoever divorces his wife and marries another woman is committing adultery against her; and if she herself divorces her husband and marries another man, she is committing adultery." By means of this teaching Jesus honored the marriage bond and declared its indissolubility as a divine institution.

Next (verses 13-16) Mark reports the attempt of the disciples to keep little children from being brought to Jesus. He rebukes the obstructionists and extends a hearty welcome to the little ones, taking them in his arms and tenderly blessing them. He adds, "I solemnly declare to y o u, whoever shall not receive the kingdom of God as a little child shall never enter it."

In verses 17-31 Mark tells the story of the rich young ruler who humbly approached Jesus with the question, "Good Teacher, what shall I do that I may inherit everlasting life?" Jesus answers, "Why do you call me good? No one is good except One—God." The Master speaks thus because the young man used the word "good" thoughtlessly. Jesus then refers him to God's perfect law, for "through the law comes the knowledge of sin." By saying, "All these things have I observed ever since I was a child" the enquirer once more reveals how shallow he is. Jesus, looking at him, loves him, not because of his lack of spiritual depth but probably because he had not fallen into gross outward sins and had gone to the best possible source to obtain an answer to his question. With affection and sympathy the Master treats this young person, and recommends to him a course of action which, if pursued, will give him the peace of mind for which he longs: Jesus says to him, "Go, sell whatever you have and give (the proceeds) to the poor, and you will have a treasure in heaven; and come, follow me." Crestfallen the wretched man walks away.

Jesus says to The Twelve, "How hard it will be for those who possess wealth to enter the kingdom of God. . . . Children how hard it is to enter the kingdom of God. It is easier for a camel to go through the eye of a needle than for a rich man to enter the kingdom of God." The disciples, in utter astonishment, say to each other, "Then who can be saved?" Jesus answers, "With men (this is) impossible but not with God, for with God all things are possible."

In response to Peter's observation, "Look, we have given up everything, and followed thee," the Master promises blessings for the present and for "the age to come." However, he also issues a warning, in order that no one may think that reward is based upon human merit. The warning is, "But many that are first shall be last, and (many) last first."

The fourth paragraph covers verses 32-34. Here begins the second part of the chapter. There is a link between paragraphs 3 and 4. According to verse 24 (see also verse 26) of the third paragraph the disciples were *amazed* or *startled* as a result of what Jesus had *said* about the difficulty of entering the kingdom of God. No less were they now *amazed* (same word in the original, fourth paragraph, verse 32) as a result of what Jesus *did*. They noticed that with unflinching determination he, taking the lead, was walking toward Jerusalem . . . in order to lay down his life as a vicarious sacrifice. Cf. 10:45. The unwavering advance of their Leader filled the hearts and minds of his followers with fear. That he knew what was coming is clear from his words, "Listen, we are going up to Jerusalem, and the Son of man shall be handed over to the chief priests and scribes." Thus he introduces his third passion-and-resurrection prediction. For the seven items that belong to this third prediction—which is far more detailed than the first and the second—and for their fulfilment, see on verses 33, 34.

In contents the opening of the fifth paragraph, which comprises verses 35-45, contrasts sharply with the preceding one. The Master's voluntary *humiliation* is replaced by his disciples' yearning for *exaltation*. James and John earnestly believe that their Master is going to be gloriously enthroned. So far, so good. But their reaction, expressed in their own words as addressed to Jesus, is, "Grant us to sit, one at your right and one at your left, in your glory." Jesus points out to them that *a.* the "greatness" for which they yearn requires sacrifice; *b.* the places at the right and left have already been fixed; and *c.* only by forgetting all about rank and by dedicating one's life to God in humble altruistic service, after Christ's own example, is true greatness attained. See especially 10:45.

How privileged were these disciples who were permitted day in, day out to listen to Christ's words, to witness the signs he performed, and to observe his behavior . . . and yet how blind they could be! But after the Master's resurrection those eyes were destined to open. He who is "the Light of the world" was able to cure blindness, spiritual as well as physical. An example of restoration of sight to a blind man is found in verses 46-52.

This final paragraph reports that Jesus and The Twelve arrived at last in Jericho. He was surrounded by a large crowd. When he was leaving that ancient city, a blind beggar, named Bartimaeus, having been informed that Jesus of Nazareth (see on 6:1) was passing by, began to cry out, "Jesus, son of David, take pity on me." When the people told him to be quiet, he cried all the more, "Son of David, take pity on me." Jesus does exactly that. He calls the blind man, lovingly asks him, "What do you want me to do for you?" and heals him, so that Bartimaeus, filled with gratitude, becomes Jesus' follower.

At this point, as well as throughout, the arrangement of Mark's Gospel is striking, for the devout people in Israel knew that, in connection with the coming of *the Messiah,* Isaiah's prophecy would be fulfilled, "Then shall the eyes of *the blind* be opened . . ." (35:5). This account is a most fitting

424

preface to "the Son of David's Triumphal Entry into Jerusalem" (11:1-11) and to the immediately following events; *see especially 12:35-37.* Mark's purpose is to indicate that "the Son of David" is not merely David's offspring; he is David's *Lord.* He is in fact "the Son of God." Everyone, therefore, should follow him, as did Bartimaeus, who followed him "in the way," the very way which for the Master led to Calvary. But the cross leads to the crown. It leads home. [519]

---

[519] In this connection see V. K. Robbins, "The Healing of Blind Bartimaeus (10:46-52) in the Marcan Theology," *JBL* (June 1973), pp. 224-243. What remains of this article after subtracting highly speculative redaction theories is very valuable.

The Work Which Thou Gavest Him to Do

Its Climax
or
Culmination

Chapter 11:1–16:8

Outline of Chapter 11

Theme: *The Work Which Thou Gavest Him To Do*

A. The Week of the Passion

11:1-11   The Triumphal Entry into Jerusalem
11:12-14   The Cursing of the Fig Tree
11:15-19   The Cleansing of the Temple
11:20-25   The Lesson from the Withered Fig Tree
11:27-33   Christ's Authority: Question and Counter-Question

CHAPTER XI

11 1 And when they were approaching Jerusalem (and came) to Bethphage and Bethany near the Mount of Olives, Jesus sent two of his disciples, 2 and said to them, "Go into the village opposite y o u, and at once as y o u enter it y o u will find a colt tied up, on which no one ever sat. Untie it and bring it here. 3 And if anyone says to y o u, 'Why are y o u doing this?' answer, 'The Lord needs it and will return it shortly.' " [520]

4 They went away and found a colt outside in the street, tied up near the door, and they untied it. 5 And some people who were standing there were asking them, "What are y o u doing, untying that colt?" 6 They answered as Jesus had directed them, and were then allowed to take it. [521] 7 They brought the colt to Jesus and laid their outer garments on it, and he took his seat on it. 8 And many people spread their outer garments on the road, while others spread leafy branches they had cut from the fields. 9 Those who went ahead and those who followed were shouting:

> Hosanna!
> Blessed (is) the One coming in the name of the Lord!
> 10 Blessed (is) the coming kingdom of our father David!
> Hosanna in the highest!

11 He entered Jerusalem and went into the temple. And having looked around at everything, since it was already late he went out to Bethany with the twelve.

11:1-11 *The Triumphal Entry into Jerusalem*
Cf. Matt. 21:1-11; Luke 19:28-40; John 12:12-19

The account of The Perean Ministry has ended, and so has the entire second division of Mark's story concerning the work which the Father gave the Mediator to do. The evangelist has told us all that he, guided by the Holy Spirit, wanted to relate concerning the Progress or Continuation of Christ's work. At this point, therefore, the narrative of The Week of the Passion begins. It covers chapters 11-15 and is followed by the story of The Resurrection, chapter 16.

The preceding paragraph of Mark's Gospel described what Jesus did when he was going out of Jericho (10:46-52). From Jericho the little party continued on its way toward Jerusalem (cf. 10:32, 33). On reasonable grounds it may be assumed that Bethany, about two miles from Jerusalem

---

520 Or: and will send it back here shortly.
521 Or: and they gave him permission.

(John 11:18), was reached before sunset on Friday, that on the sabbath (Friday sunset to Saturday sunset) Jesus enjoyed the sabbath rest with his friends, that on Saturday evening a supper was given in his honor at the home of "Simon the leper" (Mark 14:3-9), and that the next day, being Sunday, the triumphal entry into Jerusalem occurred.

Beginning, then, with Saturday evening, the main events in the conclusion of the story of Jesus, as recorded by Mark, are as follows:

Saturday evening

Supper in Bethany at the home of Simon the leper (14:3-9).

Sunday

Triumphal Entry into Jerusalem and return to Bethany (11:1-11).

Monday

Cursing of the fig tree, cleansing of the temple, and exit from the city (11:12-19).

Tuesday

Conversation between Peter and Jesus, who teaches The Twelve the lesson of the withered fig tree.

Confrontation between Jesus and his enemies, who ask him a series of questions which he answers, concluding with a question of his own. Parable of the Wicked Tenants.

Denunciation of the scribes.

Observation in the temple regarding a widow's offering.

Prediction of Jerusalem's destruction, the great tribulation, and the second coming.

Collusion for the purpose of killing Jesus.

For this entire series of events, from "Conversation" through "Collusion" see 11:20-14:2.

Wednesday

No events reported, unless the agreement between Judas and the chief priests (14:10, 11) took place on that day, but this may also have occurred a little earlier.

Thursday

(including the night from Thursday to Friday)

Preparation for the Passover.

Celebration of this feast; prediction regarding the betrayer.

Institution of the Lord's Supper.

Departure for Gethsemane; prediction that all will forsake Jesus and that Peter will deny him thrice.

Experiences in the garden of Gethsemane: Jesus' agony, prayers, betrayal by Judas, seizure, desertion by all.

Episode of the young man who fled.

Denial by Peter, in connection with Jesus' trial before the Sanhedrin resulting in

Condemnation.

> For all these events, from "Preparation" to "Condemnation" see 14:12-72.

Friday

Trial before Pilate.

The people's choice of Barabbas for release.

Jesus sentenced to be crucified; the scourging.

Mockery by the soldiers.

Simon of Cyrene forced to carry the cross.

Crucifixion of Jesus between two criminals.

Calvary Scenes: bystanders blaspheme, chief priests and scribes scoff, robbers rail, women watch.

Calvary Signs: from noon until 3 o'clock darkness over the entire land. At three o'clock: Christ's "loud voice," the veil of the temple rent from top to bottom, the testimony of the centurion: all this in connection with

Jesus' Death.

Jesus' Entombment.

> See Mark 15 for all of these "Good Friday" events, from "Trial" to "Tomb."

Saturday

No events reported in Mark; but see Matt. 27:62-66.

Sunday

Jesus' Resurrection. A "young man" dressed in a white robe tells women who had come to anoint the body, "He is risen . . . Go, tell his disciples and Peter . . ." (16:1-8). For post-resurrection "appearances" see the disputed verses 9-20.

* * *

For the arrangement of the various items pertaining to Christ's Triumphal Entry, showing how these items are distributed among the four Gospels and what each of them contributes, see the first 9 points in either N.T.C. on Matthew, pp. 761, 762; or N.T.C. on John, Vol. II, pp. 184-186.

*   *   *

1, 2. And when they were approaching Jerusalem (and came) to Beth-phage and Bethany near [522] **the Mount of Olives, Jesus sent two of his disciples, and said to them, Go into the village, opposite y o u, and at once as y o u enter it y o u will find a colt tied up, on which no one ever sat. Untie it and bring it here.**

Jesus and The Twelve are now approaching Jerusalem. They have reached a point not far away from the villages of Bethphage and Bethany. [523] Bethany is situated on the eastern slope of Mt. Olivet, and Bethphage—exact location unknown—has by tradition been located northwest of Bethany.

It would seem that from Bethany—or, if one prefers, from Mt. Olivet's eastern slope—Jesus this Sunday morning sends two of his disciples to Bethphage. His instruction was, "Go into the village opposite—or: over against—y o u," hence, "just ahead of y o u." [524] He assures them that immediately upon entering the village they will find a colt tied up.

What kind of colt? Of a camel, a horse, a donkey? It is natural to expect "of a donkey." Cf. Gen. 49:11; Judg. 10:4; 12:14. Besides, from Matt. 21:5 we know that this answer is correct and in harmony with the prophecy of Zech. 9:9 (according to the Hebrew). See N.T.C. on Matthew, p. 764, footnote 722. And for a discussion of the problem that arises from the fact that Matthew mentions two animals, Mark and Luke only one, see the same commentary, pp. 763, 765.

It will be a colt "upon which no one ever sat," hence, an unbroken or unbacked colt, by God reserved for sacred use. Cf. Num. 19:2; Deut. 21:3; I Sam. 6:7. Is not this also in line with the fact that Mary, too, was still "unused" (cf. Rom. 1:26, 27), still a virgin, when Jesus was conceived within her womb and even at his birth? See Matt. 1:25; Luke 1:34. The tomb, too, in which the body of the dead Jesus was laid had never been used (Luke 23:53). We notice, therefore, that there is nothing haphazard about the

---

[522] πρός followed by acc. in the sense of "near" or "at," as in verse 4. Cf. the use of this preposition in Luke 22:56.

[523] The order in which the two villages are mentioned is logical, *for Jerusalem has been mentioned first*. Bethphage was nearest to Jerusalem; a little farther east lay Bethany. On the other hand, for those starting out from Bethany the order was Bethany, Bethphage, Jerusalem.

[524] For more on ἀντί in composition and as an independent preposition see above on 10:45, footnote 507.

triumphal entry. Everything has been carefully planned and is orderly and appropriate, exactly as it should be.

How did Jesus know that the two disciples would find everything as he had predicted? The possibility that this knowledge had come to him in a very natural way, the owners of the colt having conveyed it to him whether directly or indirectly, cannot be entirely ruled out. Nevertheless, in view of the somewhat similar prediction recorded in 14:13, the theory that this bit of information had reached Christ's human consciousness in a supernatural manner may well be preferable. Note also that Luke 19:33 can be interpreted as meaning that there had been no previous understanding with respect to this incident between Jesus and the owners of the colt. However that may be, the fact as such that Jesus did at times receive information in ways which surpass human comprehension is clear from such passages as Matt. 17:27; John 1:48; 2:4, 25. See also on Mark 10:33, 34.

The two disciples are told to untie the colt and bring it to Jesus. The instruction continues as follows: 3. **And if anyone says to y o u, Why are y o u doing this? answer, The Lord needs it and will return it shortly** [literally: **and will send it back here shortly**].

This is one of the most controversial passages of Mark's Gospel. The argument centers around two closely related questions: *a.* What is the meaning of the words here translated "and will send it back here shortly"? And *b.* Who is the *kurios* mentioned here? Should we render this word "Lord" or "lord"? If "Lord," is the reference to the Triune God, the Jehovah of the Old Testament, or is Jesus referring to himself? There are, however, also those who prefer to spell the English equivalent of *kurios* with a small letter "l" and who accordingly accept the theory that the reference is to the owner of the colt. [525]

Now there can be no question about the fact that the Greek word *kurios*, as used in the New Testament and elsewhere, has a variety of meanings—Sir, owner, master, Lord (the reference being to God or Jehovah), Lord (the reference being to Jesus)—, but in the present case we shall limit ourselves to the question, "Here in Mark 11:3 does the word refer to the owner of the colt or to Jesus?"

From the information supplied in the footnote it has become evident that by far the most *commentators* prefer the rendering "Lord." They interpret

---

[525] Thus, for example, Vincent Taylor, *op. cit.,* p. 455; and M. H. Bolkestein, *op. cit.,* pp. 251, 252. On the other hand, W. C. Allen, *The Gospel according to Saint Mark,* London, 1915, p. 142, interprets the title as a reference to God, as in Mark 5:19. A. B. Bruce, *op. cit.,* p. 416; C. R. Erdman, *op. cit.,* p. 155; E. P. Gould, *op. cit.,* p. 207; J. Schmid, *op. cit.,* p. 205; H. B. Swete, *op. cit.,* p. 248; and J. A. C. Van Leeuwen, *op. cit.,* p. 136, are among the many who believe that the reference is to Jesus himself. So does F. C. Grant, *op. cit.,* p. 825, but he regards the title "Lord" as early church interpretation.

the entire passage to mean that Jesus is here instructing the two disciples, who while engaged in untying the colt are presumably asked, "Why are y o u doing this?" to answer, in substance, "The Lord—that is Jesus—needs this colt and will send it back to Bethphage as soon as he has reached Jerusalem."

With slight variations—for example, some substitute "Master" for "Lord"—*translators,* too, are well-nigh unanimous in supporting this view. See A.R.V., Beck, Berkeley, Dutch (both Staten and Nieuwe Vertaling), Goodspeed, Jerusalem Bible, N.A.S., N.E.B., N.I.V., Norlie, Phillips, R.S.V., Weymouth, Williams). How, then, is it that the opposite view, according to which *kurios* refers to the owner of the colt, has found defenders?

The main reason given by those who adopt this interpretation is that, as they see it, not only is *kurios,* as a name for Jesus, not used anywhere else by Mark or by Matthew, but also the acceptance of Jesus as "Lord" is of later date, reflected in the Gospels written last of all, Luke and John. The argument continues along this line: Faith in Jesus as "Lord," and addressing him as such, was not current in the primitive Jerusalem church. Jesus, during the state of his humiliation, did not regard himself as Lord, nor was he called "Lord." That was a later development. It arose after the belief in his resurrection had become firmly established.

Answer:

a. Only by very specious reasoning is it possible to interpret *kurios* here in Mark 11:3 as having reference to anyone else than Jesus. It should be borne in mind that according to the context the two disciples are pictured as untying the colt. They will presumably be interrupted by the shocked owners (cf. Luke 19:33), but their explanation must amount to: "We are doing this because the Lord Jesus needs it. However he will not keep the colt any longer than needed but will see to it that it is speedily returned."— According to Matt. 21:3 the owners, having received this assurance, will then allow the colt to be taken away.

Now this explanation makes sense. Those who favor the opposite view have failed so far to supply an equally reasonable explanation of their view. Let the reader see this for himself by carefully examining Vincent Taylor's treatment and—be it said to his credit!—the difficulties pertaining to it, *which he himself admits!*

b. Though Mark 11:3 and Matt. 21:3 are in perfect harmony, the one supplementing the other, it is useless to attempt to make them say the same thing, as is sometimes done. The phrase "back here" in Mark but not in Matthew makes identification impossible. [526]

---

[526] Even the use of the same verb ἀποστέλλω, present (futuristic) in Mark, but future, ἀποστελεῖ, in Matthew, does not change this fact.

c. Passages such as Matt. 7:21-23, "Not everyone who says to me, Lord, Lord, will enter the kingdom of heaven . . ."; Mark 12:35-37 (cf. Matt. 22:41-46; Luke 20:41-44), see on that passage; I Cor. 16:22, "Maranatha," meaning "O Lord, come!" and, because it is Aramaic, proving that the ascription of the appellation "Lord" to Jesus goes back to the earliest, still Aramaic speaking church; and Gal. 1:18, 19, where in an early Jerusalem context James is called "the brother of the Lord," demonstrate that the theory according to which the designation "Lord" for Jesus was a later development is erroneous. The explanation adopted by most commentators must therefore be considered correct.

In the heat of the discussion regarding the meaning of *kurios* in Mark 11:3 the practical lesson is apt to be overlooked. That lesson is this: If even the Lord Jesus, who was and is God as well as man, and has a right to claim for himself anything and everything on earth, returned the colt he had "borrowed," should not his followers return what was lent or entrusted to them? The reference is not only to the obligation of returning borrowed books, money, clothes, etc., but also to that of yielding hearts and lives to the One who gave them. Must "stewardship" become an empty term? See I Cor. 4:1, 2; 6:20; 15:50—16:1; II Cor. 8:8, 9; I Peter 4:10.

Everything turned out exactly as Jesus had predicted: **4-6. They went away and found a colt outside in the street, tied up near the door, and they untied it. And some people who were standing there were asking, What are y o u doing, untying that colt? They answered as Jesus had directed them, and were then allowed to take it.** Immediately upon entering the village what did the two disciples see? The colt, tied up near a door! It was the door at the end of the corridor leading from the outer court (of the house) to the outside.

As the two men started to unhitch the colt, some of the bystanders—the owners (Luke 19:33)—understandably protested. They asked, "What are y o u doing, untying that colt?" But when, in accordance with Christ's instruction (verse 3), the disciples were heard to say, "The Lord needs it and will send it back here shortly," objections quickly vanished. The mere mention of the fact that Jesus needed the colt was enough to secure immediate and unqualified assent. [527]

---

527 Vocabulary and grammar: verse 4: πρός, *near*, as in verse 1: ἄμφοδον (here ἐπὶ τοῦ ἀμφόδου), a combination of ἀμφί and ὁδός originally perhaps a road surrounding something. There is evidence for the meaning: a quarter, ward, district, or precinct (Lat. vicus; M. E. vick, German weich. Dutch wijk) of a city. See M.M., p. 28. It was called ἄμφοδον perhaps because it was surrounded and crossed by streets. Here in Mark 11:4 it probably simply means *street* (as in an Acts 19:28 variant), not necessarily "a street around a house." Words have histories. They undergo change in meanings, development,

A very important practical application must not escape our attention. It is clear from this passage—and from many others; e.g., Mark 15:40—16:1; Luke 6:13; 10:1; John 12:19; John 19:38—20:1—that in addition to The Twelve Jesus had many other disciples, men and women who stood ready to serve him in various ways. There must have been a large number of supporters in Judea, Galilee, Perea, and wherever the Lord went. Whether it was a place of lodging, a colt, a room in which to celebrate the Passover, or even at last a tomb, whatever it was that he needed, if they had it these friends were ready to provide it. That one word, "The Lord needs it" was all that was required.

Today, too, such a broad body of true followers of the Lord and supporters of his causes is urgently needed, and this not only to follow directions that are handed down to them from "the top," the ecclesiastical authorities, but also to act independently: to pray, to study, to guide, to support the poor by word and deed, to encourage the fearful, to bear testimony concerning the goodness of God in providing salvation for sinners, etc. etc. These tasks should be performed willingly, eagerly, and without any thought of acclaim or promotion. They should be undertaken in the spirit of the poem *Your Mission* by Ellen M. H. Gates, beginning with the lines:

> "If you cannot on the ocean
> 　Sail among the swiftest fleet,
> Rocking on the highest billows,
> 　Laughing at the storms you meet,
> You can stand among the sailors
> 　Anchored still within the bay,
> You can lend a hand to help them
> 　As they launch their boats away."
>
> 　　　　　See A. L. Byers and Eva R. Johnson
> 　　　　　(editors and compilers), *Treasures*
> 　　　　　*of Poetry,* Anderson, Ind., 1913, p. 267.

Permission having been obtained by the two men, **7, 8. They brought the colt to Jesus and laid their outer garments on it, and he took his seat on it. And many people spread their outer garments on the road, while others spread leafy branches they had cut from the fields.** The two now *a.* brought the colt to Jesus, *b.*—in conjunction perhaps with the other ten disciples— placed their long, thin, quadrangular robes on the colt so as to provide as comfortable a seat as possible for Jesus; and *c.* mounted him on the colt (Luke 19:35), he himself co-operating by taking his seat on it.

---

ramification, so that with the passage of time not every word-component retains its full meaning.

Verse 5: ἐστηκότων, gen. pl. masc. perf. participle of ἴστημι.

Verse 6: ἀφῆκαν, third per. pl. aor. indic. active of ἀφίημι. Those who stood by let the disciples have the colt; they released it to them.

By this time a large crowd, accompanying Jesus from Bethany, not wishing to be outdone by The Twelve, began to carpet the road with their outer garments or with leafy branches cut from the fields. [528]

At this point it is important to take note of the fact that the crowd that accompanied Jesus as he started out from Bethany does not remain the only one that participates in the activities pertaining to the triumphal entry. A caravan of pilgrims had arrived at Jerusalem previously. Having heard that Jesus had raised Lazarus from the dead and was now on his way toward the city, these people came pouring out of the eastern gate to meet him. With fronds cut from palm trees they go forth to welcome Jesus (John 12:1, 12, 13a, 18). Having done so they turn around and, as it were, lead Jesus down the western slope of the mount of Olives and so into the city. The crowd from Bethany continues to follow. This explains Mark's mention of the two crowds. **9, 10. Those who went ahead and those who followed were shouting:**

> Hosanna!
> Blessed (is) the One coming in the name of the Lord!
> Blessed (is) the coming kingdom of our father David!
> Hosanna in the highest!

We must try to get into the spirit of the occasion when these two crowds met. How impetuous and exuberant their enthusiasm! How unrestrained and tumultuous their shouting!

What exactly did they shout and what was its meaning? "Hosanna" means "save now," or "save, pray." The attitude of the people toward God was perhaps about as follows: "We beseech thee, O Lord, save now, grant victory and prosperity at this time, since because of thy goodness the appropriate moment has arrived." Hence, in this "Hosanna" exclamation, the two elements: supplication and adoration, or if one prefers: prayer and praise, are combined. It is clear that the source of Mark 11:9, 10 is Ps. 118 (LXX Ps. 117), which from beginning to end is filled with prayer and praise; see especially verses 22-26a. It is in essence a Hallel Psalm, one of the series Ps. 113-118, sung at Passover. See N.T.C. on John, Vol. I, p. 121. It is also one of the six Psalms most often quoted or referred to in the New Testament; the others being Pss. 2; 22; 69; 89; and 110.

Ps. 118 is distinctly Messianic. It speaks about the stone rejected by the

---

528 Verse 7: φέρουσι literally, *they bring;* and ἐπιβάλλουσι, *they throw—put* or *lay—on,* but these are examples of vivid historical presents so frequent especially in Mark's Gospel. In such cases we would as a rule use the past tense. See above, Introduction V, footnote 5, under *d.*

Verse 8: ἔστρωσαν, third per. pl. aor. active indic. of στρωννύω, *to spread* (out). Cf. *strew,* (light dispersing) *star.*

στιβάς = στοιβάς, *leafy bough, branch;* in the New Testament occurring only here.

builders but destined to become the cornerstone. See on Mark 12:10; cf. Matt. 21:42; Luke 20:17; Acts 4:11; and I Peter 2:7.

As to "Blessed (is) the One coming in the name of the Lord!" this is a quotation from Ps. 118:26. Combined with "the Son of David," as in Matt. 21:9, it must refer to Jesus as the Messiah. It was deplorable, however, that by far the most of these people did not go one step farther: they should have combined Ps. 118 with Isa. 53 and with Zech. 9:9; 13:1. Then they would have recognized in Jesus the Messiah who saves his people *from their sins* (Matt. 1:21).

As to "Blessed (is) the coming kingdom of our father David!" a clause preserved by Mark alone, though it is true that Jesus had often referred to "the kingdom of God" or "the kingdom of heaven," and had linked this phrase with his own coming to earth (Mark 1:14, 15), and with the near at hand manifestation of his power and glory (9:1), and though he had even taught his disciples to pray, "Thy kingdom come" (Matt. 6:10), it is hard to believe that the crowd's mention of "the coming kingdom of *our father David*" was entirely pure and wholesome.

A few facts must be borne in mind in this connection:

a. These people were "pilgrims" on their way to celebrate Passover, the very festival that reminded every Jew of the deliverance of their ancestors from Egyptian bondage. At such an occasion the thought, "How long will it be before we ourselves are delivered from foreign oppression?" occupied everybody's mind.

b. The possibility that among this huge crowd, containing many Galileans, there were those who had intended on a former occasion "to take Jesus by force in order that they might make him king" (John 6:15) cannot be considered remote.

c. The attempt to make Jesus an earthly king had been made because Jesus a few moments before had by means of a miracle fed the hungry multitude. And now, a few days before Christ's death on the cross, an even more astounding miracle—raising Lazarus from the dead—was one of the main reasons for the present vociferous adulation by this double crowd, as John 12:17, 18 makes clear.

We cannot be far amiss, therefore, when we state that the cry, "Blessed (is) the coming kingdom of our father David" was, at least to a considerable extent, an expression of the hope of national restoration, the revival of the Davidic kingdom conceived of in an earthly, political sense.

Finally, as to "Hosanna in the highest!" this shows that Messiah was regarded as a gift from God, the One who dwells in the highest heaven and is worthy of the prayers and the praises of all, including even the angels. One cannot help thinking of Ps. 148:1, 2 and of Luke 2:14.

When the people hailed Jesus as "the Son of David" (Matt. 21:9), that is, the Messiah, they were right, and those who were going to find fault with the children (Matt. 21:15) or with the disciples (Luke 19:39) for thus addressing him, were wrong and worthy of being rebuked. But when the crowds in general failed to discern the spiritual nature of his messiahship, they were wrong. Their tragic mistake was committed with tragic results for themselves. How this failure to accept Jesus for what he really was must have hurt him. It is not surprising therefore that Luke pictures a weeping King in the midst of a shouting multitude (19:39-44), nor is it strange that, a little later, when the crowds begin to understand that Jesus is not the kind of Messiah they had expected, they, at the urging of their leaders, were shouting, "Crucify (him)."

There was, moreover, no excuse for this deplorable misunderstanding on the part of the people and their leaders.

a. The very fact that Jesus was riding into Jerusalem not on a high-spirited war steed or prancing white stallion but on a colt, the foal of an ass, an animal associated with the pursuits of peace, should have been sufficient to show that it was as the Prince of Peace that he had come.

b. Besides, in doing so he was fulfilling a prophecy in which he was associated with peace, meekness, and salvation (Zech. 9:9).

c. Again, in several other prophecies, too, the peaceful character of the Messiah had been set forth (Isa. 9:6, 7; 35:5, 6; 40:11; 42:1-4; 60:1-3; 61, the entire chapter but see especially verses 1-3).

d. Then there was Isa. 53, in which in a most striking and unforgettable manner the Messiah was portrayed as the One who would by means of substitutionary suffering and death, make atonement for the sins of his people.

e. Finally, during his entire ministry did not this Son of David reveal himself as being filled with thoughts of peace? Did not his heart go out to the multitudes? Did he not on every occasion show tenderness toward the sick, the oppressed, the weak, the poor, the little ones, the widows, etc.? Did he not again and again urge sinners to come to him and find real and lasting peace? See Matt. 11:28-30; 12:17-21; 23:37; Luke 12:32; John 10:14-16, to mention only a few passages out of the many that could be cited.

Never shall we be able to understand Palm Sunday unless we perceive that, viewed from the aspect of many of the shouters, it was a *Tragedy!*

Nevertheless, it was also a *Triumph,* namely, of Christ's love! Did he not deliberately evoke a demonstration? He fully realized that the enthusiasm of the masses would enrage the hostile leaders in Jerusalem, so that they will now carry out their plot to put him to death. But he had actually come from heaven to die, to die the most cruel and painful death—in fact, eternal death—in the place of those given to him by the Father! So intensely did he love sinners that he came from heaven to earth—yes, to *hell* on earth—in

439

order to save them! From the aspect of Jesus, therefore, and of all those who, by sovereign grace, adored him for what he *really* was and is, Palm Sunday was a *Triumph!*

11. He entered Jerusalem and went into the temple. And having looked around at everything, since it was already late he went out to Bethany with the twelve. What happened at the very moment when the Lord entered Jerusalem, and perhaps shortly afterward, is related in Matt. 21:10, 11; see N.T.C. on that passage. Mark takes up the story again when it was already late [529] in the day, that is, late Sunday evening. He makes mention of only a brief visit to the temple. For Jesus' presence there see also 11:15 f., 27; 12:35; 13:1, 3; 14:49. Although the word used here for "temple" is all-inclusive—it may embrace the entire temple complex—, this does not mean that Jesus actually entered every part of it. The reference here is probably to the spacious court of the Gentiles and its adjoining porches. See the diagram, p. 448.

While in the temple Jesus "looked around at [530] everything." He made a quick, all-around, sweeping survey. Nothing escaped his purview. He gathered the impressions that would lead to actions on the following day. Since it was already late this Sunday evening, he leaves the city in order, in the company of The Twelve, to spend the night in Bethany. See also on verse 19 and cf. Matt. 21:17. He knows that the Jewish authorities are inflamed against him, and also that his time to die has not yet arrived. So, for both of these reasons, he cannot during this night remain in Jerusalem. Also, by leaving the city he will escape the hurly-burly of the crowds, will have opportunity for prayer and meditation, and perhaps even for some moments of fellowship with his disciples.

---

12 On the following day, as they were leaving Bethany, he was hungry.   13 And noticing in the distance a fig tree in leaf, he went (to see) if he could perhaps find anything on it. When he reached it, however, he found nothing but leaves, for it was not the season for figs.   14 He spoke up and said to it, "Never again may anyone eat fruit from you!" And his disciples were listening.

11:12-14 *The Cursing of the Fig Tree*
Cf. Matt. 21:18, 19

While the narrative of Christ's triumphal entry is found in all four Gospels, that of the cursing of the fig tree is found only in Matthew and Mark. The former treats this story topically, the latter chronologically. For more on this see N.T.C. on Matthew, pp. 273-275. When Mark 11:12-14 is compared with Matt. 21:18, 19, the following variations come to light:

---

529 ὀψίας ἤδη οὔσης τῆς ὥρας, genit. absolute; literally, "the hour being already late."
530 Same Greek participle as in 3:5; see footnote 105.

a. Matthew states, "Now in the morning, when he was returning to the city . . ."; Mark, "On the following day, as they were leaving Bethany. . . ." However, the fact that Jesus was returning from Bethany to Jerusalem is clear from the immediately preceding accounts in both cases.

b. According to Matthew, Jesus saw a fig tree "by the side of the road." As Mark records the incident, from a distance Jesus noticed "a fig tree in leaf."

c. The interesting detail that Jesus "went (to see) if he could perhaps find anything on it" is reported only by Mark.

d. Though both Gospels inform the reader that Jesus went up to the tree and found nothing on it but leaves, it is Mark who adds, "for it was not the season for figs."

e. The difference between the words of the curse as found in the two stories is slight. According to Matthew, Jesus said, "Never again let there be fruit from you"; according to Mark, "Never again may anyone eat fruit from you." The two are in perfect harmony.

f. Finally, while Matthew calls attention to the fact that the process of withering began at once, a fact not denied by Mark, the latter directs our attention to The Twelve, stating, "And his disciples were listening."

What has been pointed out before can be repeated here: the Gospel-writers were not mere copyists; each tells the story in his own way. The two do not conflict in any way. By supplementing each other they enrich the reader.

12. On the following day, [531] as they were leaving Bethany, he was hungry. [532] If it was at the home of his friends that Jesus had spent the night of Sunday to Monday, it is not clear why he should be hungry this Monday morning. Had he arisen very early, before breakfast (cf. 1:35)? Or had he and The Twelve spent the night under the stars that shone on the slopes in the vicinity of the village?

How thoroughly human is this Jesus, how close to us: even becoming hungry at times. Cf. Matt. 4:2; Heb. 4:15. This, too, was part of Christ's humiliation in the place of and for the sake of his people (II Cor. 8:9; Ga. 3:13; Phil. 2:8). Very effectively and beautifully the inspired author of Hebrews makes clear the comfort that can be derived from what is here revealed with reference to Christ (4:15). Consider also the poetic lines:

"Hast thou been hungry, child of mine?
I, too, have needed bread."

13. And noticing in the distance a fig tree in leaf, he went (to see) if he

---

[531] τῇ ἐπαύριον, supply ἡμέρᾳ. ἐπαύριον = ἐπ, αὔριον, on the morrow. With αὔριον cf. *Aurora*, the dawn. The incident took place, therefore, when the following day dawned.

[532] ἐπείνασε third per. aor. indic. of πεινάω, to be hungry. Cf. I Cor. 4:11; Phil. 4:12. Cf. *penury*. In Matt. 5:6 the verb is used in the sense of *to long for*.

could perhaps find anything on it.[533] But was not Jesus omniscient? The present passage seems to imply that the Master would at times gather information in ways similar to ours. At other times his knowledge was wholly supernatural. This subject has been discussed earlier. See on 2:8; 5:32; 9:33, 34; 10:33, 34; 11:1, 2. See also on 13:32.

Continued: **When he reached it, however, he found nothing but leaves, for it was not the season for figs.** In the region referred to here in Mark, the early or smaller figs, growing from the sprouts of the previous year, begin to appear at the end of March and are ripe in May or June. The later and much larger figs that develop on the new or spring shoots are gathered from August to October. It is important to point out that the earlier figs, with which we are here concerned, begin to appear simultaneously with the leaves. Sometimes, in fact, they even precede the leaves.

Passover (about April) was at hand. Accordingly, the time when either the earlier or the later figs are ripe had not yet arrived. It was therefore "not the season for figs." But Jesus notices that this particular tree, growing by the side of the road and thus probably in a sheltered place (Matt. 21:19), was something special. It had leaves, was most likely in full foliage, and could therefore be expected to have fruit. Yet, it had nothing but leaves! It promised much but provided nothing!

14. He spoke up[534] **and said to it, Never again may anyone eat**[535] **fruit from you!** It is impossible to believe that the curse which the Lord pronounced upon this tree was an act of punishing it, as if the tree as such was responsible for not bearing fruit, and as if, for this reason, Jesus was angry with it. The real explanation lies deeper. The pretentious but barren tree was a fit emblem of Israel. See Luke 13:6-9 (cf. Isa. 5). Jesus himself would interpret the figure the next day (Tuesday); see on Matt. 21:43. In fact, the disciples did not even have to wait until the next day for the explanation: The pretentious fig tree had its counterpart in the temple where on this very day (Monday) a lively business was being transacted so that sacrifices might be made, while at the same time the priests were plotting to put to death the

---

533 *συκῆ* (acc. *ῆν*) fig tree. Cf. *sycamore. φύλλον* (pl.-*α*), leaf. Cf. foliage. Note *εἰ ἄρα* with future indic.; hence, "if haply he might find. . . ." This resembles an indirect question. Cf. Acts 8:22: "if perhaps . . ."; and 17:27: "if haply they might feel after him, and find him" (A.V.).

534 For *ἀποκριθεὶς* see on 9:5, footnote 391; and on 10:51, footnote 515.

535 Note the double negation *Μηκέτι εἰς τὸν αἰῶνα . . . μηδεὶς*; literally, "Never . . . no one . . . ," where we would say "Never . . . anyone." Cf. South African: "Laat *niemand* ooit in der ewigheid van jou 'n vrug eet *nie*." See also the double negative (with subjunctive) in Matt. 21:19. For more on Mark's double negatives see Introduction IV, footnote 5 *h*. Note also *φάγοι*, third per. sing. aor. optative of *ἐσθίω*. With such an optative one must be very careful. It is by no means "a mere wish." It has here the force

very One apart from whom these offerings had no meaning whatever. Plenty of leaves but no fruit. Bustling religious (?) activity, but no sincerity and truth, tremendous promise but a very poor performance! In cursing the fig tree and in cleansing the temple Jesus performed *two* symbolic and prophetic acts, with *one* meaning. He was predicting the downfall of unfruitful Israel. Not that he was "through with the Jews," but that in the place of Israel an international and everlasting kingdom would be established, a nation bringing forth not just leaves but fruits, and gathered from both Jews and Gentiles.

And his disciples were listening. They were deeply impressed. This very Jesus, whose heart was accustomed to go out to the multitudes, the One who yearned to comfort and cheer, to help and heal, to seek and save, was actually heard to pronounce a withering curse upon a fig tree! Did these men even at this time surmise the meaning of this curse? Did they intuitively guess that they had been witnessing *an acted parable,* one somewhat similar to those acted out by some of the Old Testament prophets? See Jer. 13:1-11; ch. 19, especially verses 1, 2, 10; Ezek. 3:1-11; 12:1-16; ch. 24; Hos. 1:1-9; 3:1-5; etc. Surely, if they had attentively read Jer. 8:13, had studied Isa. 5, and taken to heart the *parable* of The Barren Fig Tree (Luke 13:6-9), they could hardly have missed the point.

One fact must not escape us. With the exception of such *multiple* miracles as are recorded in 1:32-34, 39; 3:10, 11; 6:53-56, and the greatest miracle of all, Christ's triumphant rising from the dead (16:1-8), *this* Gospel records 18 miracles. Of these 18 the blasting of the fig tree is the last.

Moreover, not only is it *last,* it is also *destructive,* in fact *totally* destructive. See verses 14, 20, 21. The miracle recorded in 5:1-20 was only *partly* destructive (5:13).

Do not these couple exceptions cause all the other miracles—those in which the divine *mercy* is displayed—to stand out all the more conspicuously? Among the many lessons taught by these signs of power and pity, are not the following two to be included? The two are: *a.* God—hence Jesus Christ (John 14:8, 9)—takes delight in showing mercy, healing, saving (Isa. 1:18; 5:1-2; 45:22; ch. 55; Ezek. 18:23, 32; 33:11; Hos. 11:8; Matt. 11:28-30; 23:37; Rev. 22:17; and *b.* "The man who, having been often reproved, hardens his neck, shall suddenly be destroyed, and this without remedy" (Prov. 29:1; cf. Isa. 1:19, 20; 5:3-7; Ezek. 18:24; Matt. 11:20-24; 23:38; Rev. 14:9-11).

---

of a command; in fact, (in the present context) of a *weighty* curse pronounced upon (or: against) this tree! A very effective curse indeed, as is clear from Mark 11:20, 21; cf. Matt. 21:19, 20. —So also in salutations the optative is not "a mere wish." See N.T.C. on I and II Thessalonians, pp. 43-45, including the footnotes there.

Miracles of Jesus Recorded in Mark

According to Mark, Jesus performed miracles on the following, as recorded in:

MARK CHAPTER	Mark alone	Mark & Matthew	Mark & Luke	Mark, Matthew & Luke	Mark, Matthew & John	All Four
1:			21-28 demoniac in synagogue	30, 31 Peter's mother-in-law; 40-45 a leper		
2:				1-12 a paralytic		
3:				1-6 a withered hand		
4:				35-41 a storm		
5:				1-20 a Gerasene demoniac; 21-24, 35-43 the daughter of Jairus; 25-34 the woman who touched Christ's robe		
6:					45-52 boisterous waves: a double miracle	30-44 5000 hungry people
7:	31-37 deaf-and-dumb man	24-30 Syrophoenician woman's daughter				
8:	22-26 the blind man of Bethsaida	1-10 4000 hungry people				
9:				14-29 an epileptic boy		
10:				46-52 Blind Bartimaeus		
11:		12-14 a barren fig tree				

Of Mark's 18 miracles 16 have parallels in one or more of the other Gospels; as follows:

MARK	PARALLELS IN		
	MATTHEW	LUKE	JOHN
1:21-28		4:31-37	
1:30, 31	8:14, 15	4:38, 39	
1:40-45	8:1-4	5:12-16	
2:1-12	9:1-8	5:17-26	
3:1-6	12:9-14	6:6-11	
4:35-41	8:18, 23-27	8:22-25	
5:1-20	8:28—9:1	8:26-39	
5:21-24, 35-43	9:18, 19, 23-26	8:40-42, 49-56	
5:25-34	9:20-22	8:43-48	
6:30-44	14:13-21	9:10-17	
6:45-52	14:22-33		6:1-14
7:24-30	15:21-28		6:15-21
8:1-10	15:32-39		
9:14-29	17:14-20	9:37-43a	
10:46-52	20:29-34	18:35-43	
11:12-14	21:18, 19		

15 They came to Jerusalem, and having entered the temple he began to drive out those buying and those selling in the temple, and he turned upside down the tables of the money-changers and the seats of those selling doves. 16 And he would not allow anyone to carry merchandise through the temple. 17 He was teaching and saying to them, "Is it not written:

'My house shall be called a house of prayer
for all the nations'?
But y o u have made it a robbers' den."

18 The chief priests and the scribes heard (this) and were looking for a way to kill him, for they were afraid of him because everybody was astonished at his teaching. 19 And whenever evening arrived, they [536] went out of the city.

11:15-19 *The Cleansing of the Temple*
Cf. Matt. 21:12-17; Luke 19:45-48
For an earlier cleansing see John 2:13-22

This striking event recorded by all three occurred on Monday of the Passion Week, after the cursing of the fig tree. The main differences in the

536 Some early texts read "he."

three accounts—variations in reporting, not conflicting items—are as follows:

It is Mark alone who states that Jesus refused to allow the temple to be used as a travel or transportation short-cut. It is also he alone who in quoting the words of Jesus derived from Isa. 56:7b includes the phrase "for all the nations." Because it was Mark's primary purpose to influence the Romans, hence the nations, while Matthew's primary objective was to reach the Jews, this difference is understandable. Luke's omission of the phrase is harder to explain. However, it must be borne in mind that his record of this event is very brief (only four verses). The omission may therefore fall into the general pattern of leaving out much in order to have room for other material (parables, etc.). Mark mentions the reaction of the Jewish leaders, who were looking for a way to destroy Jesus, a fact noted also by Luke. And Mark indicates that Jesus' evening departure from the city was customary during Passion Week.

Matthew pictures the compassion and healing power of Jesus directed toward the blind and the lame; also his defense of the children's hosannas, sincere and joyful acclamations that were resented by the religious authorities.

Luke reports that Jesus was daily teaching in the temple, and that during the early days of this week the opponents' desire to kill Jesus was thwarted by their fear of the people.

For the arguments against identifying this temple cleansing with the one recorded in John 2 see N.T.C. on John, Vol. I, p. 120.

15. They came to Jerusalem, and having entered the temple he began to drive out those buying and those selling in the temple, and he turned upside down the tables of the money-changers and the seats of those selling doves.

From the Mt. of Olives Jesus had gone to Jerusalem, had spent the night in Bethany, and was back in Jerusalem now. Here he enters the temple. The summit of nearby Mt. Olivet is about 250 feet higher than the hill on which the temple stood. Between Olivet, to the east, and the city lies the Kidron Valley.

Description of the Temple

In order to grasp the meaning of the temple cleansing and of many other New Testament references to this building, note the following *main* facts:

It was David who conceived in his heart to build a temple for the Lord. But for the reason stated in I Chron. 28:3 not to David but to his son Solomon was given the privilege to build it. He began to do so in the fourth year of his reign, hence in or about the year 969 B.C. See I Kings 6:1. It was finished seven years later (I Kings 6:38). Cedar and cypress wood from Lebanon, and white hard limestone were used in its construction. Because the level area of Moriah, on which it was built, was too small, the foundation had to be laid very deep and the space between hilltop and outer wall filled in. For an account of the furniture of this temple and of the manner in which it was dedicated see I Kings 6-8. This temple experienced stress and strain. In the course of the centuries it was plundered, renovated, desecrated, purged. See I Kings 14:26; 15:18; II Kings 14:14; 15:35; 16:17 f.; 23:4 f. Its treasures were carried to Babylon (II Kings 24:13). Finally, about the year 586 B.C. the Chaldean army destroyed Jerusalem, including Solomon's beautiful temple.

About fifty years later, at the return of a remnant from Babylonian captivity, an altar for a new temple was immediately built (Ezra 3:3). Sometime later work was begun in earnest on the building itself. It was completed about twenty years after the return. However, since it became clear that it would not be nearly as imposing and beautiful a structure as that of Solomon, the older people, who had known that first building, wept (Ezra 3:12, 13). It was this temple that was plundered and desecrated by Antiochus Epiphanes in 168 B.C. Approximately three years later it was cleansed and rededicated by Judas Maccabaeas. Pompey captured and entered this temple but did not destroy it. However, Crassus deprived it of its treasures in 54, 53 B.C.

Herod the Great altered and enlarged the temple complex. He expanded and beautified it to such an extent that the result could be called a new temple, though devout Jews probably refused to consider it such. In an eloquent address to the people the king, if we can trust Josephus, divulged his plan "to make a thankful return, after the most pious manner, to God, for the blessings I have received from him, who has given me this kingdom, and to do this by making his temple as complete as I am able." He began to build it about the year 19 B.C. Long after his death it had not yet been entirely completed. See John 2:20. The grandeur and beauty of the temple which Herod started to build and on which he had made very considerable progress is evident from Mark 13:1, 2; cf. Matt. 24:1, 2; Luke 21:5, 6. See also Matt. 4:5; Luke 4:9. It is interesting to note that this elaborate structure was not finished until . . . just a few years before it was destroyed by the Romans, A.D. 70.

Here follows a brief description of Herod's temple complex. It should be studied in connection with the diagram. The entire huge area on which it stood—a square measuring not much less than a thousand feet on each side—was enclosed by a massive outer wall. Those coming from the north— for example from the suburb of Bethesda—could enter by the north gate. The east wall overlooked the Kidron Valley. By way of what in later years was called the Golden Gate one was able from the temple area to cross the brook, and thus go to the Garden of Gethsemane, Bethany, and the Mount

GROUND PLAN OF THE TEMPLE
IN THE DAYS OF JESUS[537]

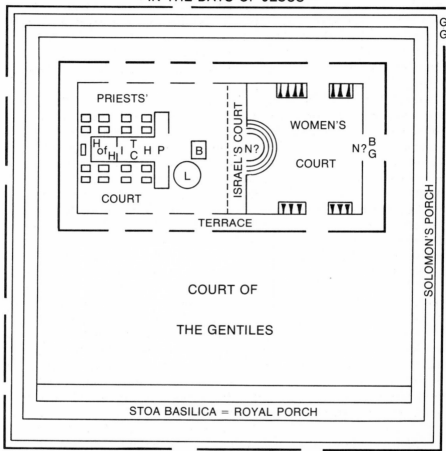

LOOKING NORTH

H = Holy Place with Table of
    Showbread, Incense Altar,
    and Candelabrum
H of H = Holy of Holies
B = Burntoffering Altar
L = Laver (Washbasin)

P = Porch

N? = Nicanor's Gate
    (location disputed)

B G = Beautiful Gate

G G = Golden Gate

of Olives; or vice versa. See Mark 11:1, 11; John 18:1. See also on Mark 11:16. Coming from the south—for example, from the Lower City—it was possible to reach the Court of the Gentiles by means of the two Gates of Huldah. One of these was a double, the other a triple gate. Of all the gates that led from or to the outside these were the most widely used. Finally, from the Upper City one was able, by means of the four western gates, to enter the temple area. Very useful also were the two bridges with which two of these western gates were linked. Their remnants have been preserved to this very day.

Lining the outer wall were rows of high pillars. Each consisted of a single block of pure white polished marble. On the east, west, and north there were three parallel rows of columns, on the south four. This meant that three sides had two parallel halls, while the Royal Porch, where according to tradition the palace of Solomon used to be, had three.

John 10:23 states, "It was winter, and Jesus was walking inside the temple, in Solomon's Porch (Portico or Colonnade)." This covered "porch" probably derived its name from the fact that of the temple which that king had built, this was in the days of Jesus the only remaining part. Cf. Acts 3:11; 5:12. It is understandable that the various ample and beautiful colonnades provided every opportunity for teaching (Mark 12:41-44 and parallels; Luke 19:47, etc.).

Beyond these colonnades—that is, farther away from the outside wall, there was the very spacious Court of the Gentiles, also extending all around. It was paved with variegated marble of the finest quality. This court was given its name because, though both Jews and Gentiles were welcome here, the latter were not allowed to proceed any farther toward the interior. In order to remind them of that restriction, the smaller area immediately enclosed by the Court of the Gentiles was surrounded by a 4½ ft. high balustrade furnished with slabs on which was written, both in Greek and in Latin, this warning:

---

537 The diagram gives *only the main features* of Herod's temple. No attempt has been made to picture the rooms lining the walls of the outer court, the additional equipment pertaining to the Priest's Court—such as the place of slaughter north of the altar, tables for preparing the sacrifices, drainage canal conducting the blood to the Kidron—and several other details. Also, there is no certainty with respect to the identity of each gate. This is especially true with respect to Nicanor's Gate, which by Edersheim and by Halberthal is placed west of the Women's Court, but by many others east of that court and identified with the Beautiful Gate.

The chief sources for our knowledge of Herod's temple, in addition to the New Testament references to it, are the Mishnaic tractate *Middoth* ("Measurements"); and Josephus, *Jewish War* V. 184-247, and *Jewish Antiquities* XV. 380-425. Also consulted were A. Edersheim, *The Temple*, London, 1908; L. Halberthal, *The Plan of the Holy Temple of Jerusalem*, Montreal, 1967; T. Kollek & M. Pearlman, *Jerusalem, A History of Forty Centuries*, New York, 1968; and several archaeological books and articles.

"Let no man of another nation enter inside the barrier and the fence around the temple. Whoever is caught will have himself to blame that his death follows."

For a picture of the recovered part of a slab with Greek lettering see Kollek and Pearlman, *op. cit.,* p. 124.

Proceeding westward from Solomon's Porch the person privileged to do so would, after crossing a portion of the Court of the Gentiles, via the Beautiful Gate enter the Women's Court. Men as well as women were allowed here. Just as "Court of the Gentiles" meant that Gentiles were not permitted any closer to the interior, so "Women's Court" was thus named in order to indicate that this was as far as women were allowed to go. It was equipped with large chambers and gave access to treasure vaults. Against the walls stood thirteen trumpet-shaped chests for gifts and dues. Mark 12:41-44 (cf. Luke 21:1-4); and John 8:20 come to mind at once.

Male Israelites were allowed to proceed even farther, namely, into "Israel's Court," a relatively narrow one. Between that and the "Priests' Court" there was only a low partition, so that by some authors these two are considered one.

It was the Priests' Court that encompassed the inner sanctuary with its Holy Place and Holy of Holies. To the east of it stood the very large altar of burnt-offering. Nearer to the sanctuary and a little farther to the south could be seen the laver, a colossal brazen reservoir that rested on the back of 12 big lions. Finally, there was the sanctuary itself. As to measurements, Josephus states that its ground floor "was 60 cubits in height, the same in length, and 20 cubits in breadth. But the 60 cubits of its length were again divided. The first portion [the Holy Place] was partitioned off at forty cubits . . . the innermost recess [Holy of Holies] measured 20 cubits."

This magnificent sanctuary must have been a marvelous sight to behold, since it was built of white marble, richly set off with gold on its front and sides. It was entered by means of a huge double-winged porch or vestibule, as indicated on the diagram. In front of the doorway to the Holy Place hung a beautifully colored Babylonian veil or curtain. There was also "the second veil," the one that separated the Holy Place from the Holy of Holies. See Matt. 27:51; Heb. 6:19; cf. 9:3; 10:20.

As it was during the old dispensation so also now, the Holy Place contained "A lampstand, a table, and an altar of incense," thus again Josephus, who adds, "But in this [that is, in the Holy of Holies] stood nothing at all. . . ." The candelabrum or seven-branched lampstand was among the temple treasures which by Titus and Vespasian were displayed in the triumphal procession which they conducted in Rome after the fall of Jerusalem, A.D. 70. See the picture in the aforementioned book, *Jerusalem, A History of Forty Centuries,* p. 131, and in many other sources.

I have purposely left to the last for special emphasis, one very important point, namely, *the height* of the various parts. Now before proceeding any further it is only proper to call attention to the fact that we cannot be entirely certain about the dimensions—mostly *length* and *breadth*—given thus far. The Bible furnishes no information on this point. Josephus and the Mishnaic tractate by no means always agree. It is not surprising, therefore, that the secondary sources—even our best textbooks—disagree among themselves on several points. See W. S. Caldecott and James Orr, *The Temple of Herod,* I.S.B.E., Vol. V. 2937-2940. The general picture is clear enough; conjecture—sometimes probable, sometimes improbable or at least fruitless—enters into the determination of many details. This holds also with respect to the *height* of the various parts.

With that reservation, it can now be pointed out that there were especially three features that made this temple unforgettable:

a. *Its vastness.*

From east to west or northwest the temple complex increased in height. From the Court of the Gentiles to that of Women there was an ascent of 14 steps; from there to the Court of Israel a rise of 15 steps. A few more upward steps would bring one to the Priests' Court; and 12 more, to the entrance of the sanctuary. Accordingly, highest of any of the buildings of this entire complex was "the temple" or "sanctuary." It soared high above the vast Court of the Gentiles. "Some of the stones in the building were forty-five cubits [67¼ feet] in length, five [7½] in height, and six [9] in breadth" (Josephus). The sanctuary, moreover, occupied the most elevated ground, and was buttressed by very formidable sub-structures. Its height was no less than sixty feet, instead of forty-five for the temple of Solomon (I Kings 6:2). To this should be added another sixty feet for the upper chamber that covered the entire sanctuary. The whole temple, with the exception of the porch, was covered with a gabled roof of cedar wood. "From its summit protruded sharp golden spikes to prevent birds from settling upon and polluting the roof" (Josephus).

From all this it follows that the best pictorial map of Herod's vast temple complex is the three-dimensional. See, for example, the reconstruction by the Comte de Vogue (*Jerusalem,* p. 100) or the Schick model, reproduced in several English and other language encyclopaedias and archaeological texts, or Lazar Halberthal's colorful drawing.

Vastness, by reminding man of his littleness, inspires awe.

b. *Its beauty.*

Says Josephus, "The exterior of the building lacked nothing that could astonish either the soul or the eyes. For, being covered on every side with massive plates of gold, the sun had no sooner risen than it radiated so fiery a flash that those straining to look at it were forced to avert their eyes as from

the solar rays. To approaching strangers it appeared from a distance like a snow-clad mountain, the reason being that whatever was not overlaid with gold was purest white" (*Jewish War* V.222). *Beauty is conducive to worship.*
　　c. *Its purpose.*

That purpose is clearly stated in I Kings 8:13, 31-61; 9:3; and especially in Isa. 56:7, for even though these passages pertain to the temple of *Solomon*, they clearly have meaning also with respect to the temple as it existed in the days of Jesus. Even the child Jesus called it "my Father's house" (Luke 2:49). And during his earthly ministry *Jesus, quoting from Isaiah, declared the temple to be a house of worship.* He said, "Is it not written: 'My house shall be called a house of prayer for all the nation. . . .' "

*　*　*　*　*

Jesus, then, has entered the Court of the Gentiles. What a sorry spectacle greets his eyes, ears, and even nostrils! He notices, as had happened also in the early part of his ministry, that this court, hence the temple, was being desecrated. It now resembled a market-place. Business was booming, lucrative too. Some men were selling oxen and sheep. At this time of the year, with Passover so close at hand and pilgrims crowding into the court from everywhere, there were many buyers. They paid high prices for these sacrificial animals. True, a worshipper could bring in an animal of his own choice. But if he did that he was taking a chance that it would not be approved. The temple merchants had paid generously for their concession, which they had bought from the priests. Some of this money finally reached the coffers of sly, wealthy Annas and of clever Caiaphas. It is therefore understandable that the tradesmen and the priestly caste were partners in this business. As Jesus enters he notices the hustle and bustle of all those buyers and sellers; also the noise, filth, and stench produced by all the animals. Could this, in any sense whatever, be called *worship?*

Notice "the buyers" and "the sellers." [538] This may be somewhat difficult to understand. *Sellers?* Yes, these were guilty of swindling the pilgrims, fleecing them. But why should the poor, innocent *buyers* be included in the number of those against whom the Lord vented his keen displeasure? The answer is probably as follows: these people were too docile. They were weaklings, like Eli. Cf. I Sam. 2:22-25; 3:13. They accepted conditions as they were. It was surely far more convenient to buy your animal in the court

---

[538] τοὺς πωλοῦντας καὶ τοὺς ἀγοράζοντας, masc. present active, acc. participles, respectively of πωλέω and ἀγοράζω; literally "the sellers and the buyers," where we would say "the buyers and the sellers." With ἀγοράζω cf. agora, forum, marketplace, and ἀγείρω to bring together. The ἀγορά is the place where *gregarious* individuals *congregate.* See also on 6:36, 37, footnote 279. For πωλέω see also on 10:21, footnote 478.

than to bring it along with you (Lev. 17:1-6; Jer. 17:26) and run the risk that it would fail to pass the official inspection. Consequently the seller's concession had become the buyer's convenience, and the receiver was about as bad as the (seller who in many cases because of the exorbitant price he charged was also the) deceiver. [539]

Among the buyers were pilgrims from countries far away. See John 12:20; Acts 2:5-13. They carried with them Greek, Roman, Egyptian, etc. currencies. But in the temple area foreign money was not accepted in payment. So in evidence were the money-changers, sitting cross-legged behind their little coin-covered tables. Also, the temple tax of half a shekel (Exod. 30:13; cf. Matt. 17:24-27) had to be paid in Jewish coin. And Jewish money was needed to fulfill the various rites of purification (Acts 21:24). So the money-changers would exchange foreign money for Jewish, charging a small fee for the favor. This business, too, was very profitable. It presented abundant opportunity for cheating the unsuspecting pilgrim.

It is not difficult to picture the righteous indignation that must have flashed from the eyes of Jesus when he drove out all who were engaged in this nefarious business, and overturned the tables of the money-changes and the seats of those selling doves. Whether also at this time, as in the first temple cleansing, he made a whip out of cords that were lying around and then let fly with that scourge, we do not know. One thing is certain: Jesus revealed himself as being indeed Lord of the temple (cf. Matt. 12:6).

In line with all this is Mark's added note: **16. And he would not allow anyone to carry** [540] **merchandise through the temple.** With the help of the diagram of Herod's temple and of the explanation that follows it, the meaning becomes clear. By means of the gates it had become rather easy and convenient to use the temple area as *a shortcut;* for example, between the city and the Mount of Olives. The sacred place was being used for a purely secular purpose. Did not even the rabbis disapprove of this? "What reverence is due to the temple? That no one go into the mountain of the house with his staff, shoes, purse, or dust on his feet. Let no one make a crossing through it, or degrade it into a place of spitting." [541] What Jesus saw was that for the sake of convenience worldly-minded people were carrying all kinds of "vessels"—objects used for profane purposes—through the temple area, thereby degrading it. Now if even the inhabitants of Europe's large cities resent seeing their cathedrals used as thoroughfares, and Americans place "No Through Traffic" signs at the entrance of some of their parks and

---

[539] Cf. the Dutch: de heler is net zo goed [of: slecht] als de steler.

[540] After $\dot{\eta}\phi\iota\epsilon$ (third per. sing. imperf. active of $\dot{\alpha}\phi\dot{\iota}\eta\mu\iota$) the infinitive would have been more usual than, as here, $\dot{\iota}\nu\alpha$ $\tau\iota\varsigma$ $\delta\iota\epsilon\nu\dot{\epsilon}\gamma\kappa\eta$ (third per. sing. aor. subj. of $\delta\iota\alpha\phi\dot{\epsilon}\rho\omega$).

[541] *Berakoth* IX.5.

university grounds, we can understand the wholly inappropriate character of the practice which Jesus here condemns.

The lesson here conveyed applies today as it did then. When the practice of "religion," so-called, becomes nothing but a means to what people are *really* interested in—such as convenience, social advancement, pecuniary gain, etc.—there is nothing left of genuine devotion. The "house of prayer" becomes a source of personal profit, not *real* profit, of course, but what is so regarded.

It is not surprising, therefore, to read, **17. He was teaching and saying to them, Is it not written:**

> **My house shall be called a house of prayer**
> **for all the nations?**

But y o u have made it a robbers' den. [542]

The quoted words are found in Isa. 56:7b. Their quotation in full—that is, including "for all the nations [or: peoples]"—is peculiar to Mark. It is clear from this that the temple was intended to be the place where God met with his people, a sanctuary for quiet, spiritual devotion, prayer, meditation, and fellowship, in connection with sacrifice. See I Kings 8:29, 30, 33; Ps. 27:4; 65:4; cf. I Sam. 1:9-18; Luke 18:10; Acts 3:1.

The second part of the statement is Christ's own comment, in which he contrasts the divine ideal for worship as described in Isa. 56:7b with the present situation, a condition that reminded him of Jer. 7:11, which he quotes. In the days of Jeremiah, too, as is proved by that prophet's famous Temple Discourse, the Jews were oppressing aliens, stealing, murdering, etc. Nevertheless, they continued to offer their sacrifices in the temple; as if such merely formalistic worship of Jehovah would do any good, and as if the very presence of the temple would protect them from the outpouring of God's wrath. It was then that Jeremiah had said, "Do not trust in lying words, saying, 'The temple of Jehovah, the temple of Jehovah, the temple of Jehovah is this,'.... Has this house that is called by my name become a den of robbers in y o u r eyes?" In the days of Christ's sojourn history was repeating itself: the temple had again become "a cave of thieves," an allusion, perhaps, to the rocky caves in the hills of Judea, where thieves and robbers would often assemble. The thieves were crowding out the Gentiles or "nations."

---

542 σπήλαιον, cave; here (robbers') den; in Rev. 6:15 the cave to which reference is made is a shelter in times of danger; in John 11:38, a tomb. Cf. *spelunker, speleologist*. The rendering "robber" or "highwayman" for ληστής suits the present context. So also in Matt. 21:13; Luke 10:30, 36; 19:46; John 10:1, 8; and II Cor. 11:26. Cf. Lucre. In the following passages the alternative meaning "revolutionary," "insurrectionist" is at least deserving of consideration: Matt. 26:55; 27:38, 44; Mark 14:48; 15:27; Luke 22:52; John 18:40.

The lessons taught by this cleansing of the temple can be summarized as follows:

a. Jesus punished degradation of religion and insisted on reverence.

b. He rebuked fraud, in the present connection especially "religious" (?) racketeering, and demanded honesty.

c. He frowned upon indifference toward those who desired to worship God in spirit and truth, and, by declaring that the temple must be a house of prayer *for all the nations,* gave his endorsement to the wonderful cause of Christian Missions. Cf. I Kings 8:41-43; Matt. 28:19.

d. By means of all this he glorified his heavenly Father. Was not the temple his Father's house?

If it be true that even in general vastness inspires *awe,* and beauty is conducive to *worship,* the conditions for awakening both of these feelings being amply present in the temple complex as has been shown, then all the more, in view of the fact that by the Lord this area had been specifically set aside for the purpose of *prayer and devotion,* it was not at all the proper place to conduct a business enterprise, a fraudulent one at that. So Jesus cleansed it.

The reaction of Christ's bitter opponents was as follows: **18. The chief priests and the scribes heard (this) and were looking for a way to kill him, for they were afraid of him because everybody was astonished at his teaching.** [543] Of course, an act as open and public as the cleansing of the temple could not remain hidden from the attention of the chief priests and the scribes, to which Luke adds "the leaders—or chief men—of the people." The entire Sanhedrin is deeply affected, is filled with vehement resentment. So these men now more than ever look for a way to bring about Jesus' death. But why do they not simply go right ahead, capture him, and kill him? Answer: because fear holds them in check, curtailing their actions against their enemy.

There must have been at least two reasons for this fear: *a.* the Hosannas of the crowds on the previous day, in honor of Jesus; and *b.* the astonishment of the people displayed as a result of his teaching. See Mark 14:49; cf. Matt.

---

543 Here, as often, Mark shows his great skill in the use of tenses. Note how the aor. ἤκουσαν, which simply records a fact, is followed by three imperfects: they were (continually) looking or seeking; they were fearing, were (constantly) afraid; and everybody—literally, the entire multitude—was being (constantly) struck with astonishment. For this last verb see on 1:22 and on 10:26. Note also πῶς followed by the (aor. active) deliberative subjunctive in an indirect question. The implied direct question was "How shall we destroy him?" It is true that ἐζήτουν can also be rendered "they began looking or seeking," but in view of 3:6 and several similar notices in the other Gospels, it is perhaps better not to introduce "began" at this point. After all, the search for a way to destroy Jesus had been going on for a long time, at least on the part of the Pharisees.

26:55; Luke 19:47; 20:1; 21:37. Note that not only in Galilee (Mark 1:22; cf. Matt. 7:28, 29) but also in Jerusalem the people were "knocked out of their senses" by the teaching of Jesus. And his enemies knew it! That is why they could not see their way clear to destroy him immediately. But they were looking for a way to change all this.

The present paragraph ends as follows: **19. And whenever evening arrived, they went out of the city.** [544] We know that Sunday evening Jesus and The Twelve had gone to Bethany (11:11). The day of the temple cleansing was Monday. That evening, too, Jesus went to Bethany and spent the night there (Matt. 21:17). The rendering "spent the night" is broad enough to leave room for either of two possibilities: *a.* He lodged with his friends in their hospitable home (see Mark 14:3; cf. Matt. 26:6-13; Luke 10:38-42; John 11:3; 12:1-8); or *b.* he spent the night under the stars somewhere in or near the village, perhaps on a slope of the Mount of Olives (see Luke 21:37).

It remains true that Sunday night, Monday night, and so also probably Tuesday night and Wednesday night, Jesus and his disciples went "out of the city," though it is impossible to be precise in every case. And did they not even go "out of the city" Thursday night? See John 13:30; 18:1, 3. Further speculation about the reason for these excursions from the city leads nowhere.

---

20 In the morning, as they were passing by, they saw the fig tree withered from the roots. 21 Peter remembered and said to him, "Rabbi, look! the fig tree you cursed has withered!" 22 In response Jesus said to them, "Have faith [545] in God! 23 I solemnly declare to y o u that whoever says to this mountain, 'Be lifted up and thrown into the sea,' and does not doubt in his heart but believes that what he says will happen, it will indeed be done for him. 24 Therefore I tell y o u, whatever y o u ask for in prayer, believing that y o u received it, it shall be y o u r s. 25 And whenever y o u stand praying, forgive if y o u have anything against anyone, that y o u r Father who (is) in heaven may also forgive y o u y o u r trespasses." [546]

11:20-25 *The Lesson from the Withered Fig Tree*
Cf. Matt. 21:20-22

Mark devotes six verses to this lesson, Matthew only three. It is Mark alone who makes clear that what is here reported occurred on Tuesday of

---

544 The imperfect ἐξεπορεύοντο, "they were going out of," or "they would go out of" favors the more usual rendering of ὅταν, namely, "whenever." The use of the aor. (instead of the imperfect) indicative ἐγένετο after ὅταν is somewhat irregular, but creates no serious problem.

545 Another reading has, "If y o u have faith . . ."

546 There is insufficient textual support for verse 26 "But if y o u do not forgive, neither will y o u r Father who (is) in heaven forgive y o u r trespasses." But see Matt. 6:15.

the Passion Week. What in Matthew is a question asked by the disciples ("How did the fig tree wither at once?") is in Mark an exclamation uttered by Peter ("Rabbi, look! the fig tree you cursed has withered!"). This presents no problem, since it is natural to assume that one disciple expressed his surprise in one way, another in a different manner. Christ's promise that by faith a person will be able to remove a mountain is found in both accounts, but most fully in Mark. To the assurance of answered prayer, also found in both Gospels, Mark adds that Jesus on the present occasion (as earlier, cf. Matt. 6:14) taught that the heart that prays must be filled with the love that forgives.

20. In the morning, as they were passing by, they saw the fig tree withered from the roots. It is now Tuesday morning. It was probably very early, for ever so many things were going to happen on that busy day. In Mark the record of Tuesday's events covers 11:20–14:2.

This morning, then, on their way back to the city the disciples notice that the fig tree on which only yesterday Jesus had pronounced a solemn sentence of doom was now irretrievably ruined. It was permanently withered, [547] all the way from the roots up; hence, "withered root and branch" (E. V. Rieu's translation).

21. Peter remembered and said to him, Rabbi, look! the fig tree you cursed has withered! Peter remembered. [548] With respect to Peter's ability to recall a word or a deed see also 14:72. The tradition according to which Mark was Peter's interpreter, thus explaining how it was possible for this evangelist even to record what went on in Peter's mind, seems to find some support here. Peter, then, recalled what had happened on the previous day with respect to this tree. As he had done previously (9:5), so also now this apostle uses the title "Rabbi" [549] in addressing Jesus. See also Matt. 26:25, 49; Mark 10:51; 14:45; John 1:50; 4:31; 6:25; 9:2; 11:8. This Semitic word is by John popularly interpreted as amounting to "Teacher." See John 1:38; 3:2. See also what Jesus says about its use (Matt. 23:7, 8). It was a title of respect originally reserved for highly honored teachers. On one recorded occasion even John the Baptist was addressed in this manner (John 3:26).

What astonished Peter—and the other disciples (Matt. 21:20)—, so that he says, "Rabbi, look!" [550] was the fact that in such a very short time,

---

547 For ἐξηραμμένην (acc. sing. fem. perf. pass. participle) here in verse 20, and for ἐξήρανται (third per. sing. perf. pass. indic. in verse 21), forms based on ξηραίνω, see on 9:18, footnote 401.

548 ἀναμνησθείς nom. sing. masc. aor. pass. participle of ἀναμιμνήσκω.

549 The word is derived from *rabh*, meaning "great one," "lord," "master." The basic meaning of *rabbi* is accordingly "my master," but the full force of this "my" was not always retained.

550 For ἴδε see on 2:24, footnote 91.

probably within twenty-four hours, the tree on which Jesus had pronounced his curse [551] had changed from a seemingly vigorous woody perennial in full foliage, to a shrunken corpse, the ghost of its former self. Not that Peter blamed Jesus for what he had done to the tree, [552] but, as the immediately following verse implies, he was unable to understand how it had been possible to bring about such a radical change, and that within so short a time.

22, 23. In response Jesus said to them, Have faith in God! [553]

For such responding when no question is asked see on verse 14.

"Have faith in God." The tense used in the original shows that abiding faith is meant. Cf. "Fear not, only believe!" (Mark 5:36; and see also John 3:16). [554]

But what is faith?

Faith is:

The soul's window through which God's love comes pouring in.

The open hand whereby man reaches out to God, the Giver.

The coupling that links man's train to God's engine.

The trunk of salvation's tree, whose root is grace, and whose fruit is good works.

Faith was:

The means of Abraham's justification.

The magnet that drew Moses away from the pleasures of Egypt, so that he threw in his lot with God's sorely afflicted people.

The force that overthrew Jericho's wall.

The secret that enabled Ruth to make her stirring confession.

The weapon that killed Goliath and destroyed Sennacherib's host.

The deciding factor in Carmel's contest.

The shield that protected Job in the midst of his trials.

---

[551] κατηράσω sec. per. sing. aor. indic. of καταράομαι.

[552] Cf. A. T. Robertson, *Word Pictures* I, p. 361: "It almost sounds as if. . . ."

[553] There is little substantial difference between "Have faith in God!" and the other reading, namely, "If y o u have faith in God. . . ." Though it is true that the former is an emphatic exhortation, and the latter a kind of prediction as to what is going to happen when the condition—namely, faith—is present, is not the exhortation implied even in the condition? For the rest, the comparative weight of the Greek manuscripts is about even. The possibility that the words, "If y o u have faith" were inserted by a scribe who remembered Matt. 17:20; 21:21; Luke 17:6, must not be overlooked. See also Vincent Taylor, *op. cit.*, p. 466. The order of the Greek words—different in Mark 11:22 than in Matt. 21:21—would seem to lend additional support to the reading adopted by almost all translators and interpreters. The most recent English translation, namely, NIV, also favors ἔχετε πίστιν θεοῦ, and translates, "Have faith in God."

[554] Note that ἔχετε πίστιν is here (Mark 11:22) followed by the objective genitive. In view of Rom. 3:22, 26 this is not strange.

The muzzle that closed the mouths of Daniel's lions.
The remedy that cured the centurion's servant and many others.

See the following passages: (respectively Gen. 15:6; Exod. 2:10, 11 ff. (cf. Heb. 11:24-26); Josh. 6:20 (cf. Heb. 11:30); Ruth 1:16, 17; I Sam. 17:45-47 and II Kings 19:14-37; I Kings 18:30-40; Job 19:23-27; Dan. 6:19-23; Matt. 8:10, 13.

Scripture also describes faith as:
Leaning on the everlasting arms.
Committing one's way to the Lord, trusting in him, knowing that he will do whatever is best.
Receiving the kingdom (or rule) of God as a little child.
Being sure of what we hope for, and being convinced of what we do not see.
The victory that overcomes the world.

For these see the following: Deut. 33:27; Ps. 37:5; Mark 10:15; Heb. 11:1; I John 5:4.
Continued: **I solemnly declare to y o u that whoever says to this mountain, Be lifted up and thrown into the sea, and does not doubt in his heart but believes that what he says will happen, it will indeed be done for him.**
For "I solemnly declare" see on 3:28. "This mountain" is the Mount of Olives; "the sea" is the Dead Sea. For this mountain literally to be lifted up and cast [555] into the sea would mean a sudden plunge of about 4,000 feet altogether. Now there would be no sense in even trying, by faith concentration, to dump Olivet into the sea. The dramatic figure, in the light of its context, which speaks of *faith* and *prayer*, must mean, therefore, that no task in harmony with God's will is impossible to be performed by those who believe and do not doubt. [556] Cf. Matt. 17:20; 21:21; Luke 17:6.
Other arguments in confirmation of the explanation here given are the following: *a.* Christ's frequent use of figurative language, examples of which occur also in Mark's Gospel (1:17; 2:20-22; 3:33-35; 5:39; 7:27; 8:15; 9:12, 13; 9:43, 45; 10:38, 39); *b.* the well-known figure of speech found in Zech. 4:7, "What are you, O great mountain? Before Zerubbabel you shall become a plain," referring to a mountain of difficulties that would disappear; and *c.* the words which immediately follow (in Mark 11:24).
We should not try in any way whatever to minimize the force of this saying and to subtract from its meaning. Both in the physical and in the

---

555 Ἄρθητι καὶ βλήθητι are sec. per. sing. aor. imperat. passives of (respectively) αἴρω and βάλλω.
556 διακριθῇ third per. sing. aor. pass. subjunctive of διακρίνω: to be of a divided mind, at odds with oneself. Cf. Matt. 21:21; Rom. 4:20; James 1:6; etc.

spiritual sphere the apostles had already been doing things that would have been considered just as "impossible" as causing a mountain to be lifted up and thrown into the sea. Had not Peter "by faith" walked on the water? See Matt. 14:29. Did not The Twelve exclaim, "Lord, even the demons are subject to us in thy name"? (Luke 10:17). A few days later was not Jesus going to promise, "I most solemnly assure y o u, he who believes in me, the works that I do will he do also, and greater (works) than these will he do, because I am going to the Father" (John 14:12)? See also Acts 2:41; 3:6-9, 16; 5:12-16; 9:36-43; 19:11, 12. In fact does not the entire book of Acts prove that what Jesus said here in Mark 11:22, 23 was true?

This also applies to verse 24. **Therefore I tell y o u, whatever y o u ask for in prayer, believing that y o u received it, it shall be y o u r s.** Several matters require our attention:

a. It is immediately apparent that verse 24 closely parallels verse 23.

Compare:

Verse 23	Verse 24
I solemnly declare to y o u	Therefore I tell y o u
whoever	whatever
does not doubt but believes	believing that y o u received it
it shall indeed be done for him	it shall be y o u r s

Hence, since verse 23 is true, "therefore" verse 24 is also true. In general the meaning of the two verses is the same.

b. In one respect the thought expressed in verse 24 is even stronger than that contained in verse 23: the person described in verse 23 believes that *what he says is going to happen;* those pictured in verse 24 are so very sure of answer to prayer that as far as they are concerned *it has already happened: they have already received* [557] it.

c. "Whatever y o u ask for in prayer" is a free rendering of what is literally "whatever y o u *pray* [or: continue to pray] for and *ask* [or: continue to ask] for." Though it is true that the first of these two verbs is generally used for prayer addressed to God, while the second is more general, that distinction is hardly relevant in the present case. If there be any distinction at all, "pray" might be considered the more general term, and "ask" might be viewed as calling attention to the several humble petitions

---

[557] Note ἐλάβετε, sec. per. pl. aor. act. indic. of λαμβάνω. For something similar see Jonah 2:9, 10; John 15:6. On the basis of the evidence of the Greek manuscripts, Grk. N.T. (A-B-M-W) ascribes a "virtually certain" value to this text—that is, to ἐλάβετε in preference to λαμβάνετε. I agree with this judgment. Also in agreement, though with slightly varying renderings, are Goodspeed, Weymouth, Williams, Beck, Berkeley, N.A.S., Jerusalem Bible, Dutch (Nieuwe Vertaling), etc. Vincent Taylor accepted it; A. T. Robertson prefers it, though he does mention a possible alternative.

that pertain to prayer. But here the two are virtually one (on the order of hendiadys); hence, "ask for in prayer."

d. If the promise of Christ, "Whatever y o u ask for . . . it shall be y o u r s" seems almost unbelievable, it should be borne in mind that such praying and asking must, of course, be in harmony with the characteristics of true prayer which Jesus reveals elsewhere; in fact, it must be in line with all of scriptural teaching. Accordingly it must be the expression of:

humble, childlike trust; note *"believing* that y o u received it," and cf. Mark 10:15; also Matt. 7:11; 18:3, 4; James 1:6.

a sincere heart and mind (Mark 12:40; cf. Matt. 6:5).

a will to persevere (Mark 13:13b; cf. Matt. 7:7; Luke 18:1-8).

a love for all concerned (Mark 12:31, 33; cf. Matt. 5:43-48; Luke 6:32-36).

submission to God's sovereign will (Mark 14:36b; Matt. 6:10b; 26:39).

This also implies that such praying is "in Christ's name," that is, it is in harmony with all that Jesus has revealed concerning himself and it rests on his merits (Mark 9:37, 41; cf. John 15:16; 16:23, 24; Eph. 4:32; 5:20; Col. 3:17).

Prayer is effective and pleasing to God only when it issues from a loving heart. This is emphasized in the passage that concludes this paragraph: **25. And whenever** [558] **y o u stand praying. . . .**

Note the following:

a. This passage strongly reminds one of the fifth petition of the Lord's Prayer, Matt. 6:12, "And forgive us our debts as we also have forgiven our debtors." See also 6:14, "For if y o u forgive men their trespasses, y o u r heavenly Father will also forgive you." There is absolutely no reason why Jesus could not have repeated here and now, in a slightly different form, what he had taught the disciples and the people in general on a previous occasion. This all the more so because by nature the sinner is disinclined to forgive. He has to be reminded of this again and again. Hence, see also Matt. 18:21-35.

---

[558] Should ὅταν here be rendered "when" or "whenever"? There is a difference of opinion with respect to this. It is impossible always to draw a sharp distinction between ὅταν and ὅτε; and even between "whenever" and "when." It is probably correct to say that when the intended meaning is definitely "whenever," the most normal Greek equivalent would be ὅταν, but this does not necessarily mean that ὅταν must *always* be rendered "whenever." See, for example, Rev. 8:1. Note also that here (Mark 11:25), as also in 3:11; 11:19, ὅταν is followed by the indicative instead of by the expected subjunctive. One way to explain this would be to say that Jesus conceives of these actions—such as standing to pray—as certain to happen, not just possible. A fact that must be borne in mind, however, is that certain fine distinctions have a tendency gradually to disappear; for example, the connection between compounds in ἀν—such as ὅταν—and the subjunctive is gradually weakening. See Vincent Taylor, *op. cit.*, p. 228.

b. "Whenever y o u stand praying . . . ." For the people of Bible times *to stand* praying was not at all unusual. In addition to the present passage see also Gen. 18:22; II Sam. 1:26; I Kings 8:22; Neh. 9:4; Matt. 6:5.

There was a vast difference between two men who prayed, as described in the parable of The Pharisee and the Tax Collector. See Luke 18:9-14. In at least one respect, however, they resembled each other: both stood up to pray. [559] Since the standing posture indicates reverence and promotes alertness, no objection can be raised against it.

But it is by no means the only prayer posture mentioned in Scripture. There is also kneeling, and there are other postures. For a summary of several, all of them appropriate, see N.T.C. on I and II Timothy and Titus, pp. 103-105.

c. Not the posture of the body but the attitude of heart and mind is what matters most of all. That is why Jesus continues: **forgive if y o u have anything against anyone, that y o u r Father who (is) in heaven may also forgive y o u y o u r trespasses.** As was pointed out above, in connection with verse 24 (see under d.), effective prayer presupposes a loving heart. The person who prays must be willing and anxious to forgive. If he lacks this disposition he has no right to assume that his own trespasses have been forgiven.

Though in the teaching not only of Paul (Rom. 3:24; Eph. 2:8; Titus 3:5) but certainly also of Christ (Matt. 5:1-6; 18:27; Luke 18:13; John 3:3, 5) salvation rests not on human accomplishments but solely on the grace and mercy of God, this does not mean that there is nothing to do for those who receive it. They must believe. Included in this faith is the eagerness to forgive. [560]

It is "y o u r Father who is in heaven" who pardons, on the basis of the Son's atonement (Eph. 4:32). Does not the very phrase "*y o u r* Father" indicate: "Think of all the blessings y o u constantly receive from him? Therefore, should not y o u r hearts also go out to those who may have injured y o u?"

d. Note "y o u r trespasses." Trespasses are deviations from the path of truth and righteousness. In committing them one *falls aside* from the path of duty. A trespass is, accordingly, a misstep. [561] Now whether these deviations are of a milder character, as in Gal. 6:1 and perhaps also Rom. 5:15, 17, 18,

---

559 The author of this commentary remembers distinctly how, when he was a child, the *men* who entered the church in order to attend the worship service, would stand up to pray silently. The prayer finished, they would sit down. I understand that in certain communities this is still the custom.

560 ἄφετε, sec. per. pl. pres. imperat. active; here in the sense of forgive. Cf. Mark 2:5.

561 On παράπτωμα see R. C. Trench *op. cit.*, par. lxvi.

or whether they are far more serious, as in Eph. 1:7; 2:1, they must be forgiven. Note, moreover, "if y o u have anything against *anyone*. . . ." Though it is probably correct to believe that Jesus was thinking first of all of the brotherhood (see Matt. 18:15-17), a comparison with Matt. 6:14—"forgive *men* their trespasses"—indicates that forgiveness must be extended also to "outsiders." Did not Jesus do the same? See Luke 23:34. And Stephen? (Acts 7:60. Cf. Eph. 5:1, 2).

Putting together all that we have learned about the fruitless fig tree (11:12-14, 20-25) we now know that:

a. Fruitlessness invites the curse (11:12-14).

b. Genuine *faith* results in answered prayer (11:20-23).

c. Therefore such faith inspires *hope,* firmly entrenched in God's infallible promise (11:24).

d. It is climaxed by *love,* which implies the forgiving spirit (11:25).

---

27 They came again to Jerusalem. And while he was walking in the temple, the chief priests and the scribes and the elders came to him, saying, 28 "By what authority are you doing these things, and who gave you the authority to do them?" 29 Jesus replied, "I have a single question to ask y o u. Answer me, and I will tell y o u by what authority I do these things: 30 The baptism of John, was it from heaven or from men? Answer me." 31 They were reasoning among themselves, "If we say, From heaven, he will say to us, Why, then, did y o u not believe him? 32 But if we say, From men. . . ." They were afraid of the people, for they all held that John was really a prophet. 33 So they answered Jesus, "We do not know." Jesus told them, "Neither do I tell y o u by what authority I do these things."

11:27-33 *Christ's Authority: Question and Counter-Question*
Cf. Matt. 21:23-27; Luke 20:1-8

The similarity between the three accounts is very striking. The main differences, none of them essential, are as follows: According to Mark the authority of Jesus was questioned while he was walking in the temple; according to Matthew, when he had entered the temple and was teaching there; and according to Luke, as he was teaching the people in the temple. All three report that Jesus was questioned by the chief priests and the elders. Mark and Luke add the scribes. The words of Jesus, "Answer me, and I will tell y o u by what authority I do these things," nearly identical in Mark and Matthew, are omitted by Luke.

For the rest, what is by many considered Mark's somewhat "rough" style—shall we call it "simple," "popular," "natural"?—is not found in Matthew and/or Luke's account. This is particularly noticeable with respect to Mark 11:32, where that evangelist does not finish his sentence. How often does not the same thing happen even today, especially in popular

463

speech? [562] Here Matthew completes the sentence by adding the words, " . . . we are afraid of the people, for they all consider John a prophet," which expression at least *implies* a conclusion. Luke, even more smoothly, adds, "all the people will stone us." [563]

The opinion would therefore seem to be warranted that there is a literary relationship between the three accounts, and that Mark's account was the earliest. [564] Fully inspired by the Holy Spirit, each evangelist, using his own style, brings us the wonderful words of life.

27, 28. They came again to Jerusalem. And while he was walking in the temple, the chief priests and the scribes and the elders came to him, saying, By what authority are you doing these things, and who gave you the authority to do them? It will be recalled that Jesus had entered the temple on the Sunday evening after the triumphal entry (verse 11), and again on Monday (verse 15), when he cleansed it. And now, Tuesday morning, Jesus, having arrived in Jerusalem, again enters the temple. We find him perhaps in the Stoa Basilica or (as in John 10:23) in Solomon's Porch. See the diagram. He is surrounded by a group of people and is teaching them. Then he walks a little farther, when another group is ready to be instructed. Or, he may even have taught as he walked. Cf. Zeno and Aristotle. While this teaching and walking was going on his opponents were approaching. Did they wait until he was through teaching? One thing is certain: these men are in an angry mood.

Who are they? Three groups are mentioned: the chief priests and the scribes and the elders, the three component parts of the Sanhedrin. See also 8:31. *The chief priests* constituted a group or order consisting of the present ruling highpriest, those who had formerly occupied this high office, and other dignitaries from whose ranks the highpriest was generally selected. The custody of the temple had been entrusted to these people, mostly Sadducees. It is not strange that *the scribes,* mostly Pharisees, are also men-

---

562 And see also Exod. 32:32; Eph. 2:1.

563 Also fitting into this pattern of smoother style in Matthew and Luke are the following items:

a. Where Mark (11:31) begins the sentence with a simple καί, both Matthew (21:25) and Luke (20:5) have οἱ δέ. See above, Introduction IV, footnote 5, under *e.*

b. Where Mark, at the beginning of 11:32, has ἀλλά, both Matthew (21:26) and Luke (20:6) have ἐὰν δέ.

c. Instead of Mark's direct discourse, "We do not know" (11:33), found also in Matthew (21:27), Luke quotes these words indirectly, by the use of an infinite (20:7). Cf. Introduction IV, footnote 5, under *g.*

d. In harmony with what was said in the Introduction IV, footnote 5 under *d.,* and on verse 7 above, footnote 528, note Mark's historical presents in 11:33. Neither Matthew (21:27) nor Luke (20:8) has them.

564 Thus also Vincent Taylor, *op. cit.,* p. 471. And see N.T.C. on Matthew, pp. 36-47.

tioned, for these were the men who studied, interpreted, and taught the law. Their teaching was done in both temple and synagogue. *The elders,* too, were present. In ancient Israel an elder was the head of a tribe or of a tribal division. In fact, every city or town of any importance soon had its ruling elders. With the establishment of the Sanhedrin the more prominent local elders became members of this august body. We might call them the Sanhedrin's "lay members."

In the abstract it is possible that in approaching—and by implication *re*proaching—Jesus, all these men acted independently and unofficially. Far more reasonable, however, is the assumption that they acted in an official capacity, having been delegated by the Sanhedrin.

Their question is clear. They want to know by what authority Jesus was doing these things, that is, who had given him this right. They were saying, "Show us your credentials!" It was an attempt to embarrass Jesus. If he admitted that he had no credentials the people could be expected to lose respect for him. On the other hand, if he considered himself authorized to do the things he had been doing, was he not arrogating to himself rights that belonged only to God? Could he not then be accused of being guilty of blasphemous behavior? By not assaulting him directly, for example by having him arrested, they reveal that they are afraid of him because of his following.

But what do they mean by "these things"? They must have been referring to recent or present activities, that is, to things he had done on Sunday or on Monday, or to what he was doing on this Tuesday. Among commentators there is general agreement that the cleansing of the temple was included in "these things." This opinion is undoubtedly correct (cf. John 2:18). But was this the only thing to which these enemies of Jesus referred? There is a wide difference of opinion among commentators. Some would include Sunday's royal entry into Jerusalem. Others say, "No," for the ovation he received at that time was not his own doing. Over against this stands the fact that he did not at all oppose the hosannas of his disciples and of the children (see Matt. 21:16; Luke 19:39, 40). The royal entry may therefore have been included in "these things." And if we bear in mind the fact that Christ's enemies ascribed his miracles to the power of Beelzebul operative within him, even the deeds of kindness to the blind and the lame (Matt. 21:14) may have been included. So was also Christ's teaching and gospel preaching in the temple (Luke 20:1, 2).

29, 30. Jesus replied, I have a single question to ask y o u. Answer me, and I will tell y o u by what authority I do these things: The baptism of John, was it from heaven or from men? Answer me.

Note: a *single* question. Theirs had been a *double* one.

When a person is verbally attacked—whether directly or, as in verse 28, by implication—, he often denies the charge, downgrades the crime, starts arguing, or produces an accusation. There are times when the best thing to do would be to admit the wrong, ask forgiveness, and make amends. For Jesus this was, of course, entirely out of the question, for he had committed no wrong.

What then? At times a charge can be effectively met by complete silence, or perhaps by a counter-charge, or, as in the present case, by a counter-question.

It has been pointed out by several interpreters that the method of answering a question by means of a counter-question was rather common in rabbinical discussions. *True, but when Jesus employs this method he in every instance vanquishes his opponents,* and *this* certainly was not true with respect to rabbis in general.

To see for himself that the statement just made is true, let the reader view the following Marcan accounts. In each of them Christ's opponents attack him, sometimes directly, then again in a veiled manner, by half-concealing their disgust inside the wrapper of a question. In each case Jesus crushes their attack. Also, his answer, *in each of these cases,* begins with a counter-question.

The opponents' attack	*Jesus' answer*
2:7	2:8-10
2:18	2:19-22
2:24	2:25-28
3:22	3:23-30
8:11	8:12, 13
10:2	10:3-12
11:27, 28	11:29-33
12:18-23	12:24-27

The same point can be established by a study of the other Gospels. And as to Mark, here again Jesus Christ stands forth as the Conquering King. See 12:34b. Let everyone submit willingly and eagerly to his rule! See Introduction III.

Now by means of the counter-question—"The baptism of John, was it from heaven or from men?"—Jesus was by no means evading the question that had been asked him, for an honest and correct answer to *his* question would unmistakably have pointed to himself as the Greater One whom John had proclaimed, and would therefore have meant that Jesus' right or authority to do these things had come from God. It was while John was baptizing that he had proclaimed Jesus as being his superior (1:4-7; cf. John 1:26, 27), and it was soon after the Lord's baptism by John that the latter had described Jesus as "the Lamb of God who is taking away the sin of the world" (John 1:29).

By means of Christ's question his enemies had been driven into a corner. Obviously they did not want to answer, "The baptism of John had a heavenly source," for they knew very well that the reply would be, "Why, then, did y o u not believe him?" On the other hand, were they to come out with what was probably that which most of them believed, or at least wanted to believe, namely, that the baptism of John was from men, the general public—perhaps especially the crowds of pilgrims that had come from Galilee—would become definitely hostile toward them, and might even stone them (Luke 20:6). Did not these people consider John a prophet? So these dignitaries start reasoning among themselves as to what to answer. Their decision was dishonest, though not surprising. They do not say, "We don't want to answer that question," which would at least have been honest, but "We do not know."

Having given this background, verses 31-33 require little further explanation: 31-33. **They were reasoning**[565] **among themselves, If we say,**[566] **From heaven,**[567] **he will say to us, Why, then, did y o u not believe him? But if we say From men.... They were afraid of the people, for they all held**[568] **that John was really**[569] **a prophet. So they answered Jesus, We do not know. Jesus told them, Neither do I tell y o u by what authority I do these things.**

An important practical lesson is taught here. Christ's opponents failed to see the truth because they hardened themselves against it. The reason why many people know so little about Jesus and about the joy of living the Christian life is that they refuse to submit themselves to his will. "An increasing knowledge of divine truth is conditioned upon humble submission of the heart and the will, to what has already been revealed" (C. R. Erdman, *op. cit.*, p. 163). Or, if one prefers, a person's epistemology depends on his theology. See John 7:17. The prayer of everyone should be: "Teach me to do thy will, for thou art my God" (Ps. 143:10).

---

565 διελογίζοντο, third per. pl. imperf. indic. of διαλογίζομαι. See on 2:6, 8; 8:16; 9:33 (footnote 423).

566 third class condition: ἐάν with aor. act. subjunctive in the protasis; aor. indic. in the apodosis.

567 From heaven = from God.

568 εἶχον, third per. pl. imperf. indic. of ἔχω, where Matt. 21:26 (direct discourse) has the present. See also Matt. 14:5; 21:46; Luke 14:18, 19; John 7:17; and Phil. 2:29. Everywhere, in these passages, the meaning is: to hold, regard, consider.

569 ὄντως, adverb based on εἰμί. The meaning is *really, actually.*

467

Summary of Chapter 11

Sunday: Christ's triumphal entry into Jerusalem. The week of the Passion begins here (verses 1-11). Jesus sends two of his disciples to a little village to fetch a colt. His predictions regarding this animal and its owners are literally fulfilled. Over it the disciples cast their outer garments and on it Jesus takes his seat. As he rides triumphantly toward and into Jerusalem, multitudes, the minds of many filled with anticipations of earthly glory, welcome him with wild enthusiasm, shouting hosannas. After a quick evening visit to the temple, Jesus and his disciples retire to Bethany.

Monday: The *cursing* of the fig tree occurred in the morning of this day (verses 12-14). Jesus was hungry. Though it was not yet the season for figs, this particular tree, growing by the side of the road, looked promising. It was in full foliage, indicating that it might at least have some early figs. But when Jesus went up to it he saw that it had nothing but leaves. So, in the hearing of his disciples, he cursed it, saying, "Never again may anyone eat fruit from you."

On that same day, upon entering the temple, Jesus noticed that its great outer court had been turned into a market-place. So he cleansed it, driving out both those who were selling and those who were buying (verses 15-19). He overturned the tables of the money-changers and the seats of those who sold doves. He refused to permit anyone to use the temple as a short-cut for travel. He said (quoting Isa. 56:7), "Is it not written: 'My house shall be called a house of prayer for all the nations?" He added, "But y o u made it a robbers' den."

By means of what the Lord did to the tree and to the temple he was predicting Israel's fall. The leaders of the Jews were very angry and were looking for an opportunity to kill him. But because of the crowds, who "were astonished at his teaching," the bitter adversaries could not see their way clear to kill him immediately.—Whenever evening arrived, Jesus and The Twelve went out of the city.

Tuesday: The *lesson* from the withered fig tree is found in verses 20-25. When the disciples, on their way back to the city noticed that the tree that had been cursed was withered root and branch, Peter, as spokesman for the rest, expressed his astonishment. Jesus assures The Twelve that no task performed in harmony with God's will is impossible for those whose faith does not waver. This faith, to be genuine, must express itself in love that is willing to forgive.

A little later this same day Jesus' authority to cleanse the temple, etc., is challenged by the Sanhedrin's representatives (verses 27-33). They ask a *double* question: *a.* "By what authority are you doing these things, and *b.* Who gave you the authority to do them?" In return, Jesus asks a *single* question, namely, "the baptism of John, was it from heaven or from men?" Jesus is referring to John's ministry, an outstanding feature of which was his baptizing. This question embarrassed Christ's opponents. They realized that the very One whom they were trying to destroy had been enthusiastically acclaimed by John. So, if they now answered "from heaven," the rejoinder would be, "Why, then, did y o u not believe him?" If they answered "from men" they feared that the people might harm—even stone (Luke)—them, for by the masses John was regarded as having been a genuine prophet. So they answered, "We do not know." Jesus told them, "Neither do I tell y o u by what authority I do these things.

Outline of Chapter 12

Theme: *The Work Which Thou Gavest Me To Do*

12:1-12   The Parable of the Wicked Tenants, and Its Sequel
12:13-37   Captious Questions and Authoritative Answers
                              also
                    Christ's Own Question
12:38-40   Denunciation of the Scribes
12:41-44   A Widow's Offering

CHAPTER XII

12   1 He began to speak to them in parables:

"A man planted a vineyard, He set a fence around it, dug a trough for the winepress, and built a tower. Then he leased the vineyard to sharecroppers, [570] and went abroad. 2 At the proper time he sent a servant to the sharecroppers to collect from them his share of the vineyard's fruit. 3 But they seized him, beat him and sent him away empty-handed. 4 Then he sent another servant to them. They struck him on the head and treated him shamefully. 5 He sent still another, and that one they killed. He sent many others; some of them they beat, others they killed. 6 He had still one other, a beloved son. He sent him last of all, saying, 'They will have regard for my son.' 7 But those sharecroppers said to each other, 'He is the heir; come on, let's kill him, and the inheritance will be ours!' 8 So they took him and killed him, and cast him out of the vineyard. 9 What then will the owner of the vineyard do? He will come and kill those sharecroppers and give the vineyard to others. 10 Have y o u never read this passage of Scripture:

> 'The stone which the builders rejected
> This became the cornerstone;
> 11 By the Lord was this done;
> And it is wonderful in our eyes'?"

12 And they were trying to arrest him, for they knew that he had spoken this parable against them. But they were afraid of the crowd. So they left him and went away.

12:1-12 *The Parable of the Wicked Tenants,*
and Its Sequel
Cf. Matt. 21:33-46; Luke 20:9-19

In its main traits the parable is the same in all three Synoptics. The minor differences present no real conflicts. The most important variations in telling the story are as follows:

a. Luke abbreviates, as he often does. He omits any mention of fence, winepress, and tower. On the other hand, he does mention one fact not found in the others: the owner of the vineyard, having gone abroad, *stays away a long time.*

b. In Matthew the servants are represented as being sent group by group;

---

570 Or "tenants"; literally "workers of the soil."

in Mark and Luke singly. However, here again we must figure with the fact that Luke abbreviates. Besides, the one servant of Mark and Luke may represent a group. And Mark also recognizes group sending ("He sent many others").

c. In Matthew and Luke what happens to the son is described as follows: "They cast him out of the vineyard and killed him." In Mark the order is reversed (". . . killed him and cast him out of the vineyard"). In other words, Matthew and Luke are giving us the historical order; Mark, the climactic, as if to say, "They killed him, and this in a most shameful manner, casting him out of the vineyard as an accursed one." Again, there is no contradiction or conflict.

d. In Matthew the question, "What will the owner of the vineyard do to these sharecroppers?" is answered by the audience, Jesus himself—as the subsequent context shows—being in thorough agreement with the answer given. Hence, in the other two Synoptics the answer is described as Christ's own. Well, it was!

e. In Luke the doom pronounced on the wicked sharecroppers evokes the audience's response, "God forbid!" Also, the passage which in Matt. 21:44 (A.V.) is probably unauthentic is authentic in Luke 20:18.

Interesting variation amid essential unity. Inspiration all along the line!

1. **He began to speak to them in parables.** Jesus was in the temple. Cf. 11:27, 28. It is still Tuesday. In fact it was probably still rather early in the day, closer to the time indicated in 11:20 than to that implied in 13:1. It will be recalled that Christ's opponents had asked him to give an account of his actions. They resolutely refused to acknowledge his greatness and authority. For such people the parabolic form of teaching had special significance. At the same time it was adapted to the needs of his true followers. See above, on 4:11, 12.

Mark uses the plural: parables. Yet in the present connection he records only one, the one about the vineyard, clearly based on Isa. 5:1-7. Matthew, on the other hand, in 21:28–22:14 presents a trilogy of closely connected parables. Therefore Mark has every right to use the plural, for he knew that Jesus at this particular time uttered more than one parable.

The parable here recorded was that of the wicked tenants or sharecroppers. It begins as follows: **A man planted a vineyard. He set a fence around it, dug a trough for the winepress, and built a tower.** This man reserved a portion of his ground for a vineyard. He planted vines in that plot, enclosed it with a fence or hedge as a protection against thieves and animals, and equipped it with a winepress and a watch-tower. The winepress generally consisted of two excavations dug into the earth and lined with stonework, or hewn out in a cliff. The upper cavity, wide and shallow, served as a receptacle for the grapes. Here they were crushed by the feet of the

472

grape-treaders (cf. Isa. 63:2, 3). Through a pipe the juice would run into the lower, narrow and deep compartment. Afterward it was put into jars (cf. Hag. 2:16). The watch-tower may have been constructed from the very stones that had been gathered when the ground set aside for the vineyard was cleared (cf. Isa. 5:2). A watchman had to be stationed in such a tower to warn of any danger from pillagers, jackals, and foxes (Song of Sol. 2:15). The tower could also be used for storage.

When the owner had thus fully prepared his vineyard, **Then he leased the vineyard to sharecroppers,** tenants or lessees who, as the parable indicates, had to give the owner a definite amount of the vintage. Having made this arrangement the owner **went abroad,** that is, "went away from home." [571]

2. At the proper time he sent a servant to the sharecroppers to collect from them his share of the vineyard's fruit. This "servant" must be distinguished from the "tenants" or "sharecroppers." The latter are the vine-growers with whom the owner has made a contract, amounting to this: "I will let y o u manage this vineyard and harvest its crop for yourselves provided that at the time of the vintage y o u give me this or that definite portion of the grapes." The servant, on the other hand, was commissioned by the owner to collect and carry to the master's home the portion of the fruit that belonged to him. Having been delegated by him, it follows that the servant was invested with the master's authority. He made his demand or request in the owner's name. The request was altogether proper, for a definite agreement had been made, and the "proper time," that is, the time of the vintage had arrived.

3. But they seized him, beat him, and sent him away empty-handed. The tenants proved to be wicked men, scoundrels, dishonest and cruel. When the servant asked for the portion of the grape harvest to which the owner had a legal claim, he was refused. Not only that, but he was even seized and beaten. When he was finally released, he returned to the owner empty-handed.

One might have expected that the owner would have responded most vigorously to the cruel treatment his servant had received, treatment which at the same time was an insult to himself. But he did not. He decided to give the sharecroppers another chance to do their duty, and still more opportunities after that, for the story continues as follows:

4, 5. Then he sent another servant to them. They struck him on the head and treated him shamefully. He sent still another, and that one they killed. He sent many others; some of them they beat, others they killed. [572]

---

571 In verse 1 ὑπολήνιον = ὑπὸ τὴν ληνόν, that which is under the winepress; hence, a pit, trough, or vessel to catch the grape juice. The word πυργός or *tower* reminds one of the German *Burg* or the Dutch *burcht* (castle, stronghold, citadel, fortress, tower).

572 Both ἔδειραν (verse 3) and δέροντες (verse 5) are forms of δέρω: to skin (cf.

The parable now reaches a dramatic climax: **6-8. He had still one other, a beloved son. He sent him last of all, saying, They will have regard for**[573] **my son. But those sharecroppers said to each other, He is the heir; come on, let's kill him, and the inheritance will be ours! So they took him and killed him, and cast him out of the vineyard.**

"Still one other, a son beloved" (cf. John 3:16)! What intense feeling—emotion, love, pathos—is implied in "He sent him last of all, saying, 'They will have regard for my son,' " meaning. "They will be ashamed of hurting him. They will respect him." So, he decided to make even this sacrifice.

But what happens? When these wicked tenants see his son approaching they begin to plot. They enter into a consultation with each other. Accordingly, what they are going to do to him is not a matter of impulse. On the contrary, it is "malice aforethought," the result of wicked deliberation, of corrupt, selfish scheming. It is premeditated murder. They reason as follows: "This is the heir. When we kill him, there will be no other heir to worry about. So the inheritance which he would have obtained will be ours." In their sinister folly they forget that the owner, the son's father, is still alive, and will certainly wreak vengeance. How blatantly foolish is sin! How absurd! "He who dwells in the heavens will laugh. The Lord will hold them in derision" (Ps. 2:4).

The villains carry out their wicked plan. When the son arrives they take him, cast him out of the vineyard and kill him. On a previous page the sequence "killed him and cast him out of the vineyard" instead of "cast him out of the vineyard and killed him" (as in Matthew and Luke) has already been commented upon.

The story is finished. Jesus has told it but has not yet explained it. So he now asks his audience, **9. What then will the owner of the vineyard do?** The answer, here in Mark presented as given by Jesus himself, is: **He will come and kill those sharecroppers and give the vineyard to others.** In other words, not the sharecroppers but the owner of the vineyard triumphs in the end. And so does his son, as will be shown. Here the meaning of the parable is surfacing. The "owner" is God, and his Son is Jesus, the Christ. This is the key to the explanation of the words which immediately follow in verses **10, 11. Have y o u never read this passage of Scripture:**

---

epidermis, dermatologist), flay, beat. The form in verse 3 is third per. pl. aor. act. indic.; the one in verse 5, the pl. pres. act. participle. Another third per. pl. aor. act. indic. is ἐκεφαλίωσαν, they struck on the head, related to κεφαλή, head (cf. *capital*).

573 The verb is ἐντραπήσονται third per. pl. fut. indic. passive of ἐντρέπω, with active or middle sense, something like: "they will turn themselves about, being ashamed of hurting"; hence, "they will stand in awe of," "will have respect or regard for." German: *"Sie werden sich vor meinem Sohne scheuen."* Dutch (Nieuwe Vertaling): *"Mijn zoon zullen zij ontzien."*

> The stone which the builders rejected
> This became the cornerstone;
> By the Lord was this done;
> And it is wonderful in our eyes?

Jesus surprises his audience, particularly his bitter opponents—the chief priests and the scribes and the elders (11:27, 28)—by reminding them of this passage from Ps. 118 (LXX 117):22, 23. There a similar transaction had been described. Builders had *rejected* a stone; meaning: leaders, prominent men of other nations, had scoffingly denigrated Israel. Nevertheless, Israel had become in a very true sense the cornerstone, the head of the nations (Ps. 147:20). This, moreover, had not happened because of Israel's own intrinsic moral and spiritual excellence or because of its own power. On the contrary, by the Lord this wonderful thing had been accomplished. Jesus now shows that the words of Ps. 118 reach their ultimate fulfilment in "the owner's son," that is, in himself, the *true* Israel. He is that stone that was being rejected by the chief priests, scribes, elders, and their followers; at Calvary, by the nation as a whole ("Crucify, crucify!"). See John 1:11. But something marvelous was going to happen: *the rejected stone would become the cornerstone:* Christ crucified would rise again triumphantly. And what about the nation, namely, the old unconverted Israel, the rejectors of the Messiah? "From y o u," says Jesus, the "kingdom of God," that is, the special kingdom privileges—the special standing in the eyes of God which this people had enjoyed during the old dispensation, to which had now been added the blessed words and works of Jesus—"will be taken away." Why? Because they had not lived up to their obligations. They had been like the sharecroppers who at the time of the vintage had refused to render to the owner that portion of the vintage that was his due. So, in the place of the old covenant people there would arise—was it not already beginning to happen?—"a nation producing its fruit," a church international, gathered from both Jews and Gentiles.

Briefly, therefore, the thrust—the one main lesson—of the parable can be expressed in the words of Ps. 2:12: "Kiss [or: pay homage to] the Son, lest he be angry, and y o u perish in the way; for soon shall his wrath be kindled. Blessed are all those who take refuge in him."

As to the subsidiary meaning of the separate items of this parable, to the extent in which a figurative meaning can be attached to them, see N.T.C. on Matthew, bottom of p. 786. In addition to what is said there, note the following:

God's precept

Among the fruit-producing growths that are frequently mentioned in Scripture three are outstanding: the olive tree, the fig tree, and the grapevine. Sometimes they are mentioned in close succession (Judg. 9:8-13; and, in a different order, Hab. 3:17). Also in connection with the events of Passion Week we are reminded of all three: the olive tree (Mount of Olives, Mark 11:1; 13:3; 14:26), the fig tree (11:12-14, 20, 21; 13:28), and the vine (vineyard, 12:1 ff.).

Their purpose was, of course, to bear fruit. In this respect they symbolize God's precept for human life: "Herein is my Father glorified that y o u bear much fruit" (John 15:8). When plants or trees do not enrich their owner with a bounteous harvest, they have failed to reach their goal. Whether they yield worthless fruit (Isa. 5:2), fruit that is unjustly withheld from the owner (the present parable), or no fruit at all (Mark 11:13, 14; Luke 13:6, 7) makes no basic difference. In all these cases God, who distributes his gifts lavishly, fails to receive his due from the hearts and lives thus symbolized. The circle is broken. The blessings poured down by him are not returned to him in the form of happy thanksgivings, surrendered hearts, rescued lives. The precept stands: Bear much fruit. Cf. Gal. 5:22.

God's patience

In the present parable, when the first servant returns to the owner empty-handed, what does the latter do? *At this point* the parable becomes very touching, and this not because it is so true to life, but because *it is not!* In fact, it far surpasses what the average person's reaction would have been. Unless a person is so very familiar with the parable that for him its keen edge has worn off, he is surprised, perhaps even somewhat shocked, to read that when this servant returns from his errand, he not only carries with him no grapes but in addition shows the evidences of the physical abuse he has received. Nevertheless, the owner does not immediately fly into a rage and punish the offenders. No, he simply sends another servant. And when that one is killed, the owner sends others. Finally, he even sends his own son, whom he dearly loves. And the owner symbolizes God!

This is the God who manifested his longsuffering at the time of the deluge (I Peter 3:20). He is the God whose throne-chariot, with its accompanying cherubs, "stood still at the door of the east gate of the house of the Lord," so reluctant was he to leave his chosen Zion (Ezek. 10:18, 19). His marvelous restraint in inflicting punishment is symbolized, in another parable, by the vinedresser's plea, "Leave that tree alone *this year also* until I dig around it and fertilize it" (Luke 13:7). He even gives notoriously corrupt "Jezebel" *time to repent* (Rev. 2:21). Touchingly Peter writes (II Peter 3:9), "He is longsuffering toward y o u, not wishing that any should perish, but that all should make room for repentance." See also Gen. 18:22-33; Isa. 1:18; 55:6, 7; Hos. 11:8; Mic. 7:18, 19; Matt. 23:37.

God's punishment

The present parable also shows that it is entirely wrong to emphasize God's love at the expense of his holiness, righteousness, and avenging wrath. Note: "He will come and kill those sharecroppers" (12:9). See also Prov. 29:1; Isa. 5:5-7; 6:1-5; Nah. 1:1-6; Zeph. 1 (the entire chapter); Matt. 23:1-36; John 15:6; Heb. 12:29; Rev. 6:12-17; 14:17-20; 18:1–19:21.

But this outpouring of wrath and punishment does not in any way imply the frustration of God's plan of salvation. Note that in the parable the owner's action—or reaction—does not cease when he has killed the wicked sharecroppers. No, he adds . . . "and give the vineyard *to others.*" The vineyard must be given away. The house must be filled (Luke 14:23). And see also Esther 4:14; Acts 13:46.

It must not be supposed that what, in its main features, is symbolically described in this parable never actually happened. On the contrary, God did indeed send his "servants"—often called by this very name—to his people Israel. In various ways these prophets were indeed scorned, wounded, and rejected (Matt. 23:29-37; Luke 6:23; 11:49-51; 13:31-35; Acts 7:52). See also N.T.C. on Matt. 5:12. But even then God did actually send his only-begotten, beloved Son (Luke 19:10; Rom. 8:32; etc.). He sent him first of all to Israel (Matt. 10:5, 6; 15:24). He, too, was rejected by the Jews (Mark 15:12, 13; John 1:11; 12:37-41; Acts 2:23; 4:10); exception: the believing · remnant destined for everlasting glory (John 1:12; Rom. 11:5). The privileges once granted to Israel were subsequently transferred to the church universal (Matt. 21:41; 28:19; Acts 13:46), a truth whose realization was already foreshadowed when Jesus walked on earth (Matt. 8:11, 12; 15:28; John 3:16; 4:41, 42; 10:16; 17:20, 21). The parable, accordingly, is not an abstraction. It pictures reality.

To a certain extent even Christ's opponents sensed this. Hence, Mark continues:

12. And they were trying to arrest him, for they knew that he had spoken this parable against them. The pronoun "they" refers to the men mentioned in 11:27: the chief priests and the scribes and the elders; that is, the body of the Sanhedrists. Some of these men were Pharisees (Matt. 21:45). Again and again they were looking for a way to arrest Jesus. Now especially, since they realized that it was against [574] *them* that Jesus had spoken the parable. They must have sensed that, as Jesus saw it, *they* were symbolized by the wicked sharecroppers, destined for destruction.

What prevented them from carrying out their plan at this particular

---

[574] Here πρός followed by the acc. means *against.* For a similar use of this preposition see Acts 6:1; 24:19; I Cor. 6:1; II Cor. 6:11; Col. 3:13; Rev. 13:6.

moment is stated in these words: **But they were afraid of the crowd.** That is not very surprising, for:

a. these people held Jesus to be a prophet (Matt. 21:46b);

b. on the preceding Sunday they had been shouting hosannas in his honor (Mark 11:8-10);

c. on a previous occasion they had tried to make him their king (John 6:15);

d. for many, Passover Week was a period during which political enthusiasm ran high, and hero worship would be difficult to control; and

e. very recently many "believers"—whether their faith was genuine or whimsical—had been added to the ranks of those who sided with the Prophet of Galilee, for he had brought back to life Lazarus, who had been dead four days (John 11:39, 43, 44; 12:10, 17-19).

Result of all this was that, for the moment at least, Christ's opponents recognized that they had not as yet found what they were looking for: a way to destroy Jesus. **So they left him and went away.**

---

13 And they sent to him some of the Pharisees and some of the Herodians, to catch him in his words. 14 They came to him and said, "Teacher, we know that you are truthful and court no one's favor, for you are not partial to anyone but truthfully teach God's way. Is it lawful to pay a poll-tax to Caesar, or not? Shall we pay or shall we not pay?"

15 But Jesus, aware of their hypocrisy, said to them, "Why put me to the test? Bring me a denarius that I may look at it." 16 So they brought it. He said to them, "Whose likeness and inscription is this?" "Caesar's," they told him. 17 Jesus said to them, "What is due to Caesar render to Caesar, and what is due to God render to God." And they were amazed at him.

18 Then some Sadducees, who say that there is no resurrection, came up to him and asked him this question, 19 "Teacher," they said, "Moses wrote for us that if a man's brother dies, leaving behind a wife but not leaving a child, that man must marry the widow and raise up children for his brother. 20 Now there were seven brothers. The first one took a wife, and when he died left no children. 21 The second took her and died, leaving no children; and so did the third. 22 None of the seven left any children. Last of all the woman herself died. 23 In the resurrection [575] whose wife shall she be, since all seven had her as wife?"

24 Jesus said to them, "Is not this the reason y o u are deceiving yourselves, that y o u know neither the Scriptures nor the power of God? 25 For when the dead rise, they neither marry nor are given in marriage, but are like the angels in heaven. 26 Now concerning the dead, that they are raised up, have y o u not read in the book of Moses, in the passage about the bush, how God spoke to him, saying, 'I am the God of Abraham and the God of Isaac and the God of Jacob'? 27 He is not the God of the dead but of the living. Y o u are badly mistaken."

28 Then one of the scribes, on hearing them arguing, came up, and recognizing how

---

575 Some manuscripts add "when they rise again."

well Jesus had answered them, asked him, "Of all the commandments which is the foremost?"

29 Jesus answered, "The foremost is, 'Hear, O Israel, the Lord our God, the Lord is one. 30 And you shall love the Lord your God with all your heart and with all your soul and with all your mind and with all your strength.' 31 The second is this, 'You shall love your neighbor as yourself.' There is no other commandment greater than these."

32 The scribe said to him, "Right! Teacher, [576] you have truthfully stated that he is one, and there is no other but he. 33 Moreover, to love him with all your heart and with all your understanding and with all your strength, and to love your neighbor as yourself, means far more than all burnt-offerings and sacrifices."

34 And when Jesus saw that he had answered wisely, he said to him, "You are not far from the kingdom of God." And from then on no one dared to ask him any more questions.

35 Now while Jesus was teaching in the temple he asked, "How can the scribes say that the Christ is the son of David? 36 David himself, moved by the Holy Spirit, declared:

> 'The Lord said to my Lord,
> Sit at my right hand
> Until I put your enemies under your feet.'

37 David himself calls him 'Lord.' How then can he be his son?" The huge crowd enjoyed listening to him.

12:13-37 *Captious Questions and Authoritative Answers*
also
Christ's Own Question
verses 13-17 Cf. Matt. 22:15-22; Luke 20:20-26
verses 18-27 Cf. Matt. 22:23-33; Luke 20:27-40
verses 28-34 Cf. Matt. 22:34-40 [577]
verses 35-37 Cf. Matt. 22:41-46; Luke 20:41-44

Is it lawful to pay a poll-tax to Caesar, or not?

This little paragraph can be divided into *a.* introduction, *b.* body, and *c.* conclusion. Mark's *introduction* is very brief: A committee consisting of Pharisees and Herodians is sent to Jesus to catch him in his words. Matthew adds that the mission of this committee was undertaken after a more or less formal decision. Lengthiest of all is Luke's introduction: the enemies watch Jesus and send spies. These spies are insincere. Their purpose, and also that of their sponsors, is to discover some pretext that would enable them to deliver Jesus to the governor.

As to number of words devoted to this incident, the *conclusion* reveals

---

576 Or "Beautiful, Teacher!"
577 Luke 10:25-28 is parallel only in a secondary sense. It parallels the summary of the law. But the circumstances are different and so is the story itself.

similar diversity. Mark is again shortest: Christ's answer results in amazement. Matthew adds that the committee left Jesus and departed. Luke reports the committee's—also the sponsors'—discomfiture, amazement, and silence. His conclusion, like his introduction, is again the lengthiest.

As to *the body* of the paragraph—the committee's question and Christ's answer—, here Matthew and Mark are closely parallel, while Luke abbreviates. Nowhere is there even a semblance of disagreement.

13. And they sent to him some of the Pharisees and some of the Herodians, to catch him in his words.

It is necessary to keep the context in mind. The Sanhedrists had bluntly questioned Jesus' authority. This attack had failed. By means of a counter-question ("The baptism of John, was it from heaven or from men?") Jesus had silenced them. Not only that, but by means of the parable of The Wicked Tenants he had predicted their doom. So, more than ever they were determined to kill him. But "they were afraid of the crowd" (12:12).

So they now decide to use the opposite method. For implied accusation they substitute adulation. At the same time they probably figured that their clever device would result in discrediting their enemy in the estimation of the people, at least of a large group.

They no longer criticize him for what he *did yesterday*—cleansing the temple—; instead, they try to "catch" [578] him in what he *says today*.

Note the combination "Pharisees and Herodians." So also in Matthew (22:16, a parallel passage), though that Gospel points out that the committee which was sent to Jesus consisted not of the veteran leaders but of the younger disciples of both of these groups. Mark does not deny this. It just happens to be a little touch which, under the guidance of the Holy Spirit, was jotted down by Matthew. According to Luke these men were "spies."

In Mark's Gospel this combination of Pharisees and Herodians was mentioned also in an earlier connection (3:6). What was said there can be repeated here: it was a strange coalition between the sanctimonious and the sacrilegious. Well, not so very strange after all, and this for the reason already stated in the explanation of 3:6; see on that passage.

The Herods were lovers of pagan art, architecture, athletics, etc. The Herodians followed in their train. Only in a very external sense did these people practice the Jewish religion. Their real philosophy was that of Hellenism. So now the two groups, Pharisees and Herodians, combine against

---

578 ἀγρεύσωσι third per. pl. aor. (here ingressive) active subjunctive of ἀγρεύω. Cf. ἄγρα (Luke 5:4, 9), a *catch* of fishes. The verb belongs to the vocabulary of fishing and hunting. In the New Testament it occurs nowhere else. The parallel passage in Matthew (22:15) uses a synonymous verb, meaning *to set a trap*. See N.T.C. on Matthew, p. 800, footnote 753. Another synonym is used by Luke (20:20), *to latch on to, grab hold of, catch*. There is, of course, no essential difference.

Jesus. Those who were—or made believe that they were—very concerned about keeping God's law, and those who were easy-going and cared little about the divine commandments, promote a common aim: getting rid of Jesus.

Each group had its own reason for wishing to destroy him. Did not his teaching imply a denunciation of the self-righteousness of the Pharisees and of the worldlimindedness of the Herodians? Besides, the Herodians cannot have been happy with Jesus' *royal* entry into Jerusalem, nor the Pharisees with his entry as "the Son of David," the Messiah. Also, both envy Jesus because, as they see it, his influence over the people is becoming too pronounced.

14. They came to him and said, Teacher, we know that you are truthful and court no one's favor, for you are not partial to anyone but truthfully teach God's way. As to "Teacher," this form of address was certainly correct. Not only do the evangelists constantly describe Jesus as such, but so do also many others (see Mark 4:38; 5:35; 9:17, 38; 10:17, 20, 35; John 3:5; etc.). In fact, Jesus himself stated that teaching was one of his main activities (Mark 14:49; cf. Matt. 26:55; Luke 21:37; John 18:20). He was the greatest Teacher ever to walk the earth. Being God's true Prophet he taught men as the Father had taught him (John 1:18; 3:34; 8:28; 12:49). It was a pity that those who now addressed him as "Teacher" did not accept his teaching.

And now the flattery. These men tell Jesus that he is truthful and that he truthfully teaches God's way. The word *way*, as here used, indicates manner of faith and conduct. "The way of God" is the manner in which God wants people to think and to live. It is his will for man's heart, mind, and behavior. They are saying, therefore, "You are a teacher on whom people can depend; you faithfully declare the will of God for doctrine and life."

In further explication of what they have in mind they say, "You court no one's favor"; literally, "and not is it a care to you concerning no one," that is, "You speak your own mind, without trying to cater to any person's likes or dislikes." Along the same line is, "You are not partial to anyone"; literally, "You do not look on anyone's countenance." They meant, "No matter to whom you speak, what you say is still the same. You do not allow yourself to be swayed by rich or poor, learned or unlearned, master or slave . . . ."579

---

579 The phraseology here used is probably typically Hebraic. For "way," as here used, see also Gen. 6:12; Ps. 1:1; Jer. 21:8. Cf. Acts 9:2; 19:9, 23; 24:14, 22. So also "looking on a person's countenance" immediately reminds one of Lev. 19:15; I Sam. 16:7; Ps. 82:2; Mal. 2:9. Cf. Acts 10:34; Eph. 6:9; Col. 3:25; James 2:1, 9. It must be admitted, however, that idioms such as these may develop in more than one language; for example, Greek as well as Hebrew. Nevertheless, when a Hebrew, or one versed in basically Hebrew

Thinking, perhaps, that by means of their kind (?) words they have completely disarmed Jesus, having dispelled any suspicion which he might otherwise have entertained with respect to their motives, they now spring their question, **Is it lawful to pay a poll-tax to Caesar, or not? Shall we pay or shall we not pay?** [580] The tribute to which the present passage refers was a capitation tax which, after the deposition of Archelaus (A.D. 6), was collected by the procurator from every adult male in Judea, and was paid directly into the imperial treasury. Since this coinage bore the image of the emperor, who ascribed divinity to himself and claimed to possess supreme authority not only in political but even in spiritual affairs (as "the highest priest."), and since, in addition to this, it reminded the Jews that they were a subject nation, it is understandable that payment of this tax was very distasteful to many a freedom-loving, devout Jew. It was in connection with the introduction of this imposition that Judas of Galilee had vehemently proclaimed, "Taxation is no better than downright slavery." He had blasted it as being no less than high treason against God. See Acts 5:37; Josephus, *Jewish War* II. 117, 118; *Jewish Antiquities* XVIII, 1-10.

The question put to Jesus was therefore a very clever scheme. If he answered affirmatively, he would be alienating ever so many devout, patriotic Jews; but a negative reply would be exposing himself to the charge of rebellion against the Roman government (cf. Luke 20:20; 23:2).

15. But Jesus, aware of their hypocrisy, said to them, Why put me to the test? Jesus was aware of *a.* their "wickedness" (Matt. 22:18), "unscrupulousness," *readiness to do anything,* no matter how wicked, to attain their purpose (Luke 20:23), and specifically (Mark) *b.* their "hypocrisy" or "duplicity." Their question, after an introduction of honeyed words, sounded like a pious request for direction in deciding what to do in a difficult matter of ethics, but their real intention was the destruction of Jesus. It is not surprising that Jesus, fully aware of their dishonesty, called them "hypocrites" (Matt. 22:18). "Why," says Jesus, "do y o u put me to the test?" See on Mark 1:13. Their action was diabolical. While feigning innocence, they thought they had lured their enemy in a trap from which, as they saw it, he would not be able to escape.

Jesus continued, **Bring me a denarius that I may look at it.** The denarius or denar, a small silver coin equal to a laborer's average wages for one day's work, was the amount fixed by law for the payment of the poll-tax. It is held by many that Christ's asking for this coin implied that he himself was so

---

conversation and literature, uses this phraseology, such use in all likelihood is rooted in ancient Hebrew idioms.

580 δῶμεν, in both cases first per. pl. aor. active subjunctive (here deliberative) of δίδωμι.

poor that he did not possess that much. To this observation some add that it showed that even his disciples did not have any denarius. But perhaps this is reading into the account something that is not really there. One could, for example, advance an entirely different explanation for this request, namely, that Jesus wanted the coin to come from the pockets of his opponents, so as to impress upon them the fact that they themselves were using this coinage, were benefiting from its use, and had accordingly accepted the resulting obligations. That explanation has in its favor that it fits into the succeeding context. But this point need not be pressed. "That I may look at it" implies that Jesus is going to direct his own attention and that of the audience to what was shown and written on this coin.

Continued: **16. So they brought it. He said to them, Whose likeness and inscription is this? Caesar's, they told him.** A denarius from the reign of the then ruling emperor Tiberius pictures on its *obverse side* the head of that ruler. On the *reverse side* he is shown seated on a throne. He is wearing a diadem and is clothed as a highpriest.

The inscriptions, with abbreviations as indicated and with V representing our present U, are as follows:

Obverse
TICAESARDIVI AVGFAVGVSTVS

Translated:
TIBERIUS CAESAR AUGUSTUS
SON OF THE DIVINE AUGUSTUS

Reverse
PONTIF MAXIM

Translated:
HIGHEST PRIEST

The tension must have been very high when **17. Jesus said to them, What is due to Caesar render to Caesar, and what is due to God render to God.** Explanation:

a. Jesus was not evading the issue, but was clearly saying, "Yes, pay the tax." Honoring God does not mean dishonoring the emperor by refusing to pay for the privileges—a relatively orderly society, police protection, good roads, courts, etc., etc.—one enjoys. At this particular time the Roman Empire had brought peace and tranquility to the people under its sway, and this to a degree seldom if ever experienced either before or afterward. Such a blessing implies a responsibility. Cf. I Tim. 2:2; I Peter 2:17. Thus, no truthful charge of sedition could be made against Jesus.

b. He was qualifying his "yes" answer by stating that the emperor should be paid (given back) only what was *his due*. Hence, the divine honor which the emperor claimed but which is due to God alone must be refused. How could the Pharisees find any fault with that? Besides, this word was a warning to all—from the most exalted emperor to the subject lowest in rank—not to claim undue honors. Cf. II Kings 18:19—19:37 (II Chron. 32:9-23; Isa. 36, 37); Dan. 4:28-32; 5; Acts 12:20-23.

c. By adding "and to God what is due to God" Jesus was stressing the fact that all the service, gratitude, glory, etc. due to God should be constantly and gladly accorded to him. Nothing must be withheld. See, for example, Ps. 29; 95; 96; 103-105; 116; John 17:4; Rom. 11:33-36; I Cor. 6:20; 10:31; 16:1, 2; II Cor. 9:15. One does not give God what is his due by plotting to destroy his beloved Son! But this was exactly what these spies and their teachers were trying to do.

d. By drawing a distinction between "what is due to Caesar" and "what is due to God" Jesus was rejecting the very claim of Caesar, a claim made on the coin and otherwise, to the effect that his was not only a physical kingdom but also a spiritual (note: "Pontifex Maximus," i.e., "Highest Priest"). Cf. John 18:36. Naturally God is Sovereign *over all* (Dan. 4:34, 35), even over the emperor. Cf. John 19:11. The emperor, to be sure, should be respected and obeyed whenever his will does not clash with the divine will. See Rom. 13:1-7. But when there is a clash the rule laid down in Acts 5:29 must be followed.

By means of this answer Jesus had discomfited his enemies. We are not surprised to read: **And they were amazed at him.** They had not expected this kind of answer. Jesus had frankly and courageously answered their question. The answer implies: Yes, the tax must be paid. There must be an adequate response to privileges enjoyed. But though the emperor must receive his due, he must not receive more than that; that is, he must not receive the divine honor he claims. At the same time, God must receive *all* the glory and honor—In all candor, who could find fault with this answer? Certainly no one.

In the resurrection whose wife shall she be?

The same interesting variety amid unity, witnessed in Mark 12:13-17 and its parallels, is again clear. Between Matthew's report and Mark's there is very little difference. Matthew alone, however, relates that question 1 and question 2 were asked "on the same day." He reports the reaction of the people to Christ's answer: "They were astounded at his teaching"; Luke has, "Well said, Teacher!" (the reaction of some scribes); also, "They no longer dared to ask him any question." Mark and Luke have in common the indication of the source of the words, "I am the God of Abraham. . . ." The words themselves are recorded in all three (direct discourse in Matthew and Mark, indirect in Luke). The source, not given in Matthew, is "the book of Moses . . . the passage about the bush." Mark alone reports that Jesus ended his argument with the Sadducees by saying, "You are badly mistaken."

Remarkable is the difference in the length of the three accounts. Often Luke's coverage is the shortest, but not in this case. Shortest of all is Matthew's. Note especially the difference in the length of the words ascribed *to Jesus*. In the original, about 60 words in Matthew, 70 in Mark, 75 in Luke. The corresponding figures in A.R.V. are: Matthew 78, Mark 97, Luke 109. Words of Jesus reported by Luke alone are: "The sons of this age marry and are given in marriage; but those who are accounted worthy to attain to that age, even to the resurrection from the dead (neither marry, etc.) . . . for they can no longer die . . . being sons of the resurrection . . . for all live to him."

18, 19. Then some Sadducees, who say that there is no resurrection, came up to him and asked him this question, Teacher, they said, Moses wrote for us that if a man's brother dies, leaving behind a wife but not leaving a child, that man must marry the widow and raise up children for his brother.

It should be emphasized that those who now approach Jesus in order to undermine his influence differed in many respects from those who had put him to the test a moment ago. On one point all the adversaries were in agreement: Jesus must be destroyed! In connection with the discussion of Mark 7:1, 2 we have given five reasons showing why it was that *the Pharisees* hated Jesus (reasons *a-e*). As to *the Sadducees,* it should be borne in mind that this was the priestly party, from whose ranks the highpriest was selected. The temple was their special domain, the very temple which "only yesterday" Jesus had cleansed! The crass materialism of the Sadducees was as repugnant to the heart of Jesus as was the pompous ceremonialism and loveless legalism of the Pharisees. As to both Pharisees and Sadducees see N.T.C. on Matthew, pp. 201-203. It is not surprising, therefore, that the Sadducees now, in turn, attack Jesus. This time, however, the attack is not an attempt to impale him on one of the horns of a dilemma, as was the case with respect to the preceding question (12:14), but rather to ridicule his faith in the afterlife.

In fact, it must be considered altogether probable that these men intended to strike a double blow. In exposing what they regarded as the foolishness of Christ's teaching regarding the glory awaiting himself and his followers on the other side of death, would they not at the same time triumph over the Pharisees, who likewise believed in a resurrection from the dead? If we are

485

permitted to assume that news of the victory of Jesus over the Pharisees (and their allies) soon reached the ears of the Sadducees—in view of Matt. 22:34 not an unreasonable assumption—, may we not also assume that the latter were already saying to each other, "We'll show the Pharisees that we can do better"? Were they perhaps already chuckling over the prospect of "killing two birds with one stone," that is, of exposing to ridicule both Jesus and the Pharisees?

For their word of address, "Teacher" see on verse 14. They continue with an appeal to the great law-giver Moses ("Moses wrote for us"). It should be borne in mind that the Sadducees regarded the Pentateuch as being higher in value than the other books of the Old Testament. They now make Deut. 25:5, 6 the springboard of their question. In that passage the law of "levirate [581] marriage" is given to Israel. According to this law, if a wife loses her husband before any male child has been born, the brother of that husband—or else the nearest of kin—must marry the widow, so that the first child born of this marriage may be counted as a child of the deceased, and the latter's line may not die out. Disobedience to this command was frowned upon (Deut. 25:7-10). Half-hearted obedience, so that a man was willing to marry the widow but not to raise offspring by her since such a child could not be counted as his own, was in the case of Onan punished with death (Gen. 38:8-10). For an interesting application of the law of levirate marriage see Ruth 4:1-8. To what extent this law was still being obeyed during Christ's sojourn on earth is not clear.

The Sadducees, then, make use of this commandment in order to show how thoroughly absurd, as they see it, is belief in the resurrection of the body. Whether the story which they are about to relate was a report on an actual event, as some commentators believe, let the reader judge for himself. I, for one, am inclined to believe that they fabricated it.

They continue: **20-23. Now there were seven brothers. The first one took a wife, and when he died left no children. The second took her and died, leaving no children; and so did the third. None of the seven left any children. Last of all the woman herself died. In the resurrection whose wife shall she be, since all seven had her as wife?** Provided that their basic assumption—namely, that married life continues in the hereafter—was correct, two husbands would have been sufficient to prove their point. But seven makes the story more interesting and might also make belief in the resurrection seem even more absurd. Think of it: when the dead arise, this woman—husband-killer?—will have seven husbands! Of course, that cannot, must not, be. She is allowed to have only one, but which one?

---

581 *Levirate* is from the Latin *levir* (for *devir;* cf. Greek δαήρ), a husband's brother; hence, brother-in-law.

It is clear, of course, that the entire representation was absurd. It was atrociously unfair; for Jesus, though believing in the doctrine of the physical resurrection, did not believe that for people who before they died had become married, this married state would continue after the resurrection. What the opponents were doing, therefore, was setting up a man of straw, to be bowled down very readily. Not the doctrine of the resurrection but the assumption from which the Sadducees were proceeding was false. In fact, it was grotesquely fictitious.

In his masterful reply Jesus does four things: He *a.* shows why it is that the Sadducees commit such a glaring error (verse 24); *b.* proves this assertion by demolishing their false assumption that marriage is resumed at the time of the resurrection (verse 25); *c.* proves the doctrine of the resurrection from Scripture (verses 26, 27a); and *d.* draws the only possible conclusion and states it, using exactly two words.

a. 24. **Jesus said to them, Is not this the reason y o u are deceiving yourselves, that y o u know neither the Scriptures nor the power of God?** Had they known the Scriptures, they would have known that there is nothing in Deut. 25:5, 6 that makes it applicable to the life hereafter, and they would also have known that the Old Testament in various passages teaches the resurrection of the body. And had they recognized the power of God (Rom. 4:17; Heb. 11:19), they would have understood that God is able to raise the dead in such a manner that marriage will not longer be needed.

The proof of this assertion, a proof that demolishes the false assumption from which the Sadducees have proceeded is now furnished:

b. 25. **For when the dead rise, they neither marry nor are given in marriage, but are like the angels in heaven.** The glorious resurrection body— Jesus says nothing about the resurrection of the wicked—is going to be immortal. Since there will be no death, the race will not have to be reproduced. Marriage, accordingly, will be a matter of the past. In not marrying and not being given in marriage the blessed will therefore resemble the angels, for they too do not marry. The saved will be like the angels *in this one respect;* yes, like the angels whose very existence the Sadducees also deny (Acts 23:8), and this in spite of the fact that the Pentateuch, accepted by them, teaches their existence (Gen. 19:1, 15; 28:12; 32:1)! Does not verse 25, taken in its entirety, and in connection with what is known of the beliefs of the Sadducees, prove that these men know neither the Scriptures nor the power of God?

Although the Sadducees ridicule a wonderful truth accepted and taught by Jesus, namely, that of the resurrection of the dead, he does not refuse to impart needed instruction to them on this very subject:

c. 26, 27a. **Now concerning the dead, that they are raised up, have y o u not read in the book of Moses, in the passage about the bush, how God**

487

spoke to him, saying, I am the God of Abraham and the God of Isaac and the God of Jacob? He is not the God of the dead but of the living. "Have y o u not read?" says Jesus. Certainly those who try to base their argument on Scripture (Deut. 25:5, 6) should know Scripture! They should be acquainted with Scripture as a whole, not just with one passage, which they then misapply. Now it is true that the Sadducees did not have the New Testament, which mentions or implies the resurrection (whether of Jesus himself or of his people, or even of all the dead) again and again (Matt. 12:39, 40; 16:21; 17:22, 23; 20:19; 21:42; 25:31 ff.; 28:1-10; Mark 16:1-8; Luke 24; John 5:28, 29; 11:24; 20; 21; Acts 2:24-36; 4:10, 11; 17:31, 32; Rom. 1:4; I Cor. 15: Phil. 3:20, 21; I Thess. 4:16; I Peter 1:3; Rev. 20:11-15, to mention but a few of all the many passages in which this doctrine is taught). But even the Old Testament is not lacking in references to the bodily resurrection. Clearest, perhaps, are Ps. 16:9-11 (interpreted by Peter in Acts 2:27, 31) and Dan. 12:2. Worthy of consideration are also Job 14:14; 19:25-27; Ps. 17:15; 73:24-26; Isa. 26:19; Ezek. 37:1-14; Hos. 6:2, 13:14 (cf. I Cor. 15:55); passages which, though not always directly teaching the resurrection of the body, may well imply belief in this truth. Take for example, Ps. 73:24-26, which clearly teaches the blessed after-death existence of the believer's soul in heaven. Does not this very existence of the soul in the intermediate state demand the resurrection of the body? Two facts certainly point in that direction: *a.* the creation of man as "body and soul" (Gen. 2:7), and *b.* this very passage, "He is not the God of the dead but of the living." Note also that Abraham surely believed in the possibility of a physical resurrection (Heb. 11:19).

Jesus, however, refers to another passage, "I am the God of Abraham . . . ," and implies that since God is not the God of the dead but of the living, the conclusion is that Abraham, Isaac, and Jacob are still alive, and are awaiting a glorious resurrection.

Mark (followed by Luke), but not Matthew, reports Jesus as saying that the quotation is found in "the book of Moses," that is, in the Pentateuch, the very book which by the Sadducees was esteemed above all others. More precisely, Jesus points out the very place in the Pentateuch where the quoted words are found, namely, "in the passage about the bush," [582] that is, "the burning bush that was not consumed." The reference is, of course, to Exod. 3:1 ff; see verse 6, and cf. verses 15, 16.

Attempts have been made to rob Christ's argument of its value. It has been said, for example, that the expression, "the God of Abraham" simply means that while Abraham was on earth he worshiped Jehovah. However, a study of the context in which Exod. 3:6 and all similar passages occur,

---

[582] This ("in the passage about") is one of the normal meanings of $\epsilon\pi\acute{\iota}$ followed by the genitive.

quickly proves that the One who reveals himself as "the God of Abraham . . ." is the unchangeable, eternal covenant God who blesses, loves, encourages, protects, etc. his people, and whose favors do not suddenly stop when a person dies but go with that person beyond death (Ps. 16:10, 11; 17:5; 73:23-26).

Another fact must be mentioned in this connection. The men with whom the immutable Jehovah (Exod. 3:6, 14; Mal. 3:6) established an everlasting covenant (Gen. 17:7) were Israelites, not Greeks. According to the Greek (and afterward also the Roman) conception, the body is merely the prison-house of the soul. See N.T.C. on I and II Thessalonians, pp. 110, 111. The Hebrew conception, product of special revelation, is entirely different. Here God deals with man as whole, not only with his soul or merely with his body. On the contrary, when God blesses his child he enriches him with physical as well as spiritual benefits (Deut. 28:1-14; Neh. 9:21-25; Ps. 104:14, 15; 107; 136; and many similar passages). He loves him body and soul. He is going to send his beloved Son in order to ransom him *completely.* The body, accordingly, shares with the soul the honor of being "the sanctuary of the Holy Spirit" (I Cor. 6:19, 20). The body is "for the Lord, and the Lord for the body" (I Cor. 6:13). God loves the entire person, and the declaration, "I am the God of Abraham and the God of Isaac and the God of Jacob" (note the triple occurrence of the word "God," mentioned separately in connection with each of the three to stress personal relationship with each) certainly implies that their bodies will not be left to the worms but will one day be gloriously resurrected. The burden of proof is entirely on the person who denies this. See also H. W. Robinson, *The People and the Book,* Oxford, 1925, p. 353 f.

Jesus now states the only possible conclusion:

d. 27b. Y o u are badly mistaken. [583] The original uses only two words to express this conclusion: one of them is *badly,* the other is *y o u-are-mistaken,* all one word in Greek. Instead of *y o u-are-mistaken,* this can be rendered *y o u-are-deceiving-yourselves.* The verb is the one also used in verse 24. If one wishes to retain the two word sentence, "Y o u blunder" (= "err badly") might not be a bad rendering. When a person departs from the Scriptures he is bound to blunder, to be badly mistaken, to wander. See also on 13:5.

Some other words and deeds of Jesus regarding the resurrection

a. He restored some from death to life: the daughter of Jairus (Mark 5:41, 42), the son of the widow of Nain (Luke 7:14, 15), and Lazarus (John 11:43, 44).

---

[583] Greek πολὺ πλανᾶσθε. For πολύ see on 9:26, footnote 411.

b. Some were raised at the moment of his death (Matt. 27:52, 53).

c. He predicted his own resurrection on the third day (Mark 8:31; 9:31; 10:34).

d. In fulfilment of these predictions, he himself rose gloriously (Matt. 28; Mark 16; Luke 24; John 20, 21).

e. With reference to the *spiritual* resurrection he said, "The hour is coming—yes, has already arrived!—when the dead shall hear the voice of the Son of God, and those who hear shall live" (John 5:25; cf. Luke 15:32).

f. With respect to the *physical* resurrection he said, "The hour is coming when all who are in the tombs shall hear his voice and shall come out: those who have done good, for the resurrection of life, and those who have practiced evil, for the resurrection of condemnation" (John 5:28, 29). Cf. Acts 24:15. Note the close connection between e. and f. in John's Gospel.

g. In every sense Jesus Christ is himself the cause of his people's resurrection: "I am the resurrection and the life; he who believes in me, though he die, yet shall he live; and everyone who lives and believes in me shall never, never die; do you believe this?" (John 11:25, 26). "Yet a little while, and the world no longer sees me, but y o u see me. Because I live, y o u too shall live" (John 14:19).

h. Filled with significance is also Christ's statement, "No one can come to me unless the Father who sent me draw him, and I will raise him up at the last day" (John 6:44). For "at the last day" see also 6:40, 54, and compare Martha's use of the same phrase (11:24).

* * * * *

Of all the commandments which is the foremost?

The present incident is reported only by Matthew and Mark. Luke has no parallel, although there are similar features in Luke 10:25 ff. It is immediately clear that as between Mark's account and Matthew's, the former is the most comprehensive by far. It includes the *Shema* ("Hear, O Israel, etc."), contains "and with all your strength" in the summary of the first commandment, and above all, describes in some detail the scribe's reaction to the words of Jesus. It even reports what, in turn, was the Master's encouraging reply to that reaction. None of this material can be found in Matthew.

On the other hand, Matthew, in his very brief report, mentions a few details not found in Mark. He leaves the impression that the scribe who now asks Jesus a question did not act solely on his own accord. He seems to have been delegated by the Pharisees in a meeting held with that purpose in view (22:34, 35). Also, according to Matthew, after Jesus had given his summary of the law he said, "On these two commandments depend the whole law and the prophets." Here Mark has Jesus saying, "There is no other commandment greater than these." The two accounts are mutually complementary.

490

28. Then one of the scribes, on hearing them arguing, came up, and recognizing how well Jesus had answered them, asked him, Of all the commandments which is the foremost? [584] Jesus had silenced the Sadducees (Matt. 22:34). His victory pleased the Pharisees, for the latter, as well as Jesus himself, believed in a bodily resurrection, a doctrine denied by the Sadducees. See Acts 23:7, 8. We can well imagine how triumphantly the Pharisees gloated over the defeat suffered by the deniers of the resurrection.

Yet, from another point of view, the Pharisees cannot have been too pleased, for they did not want Jesus' influence with the general public to be strengthened. They still wanted to kill him! So, once again they decided to put him to the test. See Matt. 22:35. [585]

For this purpose they select a certain scribe, a law expert. We receive a favorable impression of him. Having learned from many previous passages in Mark's Gospel how very hostile most scribes and Pharisees were toward Jesus (2:7; 3:2, 6, 22; 7:1, 2, 5; 8:31; 10:33; 11:18; 12:13), and how he, in turn, condemns them, a fact of which we are reminded again in the present chapter (see verses 38-40), we find it surprising that this not unfriendly scribe was chosen to represent the Pharisees in testing Jesus. Was it because they did not really know this man? Or did they indeed know him rather thoroughly, and did they send him, thinking, "*him* Jesus will not suspect, and we may still be able to trip up our enemy because of the *answer* he will give"? We do not know.

What we know is that this man, too, had taken note of the fact that Jesus had answered the Sadducees very well. Is it not possible that his own motivation and that of those who put him forward did not entirely coincide; that is, that with him approval had triumphed over misgiving and a desire to discredit?

---

584 συζητούντων, gen. pl. masc. pres. participle of συζητέω. See on 8:11, footnote 368. Note the three aorist participles: προσελθών, ἀκούσας, ἰδών. The *temporal* order is actually: having heard, having recognized, and having come up, he asked him.

585 Is it necessary, with some interpreters—e.g., Lenski, *op. cit.*, p. 336—, to assign a favorable meaning to πειράζων in this parallel passage? The verb has no such connotation in Matt. 4:1, 3; 16:1; 19:3; 22:18; or in Mark 1:13; 8:11; 10:2; 12:15. Assigning a milder meaning to the participle as used in Matt. 22:35—for example, "attempting to discover whether he was able to give the right answer," but *not* "attempting to catch him in a trap with the ultimate aim of destroying him"—results from the fact that, literally interpreted, the "testing" of which Matt. 22:35 speaks is ascribed to the noble law expert (or scribe) himself. Note the singular. A possibility would be to regard the language as an abbreviated expression—see N.T.C. on John, Vol. I, p. 206—, the full meaning being "and one of them a law expert, asked him a question, (by means of which those who sent him were) testing him," the words between parentheses being implied. Since even then the agent did the actual testing, a change from sing. to pl. would not be necessary. Both in ordinary speech and in literature such abbreviated expressions are not at all exceptional. Whatever the answer be, it is very improbable that the bitter opponents of Jesus had suddenly become friendly toward Jesus.

The question asked by this scribe, this expert in the knowledge of the whole body of Jewish religious literature—God's written law and its oral interpretation and application—, could be expected of him. The rabbis, devoted to hairsplitting legalism, carried on lengthy debates about the commandments, arguing whether a particular one was great or small, heavy or light. It was natural, therefore, that they debated the question, "Which of the 613 commandments, 248 of them positive, 365 negative [according to their count] is foremost of all?" [586]

Among the Jews two contrary tendencies were at work. One was to *analyze* the law, dividing it into ever so many hairsplitting ramifications. A good example is Matt. 5:33-37; 23:16-18. The other tendency was the very opposite, namely, to *synthesize,* that is, to express the summary of the law in one brief sentence. Even before the time of Jesus several famous rabbis had tried to do this, with varying success.

In a way this latter attempt was excellent. Religion is, after all, a matter of selecting the right priorities. If that is not done, it easily degenerates into majoring on minors. In Matt. 23:23 Jesus very concisely contrasts the good way with the bad: "Woe to y o u, scribes and Pharisees, hypocrites! because y o u tithe mint, dill, and cummin, but have neglected the more important requirements of the law: justice and mercy and faithfulness."

29-31. Jesus answered, The foremost is, Hear, O Israel, the Lord our God, the Lord is one. And you shall love the Lord your God with all your heart and with all your soul and with all your mind and with all your strength. The second is this, You shall love your neighbor as yourself. There is no other commandment greater than these.

Jesus here teaches that:

a. The whole duty of man, the whole moral-spiritual law, can be summed up in one word: *love.* Cf. Rom. 13:9, 10; I Cor. 13.

b. This love must be directed first of all toward God. In this connection Mark reports that Jesus began his summary of the law by quoting Deut. 6:4, 5: "Hear, O Israel, the Lord our God, the Lord is one. And you shall love the Lord your God with all your heart. . . ." In the original Hebrew, the first word of this quotation is *Sh^ema',* [587] meaning "Hear." In English literature the Hebrew form is often transliterated *Shema,* and the entire quotation is generally called "the Shema." Today, the ancient custom of beginning the synagogue service with the recitation of the Shema is still being observed.

---

[586] Note the meaning of $\pi\rho\dot{\omega}\tau\eta$ in $\pi\rho\dot{\omega}\tau\eta$ $\dot{\epsilon}\nu\tau o\lambda\dot{\eta}$. As in Eph. 6:2, so also here, the sense is probably *the commandment of greatest significance.* That interpretation also brings the question into harmony with its wording in Matt. 22:36. For the meaning of $\dot{\epsilon}\nu\tau o\lambda\dot{\eta}$ see above, on 7:8, footnote 319.

[587] This form is the Qal imper. sing. masc. of the verb *shāma'.*

This holds, too, with respect to the Jewish *phylacteries.* These contain the Shema in its longer form (Deut. 6:4-9; 11:13-21). For more on this see N.T.C. on Matthew, p. 823.

Finally, we should make mention of the *mezuzah,* a rectangular piece of inscribed parchment enclosed in a metal or wooden case, and attached to the upper section of a Jewish dwelling's right hand door post. The inscribed material consists of the Shema in its longer form. It is written in twenty-two lines, in accordance with definite rules.

It is readily understood that the Shema was and is the very foundation of monotheism. Not only that, but it stresses the fact that this one and only God wants to the loved! This is in harmony with the fact that he himself is a loving God. This is a truth taught not only in the *New* Testament (John 3:16; Rom. 5:8; 8:32; etc.) but also, either directly or by implication, in such *Old* Testament passages as Deut. 33:27; Ps. 27:10; 87:2; 103:8-14; 145:8, 9; 146:8; 147:1-3; Prov. 3:12; Isa. 1:18; 55:7; Jer. 31:31-34; Hos. 11:8; Jon. 4:11; Mic. 7:18-20; etc.

c. Heart, soul, mind, and strength must co-operate in loving God. The *heart* is the hub of the wheel of man's existence, the mainspring of all his thoughts, words, and deeds (Prov. 4:23). The *soul*—the word used in the original has a variety of meanings (see on 8:12, footnote 370)—is here probably the seat of man's emotional activity; the *mind* is not only the seat and center of his purely intellectual life but also of his dispositions and attitudes. In the Hebrew original (and also in the LXX) of Deut. 6:5 the reading is "heart, soul, and might (or power)." Mark 12:30 has "heart, soul, mind, and *strength.*" Cf. Luke 10:27. No essential difference is intended. We must not begin to over-analyze. What is meant in all these passages is that man should love God with all the "faculties" with which God has endowed him.

d. Moreover, man must use all these powers *to the full.* Note fourfold "all . . . all . . . all . . . all." The point is that God's wholehearted love must not be answered in a halfhearted manner. When God loves, he loves the world; when he gives, he gives his Son, hence himself. See N.T.C. on John 3:16. He gives him up. He does not spare him (Rom. 8:32). Greater love, [588] more marvelous self-giving, is impossible (John 15:13; Rom. 5:6-10; II Cor. 8:9). Surely, *the response* to such love must not be less than that indicated in Rom. 11:33-36; I Cor. 6:20; 10:31; II Cor. 9:15; Eph. 5:1, 2; Col. 3:12-17.

e. This love must be directed not only toward God (Deut. 6:5) but also

---

588 In the original "you shall love" is ἀγαπήσεις. Is there a distinction between ἀγαπάω and φιλέω; and if so, what is that distinction? See on 10:21, footnote 475.

toward man (Lev. 19:18). The question whether or not Jesus was the first to combine these two passages, [589] which in the Old Testament are separated, is not very important. If this point is pressed, the objection might be raised, "What about the author of *The Testament of the Twelve Patriarchs,* where Issachar (5:2) is introduced as saying, 'Love the Lord and love your neighbor' "? It should be pointed out, however, that Issachar's statement is not nearly as full as is Mark 12:29-31, and besides, that it is hard to determine how much in this writing, falsely ascribed to the twelve patriarchs, is original and how much is Christian interpolation. A stronger argument for the position that Jesus may not have been the first to combine these two Old Testament passages into one is found in Luke 10:27. But this does not necessarily imply that the combination of Deut. 6:5 with Lev. 19:18 originated with the "lawyer" there mentioned. There are those—for example, C. G. Montefiore, *The Synoptic Gospels,* London, 1927, Vol. II, p. 464—who believe that "the combination was apparently a commonplace, equally familiar to Christian and to Jew." That, too, cannot be proved.

What is, however, far more important is that Jesus, not only by word but also by very deed, was the first to set forth the true meaning of perfect love toward God united with perfect love toward man. "When two say the same thing, they may not actually be saying the same thing." What a vast contrast between the two speakers in Mark 12:30, 31 and Luke 10:27! Yet, both say essentially the same thing. The context of these two passages indicates Christ's big-heartedness and the lawyer's small-mindedness.

f. The second commandment resembles the first in this respect: both require love. Moreover, love toward the neighbor, who is God's image bearer, flows forth from love toward God (I John 4:20, 21; cf. Matt. 5:43; 7:12; 19:19). Conversely, the love which from the heart of God radiates toward his children, helps them to love their fellows (Eph. 4:32—5:2).

g. "Love your neighbor *as yourself.*" Man has been created with love for himself. That love for self should be the measure whereby he decides how to love his neighbor. This is a very practical precept, a rule of thumb. And that "neighbor," moreover, is anyone who has been providentially placed in his path for sympathy and help. A person should really never ask, "And who is my neighbor?" Instead, be himself *should be* a true neighbor to those in need, even though they be his enemies. See Matt. 5:43-48; Luke 10:30-37.

h. Jesus brings his answer to a climax by declaring, "There is no other command greater than these." And why are these two commandments the greatest?

First, faith and hope *take,* love *gives.* Faith appropriates the salvation that

---

[589] The position taken by W. Barclay, *op. cit.,* p. 309.

is in Christ. Hope accepts the promise of the future inheritance. Love, however, means *self-giving, self-impartation.*

Secondly, all other virtues are included in love. See I Cor. 13. According to that chapter active, intelligent, voluntary love implies patience, kindness, and humility (verse 4), unselfishness (verse 5), faith and hope (verse 7).

Thirdly, human love, in its noblest expression, is patterned after God, for "God is love." The all-surpassing character of love is clearly taught in Scripture (Col. 3:14; I Peter 4:8; I John 3:14; 4:8).

32, 33. The scribe said to him, Right! Teacher, you have truthfully stated that he is one, and there is no other but he. Moreover, to love him with all your heart and with all your understanding and with all your strength, and to love your neighbor as yourself, means far more than all burnt-offerings and sacrifices.

It was with delighted, unqualified approval that this scribe accepted the answer given by Jesus. The law-expert's reaction begins with an exclamation, "Right! Teacher. . . ." [590] For "Right!" one might substitute "Excellent!" or even "Beautiful!" For "Teacher" see on 12:14. It is clear that the words of Jesus had made a very deep impression upon this man, and that he is honest enough to admit it, even doing this with joy and enthusiasm. He adds that Jesus had spoken "truthfully," and he then virtually repeats what the Master had just said.

The variations between Christ's own words and their near-repetition by the scribe are very slight. The scribe does not permit himself the privilege of uttering the Sacred Name. He substitutes "understanding" [591] for "mind," and leaves out "soul."

The man also adds something, namely, that such love as here described "means far more than all burnt-offerings [592] and sacrifices." The first term refers to offerings that were wholly consumed by fire (cf. Lev. 1:9). The second may indicate offerings or sacrifices in general; in the present case the reference is most likely to "all other sacrifices."

It would seem that this man was rather thoroughly at home in the Scriptures. At least what he says here is the very truth emphasized and constantly repeated in the Old Testament. See especially the following passages: I Sam. 15:22; Ps. 40:6, 7; 51:16, 17; Isa. 1:10-17; Hos. 6:6; Mic. 6:6-8.

34. And when Jesus saw that he had answered wisely, he said to him, You

---

590 Because of its position in the sentence it is better to regard καλῶς as an exclamation than to construe it with εἶπες, and then to translate "Well said."

591 συνέσεως, gen. sing. of σύνεσις, related to συνίημι, to put (two and two) together, to understand. Accordingly, σύνεσις means understanding, comprehension, insight.

592 ὁλοκαύτωμα from ὅλος (whole) and καίω, to burn.

are not far from the kingdom of God. We really know very little about this specialist in Jewish law. Had he been favorably inclined toward the Lord from the very beginning of the present incident, and perhaps even earlier? Or had he been hostile at first, and had his unfavorable attitude melted in the presence of Jesus and because of the latter's succinct and beautiful summary of God's law? Whatever may have been the case, it is clear from verses 32, 33 that he warmly endorsed the answer Jesus had given. So Jesus, in turn, encourages the scribe. The Teacher saw that the man had answered wisely, that is, as a person who *had a mind* [593] and used it to good advantage.

So Jesus encouraged him by saying, "You are not far from the kingdom of God." Were other scribes still immersed in thousands of hairsplitting legal trivialities (Mark 7:3, 4; cf. Matt. 23:23), as if their observance was necessary for entrance into the kingdom? Not—at least, no longer—this one. He understood that the key that unlocked the door of the kingdom was LOVE; God's own love for sinners, their all-out love for him and for the neighbor created as his image-bearer. If this scribe would now, by God's grace and power, take one more step, namely, actually come to—that is, believe in—Jesus as his Savior and Lord (Matt. 11:28-30; John 6:35), he would have advanced from a position of being "not far from" to one of being "inside" the kingdom of God. Of one thing there can be no question: by means of this very word of encouragement, "You are not far from the kingdom of God," Jesus was urging him to enter that kingdom. [594]

What has just been said introduces us to the subject of

Jesus, the Great Encourager

We have seen how he encouraged the scribe by telling him that he was not far from the kingdom of God. The conversations and discourses of the Lord are full of similar encouragements. Leaving out such words as were spoken in *immediate* connection with healings (for example, "Your faith has healed you"), note the following, all of them taken from Mark's Gospel:

"I will make y o u become fishers of men" (1:17).

"Son, your sins are forgiven" (2:5).

"Here are my mother and my brothers" (3:35).

"Fear not, only believe" (5:36).

"Take courage, it is I; do not be afraid" (6:50).

"Let the little children come to me, and stop hindering them, for to such belongs the kingdom of God" (10:14).

---

[593] The adverb νουνεχῶς, occurring only here in the New Testament, is the equivalent of νουνεχόντως. See M.M., pp. 430, 431.

[594] A fact that is also pointed out by Lenski; *op. cit.*, p. 341.

"There is no one who has given up house or brothers . . . who shall not receive a hundredfold . . ." (10:29, 30).

"Whatever y o u ask in prayer, believing that y o u received it, it shall be y o u r s" (11:24).

"Whenever y o u are arrested and taken to trial, do not worry beforehand about what y o u should say. On the contrary, whatever is given y o u at that time, that y o u must say, for it is not y o u who are speaking but the Holy Spirit" (13:11).

"But he that endures to the end, he shall be saved." (13:13).

All this in addition to the numerous similar words of comfort and encouragement found in the other Gospels. For just a few among the many see Matt. 5:1-16; 11:28-30; 14:27; Luke 6:23, 12:32; 22:31, 32; 23:43; John, the entire fourteenth chapter; 15:11; 16:24, 33; etc.

This is not to say that our Lord limited himself to words of encouragement. Definitely not. When denunciation or sharp reproof was in order, he supplied it. See, for example, Mark 4:28, 29; 7:6-13; 9:19; 12:38, 39; and see especially Matt. 23. The emphasis, however, was on the positive, a hint for every preacher and witness-bearer.

To be sure, sin must be exposed in all its horror. Without the knowledge of sin there is no salvation. The preacher who fails to describe sin as it truly is—defiance of God's holy will—, and who neglects to point out again and again what are its terrible consequences, is not a true interpreter of the Word of God. On the other hand, the pulpiteer who neglects to address words of comfort to penitents, and to encourage them with messages of cheer taken from or based on Scripture, is not true to the maxim, engraved on many a pulpit, "Sir, we would see Jesus" (John 12:21).

* * * * *

And from then on no one dared to ask him any more questions. Something similar is reported in Luke 20:40 and in Matt. 22:46. A possible explanation would be that after the second question, the one touching the resurrection, the Sadducees had been silenced so effectually that they lacked the courage to ask any more questions (Luke 20:40). After the third question, "Of all the commandments which is the foremost?" the same timidity smote the Pharisees (Mark 12:34), a fact not reported by Matthew until after he had related how Jesus had embarrassed his opponents with his own question (22:46). Thus interpreted, there is no contradiction between these three somewhat similar statements.

The main fact is that Jesus had completely crushed the opposition, and in the process of doing this had even succeeded in drawing a member of a largely hostile group closer to his own side.

Christ's Own Question: Whose Son Is the Christ?

The record of this incident is found in Matthew, Mark, and Luke. Between the latter two there is, as often, a close resemblance. Matthew's account is much longer. Mark informs us that it was "while Jesus was teaching in the temple" that he raised the question here reported. We may assume that it was still Tuesday. In view of the fact that so much had already happened on that day, the present confrontation probably took place in the afternoon.

Those present were Jesus and his disciples (cf. Matt. 23:1; Luke 20:45), Pharisees (Matt. 22:41), among whom were several scribes (Mark 12:35), and a huge crowd (Mark 12:37b).

The main difference between Matthew, on the one hand, and on the other Mark and Luke, is that it is Matthew alone who records this incident from its very beginning. If the following harmony is accepted, there is no conflict between the three accounts:

Matthew 22	*Mark 12*
41, 42 Now while the Pharisees were gathered together, Jesus asked them, What is y o u r opinion of the Christ? Whose son is he?" They said to him, "David's."	35 Now while Jesus was teaching in the temple, he asked, "How can the scribes say that Christ is the son of David?" Cf. *Luke* 20:41, 42.
43 He said to them, "How then does David in the Spirit call him Lord, saying:	36 David himself, moved by the Holy Spirit, declared: saying:

Matt. 22:44, 45; Mark 12:36 (continued); *Luke 20:42* (continued)

> The Lord said to my Lord,
> Sit at my right hand
> ETC.

A few slight variations are: *a.* While Matthew and Mark ascribe the words of David to their source, namely, the (Holy) Spirit, Luke informs the reader that this quotation is found in "the book of Psalms." Also, Luke substitutes "a stool for your feet" for Matthew's and Mark's "under your feet."

As for the reaction of the audience to the words of Jesus, Luke is silent; Mark writes, "The huge crowd enjoyed listening to him"; and Matthew, "And no one was able to say a word in reply, nor from that day on did anyone dare to ask him another question."

*   *   *   *

35. Now while Jesus was teaching in the temple he asked, How can the scribes say that the Christ is the son of David?

At first glance there seems to be no connection between this paragraph and the immediately preceding one. Mark states only that the incident now related occurred in the temple. Nevertheless, over against his vagueness as to some of the circumstances, it is but fair to state that there is, after all, a probable link between verses 28-34 and verses 35-37. A moment ago, in his summary of the law, Jesus had placed all the emphasis on *love,* as being the fulfilment of the Decalog. And now he is putting this love into practice by directing the attention of his audience to faith in himself, for apart from such faith—and from the right conception about the Christ—no scribe (or anyone else) can be saved. Although we know that most of those to whom the Master's question was addressed continued to harden themselves, is it not possible that the man to whom Jesus had said, "You are not far from the kingdom" (12:34) was brought completely into the kingdom when he pondered Christ's question? Not all scribes were equally bad. Not all the Jewish leaders permanently rejected Jesus. See Mark 15:42-46; cf. Matt. 27:57; Luke 23:50, 51; John 19:38, 39. But regardless of all this, nothing can detract from the fact that Jesus, in causing this kind of audience (remember 12:13!) to come face to face with the question "Whose son is Christ?" (implied), is revealing his marvelous love. He is conversing with these men publicly *for the very last time,* and therefore asks the most important question of all.

It is clear that the Master is referring to himself when he says "the Christ." The question is, however, so phrased (namely, in the third person) that the Pharisees are able to give a ready answer without affirming that Jesus is himself the Christ. In fact, the idea that Jesus would be the Christ was repugnant to them. The expected *Messiah* (of which "Christ" is the Greek translation) was, indeed, the Son of David. This they knew, and this they taught (12:35; John 7:42). Moreover, in so far they were correct, for that is the teaching of Scripture (II Sam. 7:12, 13; Ps. 78:68-72; 89:3, 4, 20, 24, 28, 34-37; Amos 9:11; Mic. 5:2; etc.). But hearing *Jesus* called "the Son of David," how they hated that! See Matt. 12:23, 24; 21:15, 16.

There was one more thing which Pharisees and scribes knew. It was this, that Jesus had made no objections to the title "Son of David." He had rebuked neither the disciples nor the children when they, by implication, had called him this. However, the air must be purified. The earthly ideas attached to the concept "Son of David" or "Messiah" must be removed. Cf. John 18:36. The time has arrived to prepare the audience for the idea that the title "Son of David" means more than was generally realized. Pharisees and scribes must learn that David's Son is also David's *Lord. David's* Son is *God's* Son. Accordingly, when Jesus now says, "How can the scribes say that the Christ is the son of David?" he means, "How can they say that the Christ is *merely* the Son of David?" After all, not only is he *man;* he is also *God!*

This truth should have been clear to the scribes, from the Old Testament.

36, 37a. David himself, moved by the Holy Spirit declared:

> The Lord said to my Lord,
> Sit at my right hand
> Until I put your enemies under your feet.

David himself calls him Lord. How then can he be his son?

Explanation:

a. The quotation is from Ps. 110 (LXX 109):1. Between, on the one hand, the original Hebrew text faithfully reproduced in the LXX Greek text, and, on the other, Mark's version, there is no *essential* difference. Whether, with the Hebrew and the LXX, one says, "until I make your enemies a (foot)stool for your feet"; or, with Mark (recording the words of Jesus) "Until I put your enemies under your feet," in both cases the figure that results is that of an enemy lying before a person in the dust, so that the conqueror's feet can be placed upon his neck. Cf. Josh. 10:24. Complete triumph over every foe is assured *by* "the Lord" *to* "the Lord."

b. Jesus ascribes this psalm (110) to David, and asserts that the latter wrote it "in," that is, "moved by" the Holy Spirit; hence, "by inspiration."

c. Jesus is here declaring that Ps. 110 is a Messianic Psalm. It was so regarded also by Peter (Acts 2:34, 35), by Paul (I Cor. 15:25), and by the author of the Epistle to the Hebrews (1:13; cf. 10:13).[595]

d. In this psalm David is making a distinction between YHWH (Jehovah) and 'Adonai. YHWH, then, is addressing David's 'Adonai; or, if one prefers, God is speaking to the Mediator. He is promising the Mediator such preeminence, power, authority, and majesty as would be proper only for One who, as to his person, from all eternity was, is now, and forever will be God. See Eph. 1:20-23; Phil. 2:5-11; Heb. 2:9; Rev. 5:1-10; 12:5.

e. Nevertheless this same exalted Lord is David's son (II Sam. 7:12, 13; Ps. 132:17). That *Jesus* satisfies this description is clear from Matt. 1; Luke 1:32; 3:23-38; Acts 2:30; Rom. 1:3; II Tim. 2:8; Rev. 5:5. Thus Christ is both God and man.

f. The words, "David himself calls him Lord. How then can he be his son?" do not mean, "the Messiah cannot be David's son," but must mean, "cannot be David's son *merely* in the sense of his descendant." He is far more than that. He is the root as well as the offspring of David (Rev. 22:16; cf. Isa. 11:1, 10).

It is as if Jesus were saying to his critics, "Y o u have found fault with me

---

595 According to S.BK., Vol. IV., p. 452 ff. the Messianic character of this psalm was also accepted by the rabbis.

for accepting the praises of those who called me 'the Son of David.' Bear in mind, then, that I am the Son of David in the most exalted sense, for David himself called me 'my Lord.' Therefore whoever rejects me is rejecting David's Lord." Yet, Jesus is not as yet *openly* telling the enemies that *he* is indeed the Christ. That will come a little later. See 14:61, 62.

g. It is comforting to know that not only according to 12:10, 11 (see on that passage) but also according to the present passage Jesus a few days before his most bitter agony was fully aware that the way of the cross would for him lead home, to the crown!

37b. The huge crowd enjoyed listening to him. The fact that just now Jesus had been criticizing the scribes did not seem to bother the large listening crowd. In fact, these people were enjoying what they heard. The statement is general, however. Throughout his ministry, whenever possible large crowds came to Jesus. At times they sought healing for themselves or for their dear ones; at other times they came mainly to listen to his words (Mark 1:22; 2:2, 13; 4:1 ff.; 6:34 10:1; cf. Matt. 7:28, 29). The two purposes were often combined (Luke 5:15; 6:17).

But enjoying a sermon or a discourse—any word whatever, coming, whether indirectly or directly, from the mouth of the Lord—is not the same as being spiritually benefited by it. So often, when we read 12:37b we forget that Mark has used these identical words (see the original) in another context, namely, in connection with the eagerness with which Herod Antipas listened to John the Baptist, the very man whom he, the "king," was about to murder! See on 6:20 above. Memory's bell should have awakened us immediately to that previous passage, and also, for that matter, to Ezekiel's experience. Was it not said with reference to him that in the estimation of his audience he was "a very lovely song of one who has a pleasant voice, and can play well on an instrument," and was not the following comment added: "for they hear your words *but do not do them*"? See Ezek. 33:31, 32; also Matt. 13:5, 6, 20, 21. Do not such people resemble the man who built his house on sand instead of on rock (Matt. 7:26, 27)? Undoubtedly among those many people who were "enjoying" what Jesus was saying there must have been at least some who a few days later were going to join their voices to the "Crucify him!" refrain.

Nevertheless, while the point just made deserves considerable emphasis, we must not forget where the main stress lies, namely, in once more pointing to Jesus as the Great and Victorious King, the One who exercised control over everything, including even audiences, while he was carrying out the task which the Father had assigned to him.

---

38 And in his teaching he was saying, "Be on y o u r guard against the scribes, who relish parading about in long, flowing robes, formal salutations in the market-places, chief

seats in the synagogues,   39 and places of honor at the banquets.   40 Those who devour widows' houses, and for show [596] offer lengthy prayers, they shall receive a heavier sentence.

12:38-40 *Denunciation of the Scribes*
Cf. Matt. 23:1-36; especially 23:6, 7a; Luke 20:45-47

Mark 12:38-40 is repeated almost word for word in Luke 20:45-47. Some of the same accusations and characterizations are also found in Matt. 23:6, 7a; and on "offering lengthy prayers" cf. Matt. 6:5-7.

One may, perhaps, consider these three verses of Mark to be a very brief summary of Christ's Fifth Great Discourse, *The Seven Woes*, found in Matt. 23.

From an attack upon the *teaching* of the scribes (12:35-37a) Jesus now proceeds to an attack upon their *practice*.

38a. And in his teaching he was saying. . . . By thus expressing himself, both here and in 4:2, Mark makes clear that what follows is no more than an extract from the Master's teaching.

> **38b-40a. Be on y o u r guard against the scribes,**
> **who relish parading about in long, flowing robes,**
> **formal salutations in the market-places,**
> **chief seats in the synagogues,**
> **and places of honor at the banquets.**
> **Those who devour widows' houses,**
> **and for show offer lengthy prayers.** . . .

Illustrations of the manner in which the scribes tried to harvest praise for themselves are now given. Nowhere does Jesus even suggest that the following description was a true picture of *every* scribe. The one sketched in 12:28-34 must have been a totally different kind of person. At a later time, too, among those who joined Christ's army, or at least defended believers' rights, there were both Pharisees and priests (Acts 5:33; 6:7; Phil. 3:1 ff.). Nevertheless, it is safe to assume that what Jesus here said was a true description of very many scribes of that day and age. They were proud, selfish, insincere, untrustworthy.

"Be on y o u r guard against them," said Jesus to his disciples, in the hearing of all the people (Luke 20:45). [597] He then lists six items with respect to which these men show their evil traits:

---

596 Or: to attract attention.

597 The durative present βλέπετε ἀπό means: continue to look away from (the scribes), avoid them, turn y o u r backs on them; hence, "Beware of," "Be on y o u r guard against," as in 8:15. Though the idiom as here used may be regarded as a Hebraism, it has been found in the papyri.

a. "who relish [598] parading about in long, flowing robes." These men are putting on airs: they walked around attired like kings or priests, [599] about to perform official functions.

b. formal salutations in the market-places. Though the word for "salutation" that is here used can indicate a friendly spoken greeting, or a written message of regards (I Cor. 16:21; Col. 4:18; II Thess. 3:17), here it has a more formidable connotation, as the immediate context in Matt. 23:7 indicates (" . . . the formal salutations in the market-places, and to have the people address them as 'rabbi.' "). What the men who are here rebuked were always longing for was not a mere token of friendliness but rather a demonstration of respect, a public recognition of their prominence.

c. chief seats in the synagogues. Those were the seats in front of the raised platform on which stood the prayer leader and the reader of the Scriptures. Thus seated, a man had the double advantage of being near the person reading or leading in prayer, and of facing the congregation and thus being able to see everybody. Besides, being ushered to such a seat was regarded as a mark of honor.

d. places of honor at the banquets. Jesus issued a warning against this very sin of seeking the best seat at a banquet or dinner (Luke 14:8). James condemned the sin of assigning the best seat to the rich, while telling the poor man to stand or else to sit on the floor near someone's footstool (2:2, 3).

e. widows' houses. The scribes here condemned are described as devouring—fattening themselves on—the houses of these lonely women. [600]

The question, "Just how did these men do this?" has been answered

---

598 The present participle $\theta\epsilon\lambda\acute{o}\nu\tau\omega\nu$, from $\theta\acute{\epsilon}\lambda\omega$, has here the meaning "relishing, taking delight in." Note that it is followed both by an infinitive and by three nouns in the accusative.

599 Though for $\sigma\tauo\lambda\acute{\eta}$ the translation "stole" here—and also in Mark 16:5; Luke 15:22; 20:46; Rev. 6:11; 7:9, 13, 14; 22:14—would not be wrong, this English word is rather ambiguous, since it can also denote *the narrow cloth band* which priests and bishops wear around their neck, and which descends from their shoulders; and it can even mean an article of feminine apparel, that is, *a long wide scarf.*

600 Why the sudden change from the genitive (or ablative) after $\beta\lambda\acute{\epsilon}\pi\epsilon\tau\epsilon$ $\mathring{a}\pi\acute{o}$ to the nominative $\kappa\alpha\tau\epsilon\sigma\theta\acute{\iota}o\nu\tau\epsilon\varsigma \ldots \kappa\alpha\acute{\iota} \ldots \pi\rho o\sigma\epsilon\upsilon\chi\acute{o}\mu\epsilon\nuo\iota$? Would not the genitive have been more natural? To solve the problem of this construction some would call $o\mathring{\iota}$ $\kappa\alpha\tau. \kappa\tau\lambda$ an anacoluthon, the agreement with $\tau\tilde{\omega}\nu$ $\theta\epsilon\lambda\acute{o}\nu\tau\omega\nu$ being merely according to sense. Luke 20:47, by using not a participle but a relative plus indicative, makes reading easier. Here in Mark some of the manuscripts have dealt similarly with the problem.

What is probably the easiest and the best—and, after all, not resulting in such an unusual Greek construction—is to regard the two substantive-participles of verse 40 as belonging to a new sentence, the subject of which is the demonstrative pronoun $o\mathring{\upsilon}\tauo\iota$, with the two participles in apposition, the predicate verb being $\lambda\acute{\eta}\mu\psi o\nu\tau\alpha\iota$, and $\kappa\rho\acute{\iota}\mu\alpha$ the latter's object.

differently. Some of the answers that have been suggested are: to funds under their control and from which they, these scribes, could draw, they asked widows to contribute more than could reasonably have been expected of them; or, they offered their help in settling estates that fell to widows, meanwhile taking for themselves more than was coming to them; or, they took unfair advantage of material support which initially had been volunteered by widows. Whatever may have been the method used, it is clear that Jesus is here condemning the crime of extortion practiced on widows, according to Scripture a most heinous wrong indeed; see on verses 41-44. The history of the church supplies many examples of this evil. Read C. Chiniquy's chapter, "The Priest, Purgatory, and the poor Widow's Cow." [601]

f. praise from men. ". . . and for show [602] offer lengthy prayers." It was for the purpose of drawing attention to themselves that the scribes offered these almost endless prayers. Cf. I Thess. 2:5, 6. All they were seeking was honor from men. . . . Or, was this really all? The close grammatical juxtaposition of "devouring widows' houses" and "offering lengthy prayers" have led some [603] to suggest that between these two activities there was a very close connection, the meaning being: they devour widows' houses and *to cover up their wickedness* they make long prayers. The longer they pray for the widows (or at least in their presence), the more they can prey upon them!—Whether there is sufficient evidence for this interpretation let everyone decide for himself. Even apart from it, the evil here condemned was scandalous. For "lengthy prayers" see N.T.C. on Matthew, pp. 323-325.

As with a crash of thunder doom is pronounced upon those hypocrites: **40b. they shall receive a heavier sentence,** more severe punishment, overflowing condemnation. For those people, the very men described here in such detail—the students, interpreters, and teachers of the law, who therefore had every reason to know that God required humility, sincerity, and love—, for them the retribution is going to be all the more severe.

* * * *

The lessons taught in this little paragraph

a. Jesus warns against the sinful craving to be somebody, that is, to be prominent, to be honored above everybody else. Greatest is he who is willing to be least, that is, to serve (Mark 10:44, 45).

---

[601] *Fifty Years in the Church of Rome,* New York, Chicago, Toronto, 1886, pp. 41-48.

[602] In John 15:22, however, the meaning of πρόφασις is *valid excuse.*

[603] See the renderings by Williams, Beck, Phillips; also Lenski, *op. cit.,* p. 348.

b. He rebukes all sham in religion. Christ's true followers are unpretentious. They resemble little children (10:15).

c. He condemns using religion for gain (11:17; I Tim. 6:5).

d. He predicts that those who, though they know God's law, persevere in these sins—that is, in the "So Big" philosophy, hypocrisy, simony—shall receive a heavier punishment (Amos 3:2; Luke 12:47, 48; Acts 8:9-24).

e. He reveals that his all-seeing eyes penetrate the veil by means of which pious frauds try to hide their real intention (Ps. 139:1-6; John 2:25; 21:17; Heb. 4:13).

f. The true solution for everyone is Ps. 139:23, 24.

---

41 And as he sat down opposite the treasury, he was watching how the crowd dropped their money into the treasury. Many rich people were dropping in large amounts. 42 But a poor widow came and dropped in two very small copper coins, worth only a fraction of a penny. 43 Calling his disciples to him he said, "I solemnly declare to y o u that this poor widow dropped more into the treasury than all the others. 44 For they all gave out of their abundance, but she out of her poverty dropped in all she had, her whole living."

12:41-44 *A Widow's Offering*
Cf. Luke 21:1-4

This happens to be one of the few units of Gospel material occurring only in Mark and Luke. See N.T.C. on Matthew, p. 21. Luke's account impresses one as being an abbreviation of Mark's, and not much besides. It is very understandable that the sympathetic and beloved physician (Col. 4:14) did not wish to omit a story that so eminently served his purpose of picturing Jesus as The Sympathetic Highpriest.

The close connection between the immediately preceding report and this one can hardly escape us. That connection is twofold: *a. temporal:* though the exact time is not indicated, it seems reasonable to infer that after Jesus had delivered his Fifth Great Discourse, The Seven Woes, reproduced in Matt. 23 and briefly summarized in Mark 12:38-40 (cf. Luke 20:45-47), he would take a brief rest during which he "watched" the people, as Mark 12:41 indicates; and *b. material:* the same loving Savior, who has just now denounced the scribes for "devouring widows' houses" (12:40), shows, by his own example, how widows should *really* be treated. One should help them, and, as here, praise them whenever such praise is in order.

41. And as he sat down opposite the treasury, he was watching how the crowd dropped their money into the treasury. The phrase "opposite the treasury" has given rise to different interpretations. See, however, the sketch of The Ground Plan of The Temple, p. 448. Consult also what was said in connection with the Women's Court, with its thirteen trumpet-shaped chests, that is, receptacles for gifts and dues, p. 450. It may well have been,

505

therefore, that Jesus had seated himself near the opening of that court, perhaps in the vicinity of The Beautiful Gate. From that spot these receptacles, [604] at least some of them, would be in full view. Jesus, then, was watching or carefully observing [605] how the people dropped their money [606] into the treasury, that is, into its receptacles.—In a sense, he has been doing this ever since, is still doing it. See Acts 5:1-11; II Cor. 9:6, 7; Heb. 4:13.

Many rich people were dropping in large amounts. By means of letters of the Hebrew alphabet each receptacle was marked, so that the people would know for what distinctive purpose the money it received would be used, whether for the temple tribute, for sacrifices, incense, wood, or whatever. Jesus noticed that many rich people were dropping in large amounts. Well, those with large holdings should give large sums. There was nothing wrong with that. The Bible makes mention of several rich men who can hardly be thought of as having ever donated large amounts to any good cause (I Sam. 25:2, 3, 10, 11; Luke 12:16-19; 16:19-21). Nevertheless, as Jesus saw it, it was not the amount of the gift that mattered most but the heart of the giver.

This becomes clear from verse 42. **But a** [607] **poor widow came and dropped in** [608] **two very small copper coins, worth only a fraction of a penny.** According to the original, this widow dropped in two *lepta,* which means a quarter. [609] A quarter of what? Of a dollar? No, of an *as* or *assarius.* And an assarius was worth only *one sixteenth of a denarius!* The denarius was a laborer's average daily wage (Matt. 18:28; 20:2, 9, 13; 22:19). Due to constantly varying monetary values it is impossible to indicate with any degree of accuracy what such coins would be worth today in American or in English money. *If* the denarius be viewed as the equivalent of 16-18 American cents, then the assarius would be worth about a cent, the "quarter" or "quadrant" only about ¼ cent, and the "lepton" merely 1/8 cent.

The little copper coins which this widow dropped into the "trumpet" were literally "thin ones." Not only were they very small, they were also very thin or light. When one thinks of a *lepton,* he should remember that our

---

604 The term γαζοφυλακεῖον consists of two parts: γάζα Persian for *treasure,* and φυλακή *guard, safeguard;* hence, a chest into which treasures or gifts could be dropped and safely kept.

605 ἐθεώρει, third per. sing. imperf. active of θεωρέω. For the fine distinctions between various New Testament words for *seeing* consult N.T.C. on John, Vol. I, p. 85, footnote 33.

606 χαλκός, see above, on 6:8.

607 μία = the indefinite article.

608 Notice striking contrast between, on the one hand, βάλλει and ἔβαλλον (verse 41), and, on the other, ἔβαλε (verse 42). The present and imperfect picture what was happening all the while. These verbal forms describe the background of the story. The constative aorist tells what the widow suddenly did.

609 Greek κοδράντης, borrowed from the Latin *quadrans.*

English word *leaf* is related to it. The two *lepta,* taken together, should be regarded as being worth no more than a fraction of a penny.

By human calculation what the widow gave was insignificant. . . . Measured by divine standard, however, her contribution was priceless, as is clear from verses 43, 44. **Calling his disciples to him he said, I solemnly declare to y o u that this poor widow dropped more into the treasury than all the others. For they all gave out of their abundance, but she out of her poverty dropped in all she had, her whole living.**

Note the following:

a. What this widow did was so important in the eyes of Jesus that he summoned his disciples, in order to rivet their attention upon it. This calling to himself of The Twelve had happened before, that is, on very important occasions (3:13; 6:7; 8:1, 34; 10:42), and this was another.

b. In line with this is the fact that the Master introduces his teaching by saying, "I solemnly declare to y o u," showing that what he was about to say was of great significance and should be taken to heart by them. See on 3:28.

c. "This poor widow dropped more into the treasury than all the others," said Jesus. In his estimation the two copper coins were sparkling diamonds. One might even say: they resembled talents which over a period of time doubled in value (Matt. 25:20, 22); yes, doubled and redoubled, for her deed and Jesus' comment have inspired thousands of people to follow her example.

d. When the question is asked, "What was it that made her gift so precious?" the answer is that all the others had given "out of their abundance,"[610] she "out of her poverty," her want or lack.[611]

Shall we say that she might at least have kept *one* of these small, thin copper coins for herself? But no, she gave both. In fact, she, knowing that God would not fail her, sacrificed everything. These two coins represented all she had to live on.[612] How did Jesus know this? For a discussion of this

---

610 ἐκ τοῦ περισσεύοντος αὐτοῖς; literally, "of what was overflowing to them." See N.T.C. on Ephesians, p. 84, footnote 25.

611 The noun ὑστέρησις, in the New Testament occurring only here and in Phil 4:11, is related to the verb ὑστερέω. See above, on 10:21, footnote 477.

612 Here (in Mark 12:44; Luke 21:4) and also in Luke 8:43 (if authentic) βίος indicates *means of subsistence, living, livelihood.* In Luke 8:14 the reference seems to be to *the present life and its pleasures;* in Luke 15:12, 30, to *property.* Somewhat similar is the meaning of βίος in I John 3:17 (and perhaps also in I John 2:16): *worldly goods, material possessions,* while in II Tim. 2:4 the reference is probably to *civilian* (as contrasted with military) *life.* In I Tim. 2:2 the reference is to *everyday life,* life as it is lived from day to day.

As to the distinction between βίος and ζωή, in general ζωή is the life by which we live, while βίος is the life which we live. In the New Testament ζωή generally points to *the*

question (the inter-action between Jesus' human and divine nature) see on 2:8; 5:32; 9:33, 34; and 11:2, 13. The point to be emphasized is that this poor widow gave most generously, spontaneously. She gave "in faith." It is for this reason that Jesus praises her so lavishly.

Lessons

a. It is not the amount of the gift that matters most, but the heart (attitude, purpose) of the giver.

b. Strikingly beautiful is what Scripture teaches with respect to the manner in which God provides for widows:

(1) God is "a father of the fatherless, and a judge of the widows" (Ps. 68:5).

They are under his special care and protection (Exod. 22:23; Deut. 10:18; Prov. 15:25; Ps. 146:9).

(2) By means of the tithe and "the forgotten sheaf" he provides for them (Deut. 14:29; 24:19-21; 26:12, 13). At the feasts which he has instituted, they too should rejoice (Deut. 16:11, 14).

(3) He blesses those who help and honor them (Isa. 1:17, 18; Jer. 7:6; 22:3, 4).

(4) He rebukes and punishes those who hurt them (Exod. 22:22; Deut. 24:17; 27:19; Job 24:3, 21; 31:16; Ps. 94:6; Zech. 7:10; Mal. 3:5).

(5) They are the objects of Christ's tender compassion, as is clear from the Gospels, expecially from the Gospel according to Luke (Mark 12:42, 43; Luke 7:11-17; 18:3, 5; 20:47; 21:2, 3).

(6) In the early church they were not forgotten. It was the neglect of certain widows which led to the appointment of the first deacons, so that in the future widows might receive better care (Acts 6:1-6). And according to James, one of the manifestations of a religion that is pure and undefiled is this: "to visit the fatherless and widows in their affliction" (James 1:27). See also I Tim. 5:3-8.

Summary of Chapter 12

"By what authority are you doing these things, and who gave you the authority to do them?" the chief priests, scribes, and elders had asked Jesus. In return he had asked them, "The baptism of John, was it from heaven or from men? Answer me." Result: embarrassment for them, because they had hardened themselves against the truth.

---

higher life, salvation, victory over sin and its consequences. For more detail on ζωή see N.T.C. on John, Vol. I, pp. 71, 72, 141, 142). On the distinction between βίος and ζωή see also R. C. Trench, *op. cit.*, par. xxvii.

So, here in chapter 12, in order to expose these leaders and at the same time to warn them, Jesus tells the parable of The Wicked Sharecroppers. These tenants not only refused to give the owner what was due to him, but even increasingly maltreated his servants. Finally, they did not shrink from killing the owner's only son, with dire consequences for themselves.

Christ's opponents caught on that, according to the meaning and intention of the parable, they themselves were definitely included among the wicked sharecroppers. So they wanted to arrest Jesus, but were afraid of the crowd (verses 1-12).

They now try to catch him in his words, his teaching. They ask him three questions, as follows:

a. "Is it lawful to pay a poll-tax to Caesar?" The question was asked by Pharisees and Herodians. Jesus answers, "What is due to Caesar render to Caesar, and what is due to God render to God."

b. "One by one marrying and then dying, seven brothers successively married the same wife; in the resurrection whose wife shall she be?" The Sadducees, who rejected the doctrine of the resurrection, asked that question. Jesus answers, "When the dead rise they neither marry nor are given in marriage . . . God is not the God of the dead but of the living."

c. "Of all the commandments which is the foremost?" a scribe asked. Answer: "The foremost is, 'Hear, O Israel, the Lord our God, the Lord is one. And you shall love the Lord your God with all your heart. . . . You shall love your neighbor as yourself." When the scribe declared perfect agreement, Jesus told him, "You are not far from the kingdom of God."

Christ's own question was, "How can the scribes say that the Christ is (merely) the *son* of David, though in Ps. 110 David, moved by the Holy Spirit, calls him his *Lord?*" Implication: This "Son of David" is no other than the Son of God; hence, he is David's Lord. All of this is found in verses 13-37.

Having just now attacked the *doctrine* of the scribes, Jesus next exposes their corrupt *practice.* His criticism is not aimed at every scribe but at the group. He brands them as being vainglorious and deceitful. At times they are even cruel to widows, "devouring widows' houses" (verses 38-40).

What then is the proper attitude toward widows? This is shown in the closing little paragraph (verses 41-44), in which Jesus praises the poor widow who dropped into the offering receptacle "two very small copper coins, worth only a fraction of a penny." It was all she had to live on. Calling his disciples to him Jesus said, "I solemnly declare to y o u that this poor widow dropped more into the treasury than all the others. For they all gave out of their abundance, but she out of her poverty dropped in all she had, her whole living."

Outline of Chapter 13

Theme: *The Work Which Thou Gavest Him To Do*

Christ's Discourse on The Last Things

13:1-4   The Occasion. The Temple's Destruction Foretold
13:5-13   The Beginning of Woes or Birth Pains
13:14-23   The Great Tribulation
13:24-27   The Coming of the Son of Man
13:28-31   The Lesson from the Fig Tree
13:32-37   The Necessity of Being Ready Always, in View of the
              Unknown Day and Hour of Christ's Coming

CHAPTER XIII

13   1 Now as he was going out of the temple, one of his disciples remarked to him, "Look, Teacher, what huge stones and what magnificent buildings!" 2 Jesus said to him, "Do you see these great buildings? There will not be left here one stone upon another that will not be thrown down."

3 And as he was sitting on the Mount of Olives facing the temple, Peter and James and John and Andrew were asking him privately, 4 "Tell us, when will this happen, and what will be the sign when all these things are about to be accomplished?"

13:1-4 *The Occasion. The Temple's Destruction Foretold*
Cf. Matt. 24:1-3; Luke 21:5-7

It was with a word of commendation for a poor but generous widow that Jesus left the temple, probably late Tuesday afternoon. This may well have been his final departure, though in view of Luke 21:37 we cannot be absolutely certain about this.

In the company of his disciples Jesus started off for the Mount of Olives. The discourse on The Last Things which he delivered at this time is found in its most complete form in Matt. 24, 25. Matt. 24:1-35 has a rather close parallel in Mark 13:1-31. Matt. 24:36 parallels Mark 13:32, and even Matt. 24:37-44 has something, though little, in common with Mark 13:33-37, as will be shown when we study the Marcan verses. The Lucan parallel of Matt. 24:1-35 is found in 21:5-33 (or more loosely in 21:5-36).

By comparing the six sections into which Mark 13 can be divided (see the Outline of Chapter 13) with the ten sections of Matt. 24, 25—see N.T.C. on Matthew, pp. 848, 849—it becomes clear that, by and large, Mark's six sections run parallel with the first six of Matthew's ten sections. When there are important variations these will be indicated in connection with the discussion of Mark's individual sections.

1. Now as he was going out of the temple, one of his disciples remarked to him, Look, Teacher, what huge stones and what magnificent buildings!

"One of the disciples," says Mark. Cf. Matthew's "his disciples," and Luke's "some," probably meaning "some of his disciples." Discrepancy hunters can add these variations to their long lists of Gospel Contradictions. In reality there is more than one way of solving this little puzzle: *a.* One

511

disciple—Peter perhaps?—, in his enthusiasm about the grandeur and beauty of the temple, may have been the first to burst into exuberance; others followed until all joined in; or *b.* the voice of the one may have been louder than that of the rest.

Again, while according to Mark, the attention of Jesus was called to "huge stones and magnificent buildings," and according to Matthew, to "buildings," Luke mentions "goodly stones and votive offerings," as the objects that gave rise to the disciples' enthusiastic exclamations. Certainly all these objects of wonder must have been included.

As to these "huge stones and magnificent buildings" that formed the temple complex, after what has already been said about these in connection with the explanation of 11:15—see *The Description of the Temple*—nothing need be added.

The reason why just at this particular moment these men were thinking of the temple may well have been that Jesus had just said, "Behold, y o u r house is left to y o u a deserted place" (Matt. 23:38; cf. Luke 13:35). Though it is probable that the expression "y o u r house" meant Jerusalem, its temple was certainly included. It is as if the disciples were saying, "Is it true that also this glorious structure is going to be entirely deserted?" In substance Jesus answers, "Not only *deserted* but totally *destroyed.*

2. Jesus said to him, Do you see these great buildings? There will not be left here one stone upon another that will not be thrown down. [613] The hyperbolic figure "not one stone upon another" spelled the totality of the predicted destruction.

As to the fulfilment, when the Jews rebelled against the Romans, Jerusalem was taken by Titus, son of the emperor Vespasian (A.D. 69-79). The temple was destroyed. It is believed that more than a million Jews, who had crowded into the city, perished. As a political unit Israel ceased to exist. As a nation specially favored by the Lord it had reached the end of the road even long before the beginning of the Jewish War.

An ex-combatant and eye-witness, Josephus, almost immediately after the struggle between the Jews and the Romans had ended, began to write his *History of the Jewish War.* On the whole his narrative may be described as trustworthy, although a definitely pro-Roman bias cannot be denied. Of the seven "books" into which this work is divided one should read especially

---

[613] Note the parallelistic construction: *a.* λίθος ἐπὶ λίθον, *b.* the rhythm of the two aor. subjunctive passives ἀφεθῇ and καταλυθῇ, and *c.* the double οὐ μή, each of these preceding the accompanying verb. Does not this type of style suggest the underlying Aramaic spoken by Jesus? Semitic languages are full of similar parallelisms. The phraseology seems to echo very early material. Matthew has not, in this instance, preserved similar rhythm (see 24:2 in the original). Luke has done so only to a certain extent. Though he uses balancing future indic. passives, he has dropped the double οὐ μή feature.

books IV-VI. A few excerpts from Josephus may illumine the fulfilment of Mark 13:2 (cf. Matt. 22:7; 24:2; Luke 21:6, 20-24), and thus also the passage itself:

"That building [the temple at Jerusalem], however, God long ago had sentenced to the flames; but now in the revolution of the time-periods the fateful day had arrived, the tenth of the month Lous, the very day on which previously it had been burned by the king of Babylon. . . . One of the soldiers, neither awaiting orders nor filled with horror of so dread an undertaking, but moved by some supernatural impulse, snatched a brand from the blazing timber and, hoisted up by one of his fellow soldiers, flung the fiery missile through a golden window. . . . When the flame rose, a scream, as poignant as the tragedy, went up from the Jews . . . now that the object which before they had guarded so closely was going to ruin" (VI. 250-253).

"While the sanctuary was burning . . . neither pity for age nor respect for rank was shown; on the contrary, children and old people, laity and priests alike were massacred" (VI. 271).

"The emperor ordered the entire city and sanctuary to be razed to the ground, except only the highest towers, Phasael, Hippicus, and Mariamne, and that part of the wall that enclosed the city on the west. . . . All the rest of the wall that surrounded the city was so completely razed to the ground as to leave future visitors to the spot no reason to believe that it had ever been inhabited" (VII. 1-3).

In addition to Josephus see also the vivid description of *The Revolt* and its results, in T. Kollek and M. Pearlman, *op. cit.,* pp. 125-135.

3, 4. And as he was sitting on the Mount of Olives facing the temple, Peter and James and John and Andrew were asking him privately, Tell us, when will this happen, and what will be the sign when all these things are about to be accomplished? The variety in the reporting is again clear. All three inform the reader that there were those who asked Jesus a question. They asked it "privately," away from the crowd. Luke merely states, "They" asked, obviously referring to the disciples. Matthew has, "The disciples came to him privately, saying [or: asking]. . . ." Mark mentions the very names of the disciples who took the lead in asking the question. They were the three—Peter, James, and John—who are seen together on more than one occasion (5:37; 9:2; 14:33), plus Andrew, Peter's brother (1:16), the one who had brought Peter (=Simon) to Christ (John 1:40-42).

Also, Mark here as often is the most descriptive. He not only states, as does Matthew, that Jesus and his disciples were sitting on the Mount of Olives, but adds the little touch, "facing the temple."

Sitting there, we can imagine how, looking across the valley, a truly fascinating view disclosed itself to the eyes of the little company. There was the roof of the temple bathed in a sea of golden glory. There were those beautiful terraced courts and also those cloisters of snowy marble which seemed to shine and sparkle in the light of the setting sun. And then to think that all this glory was about to perish! The minds of the disciples reeled and staggered when they pondered that mysterious and awesome prediction.

All this glory! "Beautiful for elevation, the joy of the whole earth, is Mount Zion . . . the city of the Great King. . . . Walk about Zion, and go round about her: count her towers. Mark well her bulwarks. Consider her palaces" (Ps. 48:2, 12, 13). This surely was true no less with respect to the greatly enlarged and lavishly adorned temple which King Herod I had started to build. See above, in connection with 11:15. "Nor has there been, either in ancient or modern times, a sacred building equal to the temple, whether for situation or magnificence." [614] Rabbinic literature is not particularly favorable to Herod. Nevertheless, concerning Herod's temple it states, "He who never saw Herod's edifice has never in his life seen a beautiful building."

We can picture the disciples riveting their eyes on "Jerusalem's pride," in deep silence and sorrow meditating on the words of doom spoken by Jesus. Finally that silence is broken by the four. Stepping up to Jesus they ask, "Tell us, when will this happen, and what will be the sign when all these things are about to be accomplished?

In the light of the immediately preceding context here in Mark, the words, "When will *this* happen. . . ?" would seem to refer to the destruction of city and temple, to that and to nothing else. Nevertheless, a second look at the phraseology—note particularly "*all* these things"—points to a broader, more comprehensive, meaning. Also, in his answer Jesus by no means limits himself to the events that were to occur about the year A.D. 70. See especially verses 6, 10, 21, 26, 27. His prophetic eyes scan the centuries that lie ahead, and he definitely includes his own glorious parousia (second coming) among the things predicted. All in all, therefore, it would seem best to regard the question as reported by Mark (and see also Luke 21:7) to be an abbreviation of that which Matthew states more fully, namely, "Tell us, when will this happen, and what will be the sign of thy coming and of the end of the age?" One might perhaps say that Matthew, with Mark's wording before him, explains it by means of amplification.

The very form in which, according to Matthew, the question is cast seems to indicate that, as these men (spokesmen for the rest of The Twelve) interpret the Master's words, Jerusalem's fall, particularly the destruction of the temple, would mean the end of the world. In this opinion they were partly mistaken, as Jesus is about to show. A lengthy period of time would

---

614 A. Edersheim, *The Temple*, p. 28.

intervene between Jerusalem's fall and the culmination of the age, the second coming. Nevertheless, the disciples were not entirely wrong: there was indeed a connection between the judgment to be executed upon the Jewish nation and the final judgment on the day of the consummation of all things. The first was a type, a foreshadowing or adumbration, of the second.

With the *prediction* of the destruction of city and temple, especially the latter, and the immediately following *question* asked by the four disciples, the *occasion* or setting has been indicated for Christ's answer, that is, for his discourse on The Last Things. As to the disciples' question about "the sign," see on verses 14 and 26.

---

5 Jesus began to say [615] to them, "Take care that no one deceives y o u. 6 Many will come in my name, saying, 'I am he,' and will mislead many. 7 And when y o u hear of wars and rumors of wars, do not be disturbed. (Such things) must happen, but (that is) not yet the end. 8 For nation will rise up in arms against nation, and kingdom against kingdom. There will be earthquakes in various places; there will be famines. But these things are (merely) the beginning of birth pains.

9 "But be on y o u r guard. They will hand y o u over to councils, and in synagogues y o u will be flogged. On my account y o u will have to appear before governors and kings, as a testimony to them. 10 And to all the nations the gospel must first be preached. 11 Whenever y o u are arrested and taken to trial, do not worry beforehand about what y o u should say. On the contrary, whatever is given y o u at that time, that y o u must say, for it is not y o u who are speaking but the Holy Spirit. 12 Brother will deliver up brother to death, (the) father (his) child, and children will rise up against (their) parents and will kill them. 13 And y o u will be hated by all for my name's sake. But he that endures to the end, he will be saved.

13:5-13 *The Beginning of Woes or Birth Pains*
Cf. Matt. 10:17-22; 24:4-14; Luke 21:8-19

There is a close resemblance between this entire section and Luke 21:8-19. The main differences are:

a. In addition to earthquakes and famines, as in Mark and Matthew, Luke mentions pestilences, terrors, and signs from heaven. Moreover, according to Luke's report, the signs and earthquakes are going to be "great." Continuing Luke's additions (b., c., d.):

b. Affliction awaits the disciples not only in synagogues but also in prisons.

c. The adversaries will be unable to contradict God's persecuted children.

d. Not a hair of their head will perish (cf. Matt. 10:30).

e. On the other hand, Luke has no parallel to Mark 13:10, nor to 13:13b. Addressing ourselves now to the first part of this section, that is, to verses

---

[615] Or: said.

5-8 of Mark's thirteenth chapter, we notice that this passage and verses 4-8 of Matthew's twenty-fourth chapter are almost identical, and that Luke 21:8-11 is a close parallel.

5-8. Jesus began to say [616] to them, Take care that no one deceives [617] y o u. Many will come in my name, saying, I am he, and will mislead many. And when y o u hear of wars and rumors of wars, do not be disturbed. [618] (Such things) must happen, but (that is) not yet the end. For nation will rise up in arms against nation, and kingdom against kingdom. There will be earthquakes [619] in various places; there will be famines. But these things are (merely) the beginning of birth pains.

Jesus now proceeds to correct his disciples' mistaken inference. He shows them that "not everything that seems to be a sign of the end of the world is in reality such a sign." In other words, there are also signs which only in a very general sense are deserving of that name. Whenever these separate happenings are interpreted as being infallible indications that the end of the age is immediately in sight, they deserve the name "mistaken signs." Thus, Jesus predicts the coming of those who will say, "I am the Christ." They will mislead many. Those who persist in being misled show that they never belonged to Christ's true flock (I John 2:19; cf. I Cor. 11:19). There have always been deceivers and deceived.

This also holds true with respect to "wars and rumors of wars" (13:7). When Jesus speaks these words, the Roman empire has been enjoying a long era of peace. But about four decades later political turmoil will upset the great realm from one end to the other, so that Rome will see four emperors in one year: Galba, Otho, Vitellus, and Vespasian. But these violent revolts and insurrections cannot by any stretch of the imagination constitute definite indications that the Lord will return immediately. This is evident at once when one considers the fact that wars and rumors of war did not cease with Jerusalem's fall. Throughout the centuries the prophecy attains fulfilment: "nation will rise up in arms against nation, and kingdom against kingdom" (verse 8a). One author counted three hundred wars in Europe

---

616 This could be another instance of the pleonastic use of ἄρχω. If so, the simple translation, "Jesus said" would suffice. See on 1:45; cf. 6:7, footnote 233.

617 πλανήση third per. sing. aor. subj. active of πλανάω, to deceive, lead astray, cause to wander. In verse 6 the same verb occurs, the form being third per. pl. fut. active indic. πλανήσουσι. Certain cellestial spheres are called "planets," that is, "wandering ones," to distinguish them from the so-called "fixed" stars. The verb occurs about forty times in the New Testament. It is especially frequent in Matthew and in the book of Revelation. In Mark it is found also in 12:24, 27; 13:6.

618 θροεῖσθε, sec. per. pl. present passive imperative of θροέω, to be disturbed, alarmed.

619 For σεισμός, pl. σεισμοί see N.T.C. on Matt. 8:24 and 21:10 (including footnote 724).

during the last three hundred years. And these wars are increasing in intensity. It is perfectly clear that when any particular war is singled out as a help for "date-fixers" another "mistaken sign" has been produced.

Jesus also speaks about "earthquakes in various places and . . . famines" (verse 8b). As was true with respect to other predicted events, so it is here. These disturbances in the physical realm are indeed foreshadowings and portrayals of that which, on a much more extensive and intensive scale, will take place in the realm of nature at the end of the age; but except in that very general sense they cannot be correctly termed signs. Not any single one of them could ever give anyone the right to make predictions with reference either to the date of Jerusalem's fall or to the time of the Parousia (Christ's second coming). It is true that during the period A.D. 60-80 famine, pestilence, fire, hurricane, and earthquake ravaged the empire, as Renan points out in *l'Antichrist*. Vesuvius erupted violently in the summer of 79, destroying Pompeii and its surroundings. But, as is already clear from the preceding sentence, these catastrophes were not limited to the decade preceding the fall of Jerusalem in the year 70. Moreover, throughout the centuries there have been violent earthquakes. Ancient historians and philosophers—such as Thucydides, Aristotle, Strabo, Seneca, Livy, and Pliny— describe similar seismic phenomena in their days. And as early as the year 1668 Robert Hooke wrote his work bearing the title, *Discourse on Earthquakes*. A certain author counted no less than seven hundred disturbances of this nature, great and small, which had occurred in the nineteenth century! Famines, too, occur constantly.

Now with respect to events such as these here described Jesus says in verse 8c, "These things are (merely) the beginning of birth pains." They mark the beginning, says Jesus. They do not mark the end. Therefore, do not be alarmed.

In spite of this clear warning which our Lord gave to his disciples, many present-day church members are filled with admiration for the minister or evangelist who speaks learnedly about "The Signs of the Times," and strives to show his audience that this or that terrible battle, serious earthquake, or devastating famine "on the basis of prophecy" is the infallible "sign" of Christ's imminent return.

To be sure, the events here indicated have significance. They are stepping stones leading to the final goal. By means of them the end of the age is both foreshadowed and brought closer, and God's eternal plan is being carried forward. Moreover, when we realize that toward the end of the present dispensation the indicated disturbances will occur together (Matt. 24:33), will probably be more numerous, extensive, and fearful than ever before (Luke 21:11, 25, 26), and are going to take place in connection with the great tribulation that will usher in the parousia, we may conclude that it would not be unreasonable to call *the final outbreak* of these terrors "concurrent or accompanying signs."

The paragraph Mark 13:9-13 is paralleled in Matthew and Luke as follows:

Mark 13	Matt. 10	Matt. 24	Luke 21
a. Christ's disciples arraigned before the authorities			
verse 9	verses 17, 18	verse 9a	verses 12, 13
b. The gospel to be proclaimed to all nations			
verse 10		verse 14	
c. The Holy Spirit equipping the disciples with words of wisdom			
verse 11	verses 19, 20		verses 14, 15
d. Family tensions			
verse 12	verse 21		verse 16
e. "Hated by all"			
verse 13a	verse 22a	verse 9b	verse 17
f. "He that endures to the end, he will be saved"			
verse 13b	verse 22b	verse 13	

9. **But be on y o u r guard. They will hand y o u over to councils, and in synagogues y o u will be flogged.** [620] **On my account y o u will have to appear** [621] **before governors and kings, as a testimony to them.**

Matt. 24:9a reads, "Then y o u will be handed over to tribulation and y o u will be put to death." Matt. 10:17, 18, "And beware of men, for they will hand y o u over to councils, and in their synagogues they will flog y o u. On my account y o u will be dragged before governors and kings for a testimony to them and to the Gentiles." Arraignment before councils, synagogues, governors, and kings, such is going to be their lot.

---

620 δαρήσεσθε, second per. pl. fut. passive indic. of δέρω; see on 12:3, 5, including footnote 572.

621 σταθήσεσθε, sec. per. pl. fut. passive indic. of ἵστημι; hence, y o u will be made to stand; meaning: y o u will have to appear.

As to councils, these probably indicate the local Jewish courts, climaxed in the Sanhedrin. It was in the synagogue that those who by the court had been convicted of this or that definite crime were scourged.

Jewish sources contain detailed regulations regarding such scourging. One judge would recite an appropriate passage from Deuteronomy or from the Psalms, a second would count the blows (see Deut. 25:1-3), a third would issue a command before each blow, etc. [622] From the book of Acts (22:19) we learn that Saul (=Paul) of Tarsus caused believers in Christ to receive this horrible punishment. After his conversion he himself was going to be similarly tortured. He was going to write, "From the Jews five times I received forty lashes less one" (II Cor. 11:24). It was the servant of the synagogue ("the attendant," Luke 4:20) who was charged with the responsibility of delivering the blows.

As to "governors," think of such procurators as Pontius Pilate, Felix, and Festus; as to "kings," of Herod Agrippa I (Acts 12:1) and of Agrippa II (Acts 25:13, 24, 26). Even Herod Antipas, who technically was not a king, is also given that title at times (Matt. 14:9; Mark 6:14). It was Pontius Pilate who sentenced Jesus to die on the cross, after he had sent him to "king" Herod Antipas (Mark 15:15; Luke 23:6-12). It was King Herod Agrippa I who killed James (son of Zebedee, and brother of the apostle John). See Acts 12:1. From Acts 25:13 it appears that Paul was brought before King Agrippa II and the procurator Festus. He gave a wonderful testimony as he had also done previously before the procurator Felix. It is understandable that such testimonies were also given before other Gentiles, namely, those who were either present or subsequently heard what had been said. Cf. Phil. 1:12, 13; 4:22. Thus the good news would continue to spread.

Thus, *a.* the initial fulfilment of this prophecy was a matter of the immediate future, as is clear from already existing conditions and attitudes; and *b.* details concerning its subsequent fulfilment are recorded in the book of Acts and in the epistles. See also Rev. 1:9; 2:8-11; 6:9-11; 12:6, 13-17; etc.

What is all-important is the fact that Jesus says this will happen "on my account." When anyone persecutes Christ's disciple he is persecuting Christ himself, a fact that was stamped so indelibly upon the mind and heart of Paul (and through him upon Luke's consciousness) that, however much the accounts of Paul's conversion may vary, the words, "Saul, Saul, why do you persecute *me?*" are found in all three (Acts 9:4, 5; 22:7, 8; 26:14, 15). That means that the persecuted one is never separated from Christ's love and from the strength and the comfort he imparts.

---

622 For further details on this see K. Schneider's article on μαστιγόω, in Th.D.N.T., Vol. IV, pp. 515-519.

10. And to all the nations the gospel must first be preached. The parallel passage, Matt. 24:14, reads, "And this gospel of the kingdom will be preached in the whole world as a testimony to all the nations, and then will come the end."

The following points deserve special attention:

a. The "gospel" indicates God's message of salvation by his grace through faith in Jesus Christ. For the special section on "What Is the Gospel?" see N.T.C. on Philippians, pp. 81-85.

b. "All the nations," "the whole world." In spite of Matt. 10:5; 15:24— which passages merely indicate that God intended to have the good tidings proclaimed first to the Jews, then to the Gentiles—, it must be maintained that from the very beginning the Gentiles were included in the divine plan of redemption. Jesus knew this. He wanted it. His sympathies were certainly just as wide as those of the inspired authors of the Old Testament books. From the very beginning salvation was intended to be for all those who, by sovereign grace, placed their trust in him, whether Jew or Gentile. John 3:16, with its "whosoever believes" doctrine expresses this exactly. For the Old Testament see not only Ps. 72:8-11, 17; 87; 96:1-10; Isa. 42:1-7 (cf. Matt. 12:15-21); 49:6-12; 52:10; 60:1-3, 6; but also Gen. 12:3; 18:18; 26:4; 28:14; to which many others could be added.

c. "*must* . . . be preached."

Matt. 24:14 stresses what *was going to happen*. In how far this prophecy has already been fulfilled, and also the extent to which it is still unfulfilled, has been described in N.T.C. on Matthew, pp. 855, 856. Our present passage, Mark 13:10, emphasizes the "must" aspect of this truth. The world-wide proclamation of the gospel is a divine *must*. It *must* occur, for this is God's will, his decree from eternity. See Eph. 1:11; 2:11-22. That decree, moreover, includes the believers' responsibility to see to it that, by strength and grace from above, God's will is carried out. Moreover, God has so commanded (Matt. 28:18-20; Luke 24:47). Also, the world sorely needs this gospel (Acts 4:12; Rom. 1:16; 3:21-24; I Cor. 1:21-24). Add to this the fact that *we have* this gospel, and more and more we are coming into possession of the tools that enable us to proclaim it—unprecedented progress in the knowledge of foreign languages and dialects; transportation and travel facilities beyond anything the world has ever known; the material means to provide missionaries, to care for them, house them, and to build chapels. We have the radio, television, and recording facilities. *The time is now!* To be sure, we are not able to look into hearts, but if lives mean anything, they seem to indicate that the gap between *a.* the curve showing those dying unsaved, and *b.* the curve, indicating those who during the same time period (week, month, year, decade) are being converted, is not narrowing but is adversely widening. This is a thought that should weigh very heavily upon the conscience of every believer. Finally, many doors are still open. *They will not always remain open.* See Matt. 24:21, 22, 29; Mark 13:19, 20; Rev. 11:7-10; 20:3, 7-9a; and cf. John 9:4.

d. "must *first* be preached." In view of verses 21, 26 and Matt. 24:3, 14, 30, this means: before Christ returns.

e. "must . . . *be preached.*" See on 14:9.

Even though the most bitter persecution of believers will not occur until just previous to the Lord's return, hard times are in store for his disciples even now. They should be mentally prepared for them. Despair, for example, in connection with the question how they should answer their tormentors, should never enter their hearts:

11. **Whenever y o u are arrested and taken to trial, do not worry beforehand about what y o u should say. On the contrary, whatever is given y o u at that time, that y o u must say, for it is not y o u who are speaking but the Holy Spirit.** How to conduct oneself before judges, including even governors and kings (see verse 9), how to address them, and what to say in defense, might well fill these men with apprehension and horror. Very strikingly Jesus says, "Do not worry beforehand," in other words, "Fight that habit. Continue to arm yourselves against it. Stop this tendency of being distracted, with y o u r mind being drawn in opposite directions, from faith to fear, and from fear to faith." [623]

The reason given is: the Holy Spirit will supply the necessary words, incontrovertible "words of wisdom" (Luke 21:14, 15). This does not mean that the mind of the persecuted apostle is a *tabula rasa* (blank tablet) and that then in some mechanical fashion God will suddenly begin to write words upon that blank space. On the contrary, neither when these witnesses are brought to trial nor when they write books or epistles will their personality be suppressed, or will the previous apostolic training which they received from Jesus be nullified. All this will be enlivened and sharpened and raised to a higher plane of activity. It is in the organic sense that what they must speak will be given to them in that hour. The Father's Spirit will be speaking in them, and that very Spirit, namely, the Holy Spirit, the third person of the Holy Trinity, will "remind them of everything" that Jesus himself said to them (John 14:26). That Spirit was at work already long before Pentecost (Ps. 51:11). But on and after Pentecost he was going to be "poured out" in all his fulness.

That this prophecy, too, was gloriously fulfilled is evident from the speeches of Peter, or Peter and John (Acts 4:8-12, 19, 20, with the effect

---

[623] προμεριμνᾶτε, sec. per. pl. pres. imperat. of προμεριμνάω. Cf. N.T.C. on Matthew, p. 349 for the basic verb μεριμνάω.

upon the audience described in 4:13, 14) and from those of Paul (Acts 21:39–22:21; 23:1, 6; 24:10-21; 26:1-23).

Confessing Jesus will create division even within the family circle: **12. Brother will deliver up brother to death, (the) father (his) child, and children will rise up against (their) parents and will kill them.** True, this last clause can also be rendered, "and cause them to be put to death." Basically, however, this makes little difference. The person who unjustly causes someone to be put to death is as guilty as if he had committed the act with his own hand. See II Sam. 11:15, cf. 12:9; I Kings 21:13, cf. verse 19; and Mark 6:27, cf. and turn back to verse 16.

Jesus here predicts that the Christ-hating son is going to hand over his own brother to be put to death; the father his child; children their parents.

History supplies numerous illustrations of the kind of fratricide, filicide, and parenticide here indicated. Because of basic religious differences, intra-family relationships were often far from ideal. Did not Cain slay his brother Abel (Gen. 4:8; Heb. 11:4)? The fact that children would at times in large numbers abandon (in the sense explained below; see on verse 13a) the faith of their fathers is implied in such passages as Josh. 24:31; Mic. 7:6; Mal. 4:6. Conversely, the parents of a son, who was born blind and who with his vision restored accepted the Healer as his Lord, behaved in a cowardly manner. They refused to join their son in his frank and precious confession. They feared expulsion from the synagogue (John 9). So sometimes it was a brother who was at fault, sometimes a father, sometimes a child.

It is clear that at bottom the cleavage took place *on account of Christ*. See verse 9. The same fact is established by verse 13a. **And y o u will be hated by all for my name's sake.** The meaning is, "Y o u *will continue* to be hated. [624]** The form of the expression may well imply that Jesus was not thinking only of what would happen to The Twelve but also of the persecutions to be endured by their successors in future years, in fact until his return. See also John 16:33; II Cor. 4:8-10; I John 3:13. The expression "hated by all" must mean, "by men in general, regardless of rank, station, race, nationality, sex, or age." Is not the same true also with respect to the use of "all" in Mark 1:37; 5:20; 11:32; Luke 3:15; John 3:26; I Tim. 2:1; and Titus 2:11? Because the world hates Christ it also hates his representatives.

There is comfort, however, in the assurance, **13b. But he that endures to the end, he will be saved.** He who remains loyal to Christ throughout the

---

[624] Periphrastic future passive, probably with durative force, as if to say: this will be going on and on throughout the ages. The original was ἔσεσθε μισούμενοι.

period of persecution will enter into glory. For himself this period of persecution will last until death delivers him from this earthly scene. For the church in general it will last until Christ's return in glory.

Note this victorious ending. Moreover, the essence of this being saved is set forth beautifully in such passages as Rev. 2:7, 17, 26, 27, 28; 3:5, 12, 20, 21; 7:9-17; 14:13; 21:1-7. In times of most bitter persecution by no means all covenant children would become untrue to the faith. In fact, not any of those who had been *truly* regenerated perish in unbelief (John 4:14; 10:28; Rom. 8:37-39; Phil. 1:6; I John 2:19). But in times of persecution many of those whose worship of God had been of a merely outward character would be quick to join the forces of the enemy, some of them even becoming "informers" against members of their own families. The truly regenerated were going to remain loyal to the very end. And "those faithful until death" would include boys and girls of tender years.

Of the traditional "ten" persecutions (from Nero to Diocletian) the last one was also the most violent. Its aim was to *terminate* the church, to destroy it once for all. Appropriately it began with the festival of *Terminalia,* Feb. 23, A.D. 303. But even this supreme effort was in vain. Tertullian was right, "Go on, rack, torture, grind us to powder: our numbers increase in proportion as y o u mow us down. The blood of Christians is their harvest seed." With Constantine—remember "in hoc signo vinces"; i.e., "in this sign you will conquer"—paganism, at least officially, met its doom, A.D. 312. Nothing, but nothing—not even Hades—can prevail against the church. That church is safe because it is what Christ calls "*my* church." [625]

---

14 "Now when y o u see 'the desolating sacrilege,' standing where he has no right to be—let him who reads understand—, then let those in Judea flee to the hills; 15 let him who (happens to be) on the housetop not go down or enter his house to get something out; 16 and let him who is in the field not go back to get his coat. 17 But woe to those who are pregnant and to those who nurse babies in those days! 18 And pray that it may not occur in winter, 19 for those will be days of tribulation, such as there has never been since (the) beginning of (the) creation which God created, until now, and never again will be. 20 And unless the Lord had cut short those days, no one would be saved. But for the sake of the elect, whom he elected for himself, he shortened the days. 21 At that time if anyone should say to y o u, 'Look, here (is) the Christ!' or 'Look, there (he is)!' do not believe (him); 22 for false Christs will arise and false prophets, and will perform signs and miracles, so as to mislead, if possible, the elect. 23 But as to yourselves, be on y o u r guard; I have told y o u everything ahead of time.

---

[625] See P. Schaff, *History of the Christian Church*, New York, 1924, Vol. II; see especially pages 31-81.

13:14-23 *The Great Tribulation*
Cf. Matt. 24:15-25; Luke 21:20-24

As for the parallel passages, Luke 21:20-24 has little to say on this subject. Nevertheless, what it does say contains points of special interest, items not—or not as clearly—found in Matthew and Mark. Jerusalem is going to be surrounded by armies (verse 20; cf. 19:43). Not only should those who are in Jerusalem get out, but also those in the country must *not enter* the city (verse 21). Predictions of punishment will be fulfilled (verse 22). Cf. Dan. 9:27b; Rom. 11:25b; I Thess. 2:16b. Similarly, the people will fall by the edge of the sword, and Jerusalem will be trampled on by the Gentiles until the times of the Gentiles are fulfilled (verse 24). It is clear that according to Luke what Jesus was predicting spanned the entire new dispensation, reaching to its very end.

Matthew's parallel (24:15-25) matches Mark's passage (13:14-23) almost exactly. The most important variations are as follows: a. While both mention "the desolating sacrilege," and contain the words, "let him who reads understand," Matthew adds "which was spoken of through Daniel the prophet." Also Mark's rather obscure phrase "standing where he ought not" is clarified by Matthew's "standing in the holy place." b. Instead of Mark's, "And pray that it may not occur in winter," Matthew reads, "Pray that y o u r flight may not occur in winter or on the sabbath." c. Where Mark has, " . . . so as to mislead, if possible, the elect," Matthew has "so as to mislead, if possible, *even* the elect." No doubt, this "even" is also implied in Mark. —Up to this point Matthew in these few cases seems to express Christ's words somewhat more fully than does Mark. But now notice d. According to Matthew's report Jesus said, "See, I have told y o u ahead of time." Mark presents this same idea in the more expanded form, "But as to yourselves, be on y o u r guard; I have told y o u everything ahead of time." Finally, e. Matthew continues for a few more verses (24:26-28) after Mark leaves off. For Matt. 24:26, 27 see also Luke 17:23, 24, and with verse 28 cf. Luke 17:37. For the rest see N.T.C. on Matt. 24:26-28, pp. 861, 862.

14. Now when y o u see "the desolating sacrilege," standing where he has no right to be—let him who reads understand—, then let those in Judea flee to the hills.

The disciples had asked, "Tell us, when will this happen, and what will be the sign when all these things are about to be accomplished (verses 3, 4)?" Jesus has already shown that many disturbances will occur (verses 5-9). These, however, do not mark the end. Instead, they are the beginning of birth pains. He has also predicted that a lengthy period of gospel proclamation will intervene before the day of his return (verse 10). He has warned his disciples to stand firm, even though the opposition against them should come from the members of their own families. He has assured them that at their trials the Holy Spirit will give them words to speak, and that, though hated by all for his name's sake, those who endure to the end will be saved (verses 11-13).

The end will come at last. The end for what? For Jerusalem? For the world in general? One fact is clear: Christ's discourse is gradually bending towards its close. In verse 26, which belongs to the next section, there is mention of "the Son of man coming in clouds with great power and glory." The "tribulation," described in verses 14-23—see especially verses 14-20—, and mentioned again in verse 24, will pave the way for the Son of man's brilliant return. . . . Nevertheless, do not verses 14-18 describe what will happen in *Judea*? A parallel passage (Luke 21:20, and cf. also verse 24) even speaks about *Jerusalem* surrounded by armies!

How, then, must we interpret these words? Among theories that deserve consideration are the following:

a. Verses 14-18 refer to the woes that were to befall Jerusalem and Judea, resulting in Jerusalem's fall, A.D. 70. The remainder of the passage (verses 19-23, at least verses 19, 20) describes "the great tribulation that will immediately precede Christ's return."

Objection. It is impossible thus to separate these verses. They are too closely connected for this manipulation. Proof: with reference to what has just been said in verses 14-18, verse 19 continues, "for *those* will be days of tribulation such as there has never been since the beginning of creation . . . *and never again will be.*"

b. The entire section, verses 14-23, being a unit, describes Jerusalem's fall. It refers to that, to nothing else.

Objection. In verse 19 the tribulation is described as has just been indicated. We know that what befell Jerusalem and Judea in A.D. 70 was indescribably horrible. Nevertheless, can it be truly maintained that it was more frightful than that which took place under Hitler, who ordered the extermination of an entire race, so that an estimated five or six million Jews were most cruelly murdered? Is it possible to forget Auschwitz, Mauthausen, and Dachau?

Besides, the fact that the tribulation here referred to cannot exclusively point to A.D. 70 is clear from verses 24, 26, for "the coming of the Son of man in clouds with great power and glory" follows this tribulation; in fact, follows it *immediately* (Matt. 24:29).

c. The entire section, verses 13-23, exclusively describes the great tribulation that will immediately precede Christ's return. It has nothing to do with Jerusalem's fall in the year A.D. 70.

Objection. As already mentioned, Mark 13:14 (cf. Luke 21:20) clearly refers to the days of woe that were going to result in the fall of Jerusalem

A.D. 70. It is impossible to interpret that verse—and in fact all of verses 14-18—as if no reference is made to Judea's impending disaster.

Now if, as we have seen, none of the aforementioned theories satisfies, what then? Answer: We are dealing here with *prophetic* passages. The only safe and sound way to interpret them is in line with other similar passages. Two—or even more—events are viewed as if they were *one*. The "prophet"— whether Isaiah, Joel, Micah, Malachi . . . Jesus Christ—views the future as a traveler beholds a distant mountain range. He sees one peak rising right behind another. And from where he stands, he describes the future exactly as he sees it. Yet, the closer one gets to the first peak, the greater the distance is seen to be between peak No. 1 and peak No. 2.

Thus, for example, Messiah's first coming with good tidings and his second coming unto judgment are combined in Isa. 11:1-4 and in 61:1, 2. So are also Pentecost and "the great and terrible day of Jehovah," in Joel 2:28-31. For other illustrations of this *prophetic foreshortening,* [626] study II Sam. 7:12-16; Mal. 3:1, 2. So also here, in Mark 13:14 ff., (at least) two momentous events are intertwined: *a.* the judgment upon Jerusalem, leading to its fall in the year A.D. 70, and *b.* the tribulation climaxed by the final judgment at the close of the world's history. Our Lord predicts the city's approaching catastrophe *as a type* of the tribulation at the end of the new dispensation. Or, stating it differently, in describing the brief period of great tribulation at the close of history, ending with the final judgment, Jesus paints in colors borrowed from the clearly foreseen destruction of Jerusalem by the Romans. [627]

It is not claimed that any exegete is able completely to untangle what is here intertwined, so as to indicate accurately for each individual passage exactly how much of its contents refers to Jerusalem's fall and how much to the final great tribulation. All that is claimed is that by following the rule here stated—that of the recognition of *prophetic foreshortening* and closely related *multiple fulfilment*—the passage is placed in its own *prophetic* category where it belongs, and is thus interpreted.

We referred in the preceding paragraph to a twofold fulfilment: *a.* in A.D. 70 and *b.* just previous to Christ's return. But the traveler of the illustration may see more than two peaks. So it is also with the prophet. In our present passage there is reference first of all to what Daniel predicted when he spoke about "the desolating sacrilege." It is called a *sacrilege* because it defames or pollutes what is holy. Because of this it *renders desolate*. See especially Dan.

---

626 For more on this see N.T.C. on Matthew, pp. 205, 206, 467, 468, 659, 660.

627 Thus also F. W. Grosheide, *Het Heilig Evangelie Volgens Mattheus (Commentaar op het Nieuwe Testament),* Kampen, 1954, pp. 355, 356; C. R. Erdman, *op. cit.,* p. 192, and many others.

11:31; 12:11. In accordance with that prophet's prediction Antiochus Epiphanes (175-164 B.C.), unaware that he was indeed fulfilling prophecy, and being thoroughly responsible for his own wicked deed, erected a pagan altar over the altar of burnt-offering, thus polluting the house of God and rendering it desolate and unusable. This had happened long ago. See I Macc. 1:54, 59. Nevertheless, Jesus says, "Now when *y o u   see* 'the desolating sacrilege.' " The implication is that a divine oracle may apply to more than one historical situation. The sacrilege that results in the desolation of city and temple takes place more than once in history. *Let the man who reads Daniel's prophecy understand this!* Just as in the past the holy places of the Lord had been desecrated, so it will happen again. And it did indeed take place when *the Roman armies,* with the image of the emperor on their standards, an image and an emperor worshiped by them [628] laid siege to the city of Jerusalem (Luke 21:20).

With respect to this second fulfilment of Daniel's prophecy other interpreters think of the attempt of emperor Caligula (Gaius Caesar) to have a statue of himself erected in the temple at Jerusalem. The contemplated desecration, which as a result of massive Jewish resistance was postponed by proconsul Petronius, was subsequently prevented by the assassination of the insane emperor (January of the year A.D. 41). [629] But to see in this episode a further fulfilment of Daniel's prophecy, and to conclude that Jesus was thinking of that mad emperor's plan, is probably wrong; for, *a.* both Daniel and Jesus predict actual events, not threats that were never carried out; and *b.* Jesus has in mind a personal agent—"standing where *he* has no right to be," [630] not just a statue.

But just as the pagan altar and the swine offered upon it in the very temple of Jehovah in the second century B.C. pointed forward to the idolatrous legions of Rome, so these in turn foreshadowed the final antichrist's desecration of all that is sacred. It is for this reason that in verses 24-26 Jesus is able to say, "But in those days, after [Matthew "immediately after"] that tribulation, the sun will be darkened, and the moon will not give

---

628 See Josephus, *Jewish War* VI. 316.

629 Read the interesting account in Josephus, *Antiquities* XVIII. 257-309.

630 Similarly rendered by Williams ("standing where he has no right to stand"); and see also A.R.V., Weymouth, N.E.B., and Dutch (Nieuwe Vertaling): "waar hij niet behoort (where he does not belong)." It is not easy to explain why the *masculine s.* ἐστηκότα (perfect participle of ἵστημι), so regarded by A. T. Robertson (*Word Pictures,* Vol. I, p. 362) and by Vincent Taylor (*op. cit.,* p. 512), but not by Lenski (*op. cit.,* p. 362), has as its antecedent the neuter τὸ βδέλυγμα. That the primary New Testament fulfilment was the desecrating and desolating Roman army is clear from Luke 21:20. Is there perhaps a special reference here to this army's *general?* See A. B. Bruce, *op. cit.,* p. 430.

her light. . . . And then they will see the Son of man coming in clouds with great power and glory."

With respect, then, to the second fulfilment of this prophecy, namely, in the days just previous to Jerusalem's fall, Jesus warns his followers that when the Roman armies are arriving, his followers in Judea should flee to the hills. By all means they must not try to enter Jerusalem. Those in the country must not try to enter the city (Luke 21:21).

When the time of bitter trial arrived, what actually happened? The Jews in general did the very opposite: they rushed into the city. This resulted in a terrible blood bath. But did Christ's followers heed his exhortation to flee to the hills? According to many commentators they did, and finally found refuge in Perean Pella. But this is a theory for which there is no undisputed historical evidence. For more on this see N.T.C. on Matthew, p. 858. Let us hope that many believers obeyed their Lord's kind and urgent warning, which continues as follows:

15, 16. Let him who (happens to be) on the housetop not go down or enter his house to get something out; and let him who is in the field not go back to get his coat.

The man who is on the flat roof, from which by an outside ladder he is able to descend in order as quickly as possible to flee to the hills, must not, after descending, go into the house to recover any of his goods. Similarly, the laborer, dressed only in his tunic, and thus working in the field, must not go back from the field into his house to get his coat, but should immediately take off for the hills. Delay, in either case, might mean being captured, turned back, or perhaps even being killed.

The sympathetic heart of our Lord, revealed on so many previous occasions as recorded in this Gospel (1:41; 2:15, 17; 5:34, 41-43; 6:50; 8:2, 3; 10:13-16, 21) is deeply affected by two additional considerations: a. the plight of women (verse 17), and b. travel difficulties during winter (verse 18). **17. But woe to those who are pregnant** [631] **and to those who nurse babies** [632] **in those days!** It is a well-known fact that even though woman, having been created last of all, has been called "the crown of God's creation," she has by no means always received the consideration due to her. Boris Pasternak, in his famous *Doctor Zhivago* [633] represents one of that novel's characters as affirming that a wife is of no greater significance than a

---

[631] ἐν γαστρὶ ἔχειν (*to have in the womb*) is idiomatic for to be *pregnant*.

[632] θηλαζούσαις is dat. pl. fem. pres. participle of θηλάζω (cf. Matt. 24:19; Luke 21:23), literally *to give suck, give the breast*. Cf. θηλή: breast.

[633] Translated from Russian, a Signet Book, paperback edition, New York, 1960, p. 251.

528

flea or a louse! Read also S. M. Zwemer's book, *Across The World of Islam.* [634] It may be objected, however, that conditions are changing, and that much has happened—not only in Turkey but also elsewhere—favorably affecting the status of women. After all, Zwemer's book was written a long time ago. Accordingly, we would direct the readers' attention also to the much more recent study by W. C. Smith, *Islam in Modern History.* [635] The author, in a most interesting, penetrating, and thought-provoking manner, discusses some of the changes in the Muslim world. Could it be that Christianity is one of the factors that must be given credit for these positive developments? On pp. 303, 304 Smith gives his answer. He also has something to say about what he considers the essence of the spiritual welfare of the Muslims, p. 305. But is not *the only real solution* the turning of these people, and of all others, to Christ and salvation in him? See John 14:6; Acts 4:12. Is it not through him alone that a woman attains her true dignity? See Eph. 5:22-23.

At a time when women in general were underrated by many, and even despised by some, it was Jesus who showed special kindness to widows (Mark 12:40-44; Luke 7:11-17; 18:1-8; 20:47—21:4); to women who were, or had been, living in sin (Luke 7:36-50; John 4:1-30); and even at the time of his final agony, to his own mother (John 19:26, 27). It is to *him*—not to modified Islam, or to this or that extremist movement—that also the women of today should turn for direction, help, and comfort.

In the present passage the Lord reveals his sympathy for women who during times of great political and social distress are pregnant or are nursing babies. What a vast difference between Menahem and the Messiah! The former was the cruel monster who, after seizing Israel's vacant throne, razed a city that refused to acknowledge him as the new ruler, and ripped open all its pregnant women (II Kings 15:16; cf. 8:12; and Amos 1:13). If anyone should maintain that this happened in barbarous times, and that surely in the enlightened 19th and 20th centuries everybody—at least in Europe and America—has been and is treating women kindly, he should read Dee Brown's *Bury My Heart at Wounded Knee.* [636]

Continued: **18. And pray that it may not occur in winter. . . .** [637] Winter is the stormy, the bad weather season. Even snow cannot be entirely ruled out. So Jesus admonished his disciples to pray that "it"—namely "y o u r

---

[634] New York, 1929. See especially chapter 6, "Womanhood under Islam."
[635] New York, 1959.
[636] See the New York, May, 1972 paperback edition, pp. 19, 288, 365, 417-419, etc.
[637] Mark, writing for readers not hampered by Jewish restrictions, did not have to retain what Jesus says in Matt. 24:20 with reference to traveling *on the sabbath.*

flight" (see Matt. 24:20)—may not occur at that time. [638] They must pray—in fact, must keep on praying—for a favorable weather situation.

But are not weather conditions brought about by the laws of nature? Answer: These so-called "laws," being scientific descriptions of that which happens, or generally happens, in the realm of nature, must not be thought of as independent forces. On the contrary, it is God who is and remains in full control. By and large, man is unable to change nature's ways. In fact, even the predictions of the experts are not always reliable. Though weather forecasting has made progress for which we should be thankful, the following is a true account. Recently, for the Boston area all forecasters predicted the worst snowstorm of the season for the next morning. So, school classes were canceled, snowplows readied. And then? . . . Not even one tiny snowflake appeared! [639]

On the other hand, Elijah *prayed,* and the rains were withheld. He *prayed again,* with the result that "the heaven gave rain, and the earth brought forth its fruit" (I Kings 17:1; 18:1; James 5:17, 18).

From what immediately follows it is evident once again that for Jesus the transition from the second to the third application of Daniel's prediction, without ever forgetting the second, was as easy as that from the first (the tribulation during the days of Antiochus Epiphanes) to the second (the distress in connection with the fall of Jerusalem): **19, 20 . . . for those will be days of tribulation, such as there has never been since (the) beginning of (the) creation which God created, until now, and never again will be. [640] And unless the Lord had cut short those days, no one would be saved. [641] But for the sake of the elect, whom he elected for himself, [642] he shortened the days.**

For the sake of his chosen ones—see N.T.C. on Eph. 1:4—, in order that

---

[638] ἵνα introduces the substance of the prayer. χειμῶνος is the gen. s. (of "time within which something happens") of χειμών. In Matt. 16:3 χειμών indicates *bad weather.*

[639] See the March 25, 1974 issue of Newsweek magazine, p. 65.

[640] γένηται, third per. s. (here futuristic) aor. subjunctive of γίνομαι.

[641] This is a second class or contrary to fact conditional sentence, referring to past time. In his decree from eternity God curtailed the period of tribulation. The sentence is entirely regular grammatically, having εἰ μή and aor. indic. in the protasis, and aor. passive indic. (ἐσώθη from σώζω) with οὐκ ἄν in the apodosis. See Gram. N.T., p. 1015. As to ἐκολόβωσε, it is the third per. s. aor. indic. active of κολοβόω, *to cut short, curtail.* Our English word *halt,* in the sense of *lame,* is related to it. It refers to the curtailment of a person's walking ability.

[642] The form ἐξελέξατο, third per. s. aor. middle indic. (so also in Eph. 1:4) of ἐκλέγω indicates that in his sovereign good pleasure God from eternity chose certain persons, both individually and in relation to each other and to Christ, not just "to go to heaven," but now and forever, first here below and then in the new heaven and earth, to live not only for themselves but also for others, *to his glory.* See I Cor. 10:31, 33; Eph. 1:3-6.

not all might have to die a violent death, the Lord decided to cut short the days of the final tribulation.

As to "tribulation," or, according to Matthew, "the great tribulation," to which Jesus here refers, care should be exercised. Rev. 7:14 also speaks about "the great tribulation." Are these two the same? The answer is: they are not. As the context in Rev. 7 indicates, the word is used there in a far more general sense. Because of his faith every genuine child of God experiences tribulation during his life on earth. See John 16:33; cf. Rom. 8:18; II Cor. 4:17; II Tim. 3:12. But in Mark 13:19, 20 (cf. Matt. 24:21, 22) Jesus is speaking about a tribulation that will characterize "those days," *a definite period of dire distress, of short duration, that will occur immediately before his return* (see verses 24-27; cf. Matt. 24:29-31). It is the brief period or "little season" mentioned also in Rev. 20:3b, 7-9a; cf. 11:7-9.

It should hardly be necessary to add that justice is not done to the concept of this tribulation, one that immediately precedes the close of the world's history and surpasses any other distress in its intensity, if it is referred *solely* to the sorrows experienced during the fall of Jerusalem.

With due regard for Vincent Taylor's Commentary, which in many respects is excellent, I must dissent from his view (*op. cit.,* p. 515) that verse 20 is not necessarily an authentic saying, one actually uttered by Jesus. He speaks of "apocalyptic speculation," foreign to Christ's teaching.

Objections:

a. The idea of the shortening of the time is found not only in such uncanonical literature as Hen. 80:2; IV Ezra 4:26; Apoc. Abr. 29:4; Apoc. Bar. 20:1 (see also S.BK.I, p. 953), but also in Dan. 12:7. While the figure 7 expresses fulness, 3½ ("a time, two times, and half a time") indicates the halving, hence shortening, of this fulness.

Entirely in line with this is Ps. 30:5:

> "For his anger lasts but a moment;
> His favor for a lifetime;
> Weeping may tarry for the night,
> But in the morning there is a joyful song."

This is by no means all. The idea that with respect to those whom he has chosen—that is the context here in Mark 13:20!—and for their sake, periods of tribulation do not last long but are shortened, is firmly fixed in the Old Testament. In addition to the passages already given see also Ps. 103:9; Isa. 26:20; 54:7, 8.

b. Since Mark's chapter 13 and its parallels contain almost all of the strictly apocalyptic teaching of our Lord that is recorded in the New Testament, comparison with his other teaching—e.g., Sermon on the Mount—, which contains very little material of this nature, seems hardly fair. On the basis of non-apocalyptical or non-eschatological discourses and say-

531

ings of Jesus to draw the conclusion that Mark 13:20 "is not necessarily an authentic saying" is unwarranted.

c. As Taylor himself admits, the Semitic character of verses 19 and 20 is unmistakable. [643] This tallies with the fact that Jesus, who addressed his disciples in Aramaic, a widely spoken Semitic tongue, may well have used this kind of language.

Deserving special study are the words "(the) creation which God created" (verse 19), and "the elect whom he elected for himself (verse 20)." Such repetition of cognates has been called "pleonastic," "redundant," "tautological." Sometimes one is given the impression that such a repetition is Mark's "poor style," which Matthew "corrects." The fact is, however, that the modifiers really add something—in fact, something of significance—to the words they modify. So, for example, even today many speak flippantly about "the whole creation," but persist in denying that God created it! The phrase "the elect" is also found in their conversation and in their literature, but often as a term of derision. These same people would scornfully reject the very suggestion that God actually chose anyone for himself from all eternity. Mark's words, accordingly, are those of a thoroughly inspired writer. Neither his nor any other Gospel writer's mode of expression is in need of "correction." The Gospels present a true and interestingly varied account of Christ's teaching as, under the guidance of the Holy Spirit, it was reflected in the consciousness of each evangelist.

Continued: 21, 22. **At that time if anyone should say to y o u, Look, here (is) the Christ! or Look, there (he is)! do not believe (him); for false Christs will arise and false prophets, and will perform signs and miracles, so as to mislead, if possible, the elect.** [644]

---

643 Note the following:

(1) The sentence structure of verse 19.

Literally it reads, "for those days will be tribulation, such as not there occurred the like from (the) beginning of (the) creation which God created until now, and never will be." This strongly reminds one of at least partly similar sentence formulation in Gen. 41:19; Exod. 9:24; Dan. 12:1.

(2) The pleonasms.

The point to be emphasized in the present connection is that Mark's style, with its repetition of cognates—see not only 13:19, 20, but also 7:13 and perhaps 12:23, a feature not entirely foreign to other language families—is thoroughly Semitic. Cf. I Kings 1:40; I Chron. 29:9, etc.

(3) Other Semitisms are:

"not would be saved all flesh" (thus literally). This is really a double Semitism ("not . . . all" for "no," and "flesh" for "person," human individual viewed as weak, frail, mortal. For "flesh" see also N.T.C. on John, Vol. I, p. 84, footnote 32; and N.T.C. on Philippians, p. 77, footnote 55.

". . . the elect." The idea of election from eternity has its roots in the Old Testament (Gen. 18:19; Ps. 105:6; 148:14; Isa. 43:20b; 65:9; Amos 3:2, etc.).

644 ἐάν . . . . . πιστεύετε is a third class or future more vivid conditional sentence, with

Clearly, the word "then" or "at that time" links this passage with the preceding (see verses 19, 20), that is, with the most severe tribulation of all, an affliction foreshadowed, to be sure, by the bitter trial that resulted in Jerusalem's fall, but going beyond that, as the connection between verses 21-23 and 24-27 clearly shows. That there were false prophets at the time of Jerusalem's fall is clear from Josephus, *Jewish Wars* VI. 285-288. [645] Far more obvious, however, is the fact that in the final analysis Jesus is here referring to what will happen during the bitter days that are going to precede his return. Then especially there will be those who claim that the Christ has

third per. s. aor. subjunctive of εἴπῃ in the protasis, and sec. per. p. imperative πιστεύετε in the apodosis.

For ἴδε see on 2:24, footnote 91.

The word used in the original for "false Christs" can be more literally rendered *pseudo-Christs* (cf. Matt. 24:24); similarly, that for "false prophets" is *pseudo-prophets* (cf. Matt. 7:15; 24:11, 24; Luke 6:26; Acts 13:6; II Peter 2:1; I John 4:1; Rev. 16:13; 19:20; 20:10). In formation it is similar to *pseudo-brothers* (II Cor. 11:26; Gal. 2:4), *pseudo-apostles* (II Cor. 11:13), *pseudo-teachers* (II Peter 2:1), *pseudo-speakers* (liars, I Tim. 4:2), and *pseudo-witnesses* (Matt. 26:60; I Cor. 15:15).

The Gospels, book of Acts, epistles, the book of Revelation are full of examples of false prophets (Matt. 28:12-15; John 9:29; Acts 2:13; 8:18, 19; Rom. 6:1; 16:17, 18; I Cor. 15:12; Gal. 1:6, 9; 3:1; 4:17; 5:2-4; Eph. 5:3-14; Phil. 3:2, 17-19; Col. 2:4, 8, 16-23; II Thess. 2:1, 2; 3:6, 14; I Tim. 1:3-7, 18-20; 4:1-5, 7; 6:20, 21; II Tim. 2:14-18; 3:1-9; 4:3, 4; Titus 1:10-16; 3:9, 10; Heb. 6:4-8; 10:26-28; James 2:17; II Peter 2:1 ff.; 3:3, 4; I John 2:18; 4:1; II John 10; III John 9, 10; Jude 4 ff.; Rev. 2:9, 14, 15, 20-24; 3:9). False prophets are the representatives of the power of *darkness* (Col. 1:13; cf. Luke 22:53; Acts 26:18; Eph. 6:12) masquerading as an angel of *light* (II Cor. 11:14).

The characterization of the false prophet as the man who lacks divine authorization and brings his own message, generally telling people what they like to hear, is rooted in the Old Testament (Isa. 30:10; Jer. 6:13; 8:10; 23:21). This is the kind of prophet who, when defeat is actually imminent, will say, "Go up and triumph" (II Chron. 18:11). He will shout, "Peace, peace!" when there is no peace (Jer. 6:14; 8:11; Ezek. 13:10). His words are "softer than oil" (Ps. 55:21; cf. John 10:1, 8).

δώσουσι (in connection with its object "signs and miracles") is probably a Hebraism; cf. Deut. 13:2 ("and he *gives* you a sign or wonder"). It seems to be equal to ποιήσουσι, which synonym replaces it here in certain important manuscripts. It is therefore not absolutely necessary, with some, to render it "give" or "furnish"; "perform" will do.

For σημεῖον see above, on 8:11, footnote 366; and for the distinction between it and τέρας see Trench, *op. cit.*, par. xci.

Though there is nothing unusual about πρός τό followed by the infinitive to express purpose—see Matt. 5:28; 6:1; 13:30; 26:12; II Cor. 3:13; Eph. 6:11—, it so happens that the present is the only occurrence of this construction in Mark. The verb ἀποπλανάω (here pres. act. infinitive ἀποπλανᾶν), meaning to *mislead, cause to wander away from*, with "the faith" either expressed, as in I Tim. 6:10, or implied, as here in Mark 13:22, in the New Testament occurs only in these two passages. For the basic πλανάω see above, on 13:5, footnote 617.

645 However, when Lenski (*op. cit.*, p. 365) connects the false prophets mentioned in *Jewish Wars* II. 258-263; and *Antiquities* XX. 169-171—and see Luke's account in Acts 21:38—with Jerusalem's fall, it should be borne in mind that the matter referred to there by Josephus and Luke took place about fifteen years previous to A.D. 70. It should be noted also in this connection that Josephus' two accounts do not entirely harmonize.

already arrived. Excitedly ("Look, here! . . . Look, there!") they will even point to the place where presumably he has landed. The pseudo-*prophet* will say that this or that other person is the Christ. The pseudo-*Christ* will say that he himself is the Christ. By means of a mighty display of *a. signs*—supernatural feats that point away from the performer to the enabler—, and *b. wonders, miracles,* or *marvels*—the same astonishing performances viewed now from the aspect of their effect upon spectators—, these deceivers will try to mislead, *if possible,* the elect; yes *even* (Matt. 24:24) them! The implication is that to successfully mislead God's elect, so that until the day of their death they would permit themselves to resemble wandering stars, is impossible. See N.T.C. on Phil. 1:6.

The comforting words, 23. **But as to yourselves, be on y o u r guard; I have told y o u everything ahead of time** [646] (cf. Matt. 24:25), remind one of Christ's similar sayings in John 13:19; 14:29; 16:4. It is for the third time that Jesus now utters the words, "Be on y o u r guard" or "Take care" (see also verses 5 and 9). This warning was indeed very appropriate, for:

a. even though it is true that the predictions span the entire dispensation, including even the tribulation immediately preceding the return, the preliminary fulfilment takes place during the lives of the apostles.

b. Jesus knew that his words would be repeated to later generations. Cf. John 10:16; 17:20.

It is incorrect, on the basis of 13:3, to limit "yourselves" to Peter, James, John, and Andrew. The broader reference (see Matt. 24:1, 3) must also be borne in mind.

Lovingly the Master provides for his disciples. When fiery trial arrives they must never be able to say, "How strange and unexpected! Why did not the Lord prepare us for this? Why did he not warn us?" Having been forewarned, the disciples will not be unduly disturbed when the prediction attains preliminary fulfilment. In fact, their faith in Jesus will then be strengthened. Was there ever kinder Shepherd?

---

24 "But in those days, after that tribulation,
  The sun will be darkened,
  And the moon will not give her light,
25 And the stars will be falling from the sky,
  And the powers (that are) in the heavens will be shaken.
26 And then they will see the Son of man coming in clouds with great power and glory. 27 And then he will send forth his angels and gather his elect from the four winds, from farthest reach of earth to farthest reach of heaven. [647]

---

[646] προείρηκα functions as first per. s. perfect indic. of προλέγω.

[647] Or, with A.V., "from the uttermost part of the earth to the uttermost part of heaven."

13:24-27 *The Coming of the Son of Man*
Cf. Matt. 24:29-31; Luke 21:25-28

Between the Matthean and the Marcan account there is a close resemblance. The main differences are as follows:

a. Instead of Mark's "And then they will see the Son of man," Matthew, he alone, mentions "*the sign* of the Son of man."

b. Matthew has retained Christ's remark, "All the tribes of the earth will mourn."

c. Matthew also shows that according to Christ's teaching the glorious return will not only be visible but also audible: "with a loud trumpet blast."

Luke's account, sometimes more closely resembling Mark's than Matthew's, sometimes vice versa, speaks about "signs in sun, moon, and stars," and, in general, emphasizes the effect which the Son of man's arrival has upon the inhabitants of the earth: the distress of nations, the fear and perplexity of men because of the things that are happening, including the roaring of the sea and its billows and the shaking of the heavenly spheres. He climaxes his account by reporting the Master's very encouraging and comforting closing exhortation (21:28).

What now follows, here in Mark 13:24-27, is deeply rooted in Old Testament prophecy. It must be interpreted in the light of that literary genre. This means that an extremely literal interpretation must be avoided. Until this prophetic picture becomes history we will probably not know how much must be taken literally, how much figuratively. That at least some of it must be interpreted literally follows from II Peter 3:10. There will indeed be "a new heaven and a new earth" (II Peter 3:13; Rev. 21:1). However, since *the prophetic background* has been indicated in some detail in N.T.C. on Matthew, and since, as already shown, the two accounts (Matt. 24:29-31 and Mark 13:24-27) resemble each other very closely, I here refer the reader to p. 862 of that volume.

What *Mark* offers in these verses can be viewed under the following headings: 1. Apocalyptic Disturbances in Celestial Spheres (verses 24, 25); 2. Arrival of the Son of Man as Deliverer (verse 26); and 3. Assembling of the Scattered Elect (verse 27).

1. *Apocalyptic Disturbances in Celestial Spheres*
24, 25. But [648] in those days, after that tribulation,
     The sun will be darkened,

---

648 Though it is true that ἀλλά does not always have an adversative meaning, here "but" makes sense: the word marks the transition from supreme distress (verse 19 f.) to abrupt and full deliverance. Cf. II Thess. 2:8a contrast 8b; Rev. 11:10 versus 11; and 20:9 over against 10, 11.

> And the moon will not give her light
> And the stars will be falling from the sky,
> And the powers (that are) in the heavens will be shaken.

The picture is very vivid, in Mark even somewhat more so than in Matthew. Note Matt. 24:29, "And the stars will fall from the sky," contrasted with Mark 13:25, "And the stars will be falling from the sky." [649] One can picture them falling one by one.

First, then, we must go back for a moment to the very last day of the fierce distress or tribulation. While the earth is drenched with the blood of the saints, all at once the sun becomes darkened. Cf. Rev. 6:12. Naturally the moon now also ceases to shed her light. The stars deviate from their orbits and race to their doom. Probably summarizing all this, the account continues, "And the powers (that are) in the heavens will be shaken."

2. *Arrival of the Son of Man as Deliverer*

26. And then they will see the Son of man coming in clouds with great power and glory. This "they" must mean "all mankind," cf. Rev. 1:7. As was pointed out above, Matt. 24:30 states, "And then the sign of the Son of man will appear in the sky," but both Mark and Luke leave out the word "sign." They simply represent Jesus as declaring that men will see "the Son of man coming" majestically. Probable solution: the very appearance of the Son of man upon clouds of glory is itself the sign, the one great, final sign from the point of view of the earth. Christ's brilliant self-manifestation will be the sign or signal that *he* is about to go forth to meet his people, while *they* ascend to meet him in the air. He comes *to deliver* the oppressed elect people (clearly implied in verses 20, 27; see also Luke 21:28). In fact, he will gather *all* the elect—both the survivors and those who had previously fallen asleep—to himself, to be with him forever.

This appearance of the Son of man in majesty is a sign in still another respect: the glorious manner of his appearance corresponds exactly with the prediction of Dan. 7:13, 14; cf. Mark 14:62. For the significance of "clouds" see N.T.C. on Matthew, p. 667. The glory that marks the Son of man's sudden and brilliant manifestation is a definite proof of the Father's delight in his Son and of the justice of the cause of him who was once "a man of sorrows and acquainted with grief" (Isa. 53:3).

Note "the Son of man," see on Mark 2:10; and note also "with great power and glory." That "power" is evident from what happens at his coming: see verses 24, 25, 27; add Rev. 14:14-16; also 20:11 (in view of Rev. 3:21; 5:7, 8, it is impossible to remove the Son from this throne). "And glory," for at his coming all his attributes—power, wisdom, holiness, love,

---

[649] Note the periphrastic future ἔσονται ... πίπτοντες.

etc.—shine forth brilliantly. This "great power and glory" is enhanced by what is stated in the next verse:

3. *Assembly of the Scattered Elect*

27. And then he will send forth his angels and gather his elect from the four winds, from farthest reach of earth to farthest reach of heaven. [650] At Christ's return, the already "departed ones," that is, the souls that had previously exchanged their earthly for their heavenly dwelling, are quickly reunited with their now glorified bodies. The "survivors," that is, those children of God that are still living on earth at Christ's return, are changed "in a moment, in the twinkling of an eye" (I Cor. 15:52). Together, all the elect, now forming one countless multitude, thus gathered "from the uttermost part of the earth to the uttermost part of heaven," accompanied by the angels who were divinely instructed to gather them, now go forth as the Bride, to meet the Bridegroom, and to be with him forevermore. See N.T.C. on I Thess. 4:13-18.

Evidence for the separate units of this representation:

a. The sending forth of the angels.

Though none of the following passages teach exactly what is stated here with respect to their task at Christ's return, Mark 13:27 (cf. Matt. 24:31) is in line with the following: Matt. 13:41, 49; Mark 8:38; Luke 9:26; 16:22; II Thess. 1:7; Heb. 1:14. See also the summary of biblical teaching on angels, N.T.C. on Matthew, pp. 694, 695.

b. his elect.

See above, on verse 20.

c. The four winds.

These represent the four points of the compass; hence, "from the four winds" means "from everywhere." See Zech. 2:6; and cf. Deut. 30:4; Isa. 11:12; Ezek. 7:2; Rev. 7:1; 20:8.

d. "from farthest reach of earth to farthest reach of heaven."

It is true that the Old Testament contains many passages which show that the scattered children of God will be gathered (Deut. 30:4; Isa. 11:11-16; 27:12, 13; Ezek. 39:27, 28; Zech. 2:6-11, etc.). But such references, though indeed helpful, merely *anticipate* or *foreshadow* what is taught here in Mark 13:27. They predict a return to the land of Canaan, and it is a known fact that the remnant did actually return. What Jesus teaches, as recorded here in Mark 13:27, is something else; namely, *the collective gathering of all the*

---

[650] Literally, "from tip of earth to tip of heaven," from one end to the other, of both earth and heaven. The ἄκρον is the tip, top, (highest) point, end; thus, the top of a staff (Heb. 11:21), finger tip (Luke 16:24). Cf. *acropolis*, the highest point or upper part (often fortified) of an ancient Greek city; e.g., that of Athens with its Parthenon.

elect to himself at his glorious return. So, if one is looking for parallel passages (in addition to Matt. 24:31), he should turn rather to Matt. 25:31-40; John 10:16; II Cor. 5:10; I Thess. 4:16, 17; and Rev. 19:6-8.

---

28 "Now from the fig tree learn this lesson: as soon as its branch becomes tender and puts forth leaves, y o u know that the summer is near. 29 So also y o u, when y o u see these things happening, know then that it is near, at the very gates. 30 I solemnly declare to y o u, this generation will certainly not pass away until all this takes place. 31 Heaven and earth will pass away, but my words will never pass away.

13:28-31 *The Lesson from the Fig Tree*
Cf. Matt. 24:32-35; Luke 21:29-33

In the present section (verses 28-31) and also in the next and final one (see especially verses 33 and 37) *admonition* to a considerable extent replaces *prediction.* True, there has been admonition before; see verses 5, 7, 9a, 11, 13, 14-16, 21, 23, but the immediately preceding section (verses 24-27) was exclusively predictive in character, causing the hortatory character of verses 28-31 to stand out all the more clearly.

Matthew's and Mark's accounts are almost identical. The slight differences can be considered stylistic. Though also Luke's report is strikingly similar, two variations deserve attention. Instead of "Now from the fig tree learn this lesson" Luke reads, "Look at the fig tree *and all the trees,*" as if to say, "What holds with respect to the fig tree is basically true also with respect to the other fruit trees." And instead of " . . . know then that *it* is near, at the very gates," Luke offers, " . . . know then that the kingdom—or kingship, rule—of God is near." This, too, may well be an interpretive variation: the "it" of the other Gospels (however applied, whether to Jerusalem's fall in A.D. 70 or to Christ's return) indicating the sudden and powerful public manifestation of God's royal rule; and therefore marking *the end* of an era, the end of the age.

28, 29. Now from the fig tree learn this lesson: as soon as its branch becomes tender and puts forth leaves, y o u know that the summer is near. So also y o u, when y o u see these things happening, know then that it is near, at the very gates. [651] The branch of a fig tree becomes soft and tender

---

[651] For συκῆ, συκῆς, see on 11:13. μάθετε is sec. per. pl. aor. imper. of μανθάνω. For more details with respect to this verb see N.T.C. on Matthew, footnote 488 on p. 504; and in the same volume footnote 547 on p. 580. παραβολή is here used in the sense of *a brief illustrative comparison* or *lesson.* See also on Mark 3:23; and N.T.C. on Matthew, pp. 23, 617, 866. A κλάδος, related to κλάω, *to break,* basically may have indicated a young, tender shoot broken off for the purpose of grafting; hence, a twig, branch. Note contrast between γένηται, third per. s. *aor.* subjunctive of γίνομαι, and ἐκφύῃ, third per. s. active *pres.* subjunctive of ἐκφύω. The first of these two verbs is what may be termed a

because of the sap that is swelling within it. It is not surprising, therefore, that soon this branch is generating leaves, and still more leaves. Now when this happens to a fig tree—or, for that matter, to the fruit trees as a whole (Luke 21:29) [652] —the disciples realize that summer is near. Similarly when, during their life-time, the disciples see "these things happening," that is, when they take note not only of constantly recurring earthquakes, famines, wars, etc., but particularly also of "the desolating sacrilege," that is, the approaching Roman armies, they should understand that the end for Jerusalem and its temple is near, so near as to be able, as it were, to walk right into the door.

So also, when at a much later time believers see the final Antichrist carrying on his work of sacrilege and desolation, they will know that the glorious day of Christ's return is close at hand. Nevertheless, in view of "when y o u see these things happening," the emphasis here in verses 28, 29 is on that which these very men (at least some of them) were to witness during their life on earth.

That even now Christ's prophetic eye was focused not only on the afflictions that were to befall and/or to threaten the Jews, including the Christians among them, during the struggle with Rome, but also on that which would happen to the Jews throughout the new dispensation until the day of his return, is clear from verse 30. **I solemnly declare to y o u, this generation will certainly not pass away** [653] **until all this takes place.** Note the

---

constative aorist. Instead of "constative" it may also be designated "historical," "normal," or "regular." As here used, it simply states a fact, regardless of the amount of time consumed in bringing it about. The term "punctiliar" is somewhat confusing, since this might be interpreted as showing that the action expressed by the verb took place in one moment or "point" of time. The second verb is a descriptive, durative, or linear present. One can almost see those leaves making their appearance, now this one, then another, etc. A φύλλον (here acc. pl. φύλλα) is a leaf. Cf. *microphyll;* also, via Latin, *foliage.* As to γινώσκετε in verse *28,* there is general agreement that this is the sec. per. pl. pres. *indic.* of γινώσκω. Is this true also with respect to γινώσκετε in verse *29?* According to several translators it is; hence, "y o u know." Others, however, in *this* case interpret it to be a sec. per. pres. *imper.;* hence, "know," "know then," "recognize," or something similar. Along this line A.V., A.R.V., N.A.S., Lenski, Dutch (Nieuwe Vertaling), etc. While allowing the possibility that the first theory may be correct, I have adopted the second, in view of the introductory exhortation implied in μάθετε. In the New Testament θέρος, summer, the season of warmth, occurs only here (in Mark 13:28 and its parallels: Matt. 24:32; Luke 21:30). Think of the *thermometer.* Finally, ἴδητε is used as the sec. per. pl. aor. subjunctive of ὁράω.

[652] H. Mulder, *Spoorzoeker in Bijbelse Landen,* Amsterdam, 1973, p. 93, is of the opinion that the fig tree is singled out here because it generally produces leaves later than other fruit trees; for example, much later than the almond tree. For another reason why the fig tree is mentioned here, in preference to other trees, see N.T.C. on Matthew, p. 866. Also the great abundance and popularity of fig trees should be taken into account.

[653] παρέλθῃ third per. s. aor. subjunctive of παρέρχομαι.

impressive introduction: "I solemnly declare." See on 3:28. Probable meaning of the passage: "This generation, namely, the Jewish people—see Deut. 32:5, 20; Ps. 12:7; 78:8, etc.—will not cease to exist until all those things which I [Jesus] predicted have happened." The expression "all this" covers the events predicted for the entire new dispensation, including even the final tribulation and the Lord's glorious return. For the arguments in defense of this interpretation and for the refutation of other theories see N.T.C. on Matthew, pp. 867-869.

The majestic closing statement, **31. Heaven and earth will pass away, but my words will never pass away,** [654] deserves all the emphasis one can give to it. The *passing away* of heaven and earth, to which Jesus refers, does not mean total annihilation but glorious renewal. The fourfold process of transformation—namely conflagration, rejuvenation, self-realization, and harmonization—by means of which this "passing away" of the outward "fashion" of this world and the birth of the new heaven and earth will be accomplished, in accordance with such passages as Isa. 11:6-9; Rom. 8:18-22; I Cor. 7:31; II Peter 3:10, 13; Rev. 21:1-5, has been described in N.T.C. on Matthew, pp. 863, 864. What Jesus here drives home is that the physical universe round about, above and beneath us—mountains, valleys, rivers, vegetation, the animal world, the sky, the soil, etc.—, *as we now see it,* no matter how firm and strong some of it may appear to be, is actually unstable, but that his own words will continue to prove their stability and worth forever and ever. The negative "will never pass away" implies a strong affirmative "will always endure." This litotes is confirmed not only by such passages as Isa. 40:8; I Peter 1:24, 25, but also by centuries of fulfilment of prophecy both before and after the birth of Christ!

---

32 "But about that day or that hour no one knows, neither the angels in heaven nor the Son, only the Father. 33 Be on y o u r guard. Keep watch, [655] for y o u do not know when is the appropriate time. 34 (It is) like a man, away on a journey, who, upon leaving his home and putting his servants [656] in charge, assigning to each his task, also ordered the doorkeeper to keep on the alert. 35 Stay on the alert, [657] therefore—because y o u do not know when the owner of the house is coming, whether in the evening, or at midnight, or when the rooster crows, or at dawn—36 lest he come suddenly and find y o u sleeping. 37 And what I am saying to y o u, I am saying to everyone: Stay on the alert."

---

654 παρελεύσονται, third per. pl. fut. indic. of παρέρχομαι (cf. verse 30).
655 Some manuscripts add: Pray.
656 Or slaves.
657 Or, both at the beginning of verse 35 and at the close of verse 37, "Be watching."

13:32-37 *The Necessity of Being Ready Always, in View of the Unknown Day and Hour of Christ's Coming*
Cf. Matt. 24:36-44; 25:13, 14; Luke 21:34-36

Verse 32 closely resembles Matt. 24:36. For the rest, Mark 13:33-37 is largely peculiar to Mark. See N.T.C. on Matthew, pp. 6, 7. As is also implied on those pages, the uniqueness is not absolute; for, *a.* "Always be watchful and ready with a view to the Son of man's return" is the central lesson not only of the present Marcan section but also of Matt. 24:37-44 (cf. 25:1-13); Luke 21:34-36; and *b.* there is even a degree of verbal resemblance between:
Mark 13:33 and Matt. 24:42; 25:13; Luke 21:36;
Mark 13:34 and Matt. 25:14; and
Mark 13:35-37 and Matt. 24:42.

32. But about that day or that hour no one knows, neither the angels in heaven nor the Son, only the Father.

The series of events that shall precede Christ's return has been described. The precise moment of that great event has however not been indicated. Neither could it have been, for that moment is known to the Father alone, and it has not pleased him to reveal it. The angels, though standing in a very close relationship to God (Isa. 6:1-3; Matt. 18:10), and though intimately associated with the events pertaining to the second coming (Matt. 13:41; 24:31; Rev. 14:19), do not know the day nor the hour. Nor, in fact, does the Son himself, viewed from the aspect of his human nature. See also on Mark 2:8; 5:32; 9:33, 34; 10:33, 34; 11:12, 13. The fact that even the Son, according to his human nature, did not know, is in harmony with Phil. 2:7, "He emptied himself." The Father, he alone, knows. This proves the futility and sinfulness of every attempt on man's part to predict the date when Jesus will return, whether that imagined date be 1843, 1844, more precisely Oct. 22, 1844, the autumn of 1914, or any later one. See Deut. 29:29. Curiosity is wonderful. For nosiness, intrusiveness, impertinence there is no excuse.

33. Be on y o u r guard. Keep watch. . . . [658] For the fourth time Jesus says, "Be on y o u r guard" or "Take care." See verses 5, 9, 23, 33. The disciples must be wide awake. They have been asking about the time when the Master's predictions would be fulfilled (verse 4). They should be far more concerned about the question how to spend their time profitably. They must take cognizance of the moral and spiritual dangers that are threatening (verses 21, 22), so that they can arm themselves against them

---

658 ἀγρυπνεῖτε = ἄγρα, a catch, chase, plus ὕπνος, sleep; hence, "chase sleep away," and so "Keep watch." See V. Taylor, *op. cit.*, p. 523. This is, however, uncertain; cf. L.N.T. (Th.), p. 9.

and can warn others. They should study the events that are taking place and are going to occur, so that they will be able to discern the fulfilment of Christ's predictions and will be strengthened in their faith (verse 23). Moreover, since it is clear that being on one's guard is a synonym of keeping watch and of staying on the alert, which in turn is associated with continuing in prayer (14:38; cf. Matt. 26:41), the conclusion is warranted that these expressions—Be on y o u r guard, Keep watch, stay on the alert—also imply, "In the midst of all circumstances be sure to ask God for wisdom and strength." [659]

Continued: for y o u do not know when is the appropriate time. [660] If the angels in heaven and even the Son do not know the exact moment of the return (verse 32), then surely puny sinners, including the apostles and all other believers, are ignorant with respect to that point. It is therefore always impossible for anyone to say, "He will not come until such and such a time; hence, we need not be prepared now." They must be ready . . . *always.*

By means of an illustration—one might even call it a parable—Jesus stresses this duty of eternal vigilance: **34. (It is) like a man away on a journey, who, upon leaving his home and putting his servants in charge, assigning to each his task, also ordered** [661] **the doorkeeper** [662] **to** [663] **keep on the alert.** [664] *To be* (constantly) *on the alert* or *watchful*—a Greek word from which the proper name Gregory (the watchful or vigilant one) is derived—means to live a sanctified life, in the consciousness of the coming judgment day. Spiritual and moral circumspection and forethought are required; preparedness is necessary. The watchful person has his loins girded and his lamps burning (Luke 12:35). It is in that condition that he looks forward to the coming of the Bridegroom. For more on this subject of watchfulness and its implications see N.T.C. on I and II Thessalonians, pp. 124, 125.

Now in the illustration it is on this command to the doorkeeper *to keep on the alert* that all the emphasis falls. The meaning of the figure is this: The absent proprietor, before leaving home, not only put his servants in charge, assigning to each his special duty, all of this as a matter of course, but in particular *ordered the doorkeeper by all means to keep on the alert.* That

---

659 Therefore, though the inclusion of "and be praying" may have insufficient textual support in Mark 13:33, the thought itself is certainly implied.

660 For the meaning of καιρός see on 1:15, footnote 32.

661 ἐνετείλατο, third per. s. aor. indic. of ἐντέλλομαι. So also in 10:3; and cf. Matt. 15:4; 17:9; 19:7; John 8:5; 14:31; Heb. 9:20; 11:22. For ἐντολή see on Mark 7:8, footnote 319.

662 θυρωρός (ὁ of a man; ἡ of a woman or girl) = θύρα (door) and ὤρα (care). See John 10:3; 18:16, 17.

663 ἵνα subfinal, "that he should keep"; hence, "to keep."

664 γρηγορῇ, third per. s. pres. subjunctive of γρηγορέω.

this is indeed the emphasis follows from the fact that both the immediately preceding context (verse 33) and the immediately following (verse 35) stress this one point. [665]

35-37. **Stay on the alert,** [666] **therefore—because y o u do not know when the owner of the house is coming, whether in the evening, or at midnight, or when the rooster crows, or at dawn—lest he come suddenly and find** [667] **y o u sleeping. And what I am saying to y o u, I am saying to everyone: Stay on the alert.**

Note the following:

a. The meaning of the illustration now surfaces. The master or owner of the house represents Christ, the Son of man. See verses 21, 26. It is he who, by means of his death and ascension is going to absent himself from the disciples for a while. But he will return, first by means of his resurrection and the outpouring of the Holy Spirit. Cf. John 16:16. Later, at the close of the present age, upon the clouds, as the Bridegroom, to take the Bride to himself to be with him forever. Cf. John 14:3; I Thess. 4:13-18. It is the latter "coming" that Jesus has in mind here. The church should be watching for it, always remaining on the alert.

b. Such *alertness* or watchfulness is the very opposite of *sleeping*. The latter indicates moral and spiritual laxity. Luke 12:45 pictures this condition vividly. So does the description of the five foolish girls, who had taken no oil in their vessels with their lamps (Matt. 25:3, 8). It means unpreparedness.

c. What are the characteristics of such watchfulness? Does it merely mean to look at the clouds every morning in order to see whether Jesus is beginning to make his appearance? Not at all. The alertness Jesus has in mind is not only eager and prayerful, it is also intelligent, continuous, and last but not least, *active*. See, for example, John 15:4, 12, 26: "Abide in me . . . love each other . . . also bear witness." Or study I Cor. 16:13, "Be watchful, stand fast in the faith, acquit yourselves like men, be strong. Let all that y o u do be done in love." Consider also John 9:4; Rom. 13:8-12; I Cor. 15:58.

d. "Y o u do not know when the owner of the house is coming," repeats the thought of verse 32, but becomes more specific, for Jesus adds, "whether in the evening, or at midnight, or when the rooster crows, or at dawn." See above, on 6:48. We are dealing here with the four so-called "watches," namely:

evening: 6-9 P.M.

---

665 So also Lenski *op. cit.*, p. 373. Among English translations of this passage I have found none better than A.R.V. and N.A.S.

666 γρηγορεῖτε (verses 35 and 37), sec. per. pl. pres. imper. of γρηγορέω.

667 εὕρῃ, third per. s. aor. act. subjunctive of εὑρίσκω.

midnight: 9 P.M.-12.
rooster crowing: 12-3 A.M.
dawn: 3-6 A.M. [668]

It should not be overlooked that the coming is in each case said to take place during one of the *night* watches; that is, at a time least expected. Cf. Matt. 24:44.

e. The words, "And what I am saying to y o u, I am saying to everyone . . ." show that the Master wanted to impress upon his disciples the fact that his admonition to be and remain on the alert—in fact, that his entire discourse—was of supreme value not only for them but also for all other believers both then and later.

What is the proper attitude with respect to the coming of the Lord? The antediluvians (Luke 17:26, 27) were alert to the present but oblivious of the future. They were so busy with present, earthly affairs that they did not bother about impending dangers.

Some of the Thessalonians (II Thess. 2:1, 2; 3:6-12) were oblivious of the present but alert to the (immediate?) future. They left their workshops. Why should they tend to earthly needs when heavenly treasures were about to descend upon them?

The only proper attitude was that of the Smyrniots (Rev. 2:8-11). They were alert to both the present and the future. They attended to their present duties with such faithfulness that they were encouraged with joyful anticipation to look forward to the day when they would receive the crown of life out of the Lord's gracious hand.

Summary of Chapter 13

In verses 1-4 *the occasion* that gave rise to the discourse on *The Last Things* is described. In harmony with Matt. 23:38 Jesus, as he was leaving the temple, predicts its total destruction. This was in reply to the disciples' expression of amazement about the beauty and grandeur of that building. Arrived on the Mount of Olives four disciples ask him, "Tell us, when will this happen, and what will be the sign when all these things are about to be accomplished?" As they saw it, Jerusalem's fall meant Christ's return and the end of the world. See Matt. 24:3. Their question resulted in the discourse.

According to verses 5-13 Jesus first of all predicts what he calls "(merely)

---

668 Adverbs of time are ὀψέ and πρωΐ; ἀλεκτοροφωνίας is a gen. showing time within which something (here rooster-crowing) happens. Some interpreters, apparently thinking that μεσονύκτιον would be improper here since it would spoil the symmetry and would have to mean "through midnight" (Lenski, *op. cit.*, p. 374), adopt the reading that has a gen. ending. But this is unnecessary: μεσονύκτιον may be regarded as a neuter adjective, used adverbially. The meaning then would be "at midnight."

the beginning of birth pains," that is, the rise of deceivers, who will say, "I am he," wars and rumors of wars, earthquakes, famines, persecutions. More definite is his statement that before the Son of man can return *the gospel must first be preached to all the nations.* Jesus also assures his followers that at their arraignments the Holy Spirit will give them words to speak, and that though hated by all, including even members of their own families, those who endure to the end will be saved.

If world-wide gospel proclamation may be considered the first definite preliminary sign, *the severe tribulation in store for the church* (verses 14-23) may be called the second. Destined to occur before—in fact, immediately before (Matt. 24:29)—the manifestation of the Son of man in clouds with great power and glory (Mark 13:26), *it is foreshadowed* by woes in store for Jerusalem, culminating in "the desolating sacrilege," that is, Jerusalem surrounded by armies (Luke 21:20), carrying idol images of their emperor upon their standards. Their approach would be the signal for those in Judea to flee to the hills. Mercifully Jesus warns those who might be tempted to flee *into* the city or even *into* their homes. To women in difficult circumstances he also reveals his sympathy. He warns his followers not to be deceived by those who say, "Look, here (is) the Christ!" or "Look, there (he is)!" Their intention to deceive (even) the elect will not succeed. For the elect's sake the days of severe tribulation will be shortened. The section closes with Christ's bracing exhortation, "But as to yourselves, be on y o u r guard. I have told y o u everything ahead of time."

Verses 24-27 record what will happen (immediately) after the tribulation: the sun will be darkened, the moon will not give her light, the stars will be falling from the sky, etc. Then suddenly, "They—all men—will see *the Son of man coming in clouds with great power and glory.*" The brilliant character of his appearance, in complete harmony with Dan. 7:13, 14, will prove that this is indeed the Messiah of prophecy, and that the wedding of the Lamb with his bride, the church, is about to take place (Eph. 5:32; Rev. 19:7). For this to happen the all-glorious Son of man will send his holy angels to gather his elect "from the four winds, from the farthest reach of earth to the farthest reach of heaven."

The lesson from the fig tree is found in verses 28-31, and may be paraphrased as follows, "As soon as its branch becomes tender and puts forth leaves, y o u know that summer is near. So also y o u, my disciples, upon seeing the series of events climaxed by the desolating sacrilege should recognize that the fall of Jerusalem is near, at the very gates." As for the Jews in general, Jesus predicts that they will not pass away from the earth as a people until "all this"—events stretching all the way to the Son of man's return—takes place. He adds, "Heaven and earth will pass away, but my words will never pass away."

545

The necessity of being ready always, in view of the unknown day and hour of Christ's coming is stressed in verses 32-37. If no one—not the angels nor even the Son—knows exactly when the return will occur, then all the more no sinful man knows this. So, preparedness at all times is required. When the owner of a house leaves on a journey, he not only puts his servants in charge, assigning to each his individual task, but specifically orders the doorkeeper to remain on the alert. Beautifully Jesus therefore ends the discourse—as reported by Mark—with these ringing words, "Stay on the alert, therefore—because y o u do not know when the owner of the house is coming, whether in the evening, or at midnight, or when the rooster crows, or at dawn—lest he come suddenly and find y o u sleeping. And what I am saying to y o u, I am saying to everyone: Stay on the alert."

Outline of Chapter 14

Theme: *The Work Which Thou Gavest Him To Do*

14:1, 2   God's Counsel versus Man's Collusion
14:3-9   The Anointing at Bethany
14:10, 11   The Agreement between Judas and the Chief Priests
14:12-21   The Passover
14:22-26   The Institution of the Lord's Supper
14:27-31   Peter's Denial Foretold
14:32-42   Gethsemane
14:43-50   The Betrayal and the Seizure of Jesus
14:51, 52   The Young Man Who Escaped
14:53-65   The Trial before the Sanhedrin
14:66-72   Peter's Threefold Denial

CHAPTER XIV

14 1 Now the feast of the Passover and the Unleavened Bread was two days off, and the chief priests and the scribes were seeking how to take Jesus into custody by some trick, and kill him; 2 for they were saying, "Not during the feast, lest there be an uproar among the people."

14:1, 2 *God's Counsel versus Man's Collusion*
Cf. Matt. 26:1-5; Luke 22:1, 2; John 11:45-53

For the reader who may have experienced some difficulty in remembering which chapters in Matthew and in Luke parallel those in Mark it will be a relief to discover that for the last three chapters of each of these Gospels the answer is simple. *Where there are corresponding sections,* the events recorded in Mark 14 are paralleled in Matt. 26 and in Luke 22; for those found in Mark 15 see Matt. 27 and Luke 23; and for those narrated in Mark 16 study Matt. 28 and Luke 24. For these three chapters, in *each* case of correspondence Mark's figure plus 12 is Matthew's figure, and Mark's figure plus 8 is Luke's figure. Cf. N.T.C. on Matthew, pp. 12-16, 28-30.

In the middle of Mark 14 and parallels is Gethsemane; the heart and center of Mark 15 and parallels is Calvary (or Golgotha); and the main theme of Mark 16 and parallels is "He is risen." The result is as follows:

	Mark	Matthew	Luke
Gethsemane	14	26	22
Calvary	15	27	23
"He is risen"	16	28	24

Even when we compare the contents of these chapters as a whole we discover remarkable similarity amid pleasing variety. This is true first of all with respect to Mark 14 and 15 and parallels. Note chart on page 550.

As to the closing chapter of each of the Synoptics, the story about the women at the empty tomb is found in Mark 16:1-8; Matt. 28:1-10; and Luke 24:1-12. Cf. John 20:1-10. Also, according to the sixth verse of each Synoptic account these women, who had come to anoint the body of Jesus, are reported to have heard the startling news, "He is risen."

Parallels of Mark 14, 15

Mark	Matthew	Luke	John, etc.	
14:1, 2	26:1-5	22:1, 2	John 11:45-53	God's Counsel versus Man's Collusion
14:3-9	26:6-13		John 12:1-8	The Anointing at Bethany
14:10, 11	26:14-16	22:3-6		The Agreement between Judas and the Chief Priests
14:12-21	26:17-25	22:7-14, 21-23	John 13:21-30	The Passover
14:22-26	26:26-30	22:15-20	I Cor. 11:23-25	The Institution of the Lord's Supper
		22:24-30		The Dispute about Greatness
14:27-31	26:31-35	22:31-34	John 13:36-38	Peter's Denial Foretold
		22:35-38		"Did y o u lack anything?"
14:32-42	26:36-46	22:39-46		Gethsemane
14:43-50	26:47-56	22:47-53	John 18:3-12	The Betrayal and the Seizure of Jesus
14:51, 52				The Young Man Who Escaped
14:53-65	26:57-68	22:54, 55, 63-71	John 18:13, 14, 19-24	The Trial before the Sanhedrin
14:66-72	26:69-75	22:56-72	John 18:15-28, 25-27	Peter's Threefold Denial
15:1	27:1, 2	23:1, 2	John 18:28	The Sanhedrin's Decision to Put Jesus to Death
	27:3-10		Acts 1:18, 19	Judas' Death by Suicide
15:2-5	27:11-14	23:3-5	John 18:33-38	Jesus Questioned by Pilate
15:6-15	27:15-26	23:13-25	John 18:39-19:16	Jesus Sentenced to Die
15:16-20	27:27-31		John 19:2, 3	The Mockery
15:21-32	27:32-44	23:26-43	John 19:19-27	Calvary: The Crucifixion of Jesus
15:33-41	27:45-56	23:44-49	John 19:28-30	Calvary: The Death of Jesus
15:42-47	27:57-61	23:50-56	John 19:38-42	The Burial of Jesus
	27:62-66			The Guard Stationed

From that point on the accounts diverge. Mark's "disputed section" (16:9-20) summarizes events reported elsewhere in greater detail and also contains some unparalleled material. It requires separate discussion at the proper place.

Matthew 28 continues his unparalleled story about The Guard (now Frightened and finally Bribed). See verses 2-4, 11-15. He ends with the climactic and only partially paralleled description of The Great Claim; The Great Commission; and The Great Comfort (verses 16-20). Cf. Mark 16:14-18; Luke 24:36-49; John 20:19-23; Acts 1:9-11.

The report of The Appearance of the Risen Savior to Cleopas and his Companion, a narrative peculiar to Luke (except for Mark 16:12, 13), covers 23 verses of that evangelist's final chapter (24:13-35). With the story of Christ's Appearance to the Disciples in Jerusalem (verses 36-49; cf. Mark 16:14; John 20:19 ff.) and that of his Ascension (verses 50-53; cf. Mark 16:19; Acts 1:9-12) "the beloved physician" closes the first of his two New Testament books.

When the Marcan captions for all three chapters are reviewed a few times, they are easily commited to memory. Once Mark's sequence has been mastered, the corresponding parallels in Matthew and Luke—when there are such parallels—are also quickly located. The formula "Mark's figure plus 12 = Matthew's figure," or "plus 8 = Luke's figure" holds throughout the three final chapters.

A blank space in any column indicates that a particular section does not occur in the Synoptic Gospel mentioned by name above that column.

Take, as an example, Mark 14:51, 52. Here both Matthew's column and Luke's have a blank space, indicating that the story about The Young Man Who Escaped is found only in Mark.

A look at the columns indicates that as far as the Gospels are concerned it is Matthew alone who reports Judas' Death by Suicide. As already mentioned, it is also the converted publican alone who tells the fascinating story of The Guard.

The Anointing at Bethany is in the Synoptics reported only by Mark and Matthew. There is, however, a parallel in John 12:1-8. The Mark-Matthew parallel holds also for The Mockery, again with what by many is considered a corresponding passage in John. There are no non-Marcan sections common to Matthew and Luke. [669]

The last three chapters of the Gospel according to Luke contain many unparalleled (or nearly unparalleled) sections: The Dispute about Greatness, "Did y o u lack anything?," Jesus before Herod, the Appearance of the Risen Savior to Cleopas and his Companion (except for Mark 16:12-13), and

---

[669] This is an embarrassment to the advocates of "Q." See N.T.C. on Matthew, pp. 21, 47, 48.

The Ascension (but see Mark 16:19; Acts 1:9-12). Even the section on Christ's Appearance to the Disciples in Jerusalem (Luke 24:36-49) is to a large extent unparalleled.

The fourth column contains several references to John's Gospel. However, the only Johannine sections indicated are those which, to some extent, parallel material that is found in the final three chapters of the Synoptics. As for the beloved disciple's own full report read John 13—21 (even better chapters 11—21). Since in the fourth Gospel chapters 14—17 cover the Upper Room Discourses and the Highpriestly Prayer, topics absent from the Synoptics, none of the indicated parallel references in the fourth column are to these chapters, but all are to John 11, 12, 13, 19, and 20. The narrative found in John 21 is unparalleled.

The Outline of John's Gospel is very simple. There are two main divisions: *a.* Christ's Public Ministry (chapters 1—12) and *b.* His Private Ministry (chapters 13—21). For the rest, see N.T.C. on John, Vol. I, p. 66, and Vol. II, pp. 134, 260, 374, 446.

All this does not mean that once we are acquainted with the sequence in which the *sections* occur in these final chapters of each Gospel, we will then be able immediately to locate any and every important *passage*. There is wide variety even *within* the individual sections. Constant reading of Scripture is necessary. Constant review not only of the section headings but also of the detailed contents of each section will be a great help. If this is done, one will, for example, soon get to know that The Seven Words of the Cross are distributed as follows:

> First Word, Luke 23:34 [670]
> Second Word, Luke 23:43
> Third Word, John 19:26, 27
> Fourth Word, Matt. 27:46; Mark 15:34
> Fifth Word, John 19:28
> Sixth Word, John 19:30
> Seventh Word, Luke 23:46

Returning, then, to Mark 14:1, 2 and its parallels, we notice the following variations in reporting:

a. In a manner characteristic of him (see N.T.C. on Matt. 19:1) Matthew reports that the incident about to be narrated occurred "when Jesus had finished all these words."

b. The time indication which in Mark and Luke proceeds from the evangelist himself, is by Matthew ascribed to Jesus: "He said to his disciples,

---

[670] Absent from some ancient manuscripts.

Y o u know that after two days the Passover is held; then the Son of man is handed over to be crucified."

c. Mark speaks of "the feast of the Passover and the Unleavened Bread," Matthew of "the Passover," Luke of "the feast of Unleavened Bread . . . which is called the Passover."

d. Matthew, he alone, represents Jesus as declaring that at this Passover "the Son of man is handed over to be crucified." Though that evangelist alone reports this, it is the background for all three accounts.

e. Though all three state that at this time—two days before Passover—Jesus' enemies were plotting his death, but were afraid of the people, Mark and Matthew add that the reason for this fear was that an arrest during the feast might cause the people to riot.

f. These same two Gospel writers, but not Luke, describe the plotters as planning to arrest Jesus "by some trick," and "not at the Festival."

g. It is Matthew alone who mentions the fact that for the purpose of planning how to bring about the death of Jesus the plotters held a special meeting in the palace of Caiaphas the highpriest.

h. According to Matthew the plotters were "the chief priests and the elders of the people"; according to Mark and Luke they were "the chief priests and the scribes." This shows that the entire Sanhedrin—chief priests, elders, and scribes—was represented; probably also, that the chief priests took the lead.

It is in the light of all this that Mark 14:1, 2 must be interpreted.

1. Now the feast of the Passover and the Unleavened Bread was two days off, and the chief priests and the scribes were seeking how to take Jesus into custody by some trick, and kill him. . . .

Note the following:

a. A reasonable assumption is that Jesus was crucified in the year A.D. 30, when the fourteenth day of Nisan fell on Thursday, and the fifteenth on Friday. In Israel the first appearance of the new moon marked the beginning of the new month. It was marked by the blowing of trumpets, sacrifices, celebrations, suspension of ordinary business, and wherever necessary by signal fires (Num. 10:10; 28:11-14; Ps. 81:3-5; Amos 8:5, 6). The important days of the month—for example, the tenth of the month Nisan, when the Passover lamb was selected, the killing of the lamb on the fourteenth, etc.—were figured from this first day, or day of the new moon, as a base. See the detailed regulations in Exod. 12:1-14; cf. Esther 3:7.

There is no good reason to believe that Jesus and his disciples ate the lamb and celebrated Passover either earlier or later than on the appointed day. The fourteenth of Nisan was the day when the lamb "had to be sacrificed" (Luke 22:7). It is also clear that immediately after the eating of the lamb and the institution of what has come to be known as "the Lord's Supper" Jesus and his disciples (with the exception of Judas, who had left earlier and for his own destination, John 13:30) went to Gethsemane (Mark 14:32; John 18:1). Here, during what we would call the night from Thursday to Friday Jesus was taken into custody. Early Friday morning the Sanhedrin "took counsel against Jesus to put him to death" (Matt. 27:1). He was led to Pilate that same morning and crucified that same day (Mark 15:1, 25). It is clear, therefore, that Jesus was crucified on Friday, the day before the sabbath (Mark 15:42, 43; Luke 23:46, 54; John 19:14, 30, 42). It was early in the morning of the day "after the sabbath"—hence on Sunday, the first day of the week—that some women went to the tomb and heard the startling news, "He is risen" (Matt. 28:1, 6; Mark 16:2, 6; Luke 24:1, 6; John 20:1).

It should be clear, therefore, that the theory according to which Jesus was crucified on Thursday is opposed by the evidence of the Gospels. [671]

The day on which the lamb was killed was followed by the seven day feast of the Unleavened Bread. [672] celebrated from the fifteenth to the twenty-first of Nisan. So close was the connection between the Passover meal proper and the immediately following Festival of the Unleavened Bread that the term "Passover" is sometimes used to cover both (see Luke 22:1).

Since the feast of the Passover etc. was "two days off," it must have been Tuesday when Christ's enemies held their meeting for the purpose of plotting how to bring about the arrest and death of Jesus.

b. The plotters were "the chief priests and the scribes"; according to Matthew, also "the elders of the people." For a description of the three groups see on 11:27, 28. But is not this shocking? A dirty plot devised by Israel's leaders? By priests, scribes, and elders? Yes, indeed!

The church, too, has had many leaders. Some were good. They remind one of Joshua the highpriest, worthy bearer of a double crown, a type of Christ (Zech. 6:9-13). They were "scribes trained for the kingdom of heaven" (Matt. 13:52), "elders who ruled well" (I Tim. 5:17).

---

[671] On this question see also N.T.C. on Matthew, p. 534. The "crucifixion on Thursday" theory was revived recently by Roger Rusk, in the March 29, 1974 issue of *Christianity Today*, pp. 720-722. It was refuted by Harold W. Hoehner in the April 26, 1974 issue, pp. 878, 881. As Hoehner points out, if Jesus had died on Thursday instead of on Friday, Pilate would have secured the sepulcher until the fourth day, not the third (Matt. 27:62-66). As to the computer which established the exact times of all the new and full moons from 1001 B.C. to A.D. 1651, and confirmed the fact that in the year A.D. 30 the fourteenth of Nisan occurred on Thursday, the fifteenth on Friday, though this information is interesting and helpful, yet as far as the date A.D. 30 is concerned it is not exactly new. See, for example, P. Schaff, *op. cit.*, Vol. I, p. 135.

[672] Note the plural τὰ ἄζυμα, probably referring to the unleavened cakes of bread, and based on the Hebrew plural *matzoth*. Besides, it must be borne in mind that this was a feast lasting *several* days and including *many* festive activities. That fact, too, may account for the plural. See N.T.C. on Matthew, pp. 792, 793.

But there were—and are—also others, genuine plotters, "prophets who make my people err" (Mic. 3:5), corrupt elders perpetrating evil "in the dark" (Ezek. 8:5-13). "When corruption invades a church, the process generally starts at the top." "No politics is as rotten as church politics."

c. These enemies were seeking how to take Jesus into custody "by some trick," [673] that is, as the context indicates, "by surprise" and "away from the crowds."

d. " . . . and kill him." The plan to kill Jesus was not new. It was of long standing (Mark 3:6; 12:7; John 5:18; 7:1, 19, 25; 8:37, 40; 11:53). We may well believe, however, that due to events of recent days the leaders were now more determined than ever to destroy Jesus. Their envy had been increased by the raising of Lazarus from the dead, causing many people to believe in Jesus (John 11:45-53), by the triumphal entry's effects upon the crowds (Mark 11:1-11), by the cleansing of the temple (11:15-18, 27, 28), by parables which the leaders knew were aimed against them (12:12), and by the woes pronounced against the scribes and Pharisees (12:38-40; cf. Matt. 23). Moreover, the expression *how . . . to kill him* stresses the fact that what bothered these leaders was especially this, that though they very passionately desired to destroy Jesus they did not know how to do this without creating more trouble for themselves. This becomes even more clear from verse 2. **for they were saying, Not during the feast, lest there be** [674] **an uproar among the people.**

The plotters realized that Jesus had many friends and adherents, especially among the thousands of Galileans attending the festivities. In case of any action against their Leader these followers might cause trouble. Significant in this connection is John 12:17-19. Bitterly Christ's enemies had complained, "Look, the world has gone after him!" The chief priests, scribes, and elders were not at all desirous of having to cope with an enthusiastic, hostile, determined, rioting Passover crowd. Were the hosanna shouts (Mark 11:9, 10) still ringing in the ears of the plotters?

They are going to wait patiently until the people have returned to their homes. Then, when all is safe, they will kill Jesus! They will do it at their convenience. . . . So they thought. But it did not turn out that way.

The true significance of the present passage is not understood unless it is read in connection with its parallel, Matt. 26:1-5. Cf. Rev. 12:1-5, 10. It is only on the background of God's decree that its meaning becomes clear.

---

673 ἐν δόλῳ probably, though not necessarily, a Hebraism. Matthew uses the simple, instrumental dative δόλῳ. The meaning is identical.

674 After the final particle μήποτε, either (as here) the future indicative (see also Matt. 7:6) or the more frequent subjunctive (as in Luke 14:12) can be used, with little if any difference in meaning. See Gram. N.T., p. 988.

"Not at the Festival," said the plotters. "At the Festival," said the Almighty. That was the divine decree, for which see also Luke 22:22; Acts 2:23; Eph. 1:11. That decree always triumphs. Illustrations:

a. Did it seem as if with the fall of man Satan had won the victory? Note the mother of all promises (Gen. 3:15).

b. "I will smite David even to the wall," said Saul (I Sam. 18:11). But God's decree concerning David, with whom the Messianic promises were bound up, was different (I Sam. 16:12, 13; 25:29; II Sam. 7:16).

c. The combined forces of wickedness were arrayed against Judah. Their purpose was to blot out the house of David and to establish their own king. There follows the triumphant Isa. 7:14!

d. At Haman's request an order was issued for the destruction of all the Jews, It was one of those "unchangeable" (?) decrees. It was sealed with the king's ring. But the Lord's promise, according to which Messiah was to be born from the Jews, had been sealed with the oath of "the King of kings." The result? Read the book of Esther.

e. Herod decides to kill the newborn "king of the Jews." So he orders all the boy babies of Bethlehem and surroundings, two years and under, to be ruthlessly slain. But the holy child was already safely on his way to Egypt. Read Matt. 2.

f. At last, however, it seemed as if Satan had actually triumphed. Was not Jesus hanging on a cross? . . . But the very cross meant Satan's doom! I Cor. 1:22-25; Col. 2:13-15; Rev. 12:10, 11.

> "Jehovah brings the counsel of the nations to nought;
> He frustrates the plans of the peoples.
> The counsel of Jehovah stands forever.
> The thoughts of his heart to all generations"
> (Ps. 33:10, 11; cf. 2:1-4).

That is the foundation upon which God's children build their hope for eternity, to the glory of God Triune!

---

3 And while he was in Bethany, reclining at table in the home of Simon the leper, there came to him a woman with an alabaster jar of very expensive perfume, made of pure nard. She broke the alabaster jar and poured out (the perfume) over his head. 4 But some were indignantly saying to each other, "Why this waste of perfume? 5 For this perfume could have been sold for more than a year's wages, [675] and (the money) given to the poor." And they were grumbling at her. 6 But Jesus said, "Leave her alone. Why are y o u bothering her? (It is) a beautiful thing she has done to me. 7 For the poor y o u always have with y o u, and whenever y o u wish, y o u can do good to them; but me

---

[675] Literally: for more than three hundred denarii.

y o u have not always. 8 She has done what she could. She has anointed my body in
advance for burial. [676]   9 I solemnly assure y o u, wherever the gospel is preached in the
whole world, also what she has done shall be told in memory of her."

14:3-9 *The Anointing at Bethany*
Cf. Matt. 26:6-13; John 12:1-8 [677]

Of the three sources that contain this story, that in John (12:1-8) is by far
the most detailed, with 142 words in the original. Mark (14:3-9) comes next,
with 124 words. The shortest is Matthew (26:6-13) with only 109. The
difference consists to a large extent in the material which Mark and/or John
add(s) to Matthew's summary, though the style also varies, as could be
expected.

Items in Mark and/or John but not in Matthew: *a*. the woman broke the jar;
b. the perfume could have been sold for more than a year's wages; *c*. the disciples were grumbling at the woman; *d*. the woman who anointed Jesus was
Mary (obviously the sister of Martha and of Lazarus; see 11:1; cf. Luke 10:42);
e. she anointed Jesus' feet, which she afterward wiped with her hair; *f*. the
house was filled with the fragrance of the ointment; and *g*. it was Judas who,
for selfish reasons, took the lead in finding fault with Mary.

The description of the perfume varies. The same variety of phraseology is
evident in connection with the stated reason why the woman did what she
did.

There are no conflicts. A moment's study reveals that even items which on
the surface may seem to clash—e.g., according to John the woman anointed
Jesus' *feet,* but according to Matthew and Mark she poured the perfume over
his *head*—actually dovetail beautifully, as will be shown.

**3. And while he was in Bethany, reclining at table in the home of Simon
the leper, there came to him a woman with an alabaster jar of very expensive
perfume, made of pure nard. She broke the alabaster jar and poured out (the
perfume) over his head.**

Here at verse 3 Mark begins to tell a new story. To do so he must *go back*
a few days, from the Tuesday of verses 1, 2 to the preceding Saturday
evening, when a supper was given at Bethany in honor of Jesus. Why does
Mark go back? Could it be because human nature *at its best,* because of what
God in his marvelous grace did for it, stands out all the more radiantly when
it is contrasted with human nature *at its worst?* Could that be the reason

---

676 Or: for the—i.e., for my—burial.
677 This story must not be confused with that of "the sinful woman" of Luke 7. For
the arguments in favor of *rejecting* this identification see N.T.C. on John, Vol. II, pp.
174, 175.

why verses 3-9, describing Mary's beautiful deed, is here inserted between
a. verses 1, 2; and *b.* 10, 11? Respectively these two surrounding sections
picture the perversity *a.* of the chief priests, scribes, etc., and *b.* of Judas, the
man who becomes their partner in crime. However that may be, what we
have in this narrative of Mary versus Jesus' enemies is a manifestation of
troth over against treachery, of wholehearted devotion versus hideous degradation.

The refreshing incident took place "while he [Jesus] was in Bethany." [678]
Present at the supper were at least fifteen men: Jesus, The Twelve, Lazarus
(John 12:2), and a certain Simon, mentioned here in verse 3 and in Matt.
26:6. The idea readily suggests itself that the supper (or "dinner" if one
prefers) was prompted by love for the Lord, specifically by gratitude for the
raising of Lazarus and for the healing of Simon, the man who had been a
leper, is still called "Simon the leper," but had presumably been healed by
Jesus. It was at the home of this Simon that the dinner was given. Martha,
the sister of Mary and Lazarus, was serving (John 12:2).

Now while the guests, according to custom, were reclining at table "there
came to him a woman." That this woman was Mary of Bethany we learn
from John 12:3. She has taken a position behind the reclining Jesus. In her
hand she holds "an alabaster jar of very costly or expensive perfume," that
is, a jar or vase of white (or perhaps delicately tinted) fine-grained gypsum.
The perfume had been extracted from pure [679] nard, that is, from the dried
root leaves of this particular Himalayan plant. That the jar contained a large
quantity of this precious and very fragrant extract is also clear from John
12:3, not less than a Roman pound (twelve ounces)!

Suddenly she breaks the jar and pours its contents down or out over [680]
Jesus. According to Matthew and Mark she pours the perfume out upon or
over his *head* (cf. Ps. 23:5); according to John she anoints his *feet*. There is
no conflict, for Matthew and Mark clearly indicate that the perfume was
poured over Christ's *body* (Matt. 26:12; Mark 14:8). Evidently there was
enough for the entire body: head, neck, shoulders, and feet. Simon's house
was filled with fragrance. Along with the perfume, Mary poured out her
heart in gratitude and devotion!

The rest of the paragraph describes the reaction on the part of *a.* "some"

---

[678] Note the two gen. absolutes: "he being in Bethany" and "he reclining at table."

[679] The meaning of πιστικός,-ή-όν both in Mark 14:3 and in John 12:3 has been much
debated. πιστικός = πιστός may well be the best interpretation. Either "pure" or
"genuine" is favored by most commentators.

[680] κατέχεε third per. s. aor. indic. of καταχέω, to pour down or out over. The gen.
αὐτοῦ κ.τ.λ. is perhaps due to κατά w. gen. (down, down from, etc.), a preposition which
with the acc. generally has an entirely different meaning (along, over, through, toward,
etc.). See Gram. N.T., pp. 511, 512; and L.N.T. (A. and G.), pp. 406-409.

(verses 4, 5) and *b*. Jesus (verses 6-9). **4, 5. But some were indignantly saying to each other, Why this waste of perfume? For this perfume could have been sold for more than a year's wages, and (the money) given to the poor. And they were grumbling at her.** The language is abrupt and vivid. It is not difficult to imagine that Peter had vividly pictured to his audience, including Mark, exactly what had occurred. The scene had impinged itself indelibly upon the apostle's recollection, and it is probably in that same form that Mark here reproduces it, popular abbreviations and all. Mark's "some" are Matthew's "disciples." It seems to have been Judas, the treasurer, who voiced the strongest objection. He quickly calculated the value of the perfume, assessing it at three hundred denarii (John 12:5), or even more (as here in Mark 14:5). Think of it: more than a year's wages gone to waste, enough to feed no less than three hundred families for one whole day, and have something left! And now all was lost. What a shame! [681]

Piously (?) Judas blurts out his opinion that the huge amount for which this perfume *could*—and as he saw it *should*—have been sold, would have been a bounteous gift *for the poor*.

Both Matthew and Mark make it clear that the other disciples chimed in. They were indignant, [682] and were grumbling [683] at Mary. "The perfume could have been sold and given [684] to the poor" was the sentiment of all.

Poor Mary! Almost wherever she looks, she meets angry glances, shocked disapproval. That the native language of love is lavishness these men do not seem to understand. Noble people, these men, especially Judas, the protector of the simple way of life, and the helper of the poor! But what he was really after is pointed out in John 12:6.

6, 7. But Jesus said, Leave her alone. Why are y o u bothering her? (It is) a beautiful thing she has done to me. For the poor y o u always have with y o u, and whenever y o u wish y o u can do good to them; but me y o u have not always. Jesus rushes to Mary's defense by saying, "Leave her alone," or "Let her be." [685] He continues literally, "Why are y o u causing trouble for her?" He calls what she did "a beautiful thing." And such it was indeed: unique in its thoughtfulness, regal in its lavishness, and marvelous in its timeliness.

---

681 For the value of a denarius see above on 6:37 and on 12:42. Shall we say that in the estimation of Judas there had been $50-$60 worth of perfume in that jar?

682 ἀγανακτοῦντες, nom. pl. masc. pres. participle of ἀγανακτέω. See above on 10:14, footnote 459.

683 ἐνεβριμῶντο third per. pl. imperf. of ἐμβριμάομαι. See on 1:43.

684 πραθῆναι and δοθῆναι, aor. inf. passives (after ἠδύνατο), stating what these men held to be a simple fact, namely, that the perfume could and should have been sold, and the proceeds given to the poor. δηναρίων is best viewed as gen. of price after πραθῆναι.

685 ἄφετε sec. per. pl. aor. imper. active of ἀφίημι, as in 10:14; see on that passage, footnote 460).

Not as if the Master were unconcerned about the poor. Far from it, as the following passages indicate: Mark 10:21; 12:42, 43; and in the other Gospels see Matt. 5:7; 6:2-4; 12:7; 19:21; Luke 6:20, 36-38; 7:22; 14:13; John 13:29. On this subject, as well as on all others, his teaching was in line with the rest of special revelation (Exod. 23:10, 11; Lev. 19:10; Prov. 14:21b, 31; Isa. 58:7; and for the New Testament see II Cor. 8:1-9; Gal. 6:2, 9, 10; II Thess. 3:13; James 5:1-6). But there would be many other opportunities to tend to the needs of the poor. On the contrary, the opportunity to show love and honor to Jesus in the state of humiliation had almost vanished. Gethsemane, Gabbatha, and Golgotha were just around the corner. What Mary had done was therefore exactly right, beautiful even.

Continued: **8. She has done what she could.** [686] **She has anointed my body in advance** [687] **for burial.** Similarly Matthew writes, "For when she poured this perfume on my body, she did it to prepare me for burial." On this difficult passage much has been written. As some see it, Jesus is saying that Mary, without realizing it herself, had anointed Jesus for his impending death and burial. Now it must be admitted that this interpretation makes sense: God's purpose is often accomplished through the deeds of human beings, even though the latter are unaware of what is actually happening. Besides, Mary may not have known that her Master's death was so close at hand. On the other hand, the fact should not be overlooked that Mary of Bethany was perhaps the best listener Jesus ever had. The woman who now *anointed* Jesus' feet was the same one who had previously been *sitting* at his feet (Luke 10:39). If even the enemies of Jesus knew about the predictions Jesus had made concerning himself (Matt. 27:63), can we not assume that Mary knew fully as much? If so, is it not probable that the thought had occurred to her, "This may well be the last opportunity I shall ever get to bestow a kindness upon Jesus; and when, according to his own prediction, his enemies kill him, will his friends be accorded the privilege of anointing his body?" The view, accordingly, that Mary's *conscious* purpose was to prepare Jesus for burial must not be ruled out. For more detail on this see N.T.C. on John, Vol. II, pp. 178-180.

Jesus concludes his defense of Mary by saying, **9. I solemnly assure y o u,** [688] **wherever the gospel is preached in the whole world, also what she has done shall be told in memory of her.** As already indicated, it was now

---

686 ἔσχε, third per. s. aor. indic. of ἔχω; here ὅ ἔσχε is an abbreviation of ὅ ἔσχε ποιῆσαι; hence, the meaning is, "She has done what she was able to (or: what she could) do."

687 προέλαβε μυρίσαι; i.e., She undertook in advance to anoint, etc., amounting to "She anointed . . . beforehand." The main verb προέλαβε is here used adverbially. Cf. its use in I Cor. 11:21.

688 See on 3:28.

Saturday evening, the day before the triumphal entry. Then on Tuesday Jesus was going to make the astounding prediction, "And to all the nations the gospel must first be preached" (13:10; cf. Matt. 24:14). For "gospel" see N.T.C. on Philippians, pp. 82-85. This gospel must be *preached*. [689] Preaching, in the religious sense, means *heralding*. Careful exposition is basic. But genuine preaching is lively, not dry; timely, not stale. It is the earnest proclamation of news initiated by God. It is not the abstract speculation of views excogitated by man. See N.T.C. on II Tim. 4:2.

But before Jesus makes the announcement about worldwide gospel preaching he *now,* that is, three days earlier, solemnly promises that wherever the joyful story travels, the deed of Mary will march hand in hand with it. The memory of Mary's noble act must be kept alive. The Master will not allow it to be forgotten. Cf. Matt. 25:34-40.

In studying this section one is prone to commit the error of becoming so filled with admiration for Mary's beautiful deed as to forget that what she did was only a reflection of the Master's own kindness toward her. Consider not only his mercy in saving her but also the tenderness he revealed when in this particular moment he rushed to her defense. After all, he knew that the hour of his own incomparably bitter suffering was fast approaching. Nevertheless, so deeply did he love his own (cf. John 13:1) that, because of his appreciation for what she had done, he was wounded deeply by the unjustified criticism to which she was subjected. His heart went out to her.

Is not the real lesson this, therefore, that God, whose image is Christ (Heb. 1:3), takes infinitely keen delight in rewarding the faithfulness of those who honor him? Whenever we enumerate his many glorious attributes, should we not also pay due attention to the fact that he is indeed "the *Rewarder* of those who diligently seek him" (Heb. 11:6)?

Note how generously and with what intense delight he rewarded:
Abraham (Gen. 22:15-18)
Ruth (Ruth 1:16, 17; 2:12; 4:13-22)
Hannah (I Sam. 1:1-20)
Ebed-melech the Ethiopian (Jer. 39:15-18)
King Hezekiah (II Kings 19)
King Jehoshaphat (II Chron. 20:1-30)
Daniel and his friends (Dan. 1:1–6:28)
"The commended centurion" (Matt. 8:5-13)
The Syrophoenician woman (Mark 7:24-30)
Those who brought their little ones to Jesus (Mark 10:13-16)
His loyal disciples, in spite of their many faults (Mark 10:23-31)
The poor widow who gave "her whole living" (Mark 12:41-44)

---

689 κηρυχθῇ third per. s. aor. subjunct. passive of κηρύσσω.

The Samaritan leper (Luke 17:11-19)

Ever so many other names could be added, but this small list should suffice to indicate what is one of the main lessons—perhaps even the main lesson—taught here in Mark 10:13-16.

---

10 And Judas Iscariot, who was one of the twelve, went to the chief priests in order to hand him over to them. 11 They were delighted to hear this and promised to give him money. So he was looking for an opportunity to betray him. [690]

14:10, 11 *The Agreement between Judas*
and the Chief Priests
Cf. Matt. 26:14-16; Luke 22:3-6

According to all three accounts Judas, "one of the twelve," goes to the chief priests (and the officers of the temple police, Luke 22:4) to discuss how he might deliver Jesus to them. The delight experienced by the leaders because of the unexpected entrance and offer of Judas is reported by both Mark and Luke. A sum of money for the betrayal is agreed upon. Afterward the traitor watched for an opportunity to hand Jesus over to these men, and (as Luke adds) to do this in the absence of a crowd.

It is Matthew alone who has transmitted to posterity the traitor's vulgarly mercenary question flung at the chief priests, etc., "What are y o u willing to give me if I hand him over to y o u?" It is also that same evangelist who makes clear that Judas leaves the conference, with the thirty pieces of silver on his person.

Mark reports, "They promised to give him money," a promise that was fulfilled at that very meeting.

Luke's account reveals the devil's part in this sordid affair, "Then Satan entered Judas." Cf. John 13:27.

10. And Judas Iscariot, who was one of the twelve, went to the chief priests in order to hand him over [691] to them.

What caused Judas to become Christ's betrayer? To the reasons given above—see on 3:19—the following should be added, at least for consideration:

a. The rebuke which Jesus administered to the disciples, including Judas, Mary's chief maligner (John 12:4, 5), may have contributed to the traitor's decision. We say, "may have," for certainty on this point is impossible. [692]

---

690 Or: how he might conveniently hand him over [or: deliver him up].

691 Literally, "that he might hand him over."

692 Even the adverb τότε (Matt. 26:14) does not make it certain, for that is a word with a very wide meaning. Temporal sequence—*then, thereupon*—does not necessarily imply cause-and-effect relationship. *Post hoc, ergo propter hoc* is faulty reasoning.

b. To his twelve privileged followers Jesus had promised dazzling rewards (Mark 10:29, 30), thrones even (Matt. 19:28). Judas must have listened with rapt attention to words such as these. But, strange to say, Jesus had also on several occasions predicted his imminent and violent death (Mark 8:31; 9:31; 10:34). In fact, most recently he had even referred to his burial, as if it were a matter pertaining to the immediate future (14:8). Is it difficult to believe that a man such as Judas was deeply disturbed by this language, and that he drew the conclusion that to remain with Jesus meant to go down in defeat with him? He should have taken to heart the words of the Master spoken earlier, "For whoever would save his life will lose it, but whoever loses his life for my sake and the gospel's sake will save it" (8:35). But, as remarked previously, though various elements must have entered into the reason why Judas betrayed the Master, basic to everything else was this disciple's utterly selfish heart as contrasted with Christ's infinitely unselfish and outgoing heart. It was the traitor's unwillingness to pray for renewal of life that ruined him. It was impenitence that destroyed him.

For his shockingly loathsome deed there was no excuse whatever. Judas was, after all, a specially privileged person. He was "one of the twelve," as all four evangelists take the trouble to point out (Matt. 26:14; Mark 14:10; Luke 22:3; John 6:70, 71). For many months Judas had been living in Christ's immediate presence, had been eating, drinking, and traveling with him. He had noticed the strength in the Master's voice when he stilled the storm, cursed the barren fig tree, and rebuked those who devoured widows' houses. But Judas had also become aware of the tenderness of that same voice when it pleaded with sinners, including Judas!, to come to him and rest. He had listened to the Savior's marvelous discourses and to the decisive and authoritative answers he had given to the many questions that had been hurled at him, sometimes with the intention of ensnaring him. Judas had watched the Great Physician in the act of tenderly restoring the handicapped, or bending down mercifully over the sick and healing them . . . and then even adding (at times), "*Your* faith has made you well." Yes, Judas had witnessed all this and much more. Cf. Matt. 13:17. And then he decided to deliver this unsurpassably powerful, wise, and compassionate Benefactor into the hands of cruel men . . . "for thirty pieces of silver."

11. They were delighted to hear this and promised to give him money. Naturally the chief priests were glad when a disciple of Jesus suddenly turned up to be their helper. Did he perhaps arrive on Tuesday evening, just as the members of the Sanhedrin were leaving, and did they then quickly reassemble? We do not know. What we do know is that they regarded the arrival of Judas and his implied offer to be a godsend.

The parallel accounts leave the impression that the business was quickly transacted. A combination of Matt. 26:14; Mark 14:11; and Luke 22:5, 6a results in the following legitimate reconstruction of what now transpired:

Judas: "What are y o u willing to give me if I hand him over to y o u?"

The chief priests: "We promise to give you thirty pieces of silver as soon as you agree to deliver him into our hands."

Judas: "I agree."

The chief priests, after weighing out the money: "Here are the thirty silver pieces." Judas takes them and departs.

This interpretation is in harmony with the psychology of the situation. The chief priests would not have allowed their golden opportunity to pass by unheeded. They knew very well that if Judas had the money "in his pocket" he would not have dared to back out before committing the deed.

As to the price paid, namely "thirty pieces of silver," these *pieces* were tantamount in value to tetradrachmas or Hebrew shekels. Thirty of them figured at 64-72 cents each add up to (a sum) slightly more or less than $20, or not much over £ 8. But with money values constantly fluctuating, it is impossible to determine with any exactness what this would amount to in present currency. For a price of a slave, gored by an ox, the Savior was sold to his enemies. See Exod. 21:32. For such a pitiful sum Judas betrayed the Master.

With the money already in his possession, Judas now feels obliged to go into action. We are therefore not surprised to read: **So he was looking for an opportunity to betray** [693] him. That opportunity would come his way very soon.

---

12 Now on the first day of the Feast of Unleavened Bread, when it was customary to sacrifice the Passover lamb, his [Jesus'] disciples asked him, "Where do you want us to go and get the Passover Supper ready for you to eat?" 13 So he sent two of his disciples and told them, "Go into the city, and a man carrying a jar of water will meet y o u. Follow him; 14 and wherever he enters, say to the owner of that house, 'The Teacher asks, Where is my guest-room, in which I may eat the Passover with my disciples?' 15 And he will show y o u a large upper room, furnished and ready. There make ready for us." 16 So off the disciples went. They came into the city, found (everything) just as he had told them, and prepared the Passover.

17 And when it was evening he arrived with the twelve. 18 While they were reclining at table and eating, Jesus said, "I solemnly swear to y o u, one of y o u will betray me—one who is eating with me." 19 They became distressed, and one by one said to him, "Surely not I?" 20 He told them, "(It is) one of the twelve, one who dips (his hand) into the bowl with me. 21 For the Son of man goes as it is written concerning him, but woe to that man by whom the Son of man is betrayed. It would have been better for that man if he had not been born."

---

693 παραδοῖ is a third per. s. aor. subjunct. form of παραδίδωμι, literally, "(he was seeking) how he might conveniently hand him over."

14:12-21 *The Passover*
Cf. Matt. 26:17-25; Luke 22:7-14; 21-23; John 13:21-30

According to all three synoptists Jesus, on the first day of the Feast of Unleavened Bread, gives instructions to disciples to reserve a room for the celebration of the Passover, and to make all the necessary preparations. They are sent to the home of a certain unnamed individual, where they make ready. During the meal Jesus suddenly shocks the little company by saying, "One of y o u will betray me, one who is eating with me." He adds, "For the Son of man goes as it is written concerning him. . . ."

The main variations are as follows:

According to Mark the instructions were given to two of Christ's disciples; according to Luke, to Peter and John. Matthew does not specify. In fact, Matt. 26:17-19 looks like a summary when compared to Mark 14:12-16. In his more detailed account "Peter's interpreter" informs his readers that the two disciples were told to go into the city, where a man carrying a jar of water would meet them. They must follow him into whatever house he enters, and must say to the owner, "The Teacher asks, 'Where is my guest-room. . . ?'" The owner will then show the two a larger upper room, furnished and ready. There they must make the necessary preparations.—All this was done, and in the evening Jesus sits down with The Twelve.

Up to this point there is very little difference between Mark's and Luke's account. In fact, Luke 22:7-14 is almost a verbatim repetition of Mark 14:12-17. However, in verse 17 Luke has "the apostles" where Matthew and Mark read "the twelve." Also in the same verse Luke says "And when the hour came," where Matthew and Mark have "(And) when it was evening." We have already called attention to the fact that according to Luke the (first) day of Unleavened Bread was the one "on which the passover lamb *had to be* sacrificed." See above, on 14:1. Where both Matthew and Mark have Jesus saying, " . . . one who dips his hand into the bowl with me," Luke (22:21) substitutes, "But look, the hand of him who betrays me is with me on the table." And in verse 23 Luke describes the disciples as asking *each other* which of them was the traitor. It is surely easy to understand that these startled men would direct their searching questions to their own hearts, to each other, and to the Lord. Every idea of contradiction is therefore unrealistic. The three accounts, though interestingly varied, are in perfect harmony.

Thus also the fact that according to Mark the disciples one by one say, "Surely not I?" whereas Matthew reports the same question in the more complete form, "Surely not I, *Lord?*"—and with reference to Judas, "Surely not I, Rabbi?"—simply means that with respect to this item it is Mark who summarizes. What he says is true, but on this particular point Matthew, who was present, has given us a more complete report.

12. **Now on the first day of the feast of Unleavened Bread, when it was customary to sacrifice the Passover lamb, his [Jesus'] disciples asked him, Where do you want us to go and get the Passover Supper ready for you to eat?**

Finally the morning of the fourteenth of Nisan arrived. When, as sometimes happens, the term "Festival of Unleavened Bread" is taken in its broadest sense, even the day on which occurred the eating of the Passover lamb is included. We are not told where Jesus and his disciples spent Wednesday, the day between the one to which reference was made in verse 1 (Tuesday), and the Passover, verses 12-21 (Thursday). [694]

Nothing is said about the purchase of a lamb. We may probably assume that this had been attended to a few days earlier. See Exod. 12:3. Further preparations had to be made however. During the afternoon the lamb must be killed in the forecourt of the temple (cf. Exod. 12:6). A room of sufficient size must be obtained, and everything in connection with this room and its furniture must be arranged. Besides, purchases must be made: of unleavened bread, bitter herbs, wine, etc. The lamb must be made ready for use, the sauce must be prepared. Since it was now probably Thursday morning, there could be no delay.

A few additional remarks are in order:

a. The words "when it was customary [695] to sacrifice the Passover lamb" are probably added by Mark for the sake of his Gentile readers.

b. " . . . us to go," indicates that at this particular moment Jesus and his disciples were not in "the city" (see verse 13). They may have been in Bethany.

c. The disciples realize that it is *their* duty to prepare the Passover for the Master. [696] It is *his* Passover. He was the Host. The disciples were privileged to eat "with him" (see verses 18, 20). They are his guests.

13, 14. **So he sent two of his disciples and told them, Go into the city, and a man carrying a jar of water will meet y o u. Follow him; and wherever he enters, say to the owner of that house, The Teacher asks, Where is my guest-room, in which I may eat the Passover with my disciples?**

In his answer Jesus now gives instructions to two of his disciples; i.e., to Peter and John, as Luke 22:8 informs us. The directions given are in a sense very definite; in another sense very indefinite. They are definite enough so

---

694 Luke 21:37 may give a hint, but this is not certain.
695 ἔθυον, the imperfect is used to indicate a custom.
696 ἑτοιμάσωμεν, aor. subjunct. after θέλεις; φάγῃς, aor. subjunct. expressing purpose, after ἵνα.

that the two men will experience no difficulty in finding the place where the supper is to be held. Yet, they are indefinite enough for the present to conceal the name of the owner and the location of his home. Is the indefiniteness due to the fact that not until evening must Judas know where the Passover will be kept, so that Jesus may indeed observe it with his disciples, and the plan of God regarding the subsequent events may be fully carried out?

However this may be, the two apostles are told that on entering the city (Jerusalem) they will be met by *a man* carrying [697] a jug [698] of water. [699] This is remarkable, for ordinarily not a man but a woman or girl would be doing this. Hence the disciples will experience no difficulty in singling out this man.

Furthermore, Jesus instructs them to follow this man into whatever house he enters. [700] It is clear that the man to be followed is not the owner, but perhaps a servant or a son. It is useless to speculate exactly who he was, though this has been done. This holds, too, with respect to the owner. All we really know is that he must have been a disciple of Jesus. Was the owner John Mark's father, then still alive? I am neither willing to say with Zahn that he was, nor with others that he was not.

The two disciples must say to the owner, "The Teacher [701] asks, Where is my guest-room, [702] in which I may eat the Passover with my disciples?" As indicated in the preceding, this is going to be Christ's own Passover. Even the guest-room is in a sense his own; that is, he asks that it be placed entirely at his disposal for the purpose of celebrating the feast, together with the disciples as his guests.

15. And he will show y o u a large upper room, furnished and ready. There make ready for us. It was the rule in Israel that if anyone at this time had space available it must be given free of charge to whatever family or group wished to make sacred use of it. Besides, the owner, being one of Christ's followers, would for that very reason be happy to accommodate the Master and his disciples.

---

697 βαστάζων, pres. participle of βαστάζω. For the various meanings of this verb see N.T.C. on Galatians, p. 232, footnote 171.

698 κεράμιον, earthenware jar, pitcher, or jug. Cf. *ceramics.*

699 ὕδατος gen. of contents.

700 The indefinite ὅπου ἐάν ("wherever he may enter") is naturally followed by the subjunctive (third per. s. aor.). The second ὅπου (ὅπου . . . φάγω) is followed by the (probably deliberative) aor. subjunct. first per. s. in a final relative clause embodying an indirect question. See Gram. N.T., p. 969.

701 For the designation "Teacher" or "Master," here used by Jesus with reference to himself, see above on 4:38b, including footnote 172; and see also on 10:17.

702 κατάλυμα. Cf. καταλύω in the sense of *to loosen, to unharness* (the pack animals); hence, to rest, to take lodging for the night. Accordingly κατάλυμα is here a guest-room.

This, then, is the famous Upper Room [703] in which Jesus celebrated his last Passover, instituted "the Lord's Supper," and delivered the beautiful and comforting discourses found in John 14-16. It was here also that he was going to offer the unforgettable prayer recorded in John 17.

The fact that this room was built on top of the house made it right for the present purpose. In such a room one could be relatively free from disturbance. It was a place for discussion, fellowship, meditation, and prayer. Also, it was ample: the thirteen were not crowded. And it was "furnished" [704] and in every respect "ready" to be used for the purpose it was going to serve.

The question may be asked, "How did Jesus know that the two men would find everything as here indicated?" For remarks with respect to this problem see on 2:8; 5:32; 9:33, 34; 11:2, 13. The interaction between Jesus' human and his divine nature is, in the final analysis, a mystery, too deep for us to comprehend.

16. So off the disciples went. They came into the city, found (everything) just as he had told them, and prepared the Passover. Peter and John found everything as predicted, and did everything as ordered. See above, on verse 12.

17, 18. And when it was evening [705] he arrived with the twelve. While they were reclining at table and eating, Jesus said, I solemnly declare to y o u, one of y o u will betray me—one who is eating with me. Though it was still what we would call Thursday when Jesus arrived, by Jewish reckoning it was already Friday. In order to obtain as complete as possible a picture of what happened in the Upper Room, the Gospel according to John will have to be consulted in addition to the Synoptics. When this is done it becomes clear that the Master did not, immediately upon arriving, predict that one of his disciples would betray him. Matthew and Mark evidently begin their account when much has already happened.

According to John's Gospel (13:1-20) Jesus has already washed the feet of his disciples, giving them a lesson in humility. Afterward he startles them by telling them that one of them is going to betray him (13:21-30). The pointing out of the betrayer occurred, according to our passage, "while they were reclining at table and eating," that is, after the meal had been proceeding for some time. For the elements that pertained to the Passover meal, as far as possible chronologically arranged, see N.T.C. on the Gospel of John,

---

703 ἀνάγαιον = ἀνά and γαῖα (γῆ), anything above the ground; in the present context *an upper room.*

704 ἐστρωμένον, acc. s. neut. perf. pass. participle of στρώννυμι; see on 11:8, footnote 528. The room was, as it were, "bestrewn" (covered, furnished) with couches.

705 ὀψίας γενομένης, gen. absolute, a rather common expression in Matthew and in Mark (also occurring in Mark 1:32; 4:35; 6:47; and 15:42). See further on 1:32.

Vol. I, p. 121. The reference is probably to item *f.* on that page. In the same commentary see also p. 242.

"One of y o u!" It came as a bolt from the blue. It was a stunning blow. What! Did the Master actually mean to say that one of their own number was going *to hand him over* to the authorities, for them to deal with as they pleased? Why, it was almost unbelievable.—Yet, the One who never told an untruth and whose very name was "the Truth" (John 8:46; 14:6) was saying this; so it must be true. Does not the Master even introduce his startling saying with "I solemnly declare to y o u"? See on Mark 3:28.

Christ's shocking announcement evoked three responses, in the form of questions, as follows: *a.* a question of *wholesome self-distrust,* "Surely not I?" That was the reaction on the part of all the disciples with the exception of Judas Iscariot. In Mark's Gospel the question in this form is found in 14:19; Christ's answer in verses 20, 21. There was also *b.* a question of *loathsome hypocrisy,* "Surely, not I, Rabbi?" That, probably after considerable hesitation, was Judas' reaction. For both his question and Christ's answer see Matt. 26:25. Finally, there was *c.* a question of *childlike confidence,* "Lord, who is it?" That was the way in which John, prompted by Peter, expressed himself. The question in this form, the events relating to it, Christ's response, and the disciples' reaction to that response, are recorded only in John 13:23-30, which also in verse 30 mentions the traitor's departure. Therefore for *b.* read N.T.C. on Matthew, pp. 907, 908, and for *c.* read N.T.C. on John, Vol. II, pp. 245-250.

Here in Mark, therefore, we are dealing only with *a.*

As to this question of wholesome self-distrust, note verse 19. **They became distressed, [706] and one by one [707] said to him, Surely not I?**

Eleven hearts—those of The Twelve minus Judas Iscariot—are filled with misgiving. Each of these eleven men feels that he could not possibly be the one meant by the Lord—and yet one never can tell. And so, one by one, each of them, caught with a certain dread of himself, asks, "Surely not I?" As to its form in the original, the question expects a negative answer, the kind of answer each ardently hopes the Master will give. **20. He told them, (It is) one of the twelve, one who dips (his hand) into the bowl with me.**

---

[706] ἤρξαντο λυπεῖσθαι. The question is, "Does the original mean *became* (= *began to be*) *distressed,* or does ἤρξαντο have the weakened, pleonastic sense, so that the correct translation would be *were distressed.* See on 1:45 and on 6:7, footnote 233. The context, according to which these men received a sudden shock, would seem to argue in favor of *became* or *began to be.* Thus also A.V., R.S.V., A.R.V., N.A.S., Williams, and Dutch (both Staten en Nieuwe Vertaling).

[707] εἷς κατὰ εἷς. There are many explanations of this idiom. Simplest would seem to be to regard the three words as a unit, and nominative in apposition with the subject "they" in ἤρξαντο.

It is clear that Jesus did not immediately allay the fear of these men or cure their self-distrust. Nor did he at once satisfy their suddenly aroused curiosity. Were not all the twelve disciples dipping morsels of food into the bowl filled with a broth consisting of mashed fruit (probably dates, figs, and raisins), water, and vinegar? Judas surely was not the only man doing this. What the Lord is doing, therefore, is this: he is emphasizing the base character of the betrayer's deed. He is saying, "Think of it, my betrayer is a man who is sharing his meal with me." As has been indicated, Jesus was himself the Host. All the others were eating *his* food. That very fact, especially in the Near East, a region where accepting someone's hospitality and then injuring him, was considered most reprehensible, should have tied the hands of all. It should have made it impossible for any of The Twelve to take any action against their Host. Think of Ps. 41:9.

The answer given by Jesus here in verse 20 served the following purposes:

a. It was a warning for Judas. Let Judas ponder what he is doing. "I know your designs, Judas," the Master seems to be saying. The revelation of this detailed knowledge should have put Judas on guard even at this late hour to return those thirty pieces of silver! Yes, in God's incomprehensible and all-comprehensive decree there is room even for solemn admonitions given to those who ultimately are lost. You ask, "How is that possible?" I answer: "I do not know, but the fact remains, nevertheless." If one does not want to accept the idea of warnings even for reprobates, he misses something of the meaning of this account. The serious character of the implied admonition increases the guilt of Judas. Before one is ready to deny the possibility of earnest warnings even for the reprobate, he should study Gen. 4:6, 7; Prov. 29:1; Luke 13:6-9, 34, 35.

b. It rivets the attention upon the depth of Christ's suffering. In a treacherous and humiliating manner he, the Lord of glory, is being handed over to his enemies. It is very important that we see this. Our reflection on the account of Christ's Passion should not become lost in all kinds of details regarding Judas and Peter and Annas and Pilate. It is, after all, the story of *his* suffering. It centers in *him,* and we must never forget to ask how all these things affected *him!*

c. It showed, once again, that Jesus was in full control of the situation. He was not taken by surprise. He knew exactly what was happening and what was going to happen, the very details.

d. It furnished an opportunity to the disciples *to examine themselves.* This point is often passed by. It is, nevertheless, very important. By giving the answer that is recorded here in Mark 14:20 Jesus did not identify the betrayer, and exactly by not identifying him the Lord was actually doing all a favor. He knew that self-examination would be the very best exercise for men such as these (remember Luke 22:24!). Let each disciple be filled with grave misgivings, with wholesome self-distrust. These men need time for self-examination. **21. For the Son of man goes as it is written concerning him, but woe to that man by whom the Son of man is betrayed. It would have been better for that man if he had not been born.** For "Son of man" see on 2:10, and on Matt. 8:20, pp. 403-407. Jesus, the One who via the path of humiliation attains to glorification, and in fact was glorious from the very beginning, *goes,* that is, lives on earth, suffers, dies, all this not as a victim of circumstances, but "as it is written concerning him," hence as predicted by the prophets (Isa. 53, etc.) and established in God's eternal decree. It was necessary for the Master to emphasize this truth once again, for it was so very difficult for the disciples to reconcile themselves with the idea of a Messiah who would die. Besides, when, on the day of tomorrow— by Jewish reckoning "today"—he dies on the cross, let the disciples reflect on this solemn statement, that they may know that this death does not mean the triumph of his enemies but rather the realization of God's gracious, sovereign, and ever victorious plan.

However, nowhere in Scripture does predestination and prophecy cancel human responsibility. So also here: the cry of sorrow and anguish, "Woe to that man by whom the Son of man is betrayed" fully maintains the guilt and establishes the doom of the traitor. Not to have been born would have been better for such a man. But he was born, and is in the process of comitting the gruesome deed. Therefore the entire statement, "It would have been better for that man if he had not been born" is an expression of unreality—a situation that can be changed only if Judas, who remains fully responsible, still repents. We know that he did not repent. Hence he faces everlasting damnation (see Matt. 25:46). What makes his guilt all the heavier is the fact that he not only planned the treachery and took the next step—volunteering to deliver Jesus to the enemy—and the next—accepting the thirty pieces of silver—but even now, in spite of Christ's impressive warnings, goes right ahead.

The rest of the story—Judas' question, "Surely not I, Rabbi?" and John's, "Lord, who is it?"—is not found in Mark; but see above, on verses 17, 18.

---

22 And while they were eating, he took bread, gave thanks and broke it. He then gave it to them and said, "Take (it); this is my body." 23 Then he took a cup and gave thanks. He gave it to them, and they all drank from it. 24 He told them, "This is my blood of the covenant, which is poured out for many. 25 I solemnly declare to y o u that from now on I will certainly not drink from this fruit of the vine until that day when I am drinking it new in the kingdom of God." 26 And when they had sung a hymn they went out to the Mount of Olives.

14:22-26 *The Institution of the Lord's Supper*
Cf. Matt. 26:26-30; Luke 22:15-20; I Cor. 11:23-25

First, a few remarks regarding Luke's account. It presents problems both
as to the Greek text and as to chronological sequence. A detailed discussion
of these problems does not belong here but in a commentary on Luke.
Accordingly, we limit ourselves to the following:

Luke is never primarily concerned with *time* sequence. The "order" (1:3)
according to which he arranges his materials is often of a different nature, so
that sayings or events apart in time but similar in thought are grouped
together. Once this is understood, most of the difficulties disappear. The
words of Jesus recorded in Luke 22:15, 16 (unparalleled) may have been
spoken at the beginning of the *Passover* meal.

As to the *Lord's Supper,* with Luke 22:17, 20 (the cup) compare Matt.
26:27, 28 and Mark 14:23, 24. With Luke 22:18 ("I will not drink until . . .") compare Matt. 26:29 and Mark 14:25. And with Luke 22:19 (the
bread) compare Matt. 26:26 and Mark 14:22.

The words that have given rise to much controversy, namely, "This is my
body" occur in all three accounts. What must be done with bread and wine is
also either distinctly stated or at least implied in all three. Peculiar to Luke
but entirely in line with the contents of the communion passages in Matthew
and Mark are such dominical words as "Take this, and divide it among
yourselves" (verse 17) and "Do this in remembrance of me" (verse 19).

The passage in which Luke represents Jesus as saying, "But behold, the
hand of him who betrays me is with me on the table" (verse 21) does not
mean that Judas partook of the Lord's Supper. It means that before the
institution of that sacrament—in other words, when Jesus reclined at table
for the passover meal—the hand of Judas and that of the Master were indeed
together on the table (cf. Mark 14:18, 20). There is, accordingly, no conflict
between Luke 22:21 and John 13:30, "So having taken the morsel, he went
out immediately and it was night."

Matthew's account and Mark's are almost identical. Matthew has "All of
y o u drink from it" where Mark has "And they all drank from it." After
"which is poured out for many" in both, Matthew adds "for the forgiveness
of sins." And for Mark's "when I am drinking it new in the kingdom of
God" Matthew substitutes "when I am drinking it new with y o u in my
Father's kingdom." Remarkable similarity, no essential difference.

22. And while they were eating, he took bread, gave thanks and broke it.
At this point Passover passes over into the Lord's Supper; for it was while,
toward the close of the Passover meal, the men were all eating freely (see on
verse 18) that Jesus instituted the new sacrament that was to replace the old.
A few more hours and the old symbol, being bloody—for it required the

572

slaying of the lamb—will have served its purpose forever, having reached its fulfilment in the blood shed on Calvary. It was time, therefore, that a new and unbloody symbol replace the old. Nevertheless, by historically linking Passover and Lord's Supper so closely together Jesus also made clear that what was essential in the first was not lost in the second. Both point to him, the only and all-sufficient sacrifice for the sins of his people. Passover pointed forward to this; the Lord's Supper points back to it.

Having taken from the table a thin slice or sheet of unleavened bread, Jesus "gave thanks" and then started to break up the slice. Though the original, in referring to the prayer, uses one word in verse 22 (literally "having blessed"; cf. Matt. 26:26), and another in verse 23 ("having given thanks"; cf. Matt. 26:27)—the first participial form occurring in connection with the bread, the second in connection with the cup—there is no essential difference. Both Luke (22:19) and Paul (I Cor. 11:24) read "having given thanks" where Matthew and Mark read "having blessed." It is not incorrect therefore, in both Mark 14:22 and 23, to adopt the rendering, "Jesus . . . gave thanks." For more on this see on 6:41. The words which the Lord used in this thanksgiving have not been revealed. To try to reconstruct them from Jewish formula prayers would serve no useful purpose. How do we even know that our Lord availed himself of these prayers?

The *breaking* of the bread, to which reference is made in all four accounts, must be considered as belonging to the very essence of the sacrament. This becomes clear in the light of that which immediately follows, namely, **He then gave it to them and said, Take (it); this is my body.** To interpret this to mean that Jesus was actually saying that these portions of bread which he handed to the disciples were identical with his physical body, or were at that moment being changed into his body, is to ignore *a.* the fact that *in his body* Jesus was standing there in front of his disciples, for all to see. He was holding in his hand the bread, and giving them the portions as he broke them off. *Body* and *bread* were clearly distinct and remained thus. Neither changed into the other, or took on the physical properties or characteristics of the other. Besides, such an interpretation also ignores *b.* the fact that during his earthly ministry the Master very frequently used symbolical language (Mark 8:15; John 2:19; 3:3; 4:14, 32; 6:51, 53-56; 11:11). It is striking that in *all* of the instances indicated by *these* references the symbolical or figurative character of our Lord's language was disregarded by those who first heard it! In *each* case also, the context makes clear that those who interpreted Christ's words literally were mistaken! Is it not high time that the implied lesson be taken to heart? Finally, there is *c:* when Jesus spoke of himself as being "the vine" (John 15:1, 5), is it not clear that he meant that what a natural vine is in relation to its branches, which find their unity, life, and fruit-bearing capacity in this plant, *that,* in a far more exalted

573

sense, Christ is to his people? Is it not clear, therefore, that the vine *represents* or *symbolizes* Jesus, the genuine Vine? Thus also he calls himself— or is called—the door, the morning star, the cornerstone, the lamb, the fountain, the rock, etc. He also refers to himself as "the bread of life" (John 6:35, 48), "the bread that came down out of heaven" (John 6:58). So, why should he not be, and be represented and symbolized by, "the broken bread"? Accordingly, the meaning of "the broken bread" and the poured out wine is correctly indicated in a Communion Form which represents Christ as saying: "Whereas otherwise you should have suffered eternal death, I give my body in death on the tree of the cross and shed my blood for you, and nourish and refresh your hungry and thirsty souls with my crucified body and shed blood to everlasting life, as certainly as this bread is broken before your eyes and this cup is given to you, and you eat and drink with your mouth in remembrance of Me." [708]

It was the desire of our Lord, therefore, that by means of the supper, here instituted, the church should remember his sacrifice and *love* him, should reflect on that sacrifice and embrace him by *faith*, and should look forward in living *hope* to his glorious return. Surely, the proper celebration of communion is a loving remembrance. It is, however, more than that. Jesus Christ is most certainly, and through his Spirit most actively, present at this genuine feast! Cf. Matt. 18:20. His followers "take" and "eat." They appropriate Christ by means of living faith, and are strengthened in this faith.

Having said all this, it will not be necessary to expatiate to any great extent on verses 23, 24. **Then he took a cup and gave thanks. He gave it to them, and they all drank from it. He told them, This is my blood of the covenant, which is poured out for many.**

Note the following:

a. Not much significance should be attached to the fact that Mark speaks of "a" cup, for in the parallel accounts Matthew's text varies, while Luke and Paul both use the definite article; hence "the cup." At the Passover it was customary to drink several cups of diluted wine. Since, as has been shown, the Lord's Supper was linked with the last part of the Passover, it is clear that the cup here mentioned reflects the final drinking that occurred at this feast. Hence both Luke and Paul speak of "the cup *after* supper." The emphasis, moreover, is never on the container. All the stress is on its contents, the wine (see on 14:25), as symbol of Christ's blood.

b. By ordering "all" his true disciples to drink this wine (Matt. 26:27),

---

[708] *Form for The Lord's Supper,* belonging to the Liturgy of the Christian Reformed Church. See *Psalter Hymnal* (Centennial Edition), *Doctrinal Standards and Liturgy of the Christian Reformed Churh,* Grand Rapids, 1959, p. 94 of the Liturgical Forms.

which they all did (Mark 14:23)—Judas had already left (John 13:27, 30)—the unity of all believers in Christ is stressed. Moreover, the practice of having one person, a priest, drink "for all" is hereby condemned. See also Luke 22:17b.

c. In all four accounts a relation is established between Christ's *blood* and his *covenant*. As reported by Matthew and Mark, Jesus said, "my blood of the covenant." The expression goes back to Exod. 24:8. See also the significant passage Lev. 17:11. And note: "Apart from the shedding of blood there is no *remission*" (Heb. 9:22; cf. Eph. 1:7); therefore also no *covenant*, no *special relation of friendship* between God and his people. Reconciliation with God always requires blood, an atoning sacrifice. And since man himself is unable to render such a sacrifice, a *substitutionary* offering, accepted by faith, is required (Isa. 53:6, 8, 10, 12; Matt. 20:28; Mark 10:45; John 3:16; 6:51; Rom. 4:19; 8:32; II Cor. 5:20, 21; Gal. 2:20; 3:13; I Peter 2:24). Thus the covenant comes into being. Scripture refers again and again to God's covenant with his people. The Lord established it with Abraham (Gen. 17:7; Ps. 105:9); hence, also with all who share Abraham's faith (Gal. 3:7, 29). [709]

d. Jesus says that his blood is poured out "for *many*," not for all. Cf. Isa. 53:12; Matt. 1:21; 20:28; Mark 10:45; John 10:11, 14, 15, 27, 28; 17:9; Acts 20:28; Rom. 8:32-35; Eph. 5:25-27. Nevertheless, "for *many*," not for just a *few*. Cf. John 1:29; 3:16; 4:42; 10:16; I John 4:14; Rev. 7:9, 10.

In both Matthew and Mark Jesus indicates that this is *certainly* the very last time that he is going to be with his disciples at this kind of supper. By means of this saying and its implications, he both predicts his imminent death and instructs them, and their followers throughout the ages, to continue until his return (cf. I Cor. 11:26) this manner of remembering him: **25. I solemnly declare to y o u that from now on I will certainly not drink** [710] **from this fruit of the vine until that day when I am drinking** [710] **it new in the kingdom of God.** Note the solemn introduction, for which see on 3:28. Jesus knew that he was about to depart from his disciples. In fact, he was going to lay down his life the very next day; or, according to Jewish time reckoning, that very day (Friday).

By speaking of "the fruit of the vine" Jesus undoubtedly refers to wine. Note close relation between "vine" and "wine" in Isa. 24:7. See also Num. 6:4; Hab. 3:17. At this time of the year (April), and under conditions then

---

[709] For more on this "covenant," its one-sidedness or two-sidedness, the relation of "covenant" to "testament," etc., see N.T.C. on Galatians, p. 134 (including footnote 98) and on Ephesians, pp. 129, 130; also the author's book, *The Covenant of Grace*, Grand Rapids, 1932.

[710] First πίω 1st per. sing. aor. subjunctive of πίνω; then πίνω, 1st per. sing. present subjunctive ("when I am drinking," or "shall be drinking").

prevailing in Judea, it is hard to think of anything but fermented grape juice, that is, *wine,* the kind of wine used at Passover; hence, diluted or paschal wine.

Note the expression "(I will certainly not drink from this fruit of the vine) until that day when I am drinking it new in the kingdom of God." For "the kingdom of God" see on 1:15. It is the kingdom in its eschatological sense that is meant here, the glorious realm of the redeemed, to which their souls ascend at death (Ps. 73:24, 25; Acts 7:56, 59; II Cor. 5:8; Phil. 1:21, 23; Heb. 12:23; Rev. 20:4, 5b, 6). At the close of the present age it will be transformed into the new heaven and earth (Rev. 21:1 ff.). There believers, body and soul then gloriously reunited, will feast forever in the company of their Lord, to praise him forevermore. Then both passover and eucharist will reach their fruition.

We see, therefore, that communion not only points back to what Jesus Christ has done for us but also forward to what he is still going to mean for us. "Drinking new wine in the kingdom of God" (or "in my Father's kingdom," Matt. 26:29) is a symbol of the glorious reunion and never-ending festivities awaiting the children of God, in fellowship with their Savior— note: "when *I* am drinking it new"—in the hereafter. Cf. Ps. 23:5; Isa. 25:6; Matt. 8:11; 22:1 ff.; Luke 14:15; Rev. 3:20; 19:9, 17. Then, too, it is he, the Victorious Lamb, who will be the Host; and his faithful ones the guests, feasting with him!

26. And when they had sung a hymn they went out to the Mount of Olives. "When they had hymned," says the original. Since, as has been shown, the Lord's Supper was the natural outgrowth of the Passover, it is probable that the hymns of praise that were lifted up to God were Pss. 115-118. These are songs of praise, thanksgiving, and trust, as anyone can see by reading them. They not only constituted a fitting conclusion to the blessings enjoyed but also a most appropriate preparation for the ordeal that was about to begin. For the entire subject of songs appropriate for the home as well as for public gatherings see N.T.C. on Eph. 5:19 and on Col. 3:16. When the meeting had been thus concluded, Jesus and his disciples, no longer twelve but eleven, went to the Mount of Olives. Specifically, they crossed the Kidron and entered the Gethsemane grove, located near the foot of that mountain. See 14:32; cf. John 18:1.

---

27 Then Jesus told them, "Y o u will all fall away, [711] for it is written,
    'I will strike down the shepherd,
    And the sheep will be scattered.'
28 But after I have been raised, I will go ahead of y o u to Galilee."

---

711 Or: become untrue (to me).

29 But Peter said to him, "Even though all may fall away, yet will not I." 30 Jesus answered, "I solemnly declare to you that today—yes, this very night—before the rooster crows twice, [712] you will deny me three times." 31 Nevertheless, with great emphasis Peter continued to insist, "Even if I have to die with you, I will certainly not deny you." Similarly spoke also all (the others).

14:27-31 *Peter's Denial Foretold*
Cf. Matt. 26:31-35; Luke 22:31-34; John 13:36-38

As has already been indicated, if the account with respect to the prediction of Peter's denial occurs in Mark 14, it can also be found in Matthew (14+12=) 26. In the present instance so very similar is Matthew's report to that of Mark—a similarity happily reflected even in the division into verses which at a much later date was applied to it—, that in order to find a certain verse in Matthew all one has to do is add 4 to the number of the verse in Mark. Accordingly, Mark 14:27 parallels Matt. 26:31; Mark 14:28 parallels Matt. 26:32, etc.

As to Mark 14:27, to "Y o u will all fall away" (or: "become untrue"), Matthew adds "this very night." On the other hand, it is Mark who in his thirtieth verse ("today—yes, this very night—") is more specific and emphatic than is Matthew in his thirty-fourth. In verse 31 Mark graphically introduces Simon's boastful assertion as follows, "Nevertheless, with great emphasis Peter continued to insist . . ." Matthew's parallel is simply, "Peter said to him."

Luke 22:31, 32 reproduces Christ's memorable words of revelation, encouragement, and admonition, addressed to Peter. In verse 33 Peter answers, "Lord, I am ready to go with you both to prison and to death." Verse 34—". . . you will deny three times that you know me"—is an interesting variation of its parallel in Matthew and Mark.

Finally, John 13:37, 38 has Peter asking, "Lord, why can't I follow you right now? I will lay down my life for you." Jesus replies, "You will lay down your life for me?" When allowance is made for word transposition and use of synonymns, the rest of the reply closely resembles its parallel in Matthew and Mark. Cf. John 13:38b with Matt. 26:34; Mark 14:30.

If we bear in mind that it was not the purpose of any of the Gospel writers to reproduce every word that was spoken, and that each in his own way and for his own purpose gave a fully inspired and true account of the events that occurred and of the words that were spoken, difficulties will begin to disappear. The various reports dovetail beautifully. At various points they supplement each other.

---

712 For omission of "twice" in some MSS. see footnote 778.

27. Then Jesus told them, "Y o u will all fall away, [713] for it is written,
I will strike down the shepherd,
And the sheep will be scattered.

For Old Testament passages based on the well-known figure of the shepherd and his sheep see Ps. 23; 79:13; 80:1; 95:7; 119:176; Isa. 40:11; 53:6; Ezek. 34:5. Similar sayings again and again issued from the lips of Jesus (Matt. 15:24; 25:31-46; Mark 6:34; Luke 12:32; John 10:11-18, 25-29). A rather detailed account of this imagery can be found in N.T.C. on John, Vol. II, pp. 97-103, 116-118.

Here in Mark 14:27 and its parallels Jesus is predicting that the disciples will all become untrue to him. They will resemble sheep that are running away from their shepherd. This will happen when Jesus, the Good Shepherd, is captured and slain.

In the momentary lapse of the disciples—their failure to show loyalty that night—Jesus sees the fulfilment of Zech. 13:7. The application of that passage to Jesus and his disciples does not present any great difficulty. It is true that in the context of Zechariah's prophecy the one who smites the shepherd is not mentioned. An order is simply issued, namely, to strike down the shepherd. On the other hand, the entire context refers repeatedly to Jehovah as being the Actor. It is he who will turn, bring, refine, try, hear, and say. Accordingly, Jesus was entirely justified in saying, " . . . for it is written 'I will strike down the shepherd.' " Similarly, it was Jehovah himself who, according to Isa. 53:6, laid upon the Mediator "all our iniquities." It was he who "bruised him," "put him to grief," "made his soul an offering for sin." Cf. Acts 8:32-35. It was God the Father who "spared not his own Son" (Rom. 8:32).

Now when a shepherd is struck down, the sheep scatter in every direction, for they have lost their rallying point. So also when Jesus is captured and subsequently crucified, his followers will panic and flee. That this prediction was indeed fulfilled in the case of Christ's disciples is clear from passages such as the following:

"And they all left him and fled" (Mark 14:50).

"Then he [Peter] started to curse and to swear, 'I don't know this man y o u're talking about' " (Mark 14:71).

"We had hoped that he was the one who was going to redeem Israel, but . . ." (Luke 24:21).

---

[713] σκανδαλισθήσεσθε, sec. per. pl. fut. indic. passive of σκανδαλίζω; see on 4:17, footnote 147. Various translations have been attempted. Some insist on the literal "be made to stumble," or simply "stumble." Others prefer "be offended," "turn against (me)," "fall away (from me)," "become untrue (to me)." The context would seem to favor the last two. See also the fine article on σκάνδαλον, σκανδαλίζω, by G. Stählin, Th.D.N.T., Vol. VII, pp. 339-358, especially p. 349.

"Jesus answered them, 'Do y o u now believe? Note well, there comes an hour—yes, it has arrived!—when y o u will be scattered, each to his own home, and y o u will leave me alone" (John 16:31, 32).

"But Thomas, one of the twelve, the one called the Twin, was not with them when Jesus came . . . He said, 'Unless I see in his hands the mark of the nails . . . I definitely will not believe' " (John 20:24, 25).

The beauty in all this is not only that Jesus here reveals that he loves them all the same, but also that his very prediction would serve the purpose of bringing the scattered sheep together again, once they reflected on the fact that their Master had lovingly forewarned them.

Christ's prediction has an optimistic climax: **28. But after I have been raised, I will go ahead** [714] **of y o u to Galilee.** In clear and unfigurative language Jesus speaks about being raised from the dead, just as he had spoken previously (8:31; 9:9, 31; 10:34). This is also another revelation of his love, for here Jesus assures them that he is going to meet them in the very region, Galilee, where their homes were, and where the Lord had originally called them to himself.

As to fulfilment, immediately after Christ's resurrection a messenger from heaven reminded the disciples of this promise (16:7). It was indeed in Galilee that the risen Savior met with these men (Matt. 28:16), with seven of them (John 21:1-23), with more than five hundred of his followers (I Cor. 15:6).

29. But Peter said to him, Even though [715] **all may fall away, yet will not I.** Matthew substitutes, "I will *never* become untrue." Peter here commits the sin of treating the words of Jesus ("Y o u will all fall away"; or: "become untrue") with disbelief. At the same time he assumes an attitude of superiority with respect to his fellow disciples. Finally, he clearly shows that he does not know himself. He has an inflated opinion of himself, is over-confident, conceited, as events are quickly going to prove.

30. Jesus answered, I solemnly declare to you that today—yes, this very night—before [716] **the rooster crows twice, you will deny** [717] **me three times.**

---

714 In the present case the verb προάγω (here προάξω, first per. s. fut. indic.) cannot have the meaning "go in front of y o u and lead y o u"; cf. 10:32. It must mean "go ahead of y o u, so as to arrive earlier and meet y o u (in Galilee)," as is clear from 16:7.

715 According to L.N.T. (A. and G.), p. 219, εἰ καί can have the meaning "even though." In the present passage most English translations have "although," "even though," "even if," or something similar. Robertson calls attention to the fact that the true text in the present passage is εἰ καί, not καὶ εἰ. He sees a distinction and takes εἰ καί to mean "and if," the matter mentioned in the clause beginning with εἰ καί being belittled. If this distinction is valid, the translation might be, "whoever else may become untrue, I certainly will not," or something similar. See N.E.B.'s rendering.

716 As in John 4:49, πρίν—here πρὶν ἤ—is followed by the infinitive. See Burton, *op. cit.*, par. 380.

717 ἀπαρνήσῃ sec. per. s. fut. middle indic., or (volitive) aor. subjunct. (same form) of ἀπαρνέομαι. For this verb see also on 8:34, footnote 381.

In comparison with verse 27 the present predication *a.* is introduced in a more solemn and impressive manner, "I solemnly declare"—see on 3:28—; *b.* is far more specific, being addressed to just one person, Peter; *c.* indicates even more precisely when it will be fulfilled, namely, "before the rooster crows twice," that is, before dawn; and *d.* describes the nature of the disloyalty trap into which that disciple will fall, namely, "deny me three times." Rooster-crowing served as a time indication. Mark 13:35 shows that it marked the third of the four watches; see on that passage; therefore, 12 midnight-3 A.M.; "crows twice" indicating the latter part of that period.

We see Jesus here as *the great Prophet*. Though Peter did not know his own heart, Jesus not only knew it but also revealed it. Note the detailed character of this knowledge: *three times*. We see Jesus also as *the great Sufferer*. How what he foresaw must have grieved him. Finally, we see him as *the great Savior*. The reference to the crowing of the rooster does double duty: *a.* It indicates the shallow character of Peter's boast. Within just a few hours, yes, *even before dawn*, Peter will publicly disown his Master! Yet, *b.* this very rooster-crowing is also a means of bringing Peter back to repentance, for Christ's reference to it becomes firmly embedded in his mind, so that at the appropriate moment this hidden memory will suddenly pull the rope that will ring the bell of Peter's conscience. See Matt. 26:74; Mark 14:72; Luke 22:60; John 18:27.

The disciple who by the Lord had been singled out for this specific prediction persists, however, in his profession of unswerving loyalty: **31. Nevertheless, with great emphasis** [718] **Peter continued to insist, Even if I have to die with you, I will certainly not deny you.** Instead of "with great emphasis continued to insist," another good translation would be "was saying vehemently." If need be, Peter is willing even to die *with* (so also Matt. 26:35; Luke 22:33) and *for* (John 13:37) Jesus. See also John 11:16. **Similarly spoke also all (the others).** They were swept off their feet by Peter's mighty boasts. They must have felt that they could not very well promise less than Peter!

Jesus predicted that *all* would become untrue to him (14:27).

All protested that this would never happen (14:31).

A little later, this very night, they *all* left him and fled (14:50).

* * *

The present section has shown that we do not know ourselves. All these disciples were very sure that they would never become ensnared into the sin

---

718 ἐκπερισσῶς, in the New Testament found only here, but compare related words in 7:37; I Thess. 3:10; 5:13 (see N.T.C. on I and II Thessalonians, p. 135, including footnote 103 in that book); also see Eph. 3:20.

of being untrue to Jesus. Yet, that is exactly what happened. In connection, then, with

The Unknown Self

the following thoughts should be emphasized:

1. The sinner does not know his inner self. This is true with respect to the unregenerate—for example, Hazael (read II Kings 8:12, 13)—, but to a certain extent even with respect to those who have been reborn. Think of Peter and the other disciples, contrasting what they *promised* with what they actually *did*. Cf. Jer. 17:9.

2. God knows the sinner thoroughly. Read Jer. 17:10; Ps. 139:1-16; Heb. 4:13. Of course, this holds also for Jesus, according to his divine nature, as indicated in John 2:24, 25; 16:30; 21:17. Christ's predictions recorded in Mark 14:27, 28, 30 were fulfilled in every respect (14:50, 62-72).

3. What, then, if anything, can man do about this situation?

a. Apart from God he can do nothing. But when by God's sovereign grace he is converted, he can and should watch his conscious thoughts, words, and deeds; for, whatever he does consciously exerts a powerful influence upon his subliminal or inner self: "For as he thinketh in his heart, so is he" (Prov. 23:7 A.V.). Important, therefore, is obedience to such exhortations as are found in Ps. 34:13; 119:35; 141:3; John 15:4, 12, 27, to mention only a few.

b. It is also true, however, that man's inner self reacts upon his outer self. And since man cannot very well directly fight those sins within himself that are hidden from his consciousness, he should ask God to do what he (man) himself cannot do. Hence, the prayer, "Clear thou me from hidden faults" (Ps. 19:12) is necessary. Very fitting is also the prayer expressed in Ps. 139:23, 24.

c. Doing this, he should not be afraid but should fully accept and derive comfort from the divine assurance, "Jehovah has laid on him [i.e., on the Messiah] the iniquity of us all" (Isa. 53:6). "Where sin increased, grace increased all the more" (Rom. 5:20).

The main lesson conveyed by the paragraph just studied (Mark 14:27-31 and its parallels) is that it "directs our heart to the love of God" (II Thess. 3:5). Was it not gracious of Jesus to say, "Simon, Simon, behold, Satan has asked to sift y o u as wheat. But I have made supplication for you, that your faith may not utterly fail. And when you have returned (to me) impart strength to your brothers"? And was it not gracious of him to tell the eleven, "But after I have been raised I will go ahead of y o u to Galilee"? Even before they were scattered he told them that they would be regathered! This is the "marvelous grace of our loving Lord," the very "grace that will pardon and cleanse *within.*" [719]

---

32 They went to a place called Gethsemane, and he said to his disciples, "Sit here while I pray." 33 And he took with him Peter and James and John, and began to be filled with horror and anguish. 34 He said to them, "I am overwhelmed with sorrow to the point of death. Stay here and keep awake." 35 And going a little farther, he was throwing himself to the ground, and was praying [720] that if it were possible this hour might pass him by. 36 He said, "Abba, Father, all things are possible with thee. Remove this cup from me; nevertheless, not what I will but what thou wilt."

37 And he came and found them sleeping. "Simon," he said to Peter, "Are you asleep? Were you not able to stay awake for a single hour? 38 Keep on the alert and keep on praying that y o u may not enter into temptation. The spirit is eager but the flesh is weak."

39 Again he went and prayed, saying the same thing. 40 Again he came and found them asleep, for their eyes were weighed down with sleep, and they did not know what to answer him. 41 And he came the third time and said to them, "Sleep on now and take y o u r rest. It is enough. The Son of man is being betrayed into the hands of sinners. 42 Get up! Let us be going. Look, my betrayer is near."

14:32-42 *Gethsemane*
Cf. Matt. 26:36-46; Luke 22:39-46

It is with profound reverence that one approaches the Gethsemane narrative. Also with due appreciation of the unique character of the event here described. This uniqueness deserves emphasis, for again and again one will hear a person who has passed through a fiery trial refer to this experience as "my Gethsemane." Better surely is the following:

"Joy is a partnership,
Grief weeps alone,
Many guests had Cana,
Gethsemane but One."
—F. L. Knowles, *Grief and Joy*

What Jesus endured in Gethsemane was never experienced by anyone else.

But why Gethsemane at all? Why could not God have arranged it in such a way that at the very entrance of the garden Jesus would immediately have been arrested, etc.? Why all the agony, the wrestlings, the prayers, the bloody sweat?

Could not the answer be as follows: to establish for all time that the obedience (both active and passive) which Jesus rendered was not forced upon him against his will but was *voluntary?* He was actually laying down his

---

[719] The words between quotation marks are from the beautiful and deservedly popular hymn by Julia H. Johnston, *Grace Greater Than Our Sin.*
[720] Or: began to pray.

life for the sheep (John 10:11, 14). That wholehearted sacrifice, in total obedience to the Father's will, was the only kind of death capable of saving the sinner (Heb. 5:7-9).

What kind of death did Jesus die? Merely physical death? Spiritual death? Eternal death? There can be no question of the fact that Jesus experienced *physical death,* separation of body and soul (Mark 15:37). Did he also undergo *spiritual death?* If by this term is meant death in sin—"to live apart from God is death"—, the answer must be a very emphatic *No.* See John 8:46; Acts 3:14; II Cor. 5:21; Heb. 4:15; 7:26; I Peter 2:22; I John 3:5. But what about *eternal death?* If by ascribing eternal death to Jesus we mean that during his entire life on earth, and especially in Gethsemane and on the cross, Jesus suffered the full equivalent of that which his people would have suffered if no one had died in their stead, the answer is, "Yes, that is indeed the kind of death Jesus suffered." To state it differently, hell, as it were, came to him in Gethsemane and on Golgotha, and he descended into it, experiencing to the full its terrors.

"He has borne for us the wrath of God under which we should have perished everlastingly, from the beginning of his incarnation to the end of his life on earth, and has fulfilled for us all obedience and righteousness of the divine law, especially when the weight of our sins and of the wrath of God pressed out of him the bloody sweat in the garden, where he was bound that we might be loosed from our sins; that afterward he suffered innumerable reproaches that we might never be confounded, and . . . humbled himself to the deepest reproach and anguish of hell, in body and soul, on the tree of the cross, when he cried out with a loud voice, *My God, my God, why hast thou forsaken me?* that we might be accepted of God, and nevermore forsaken of him. . . ." [721]

Those who object to this representation should ask themselves in all seriousness whether One who did not actually descend into the terrors of hell as our Substitute can be our Savior. If *he* did not suffer that punishment, does it not follow that this is in store for *us?*

* * *

Luke's account, even with the retention of 22:43, 44, [722] is much shorter than that of either Matthew or Mark. Luke does not mention the fact that in

---

[721] Quoted from Psalter Hymnal (Centennial Edition), Doctrinal Standards and Liturgy of the Christian Reformed Church, Grand Rapids, 1959, p. 93, Lord's Supper Form.

[722] For detailed discussion of the textual problem the reader should consult commentaries on Luke. Briefly, those who reject this passage about an angel who came and strengthened Jesus, and about the Master's sweat becoming like thick drops of blood, present the following reasons for this rejection: *a.* this passage is missing from Codex

Gethsemane Jesus prayed more than once. However, this is no reason for positing a conflict between Luke and the others. Luke 22:42 states the very essence of Christ's prayers at this time, as is clear from both Matthew and Mark. Luke's additions—with reference to *the angel* and *the thick drops of blood*—harmonize very well with that which the other Gospels report with respect to the Sufferer's agony. God be praised for having given us Luke's account as well as those of Matthew and Mark!

As to Matthew and Mark, their reports are almost identical from start to finish. The main differences are as follows:

a. While both Matthew (26:39) and Mark (14:36), by means of direct discourse, report Christ's first prayer in Gethsemane, Mark, before doing so, introduces this prayer by means of indirect discourse (verse 35b). In the introduction note the word *hour;* in the prayer itself "cup."

b. It is true that the prayer reported in Matt. 26:39 and the one found in 26:42 are essentially the same, for in both Jesus prays that if possible the cup may pass him by, and submits himself completely to the Father's will. It is that essential sameness in essence which Mark is declaring (14:39). But within this essential oneness there was, nevertheless, room for a degree of difference *in emphasis*. The words of the two prayers are not exactly identical. It is Matthew who brings out the distinction. See N.T.C. on Matt. 26:42, p. 919. There is no conflict.

c. In connection with Christ's second return to the sleeping disciples Mark adds, "They did not know how to answer him" (14:40).

* * * *

Vaticanus and from other important manuscripts; *b*. it looks like a scribal embellishment of Luke's text; *c*. it may be considered a Western interpolation; and *d*. it is out of harmony with the contents of the immediately preceding verse.

On the other hand, those who take the opposite view answer: *a*. the passage is present in Codex Sinaiticus and is supported by several other witnesses, some of them early; *b*. it is especially Luke who throughout his Gospel and book of Acts mentions angels again and again (see any good Concordance and note frequency of the word "angel" in Luke's writings as compared with its frequency in the other Gospels); *c*. Luke also shows that Jesus himself was very conscious of the presence and work of angels; *d*. the question is legitimate whether the omission of verses 43, 44 from several important manuscripts, etc., may not be ascribed to a theological bias, namely, the *mistaken* belief that what is reported here, being supposedly out of harmony with the doctrine of Christ's deity, was therefore a legitimate basis of appeal for the Arians; and *d*. the passage is entirely in line with Heb. 5:7, 8. In both cases the fact that, in a sense, Christ's human nature, though entirely without sin, needed strengthening, is held before us. Besides, as to the reasoning of those who reject the passage, are not some of their arguments of a purely subjective character?—I believe the passage should be retained.

In Gethsemane Jesus agonized

32. They went to a place called Gethsemane, and he said to his disciples, Sit here while [723] **I pray.** Just where was Gethsemane? This "oil press" garden must have been somewhere in the general area across the Kedron (John 18:1) and on the slope of the Mt. of Olives (Luke 22:39). But *exactly* where, and how far up the slope? Is the present so-called Franciscan Garden the real spot where Jesus agonized and prayed? Or does the Russian Gethsemane, higher up the hill, have a better claim to authenticity? And what about the Armenian Gethsemane? One fact is often forgotten. Says Josephus (*Jewish War* VI.5), "Meanwhile the Romans, though sorely harassed in the gathering of timber, had completed their earthworks in twenty-one days, having, as previously stated [see V. 522, 523], cleared (of trees) the entire district around the town to a distance of ninety furlongs [about eleven miles or eighteen kilometers]." In his very interesting book *Spoorzoeker in Bijbelse Landen* (Combing Biblical Lands, Amsterdam, 1973, pp. 121, 122) Dr. H. Mulder, who himself lived in this vicinity for a while, states, "It is impossible that in the days of Jesus and his disciples these very trees [the ones shown to visitors today] were yielding fruit to the then owner. . . . To be sure, the trees of today, attended by the monks, are very, very old [Dutch "stokoud"]. But even five hundred or seven hundred years is quite an age for a tree!"

Wherever it was, the point which Mark brings out is that near the entrance of this quiet place—an ideal spot for resting, sleeping, praying, and teaching—, a grove probably belonging to one of Christ's followers, Jesus left eight of his disciples. He told them to remain there while he himself was praying.

33. And he took with him Peter and James and John. . . . Also at other occasions (5:37; 9:2) these same three men were selected by the Master to be with him. Why just these three? See on 5:37. That, in proceeding farther into the grove, Jesus would take some of his disciples with him is not strange. Being human himself, he stood in need not only of food, drink, clothing, shelter, and sleep, but also of human fellowship. Cf. Heb. 4:15. He

---

[723] In this passage does ἕως mean "while" or "until"? Grammars do not agree. Contrast Burton, *op. cit.,* par. 325 ("properly *until*"), and Gram. N.T., p. 976 ("while"). "While" would seem the most natural. If "until," then the translation would have to be "until I have prayed," for Jesus would hardly tell the disciples to sit at a certain place *until* he prays (or starts praying). Lenski, *op. cit.,* p. 399, has "until" in his translation but "while" in his explanation. However, on the same page he imparts some very interesting information about Gethsemane. Among commentaries on Mark that are read or consulted Bible students should be sure to include that of Lenski.—Moreover, the ἕως rule (see footnote 286) is flexible.

needed these men. Even more, they needed him! . . . and began [724] to be
filled with horror and anguish. The words " . . . filled with anguish" [725] are
used by both Matthew and Mark. In Matt. 26:37 the first verb is "(filled
with) sorrow"; in Mark 14:33 "(filled with) horror." [726] All the waves and
the billows of distress came pouring over his soul. Cf. Ps. 42:7b. Why this
terror and dismay? Was it because he knew that even now Judas was
approaching—or preparing to approach—in order to deliver him to his
enemies? Was it because he was painfully aware that Peter would deny him,
that the Sanhedrin would condemn him, Pilate sentence him, his enemies
ridicule him, and the soldiers crucify him? No doubt all that was included.
However, as the story develops we notice that it was especially this one
thought, namely, that he, a most tender and sensitive soul, is more and more
being driven into isolation. Many of the people have already left him (John
6:66). His disciples are going to forsake him (Mark 14:50). Worst of all, on
the cross he will be crying out, "My God, my God, why has *thou* forsaken
me?" (15:34). Did he, perhaps, here in Gethsemane see this tidal wave of
God's wrath because of our sin coming?

34. **He said to them, I am overwhelmed with sorrow to the point of
death.** Literally the original reads, "Overwhelmed is my soul [727] to the point
of death." By means of the forward position of the word "overwhelmed"
Jesus shows where he wishes to place the emphasis. To be sure, he had been
a curse-bearer throughout the days of his humiliation, but now he was
becoming overwhelmed with the curse, was more than ever before becoming
a curse for those who place their trust in him (Gal. 3:13). This consciousness
would not again leave him until he was able to say, "It is finished" (John
19:30). He knew that he was giving his life as a ransom for many (Mark
10:45; cf. Matt. 20:28); that he, the sinless One, was "being made sin," that
is, the vicarious bearer of God's wrath (II Cor. 5:21). It is not surprising that

---

[724] For ἤρξατο, third per. s. aor. indic. middle of ἄρχω see on 1:45 and on 6:7,
footnote 233. Though in 6:7; 13:5 and perhaps a few other passages there could be a
pleonastic use of this verb, this is not at all probable here. Gethsemane was unique. The
account leaves the definite impression (see especially verses 33, 34) that the suffering
which Jesus now began to experience was more intense than anything he had borne
previously.

[725] Both ἐκθαμβεῖσθαι and ἀδημονεῖν are present infinitives after ἤρξατο. The verb
ἀδημονέω is of uncertain derivation. The etymology "to be away from home" cannot be
proved. See also N.T.C. on Philippians, pp. 140, 141.

[726] Another good translation of ἤρξατο ἐκθαμβεῖσθαι is "began to be greatly amazed."
See on 9:15.

[727] See above, on 8:12, footnote 370; also on 10:45. The "soul" is here the self (cf. I
Tim. 2:6), with emphasis on the emotional.

he said to his three closest disciples, **Stay here and keep awake.** [728] Did they do so? See verses 37 and 39.

The anguish of death—not just physical death but eternal death in the place of his people, to atone for their sins—was coming upon Jesus, now more than ever before. That is why he speaks of "sorrow to the point of death." And he bore it—all alone!

In Gethsemane Jesus agonized and prayed

35. And going a little farther, he was throwing himself to the ground, and was praying that if it were possible this hour might pass him by.

Consider the beautiful lines by William B. Tappan:

> 'Tis midnight; and on Olive's brow
> The star is dimmed that lately shone.
> 'Tis midnight; in the garden now
> The suff'ring Savior prays alone.

The agony continues and even intensifies. But now the story of Christ's *agonizing* shifts into that of his *praying* (already briefly introduced in verse 32). Jesus wishes to be all by himself during his prayer. Hence, he now leaves even the three behind. Yet not far behind, for he desires to retain the possibility of contact with them. According to Luke 22:41 he withdrew from—or beyond—them about a stone's throw.

In a very picturesque manner [729] Mark describes what happened: Jesus was throwing himself to the ground and was praying. " . . . began to pray" is also possible. [730] The substance of his prayer was that if it were possible this hour might pass him by.

Note "this hour." It is not true that whenever Jesus uses this or a similar expression he always has reference to the same event. What is true is that "the hour" in the phraseology of Jesus means "the predestined moment, season, or time," for something to happen. Thus, there was a proper time, a predestined moment, for Jesus to perform a certain sign (John 2:4), a predestined season for him to awaken those spiritually dead (John 5:25), a predestined time (still future) for him to raise all the physically dead (John

---

[728] Though both of these actions—remaining and keeping awake—are durative in character, it is only with respect to the second verb that the emphasis falls on this continuation. Hence μείνατε is *aorist* imper., the action being indicated as a simple fact, an order to be obeyed, but γρηγορεῖτε is *present* imper. For γρηγορέω also see on 13:34 and on 14:38.

[729] Note the imperfects ἔπιπτε and προσηύχετο.

[730] For prayer postures and their significance see N.T.C. on I and II Timothy and Titus, pp. 103, 104.

5:28). And so also there was a predestined "hour" for the Son of man to depart from this world (John 13:1) and, by means of his death and resurrection, to be glorified (John 12:23; 17:1). Jesus was a strong believer in the doctrine of divine predestination, never for a moment accepting it at the expense of the doctrine of human responsibility! See Luke 22:22.

He is in deep agony, probably, as was indicated previously, because he sees more sharply now than ever before the woes that await him. So he prays that this hour, this time of indescribably bitter pain and anguish, may pass him by. [731]

The actual words of the prayer are now given: **36. He said, Abba, Father, all things are possible with thee. Remove this cup from me; nevertheless, not what I will but what thou wilt.** Note the following:

a. It is not necessary to believe that Jesus, in addressing his Father, used two words: the Aramaic *Abba* and the Greek *Patēr,* both with the same meaning, namely, "Father." He probably said "Abba," a word which Mark, writing mainly for non-Jews, immediately translates into the language with which his readers are better acquainted, Greek.

b. "All things are possible with thee." Jesus here very properly appeals to the fact that the Father, whom he is addressing, is able to do whatever he wants to do. It is, accordingly, in the spirit of complete confidence and submission that he makes his petition.

c. "Remove this cup from me." This cup means "this terrible, impending experience," climaxed by the cross and complete abandonment (Mark 15: 34). For "cup" see further on 10:38.

d. "Nevertheless, not what I will but what thou wilt." The completely sinless, in fact exemplary, nature of the supplication appears from the fact that the clause, "Remove this cup from me," is immediately modified by "nevertheless, not what I will but [732] what thou wilt." It is clear that Jesus is submitting himself entirely to the will of the Father.

That the soul of our Lord was indeed filled with excruciating anguish as he prayed this prayer is clear from Luke 22:43, 44, "There appeared to him an angel from heaven, strengthening him. And being in anguish, he prayed very fervently; and his sweat became like thick drops of blood, falling down upon the ground." [733] It was indeed "with strong crying and tears" (Heb. 5:7) that he was offering up his prayers and supplications.

After the first prayer Jesus returned to the three men who had been exhorted to keep awake: **37. And he came and found them sleeping. Simon,**

---

[731] παρέλθῃ third per. s. aor. subjunct. of παρέρχομαι as in 13:30.

[732] Note the strong adversatives. The sec. per. s. aor. imperat. of παραφέρω, namely, παρένεγκε is balanced by ἀλλά . . . ἀλλά.

[733] For the textual question see above, footnote 722.

he said to Peter, Are you asleep? Were [734] you not able to stay awake for a single hour? Sleeping at this hour, probably past midnight, was natural, especially after the exciting experiences in the Upper Room (the washing of the disciples' feet, the revelation that one of The Twelve was going to betray his Master, the departure of Judas, the institution of the Lord's Supper) and afterward ("All of y o u will become untrue to me," Peter's protest, etc.). Nevertheless, these men should have stayed awake. They could have, had they only prayed for strength to do so. Though Christ's gentle reprimand concerned all three—note the plural—yet it was addressed particularly to Peter, no doubt because in the matter of pledging his loyalty and even boasting about it he had taken the lead.

This was the same Peter who on the way to Gethsemane and even while still in the Upper Room had made boasts such as these:
"Even though all may fall away, yet will not I" (Mark 14:29).
"Even if I have to die with you, I will certainly not deny you" (14:31).
"Lord, with you I am ready to go both to prison and to death" (Luke 22:33).
"Lord, I will lay down my life for you" (John 13:37).
And now, here he is . . . sound asleep, even though Jesus had urged him to pray so as to be able to remain awake!

Jesus continues, 38. **Keep on the alert and keep on praying that y o u may not enter into temptation.** [735] The context clearly indicates that here a slightly different meaning must be assigned to the same Greek word that was used also in verses 34, 37. "Keep (or: stay) awake" becomes "Keep on the alert," or "Remain watchful." The reason for the change is the clause "that y o u may not enter into temptation." A person may be wide awake physically and may still succumb to temptation, but if he remains awake spiritually, that is, if with heart and mind he remains "on the alert" or "watchful," he will overcome temptation. See N.T.C. on Matt. 6:13. The temptation for the disciples was to become untrue to Jesus. We already know that they, definitely including Peter, did not remain alert, did not make earnest work of prayer, and therefore did, indeed, succumb to temptation. Jesus adds: **The spirit is eager but the flesh is weak.** If in this nightly hour Jesus experienced the weakness of his own human nature, hence the need of prayer, we may be sure that this was far more seriously true in the

---

734 Note striking contrast here between the present and the aorist: "*Are* you asleep . . . *were* you not able (or: Did you not have the strength) . . ."

735 Note the sec. per. pl. pres. imperatives, durative in character: γρηγορεῖτε and προσεύχεσθε. ἵνα μή is negat. final: "lest" or "that . . . not." ἔλθητε (another reading has εἰσέλθητε): sec. per. pl. aor. subjunct., an illustration of the non-literal use of ἔρχομαι followed by εἰς, (that y o u may not) *enter*, that is, seek or sinfully expose yourselves to (temptation). The aorist summarizes the entering action.

case of the disciples. In the present passage "spirit" indicates man's invisible entity viewed in its relation to God. As such it is the recipient of God's favor and the means whereby man worships God. See further on 8:12, including footnote 370. "Flesh," as here meant, is the human nature considered from the aspect of its frailty and needs, both physical and psychical. See N.T.C. on Philippians, p. 77, footnote 55. Cf. Isa. 40:6; I Cor. 1:29; Gal. 2:16. This use of "flesh" must not be confused with that according to which "flesh" indicates the human nature regarded as the seat of sinful desire (Rom. 7:25; 8:4-9; etc.). To the disciples, borne down with sleep, it was a battle between their "spirit" which was eager to do what was right and thus to remain "on guard" against temptation, and their "flesh" which, because of its weakness, was prone to yield to Satan's desires.

39. Again he went and prayed, [736] saying the same thing. Though Jesus did not utter exactly the same words, he did say what amounted to *substantially* (though not precisely) the same *thing*. [737] For the difference in wording and emphasis see N.T.C. on Matthew, p. 919.

40. Again he came and found them asleep, for their eyes were weighed down with sleep, and they did not know what to answer him. [738] Their drowsiness had once again gained the victory over their desire to stay awake and remain on the alert. Their eyes were weighed down with sleep, for their hearts had not been filled with prayer. So all alone Jesus must fight the battle. No help of any kind does he receive from men, not even from these three!

Though the Master spoke to them, they did not know what to say in return. To a certain extent these three men were reliving a previous experience. Read the story of the Master's Transfiguration. Note especially Mark 9:6 and Luke 9:32. But here in Gethsemane, in addition to being weighed down with sleep, were Peter, James, and John perhaps also somewhat oppressed with shame, sensing, however vaguely, that if they had obeyed the exhortation to keep on praying they would not have fallen asleep?

Again Jesus leaves the three and is in communion with his Father. Mark takes up the story when for the third time the Suffering Servant returns to his disciples:

In Gethsemane Jesus prayed and kept watch

---

[736] Lenski, *op. cit.*, p. 404, calls προσηύξατο "the imperfect." It happens to be an aorist. Verse 35 has the imperfect προσηύχετο.

[737] λόγος acc.-ον probably here used in the sense of the Hebrew *dābhār*.

[738] ἦσαν . . . καταβαρονόμενοι, periphrastic imperfect. ἤδεισαν, third per. pl. pluperf. with sense of imperfect. ἀποκριθῶσι, the deliberative subjunctive of the direct question is retained in the indirect question.

With respect to the final two verses of this section there is great diversity of opinion among commentators. With very slight alteration I have adopted the rendering of verse 41 that is found in A.V. and A.R.V.: [739]

41. And he came the third time and said to them, Sleep on now and take y o u r rest. No longer does Jesus reprove these men. No longer does he say to Simon, "Were you not able to stay awake for a single hour?" No longer does he even tell all three to keep on the alert and keep on praying. In reading the words of verse 41 we receive the definite impression that for Jesus the Gethsemane struggle is over. The victory has been won. In his heart there is perfect peace. He has been strengthened by an angel (Luke 22:43) and through his own prayers. To be sure, the three men had failed him. But never, no never will his love fail them.

So what verse 41 pictures to us is the Good Shepherd tenderly watching over his own, that is, over these very men who have sinfully neglected to watch with him! According to Mark, Jesus added **It is enough.** [740] It may well be impossible to determine exactly what he had in mind when he said this. Could he have meant, "There have been enough attempts to keep y o u awake and watching"? "Enough reproof"? But these are guesses. We do not know. **The Son of man is being betrayed into the hands of sinners.**

The vigil was of short duration. After just a little while Jesus could see the approaching band. He now rouses the three men by saying: **42. Get up! Let us be going. Look, my betrayer is near.** [741] Going where? Away as far as possible from the approaching band? Fleeing? No, the very opposite: going forward to meet those who have come to arrest Jesus; yes, to meet them, including Judas!

---

43 And immediately, while he [Jesus] was still speaking, Judas, one of the twelve, arrived, and with him a crowd (armed) with swords and clubs, from the chief priests and the scribes and the elders.   44 Now he who was betraying him had given them a signal, saying, "The one I kiss is the man; grab him and lead him away under guard." [742] 45 And when he came, he immediately stepped up to him, saying, "Rabbi," and kissed

---

739 The original—here rendered, "Sleep on now and take y o u r rest"—is Καθεύδετε τὸ λοιπὸν καὶ ἀναπαύεσθε (Matt. 26:45 and Mark 14:41). Reasons for rejecting other translations are given in N.T.C. on Matthew, p. 920, footnote 848.

740 ἀπέχει, third per. s. pres. indic. of ἀπέχω, here used impersonally; cf. use in 7:6: "is (far) from." Also see Matt. 6:2, 5, 16, where the meaning seems to be *to receive in full*. See also N.T.C. on Phil. 4:18. In Acts 15:20, 29; I Thess. 4:3; 5:22; I Tim. 4:3; and I Peter 2:11 the sense is *abstain from;* and in Philem. 15: *was parted from.*

741 In "Get up . . . Let us be going" we have the combination of a sec. per. pl. pres. imperat. and a first per. pl. pres. hortative subjunctive. "My betrayer," literally: the one (who is) betraying me. Finally, ἤγγικε is third per. s. perf. indic. of ἐγγίζω, and has the usual meaning *has come near*, hence *is near.*

742 Or: safely.

him fervently. [743]   46 They laid their hands on Jesus and arrested him.   47 And one of the bystanders drew his sword and struck the highpriest's servant, cutting off his ear.

48 Jesus answered and said to them, "As against a robber [744] did y o u come out, with swords and clubs to seize me?   49 Every day I was with y o u in the temple teaching, and y o u did not arrest me. But (this happened) in order that the scriptures might be fulfilled."   50 And they all left him and fled.

14:43-50 *The Betrayal and Seizure of Jesus*
Cf. Matt. 26:47-56; Luke 22:47-53; John 18:2-12

The story here told is found in all four Gospels. By far the longest reports are those in Matthew and in John, of approximately equal length. Covering about two-thirds as much space as either of these are the accounts, also nearly equal in size, found in Mark and in Luke.

Leaving out minor details, the main variations are as follows:

Though Matthew and Mark, as often, run closely parallel, Matthew contains one important item not found in Mark, namely, the expostulation which Jesus addressed to the man [Peter, according to John 18:10] who had struck the highpriest's servant and had cut off his ear. This reprimand, found in Matt. 26:52-54, ends, as not unusual in Matthew, with a reference to fulfilment of prophecy.

As to Mark, except for the mention of "scribes" (14:43) and the words, "and lead him away under guard" (14:44), this evangelist reports nothing that cannot be found in Matthew. But is not the very brevity of Mark's account—it is almost all *action*—an element that contributes to its sparkling vividness?

Luke's account contains the following items not found elsewhere: *a.* "Judas, are you betraying the Son of man with a kiss?"; *b.* "Lord, shall we smite with a sword?"; *c.* "Jesus touched the man's ear and healed him"; and *d.* "But this is y o u r hour and the power of darkness."

Peculiar (either entirely or to a large extent) to John are the following bits of information:

a. "Judas knew this place [Gethsemane], for Jesus often met there with his disciples"; *b.* "So Judas took the cohort and some officers from the chief priests and the Pharisees, and went there with torches and lanterns and weapons." *c.* the story showing how Jesus took the initiative, advanced up to the group and said, "For whom are y o u looking?" When the commander and others with him answered, "For Jesus, the Nazarene," Jesus answered, "I am he." "They lurched backward and fell to the ground." Jesus repeated his question and received the same answer. Jesus answered, "I told y o u

---

[743] Or: again and again.
[744] Or: insurrectionist, revolutionist, rebel.

that I am he. Therefore if y o u are looking for me, let these men go their way." By inspiration John sees in this incident the fulfilment of words spoken earlier by Jesus. See N.T.C. on John, Vol. II, p. 380. *d.* John informs us that the name of the servant whose right ear Peter had struck off with the sword was Malchus, and that Jesus responded to Peter's rash deed by saying, "Put your sword into the sheath. The cup the Father has given me, shall I not drink it?"

* * *

Though the story, as always, is definitely and basically that about *Jesus,* what was done to *him* and how *he* reacted, on the surface the actors in this very dramatic happening are brought to the forefront in the following order: Judas (verses 43-45), the band that came to arrest Jesus (verse 46), one of the bystanders (Peter, verse 47), Jesus (verses 48, 49), and the disciples (verse 50).

Judas

43. And immediately, while he [Jesus] was still speaking, Judas, one of the twelve, arrived, and with him a crowd (armed) with swords and clubs, from the chief priests and the scribes and the elders.

"So, having taken the morsel, Judas went out immediately, and it was night." So reads John 13:30. Where did he go? He must have hurried off to the chief priests, etc., the men who had hired him. Was he afraid that once his treachery became known the alarm would spread and from everywhere friends of Jesus—think especially of the many from Galilee, now in the city—would gather in his defense? "Act quickly," he must have told the Jewish authorities, "preferably by night, when no crowds are around. Act tonight." The authorities had been waiting for him. So busy were they with this plot to destroy Jesus that, as explained in N.T.C. on John, Vol. II, pp. 401-404 (on John 18:28), they had not yet partaken of the Passover meal. The probable whereabouts of Jesus had to be ascertained; a posse had to be organized; the temple police must be notified; permission must be obtained, whether from Pilate, which in view of Matt. 27:62-65 seems probable, or from the Roman "chiliarch," so that a group of soldiers could accompany the temple police; all the members of the Sanhedrin must be alerted; Annas must not be left in the dark; lanterns, swords, and clubs must be collected; the need of secrecy must be emphasized to all those who are "in" on this; etc. etc.

Finally, then, all is in readiness. Now to find Jesus. Judas did not know for certain where the group might have gone after leaving the Upper Room, but since he knew that Gethsemane was the place often visited by the Master and his disciples (John 18:2), the traitor was able to make a good guess, one that proved to be correct. So, while Jesus was still talking to the three disciples, Judas was seen entering the grove. "Judas, one of the twelve," says the text, to emphasize the terrible character of the crime this man was committing. See on verse 10 and note repetition of "one of the twelve" in verse 20. Since he was "one of the twelve," it would be impossible to mention all the privileges that had been bestowed upon him during the many days, weeks, and months he had spent in Christ's immediate company. Such confidence had the other eleven resposed in this same Judas that they had even made him their treasurer. And now he was proving himself totally unworthy of all these honors and advantages, of all this trust. A shameless, disgusting quisling he had become, a wretched turncoat, one who for the paltry sum of thirty pieces of silver was delivering over to the enemy the greatest Benefactor whose feet ever trod this earth, even the Mediator, both God and man, the Lord Jesus Christ.

No one knows exactly how the crowd that accompanied Judas was arranged, if it be even correct to speak about any order or arrangement. If any guess be permissible it would be as follows:

In front Judas. This, at least, seems rather well established. The crowd is said to be "with him." Besides, he is the one who is going to "step up to Jesus" (verse 45), to point him out to the others. The highpriest's personal servant, Malchus, must also have been near the front (14:47; Luke 18:10) and so were also probably the temple police, Levites (14:49; cf. John 18:3). The detachment of soldiers, together with their commander, cannot have been far behind (John 18:3, 12). John 18:3 mentions a "cohort," probably obtained from the tower of Antonia, situated at the northwest corner of the temple area. Though a cohort at full strength consisted of six hundred men (the tenth of a legion), the Roman authorities would probably not have depleted their garrison to that extent. At any rate, the band must have been rather large.

But why Roman legionaries at all? Would not the temple police have sufficed? The answer is that the Sanhedrin had learned that these officers could not always be relied on. Who knows, they might even side with Jesus, as had happened once before. See John 7:32, 45. Hence, it was felt that a detachment of soldiers was also needed. And because the Roman authorities themselves were very desirous of preventing trouble in Jerusalem, especially during Passover, when there was always danger of Jewish rebellion, the requested legionaries were quickly obtained.

Perhaps somewhat farther toward the back were members of the Sanhedrin (Luke 22:52). Whether any others were present we cannot be certain. Even Matt. 26:55 does not necessarily imply this.

The force that had been commissioned to capture Jesus was well equipped. The men carried swords and clubs. As to the first, these were probably the short swords carried by the heavily armed Roman soldier. See N.T.C. on Ephesians, p. 279, including footnote 177. The clubs or cudgels, we may assume, were in the hands of the temple police. Absolute certainty in such matters is not possible. Words have histories, which in the present case means that the term used in the original for "swords" may at times have a more general meaning. It was not always used to distinguish these weapons from the broadswords. Also, we cannot be entirely certain that none but soldiers carried swords. Did not even Peter have a sword? See verse 47. All we really know is that those who came to arrest Jesus carried swords and clubs. Their distribution is not definitely indicated, though it is natural to think of soldiers equipped with swords. The Gospel of John also mentions "torches and lanterns." Torches and lanterns—to search for the Light of the world. And it was full moon! Swords and cudgels—to subdue the Prince of Peace. For the Man of Sorrows the very sight of this band of ruffians, which considered him their quarry, meant indescribable suffering.—And to think that the men who were supposed to be leaders in Israel, highly religious and devout, chief priests and scribes and elders, together composing the Sanhedrin, had sent this force. Instead of welcoming Jesus as the long-expected Messiah, they were sending a posse to capture him, with the ultimate purpose of having him brought before the authorities that he might be sentenced to death! For more on chief priests, scribes, and elders, see above, on 14:1.

44, 45. Now he who was betraying him had given them a signal, [745] saying, The one I kiss is the man; grab him and lead him away under guard. And when he came, he immediately stepped up to him, saying, Rabbi, and kissed him fervently. There are those who say that a kiss was the customary way of greeting a rabbi. However that may be, we may be sure that then as well as today—though more so in certain regions of the globe than in others—a kiss was the symbol of friendship and affection. As used by Judas, however, it was the prearranged signal for the arresting band to grab Jesus and, as Mark adds, to lead him away "safely" or "under guard" (cf. Acts 16:23). To be sure, Judas already has his money (Matt. 26:15), but he also knows that he will not be able to keep it until he has made sure that the one he is betraying is actually in the hands of the Sanhedrin.

So, having arrived in Gethsemane, in front of the posse that had been dispatched to arrest Jesus, Judas, on seeing Jesus, steps forward to a position directly in front of him. He then greets him by saying "Rabbi," or, as Matthew has it, "Hello, Rabbi." Does the fact that Judas addresses Jesus

---

745 σύσσημον, in the New Testament only here. For the occurrence of this word elsewhere see M.M., p. 617.

thus and not as "Lord," indicate disrespect? We must be very careful here. It is true that at the Passover meal, when all the other disciples said, "Surely not I, Lord?" but Judas alone said, "Surely not I, Rabbi" (respectively Matt. 26:22 and 25), the contrast between the two modes of address is so obvious that it may well have been intentional. In the present case, however, there is no basis for any comparison. On the whole it remains true that "Rabbi," in addressing Jesus, was very common, especially during the earlier and middle part of Jesus' ministry (Mark 9:5; John 1:38, 49; 3:2; 4:31; 6:25; 9:2). Nathanael certainly did not show any lack of respect when he thus addressed Jesus; rather the opposite, as the context indicates (John 1:49). And even during the latter part of his ministry the term was not in disuse (John 11:8), and Jesus himself approved of it (Matt. 23:8). All we can safely say is that there is some evidence for the fact that, with the increase of reverence for Jesus, "Lord" was gradually substituted for "Rabbi." See N.T.C. on John, Vol. I, p. 103, footnote 44. After Christ's resurrection "Rabbi" disappears, and "Lord" is used with great regularity. In the present instance (Mark 14:45) it is probably best to concentrate rather on what Judas *did* instead of on what he *said*.

And what he did has caused all later generations to recoil with horror at the mere mention of his name. Embracing Jesus he kissed him—probably fervently or repeatedly. [746]

For the striking response of Jesus see Matt. 26:50 ("Friend, for this are you here?"), and see N.T.C. on that passage. And do not forget Luke 22:48 ("Judas, are you betraying the Son of man with a kiss?"). It is clear that even at this very late moment Jesus was earnestly warning Judas. For his everlasting perdition he had only himself to blame!

The band that came to arrest Jesus

46. They laid their hands on Jesus and arrested him. For the details see John 18:4-9 and N.T.C. on those verses. John 18:3, 12 shows that the arrest was made by *a.* the soldiers and their chiliarch (commander) and *b.* the temple guards. Gentiles and Jews combine against Jesus. Cf. Acts 4:27. John's Gospel, moreover, makes it clear that before allowing himself to be bound Jesus demonstrated his power over his captors, proving that he voluntarily surrendered himself to them, in line with John 10:11b, 15b. In this capture it was the Captive who triumphed!

---

[746] It is a well-known fact that the prefixes in such compounds as the one here used—κατεφίλησε—often lose their intensive force. Nevertheless, the use of the simple form of the verb in verse 44—φιλήσω first per. sing. aor. subjunctive of φιλέω—contrasted with the compound form in the next verse, probably points to the strengthened connotation in this second case.

One of the bystanders

47. **And one of the bystanders drew his sword and struck the highpriest's servant, cutting off his ear.** [747] By this time the eight disciples have joined Jesus. See verse 50 and cf. Luke 22:49. One of those standing near goes into action. Although the incident is related in all four Gospels, only John (18:10) mentions the names of the two persons who (in addition to Jesus himself) figured most prominently in it. These two were Peter and Malchus, the highpriest's servant. The reason why John alone mentions these two names may well have been that when he published his Gospel it was no longer possible to punish the assailant.

That assailant or "bystander" was Simon Peter. Emboldened perhaps by the marvelous triumph of Jesus over the men who had come to capture him—at first the would-be captors, at the word of Jesus, had lurched backward and fallen to the ground (John 18:6)—, and impelled by his own previous boasts (Matt. 26:33, 35; Mark 14:29, 31; Luke 22:33; John 13:37), Simon drew his short sword from its scabbard. Then he sprang at Malchus and, probably because the servant saw what was coming and quickly jumped aside, cut off his ear. Peter probably still believed that the Messiah must not die. Cf. Matt. 16:22.

Mark says nothing about Jesus' reaction to Peter's rash action. What did the Master *say* about it? See Matt. 26:52-54. What did he *do* about it? See Luke 22:51.

The attention is now focused entirely upon

Jesus

48, 49. **Jesus answered and said to them, As against a robber [or: rebel] did y o u come out, with swords and clubs to seize me? Every day I was with y o u in the temple teaching, and y o u did not arrest me.**

As has been pointed out earlier, the word "answered" does not always mean "replied verbally to a question"; it may also mean, as here, "reacted to a situation." Right then and there Jesus, though bound, addressed the crowds. The venerable members of the Sanhedrin were also present (Luke 22:52). See above, on 14:43. Of course, they had no business being here during this sacred night, but were so anxious to see whether their sinister plot against the enemy would succeed that they were actually to be seen

---

747 σπασάμενος, nom. s. masc. aor. middle particple of σπάω. ἔπαισε, third per. s. aor. act. indic. of παίω. ἀφεῖλε, third per. s. aor. act. indic. of ἀφαιρέω. ὠτάριον and ὠτίον (Matt. 26:51) are diminutives of οὖς (outer) ear. Probably by this time these diminutives had lost most or all of their diminutive force. See above, Introduction IV, footnote 5; and also see on Mark 3:9, footnote 108.

among this crowd, probably in the rear. See N.T.C. on John, Vol. II, pp. 403, 404. Jesus, then, pointed out to the crowds—to all those who had come to arrest him and all those who gloated over his capture—how cowardly and perfidiously they were behaving. They had come out against him with an army, equipped with swords and clubs, as if he were a highwayman or, as the text can also be rendered, an insurrectionist, rebel, or revolutionary. In reality he was and had been a quiet, peaceful Prophet, sitting day by day in the temple, teaching the people. His life had been an open book. Had he been guilty of any crimes, those in charge of law and order would have had every chance to seize him.

If anyone wishes to know what kind of person this Jesus had proved himself to be during the slightly more than three years of his public ministry, let him read such passages as Mark 1:39; 10:13-16; and see also Matt. 4:23-25; 11:25-30; 12:18-21; Luke 22:49-51; 24:19; John 6:15; 18:11, 36, 37; Acts 2:22. To say, as some have done, that Jesus was "harmless" is putting it too mildly. He was and is "the Savior of the world" (John 4:42; I John 4:14), the world's greatest Benefactor. How absurd and hypocritical it was for the foe in the hour of darkness to pounce upon this Good Shepherd, from whom no one who heeded his message had anything to fear, and who even taught people to love their enemies! See Matt. 5:44.

By addressing the crowds in this manner Jesus was in reality doing them a favor. He was exposing their guilt. Is it not true that it takes confession of guilt to bring about salvation? Though it is a fact that by far the most of those who heard Jesus speak these words hardened themselves in sin, we have no right to conclude that the message, together with other messages that followed (for example, the seven words from the cross, Peter's Pentecost address, etc.), was completely ineffective. See, for example, Acts 6:7. The impression left upon us by these words of our Lord is that they were spoken in a calm and earnest manner. To be sure, Jesus rebukes, but at the same time he is even now seeking the lost, that he may save them.

He adds: **But (this happened) in order that the scriptures might be fulfilled.** Had it not been for God's eternal decree for man's salvation, a decree reflected in the prophets (Isa. 53:7, 10, 12; Jer. 23:6; Dan. 9:26; Zech. 11:12; 13:1; etc.), these captors could have accomplished nothing at all! Cf. John 19:11.

The Disciples

50. And they all left him and fled. As was indicated previously, verse 27 is being fulfilled here. Notice: *all,* not only the eight but also the three; not only two of the three (James and John) but even Peter, in spite of his grandiloquent boasts and tremendous promises. It is but fair to add that a little later two (Peter and John) recovered themselves, turned around and started following at a safe distance (see verse 54; cf. John 18:15). It is, however, also only fair to add that for Peter this "following..." had disastrous results (verse 66 f.).

All these eleven disciples heaped shame upon themselves. Peter's case was especially bad. Somewhat later Thomas, too, failed miserably (John 20: 24 f.). Best of all is John. See John 18:15, 16. Not only does he enter the highpriest's palace, where Jesus was tried, but we even see him—of all the eleven disciples *him alone,* as far as the record goes!—at the cross (John 19:25-27). Was he perhaps the one who had boasted least? There is a lesson here!

The main lesson, nevertheless, is not connected with Peter or Thomas or John. Our eyes should be riveted on the Lamb of God who was taking away the sin of the world. Forsaken by all, in order that all who believe in him would never be forsaken! Voluntarily Jesus entered into this state of desertion, abandonment. It was to become an increasing horror. The climax is reached in Mark 15:34.

---

51 And a certain young man, with only a linen cloth thrown about his body, was following him; and they seized him.   52 He left the linen cloth behind, and escaped naked.

14:51, 52 *The Young Man Who Escaped*

This incident is reported only by Mark. It covers only two verses. There is no need to reprint them in bold type.

Before summarizing what I, along with many others, believe to be the true meaning of this short report, let me briefly tell the reader what two advocates of "redaction criticism" [748] have done with it. In order not to be guilty even in the slightest degree of misrepresenting their view we urge the readers to read the article itself. The two authors, who have spent much labor on it, deserve that much consideration.

Briefly, then, they affirm that what is here presented by whoever it was that wrote it makes no sense as an actual, historical incident. On a night in early spring no person in that climate would go outside wearing only one piece of clothing. Also, when these verses are taken literally, they would be the report of a trivial incident, one in which the Marcan author would not have been interested.

---

748 R. Scroggs and K. I. Groff, "Baptism in Mark: Dying and Rising With Christ," JBL 92 (Dec. 1973), pp. 531-548.—The basic idea, namely, that there is a connection between Mark 14:51, 52 and 16:5, has also been accepted by others. See S. E. Johnson, *op. cit.,* p. 238.

What then? According to the composers of the article, Mark 14:51, 52 must be interpreted symbolically. Also, it should be studied in connection with 16:5, which informs us that some women, having entered the tomb early Sunday morning, saw a young man dressed in a white robe. The two young men—the one of 14:51, 52 and the one of 16:5—are really one and the same person. His nakedness and flight in 14:51, 52 symbolizes dying with Christ. His reappearance (16:5) in a bright new garment indicates rising with Christ. In 14:51, 52 he is symbolically baptized; in 16:5 he emerges in his sparkling new baptismal robe.

Objections:

a. Why should it be unnatural for a *young* man, who is in a hurry, to rush outside even at this time of the year, with only a piece of linen cloth wrapped around himself? In similar circumstances, do not things of this character happen frequently?

b. If, as accepted by many, this dramatic near-capture befell the author himself, would it have been considered "trivial" *by him*?

c. Nowhere does Scripture establish any connection between the young man of 14:51, 52 and the young man of 16:5. Then what right have we to do so? Matthew (28:5) calls this "young man" an *angel*. Luke speaks of "two men in dazzling apparel" (24:4), "angels" (verse 23).

d. Neither in Mark 14 nor in 16:1-8 is anything said about *baptism*. What right, then, have we to inject a reference to baptism into these passages?

e. The account reads as if it were a report of an actual, literal, historical happening. The style is the same as in the immediately preceding context (verses 43-50, Jesus' betrayal and seizure) and in the immediately following (verses 53-65, his trial before the Sanhedrin). If these two passages record what actually happened, why not verses 51, 52?

Having disposed of the "redaction criticism" theory, what do I believe to be the true explanation? First of all, in a footnote [749] I briefly summarize the various views respectively advanced by several commentators. Anyone interested can read them.

---

[749] *First,* there are those who either say, "The young man was not Mark," or simply "We do not know who he was."

a. Lenski rejects every effort to identify the young man of 14:51, 52, and believes that the incident simply shows the temper of the captors of Jesus (*op. cit.,* pp. 410, 411).

b. With respect to the young man's identity Bolkestein (*op. cit.,* p. 334) also simply states, "We do not know."

c. Swete (*op. cit.,* p. 354), though remaining non-committal with respect to the identity of the young man, states that the theory that he resided in the house of the Upper Room and the view that he was the evangelist himself, are not incompatible.

d. Taylor (*op. cit.,* pp. 561, 562) thinks that the young man was probably not Mark. If Mark, there would have been more details.

Secondly, there are those—the majority by far—who either *lean toward* the position that the young man was Mark, or rather positively so *assert.*

Secondly, I here present my own view. Certainty with respect to the young man's identity is impossible. Nevertheless, the probability that he was Mark, a position already stated in *Introduction I,* would seem to have the following evidence on its side:

a. Neither Matthew nor Luke has retained this item. It does not appear to have been of special interest to them. But to Mark, to him alone, it was of sufficient importance to be included in his Gospel. This is understandable if he himself was that young man.

b. The apostle John, too, refers to himself without mentioning his name (John 18:15, 16; 19:26, 27; 20:2-8; 21:7, 20, 23, 24).

c. By itself the item is rather insignificant, except if it refers to what the author, Mark, himself experienced that solemn night.

To the reconstructed story as found in *Introduction I* it is necessary to add that several modifications are possible and have actually been suggested by various authors; for example:

a. Granted that the young man was awakened by the departure of Jesus and the eleven from the house with the Upper Room, when did his near-capture occur? *If* there is a close temporal connection between verses 51, 52 and the immediately preceding verse ("And they all left him and fled"), then it occurred in connection with the flight of the eleven. *They* fled. *He* did not, and consequently was pursued and barely escaped. If there is no such temporal connection, the near-capture may have occurred earlier. We just do not know.

b. It is also possible that the young man was awakened from his sleep— assuming that he slept!—a little later. The situation may have been as follows: Judas and his band arrived at Mark's house, thinking that Jesus was

---

a. Van Leeuwen (*op. cit.,* pp. 187, 188) opines that Mark is a guess that may well be correct.

b. Gould (*op. cit.,* p. 276) thinks that the very failure of the author to mention the name of this young man, plus the mention of the incident at all, may well point to Mark.

c. Robertson (*Word Pictures,* Vol. I, p. 386) also leans toward the theory that the young man was Mark, in whose house the group had probably observed the Passover meal.

d. Among others who are of the same opinion, with certain reservations, are M.-J. Lagrange, *Evangile selon Saint Marc,* Paris, pp. 396, 397; and A. E. J. Rawlinson, *St. Mark,* London, 1925, pp. 215, 216.

e. Th. Zahn, *Introduction to the New Testament,* English tr. Edinburgh, 1909, p. 494, leans strongly toward Mark. So does Barclay, *op. cit.,* p. 365.

f. Cole, also leaning toward Mark, very aptly adds, "It seems unnecessary and unfair to spiritualize an incident like this; it is stated as a plain fact, and as such it must be accepted, whatever spiritual lessons we may then see fit to associate with the event" (*op. cit.,* p. 224).

Thirdly, the following views with respect to the identity of the young man have not found much support: the apostle Paul (Ewald), the apostle John (Ambrose), James, the brother of Jesus (Epiphanius). This holds too with respect to the idea of F. C. Grant (*op. cit.,* p. 886) that Mark 14:51, 52 was suggested by Amos 2:16.

still there. The commotion caused by their disappointment awakens Mark. With the linen quickly wrapped around himself he, sensing what is happening, rushes out in order to warn the already departed Jesus. He arrives in Gethsemane just as the eleven are fleeing and Jesus is being led away. As he is following Jesus, the near-capture occurs.

c. We are not at all certain that the house with the Upper Room was the one mentioned in Acts 12:12. It may have been, but a possibility is not necessarily a fact. If it was not, then this, too, would affect the course of events at least to some extent. All further speculation would be useless.

What is certain, however, is that the escape of the young man, whom most commentators, not without reason, consider to have been John Mark, was dramatic. His would-be captors grabbed him and would have captured him had it not been for his amazing dexterity shown in disengaging himself, in a flash, from his linen cloth, shirt, sheet, or whatever it was. [750]

The contents of 14:51, 52 having now been treated as referring to an actual, historical incident, something that was in all probability experienced by the author of the book, namely, John Mark, is it possible, without doing violence to sober exegesis, to derive any lessons from this passage or from 14:43-52 as a whole?

The answer might well be that what stands out is:

a. The unshakable and majestic composure of Jesus (14:48, 49; Luke 22:48, 51; John 18:4, 5, 8) over against the fear and nervousness of those around him: captors lurch backward and fall to the ground (John 18:6); disciples flee (Mark 14:50).

b. His willingness to be isolated for the sake of his people. All left him and fled: the eleven, including even Peter; also the young man of Mark 14:51, 52. *Alone* he faces his enemies, *alone* he suffers, and *alone* he is going to lay down his life, in order that all those who accept him as their Savior and Lord may never be alone. Hallelujah, what a Savior!

---

53 They led Jesus away to the highpriest; and all the chief priests and the elders and the scribes were assembled. 54 And from a distance Peter followed right into the highpriest's courtyard. There he was sitting with the officers and warming himself near the fire. 55 Now the chief priests and the entire Sanhedrin were seeking to obtain evidence against Jesus to put him to death, but were not finding any. 56 For, though many were bearing false testimony against him, their testimonies did not agree. [751]

---

750 συνδών. The word occurring here (in verse 51 and again in verse 52) is also found in Matt. 27:59 and its parallels: Mark 15:46; Luke 23:53, where it indicates the linen cloth in which the body of Jesus was wrapped. "Sindon," though archaic, is still a good English word. It indicates a fine fabric, especially one of linen. Was the young man's sindon a shirt, tunic, bed-sheet? We do not know. περιβεβλημένος, nom. masc. s. perf. passive participle of περιβάλλω. συνηκολούθει, third per. s. imperfect indic. of συνακολουθέω. Cf. acolyte. ἔφυγε, third per. s. aor. of φεύγω.

751 Literally: were not equal. So also in verse 59.

57 Then some stood up and were giving this false testimony against him: 58 "We heard him saying, 'I will destroy this temple made by (human) hands, and in three days I will build another not made by (human) hands.'" 59 But not even so did their testimony agree.

60 Then the highpriest arose, came forward and asked Jesus, "You don't answer? What is it that these men are testifying against you?" 61 But he remained silent and did not answer. [752] Again the highpriest was questioning him, saying, "Are you the Christ, the Son of the Blessed?" 62 Jesus said, "I am, and y o u will see

the Son of man
sitting at the right hand of the Power
and coming with the clouds of heaven."

63 Then the highpriest tore his clothes and asked, "What need do we still have of witnesses? 64 Y o u have heard his blasphemy. What do y o u think?" They all condemned him as being worthy of death. 65 And some began to spit at him, to blindfold him, to strike him with their fists, and to say to him, "Prophesy!" and the officers received him with blows. [753]

14:53-65 *The Trial before the Sanhedrin*
Cf. Matt. 26:57-68; Luke 22:54, 55, 63-65; [754] John 18:24 [755]

A comparison of the Matthew-Mark parallels reveals the following:

Mark 14:53 mentions all three of the Sanhedrin's component groups; Matthew 26:57 omits the chief priests.

While both Gospels mention the fact that Peter was sitting with the officers, Matthew (verse 58) adds "to see the outcome"; Mark (verse 54), "warming himself near the fire."

The testimony of the false witnesses—Matthew "two," Mark "some"—is more fully reproduced in Mark (verse 58) than in Matthew (verse 61). Moreover, Mark adds, "But not even so did their testimony agree."

Matthew's " . . . whether you are the Christ, the Son of God" (verse 63) parallels Mark's " . . . Are you the Christ, the Son of the Blessed?" (verse 61). Moreover, it is Matthew alone who informs us that the highpriest was putting Jesus under oath.

Matthew (verse 67) omits Mark's item (verse 65) that during the mockery Jesus was blindfolded.

Luke 22:54, 55 may be called an abbreviated reproduction of Mark

---

752 Or: and answered nothing.

753 Or: slaps in the face.

754 Strictly speaking, verses 66-71 of Luke 22 do not belong here, for they record what happened early in the morning. They constitute a parallel to Mark 14:53-65 and to Matt. 26:57-68 only in the sense that certain passages in this Luke portion closely resemble the Matthew and Mark references. This simply means that certain questions asked during the night were repeated during the early morning trial.

755 As to John 18, only verse 24, "Then Annas sent him bound to Caiaphas the highpriest" belongs here. John 18:12-14, 19-23 do not belong here but describe Christ's preliminary hearing before Annas, as is explained in N.T.C. on John, Vol. II, pp. 385-387.

14:53, 54. With very little change Luke 22:63, 64 reproduces Mark 14:65. Note, however, Mark's "spit at him," where Luke has "mocked him." In verse 65 Luke adds, "And they were saying many other insulting things to him."

* * * *

To understand Mark 14:53-65 and that which follows in chapter 15 it is necessary to bear in mind that Jesus had to undergo two trials. The first has often been called the ecclesiastical trial; the second, the civil. The first contained three stages, and so did the second. The three stages of the so-called ecclesiastical trial were: *a.* the preliminary hearing before Annas (John 18:12-14, 19-23); *b.* the trial before the Sanhedrin, that is, before the highpriest, the chief priests, elders, and scribes (Mark 14:53); and *c.* the trial before the same body just after daybreak (Mark 15:1). The three stages in the trial before the civil authorities were: *a.* the trial before Pilate, *b.* that before Herod, and *c.* that before Pilate resumed. Just as it is true that the preliminary hearing before Annas is found only in John's Gospel, so also Christ's appearance before Herod is recorded only by Luke (23:6-12).

In our present paragraph (Mark 14:53-65), therefore, it is assumed that the preliminary hearing before Annas has been held.

53. They led Jesus away to the highpriest; and all the chief priests and the elders and the scribes were assembled. As Matt. 26:3 informs us, the highpriest was Caiaphas. He occupied that office from A.D. 18-36, and was son-in-law of Annas (John 18:13). He was a rude and sly manipulator, and opportunist, who did not know the meaning of fairness or justice and who was bent on having his own way "by hook or by crook" (Matt. 26:3, 4; John 11:49). He did not shrink from shedding innocent blood. What he himself ardently craved for selfish purposes, he made to look as if it were the one thing needful for the welfare of the people. In order to bring about the condemnation of Jesus, who had aroused his envy (Matt. 27:18), he was willing to use devices which were the product of clever calculation and unprecedented boldness. He was a hypocrite, as will become evident (see below, on verse 63).

Note that we are distinctly told that "all the chief priests and the elders and the scribes were assembled." Accordingly, this must have been an assembly of the Sanhedrin, not just a few members but a goodly number being present. For "chief priests, elders, and scribes" (or: "scribes and elders") cf. 14:43 and see on 14:1. It is to the palace of (Annas, John 18:13, 15, 24, and of) Caiaphas (see N.T.C. on John, Vol. II, p. 391) that Jesus was led.

54. And from a distance Peter followed right into the highpriest's court-

yard. There he was sitting with the officers and warming himself [756] near [757] the fire. Though all the disciples had fled, two—Peter and "another disciple"—soon rallied and began to follow the band that was leading Jesus to the highpriest's palace. In the case of Peter, "following Jesus" was probably prompted, in part, by the loud boasts he had uttered, as recorded in verses 29 and 31; in part also, by sheer curiosity, as Matt. 26:58 states, and perhaps we should add, in part by love for his Master. How this disciple secured admission to the palace is described in John 18:15, 16. Peter, then, having been allowed to enter the palace by its outer gate, walked through the archway that led to the unroofed courtyard, where he sat down with the palace servants and the temple guards (policemen), warming himself near the fire. By this time most of the soldiers, having delivered their prisoner, had probably returned to the fortress of Antonia. The record of Peter's first denial, which here in verse 54 is merely introduced, is found in 66-68; Matt. 26:69, 70; Luke 22:54-57; and John 18:15-18. The story now returns to Christ's trial before the Sanhedrin.

55, 56. Now the chief priests and the entire Sanhedrin were seeking to obtain evidence against Jesus to put him to death, but were not finding any. For, though many were bearing false testimony against him, their testimonies did not agree. [758]

It is clear as daylight that by means of these verses, and others like them, Scripture blames "the chief priests and the entire Sanhedrin" for the death of Jesus.

Not the masses but the leaders—chief priests, Pharisees, Caiaphas—are mentioned in John 11:53 as the ones who plotted Christ's death. Jesus uttered his *Seven Woes* (Matt. 23) not against the mob but against "scribes and Pharisees, hypocrites." When Pilate at Jesus' trial before him said to the multitude, "I am bringing him out to y o u in order that y o u may know that I find no crime in him," it was the chief priests and their officers who shouted "crucify (him), crucify (him)" (John 19:6; cf. verses 15, 16). The priest-ridden mob followed the example of the leaders, as Matt. 27:20-23 makes very clear. See also Matt. 27:25; Acts 3:13-15; 4:27; I Thess. 2:14, 15. It is as the passage now under study (Mark 14:55, 56) clearly attests, blame for the murder of Jesus rests especially on the religious leaders of that day. Nevertheless, by no means is it possible, on scriptural grounds, entirely to excuse those who followed the example of these leaders. Rather, all those who took part in the crime or were in agreement with it share the blame.

---

[756] Note pleasing contrast between ἠκολούθησε, aorist, and ἦν συγκαθήμενος . . . καὶ θερμαινόμενος, periphrastic imperfects.

[757] Note πρός in the sense of *near*, as in 11:1.

[758] Mark's account is very vivid. Note the imperfects: were seeking, were not finding (verse 55), were bearing false testimony (verse 56 and again in the next verse).

This firm belief, moreover, is not a manifestation of hostility toward Jews (anti-Semitism). The very opposite is the truth. It is because we love the Jews that we desire to become the means in God's hand to bring them to Christ, and thus also into the fellowship of the church. We feel for these people. In fact, in a sense we stand where they stand, for we made common cause with them against Jesus. Not that we plotted his death, as did *their* ancestors. Yet it remains true that we, yes even we ourselves, killed Jesus, for our sins nailed him to the cross. But by that very crucified and risen Christ we were saved. [759]

Opposition against this view has arisen from many sides. Ecumenical assemblies have published "declarations" exculpating the Jews from responsibility for the death of Jesus. Some of these decrees have been good, some hardly in keeping with historical facts. Moreover, the Jews themselves, as could be expected, have gone even farther in striving to absolve themselves from blame. Thus, Haim Cohn, an internationally famous specialist in Jewish legal tradition, argues [760] that Annas and Caiaphas, "did all that they possibly and humanly could to save Jesus, whom they dearly loved and cherished as one of their own." And Hugh J. Schonfield states that the only way for the church once and for all to remove the stigma from the Jews is to renounce the absolute reliability of the sacred documents. [761]

From an entirely different direction doubt has also been cast upon the contents of Mark 14:55, 56. In connection with "Now the chief priests and the entire Sanhedrin were seeking to obtain evidence against Jesus to put him to death. . . ." Taylor [762] remarks that apparently Mark thought of the meeting as a full session of the council, but that it is doubtful that it actually had this character, especially if it was a night session. He then defends the view that Luke (22:66-71) is not in agreement with Mark's position and teaches that the trial took place on the following morning. Now it is indeed true that the *night* session of the Sanhedrin, introduced in Mark 14:53, 54, 55, especially in its confrontation between Jesus and the highpriest (verses 61-64a; cf. Matt. 26:63-65), resembles the *early morning* session as pictured in Luke 22:69-71. Shall we say, then, that Mark errs, ascribing to a night session that which actually happened "when day came" (Luke 22:66)? Not at all. There is a problem here, but the ascription of an error to Mark by no means solves that problem. After all, the two sessions are not the same. At night it was the *highpriest* who asked Jesus, "Are you the Christ?" (Mark

---

759 With little change the last two paragraphs—beginning with "Not the masses"—were taken from my booklet *Israel in Prophecy*, Grand Rapids, 1972, See pp. 13, 14.
760 In his book, *The Trial and Death of Jesus*, 1971.
761 *The Passover Plot*, New York, 1965, pp. 140, 142.
762 *Op. cit.*, p. 565.

14:61). In the early morning session *"they all* said, 'Are you the Son of God, then?' " (Luke 22:70; cf. verse 66). In their respective commentaries on Luke 22:66 f. many commentators—including A. Plummer, R. C. H. Lenski, and N. Geldenhuys—point out this difference, and explain why it was deemed necessary to hold a morning session. We may rest assured, therefore, that there are no real contradictions.

For the absolutely sinless One to be subjected to a trial conducted by sinful men was in itself a deep humiliation. To be tried by *such* men, under *such* circumstances made it infinitely worse. Greedy, serpent-like, vindictive Annas (see on John 18:13), rude, sly, hypocritical Caiaphas (see on John 11:49, 50), crafty superstitious, self-seeking Pilate (see on John 18:29); and immoral, ambitious, superficial Herod Antipas; these were his judges!

In reality, the entire trial was a farce. It was a mis-trial. There was no intention at all of giving Jesus a fair hearing in order that it might be discovered, in strict conformity with the laws of evidence, whether or not the charges against him were just or unfounded. In the annals of juris-prudence no travesty of justice ever took place that was more shocking than this one. Moreover, in order to reach this conclusion it is not at all necessary to make a close study of all the technical points with reference to Jewish law of that day. It has been emphasized by various authors that the trial of Jesus was illegal on several technical grounds, such as the following: *a.* No trial for life was allowed during the night. Yet, Jesus was tried and condemned during the hours of 1-3 A.M. Friday, and executed on the Feast, which was forbidden. According to Pharisaic law, no hearings in a case involving capital punishment could even be initiated on the eve of a major festival like Passover. No conviction was allowed at night. To execute a sentence on the day of one of the great feasts was contrary to the established regulations. [763] *b.* The arrest of Jesus was effected as a result of a bribe, namely, the blood-money which Judas received. *c.* Jesus was asked to incriminate himself. *d.* In cases of capital punishment, Jewish law did not permit the sentence to be pronounced until the day after the accused had been convicted. Such and similar points of law have been mentioned again and again and used as arguments to prove the illegality of the entire procedure against Jesus of Nazareth.

Attempts have also been made to refute them, one by one, as if the Jewish authorities, also in their procedure against Jesus, acted strictly in accordance with legal regulations, and were uninfluenced by subjective considerations such as envy and malice. But all such attempts have failed miserably. With respect to law, order, and justice, as practiced by the Jewish leaders of the

---

[763] See Mishna, *Sanhedrin* IV.1.

first century A.D., history supplies the answer. Did the Jews really proceed in a legal manner when they murdered Stephen? Read Acts 6:8-15; 7:54, 58, 59. Did they show a painstaking regard for justice when they killed James, the Lord's brother? Study Josephus, *Jewish Antiquities* XX.200. Add to this the fifth century A.D. compilation of Jewish traditions about Jesus. It is called *Toledoth Jeshu* and it clearly charges the Jerusalem priesthood with responsibility for the conviction of Jesus. The truth is that the hair-splitting casuistry of rabbinic law had discovered all kinds of ways to circumvent its own regulations. All Caiaphas had to do was to say that the trial of Jesus at this time and under these conditions was in the interest of the people and of religion. [764]

To any fair-minded individual it must be evident at once that all these legal technicalities were but so many details. They do not touch the heart of the matter. The main point is nothing less than this: *it had been decided long ago that Jesus must be put to death* (see on Mark 14:1). *And the motive behind this decision was envy* (15:10). The Jewish leaders just could not "take" it that they were beginning to lose their hold upon the people and that Jesus of Nazareth had denounced and exposed them publicly. They were filled with rage because the new prophet had laid bare their hidden motives, and had called the temple court from which they derived much of their profit *a den of thieves*. On the surface, the dignified chief priests, elders, and scribes might try to put on an act by the seeming imperviousness of their demeanor; underneath they were vengefully nettled, convulsively agitated. They were thirsting for blood!

Hence, this is not a trial but a legal farce, a detestable plot, and the entire plot is *their own. They* devised it and *they* see to it that it is carried out. *Their* officers take part in the arrest of Jesus. *They* themselves were present! *They* seek the witnesses—*false* witnesses, of course—against Jesus, in order that *they* may put him to death (Matt. 26:59). *They* all condemn him as being deserving of death (Mark 14:64). "*They* (by means of *their* underlings) bind him and lead him away" (Mark 15:1). *They* deliver him to Pilate (John 18:28). Before Pilate *they* stir up the people to get Barabbas released in order that Jesus may be destroyed (Matt. 27:20). *They* intimidate Pilate, until at last the latter delivers Jesus up, to be crucified (John 19:12, 16). And even when he hangs upon the cross, *they* mock him, saying, "He saved others, himself he cannot save" (Mark 15:31).

---

[764] See G. Dalman, *Jesus-Jeshua*, New York, 1929, pp. 98-100. S. Rosenblatt, who in his article, "The Crucifixion of Jesus from the Standpoint of Pharisaic Law," *JBL* 75 (Dec. 1956), pp. 315-321, denies the account of the trial of Jesus as presented in the Gospels, nevertheless admits (p. 319) that "although the details of the trial given in the New Testament were definitely contrary to Pharisaic law, a way of removing an undesirable enemy is usually found when the will is there." That is exactly the point.

Note well that according to our passage the people who were supposed to be neutral judges "were themselves seeking evidence against Jesus to put him to death." Ostensibly they were gathered for the purpose of investigation; in reality they were bent on annihilation. In their search they were never successful. To be sure some so-called witnesses showed up, but their testimony was *false*. Moreover, as both verse 56 and verse 59 prove, their testimony *did not agree*.

57-59. Then some stood up and were giving this false testimony [765] **against him: We heard him saying, I will destroy this temple** [766] **made by (human) hands, and in three days I will build another not made by (human) hands. But not even so did their testimony agree.** The allusion is to the veiled saying of Jesus reported in John 2:19, "Break down this temple, and in three days I will build it up." The Jews who had first heard Jesus say this had misinterpreted it, as if Jesus referred to nothing else than the physical structure he had just cleansed (John 2:20). "But he was speaking about the sanctuary of his body" (verse 21). For explanation see N.T.C. on John, Vol. I, p. 125.

Now what did these two false witnesses do? In addition to misinterpreting they also misquote. In fact, they made themselves guilty of the following falsehoods:

a. They said that they had heard Jesus say that he—*he himself*—would destroy the temple. Jesus never said that. Instead he had spoken about the Jews destroying their own temple.

b. They said that Jesus had contrasted "the temple made by (human) hands" with another "not made by (human) hands." These modifiers cannot be found in the language used by Jesus.

c. Their implication was that Jesus was a defamer of the temple, which was the very opposite of the truth. See Mark 11:17; Luke 2:49.

It is not at all surprising that when these two witnesses presented their garbled account of a saying of Jesus there were details with respect to which even they were not in agreement. They were simply "all mixed up," and this not innocently but with evil intent.

60. Then the highpriest arose, came forward and asked Jesus, You don't answer? What is it that these men are testifying against you? [767]

---

765 Same verb as in verse 56. The imperfect tense—ἐψευδομαρτύρουν—continues.

766 Or *sanctuary*, but the distinction between ἱερόν, the entire temple complex, and ναός, the Holy Place and Holy of holies, though valid at times, cannot always be pressed; particularly not in connection with John 2:20. See N.T.C. on Matthew, p. 944.

767 εἰς μέσον, into the midst; here (came) *forward*. See L.N.T. (A. and G.), p. 508; and see also on 3:3. ἀποκρίνῃ, (verse 60), sec. per. s. pres. indic. of ἀποκρίνομαι. ἀπεκρίνατο, (verse 61), third per. s. aor. indic. of the same verb. Note also the double occurrence—first in the question of verse 60; then in the statement of verse 61—of the double negative: οὐκ . . . οὐδέν. For the double negative in Mark see *Introduction IV*, footnote 5, under h.

The question inevitably occurs, "But if these leaders had already made up their minds with respect to the question, 'What shall we do with Jesus?' why did they at all search for witnesses?" Probably to be able to justify their action before others; for example, before Pilate and the general public; or to satisfy a legal requirement. Perhaps even to soothe their own consciences? The remark made by G. C. Morgan may well be true: "They must find witnesses; they must have some reason for the thing they do. This was the unconscious compliment which devilish falsehood paid to the ascendency of truth." [768]

Of course, Jesus could have exposed the totally unwarranted character of the accusation, "I will destroy this temple. . . ." He could have shown that it was both a misinterpretation and a distortion of what he had said. But he knows very well that the purpose of this trial is not to vindicate the right, but rather to cause the wrong to triumph. So he remains silent. This irritates Caiaphas. That presiding officer has taken it upon himself to go way beyond presiding over a meeting. Instead, he is using this session of the Sanhedrin as a tool for the realization of his own pronounced intention (verse 55 and John 11:49-50) to destroy Jesus. So, visibly agitated, he rises from his seat and asks Jesus the question of verse 60. As if to say, "A serious charge is this. It certainly requires an answer!" 61. **But he remained silent and did not answer.** He is fulfilling the prophecy of Isa. 42:1-4; Matt. 12:18-21; and even more specifically, of Isa. 53:7 ("He opened not his mouth"). See also I Kings 19:11, 12; Isa. 57:15; Zech. 9:9; Matt. 5:7-9; 21:5; Luke 23:24. For similar behavior on the part of Jesus on this day—it is already Friday—see Mark 15:5; Luke 23:9b. But not only was he fulfilling prophecy; he was in so doing also suffering intensely because of this assault on himself—"the Truth"—by Satan, "the father of the lie" (John 8:44).

When it seemed as if the trial would turn out to be a failure, Caiaphas all of a sudden leaps to the rescue by as it were waiving all secondary considerations and asking the main question, the one which had been on the minds of the leaders for a long time. Mark reports this dramatic development in these words: **Again the highpriest was questioning him, saying, Are you the Christ, the Son of the Blessed?** That was the clincher, the decisive question. Did this question suddenly suggest itself to his mind, or had he thought of it previously and kept it in reserve, to be used if necessary? According to Matt.

Nevertheless, it is probably incorrect to place great emphasis on this double negative. The parallel passage in Matthew has the simple negative (26:62), and even this only in the question. It is entirely possible, therefore, that Mark's two double negatives represent his own popular style, his thoroughly legitimate manner of reporting. If that be true, "You don't answer?" and "He did not answer" may well suffice. Cf. also the French *Ne réponds-tu rien?* and the South African *Antwoord U niks nie?*

[768] *Op. cit.*, p. 308.

26:63, in order to emphasize the ominous gravity of the question and the impossibility of refusing an answer, the highpriest places Jesus "under oath," the weightiest oath of all, namely, "by the living God." He demands a clear and straightforward reply to the question, "Do you really claim to be the long-expected Messiah?" Now it cannot be said that up to this time Jesus had never revealed himself as such. In his conversation with the Samaritan woman had he not very definitely declared himself to be indeed the Messiah? See John 4:25, 26. Had he not defended those who addressed him as "the Son of David" (Matt. 21:15, 16)? Had he not, by implication, referred to himself as "the stone rejected by the builders but made the cornerstone" (Mark 12:10)? Had he not pointed to himself as "the Son of man" coming in clouds with great power and glory (13:26)?

All of this is true. But it could be argued that a declaration made in Samaria did not necessarily reach the Jews; that Matt. 21:15, 16 was not a direct claim but only a reflection on an exclamation made by others; that Mark 12:1-11 is parabolic, hence not direct; and that the term "Son of man" was not interpreted in the same way by everybody. It can even be added that there were definite reasons why during the earlier part of his ministry Jesus did not *openly* declare to the Jews, "I am the Messiah." See on Matt. 8:4; 9:30; 16:20; 17:9; Mark 1:44, 45. They would certainly have misunderstood it. See John 6:15. But now that the events that were happening with reference to him were making it clear that his messiahship was that of the Suffering Servant, as he had himself declared again and again to his disciples (Mark 8:31; 9:12, 31; 10: 33, 34; John 3:14), the moment had also arrived to come forth with a very clear statement, made before the highest authorities of the Jewish nation. Accordingly, when Caiaphas asked what he must have considered a question that would drive his enemy into a corner, he was actually in the providence of God giving the Son of man the opportunity for which he was looking.

We are not surprised therefore that, without the least hesitancy, in answer to the highpriest's question, "Are you the Christ, the Son of the Blessed [769] (out of reverence, whether real or feigned, substituted for "the Son of God")," 62. **Jesus said, I am, and y o u will see**

> **the Son of man**
> **sitting at the right hand of the Power**
> **and coming with the clouds of heaven.**

That is the way in which Daniel had seen the coming Redeemer (Dan. 7:13, 14). It was thus that David sang of him (Ps. 110:1), and thus also that Jesus

---

[769] For the designation εὐλογητός see also Luke 1:68; Rom. 1:25; 9:5; II Cor. 1:3; 11:31; Eph. 1:3; I Peter 1:3. It is always used to indicate Deity. In Rom. 9:5 ("Christ, who is God over all") it ascribes godhead, in the most exalted sense, to Christ.

had himself described himself (see on Mark 8:38; 12:35-37; 13:26), be it previously only to his disciples. Jesus is looking down history's lane. He sees the miracles of Calvary, the resurrection, the ascension, the coronation at the Father's right hand ("the right hand of the Power," that is, "of the Almighty"). Pentecost, the glorious return on the clouds of heaven, the judgment day, all rolled into one, manifesting his power and glory. On the final day of judgment he, even Jesus, will be the Judge, and these very men—Caiaphas and his partners—will have to answer for the crime they are now committing. Christ's prophecy is also a warning!

The following items deserve special attention:

a. Jesus said, "I am," meaning, "I am indeed the Christ, the Son of the Blessed." This, in turn, sheds light on the meaning of the Matthean parallel "You said (it)," which can, therefore, mean no less than the majestic, affirmative declaration, "Yes, I am." That the Gospel of Mark very definitely describes Jesus as being the Messiah, even the Son of God, in the most exalted sense of that term, has been shown in detail in N.T.C. on Matthew, pp. 58-60.

b. As to "the Son of man," the One who from (and by means of) suffering attains to glory, but was glorious from all eternity, see above on 2:10; also, for a more complete study, see N.T.C. on Matt. 8:20 (pp. 403-407 of that commentary).

c. The grammatical construction of "at the right hand" has been explained in connection with Mark 10:37, see footnote 499. For the idea of Christ's session at the Father's right hand, see also Acts 2:33; Heb. 2:9; Rev. 12:5; and N.T.C. on Eph. 1:20-23; and Phil. 2:9-11.

d. The phrase "coming with the clouds of heaven"—see also Dan. 7:13; Joel 2:2; Zeph. 1:15; Rev. 1:7; 14:14-16—reminds us of the fact that Scripture frequently associates "a cloud" or "clouds" with the idea of judgment, God's coming in order to punish the wicked. This, however, is by no means always the case. In fact, sometimes it is God's love, mercy, and grace that are emphasized (Exod. 34:5-7), though even then punitive justice is not left out of the description. On clouds see also Mark 13:26 and N.T.C. on Matthew, p. 667.

63, 64. Then the highpriest tore his clothes and asked, What need do we still have of witnesses? Y o u have heard his blasphemy. What do y o u think? [770]

Here the hypocrisy of the highpriest becomes very clear. He acts as if he is overwhelmed with grief, as was Reuben when, on returning to the pit, he noticed that Joseph was no longer there (Gen. 37:29). See also Gen. 37:34;

---

770 διαρρήξας, nom. s. masc. aor. participle of διαρρήγνυμι. τι ὑμῖν φαίνεται; What does it seem to y o u? = How does it strike y o u? What do y o u think (of it)?

44:13; Josh. 7:6; II Sam. 13:31; I Kings 21:27; II Kings 5:7, 8; 18:37; Esther 4:1; Acts 14:14, to mention only a few from among many instances of tearing one's clothes in token of poignant grief or overwhelming sorrow. In reality Caiaphas must have been filled with fiendish glee.

When a highpriest tore his clothes, he had to do this in a certain, definitely prescribed way. The exact method to be followed has been preserved in the Talmud. [771]

As he did this he asked his audience, "What need do we still have of witnesses?" In other words, "Why continue to search for witnesses when all of us are witnesses?" When he adds, "Y o u have heard his blasphemy," he is using the word *blasphemy* in its gravest sense: unjustly he has claimed for himself prerogatives that belong to God alone. Representing oneself as the fulfilment of Daniel's prophecy, such a claim could be made only by God. Hence, either *a.* Jesus was indeed divine, "the Son of God" in the fullest sense of that term, or else *b.* he was guilty of blasphemy. And such blasphemy was punishable by death (Lev. 24:16). Caiaphas has chosen the second alternative.

He continues, "What do y o u think?" Mark, using indirect discourse, reproduces the reaction of the judges as follows, **They all condemned him as being worthy of death.** Matthew, using direct discourse, writes, "They answered, 'Deserving of death is he.' " The verdict was unanimous. We assume that one member was absent (Luke 23:50, 51). There may have been others.

This unanimous *verdict* was not as yet a formal *sentence.* Declaring a person guilty and sentencing him are two different matters. In order to create at least a semblance of legality, a short period of time must elapse between these two actions. As was pointed out earlier, according to existing regulations that interval should have been a day. But as the Sanhedrists see it, such a prolonged delay would have been too dangerous. It could have given the friends of Jesus enough time to organize a revolt in his behalf. *Now* is the time to act. Early in the morning the Sanhedrin will have to be convened once more. See on 15:1. That will be for the purpose of sentencing. And even that action will not be final. It must still be approved by Pilate, the governor.

65. And some began to spit at him, to blindfold him, to strike him with their fists, and to say to him, Prophesy! and the officers received him with blows. [772]

---

771 See S.BK., Vol. I, p. 1007 f.
772 As in verses 19 and 33, so also here there is good reason to retain the translation *began* for ἤρξαντο, for a new stage has arrived in the afflictions suffered by Jesus: the verdict has been announced. But see also on 1:45 and 6:7, footnote 233. "Began," in

The venerable(?) members of the Sanhedrin now show their real cruel, vengeful, sadistic character. Utterly mean are they, inhuman, base, contemptible! Even if we make allowance for the possibility that the cruelty to which Jesus was now subjected was the action of the "underlings," and not directly of the priests, etc., it remains true that it was carried out with the wholehearted permission and co-operation of the members of the Sanhedrin. In fact, it is possible that the sequence "And some . . . and the officers" implies that a distinction is being drawn between what some—not all!—of the Sanhedrists did, and what the officers (temple guards, etc.) did. If that distinction should be correct, [773] then these guards, who caught (or "received") Jesus with blows, were simply following the example of their superiors, and "being emboldened" by them (Swete).

The cruelty reached its climax when with their fists these wicked men struck their blindfolded prisoner in the face, and then shouted, "Prophesy," meaning, as Matthew and Luke explain, "Prophesy to us, Christ, who is it that hit you?"

What stands out in this story is the fortitude of Jesus, his majestic calmness and deep-seated, firmly anchored confidence, over against the haunting fear of his venomous adversaries. Note how "scared" these adversaries are, even though for the moment they seem to be victorious. Not only now but also shortly before these happenings, and again after Christ's resurrection, they are never sure of themselves. They are always beset by harrowing fears: fear of the Romans ("The Romans may come," John 11:47, 48), of the crowds ("the people may riot," Mark 14:2), of the disciples (" the disciples may come by night," Matt. 27:62-64), and of news ("this thing must not spread any further among the people," Acts 4:17). And was not the blustery, bullying behavior of the highpriest this very night proof of feverish inner agitation, of morbid, undulating restlessness?

Over against all that stands Jesus' majestic, calm, and eloquent declaration, "I am (indeed the Son of the Blessed), and y o u will see the Son of man sitting at the right hand of the Power and coming with the clouds of heaven." It is he who is the real Victor. It is he who is fully at rest. It is he who imparts rest to all who repose their trust in him. It is he who is still saying, "Come to me all who are weary and burdened, and I will give y o u rest. Take my yoke upon y o u and learn from me, for I am meek and lowly

---

turn governs four pres. (durative) infinitives: *to spit (at), to blindfold, to strike,* and *to say.* Literally περικαλύπτειν means *to put a veil around;* hence, *to cover,* and (since the veil is put around the face) *to blindfold.*

[773] The reason why it is best to express ourselves cautiously on this point is Luke 22:63 which, as many interpret it, ascribes the mocking, beating, blindfolding, etc., to "the men who were guarding Jesus," the underlings, and not to the Sanhedrists themselves.

in heart, and y o u will find rest for y o u r souls. For my yoke is kindly, and my burden is light."

---

66 Now while Peter was below in the courtyard, one of the highpriest's servant-girls came, 67 and seeing Peter warming himself, took a close look at him, and said, "You, too, were with Jesus the Nazarene." 68 But he denied (it). "I don't know or understand what you're talking about," he said, and he went out into the entryway. And a rooster crowed. [774]

69 When the servant-girl (there) saw him, she, in turn, told the bystanders, "This fellow is one of them." 70 But again he proceeded to deny (it).

And again, a little later, those who were standing around were saying to Peter, "Certainly you are one of them, for you are a Galilean!" 71 Then he started to curse and to swear, "I don't know this man y o u're talking about." 72 At once a rooster crowed the second time. [775] And Peter recalled the word Jesus had spoken to him, "Before the rooster crows twice, [776] you will deny me thrice." And when he reflected on this he wept.

14:66-72 *Peter's Threefold Denial*
Cf. Matt. 26:69-75; Luke 22:56-62; John 18:15-18, 25-27

The story is found in all four Gospels. However, since John, without in any way being in conflict with the Synoptics, has his own arrangement, for his contribution we refer to N.T.C. on John, Vol. II, pp. 388-394, 399, 400.

As to the Synoptics, though the story is basically the same in all three and there are no contradictions, each Gospel presents the story in its own way. Omitting minor points, note the following interesting variations:

In connection with the first denial—Matt. 26:58, 69, 70; Mark 14:54, 66-68; Luke 22:54-57—at the outset Mark's account, not surprisingly, is somewhat more vivid and detailed than are the others. The portress was "one of the highpriest's servant-girls." She "took a close look at Peter." What this girl said to Peter, and how he replied, is substantially the same in all the accounts. (However, according to Matthew and Mark, Peter said, "I don't know *what* . . ."; according to Luke, "I don't know *him*.") Luke adds that the girl saw Peter "as he sat in the light."

With respect to the second denial—Matt. 26:71, 72; Mark 14:69, 70a; Luke 22:58—Mark has "He proceeded to deny it." Matthew adds "with an oath." According to Luke's report at least one male bystander chimed in with what the portresses were saying to Peter, which amounted to "This fellow is one of them."

As to the third denial and the conclusion of the story—Matt. 26:73-75;

---

774 Grk. N.T. (A-B-M-W) ascribes dubious textual validity to these words. But see footnote 778.

775 Some MSS. omit "the second time." But see footnote 778.

776 Some MSS. omit "twice." But see footnote 778.

Mark 14:70b-72; Luke 22:59-62—Mark reports that those who are standing around were saying to Peter, "Certainly you are one of them, for you are (Luke: he is) a Galilean." Here Matthew has, " . . . for your accent gives you away." All report what the crowing of the rooster did to Peter's memory. Mark ends the story with, "And when he [Peter] reflected on this he wept" (exact translation is in dispute); Matthew and Luke, "He went outside and wept bitterly." Luke shows that there was an interval of about an hour between the second and the third denials. He also informs us that in connection with the crowing of the rooster, "the Lord turned and looked at Peter."

The First Denial

Let no one say that Peter was a man completely lacking in courage. On the contrary, a careful examination of the Gospels indicates that among all the disciples he was one of the most daring. Was it not Peter who said, "Lord, if it be thou, bid me to come to thee on the water" (Matt. 14:28)? Was it not he also who boldly declared, "Thou art the Christ" (Mark 8:29)? Was it not he who, all by himself taking on the entire mob that had come to Gethsemane to capture Jesus, had drawn his sword and had struck the highpriest's servant, cutting off his right ear (Mark 14:47; cf. Luke 22:50; John 18:10)? And after Christ's resurrection was it not Peter who had uttered the unforgettable words of Acts 2:36, "Let all the house of Israel therefore be assured of this, that God has made him both Lord and Christ, this Jesus *whom y o u crucified*"? Of Acts 4:10, "Let it be known to y o u all, even to all the people of Israel, that in the name of Jesus Christ of Nazareth, *whom y o u crucified,* does this man stand before you completely healed"? Of Acts 4:20, "We cannot but speak the things we saw and heard"? And of Acts 5:29, "We must obey God rather than men"?

Yes, Peter was definitely a man of great courage. But when he forgot for a moment that both for the possession and for the exercise of this gift he was dependent entirely upon God, even Peter failed. When he looked away from Jesus he was no longer "Peter the man of courage." This, too, can be illustrated by examples from his life both before Christ's resurrection (Matt. 14:30, 31; Mark 14:50) and afterward (Gal. 2:11-14a).

This same lesson is illustrated in the story of Peter's three denials. He failed because he let go of Christ's hand. He was restored because Jesus held him fast in his hand (Luke 22:31, 32). Peter's life is a vivid illustration of Paul's memorable passage, "For by grace y o u have been saved, through faith; and this not of yourselves, (it is) the gift of God" (Eph. 2:8).

The background of the first denial has already been indicated; see above on 14:54. The story is continued here in verses **66, 67. Now while Peter was** below in the courtyard, one of the highpriest's servant-girls came, and seeing Peter warming himself, took a close look at him and said, You too were with Jesus the Nazarene. [777]

Note: "below in the courtyard," where Matthew has "outside in the courtyard." These two ways of describing the courtyard cannot be understood apart from the knowledge of an Oriental palace or house of the well-to-do. Such a house looks into its own interior: that is, its rooms are built around an *open* courtyard. An arched passage leads from the heavy outside *door* or (better) *gate* into this inner court. In this passage there is a place (in some houses a little room) for the gate-keeper. Sometimes, as also in the present instance, the court was *lower* than the rooms which ranged around it. It is not entirely impossible that the room to which Jesus had been led was a kind of gallery, from which what happened in the court could be seen and heard. This theory has its objections, however. One might ask, "Would not the loud conversations of the men who stood in the open courtyard have been a cause of annoyance to the priests who conducted the trial?"

When John had been admitted by the gate-keeper, he secured admission for Peter also. John "spoke to the girl who kept the gate."

It would seem that the very moment when Peter had entered the palace, the portress, viewing him from her nook in the vestibule, had her suspicions. The fact that she had admitted him at the request of John seemed to indicate that Peter too was a disciple of Jesus. The uneasiness that could be read on his face confirms her suspicions. So, about to be relieved by another gate-keeper, she walks toward Peter, who has already entered the open courtyard, and who in the light of the fire by which he is warming himself is clearly visible (Luke 22:56). She fixes her eyes on him. Then, stepping even closer, she says to him, "You too were with Jesus the Nazarene." That the words she uses are reported somewhat differently in John's Gospel presents no difficulty. It must not be taken for granted that either—or any—Gospel, all by itself, reports all the words spoken by this girl. Her accusing jabber may have included all the following lines: "You surely are not also one of this man's disciples, are you?—Why, I'm sure you were also with Jesus the Nazarene."

68. But he denied (it). I don't know or understand what you're talking about, he said, and he went out into the entryway. Peter evidently has been floored. The suddenness and boldness of the servant-girl's incriminating remark catches him off guard. In spite of all his loud and repeated promises

777 For "the Nazarene" see N.T.C. on 1:24; also on Matt. 2:23; 26:71; and on John 1:46.

of unswerving loyalty to Jesus, promises made only a few hours earlier, he is now thoroughly frightened. One might say: he panics. Evidently he had failed to take to heart Christ's admonition recorded in 14:38. So he tries to make the girl believe that he doesn't know or understand what she is talking about, and in his frustration he makes for the entryway, hoping that for him it will be an exit.

The man who had been warming himself by the fire suddenly discovers that matters are becoming "too hot" for him. He is probably afraid that at any moment an underling—whether temple guard or palace servant—will grab him and make him a prisoner. The fear that someone might even recognize him as the person who slashed off the ear of the highpriest's servant may have made things even worse for him. "I must escape," he says to himself, "and that as quickly as possible."

And a rooster crowed.—Did it really? The Greek text presents a problem. But the argument for the retention of these words is not as weak as some seem to think. [778]

However, is it not true that, according to Matthew's report, Jesus had said, "This very night, before the rooster crows, you will deny me three times" (26:34)? But if (here in Mark 14:68) the words "And a rooster crowed" are authentic, Peter has denied the Master only once, not three times, before that rooster crowed. Possible solutions:

a. Simply omit the words "And a rooster crowed" from the text of Mark 14:68. Many modern translations do this. When this is done without even informing the reader by means of a note that there is doubt about the right to exclude these words, is this fair?

b. Include the words in dispute but state that this first rooster-crowing had not registered, as is shown by the fact that there is no further reference to it in the text.

c. Recognize the fact that between 12 midnight and 3 A.M. there was nothing to stop a rooster from crowing—hence, Mark 14:68—, but that the reference in Christ's prediction as well as in the fulfilment—hence, in Matt.

---

[778] It cannot be questioned that the manuscripts which omit the words in dispute are weighty. Therefore many modern translators and commentators reject "And a rooster crowed." See, however, the discussion in V. Taylor, *op. cit.*, p. 574. The fact that Mark's report seems to require the *inclusion* of the words—note verses 30 and 72—should receive at least as much consideration as does their omission from verse 68 in important manuscripts. Why speak about a *second* rooster-crowing if there has been no *first*? Is it not possible that a scribe, thinking that the mention of rooster-crowing in Mark 14:68 was in conflict with the story as presented by Matthew, etc., started the process of omitting it? May not something similar account for the omission of "twice" from verses 30 and 72, and of "the second time" from verse 72? It is easier in these cases to explain omission from the true text than interpolation into it.

26:34, 74; Luke 22:34, 60; John 13:38; 18:27, *and also in Mark 14:30, 72,*
is to the rooster-crowing that marked *the end* of the 12 (midnight) - 3 A.M.
period. See on Mark 13:35.

This would mean that when Jesus predicted Peter's three manifestations
of unfaithfulness he meant, "I solemnly declare to you: this very night,
before the rooster crows, that is, crows for the second time, you will deny
me three times."

If either *b.* or *c.* is adopted the problem may well have been solved.
Perhaps *b.* and *c.* should be combined. As footnote 778 indicates, there is
good reason, in agreement with A. V., Moffatt, Weymouth, Beck, Phillipps,
and Berkeley Version, to allow the disputed words of Mark 14:72 to stand.

The Second Denial

**69, 70a. When the servant-girl (there) saw him, she, in turn, told the
bystanders, This fellow is one of them. But again he proceeded to deny (it).**
The second denial follows closely upon the first. In his frustration resulting
from the first embarrassment Peter tried to get out of the building. However,
the portresses are unwilling to let him out. So he gets no farther than the
entranceway or vestibule which via the gate leads to the outside. Several
people are standing around. It seems that the portress who is about to go off
duty has already told the news about Peter to the girl who has come to
relieve her. So this second girl (cf. Matt. 26:71 and Mark 14:69) now says to
those standing around, "This fellow is one of them" (as Mark has it); "This
fellow was with Jesus the Nazarene" (Matthew's way of stating the same
thing).

There are those who see a contradiction between Mark and Matthew at
this point. [779] As they see it, according to Mark's representation there is
only one portress: the girl of verses 66, 67 is also the one of verse 69. But
according to Matt. 26:71 the girl who is mentioned in connection with
Peter's second denial is "another girl." Now it should be frankly admitted
that Mark 14:69 can indeed be read in such a way that there would be a
conflict. It can be read to mean: "And the servant-girl (mentioned a moment
ago) seeing him said again to the bystanders, 'This fellow is one of them.' "
This, however, does not make Mark's account any more intelligible, for as *he*
tells the story the girl has not yet been speaking to those standing around; so
how could she speak to them *again?* But by thus rendering the passage are
we not creating both a difficulty and a conflict where there need not be one?

---

[779] So, for example, V. Taylor, *op. cit.,* pp. 574, 575. In fact, the contradiction he
sees reaches even farther than this, but this we can ignore, since portresses and male
bystanders must not be confused.

Is it really so certain that throughout the report Mark *must* have been thinking of *only one* portress? Is it not true that while Matthew, by saying "a servant-girl . . . another girl," makes clear that the words of *two* girls are reported in this story, Mark may be doing the same thing by referring to *girls* in the plural: "*one of* the highpriests's servant-girls came and . . . said . . ." (verses 66, 67), a (not the only possible) natural sequel being "*another* servant-girl said. . . ." Also, when Mark continues, "He [Peter] went out into the entryway . . . when the servant-girl saw him," is not "When the servant-girl *who was there* saw him" a reasonable interpretation? And since it has already been shown that the word *again* creates a difficulty even for those who accept only one servant-girl, is not the proposed translation—which substitutes "in turn" [780] for "again"—better all around? It is clear at any rate that here again a Gospel contradiction cannot be proved.

The fact that at least one male bystander now chimes in with what the two girls are saying does not make matters any easier for Peter. Again Peter proceeded to deny [781] that he knew Jesus. According to Matthew this time his denial was accompanied by an oath.

*The Third Denial
and the Conclusion of the Story*

70b, 71. And again, a little later, those who were standing around were saying to Peter, Certainly you are one of them, for you are a Galilean!

We have noticed that even during the second denial interest in Peter's case was no longer confined to the portresses. And now the bystanders *again* express themselves. The reason for this was as follows: Having been refused exit, Peter returns to the open courtyard. An hour elapses (Luke 22:59). It would seem, therefore, that the first two denials took place during Christ's appearance before Annas. Now the situation changes somewhat: Jesus has been brought before Caiaphas and the entire Sanhedrin. Christ's first trial before this body is almost over.

During the interval of an hour the news about Peter has been spreading. Now the palace servants and the officers, the men who are standing around the fire with Peter, begin to tell him that he is one of Christ's disciples, and that his very accent or brogue identifies him as a Galilean. Cf. Matt. 26:73. A comparison of the Gospel accounts shows that some people are talking *to* Peter; others, *about* him. Accusations are flying in from every side. This was enough to get anyone excited, especially excitable Simon! As if all this were

---

[780] This is a legitimate translation of πάλιν. See John 12:22 t.r.

[781] Note the imperfect ἠρνεῖτο, which is a vivid description of what was happening, and may indicate (though not necessarily) that the action continued for some time.

not enough, a relative of Malchus blurts out, "Did I not see you in the garden with Jesus?" For this story see N.T.C. on John, Vol. II, pp. 399, 400. **Then he started to curse and to swear, I don't know this man y o u're talking about.** Angry and excited Peter now begins to call down curses on himself and to swear that he doesn't even know Jesus. He must have said something like, "May God do this or that to me if it be true that I am or ever was a disciple of Jesus." He stands there invoking on himself one curse after another. And the louder this Galilean talks, the more, without realizing it, he is saying to all those standing around, "I'm a liar."

In his infinite and tender mercy the Lord, who in his sovereign providence controls all things, including even roosters, comes to the rescue: **72. At once a rooster crowed the second time. And Peter recalled the word Jesus had spoken to him, Before the rooster crows twice, you will deny me thrice. And when he reflected on this he wept.** [782]

Note the following:

a. Mark's representation "At once a rooster crowed the second time," and Matthew's "At once a rooster crowed" are not in conflict. Neither is there any real contradiction between Mark's "Before the rooster crows twice you will deny me thrice" and Matthew's "This very night, before the rooster crows, you will deny me three times." See on verse 68.

b. How was it that Peter recalled the word spoken to him? From Luke 22:61 we gather that at the very moment when the rooster crowed, or at least very nearly at that moment, someone was looking straight into Peter's eyes. It was Jesus, his face very likely still black and blue because of the blows it had received. It would seem that the Master, his trial ended, was being led across the court to his prison cell, from which within a few hours he would emerge once more to face the Sanhedrin.

When Peter heard the crowing of the rooster, and saw Jesus looking at him, with eyes full of pain, yet also of pardon, his memory of Christ's warning prediction was suddenly awakened.—In this connection we must not forget that "the look of Jesus would have been wasted on Peter, if it had not been that Peter was looking at Jesus." [783]

c. The original of the words, "And when he reflected on this he wept" has given rise to much discussion. See footnote. [784] The A.V. rendering is probably still the best.

---

782 For the textual problems in connection with this verse see above, on verse 68, footnote 778. Though it is true that Mark uses the imperfect ἔκλαιε, it is not necessary to translate "He continued to weep," since the very idea of weeping already implies continuity.

783 G. Campbell Morgan, op. cit., p. 312.

784 Of the various renderings that have been proposed the most simple and perhaps the best would seem to be to interpret ἐπιβαλών (nom. sing. masc. aor. participle of

d. When we review the entire story it becomes clear that the following lessons are taught here (and there may be others):

First of all, how deceitful is man's heart! See above, on 14:31: *The Unknown Self.*

Secondly, how Christ must have suffered! No doubt much more because of these denials by a highly favored disciple and friend than because of the blows and the mockery inflicted ọn him by his declared enemies. See Ps. 55:12-14.

Finally, how God's grace and the Savior's forgiving love are here revealed! See Isa. 1:18; 53:6; 55:6, 7.

Summary of Chapter 14

There is a close connection between chapters 13 and 14. According to 13:32 Jesus said, "But about that day or that hour no one knows. . . ." He knew that his times were in the Father's hand. Cf. Ps. 31:15. But the venerable members of the Jewish supreme court seemed to have been of the opinion that they themselves were in control, and had the power to determine the day of Christ's death. See 14:2.

There is also another obvious connection. Chapter 13 contains an admonition which Jesus repeats several times in one form or another, namely, "Stay on the alert" ("Be watchful"). See verses 23, 33, 35, 37. This word of warning is repeated in 14:38. But according to 14:37, 40, 41 this is exactly what Peter, James, and John failed to do.

As to the contents, chapter 14 is divided into 11 very unequal sections, as follows:

1. "Not during the feast," said the plotters. "During the feast (Passover)," said the Almighty, echoed by Jesus. And so it happened (verses 1, 2).

2. In connection with Mary of Bethany's generous, thoughtful, and timely deed of anointing Jesus, we are shocked by the disciples' inexcusable criticism, "Why this waste of perfume?" What is especially striking is the emphatic manner in which Jesus rushes to Mary's defense with the words, "Wherever the gospel is preached in the whole world, also what she has done will be told in memory of her" (verses 3-9).

ἐπιβάλλω) as meaning *putting to, applying to,* and then to supply τὸν νοῦν (or something similar), resulting in the sense *applying the mind to, reflecting on, thinking on.* Thus also A.V., A.R.V., Gould, Robertson, Erdman. Both Bruce and Swete, after mentioning several other possibilities, finally retain two, though not the same two. The *one* retained by both is *thinking on.* The rendering "He burst into tears," or "broke down and wept," preferred by some, rests on the idea that ἐπιβάλλω indicates violent action (as in Mark 4:37). See F. Hauck, Th.D.N.T., Vol. I, p. 529. Such violent action, however, is not always implied (see Mark 11:7; Luke 9:62). And when it is implied, the object (direct, indirect, or both) is mentioned. *Mark 14:72 is different.*

3. Mary receives the Master's everlasting praise. Judas receives money from the Jewish leaders. Having received it he now looks for an opportunity to betray Jesus (verses 10, 11).

4. Mark now relates how Jesus sent two of his disciples *a.* to secure a room to celebrate Passover with his disciples, and *b.* to make the necessary preparations. The Master's predictions with respect to the two disciples' experiences in Jerusalem in search for a room are fulfilled in every respect.

It was Thursday evening, during the Passover meal, that Jesus declared, "One of y o u will betray me—one who is eating with me." Since all the disciples were eating with Jesus, they, one by one, said to him, "Surely not I?" All the disciples were given an opportunity to examine themselves. Note the combination of divine sovereignty and human responsibility in Christ's words, "The Son of man goes as it is written concerning him, but woe to that man by whom the Son of man is betrayed" (verses 12-21).

5. Toward the end of the Passover meal Jesus instituted "the Lord's Supper." It signifies that because of what Jesus did for his people in what is now *the past* they should give him their *love;* also, that because whenever the supper is truly celebrated he is *present* with those who partake of it, they should embrace him as the object of their *faith;* and finally that, in view of his promise with respect to the *future*—a promise made when he instituted the supper—, they should look forward with living, firmly anchored *hope* to everlasting communion with him in the mansions above (verses 22-26).

6. On the way to the Mount of Olives (as even before, in the Upper Room) Jesus predicted that all his disciples would become untrue to him, in fulfilment of Zech. 13:7. All protest and profess their unflinching loyalty; especially Peter. Jesus said to him, "I solemnly declare to you that today—yes, this very night—before the rooster crows twice, you will deny me thrice." Paragraph 11 shows that this was exactly what also happened (verses 27-31).

7. In Gethsemane Jesus *a.* agonized; *b.* agonized and prayed; *c.* prayed and kept watch. Three times he prayed, the substance of his prayer being, "Father, remove this cup from me; nevertheless, not what I will but what thou wilt." After his third prayer, on returning to his disciples and finding them still (or: again) sleeping, he stood there, tenderly keeping watch over them and saying, "Sleep on now and take y o u r rest. It is enough."

Shortly afterward he added, "Get up! Let us be going. Look, my betrayer is near" (verses 32-42).

8. By means of a kiss (or kisses) Judas identified and thus betrayed Jesus to a detachment of soldiers, temple-police, and Sanhedrists, all of them well equipped. Peter draws his sword and strikes the highpriest's servant, cutting off his ear. Jesus exposes the folly and guilt of his captors. In fulfilment of his prediction all the disciples flee. What is especially significant is the fact

that Jesus allows himself to be seized, bound, and led away. The "Victim" is obviously the "Victor." In fulfilment of Isa. 53, he is surrendering his life as an offering in exchange for many (verses 43-50).

9. Though Jesus' captors did not catch any of the disciples—and probably did not even try (John 18:8, 9)—, they did try to capture a certain "young man" who, with only a linen cloth thrown around his body, was following Jesus. As they seized this young man, he left the linen cloth behind and escaped naked. In the opinion of many Mark is narrating his own unforgettable experience (verses 51, 52).

10. Before the Sanhedrin Jesus, in answer to the highpriest's question, declares himself to be the Messiah, the One who is about to be gloriously exalted (Ps. 110:1), and who one day, in fulfilment of Dan. 7:13, 14, will appear upon the clouds of heaven, clothed with dominion and majesty. The nervous highpriest, who had failed to elicit from witnesses damaging testimony on which they could agree, now tears his clothes and asks, "What need do we still have of witnesses? Y o u have heard his blasphemy. What do y o u think?" They all condemn him as being worthy of death. Mockery and cruelty follow (verses 53-65).

11. The background of Peter's first denial is indicated in 14:54. The story is continued here. The first denial takes place in the courtyard of the highpriest's palace, where Peter is warming himself in the presence of the palace servants and temple guards. A portress takes a close look at him and exclaims, "You too were with Jesus the Nazarene." The next denial occurs, in all probability, as Peter is trying to escape to the outside. The portress who had come to relieve the first one tells the bystanders, "This fellow is one of them." Since Peter apparently was not allowed to make his exit, he returns to the courtyard. Here, about an hour later (according to Luke) those standing around are saying to Peter, "Certainly you are one of them, for you are a Galilean."

Whenever he is accused Peter denies any connection with Jesus. The third time "he started to curse and to swear, 'I don't know this man y o u're talking about.' " It was then that the rooster crowed.

There had been rooster-crowing before, after the first denial. But the rooster-crowing immediately after the third denial was the significant one. When the rooster crowed this second time, Peter recalled the word Jesus had spoken to him, "Before the rooster crows twice, you will deny me thrice."

When he reflected on that which, in spite of all his earlier promises and boasts, he had done, and on what Jesus really meant to him and had done for him, he wept! (verses 66-72).

624

Outline of Chapter 15

Theme: *The Work Which Thou Gavest Him To Do*

15:1   The Sanhedrin's Decision to Put Jesus to Death
                    Jesus Brought before Pilate
15:2-5   Jesus Questioned by Pilate
15:6-15   Jesus Sentenced to Die
15:16-20 The Mockery
15:21-32 Calvary: The Crucifixion of Jesus
15:33-41 Calvary: The Death of Jesus
15:42-47 The Burial of Jesus

CHAPTER XV

15 1 Very early in the morning the chief priests, together with the elders and the scribes, that is, the entire Sanhedrin, passed a resolution. They bound Jesus, led him away, and delivered him to Pilate.

15:1 *The Sanhedrin's Decision to Put Jesus to Death*
Jesus Brought before Pilate
Cf. Matt. 27:1, 2; Luke 22:66; 23:1; John 18:28

From about three o'clock (see 13:35; 14:72) until daybreak Jesus must have been held in imprisonment somewhere in the palace of Caiaphas. Then 1. **Very early in the morning** there was another meeting: **the chief priests, together with the elders and the scribes, that is, the entire Sanhedrin, passed a resolution.** Note that the same three groups are mentioned as in 8:31; 14:43, 53. See on 14:1. It was to the priesthood that the care of the temple had been especially entrusted. This may account for the wording here "the chief priests, *together with* the elders and the scribes." The main reason for the early morning meeting may well have been to give a semblance of legality to the action against Jesus. For explanation of this point see above, on 14:55, 56. Note especially point *d.* mentioned there. Though not an entire day, as required, would intervene between conviction and sentencing, there would at least be a brief interval and a second meeting, one during which Caiaphas could afford to relax somewhat, allowing others to question Jesus and to repeat their verdict of a few hours earlier (Luke 22:66-71).

In view of the fact that Mark's expression, indicating what was *reconfirmed* at this dawn session, is immediately followed by drastic *action* against Jesus, it is probably correct to say that what Mark means in verse 1 is that the Sanhedrin "passed a resolution," [785] and not simply "held a consultation." The "resolution" or "sentence" was that Jesus be put to death. However, since the Sanhedrin was well aware of the fact that this sentence, in order to be carried out, must be confirmed by the Romans, there follows: **They bound Jesus, led him away, and delivered him to Pilate.** [786]

---

785 συμβούλιον ποιήσαντες (nom. pl. masc. aor. participle of ποιέω).
786 δήσαντες, same construction as the preceding participle. ἀπήνεγκαν, third per. pl. aor. indic. of ἀποφέρω.

The *binding* of Jesus had also occurred earlier (John 18:12, 24). He had come to make men free (John 8:36; Gal. 5:1). This was included in the work which the Father had given him to do. In order to accomplish this, he himself had to be bound.

Thus bound, he was handed over to Pilate the governor, as he had predicted (10:33). John 18:28 states that Jesus was led to the governor's residence or praetorium. The language used in Luke 23:7, the fact that according to Mark 15:8 those who wanted to see Pilate had to *ascend* in order to do so, the mention of "the stone platform" in John 19:13, and the fact that Pilate was not a friend of Herod (Luke 23:12) make it well-nigh impossible to believe that the meaning of Mark 15:1 would be that Jesus was brought to Herod's palace. The reference must be to the fortress of Antonia at the northwest corner of the temple area. Pilate had rooms in this fortress, in close proximity to the garrison (Mark 15:16), though his main residence was in Caesarea. Supported by his soldiers he was now in Jerusalem in order, at the politically dangerous season of the Passover, to preserve the peace.

Pontius Pilate [787] was the fifth procurator of Samaria and Judea. He was under the authority of Syria's legate. Many reports have come down to us about him. Estimates of his character range all the way from that of Philo who, quoting a letter from Agrippa I to Caligula, calls him "inflexible, merciless, and obstinate," a man who repeatedly inflicted punishment without previous trial and committed ever so many acts of cruelty; to that of the Copts and Abyssinians who rank him among the saints! One thing is certain: he exercised little common sense in handling the delicate problem of the strained relations between the Jews and their Roman conquerors. In fact, it would almost seem as if he enjoyed annoying the Jews: using the temple treasure to pay for an aqueduct, bringing Roman standards into Jerusalem, and even defiling the temple with golden shields inscribed with the images and names of Roman deities.

The incident which led to Pilate's removal from office was his interference with a mob of fanatics who, under the leadership of a false prophet, were at the point of ascending Mt. Gerizim in order to find the sacred vessels which, as they thought, Moses had hidden there. Pilate's cavalry attacked them, killing many of them. Upon complaint by the Samaritans, Pilate was then removed from office. He started out for Rome in order to answer the charges that had been leveled against him. Before he reached Rome, the emperor

---

[787] Sources on Pilate are, first of all, *The Gospels;* then Philo, *De Legationem ad Caium* XXXVIII; Josephus, *Antiquities* XVIII. 55-64; 85-89; Josephus, *The Jewish War* II.169-177; Tacitus, *Annals* XV.xliv; and Eusebius, *Ecclesiastical History* I.ix, x; II.ii, vii. See also G. A. Müller, *Pontius Pilatus der fünfte Prokurator von Judäa*, Stuttgart, 1888; and P. L. Maier, *Pontius Pilate*, Garden City, New York, 1968.

(Tiberius) had died. An unconfirmed story, related by Eusebius, states that Pilate "was forced to become his own slayer."

From the Gospels we gather that he was *proud* (see N.T.C. on John 19:10); and *cruel* (Luke 13:1). He was probably just as *superstitious* as his wife (Matt. 27:19). Above all, as all the accounts of the trial of Jesus before him indicate, he was a *self-seeker*, wishing to stand well with the emperor. He thoroughly hated the Jews who, as he saw it, were always causing him trouble upon trouble. That he was *utterly* devoid of any remnant of human sympathy and any sense of justice cannot be proved. In fact, there are passages which seem to point in the opposite direction. At any rate, though his guilt was great, it was not as great as that of Annas and Caiaphas, cf. John 19:11.

---

2 Pilate questioned him, saying, "You are the king of the Jews?" Answering he said to him, "You said (it)." 3 And the chief priests were accusing him of many things. [788] 4 So Pilate was again questioning him, saying, "Don't you answer at all? You hear how many accusations they are bringing against you." 5 But Jesus never answered at all, so that Pilate was amazed.

15:2-5 *Jesus Questioned by Pilate*
Cf. Matt. 27:11-14; Luke 23:2-5; John 18:33-38

The story started in verse 1 is now continued. By combining the Gospel accounts one gains the impression that from start almost to finish Pilate did everything in his power to get rid of the case. He had no love for the Jews. He hated to please them and to grant their request with respect to Jesus. Yet, on the other hand, deep down in his heart he was afraid of them and of the possibility that they might use their influence to hurt him. Up to a point he is willing to do what justice demands, but only up to a point. When his *position* is threatened, he surrenders.

In harmony with this attitude on the part of Pilate the story begins to unfold as follows:

a. Pilate asks those who have brought Jesus to him, "What charges do y o u prefer against this man?" When they fail to bring any charges, he tries to return the prisoner to them: "Take him yourselves, and judge him according to y o u r own law." However, the Jews then make clear that they desire nothing less than the prisoner's *death*. In this connection the apostle John sees the fulfilment of earlier sayings of Jesus regarding the manner in which he was going to die (John 18:28-32). John undoubtedly had in mind such sayings as are found in Matt. 20:19; 26:2; Mark 10:33; John 3:14; 8:28; 12:32, 33.

---

788 Or: harshly.

b. The Jews now understand that they wiil have to make definite charges. So they quickly advance three of them: Jesus perverts the nation; he forbids us to pay tribute to Caesar; and he claims that he himself is king (Luke 23:2). In reality these three charges amounted to *one:* "This man is a revolutionary, a seditionist, a politically dangerous person." Pilate could not afford to allow such an alleged claim to kingship to remain unexamined. So he takes Jesus with him inside the praetorium to examine him on this matter (John 18:33a).

c. At this point our present passage (Mark 15:2a; cf. Matt. 27:11a; Luke 23:3a; John 18:33b) takes up the story. Pilate asks Jesus, "You are the king of the Jews?"

d. Jesus explains to Pilate in which sense he is and in which sense he is not a king (John 18:34-37).

e. The other Gospels simply report that Jesus answered Pilate's question affirmatively (Mark 15:2b; cf. Matt. 27:11b; Luke 23:3b).

f. Having examined Jesus, Pilate steps outside (on the porch) again and declares to the Jews (the chief priests and the multitude), "No crime whatever do I find in him" (John 18:38b; cf. Luke 23:4).

g. The chief priests accuse Jesus of many things (Mark 15:3; cf. Matt. 27:12a), no doubt reiterating the earlier charges (see b. above) and adding others.

h. To the consternation and amazement of Pilate, Jesus remains silent (Mark 15:4, 5; cf. Matt. 27:12b-14).

i. One of the many charges now made is, "He stirs up the people, teaching throughout all Judea, from Galilee even to this palace." The mention of Galilee is music to Pilate's ears, for to him it means that he may be able to turn the case over to the tetrarch Herod Antipas, now in Jerusalem (Luke 23:5-12).

From the above it follows that Mark's narrative covers points c, e, g, and h. To understand the Marcan account the other points (especially a, b, d, and f) will have to be borne in mind.

The closest parallel to Mark 15:2-5 is Matt. 27:11-14. The resemblance is so very close that nothing further needs to be said about it.

2. **Pilate questioned him, saying, You are king of the Jews?** It is clear that though the Sanhedrin had accused Jesus of blasphemy, before Pilate the Jewish leaders do not immediately press this charge. They must have been of the opinion—and rightly so—that a more definitely political accusation would have a better chance to be considered legally valid from the aspect of Roman jurisprudence. Besides, they may have felt that a strictly religious charge would make little impression on a pagan. This does not mean, however, that they have altogether discarded the idea of ever bringing this religious indictment to the attention of the governor. They did in fact do

this very thing (John 19:7), but for the present they hold it in abeyance.

When Pilate now asked Jesus, "You are the king of the Jews?" he asked it because he felt that for his own protection he had to do this, and not because he himself believed the charge.

The pronoun "You" is not only spelled out but heads the question. Great emphasis is placed on it, as if Pilate were saying, "*You* are the king of the Jews? How ridiculous!" Continued: **Answering he said to him, You said (it).** This can mean no less than, "It is even as you have stated." For proof see a similar expression in Matt. 26:25, and cf. John 18:36, 37. In both of these other cases the context clearly establishes the fact that the answer of Jesus was an affirmation.

At this point (see f. above) Pilate steps outside the praetorium again and from his elevated tribunal declares to the chief priests and the multitude, "No crime whatever do I find in him," that is, no legitimate basis for any accusation.

There follows (see point g. above): 3. **And the chief priests were accusing him of many things.** [789] Note that the chief priests are again in the forefront of the accusers. See on 15:1. For their "many charges" see Luke 23:2, 5. —Jesus remained silent. [790]

4. So Pilate was again questioning [791] him, saying, **Don't you answer at all? You hear how many accusations they are bringing against you.** This is almost a repetition of Mark 14:60; cf. Matt. 26:62. It would seem that both Caiaphas and Pilate proceeded from the assumption that an accused person is guilty unless he can prove himself to be innocent.

5. **But Jesus never answered at all, so that Pilate was amazed.** The governor is confronted with a double contrast: a. Between Jesus and ever so many other accused persons who had appeared before him, and had probably been very vocal and excited in defending themselves; and b. between the boisterous, troublesome, aggressive person as Jesus had been pictured by the chief priests and the elders, and the quiet, dignified, serene individual who was now standing before him.

---

789 Instead of "of many things" another possibility is "harshly" (thus, for example, N.A.S.). See above on 9:26, footnote 411. But "were accusing—or: began to accuse—him of *many things*" harmonizes with verse 4: "You hear how *many accusations* they are bringing against you."

790 Mark 15:3b in A.V. reads "but he answered nothing." But the reading αὐτὸς δὲ οὐδὲν ἀπεκρίνατο is generally rejected, because of insufficient manuscript support. V. Taylor, however, thinks that it may, after all, be authentic. I agree that this possibility must be granted. Without it something seems to be lacking between verses 3 and 4. But however this may be, Pilate's question (verse 4) lacks meaning apart from the implied silence of Jesus, a silence confirmed by Matt. 27:12b.

791 Note κατηγόρουν in verse 3 and ἐπηρώτα in verse 4, both imperfect and probably also both iterative.

Just exactly why it was that Jesus remained silent has not been revealed. The following possible reasons, however, deserve consideration:

a. He "opened not his mouth" in fulfilment of prophecy (Isa. 42:1-4; 53:7; 57:15; Zech. 9:9). See also I Kings 19:11, 12; Matt. 5:7-9; 12:18-21; 21:5.

b. Pilate did not deserve an answer, for he knew very well that Jesus was innocent. The governor had declared this openly (John 18:38b; cf. Luke 23:4). He should have acquitted Jesus.

c. The Jewish leaders knew very well that they were lying. Not once during his ministry had Jesus spoken or acted as a political rebel. Rather, the very opposite (Mark 12:17; John 6:15).

On four separate occasions during the last several hours of his life Jesus "opened not his mouth": before Caiaphas (Mark 14:60, 61), before Pilate (Mark 15:4, 5), before Herod (Luke 23:9b), and again before Pilate (John 19:9b). These silences spoke louder than words. They were in reality condemnations of his tormentors. And they were proofs of his identity as the Messiah.

---

6 Now at a feast it was customary to release to the people any one prisoner whom they asked for. 7 And among the rebels in prison, who had committed murder in the insurrection, there was a man called Barabbas. 8 So the crowd came up and asked [792] (Pilate) to do as he had been accustomed to do for them. 9 Pilate asked them, "Do y o u want me to release to y o u the king of the Jews?" 10 For he was aware that because of envy the chief priests had handed him over (to him). 11 But the chief priests stirred up the mob (to get) him to release to them Barabbas instead (of Jesus). 12 Replying, Pilate said to them, "What, then, do y o u want me to do with the one whom y o u call 'the king of the Jews'?" 13 "Crucify him!" they shouted back. 14 But Pilate said to them, "Why? What wrong has he done?" All the louder they were screaming, "Let him be crucified!" 15 So Pilate, anxious to satisfy the crowd, released Barabbas to them; and he had Jesus flogged and handed him over to be crucified.

15:6-15 *Jesus Sentenced to Die*
Cf. Matt. 27:15-26; Luke 23:13-25; John 18:39—19:16

Without material conflicts each evangelist tells the story in his own way. Common to Matthew and Mark is the following: At a (or "the") feast it was customary for the governor to release to the crowd any one prisoner whom they wanted. So, realizing that because of envy Jesus had been delivered to him, Pilate allows the people to choose between Jesus and the prisoner Barabbas. The chief priests persuade the people to ask that not Jesus but Barabbas be released. "What then do y o u want me to do (or: shall I do)

---

792 Or: began to ask.

with the one whom y o u call the king of the Jews?" (thus Mark); "with Jesus, who is called the Christ?" (thus Matthew). They shout back, "Let him be crucified." Pilate asks, "Why? What wrong has he done?" All the louder the people answer or scream, "Let him be crucified." Pilate releases Barabbas and orders Jesus to be flogged, a punishment which was generally followed by crucifixion.

The most important variations are as follows: Mark describes Barabbas as a rebel and murderer (15:7); Matthew calls him "a notorious prisoner" (27:16); John, "a robber" (18:40). While both Matthew and Mark clearly imply that the choice between Jesus and Barabbas was left to the people, Mark adds that the people took the initiative in seeing to it that as usual, so also now, a prisoner was released (15:8). Also, according to Mark, Pilate suggests that the people choose "the king of the Jews" for release (15:9).

Matthew adds that while the people were considering whom to choose for release, Pilate received a message from his wife informing him about her dream and warning him not to do anything with "that righteous man" (27:19). At the close of the story as told by Matthew, Pilate washes his hands and declares his innocence "of the blood of this man." The people reply, "Let his blood be upon us and upon our children" (27:24, 25).

Luke states that when Jesus returned from Herod (23:6-12), Pilate informed the Jewish authorities that since neither he himself nor Herod had found the accused guilty of any charge, he would be punished ("chastised") and released (23:22). Luke presents an abbreviated account of the *Jesus versus Barabbas* incident (23:18b, 19, 25a). His story ends as does that of Matthew and Mark: Barabbas is released; Jesus is delivered to the will of the chief priests and the people (23:24, 25). The innocence of Jesus, definitely implied by all four evangelists, is affirmed in no uncertain language by Luke, and this repeatedly (verses 4, 14, 15, 22). Luke's account, too, emphasizes even more strongly than do the others how earnestly and strenuously Pilate tried to persuade the people to agree with his suggestion that Jesus should be "chastised" and released (verses 16, 22).

Pilate's assertion "I find no crime in him" also occurs more than once in John's Gospel (18:38; 19:4, 6). Here, too, the story *Jesus versus Barabbas* is presented in abbreviated form (18:39, 40). Distinctive of John's account are the "Ecce homo" and the "Ecce rex vester" incidents (19:5, 14). But most of all we are indebted to John's Gospel for showing us what finally moved Pilate to yield to the will of the chief priests and the people:

"So Jesus came outside, still wearing the thorny crown and the purple robe. And he said to them, 'Look! The man!' Then when the chief priests and the officers saw him, they cried out, saying, 'Crucify (him), crucify (him)!' Pilate said to them, 'Take him yourselves and crucify (him); for I, on my part, do not find any crime in him.' The Jews answered him, 'We have a

633

law, and according to that law he ought to die, because he made himself the Son of God.'

"Now when Pilate heard this word, he was even more afraid, and he entered into the governor's residence again, and said to Jesus, 'Where do you come from?' But Jesus gave him no answer. So Pilate said to him, 'To *me* you do not speak? Don't you realize that I have the authority to release you and that I have the authority to crucify you?' Jesus answered, 'You would have no authority at all over me if it had not been given to you from above. Therefore the one who delivered me up to you has the greater sin.'

"As a result of this, Pilate was making efforts to release him. But the Jews kept shouting, 'If you release this man, you are no friend of the emperor. Whoever makes himself king rebels against the emperor.'

"Then Pilate, on hearing these words, led Jesus out, and sat down on the judgment seat, in a place called The Stone Pavement, in Aramaic: Gabbatha. Now it was the Preparation of the Passover. The hour was about the sixth. And he said to the Jews, 'Look! Y o u r king!' Then they cried out, 'Away with him, away with him, crucify him!' Pilate said to them, 'Y o u r *king* shall I crucify?' Answered the chief priests, 'We have no king but the emperor.' So he then handed him over to them in order to be crucified" (19:5-16).

* * * *

6. **Now at a feast it was customary to release to the people any one prisoner whom they asked for.** [793] Whether the reference here is to any of the great religious festivals or exclusively to the Passover is not clear, though the idea of setting a prisoner free would seem to be most appropriate in connection with Passover, the commemoration of the deliverance of the Israelites from the house of bondage. And see also John 18:39, "But y o u have a custom that I release a man for y o u *at the Passover.*" One thing is clear: Pilate at this particular moment is most willing to release a prisoner; for, as he sees it, this may be a way to get Jesus off his hands.

---

793 ἀπέλυε, third per. s. imperfect of ἀπολύω. This is the customary or iterative imperfect, the imperfect of repeated action. δέσμιος, one bound, a prisoner; related to δέω, to bind, tie. See the aor. active participle of this verb in verse 1, footnote 786. Cf. *diadem*, a garland *bound around* the head. The word prisoner, used here in 15:6 and its parallel Matt. 27:15; 16, occurs also in Acts 16:25, 27 (those imprisoned in the Philippian jail). It is used in connection with Paul (Acts 23:18; 25:14, 27; 28:17). Paul calls himself "the prisoner of Christ Jesus" (Eph. 3:1; cf. 4:1; II Tim. 1:8; Philem. 1, 9). Hebrews refers to "those in bonds" (10:34; 13:3).

παρῃτοῦντο, third per. pl. imperf. of παραιτέομαι. Here in Mark 15:6 the meaning is *to ask for*. Other meanings: *to excuse* (Luke 14:18b, 19, "consider me excused"); *refuse* (I Tim. 4:7; 5:11; Heb. 12:25); *entreat that not* (Heb. 12:19).

7. **And among the rebels in prison, who had commited murder in the insurrection, there was a man called Barabbas.** [794] We know very little about this man except what is stated here and in parallel passages. He may well have been a fanatic patriot. The country was full of them. Was he perhaps a dagger-bearer, one ready at any time to bid defiance to Roman oppression? Note "*the* insurrection." The one familiar to Mark? To the readers? To both? Or simply, the particular insurrection in which these men had been involved? We do not know.

8. **So the crowd came up and asked (Pilate) to do as he had been accustomed to do for them.** Note "came up," probably up the steps leading to Pilate's elevated quarters in the Tower of Antonia. Though the original may also be translated "and began [795] to ask," in the present case the simple "asked" is probably sufficient. We are not told who were in the committee that made this request, and it is useless to guess, except to say that all or most of them must have been Pilate's own subjects. To conclude from this that all those who at this early hour were gathered in front of "the governor's palace" must have been inhabitants of Jerusalem and surroundings is deriving too much from too little.

9. **Pilate asked them, Do y o u want me to release [796] to y o u the king of the Jews?** As is clear throughout and was mentioned earlier, Pilate wishes to shake off the responsibility of making a decision with respect to Jesus. In the first place, he is not favorably inclined toward the Jews, and an added reason for his disinclination to grant the earlier request, namely, that he sentence Jesus to death (John 18:30, 31; cf. Mark 14:64; 15:1, 3, 4), is mentioned in verse 10, as will be shown in a moment. So, in the present request for the release of a prisoner he sees an opportunity to disengage himself from this case. It is therefore clear that his questions, "Do y o u want me to release to y o u the king of the Jews?"—this title being uttered contemptuously—is really a suggestion that the Jews should ask for the release of Jesus.

Of course, the very idea that Jesus, whom Pilate has already declared innocent, is here treated as if he were in a class with a reckless bandit, a

---

794 In this verse note στασιαστής, one who rises (stands up) against, a rebel; στάσις, an uprising, rebellion; cf. German *Aufstand*, Dutch *opstand;* δεδεμένος (nom. s. masc. perf. passive participle of δέω) one bound, a prisoner; πεποιήκεισαν, third per. pl. plup. active of ποιέω: to do, commit.

795 ἤρξατο (from ἄρχω); see on 1:45 and on 6:7, footnote 233.

796 For θέλω without ἵνα see also 10:36, 51; 14:12. There is a tendency not only in Greek but in language generally to omit words that are not felt to be strictly necessary. Usually the longer and the shorter form of expression exist side by side for a while. Thus also in English "in order to" often becomes "to," and many a "that" is today simply omitted. ἀπολύσω is first per. s. aor. subjunctive (here deliberative) of ἀπολύω.

convicted revolutionist and murderer, is shocking. The suggestion that the
chief priests and the people in general choose between Jesus and Barabbas, as
if both were condemned criminals, one of whom could now become the
object of Pilate's and of the mob's mercy, was outrageously unfair. The fact
that Jesus submitted to this outrage instead of requesting "more than twelve
legions of angels" to destroy his enemies shows with what earnestness and
devotion he applied himself to the task which the Father had assigned to
him.

As to Pilate, his purpose in saying, "Do y o u want me to release to
y o u the king of the Jews?" was that he had decided to let Jesus go (Acts
3:13) . . . that is, *if* he could do this without what he considered loss to
himself. **10. For he was aware that because of envy the chief priests had
handed him over** [797] **(to him).**

Pilate knew that there was no objective ground, no just cause for the plot
of the Jewish leaders to put Jesus to death. He knew that these men were
being devoured by envy. For more on *envy* see N.T.C. on I and II Timothy
and Titus, p. 388, where one can also find several Biblical illustrations of this
sinful characteristic. Envy is the displeasure aroused by seeing someone else
having what you do not want him to have. So, for example, the leaders
envied Jesus because of his fame and following, his ability to perform
miracles, etc.

Surely, now Pilate is going to have his way. Why, even *the leaders* cannot
with any consistency ask for the release of a proved, condemned, violent,
murderous insurrectionist, since just a little while ago they have accused
Jesus of insurrection, a man whose guilt in this respect has not even been
proved; in fact, has been disproved.—And as to *the crowds*, Pilate "knows"
how *they* will vote! . . . And then, as Matt. 27:19 relates, there was a sudden
interruption. A message arrives from the governor's wife, stating, "Don't
have anything to do with this righteous man; for this very day I have
suffered much in a dream because of him." For the details see N.T.C. on
Matthew, pp. 953, 954.

While Pilate was being kept busy with the message from his wife, the chief
priests took full advantage of the situation: **11. But the chief priests stirred
up the mob (to get) him to release to them Barabbas instead (of Jesus).** [798]

---

[797] παραδεδώκεισαν, another pluperfect form, this one derived from παραδίδωμι.
Barabbas *had committed* murder and as a result *had been bound*, that is, imprisoned and
was now still a prisoner. Because of envy the chief priests *had handed Jesus over* (to
Pilate). All of these *antecedent actions* form the background for *a.* Pilate's suggestion
(verse 9) that the people ask for the release of Jesus (verse 9) and *b.* the chief priests'
demand (verse 11) that they ask for the release of Barabbas.

[798] ἀνέσεισαν, third per. pl. aor. indic. act. of ἀνασείω = ἀνά, up; plus σείω, to stir,
shake, agitate; a σεισμός being an earthquake; cf. *seismograph.* ἀπολύσῃ (after ἵνα), third

636

Did they recount all the crimes which Pilate had previously committed against the Jewish nation? And did they intimidate those who at first were inclined to choose Jesus? If they did, it would not have been the first time; see John 7:13; 9:22; 19:38; nor would it be the last; see John 20:19; Acts 4:18.

What is implied in Mark is fully stated in Matt. 27:21: "So when the governor asked them, Which of the two do y o u want me to release to y o u? they said, Barabbas." Mark continues: **12. Replying, Pilate said to them, What, then, do y o u want** [799] **me to do with** [800] **the one whom y o u call** [801] **the king of the Jews?** The governor, apparently not realizing what the chief priests had been doing, must have been fully confident that the people would ask for the release of Jesus. When instead, they demanded the release of Barabbas, Pilate was becoming desperate. He did not want to sentence Jesus to death. Yet, it was becoming more and more clear to him that this by now had become the desire of the fickle multitude. When the prophet of Galilee was still healing the sick, raising the dead, cleansing the lepers, holding the multitudes spellbound by means of his marvelous discourses, he was popular. When he rode into Jerusalem, he was applauded. But now that he is seemingly helpless, and the leaders have used their strongest arguments to persuade the people to demand his crucifixion, they turn their backs on him. As to Pilate, when he asked, "Then what do y o u want me to do with the one whom y o u call 'the king of the Jews?' " his own immediate answer should have been, "Since he is innocent I will order his immediate and definite release." In fact, the judge should not even have asked the question at all. He knew the answer. **13. Crucify him! they shouted back.** [802]

The people reacted angrily to Pilate's assumption that they regarded Jesus as their king. In this connection it should not escape us that by demanding Christ's crucifixion they were beginning to fulfil his own prediction. See Matt. 20:19; 26:2; John 3:14; 12:32.

---

per. sing. aor. subj. active of ἀπολύω, to release, as in verses 6, 9, 15; elsewhere: to send away, 6:36, 45; 8:3, 9; to divorce, 10:2-12.

[799] In certain important manuscripts θέλετε is lacking, resulting in "What, then, am I to do with . . . ?" The resultant meaning is about the same. On θέλω without ἵνα see above, on 15:9.

[800] For the idiom ποιεῖν with double acc. see L.N.T. (A. and G.), p. 688. Note ποιήσω, first per. s. aor. (deliberative) subjunctive.

[801] Though ὅν λέγετε, too, is uncertain, in favor of retaining it is the fact that then Pilate puts the burden of calling Jesus "the king of the Jews" upon the Jews themselves. On the other hand, Pilate may well have used the term himself, sarcastically.

[802] Cf. 11:3, "He will send it *back*—or return it—shortly." Either "back" or "again" (for πάλιν) also makes good sense in John 4:46; Acts 11:10; Phil. 1:26; Gal. 1:17. For more on πάλιν see on 14:69, footnote 780.

The contrast between the jubilations of the preceding Sunday and the execrations of Good Friday create a problem. The question is often asked, "How was it possible for the crowd to cheer Jesus on Sunday and to sneer at him five days later?" The usual answer is, "But this was not the same crowd. The *hosanna shouters* were Galilean pilgrims; the *Crucify him* screamers were Jerusalemites or at least Judeans."

Whatever element of truth (see verse 8) there may be in that solution, it is *not fully* satisfactory. Unbiased reading of the Triumphal Entry accounts (Matt. 21:8-11; Mark 11:7-10; Luke 19:36-38; and John 12:9-18) does not leave one with the impression that all these Sunday enthusiasts were Galilean pilgrims. See, for example, John 12:17. Though we must make allowance for the figure of speech called hyperbole, we will probably have to agree with the conclusion of the Pharisees, "Look, *the world* has gone after him!" (John 12:19). Similarly, it would be difficult to defend the proposition that on the following Friday none but Pilate's subjects were screaming "Crucify him." Admittedly many of them may well have been exactly that. But to exclude from Calvary a goodly number of people who, in order to participate in the feast, had come from elsewhere, including Galilee, would amount to doing injustice to the probabilities. As well as there were Galilean women in that crowd (Mark 15:40, 41) there must have been Galilean men also. With respect to variety of visitors, Passover probably resembled Pentecost. See Acts 2:5-11. Eagerness to see what was going on at Calvary must have been widespread. Curiosity does not recognize ethnic boundaries. And as concerns the attitude of the people, including the Jerusalemites, toward Jesus during the days intervening between the Triumphal Entry and Good Friday, "the huge crowd [regardless of where they came from] enjoyed listening to him" (Mark 12:37). It would seem therefore that the only logical conclusion is that on the part of many a change of attitude had actually taken place. [803]

How must we account for this? The fickleness or instability of the human heart and mind apart from regenerating grace enters into the answer. Other factors deserving consideration are:

a. The pressure exerted upon the crowd by the chief priests. We are distinctly told, "But the chief priests stirred up the mob to get him [Pilate] to release to them Barabbas instead (of Jesus)." Read Mark 15:11; cf. Matt. 27:20. It was hard to resist such pressure. See John 9:22; 12:42; cf. 20:19.

b. The fact that in the end Jesus did not prove to be the kind of Messiah the people desired and were expecting.

c. Sinful ignorance of Scripture. With increasing clarity the Old Testa-

---

[803] For this "change of attitude" see also V. Taylor, *op. cit.*, p. 581.

ment draws the picture of the coming Redeemer: Gen. 3:15; II Sam. 7:12, 13; Ps. 72; 118:22, 23; Isa. 7:14; 9:6; 11:1-10; 35:5, 6; 42:1-4; 53; 60:1-3; Jer. 23:6; 31:31-34; Mic. 4:1-5; 5:2; 7:18-20; Hag. 2:1-9; Zech. 3:8; 6:9-13; 9:9, 10; 13:1; Mal. 3:1-4, to mention only a few of the many messianic prophecies. These predictions associate with Messiah: peace, pardon, healing, righteousness, vicarious suffering, spiritual cleansing.

The lesson is obvious: Do not neglect the prayerful study of the Scriptures! And do not neglect to take the Bible's precious truths to heart!

14. But Pilate said to them, Why? [804] **What wrong has he done?** It is rewarding to count the number of times the governor uttered the words, "I do not find any crime in him," or something similar, as here. In addition to the passages from Luke and John, already mentioned, and the clear implication of the present Marcan passage, see also Matt. 27:23, 24. Even when due allowance is made for parallel (duplicate) passages, the fact remains that Pilate stresses and constantly re-iterates the truth that in Jesus there is no cause of indictment. And by means of Pilate it was God himself who declared his Son's complete innocence, his perfect righteousness. Nevertheless, in a few more moments this same Pilate is going to succumb to the persistent clamor of the Jews, and is going to sentence Jesus to die the accursed death of crucifixion. "No guilt in him . . . no guilt in him . . . no guilt in him . . . no guilt in him. . . . So then he handed him over in order to be crucified." Thus reads the sacred record. But how could a righteous God permit this? There is only *one* solution. It is found in Isa. 53:6, 8, "Jehovah has laid on him the iniquity of us all. . . . He was cut off out of the land of the living for the transgression of my people to whom the stroke was due." Cf. Gal. 3:13.

In answer to Pilate's question the people did not even say, "He did this" or, "He did that." They followed what must have been for them the easier course: **All the louder they were screaming, Let him be crucified!** Over and over again these terrible words are yelled until they become a monotonous refrain, an eery, ominous chant: "Let him be crucified. . . . Let him be crucified. . . ." The crowd has become a riotous mob, an emotion-charged screaming rabble.

Matthew (27:24) continues as follows: "So when Pilate saw that he was not getting anywhere, and that on the contrary a riot was starting, he took water and washed his hands in front of the crowd, saying, Innocent am I of the blood of this man." Mark skips this incident and continues with **15. So Pilate, anxious to satisfy the crowd, released Barabbas to them; and he had**

---

804 By no means does γάρ always mean *for* or *because*. It can also be strongly confirmatory or exclamatory: Yes, indeed! Certainly! There! What! Why! (cf. John 7:41; Acts 8:31; I Cor. 9:10; 11:22; Gal. 1:10; Phil. 1:18).

Jesus flogged and handed him over to be crucified. As was mentioned previously, what turned the scale so that Pilate finally decided to yield to the mob's clamor was the frightening and diabolical outcry, "If you release this man [Jesus], you are no friend of the emperor. Whoever makes himself king rebels against the emperor" (John 19:12). It was this outcry that floored the governor. In his feverish imagination he saw how he was about to lose his prestige, position, possessions, freedom, even his life perhaps.

Pilate understood immediately that the people's angry statement *implied* much more than it *expressed*. It implied: "We will lodge a complaint against you. We will tell the emperor that you condone high treason against the government; that you have released a man who was guilty of continuous sedition, and who allowed himself to be called *king*. We will accuse you of 'softness toward rebels.' Then where will *you* be?"

Mark summarizes by simply stating that Pilate, anxious to satisfy [805] the crowd, released Barabbas to them. He continues literally, "And having flogged Jesus, he handed him over that he should be crucified." "Having flogged" means "having caused him to be flogged." Cf. 6:16: "the man whom I beheaded."

Flogging [806] generally preceded crucifixion, though, as John 19:4-6 (see N.T.C. on that passage) indicates, that was not Pilate's immediate intention in the present case. It is clear from that passage that Mark summarizes. None of the Gospel-writers is attempting to give a complete account. The Roman scourge consisted of a short wooden handle to which several thongs were attached, the ends equipped with pieces of lead or brass and with sharply pointed bits of bone. The stripes were laid especially on the victim's back, bared and bent. Generally two men were employed to administer this punishment, one lashing the victim from one side, one from the other side, with the result that the flesh was at times lacerated to such an extent that deep-seated veins and arteries, sometimes even entrails and inner organs, were exposed. Such flogging, from which Roman citizens were exempt (cf. Acts 16:37), often resulted in death.

One can picture Jesus after the scourging, covered with horrible bruises and lacerations, with wales and welts. It is no surprise that Simon of Cyrene was compelled to bear the cross after Jesus had carried it a short distance (15:21; cf. Matt. 27:32; Luke 23:26; John 19:16, 17). Scourging was

---

805 Note τὸ ἱκανὸν ποιῆσαι. For this see above, on Mark 10:46, footnote 509. Cf. the Latin: "Pilatus igitur volens turbae satisfacere (from *satis facere*). . . ."

806 The aor. participle φραγελλώσας of φραγελλόω, is another reminder of the fact that Mark is writing to Romans; cf. *flagello*. The Greek word is therefore probably a loanword from the Latin.

hideous torture. It must, however, be borne in mind that the suffering of the Man of Sorrows was not only intense but also vicarious:

"He was wounded for our transgressions, he was bruised for our iniquities; the chastisement of our peace was upon him; *and with his stripes we are healed*" (Isa. 53:5; I Peter 2:24).

For the believer it is a comfort to know that back of Pilate stood God himself. The responsibility for the sinful act, to be sure, remained with Pilate and with those who pressured him into delivering Jesus to be crucified. [807] But the actions of all these sinners were included in the all-comprehensive, eternal decree of God: "This man, having been handed over (to y o u) by the predetermined purpose and foreknowledge of God, y o u, by the hand of lawless men, have crucified and slain" (Acts 2:23). "Therefore, there is now no condemnation for those who are in Christ Jesus" (Rom. 8:1).

Pilate had tried again and again to bypass Jesus. He discovered that this was entirely impossible. He was forced to take a stand, and he took the wrong stand.

The impossibility of evading Jesus is by himself expressed in these words.

a. (Negatively) "He who is not with me is against me" (Matt. 12:30).

b. (Positively) "He who is not against us is for us" (Mark 9:40).

In the great day of judgment there will just be two groups, not three. There will be no middle ground. See Matt. 25:31-46. The decisive moment to choose is always NOW: "Today, O that y o u would listen to his voice" (Ps. 95:7; Heb. 3:7, 15).

---

16 Then the soldiers led him away inside the palace, that is, the governor's headquarters, and called together the whole band. 17 And they dressed him in a purple robe; and having woven a crown of thorns, they set it on his head. 18 And they began to salute him, "Hail, king of the Jews!" 19 They were repeatedly striking him on the head with a stick, spitting on him, and on bended knee doing him homage. 20 And when they had finished mocking him, they took off the purple robe and put his own clothes on him (again). Then they led him away for crucifixion.

15:16-20 *The Mockery*
Cf. Matt. 27:27-31; John 19:2, 3

This section is not paralleled in Luke. As to the extent to which the individual items, as presented by Matthew, Mark, and John, parallel each other see N.T.C. on Matthew, the columns on pp. 958, 959.

---

807 ἵνα σταυρωθῇ, that he should be crucified = to be crucified.

16. Then the soldiers led him away inside the palace, [808] that [809] is, the governor's headquarters, [810] and called together the whole band.

Note the words, "The soldiers led him away." From Thursday night until Friday morning about nine o'clock (see Mark 15:25) Jesus permitted himself to be "led," "led away," "sent," "brought," etc. This means that he allowed himself to be passed from one individual or group to another, as a captive.

To appreciate more fully what is meant by Isa. 53:7—"As a lamb *he was led* to the slaughter"—study the following table (not necessarily complete):

Jesus was led

	From Gethsemane	Matthew	Mark	Luke	John
1	to Annas				18:13
2	to Caiaphas	26:57	14:53	22:54	18:24
3	to Pilate	27:2	15:1	23:1	18:28
4	to Herod			23:7	
5	to Pilate			23:11	
6	to inside the praet.	27:27	15:16		18:33
7	outside before the crowds				19:5
8	to inside the praet.				19:9
9	outside before the crowds				19:13
10	to Calvary	27:31	15:20	23:26	19:17

808 Greek αὐλή, a word about which there has been much dispute. Because of the context in each individual case, the following meanings are probably correct:

a. *sheepfold:* John 10:1, 16. The context has reference to shepherds and their sheep. The meaning "sheepfold" is therefore natural.

b. *court, courtyard:* Matt. 26:58, 69; Mark 14:54, 66; Luke 22:55; John 18:15. In all these cases Peter is represented as being with the temple police and the palace servants, warming himself near the fire in an "open" or "roofless" place, one that is represented as being "lower" than the rest of the house or palace. Hence, the natural meaning is "court" or "courtyard." Rev. 11:1, 2 makes a distinction between the inner temple and naturally the "outer court."

c. *house, palace:* Matt. 26:3; Mark 15:16; Luke 11:21. Respectively, the argument for "house" or "palace" is as follows: A courtyard, with servants passing in and out, would not have suited the context of Matt. 26:3. The expressed synonym "praetorium" indicates that more than a courtyard is meant in Mark 15:16. And the owner of a house or palace (Luke 11:21) would guard more than his courtyard; besides his "possessions" would not be confined to that area.

809 The neuter relative pronoun ὅ is employed in explanations of words (often, but not always, foreign words). See, besides our passage, also Mark 3:17; 5:41; 7:11, 34; 12:42; 15:22, 34; and in other New Testament books: Matt. 1:23; 27:33; John 1:38, 41 f.; 19:17; Acts 4:36; Eph. 5:5; Col. 1:24; 3:14; Heb. 7:2.

810 Literally, "the praetorium," another Latin loanword.

The soldiers, as many as were available—note "the whole band," literally "the entire cohort," though this does not necessarily mean a full cohort of six hundred men—now gather around Jesus in order to make sport of him. They desire to gratify their sadistic urges. They wish to have some fun with this "King of the Jews." These soldiers, though Roman in the sense that they were in the service of the Roman government, were probably recruited from the province of Syria; and if so, were able to converse in the Aramaic language, spoken also by the Jews, and were acquainted with Jewish ways. They probably regarded Jesus as a fake claimant to the royal throne, a person who deserved nothing better than to be mocked.

To say that this mockery had been ordered by Pilate (thus Lenski) is unwarranted. Nowhere does the record support that interpretation. It was Pilate who had ordered the *scourging*. Though it is true that he could and should have prevented the mockery, and was therefore partly responsible for it, we have no right to say that he ordered it.

17-19. And they dressed him in a purple robe; and having woven a crown of thorns, they set it on his head. And they began to salute him, Hail, king of the Jews! They were repeatedly striking him on the head with a stick, spitting on him, and on bended knee doing him homage.

This mockery should be compared to what Jesus had already endured in the house of Caiaphas, just a few hours earlier. See Mark 14:65; cf. Matt. 26:67; Luke 22:63-65.

In summary, the entire picture is as follows. The soldiers, having stripped Jesus of his outer garments, throw a "royal" robe around him. They weave a crown of thorns and set it on his head. Moreover, since a king must also wield a scepter, they thrust a stick into his right hand. This item is mentioned in so many words by Matthew and is implied by Mark. Then, one by one, they kneel down in front of him in mock adoration, saying, "Hail, king of the Jews." They spit on him and hit him on the head with his own "scepter."

Note the separate items mentioned by Mark:

a. *They robed him in purple.*

As Matthew indicates, they first disrobed him. This had been done once before, just before he was scourged (Mark 15:15). How terribly it must have hurt him when the robe had been cast around his scourged body. And now again they strip him and then throw around him what was probably a discarded and faded soldier's mantle of a "purple" (so also John 19:2b) hue, representing the royal purple. Here Matthew uses the synonym "scarlet." Since the robe must have been faded, its color did not stand out very clearly, and could therefore be considered either "purple" or "scarlet." Again, how throwing this robe around the scourged Savior must have hurt him!

b. *They crowned him with a crown of thorns.*

643

Somewhere in the vicinity of the praetorium the soldiers find some thorny twigs. Whether the plant from which they obtained these twigs was the *Spina Christi* or *Palinrus Shrub,* as some think, is not known. It has been pointed out by botanists that few countries of the size of Palestine have so many varieties of prickly plants. The identity of the species is of little importance. Far more significant is the fact that thorns and thistles are mentioned in Gen. 3:18 in connection with Adam's fall. Here in Mark 15:17b and its parallels Jesus is pictured as bearing the curse that lies upon nature, in order to deliver nature and us from it. With fiendish cruelty the soldiers, having made "a crown" out of these thorny twigs, press it down upon Christ's head. It represented not an imperial wreath but a crown such as would be appropriate for a "king of the Jews." Those who were engaged in this bit of fun wanted to mock Jesus. They also wanted to torture him. The crown of thorns satisfied both purposes. Rivulets of blood must have started to run down his face, neck, and other parts of his body. Did his molesters realize that they were doing this to him who is "King of kings and Lord of lords"?

c. *They mockingly adored him.*

"Hail, king of the Jews," a soldier would say, as on bended knee he was doing him homage. Then another would take his turn, and still another, until all those many soldiers had taken their turn.

d. *They hit him.*

Before any of these mockers vacated his position in front of Jesus, he would remove the stick from the hand of the victim and strike him on the head with it, as if to say, "What a king you are! One that gets hit over the head with his own scepter!" And as the fiend hits Jesus, the thorny spikes are driven deeper into the flesh.

e. *They spat on him.*

They descend to a level lower than the beasts. Gleefully—for they're having fun—each soldier, when his turn comes around, after getting up from his knees spits into the face of God's only begotten and beloved Son!

In studying this passage a few practical lessons stand out:

a. How darkened man's mind! These men think they are doing all this to a false claimant to an earthly throne. They have no conception of the fact that they are doing it to the rightful owner of the universe, the "King of kings and Lord of lords."

b. How depraved man's heart! Hellish cruelty is displayed here. Unbridled sadism triumphs. And what an empty triumph! One that makes the soul of the perpetrator more wretched than ever (Isa. 48:22; 57:21; contrast Isa. 26:3; Ps. 119:165).

c. How dependable God's Word! What had been predicted is here being fulfilled (Ps. 22:6, 7; Isa. 53:3, 5, 7, 8, 10; Mark 10:34). That very fact must have imparted comfort to the heart and mind of Christ.

d. How durable Christ's purpose! He bore it all without complaining. He did this because he knew that he was accomplishing the work which the Father had given him to do (John 17:4). For our sake he became poor that we through his poverty might become rich (see II Cor. 8:9).

20. And when they had finished mocking him, they took off the purple robe and put his own clothes on him (again). Then they led him away for crucifixion. [811] Finally the soldiers have all had their turn. According to John 19:4 ff. Pilate now enters into the picture again. He brings Jesus out before the crowd, the sorely afflicted one still wearing the thorny crown and the purple robe. A pathetic spectacle is exposed to the view of the public: blood-streaked Jesus, covered with gashing wounds. "Look! The man!" says the governor, in order to arouse the people's sympathy and to testify once again that he, Pilate, finds no crime in him. But this effort on the part of the judge fails as tragically as have all the previous ones. When the chief priests and the officers see Jesus they cry out, "Crucify . . . crucify!" They now use their final argument, the one which up to this time they have held in abeyance, namely, "We have a law, and according to that law he ought to die, because he made himself the Son of God." Having re-examined Jesus and all the while still trying to release him, Pilate finally surrenders to the wishes of the chief priests and the mob. He does so for the reason stated previously (and see John 19:12).

The soldiers' game having ended somewhat earlier, these men now remove their victim's royal accouterments and put his own clothes on him again. Then they lead him away to be crucified.

---

21 And they forced a certain bypasser, who was coming from the country, a Cyrenian, Simon, the father of Alexander and Rufus, to carry his cross.   22 And they brought Jesus to the place (called) Golgotha, which, translated, is Place of a Skull.   23 They offered him wine flavored with myrrh, but he refused to accept it.   24 And they crucified him, and divided his garments, casting lots for them (to determine) who should take what.

25 Now it was the third hour [812] when they crucified him.   26 The superscription stating the charge against him read,

THE KING OF THE JEWS

27 And with him they crucified two robbers, one on his right and one on his left. 29 [813] And those who passed by were blaspheming him, shaking their heads and saying,

---

811 Points of vocabulary and grammar in this passage: ἐνέπαιξαν, third per. pl. aor. act. indic. of ἐμπαίζω, to play with, mock. Cf. Matt. 27:31. Note the aor. where English uses the pluperfect, Grm. N.T., p. 840; E. D. Burton, *op. cit.*, pp. 22, 23. Verbs of clothing and unclothing usually (not always) have two accusatives: one of the person, one of the clothes, Gram. N.T., p. 483. Note also the vivid historical present ἐξάγουσι here in verse 20, after the imperfects in verse 19.

812 Or: 9 A.M.

813 There is insufficient textual support for verse 28: and the scripture was fulfilled which says, "He was reckoned with the transgressors."

645

"Aha! You who destroy the temple and rebuild it in three days,   30 save yourself and come down from the cross."   31 Similarly also the chief priests, mocking (him) among themselves, along with the scribes, were saying, "Others he saved, himself he cannot save!   32 Let the Christ, the king of Israel, now come down from the cross, that we may see and believe!" And those crucified with him were also heaping insults on him.

15:21-32 *Calvary: The Crucifixion of Jesus*
Cf. Matt. 27:32-44; Luke 23:26-43; John 19:17-27

The story of Christ's crucifixion is told by all four evangelists in some detail. Mark's account is the shortest. Slightly longer is Matthew's. Luke's report is almost twice the length of Mark's. John's is about as much longer than Matthew's as it is shorter than Luke's. If we assign the convenient figure 10 to the length of Matthew's account of the crucifixion, Mark's would be 9, Luke's 17, and John's 13½.

Omitting minor details, the contents of the four accounts may be briefly summarized and compared as follows:

The resemblance between Matthew (27:32-44) and Mark (15:21-32) is very close. Both record that Simon of Cyrene was forced to carry Christ's cross. Arrived at Golgotha Jesus was offered a drink (probably to deaden the sense of pain), but he refused it. Having been crucified, his clothes were divided by lot among the soldiers. Over his head was placed the indictment against him: it described him as "the king of the Jews." Two robbers were crucified with Jesus, one on either side of him. Bypassers blasphemed him, taunting him to come down from the cross. Chief priests and scribes were scoffing among themselves. "Others he saved," they said, "himself he cannot save. . . ." The robbers who had been crucified with him were reviling him.

The main variations between Matthew's report and Mark's, aside from the wording of the superscription, which is somewhat different in each of the four Gospels, are as follows:

Matthew states that it was while the procession was coming out of the city that Simon of Cyrene was pressed into service. When Jesus had been crucified, the soldiers, sitting down, were keeping watch over him. To the words of mockery uttered by the chief priests, etc., Matthew adds those found in 27:43, "He has placed his trust in God. . . ."

Mark informs his (Roman) leaders that "a Cyrenian, Simon," was coming "from the country" (so also Luke) when the soldiers forced him to bear Christ's cross, and that this Simon was the father of Alexander and Rufus (probably of Rome; see Rom. 16:13). He also states that it was "the third hour" when Jesus was crucified.

As to *Luke,* the main specific features of his contribution (23:26-43) are the following: Jesus' address to Jerusalem's weeping women, the story of the impenitent criminal and the penitent one, and (verses 34, 43) the first two

646

words from the cross. This evangelist adds that the soldiers joined in the mockery and offered Christ vinegar.

According to *John* (19:17-27) at first Jesus himself carried the cross. In fact, John says nothing about Simon of Cyrene. The "title" that had been affixed to the cross was written in Aramaic, Latin, and Greek. Many of the Jews read it, for the place where Jesus was crucified was near the city. John reports the objection of the chief priests to the wording of the title, and also Pilate's answer. This evangelist goes into some detail in describing the manner in which the garments of Jesus, including the seamless tunic, were divided. He has preserved for us the third word from the cross (verse 27).

*   *   *   *

Though in the Passion story the center of interest is always Jesus himself, what *he* did, said, or endured, our attention is here also fixed upon five subsidiary persons or groups:

a. *Simon of Cyrene* renders a service to Jesus (verse 21).

b. Arrived at Golgotha *the legionaries* or soldiers offer Jesus drugged wine, which he refuses. Having crucified him between two robbers, and having affixed a label above his head, they cast lots for the division of his clothes (verses 22-27).

c. *Bypassers* blaspheme (verses 29, 30).

d. *Scribes* (and their companions) scoff (verses 31, 32a).

e. *Robbers* revile (verse 32b).

With the exception of verse 21, the entire section (Mark 15:21-32) relates what happened to Jesus from nine o'clock A.M. (cf. 15:25) until noon (cf. 15:33) on Good Friday.

Simon of Cyrene

In reality what is said in verse 21 might also have been included under the next heading, because Simon did not act of his own accord. By the soldiers he was forced to do what he did. But since the New Testament and early tradition place such emphasis on him and (probably) his family, a separate caption is given to verse 21. **And they forced** [814] **a certain bypasser, who**

---

814 ἀγγαρεύουσι, third per. pl. pres. indic. of ἀγγαρεύω, also occurring in the parallel passage Matt. 27:32 and in Matt. 5:41. The ἄγγαρος was originally a Persian messenger or courier. To him had been given the authority to press into service men, horses, etc. This is, accordingly, a Persian word, a term pertaining to its postal service. The Persians may have derived it from the Babylonians. It is not strange that the meaning of the word gradually broadened, so that not only pressing into service to expedite the mail but forcing a person to render any kind of service was covered by it. See also N.T.C. on Matthew, p. 311.

was coming from the country, a Cyrenian, Simon, the father of Alexander and Rufus, to carry his cross. As was customary and according to law, the execution was carried out outside the city (Exod. 29:14; Lev. 4:12, 21; 9:11; 16:27; Num. 15:35; 19:3; cf. John 19:20; Heb. 13:12, 13). Those condemned to be crucified had to carry their own cross. Commentators are divided on the question whether this refers to the crossbeam alone, the upright having already been set in place on Golgotha, or to the entire cross. Since there is nothing in text or context that suggests otherwise, it is here assumed that the latter position—the entire cross—is correct.

In the light of the fact that the title of indictment was written above Christ's head, it is well-nigh certain that artists are correct in their preference for the dagger-type or Latin cross: † . For the reasons why death by crucifixion must be considered a curse see N.T.C. on the Gospel of John, Vol. II, p. 425.

Jesus, too, carried his own cross (John 19:16, 17), but not for long. Sheer physical exhaustion made it impossible for him to carry it very far. Consider what he had already endured within the last fifteen hours: the tense atmosphere of the Upper Room, the betrayal by Judas, the agonies of Gethsemane, the desertion by his disciples, the torture of a totally hypocritical trial before the Sanhedrin, the mockery in the palace of Caiaphas, the denial by his most prominent disciple, the trial before an unjust judge, the terrible ordeal of being scourged, the pronunciation of the death sentence upon him, and the seven-itemed abuse by the soldiers in the praetorium! Humanly speaking, is it not a wonder that he was able to carry the cross any distance at all?

When Jesus succumbed beneath his load, the legionaries, exercising their right of "requisitioning" or "making demands on" people, forced Simon, a Cyrenian or man from Cyrene—located on a plateau, ten miles from the Mediterranean Sea, in what is now Libya (west of Egypt)—to carry Christ's cross for the rest of the distance. The theory that Simon could not have been a Jew, because he gave his sons Greek names (verse 21), is without merit, since many Jews followed that practice. Besides, in Cyrene there was a large colony of Jews (Acts 2:10; 6:9; 11:20; 13:1). The further speculation that the man must have been a farmer, because on this particular Friday morning he came "from the country," is also without any basis. Even today many people besides farmers have business or social connections in the country. Some even live there!

The following reconstruction, though not certain, is however probable. Simon, a Jew, has come to Jerusalem to attend one of the great festivals (in this case Passover), as was the custom of many Jews, including those from Cyrene (Acts 2:10). There was even a Cyrenian synagogue in Jerusalem (Acts 6:9).

Now on this particular Friday, returning to the city from a visit to the country, Simon is pressed into service by the soldiers who are leading Jesus to Calvary, perhaps (but this is by no means certain) along the Via Dolorosa (Sorrowful Way), and are just now coming through the gate out of the city. So—reluctantly at first?—Simon carries Christ's cross, arrives at Calvary, and witnesses what happens there. The behavior of Jesus and his words from the cross leave such an impression on Simon that he becomes a Christian. Subsequently he and his family are living in Rome. He may have been living there before, but in any event he was a Cyrenian by birth. (Among the early Christians there were many Cyrenians, Acts 11:19; 13:1).

Mark, writing to the Romans, mentions "Simon, the father of Alexander and Rufus," as if to say, "people with whom y o u, in Rome, are well acquainted." Paul, in his letter to the Romans (16:13), writes, "Greet Rufus, outstanding in the Lord, and his mother and mine." Evidently the mother of Rufus—hence, the wife of Simon—had rendered some motherly service to Paul.

If this reconstruction is factual, then the service which Simon rendered, though initially "forced," turned out to be a genuine blessing for himself, his family, and many others.

The Legionaries

22. **And they brought Jesus to the place (called) Golgotha, which, translated, is** [815] **Place of the Skull.**

The name *Golgotha* is basically Aramaic. It is a Greek transliteration of Aramaic *golgoltha;* cf. Hebrew *golgoleth.* The name means *skull.* The Greek word for Skull is *Kranion* (cf. *cranium*). In the Vulgate (Jerome's Latin version of the Bible) *Kranion* was rendered *Calvaria;* cf. "Calvary."

Why was this name—Place of the (or *a*) Skull—given to it? Because it looked like a skull? Because a skull was found there? Precisely where was Golgotha? Is it possible to point out its exact location today? On all this see N.T.C. on John, Vol. II, p. 426.

The procession arrived at "the Place of the Skull." Though today it may well be impossible to point out the exact spot where Jesus was crucified, the Church of the Holy Sepulchre has tradition on its side. Not too much can be made of this, however, for the "tradition" is rather late (fourth century

---

815 ὅ ἐστιν μεθερμηνευόμενον. For ὅ in such connections see above, on 15:16, footnote 809. The verb from which the pres. pass. participle is derived is μεθερμηνεύω, meaning: to translate, interpret. The entire phrase may be rendered "which, translated, is," or simply "which means." *Hermeneutics* is the art of *interpretation.* See also Matt. 1:23; Mark 5:41; 15:34; Acts 4:36; and cf. John 1:38, 42; Acts 13:8. For more on this verb see N.T.C. on John, Vol. I, p. 103.

A.D.). Within the large space covered by this church there is room for the site of the crosses and also for that of the tomb in which Joseph of Arimathea laid Jesus' body. The place of execution and the tomb were very close to each other (John 19:41, 42). "Skull's Place" was "outside the gate" as it existed at that time (Matt. 27:32; Heb. 13:12). [816]

23. They offered [817] **him wine flavored with myrrh,** [818] **but he refused to accept it.**

That the wine which the soldiers tried to give Jesus was mixed with something bitter appears from Matthew's account. Here in Mark it becomes clear that this bitter substance was myrrh. They offered Jesus this "myrrhed" wine. He tasted it (Matt. 27:34), and then refused it. Had the sympathetic women of Jerusalem (cf. Luke 23:27) prepared this drink in order to lessen the pain of the sufferers? However that may be, the reason why Jesus rejected it was probably because he wanted his mind to be clear when he spoke from the cross and because he wished to endure to the full the pain that was in store for him, in order to be his people's perfect Substitute.

24a. And they crucified him . . . .

Using the vivid present tense, Mark simply writes, "And they crucify him." Nevertheless, in English it is entirely correct to substitute the past tense for this historical present. Note how few words—in the original only three: "And they-crucified him"—are used to indicate this enormously significant event! With this marvelous restraint we might compare the manner in which Scripture tells the story of the creation of the billions of stars: "and the-stars" (Gen. 1:16b).

The pronoun "they" (in "And they crucified him") refers to *the soldiers,* as is clear from verse 16. The mode of execution to which reference is made existed in many nations, including the Roman Empire. Rome generally (not always!) reserved this form of punishment for slaves and those who had been convicted of the grossest crimes.

It has been well said that the person who was crucified "died a thousand deaths." Large nails were driven through hands and feet (John 20:25; cf. Luke 24:40). Among the horrors which one suffered while thus suspended (with the feet resting upon a little tablet, not very far away from the ground) were the following: severe inflammation, the swelling of the wounds in the region of the nails, unbearable pain from torn tendons, fearful discomfort

---

816 For "Gordon's Calvary" see G. A. Turner, *Historical Geography of the Holy Land,* Grand Rapids, 1973, p. 336. Excellent are also the observations of H. Mulder, *Spoorzoeker,* p. 157. For the location of the Church of the Holy Sepulchre see L. H. Grollenberg, *op. cit.,* map 33 on p. 115.

817 ἐδίδουν, conative imperfect: offered, tried to give.

818 ἐσμυρνισμένον, acc. s. masc. perf. pass. participle of σμυρνίζω.

from the strained position of the body, throbbing headache, and burning thirst (John 19:28).

In the case of Jesus the emphasis, however, should not be placed on this physical torture which he endured. It has been said that only the damned in hell know what Jesus suffered when he died on the cross. In a sense this is true, for they, too, suffer eternal death. One should add, however, that *they* have never been in heaven. The Son of God, on the other hand, descended from the regions of infinite delight in the closest possible fellowship with his Father (John 1:1; 17:5) to the abysmal depths of hell. On the cross he cried out, "My God, my God, why hast thou forsaken me?" (Mark 15:34).

24b. and divided his garments, casting lots for them (to determine) who should take what.

Having crucified him, the legionaries, as was their custom, divided his garments by casting lots. In all probability by means of throwing of dice the four pieces—headgear, sandals, belt, and outer garment—were divided among the four (John 19:23) soldiers. The seamless tunic, all of one piece, woven all the way from top to bottom, was also put into the lottery, all of this in accordance with the prophecy of Ps. 22:18 (LXX Ps. 21:19), which, as is clear, Mark has in mind, though the fulfilment formula is not found in Mark but in John 19:23, 24. See N.T.C. on that passage for further details.

Note the total indifference, on the part of these soldiers, to Christ on the cross. They certainly should have paid closer attention to him, to his attitude, his words, etc. At least on one of them, the centurion, such things and other circumstances made a very deep impression (15:39). And, as Matthew informs us, even the soldiers who were with the centurion, were *somewhat* similarly affected (27:54), but that effect was not produced immediately.

Right now soldiers were throwing dice while the Lamb of God was taking away the sin of the world (John 1:29). Nevertheless, it is but fair to add that Luke 23:34 ("they do not know what they are doing") was applicable to them in a higher degree than it applies to us today, after all these years during which the light of the gospel has been spreading.

Poor, poor soldiers! How much did they take home from Calvary? A few pieces of clothing! No truly penitent hearts, no renewed visions, no changed lives, no Savior? Even today, how much—or how little—do some people carry home with them from the church service, the Bible class, the hymn sing, the revival meeting? Each individual should answer this question for himself. Does not Christ's own parable of The Sower apply here? See above, on 4:1-20. And let us remember Luke 12:48.

25. Now it was the third hour when they crucified him.

Much has been written with reference to this brief note of time. Bible critics cite this passage as proof-positive that Scripture contains errors and contradictions. Does not John 19:14 state that Pilate sentenced Jesus to die when it was about the sixth hour? Surely, Jesus was *sentenced* before he was *crucified*. Yet, according to John (say the critics), the sentencing took place *at noon* ("the sixth hour").

It has been shown, however, that in other passages the author of the Fourth Gospel in all probability used *the Roman civil day time computation.* See N.T.C. on John 1:39; 4:6; 4:52. If there, why not here? Now the two statements—the one from John, namely, that Jesus was sentenced at *about six o'clock* in the morning; and the one from Mark, that he was actually nailed to the cross at *nine o'clock in the morning,* can hardly be said to be in hopeless conflict with each other. It must be borne in mind that John does not say *six o'clock* but *about* six o'clock. Let us suppose that it was actually half past six. We grant that even this leaves a difficulty, but the difficulty is not great. It is difficult for us to understand how the trial before Pilate (in reality the Pilate-Herod-Pilate trial) was so speedy, how everything transpired so rapidly. On the other hand, does it not seem probable that the Sanhedrin had been doing all in its power to *rush* Pilate to a decision? Is it not true that this august body had been rushing the case from the very moment when Jesus was captured? The morning meeting of the Sanhedrin may have been *very* early, indeed! It may have taken only a few minutes. The real decision had been agreed on long before.

Once the sentence had been pronounced by Pilate, the heat was off. So, three hours intervened between the sentencing and the crucifixion; or, let us say two hours and a half (in case the sentence was pronounced at 6:30 A.M., "*about* six o'clock"). Why so much time elapsed between the two events we do not know.

26. **The superscripture stating the charge** [819] **against him read,**

THE KING OF THE JEWS

Pilate had caused a notice or label to be written on the cross, above Jesus' head. In John's Gospel (19:19, 20) this notice is called a "title," in Matthew's (27:37), a "charge," "accusation" or "indictment," and in Mark's (15:26) and Luke's (23:38) a "superscription." With respect to this written notice critics have discovered another contradiction in the Bible. They point to the fact that the words of which it was composed differ in all four Gospels. But there is more than one possible way in which this attack upon Scripture can be refuted. First, it must be considered possible that each Gospel writer gives the gist of the superscription as he sees it. The full wording may have been "This is Jesus of Nazareth the King of the Jews." So Matthew says that the charge read: "This is Jesus the King of the Jews";

---

819 αἰτίας, objective genitive.

Mark states the superscription was: "the King of the Jews"; Luke's version is: "This is the King of the Jews"; and John, who was himself present and must have seen it, says that the title was: "Jesus of Nazareth the King of the Jews." It certainly was not necessary for each evangelist to write down all the words. Another possibility is this: since the superscription was written in three languages, Aramaic, Latin, and Greek, in one, two, or even all three of these—but differently in each case—it may have been abbreviated.

The four agree in informing the reader that on this superscription Pilate called Jesus "the king of the Jews." Why did the governor word it thus? *Negatively,* because he did *not* want to write, "Jesus *who claimed* to be the King of the Jews," for he had proclaimed again and again that Jesus was innocent of this charge which the Jew's had preferred against him. Therefore the governor absolutely refused to yield to the subsequent demand of the chief priests that he change the wording of the superscription. See John 19:21, 22. It is impossible to state *positively* why Pilate worded the superscription as he did. Did he do it to bestow honor on Jesus? One would like to think so. Yet, honoring Jesus, on the one hand, and on the other, allowing him to be mocked, and ordering him to be scourged and crucified, hardly go hand in hand. What then? Although we cannot be sure, perhaps the true answer is as follows: Pilate hated the Jews, especially their leaders. He was keenly aware that just now they had won a victory over him; for, as he probably saw it, they had forced him to sentence Jesus to be crucified. So, now he is mocking them. By means of the superscription he is saying, "Here is Jesus, the King of the Jews, the only king they have been able to produce, a king crucified at their own urgent request!"

All this does not take away the fact that although Pilate may have purposely worded the superscription as he did in order, negatively, to tell the Jews, "I do not at all believe the charge you brought against him," and positively, to mock them, God Almighty is also speaking in and through this same superscription. He is making a proclamation to one and all. Bear in mind the three languages in which the notice was written. He is saying, "This is Jesus, King of the Jews indeed; and not only this, but by means of this very cross he is King of kings and Lord of lords."

27. **And with him they crucified two robbers, one on his right and one on his left.** [820] The two men who were crucified with Jesus were "robbers," or, as the word can also be translated "revolutionaries," though, in view of Luke 23:33, "robbers" may be the best rendering here. [821] It was a gross injustice

---

[820] For the explanation of the Greek idiom here used— . . . $\dot{\epsilon}\kappa$ $\delta\epsilon\xi\iota\hat{\omega}\nu$ $\kappa\alpha\grave{\iota}$ . . . $\dot{\epsilon}\xi$ $\epsilon\dot{\upsilon}\omega\nu\dot{\upsilon}\mu\omega\nu$—see above, on 10:37, footnote 499.

[821] See on 11:17, footnote 542; also K. H. Rengstorf's article on this word in Th.D.N.T., Vol. IV., pp. 257-262. He points out that the $\lambda\eta\sigma\tau\dot{\eta}\varsigma$ is always one who ruthlessly uses force in seeking to obtain the goods of others.

that Jesus was crucified between these two criminals, as if he, too, were a criminal. Nevertheless, viewed in the light of God's providence, it was also an honor. Is it not true that Jesus came to earth in order to seek and save the lost (Luke 19:10)? Was he not "the Friend of publicans and sinners" (Matt. 11:19)? See also N.T.C. on John 3:16 and on I Tim. 1:15.

By causing Jesus to be crucified between these two culprits did Pilate intend to insult the Jews even more? Did he intend to say, "Such is y o u r king, O Jews, one who is not any better than a bandit, and therefore deserves to be crucified between two of them"? However that may have been, one thing is certain, the prophecy of Isa. 53:12—"He was reckoned with the transgressors"—was here being fulfilled. [822] And, in view of Luke 23:39-43, fulfilled gloriously.

Bypassers

29, 30. And those who passed by were blaspheming him, shaking [823] **their heads and saying, Aha! You who destroy the temple and rebuild it in three days, save yourself and come down from the cross.**

In rapid succession Mark now describes how three groups—*a.* bypassers, *b.* chief priests and scribes, and *c.* robbers—reacted toward Jesus. First, then, the bypassers (or passers-by). The word "bypasser" literally translates the Greek original, conveying its meaning exactly. If, as some believe, Calvary even then was located at the conjunction of roads—cf. The Church of the Holy Sepulchre—then the expression "the bypassers" begins to make real sense. Not everyone belonged to the multitudes (Luke 23:48) that were going *to* Calvary that day, to watch everything that happened there from beginning to end. There were also those who merely "passed by." On their way elsewhere they stop long enough to take in the scene. They center their attention on the One nailed to the central cross, about whom they have heard so much already. They shake their heads in contempt and arrogance. Cf. Ps. 22:7b; Isa. 37:22; Lam. 2:15. Then they begin to hurl abuse at him. They are actually *blaspheming* him, as the original states. For the meaning of this word and its cognates see on 2:7; 3:28, and note that here in 15:29 it is used not in a general sense, but in its most terrible sense of mocking the very Son of God. This is nothing short of "defiant irreverence."

The words which they use will bear this out. As they shake their heads they are saying, "Aha!" We may be thankful that Mark, in his vivid account, has preserved this little touch. What does this "Aha!" mean? It is an exclamation in which glee, scorn, and sense of victory are mingled. But what

---

[822] This does not contradict what was said above, in footnote 813.

[823] κινοῦντες, pres. act. participle of κινέω, to move, shake. Cf. *cinema, kinetic.*

a premature "Aha!" this is! The shouters are forgetting the maxim, "Let not the man who girds on his armor boast as the man who puts it off" (I Kings 20:11). They remind one of the enormous, heavily armored giant Goliath, who roared at the callow (?) stripling David, "Come over here and I'll give your flesh to the birds of the heavens and the beasts of the field." . . . It was his last speech! See I Sam. 17:41-49. They also bring back to mind Haman:

> "Make thou a gallows fifty cubits high,
> And thereon tomorrow let this Hebrew die!"
> C. M. Cady, in
> Wm. B. Bradbury's cantata *Esther*
> (based on Esther 5:14)

It was *Haman himself* who was hanged on the fifty cubits high gallows (or impaled on this high stake, if one prefers that translation). See Esther 7:9, 10.

Instead of yelling "Aha!" the sneering blasphemers should have said "Woe to us." Why? Because right here and now the victory was being won on the cross by the One they despised, and *they* were being defeated. Unless they repented, what awaited them was the day when they would be crying to the mountains and to the rocks, "Fall on us and hide us from the face of him who sits on the throne and from the wrath of the Lamb! For the great day of their wrath has come, and who is able to stand?" (Rev. 6:15-17).

These scoffers continue, "You who destroy the temple and rebuild it in three days. . . ." They too, therefore, as well as the false witnesses of 14:57, 58 (see on that passage), have picked up the slanderous misquotation plus misinterpretation of Christ's saying (John 2:19), and have accepted it as if it were the very truth. They are now using it, and adding, "Save yourself and come down from the cross." Scornfully they exclaim that the way for the crucified One to prove his lofty claims will be for him to descend from the cross. They imply that it is weakness that keeps them there. Actually, however, it was strength, the strength of his love for sinners. It was exactly because Jesus *did not* come down from the cross that he is our Savior. But these bypassers have made up their minds to defy the testimony of all the miracles, all the mercy shown to those in need, all the marvelous discourses, yes, the entire beautiful life of the Son of God on earth. All of this they have rejected. They prefer to jeer, to blaspheme!

Chief Priests and Scribes

31, 32a. **Similarly also the chief priests, mocking (him) among themselves, along with the scribes, were saying, Others he saved, himself he cannot save! Let the Christ, the king of Israel, now come down from the cross, that we may see and believe.**

655

So delighted were the members of the Sanhedrin with the fact that their archenemy was now hanging on a cross that they—these chief priests, scribes, and (according to Matt. 27:41) elders (for the meaning of all three see on Mark 11:27, 28)—lose every bit of dignity, and join the bypassers in giving expression to their contempt of Jesus. "Similarly," writes Mark; and in several respects the words of the leaders were indeed similar to those of the ones who passed by. Both mock. Both are convinced that the victim's remaining on the cross is due to his weakness, his utter inability to rescue himself. Both bid him to prove his claims by coming down from the cross.

Nevertheless, there is also a rather striking difference. The bypassers had addressed Jesus directly, using the second person singular. See verses 29, 30. But not once in the narrative of Christ's crucifixion—whether in Matthew, Mark, or Luke—do the leaders address Jesus directly. Each time they talk *about* him, to each other. They never talk *to* him. So thoroughly do they hate him. Matthew and Mark relate that these Sanhedrists, in their conversation with each other about their enemy *mocked* him. And so they did indeed! Luke uses a different word, however. He shows that this mockery was of the worst possible kind. Their ridicule was mingled with hatred and envy. Says Luke, "They turned up their noses at him," that is, they *sneered,* they *scoffed* (23:35).

When they now say, "others he saved; himself he cannot save," they do not deny that the miracles he had performed in the interest of others were real. Not at all. They had admitted their genuine character before (John 11:47). Only, they had ascribed his power to perform them to Satan (Mark 3:22). The conclusion they draw is that now that Beelzebul is not able and/or willing to help him any more, he is completely powerless. They too refuse to admit that it was the power of his love for sinners that kept him on that cross.

With derision they refer to the fact that he had claimed to be "the Christ, the king of Israel." Well, he did indeed make that double claim (14:62–15:2). Moreover, he had accepted royal honor implied in that and similar titles when others bestowed that honor on him. In fact he had even ascribed to himself royal authority over everything (Matt. 11:27; 25:34), and he was going to do this again (Matt. 28:18). But these leaders were deliberately misrepresenting him; for whenever, either in word or action, the people had tried to make of him an earthly king, a ruler who had come to deliver the Jews from the yoke of the Romans, he had quickly walked as far as possible away from that error. See John 6:15; cf. 18:36.

When to the words "Let the Christ, the king of Israel, now come down from the cross" the chief priests and scribes add these others: "that we may see and believe," they are uttering a gross untruth. If healing all kinds of diseases, restoring sight to those born blind, cleansing lepers, and even raising the dead, if these works of power and grace, all of them performed in fulfilment of prophecy!, did not cause them to believe in Jesus, but rather hardened their hearts so that they hated him for it, would a descent from the cross have caused them to accept him as their Lord and Savior? Of course not! We are reminded of the words found in the parable of The Rich Man and Lazarus: "If they do not listen to Moses and the prophets, they will not be convinced even if someone rises from the dead" (Luke 16:31).

Robbers

32b. And those crucified with him were also heaping insults [824] on him.
Bypassers and Sanhedrists were agreed that if Jesus wanted to prove that he was indeed what he claimed to be he should save himself. The robbers are carried away by this argument. They too in the same manner begin to revile him. It must be emphasized that according to the plain language of Scripture *both* robbers were at first heaping abuse on Jesus in this manner. The language of one of these men is reported in Luke 23:39. He said, "Aren't you the Christ? Save yourself and us." Even the military joined in this type of mockery (Luke 23:36, 37). The insults were coming from almost every side. Legionaries, bypassers, chief priests, scribes, elders, robbers, and multitudes of other spectators deride him.

In the midst of it all Jesus remains silent. He offers not one word of rebuke. Peter puts it beautifully when he says, "who, while being reviled, did not revile in return; while suffering, never threatened, but continued to entrust himself to him who judges righteously; who himself bore our sins in his body on the cross, that we might die to sin and live to righteousness; for by his wounds y o u were healed" (I Peter 2:23, 24).

---

824 ὠνείδιζον, third per. pl. imperfect of ὀνειδίζω, to heap abuse or insults upon, rebuke, reproach, reprove, revile, chide, find fault with. See also the parallel (Matt. 27:44).

The meaning will become clear from the other New Testament passages in which this verb is used:

"Blessed are y o u whenever people heap insults upon y o u" (Matt. 5:11).

"Then he began to reproach the cities" (Matt. 11:20).

"He rebuked them for their lack of faith" (Mark 16:14).

"Blessed are y o u whenever men revile y o u" (Luke 6:22).

"The reproaches of those approaching you fell upon me" (Rom. 15:3).

" . . . who gives generously to all, without reproaching" (James 1:5).

"If y o u are reproached because of the name of Christ, blessed (are y o u)" (I Peter 4:14).

The suggested renderings are by no means the only good ones.

The root of the word seems to be *nid* (preceded by euphonic ὀ), but whether or not the Dutch word *nijdig* (angry), somewhat related in meaning, belongs to the same etymological family I do not know.

Is it not possible—probable even—that this calm and majestic behavior of our Lord, coupled with the prayer, "Father, forgive them, for they do not know what they are doing" (Luke 23:34), was used by God as a means to lead one of these two robbers to repentance? For that story see Luke 23:39-43.

33 Now when the sixth hour [825] had come there was darkness over the whole land until the ninth hour.   34 And at the ninth hour Jesus cried out with a loud voice,

"Eloi, Eloi, lema sabachthani?"

which means

"My God, my God, why hast thou forsaken me?"

35 When some of the bystandards heard this they said, "Listen! he's calling Elijah." 36 Someone ran, filled a sponge with sour wine, put it on a stick, and gave him a drink, saying "Allow (me), let us see whether Elijah is coming to take him down." [826] 37 Then, with a loud cry, Jesus breathed his last.

38 And the curtain of the sanctuary was torn in two from top to bottom.   39 Now when the centurion, who stood facing him, saw that he thus cried out and died, he said, "Surely, this man was God's Son."

40 Watching from a distance there were women. Among them were Mary Magdalene, Mary the (mother) of James the Less and of Joses, and Salome.   41 When he was in Galilee these women used to follow him and to minister to his needs. And there were also many other women who had come up with him to Jerusalem.

15:33-41 *Calvary: the Death of Jesus*
Cf. Matt. 27:45-56; Luke 23:44-49; John 19:25, 28-30

The Gospel sections which describe "Calvary: the Death of Jesus" (Mark 15:33-41 and parallels) vary considerably in length. Stated in round figures, the number of words devoted to this theme in each Gospel (in the Greek text) is:

Matthew	Mark	Luke	John
200	150	100	70 [827]

With one major difference Matthew's account and Mark's are almost identical in contents. This resemblance is especially striking in Mark 15:33-37 and its parallel Matt. 27:45-50 ("From darkness to death"). We reserve for later remarks with respect to the slight differences in the wording of *a.* the cry of agony, and *b.* Christ's dying act. The problem in connection with Mark 15:36b also requires special attention.

A considerable degree of similarity is also apparent in connection with the

---

825 Or: 12 noon.

826 Alternate translation for everything after *saying:* "Let us see whether Elijah is coming to take him down."

827 More accurate for Matthew, Mark, Luke, and John, respectively in that order, are the figures 196, 150, 95, and 70. If John 19:26, 27 is added, the last figure increases to 109.

description of the women "watching from a distance" (Mark 15:40, 41; cf. Matt. 27:55, 56). Matthew immediately introduces these friends of Jesus as those "who had followed him from Galilee, ministering to his needs." Mark reserves this description for the end of the passage and adds a few words to it. Also, for Matthew's descriptive appellation "the mother of the sons of Zebedee" Mark substitutes her name "Salome." For the rest, what is said about the women varies little in these two Gospels.

The major difference between the two accounts is in the middle part (Mark 15:38, 39 and its parallel Matt. 27:51-54), where, immediately after the mention of Jesus' death, Matthew relates several "signs" or amazing incidents that occurred. Of all of them Mark records only the rending of the veil and the centurion's confession.

Luke, in his brief account, adds the words "the sun being darkened" (literally "eclipsed") to that which Matthew and Mark relate with reference to the three hours of darkness. Even before Luke records how Jesus died he already states "and the curtain of the temple was torn in two" (verse 45). He has preserved and transmitted to the church the touchingly beautiful seventh word from the cross (verse 46). With reference to the fourth word, the cry of agony, and the events that took place in connection with it, Luke is silent. He gives his own version of the centurion's confession (verse 47); relates that after Jesus' death the deeply moved multitude went home "beating their breasts" (verse 48); and, without mentioning their names, briefly summarizes what Matthew and Mark say about the women who had come from Galilee (verse 49).

As to John, among the women standing "near the cross" he includes Jesus' mother Mary (19:25). In verses 26, 27, which might be considered for inclusion in the general parallel, "the disciple whom Jesus loved" records the fifth and sixth words from the cross ("I thirst" and "It is finished"). He describes Christ's death in these words, "He bowed his head and gave up his spirit."

* * * *

Darkness

33. **Now when the sixth hour had come there was darkness over the whole land until the ninth hour.** From nine o'clock until noon Calvary had been a very busy place. The soldiers had performed their various tasks, as was shown in verses 22-27. Bypassers had blasphemed. Chief priests and scribes had scoffed. Robbers had reviled, though one of them had repented. Jesus had uttered his first three words. Then, at twelve o'clock, something of a very dramatic character takes place. Suddenly the land becomes dark. Cf. Amos 8:9. The very fact that this darkness is mentioned shows that it must

have been intense and unforgettable. Moreover, it occurred when least expected, at high noon, and lasted three hours.

Much has been written about this darkness. What caused it? How extensive was it? Did it have any meaning? As to the first, very little information is given. We are safe in saying, "God brought it about." That is far better than to say that either the devil or Nature caused it. But when the further question is asked, "By what means did God bring it about?" a completely satisfactory answer cannot be given. A sudden thunderstorm, even if it lasted three hours, would not have covered the entire country and would probably not have been singled out for special mention. A black sirocco storm from the desert is not generally known to cause such darkness. To be sure, Luke 23:44, 45 may seem to supply the answer for which we are looking. Does it not say, "the sun being eclipsed"? But, first of all, the reading is not entirely certain. There are several variants. Secondly, granted that "eclipsed" is the right word, this cannot refer to an eclipse in the technical, astronomical sense, for that is impossible at the time of Passover (full moon). Besides, such an eclipse would hardly last three hours! But if the term be taken in a broader sense, namely, "darkened," we are back to where we were: darkened by what? The best answer may well be to regard what happened here as a special act of God, a miracle, and to enquire no further as to any secondary means.

How extensive was it? Here, too, we must abstain from giving a definite answer. It will not do to say that when the light of the sun is shut off half of the globe must be darkened. The light of the sun could be shut off for a certain country or region. See Exod. 10:22, 23. Luther, Calvin, Zahn, Ridderbos, etc. prefer the translation "land" for 15:33. Even if the translation "land" instead of "earth" should be correct, which may well be the case, the fact must not be ignored that the darkness "covered *all* the land," and was therefore very extensive.

As to the third question, "Did it have any meaning?" here a positive answer is certainly in order. Yes, it did have a very important meaning. The darkness meant judgment, the judgment of God upon our sins, his wrath as it were burning itself out in the very heart of Jesus, so that he, as our Substitute, suffered most intense agony, indescribable woe, terrible isolation or forsakenness. Hell came to Calvary that day, and the Savior descended into it and bore its horrors in our stead. How do we know that this answer is correct? Note the following:

a. Darkness in Scripture is very often a symbol of judgment. See Isa. 5:30; 60:2; Joel 2:30, 31; Amos 5:18, 20; Zeph. 1:14-18; Matt. 24:29, 30; Acts 2:20; II Peter 2:17; Rev. 6:12-17.

b. With a view to his impending death the Savior had himself stated that

660

he was giving and was about to give his life as "a ransom for many" (Mark 10:45; cf. Matt. 20:28; 26:28).

c. The agony suffered by our Lord during these three hours was such that he finally uttered the explanatory words of verse 34, to which we now turn:

The Cry of Agony

34. And at the ninth hour Jesus cried out with a loud voice,
Eloi, Eloi, lema sabachthani?
which means [828]
My God, my God, why hast thou forsaken me?

In uttering this cry Jesus was using words taken from the Old Testament, in this case from Ps. 22:1 (22:2 in the original). It should not escape our attention that often during his earthly ministry Jesus drew his strength from the Old Testament. Careful study of *those* references given in N.T.C. on Matthew, pp. 80, 81 which indicate dominical sayings (not all of them do) will make this clear. But even during the final hours of his life on earth before he died, Jesus made use of passages from the sacred writings again and again:

Sayings of Jesus	*Old Testament References*
Matt. 26:31; Mark 14:27	Zech. 13:7
Matt. 26:64; Mark 14:62;	
Luke 21:27; 22:69	Ps. 110:1; Dan. 7:13, 14
Matt. 27:46; Mark 15:34	Ps. 22:1
Luke 22:37	Isa. 53:12
Luke 23:30	Hos. 10:8
Luke 23:46	Ps. 31:5
John 19:28	Ps. 22:15; 69:21

The link between the darkness and the cry is very close: the first is a symbol of the agonizing content of the second. This, then, is the fourth word from the cross, the only one reported by Matthew and Mark. It issued from the mouth of the Savior shortly before he breathed his last.

In the Gospels what happened between twelve o'clock and three o'clock is a blank. All we know is that during these three hours of intense darkness Jesus suffered indescribable agonies. He was being "made sin" for us (II Cor. 5:21), "a curse" (Gal. 3:13). He was being "wounded for our transgressions

---

[828] The idea that Jesus was indeed "forsaken" by his Father, as is clearly implied in the cry of agony, is by no means inconsistent with the love of God, as V. Taylor maintains, *op. cit.*, p. 594. For "which means" see on 15:22, footnote 815.

and bruised for our iniquities." Jehovah was laying on him "the iniquity of us all," etc. (Isa. 53).

To be sure, this happened throughout the period of his humiliation, from conception to death and burial, but *especially* in Gethsemane, Gabbatha, and Golgotha.

The question has been asked, "But how could God forsake God?" The answer must be that God the Father deserted his Son's human nature, and even this in a limited, though very real and agonizing, sense. The meaning cannot be that there was ever a time when God the Father stopped loving his Son. Nor can it mean that the Son ever rejected his Father. Far from it. He kept on calling him "*My* God, *my* God." And for that very reason we may be sure that the Father loved him as much as ever.

How, then, can we ascribe any sensible meaning to this utterance of deep distress? Perhaps an illustration may be of some help, though it should be added immediately that no analogy taken from things that happen to humans on earth can ever begin to do justice to the Son of God's unique experience. Nevertheless, the illustration may be helpful in some slight degree. Here, let us say, is a child that is very sick. He is still too young to understand why he has to be taken to the hospital, and especially why, while there, he may have to be in the Intensive Care Unit, where his parents cannot always be with him. His parents love him as much as ever. But there may be moments when the child misses the presence of his father or mother so much that he experiences profound anguish. So also the Mediator. His soul reaches out for the One whom he calls "my God," but his God does not answer him. Is not that exactly the manner in which the cry of agony is interpreted in the context of Ps. 22? Note:

"My God, my God, why hast thou forsaken me?
Why art thou so far from helping me, and from the words of my groaning?
O my God, I cry in the daytime, but thou answerest not;
And by night, but I find no rest."

For the Sufferer with a superbly sensitive soul this terrible isolation must have been agonizing indeed. This all the more in view of the fact that only several hours earlier he had said to his disciples, "Note well, there comes an hour—yes, it has arrived—when y o u will be scattered, each to his own home, and y o u will leave me alone. *Yet I am not alone, for the Father is with me*" (John 16:32). And a little later he had added, in his touchingly beautiful Highpriestly Prayer, "And now Father, glorify thou me in thine own presence with the glory which I had with thee before the world existed" (John 17:5). And now the Father does not answer, but leaves him in the hands of his adversaries. Reflect again on all the abuse and the suffering Jesus had already endured this very night. Is it any wonder that he now cries out, "My God, my God, why has thou forsaken me?" His God and Father would not have abandoned him to his tormentors if it had not been necessary. But it *was* necessary, in order that he might fully undergo the punishment due to his people's sins.

The Mockery
and
The Sympathy

35, 36. When some of the bystanders heard this they said, Listen! he's calling Elijah. Someone ran, filled a sponge with sour wine, put it on a stick, and gave him a drink, saying, Allow (me), let us see whether Elijah is coming to take him down. It was with a loud voice that Jesus had uttered the fourth word from the cross. Those who heard it must have understood, even though not all recognized the words as fulfilment of prophecy, the prophecy of Psalm 22, of which here at Calvary so many passages had already been, or were being, fulfilled (see verses 1, 2, 7, 8, 12-14, 16-18). But so loud and clear was the voice that there could be no mistake about *what* Jesus just now had said. At least, all those who knew Aramaic and Hebrew understood.

What is described, then, here in verse 35, is the mockery of those heartless persons who tried to make others believe that they had heard Jesus cry to Elijah for help. Of course, they knew better. But the resemblance between either the Hebrew "Eli" or the Aramaic "Eloi" and the name of the Old Testament prophet was probably close enough so that *perverted minds and lips* could turn that similarity into a coarse joke. [829] Moreover, was it not a Jewish belief that Elijah would introduce the Messiah and live beside him for a while as his assistant and the rescuer of those who were about to perish?

But though these mockers were having their fun, there was One who had heard the cry of anguish and immediately answered it. That was God the Father, who right here and now put an end to the brunt of his Son's anguish, so that the Sufferer was permitted to seek some relief for his parched lips and throat, this too in fulfilment of Ps. 22, this time verse 15. So Jesus utters the fifth word, "I am thirsty" (John 19:28). Immediately someone—no doubt a soldier, acting under order of the centurion—took a sponge, filled it

---

[829] Several commentators are of the opinion that Jesus must have uttered his cry of agony in Hebrew—hence, "Eli, Eli" as in Matt. 27:46—, since the Aramaic "Eloi, Eloi" could not have provided a basis of confusion with Eliyyâhû (Elijah). So, for example, V. Taylor, *op. cit.*, p. 593. *This opinion may be correct.* However, it is not necessarily right. It has not been proved that people with perverted minds and hearts, determined to ridicule Jesus, would be unable to connect even Eloi with Elijah. It must be granted that since Jesus was making use of Ps. 22 he may for once have made an exception and have spoken Hebrew. However, he generally spoke Aramaic, which is especially evident from Mark's Gospel. See 3:17; 5:41; 7:11; 7:34; 14:36.

with sour wine or vinegar, the kind of cheap wine which the soldiers drank and which was good for quenching thirst—put the sponge on a stick, and brought it to the mouth of Jesus. For details on this see N.T.C. on John, Vol. II, p. 435.

Not all men standing near the cross that day were equally hardened. Whoever it was that gave the order that was here being carried out—it has been assumed that it was the centurion—was showing genuine sympathy. But this was by no means the sentiment of all. The heartless ones continued their jesting.

According to Matt. 27:49 these mockers shouted, "Hold off," or "Stop," "Let be." They continued, "Let us see whether Elijah is coming to rescue him." Mark abbreviates. The opposition to what the soldier is in the process of doing, by Matthew expressed in so many words, is implied by Mark. Here in 15:36b the soldier probably reacts to this opposing clamor. What he is saying can be interpreted in either of two ways, with very little, if any, resultant difference. In reply to the bystanders he is either saying:

a. "Allow (me)," meaning, "Allow me to give him this drink." Continued: "Let us see whether Elijah is coming to take him down"; or simply:

b. "Let us see whether Elijah is coming to take him down." The reason why I, by a small margin, prefer a. is given in the footnote. Either way the soldier (or whoever he was) is going right ahead with what he started out to do, and is telling the people, whether directly or indirectly, to concentrate their attention not on him but on Jesus, with a view to seeing whether Elijah is coming to take him down. In other words, he joins the bystanders in their mockery. Cf. Luke 23:36, 37. [830]

---

[830] The interpretations of Mark 15:35b are legion. Some see a contradiction between Matthew and Mark. They believe that Matthew was correcting Mark. See, for example, V. Taylor, *op. cit.*, pp. 594, 595. But Matthew tells us what heartless bystanders are saying to the soldier, while Mark probably relates how the soldier reacted. Thus interpreted there is no conflict.

Most translators have adopted a *two* concept English equivalent for Ἄφες (Ἄφετε) ἴδωμεν. Thus, in both Matt. 27:49 and Mark 15:36 they favor the rendering "Wait; let us see" (Williams, R.S.V.); "Let be; let us see" (A.R.V.); "Hold on! Let us see" (Berkeley).

Others in harmony with L.N.T. (A. and G.), p. 126, treat the two Greek words as *one* concept, and in both passages (Matt. 27:49 and Mark 15:36) simply translate: "Let us see," assigning no separate meaning to the form of ἀφίημι, but allowing it to coalesce with ἴδωμεν. Thus N.A.S., Beck, N.E.B., Goodspeed.

This, too, cannot be considered incorrect. It should be noted, however, that it is not absolutely necessary to assign the same meaning to Ἄφες in Matt. 27:49 as to Ἄφετε in Mark 15:36. It should be borne in mind that ἀφίημι has a wide range of meanings: let go, utter, send away, divorce, pardon, leave off, stop, abandon, tolerate, permit, allow, etc.

In harmony with this fact and with the observation made previously, namely, that the two situations pictured respectively in Matt. 27:49 and in Mark 15:36 are probably different, A. B. Bruce, *op. cit.*, p. 450 calls attention to the following: In Matt. 27:49 some are saying to the friendly person who gives Jesus a drink, "Stop, don't give him the

Death

37. Then, with a loud cry, Jesus breathed his last. Note "with a loud cry." Cf. Matt. 27:50; Luke 23:46. This shows that the Sufferer did not just allow his life to ebb away. He died voluntarily. He *gave* his life, *poured it out, laid it down* (Isa. 53:12; John 10:11, 15). He *yielded, gave up* his spirit (Matt. 27:50; John 19:30). Jesus knew exactly what he was doing when he thus offered himself as a voluntary sacrifice. This is clear from his two last words: the sixth, "It is finished" (John 19:30), meaning that the work which the Father had given him to do had now been accomplished; that he had now given his life as a ransom for many (Mark 10:45; cf. Matt. 20:28); and the seventh, "Father into thy hands I commend my spirit" (Luke 23:46), proving that he had fully regained the consciousness of the Father's loving presence and was entrusting his spirit to the Father's loving care. Thus he returned to the glory which he had with the Father from eternity (John 17:5, 24; cf. Prov. 8:30). The Father welcomed him back to glory, and on the morning of the resurrection restored his Son's spirit to his body, nevermore to die. It is comforting to know that when Jesus went to Paradise he did not go alone, but carried with him the soul of the penitent robber (Luke 23:43). [831]

The Curtain of the Sanctuary

38. And the curtain of the sanctuary was torn in two from top to bottom. On the basis of Heb. 6:19; 9:3; and 10:20 it is natural to think of this curtain as the inner one, "the second veil," the one that separated the Holy Place from the Holy of holies. This inner curtain is the one described in Exod. 26:31-33; 36:35; II Chron. 3:14. As pictured in these passages, strands of blue, purple, and scarlet were interwoven into a white linen fabric, in such a manner that these colors formed a mass of cherubim, the guardian angels of God's holiness, symbolically as it were barring the way into the holy of holies. A description of the curtain in the Herodian temple is given in Josephus, *Jewish War* V.212-214.

---

drink." In Mark 15:36 the man who brought the drink is saying to the bystanders, "Allow me (to give him the drink)."

In order to bring out this distinction I have purposely rendered Ἄφετε here in Mark 15:36 differently than Ἄφες in Matt. 27:49, though, along with Bruce, I admit that other translators and interpreters who translate these forms of ἀφίημι identically in both passages (whether along the line of Williams, etc., or of N.A.S., etc.) are not necessarily wrong in doing so.

831 On the basis of ἐξέπνευσεν here in verse 37 to draw a sharp distinction between ψυχή and πνεῦμα, and to base on it a plea for trichotomy, is unwarranted. See above, on 8:12, footnote 370.

At the moment of Christ's death this curtain was suddenly sliced in two from top to bottom. This happened at three o'clock, when priests must have been busy in the temple. How did it come about? Not through natural wear, for in that case there would probably have been rents all over, and the tearing would more likely have been from the bottom up. Nor is it at all probable that Matthew, who immediately afterward mentions an earthquake (27:51), is trying to convey the idea that this splitting in two of the curtain was caused by the earthquake. Had that been his intention, would he not have mentioned the earthquake before the tearing of the curtain? What happened must be regarded as a miracle. Any secondary means that may have been used to effect it are not mentioned, and it would be futile to speculate. As to the symbolic significance, this is made clear by two considerations: first, it occurred exactly at the moment when Jesus died; secondly, it is explained in Heb. 10:19, 20: through the death of Christ, symbolized by the tearing of the curtain, the way into "the holy of holies," that is, heaven, is opened to all those who take refuge in him. For the practical lesson see Heb. 4:16. More may be implied, but by limiting the interpretation to this we are on safe ground.

The Centurion

39. Now when the centurion, who stood facing him, saw that he thus cried out and died, he said, Surely, this man was God's Son.

The centurion had seen how Jesus had been conducting himself in the midst of all the wicked taunts and mockeries. And now there was that loud cry. It was a cry of confidence, a cry by means of which Jesus voluntarily surrendered himself to him whom even now he calls his Father. Also, the centurion must have heard how the Jewish leaders, speaking among themselves, had scoffed at Jesus' claim that he was the Son of God. See on Matt. 27:43. Had he also, perhaps, heard how Pilate had examined Jesus with respect to this very point (John 19:7 ff.)? Besides all this, the centurion had seen and must have felt how nature reacted to the death of Jesus. Think of the earthquake, the splitting of the rocks and the opening of the tombs. Cf. Matt. 27:51, 52, 54.

The centurion, then combines all these impressions, though Mark emphasizes the impression made on this man by the manner in which Jesus himself died! Standing *right opposite* Jesus, the centurion had observed him very carefully.

This legionary was in all likelihood not a Jew. His heart had not been hardened against Jesus, as had the hearts of many of the Jews, especially their leaders. So, when all was over he is heard to exclaim, "Surely this man was God's Son." Whether by this time his knowledge of Christ had advanced to the point where he confessed Jesus to be in a unique sense "the" Son of God, has not been revealed. As far as Greek grammar is concerned, it gives us no information on that point. [832] Legend says that this man became a Christian. Let us hope that he did. Luke states that the centurion "glorified God and said, 'Certainly, this was a righteous man.' " There is no contradiction here. He may very well have said both.

Matthew informs us that not only the centurion but even the soldiers under him were similarly affected. Here, again, there is no contradiction. It is true that the soldiers had been mocking (Luke 23:36). But that was before the earthquake had occurred, with its effect on rocks and tombs. The men who had crucified Jesus may certainly have changed their minds. Did not one of the robbers also mock at first and then repent? According to Luke 23:48 even the multitude in general was at last deeply impressed and "returned smiting their breasts."

Ministering Women

40 41. **Watching from a distance there were women. Among them were Mary Magdalene, Mary the (mother) of James the Less and of Joses, and Salome. When he was in Galilee these women used to follow him and to minister to his needs. And there were also many other women who had come up with him to Jerusalem.**

As to the identity of the women here mentioned—we are told that there were *many* others—it is very well possible that the two lists (Matt. 27:56; Mark 15:40) indicate the same three persons. If this be true, the three would be: *a.* Mary Magdalene, so named in both lists; *b.* Mary the mother of James the Less and of Joses; and *c.* Salome = the mother of the sons of Zebedee. In fact, it is even possible that the list in John 19:25 has reference to the same individuals plus Mary, the mother of Jesus. John's list in all probability refers to four women, not three. Is it not possible that the reason why John mentions the presence of Christ's mother, but Matthew and Mark do not, was that the author of the fourth Gospel, in distinction from the others, describes the situation as it was before the disciple whom Jesus loved had taken Mary to his home (John 19:27)? The three other women mentioned in John's list would then be the same as those referred to in Matthew and Mark; namely, *a.* his [Christ's] mother's sister = Salome = the mother of the sons of Zebedee; *b.* Mary the (*wife* probably) of Clopas = the mother of James the Less and of Joses; and *c.* Mary Magdalene. For more on this and on the

---

[832] The Greek has no definite articles here, but simply says υἱός. On the other hand, with proper nouns and titles, forms without the article can still be definite. They may be either definite or indefinite.

references to the four in the New Testament see N.T.C. on John, Vol. II, pp. 431, 432.

Taking the three names according to the order given here in Mark we note that "Mary Magdalene" was from Magdala, located on the southwestern shore of the Sea of Galilee. The Lord had delivered her from a bad case of demon-possession (Luke 8:2). She is the Mary who, after Christ's resurrection, "stood at the tomb weeping" when Jesus, whom she took to be the gardener, appeared to her (John 20:11-18). She is definitely *not* the sinful woman of Luke 7. About "Mary the mother of James the Less and of Joses" we know only that. together with Mary Magdalene, she was present also at Christ's burial (Matt. 27:61; Mark 15:47; cf. Luke 23:55), and was one of the women who went out very early on Sunday morning to anoint Christ's body (Matt. 28:1; Mark 16:1). In that same group of women was also Salome (Mark 16:1). This "mother of the sons of Zebedee" is also mentioned in Matt. 20:20, 21.

Notable women were these, and this for at least three reasons:

a. With the exception of John none of the other disciples who belong to the group of twelve is reported to have been present at Calvary, but these women were present! They displayed rare courage.

b. We are distinctly told that they were women who had followed Jesus from Galilee to Jerusalem and had been in the habit of ministering to his needs. Cf. Luke 8:2, 3. They had given evidence of hearts filled with love and sympathy.

c. Being witnesses of Christ's death, burial, and resurrection appearance, they were qualified witnesses of facts of redemption on which, under God, the church depends for its faith.

---

42 When evening had already fallen, then, since it was Preparation Day, [833] that is, the day before the sabbath,   43 Joseph of Arimathea, a distinguished member of the council, who was also himself constantly waiting for the kingdom of God, came (forward). He summoned up courage, went to Pilate and asked for the body of Jesus.   44 Pilate was surprised to hear that he was already dead. So, summoning the centurion, he asked whether Jesus had already died.   45 When he was so informed by the centurion, he granted the body to Joseph.   46 Then he bought a linen cloth, took him down, wrapped him in the linen cloth, and laid him in a tomb that was cut out of the rock. He rolled a stone in front of the entrance of the tomb.   47 Mary Magdalene and Mary the (mother) of Joses were looking on (to see) where he was laid.

15:42-47 *The Burial of Jesus*
Cf. Matt. 27:57-61; Luke 23:50-56; John 19:38-42

42, 43. When evening had already fallen, then, since it was Preparation Day, that is, the day before the sabbath, Joseph of Arimathea, a distin-

---

[833] Or: Friday.

guished member of the council, who was also himself constantly waiting for the kingdom of God, came (forward). He summoned up courage, went to Pilate, and asked for the body of Jesus. [834]

The struggle is over. The battle has been won. The work which the Father gave the Son to do is finished (John 17:4; 19:30). The body of Jesus, though still on the cross, suffers no more pain, for his spirit has entered Paradise (Luke 23:43). It is quiet on Calvary now. Most of the people have left. In fact, evening has fallen, as our passage states.

According to the ancient Hebrew way of speaking there were "two evenings" (cf. Exod. 12:6 in the original). The first "evening" which we would call "afternoon" began at 3 P.M., the second at 6 P.M. Something of this is probably reflected in the phrase "When evening fell," for we cannot imagine that Joseph of Arimathea, a Jew, would have approached Pilate on Friday, 6 P.M., asking for the body of Jesus when the sabbath was beginning. Much sooner than this he must have started to make preparations. It was against the law to leave a dead body on a tree overnight (Deut. 21:23). This would have been all the more reprehensible if by doing so, the body would be hanging on a tree or cross on the sabbath. Moreover, this was the sabbath of the Passover week. Great, indeed, was that sabbath (John 19:31)! Besides all this, as has been pointed out earlier (see on Mark 5:38), it was customary to bury a person very soon after death had occurred. For all these reasons it is clear that if the body of Jesus was going to be buried at all, it had to be done now, that is, sometime before 6 P.M. There could be no delay, as especially *Mark* points out, for in order to emphasize this fact, he *alone* among the evangelists states that evening had *already* fallen.

But who was going to take care of this? The disciples, let it be borne in mind, had fled (Matt. 26:56). To be sure, John had retraced his steps and had even been standing among the spectators at Calvary, but not for long (John 19:27). The care of Mary, the mother of Jesus, had been entrusted to him and he had taken her to his home. He did, however, return to Calvary, for he saw the spear thrust (John 19:35), but we can well understand that he had had no time to make preparations for Jesus' burial.

It is at this point that Joseph of Arimathea enters into the picture. What kind of a man was he? He was:

---

[834] Notes on vocabulary and grammar: ὀψίας γενομένης, gen. absolute; see on 1:32 and on 14:17, footnote 705. παρασκευή, cf. παρασκευάζω, to prepare. Friday was called Preparation Day because on that day everything had to be prepared for the sabbath. Even in modern Greek Friday is called παρασκευή. εὐσχήμων = εὖ good, and σχῆμα figure, form; hence, possessing a good figure, graceful, shapely, comely (I Cor. 7:35; 12:24), but here: of good standing, prominent, respectable, distinguished, noble. ἦν προσδεχόμενος, periphrastic imperfect: was constantly waiting for. τολμήσας, aor. active participle: "having summoned up courage (he went)" or (used adverbially) "he went bravely." ἠτήσατο, third per. s. aor. middle indic. of αἰτέω, as in 6:25. See on that passage, footnote 262.

a. a man of Arimathea, that is, Ramah (= "height"). It was the city of Samuel. It was anciently located in the tribe of Ephraim and known also as Ramathaim-zophim (I Sam. 1:1).

b. a distinguished member of the council, that is, of the Jewish Supreme Court, the Sanhedrin. Note: not just a member but a *prominent* one, one whose counsel must have been eagerly sought, one whose word carried weight.

c. rich (Matt. 27:57a). To be sure, Jesus blessed the poor (Luke 6:20). He considered it his duty and joy to preach good tidings to the poor (Luke 4:18), in fulfilment of Isa. 61:1 f. He wanted John the Baptist to know that the poor were hearing the gospel (Luke 7:22). He also pointed out the peril of earthly riches (Mark 10:23-27). But all this does not mean that in the kingdom of God there is no room for the rich. Abraham, Barnabas, Nicodemus, Lazarus and his sisters Martha and Mary, the mother of John Mark, and Lydia must have been rather well-to-do. So was Joseph of Arimathea. But by God's sovereign grace they all were—or became—willing and eager to contribute generously to the cause of God and his kingdom.

d. constantly waiting for the kingdom of God; that is, in harmony with Christ's own message (Matt. 11:4-6, 12) he believed that the reign of God in human hearts and lives was being established and was going to be established more and more. In a sense this man had become a disciple of Jesus (Matt. 27:57b). The work of God had begun in him (cf. Phil. 1:6). As a result, he wanted to do what was right, and had not consented to the decision and deed of the Sanhedrin in condemning Jesus to death (Luke 23:50, 51a). Had he perhaps remained at home when the Sanhedrin's dreadful meetings took place? In view of Mark 14:64; 15:1 that may well have been the case.

e. up to this moment a *secret* disciple. Note John 19:38, "Joseph of Arimathea, a disciple of Jesus *but a secret one for fear of the Jews.*" By all means read John 12:42, which is the best commentary. Add John 9:22 and read N.T.C. on that passage.

But now, because of God's sovereign grace, there was a change, a very significant change, brought about undoubtedly by various factors; such as the man's conscience, the memory of the words and works of Jesus in previous days, and perhaps especially the words of the Master as he was dying on the cross and the miracles of Calvary.

What did he now do?

a. He came (forward). Though no further explanation of this word (literally "having come") is given, it could well mean that he stepped up to the centurion, who had not yet left, and told him that he desired to assume responsibility for the body of Jesus: to take it down from the cross and to give it an honorable burial.

b. He summoned up courage, went to Pilate, and asked for the body of

Jesus. This act did indeed take courage. It should be borne in mind that Pilate hated the Jews and had but a little while ago refused their request to change the wording of the superscription (John 19:21). Note especially his blunt reply (verse 22). Besides, by means of what Joseph of Arimathea was now doing he was openly professing before the entire world, including the entire Sanhedrin!, that he was a believer in Jesus Christ. Contrast the behavior of the eleven. It would seem that only one of them even witnessed how Jesus died for them. And do not forget the passages to which reference has been made: John 9:22; 12:42, to which add 12:10.

With far more interesting and vivid details than are provided by the other three evangelists Mark continues: 44, 45. **Pilate was surprised to hear that he was already dead. So, summoning the centurion, he asked whether Jesus had already died. When he was so informed by the centurion, he granted the body to Joseph.** [835]

In view of the fact that death by crucifixion was generally a very slow process, Pilate could hardly believe that Jesus had already died. So before deciding whether or not to grant Joseph's request he called in the centurion. Having been assured by him that Jesus had actually died, he gave the body to Joseph. Granting permission to relatives or even, as in this case, to friends, to take charge of the body of a crucified person was not anything unusual.

46. Then he bought a linen cloth, took him down, wrapped him in the linen cloth, and laid him in a tomb that was cut out of rock. He rolled a stone in front of the entrance of the tomb. [836]

For the interpretation of this passage see the detailed explanation in N.T.C. on John 19:40-42, Vol. II, pp. 442-444, beginning with the words "Pilate having ascertained" (p. 442) and continuing up to the Synthesis on p. 444.

Lessons based on 15:42-46

a. Fruits of the cross are not only *initial conversions* but also *later transformations*, so that faith concealed becomes faith revealed, as in the

---

835 ἐθαύμασεν εἰ, he was surprised that. See L.N.T. (A. and G.), p. 353. Note also the perfect τέθνηκε, had died, hence "was dead." And cf. ἀπέθανε, the aor. of ἀποθνῄσκω. Because this word is preceded by πάλαι, the translation "had already died" would seem to be the best. ἐδωρήσατο, third per. s. aor. indic. of δωρέομαι, to give, grant, present. πτῶμα (cf. πίπτω), that which has fallen; hence, dead body, corpse.

836 συνδών; see on 14:51, 52, footnote 750. καθελών, masc. s. aor. participle of καθαιρέω, to take down. ἐνείλησε, third per. s. aor. indic. of ἐνειλέω, to wrap in, envelope; in the New Testament found only here. ἔθηκε, third per. s. aor. indic. active of τίθημι. μνημεῖον, tomb, sepulchre, memorial, monument, related to μιμνήσκω, to remind. Another word for grave or tomb is τάφος (Matt. 27:61, 64, 66; 28:1). On Sunday morning, when the *grave* was empty, the "memorial" (μνημεῖον) remains! See the fine

case of Joseph of Arimathea and of the woman who touched Christ's garment (Mark 5:25-34). We sometimes forget this!

b. The gospel touches both rich and poor. It is for all.

c. Joseph of Arimathea realized that he "had come to the kingdom for such a time as this" (Esther 4:14). By God's grace he saw his opportunity and made the most of it.

d. Prophecy was again being beautifully fulfilled. See Isa. 53:9.

e. So intensely does the Father love his Son that as quickly as ever possible he changes Jesus' state of humiliation to that of exaltation. Granted that the burial belongs to the former, does not the fact that there was no corruption in the grave and the additional fact that it was a new grave provided by a man who was rich in earthly and now also in heavenly goods guarantee the glory that was about to burst forth? If, then, the Father so loved his Son, should not we?

* * * * *

47. Mary Magdalene and Mary the (mother) of Joses were looking on (to see) where he was laid. [837] See what is said about these loyal women in verse 40. Note that according to that verse the second Mary had two sons: James the Less and Joses. Here in verse 47 she is mentioned in connection with one of these two; in 16:1 with the other. The Father in heaven took care that at every step there were faithful witnesses. In the present case simply to say that these two women "saw" where Jesus was laid fails to bring out the full picturesque description. They were watching, were observing . . . carefully, intently, devoutly. [838]

Summary of Chapter 15

As 14:64 indicated, by the Sanhedrin Jesus had been condemned as being worthy of death. The seven sections of the present chapter continue the story.

1. On the surface the reconvening of the Jewish supreme council would seem superfluous. The reason why it was nevertheless reconvened was probably to give a semblance of legality to the action against Jesus. In a case of capital punishment Jewish law did not permit the sentence to be pronounced until a day after the accused had been convicted. So now, at early

---

remarks on this in H. Mulder, *Spoorzoeker*, pp. 157, 158. λελατομημένον, perf. passive participle of λατομέω, to hew out of stones. A λατόμος is a stone-cutter. A λᾶς is a stone, cf. *lapidary, lapis lazuli;* τέμνω means to cut.

[837] ἐθεώρουν, third per. pl. imperf. active of θεωρέω. τέθειται, third per. s. perf. indic. passive of τίθημι.

[838] The Greek New Testament uses several synonyms for *seeing.* Study N.T.C. on John, Vol. I, p. 85, footnote 33.

dawn, the sanhedrists pass a resolution condemning Jesus to death. Then they bind him, lead him away, and deliver him to Pilate for confirmation and execution of the sentence (verse 1).

2. The chief priests, having been compelled by Pilate to present definite charges against Jesus, come up with several, all of them amounting to the accusation that Jesus was a revolutionary, a man who wanted to be king. So Pilate questions Jesus on this score. Jesus refuses to answer, so that Pilate was amazed (verses 2-5).

3. Pilate is anxious to get rid of the obligation to make a decision regarding Jesus. He sees an opportunity to shift the responsibility to the people when their representatives ascend the steps to his quarters in order to demand that he, as usual at the feast, release a prisoner. Pilate suggests two names, one to be selected by the people for release. The two were Jesus and Barabbas, the latter a convicted and imprisoned revolutionist and murderer. The governor suggests that Jesus be chosen for release. He is thoroughly aware of the fact that it was because of envy that the chief priests had delivered Jesus to him. But while Pilate was busy pondering a message from his wife, urging him to refrain from any action with reference to "this righteous man" (Matt. 27:19), the chief priests make the most of their opportunity. They persuade the masses to request the release not of Jesus but of Barabbas. Thoroughly frustrated, Pilate now asks, "What, then, do y o u want me to do with the one whom y o u call 'the king of the Jews?' " They shout back, "Crucify him." Again and again Pilate loudly proclaims his conviction that Jesus is innocent. At last, however, because of fear as to what may happen to him if he does not comply with the people's wishes (see John 19:12), he orders Jesus to be scourged and crucified (verses 6-15).

4. The soldiers now gather around Jesus to make sport of him. They strip him of his outer garments, throw an imitation "royal" purple robe—really only a faded soldier's mantle—around him, press down on his head a crown of thorns, thrust a stick in his hand for a scepter, and then one by one they kneel down in front of him in mock adoration. They salute him, spit on him, and hit him on the head with his own "scepter." Finished, they remove the purple robe, put his own clothes on him again, and lead him away for crucifixion (verses 16-20).

5. As John 19:16, 17 indicates, at first Jesus carried his own cross. But sheer physical exhaustion made it impossible for him to carry it very far. When he succumbed beneath his load, the legionaries, exercising their right of requisitioning, forced Simon of Cyrene to carry the cross. Mark reminds his readers that this Simon was the father of Alexander and Rufus, people with whom Mark's Roman readers were probably well acquainted. See Rom. 16:13.

Arrived at Golgotha, Jesus is offered wine flavored with myrrh, which he refuses to drink. The soldiers divide his garments, casting lots for them to determine who should take what. At nine o'clock A.M., on "Good Friday," they crucified Jesus. The superscription stating the charge read

THE KING OF THE JEWS

With him were crucified two robbers, one on his right and one on his left. Bypassers blasphemed. They shook their heads and said "Aha!" (reported only by Mark), continuing "You who destroy the temple and rebuild it in three days, save yourself and come down from the cross." Chief priests and scribes scoffed. However, they do not address him; they speak to each other about him. Their ridicule of him was mingled with hatred and envy. "Others he saved, himself he cannot save," they sneered. And they added, "Let the Christ, the king of Israel now come down from the cross, that we may see and believe." Those crucified with him were also heaping insults upon him. That one of the two robbers repented and was saved is not recorded by Mark but by Luke (23:39-43). As far as reported by Mark, all of this material is found in verses 21-32.

6. This section records Christ's cry of agony, "Eloi, Eloi, lema sabachthani," and has an account of the mockery that followed. When Jesus uttered his fifth word from the cross, namely, "I am thirsty" (John 19:28), an order was issued—probably by the sympathetic centurion—to give him a drink. When someone—probably a soldier—immediately took a sponge, filled it with sour wine or vinegar, put the sponge on a stick, and brought it to the mouth of Jesus, heartless mockers shouted, "Hold off" (or "Let be"). They continued, "Let us see whether *Elijah*—a play on the word *Eli* (Hebrew) or *Eloi* (Aramaic)—is coming to rescue him." According to Mark 15:36b the soldier reacts to this clamor, and says, "Allow me," that is, "Allow me to complete what I am doing," and then "let us see whether Elijah is coming to take him down." See the interpretation for the various possibilities of explaining what the soldier said.

After having accepted the offered drink, Jesus, with a loud cry (Luke 23:46), breathed his last. The curtain of the sanctuary was torn in two from top to bottom. And the centurion cried out, "Surely, this man was God's Son." Mark closes this section by calling attention to some ever faithful women who had been ministering to Jesus in Galilee, had come down with him to Jerusalem, and were now standing here, tenderly and faithfully watching the Calvary scenes (verses 33-41).

7. Since it was against the law (see Deut. 21:23) to leave a dead body on a cross overnight, especially if the next day was a sabbath, Joseph of Arimathea, realizing that the next day, which by Jewish reckoning would begin very soon (perhaps within a couple of hours), was not only a sabbath but the most sacred sabbath of all, the one of Passover week, decided to take

674

charge of Jesus' body. Joseph was a distinguished member of the sanhedrin. He was rich. See Isa. 53:9, which was being fulfilled. And he was a disciple of Jesus. However, up to this moment he had never ventured to confess Jesus publicly. But now, as a result of the operation of God's sovereign grace in his heart, he summoned courage and came out openly for the Crucified One. Boldly he went to Pilate and asked for the body of Jesus. The governor, having been assured by the centurion that Jesus had actually died, granted the request. With the co-operation of Nicodemus, as we learn from John 19:38-42, Joseph then took down the body, wrapped it in a linen cloth, and laid it in a tomb that had been cut out of rock. He rolled a huge stone in front of the tomb's entrance. And again, the faithful women disciples were watching. They saw where Jesus was laid (verses 42-47).

Outline of Chapter 16

Theme: *The Work Which Thou Gavest Him To Do*

B. The Resurrection

16:1-8   The Lord Risen; The Women Surprised

THE PROBLEM WITH RESPECT TO MARK 16:9-20
BRIEF NOTES ON THE LONG ENDING (Mark 16:9-20)

16:9-11   Christ's Appearance to Mary Magdalene
16:12, 13 His Appearance to Two Disciples
16:14-18 The Great Commission and The Signs
16:19, 20 Christ's Ascension

CHAPTER XVI

16 1 Now when the sabbath was past, Mary Magdalene, Mary the (mother) of James, and Salome bought spices, that they might come and anoint him. 2 Very early on the first day of the week, when the sun was risen, they were coming to the tomb. 3 And they were saying to each other, "Who will roll away the stone for us from the entrance of the tomb?" 4 But looking up, they saw that the stone had been rolled away. (They had been alarmed about the stone) for it was very large. [839] 5 And as they entered the tomb, they saw a young man dressed in a white robe sitting at the right, and they were alarmed. [840] 6 He said to them, "Do not be alarmed. Y o u are looking for Jesus the Nazarene, who was crucified. He is risen. He is not here. Look, here is the place where they laid him. 7 But go, tell his disciples and Peter, 'He is going ahead of y o u into Galilee. There y o u will see him, as he told y o u.' "

8 And they went out and fled from the tomb, for trembling and astonishment were holding them in their grip; and they said nothing to anybody, for they were afraid.

16:1-8 *The Lord Risen; The Women Surprised*
Cf. Matt. 28:1-8; Luke 24:1-12; John 20:1-10

Mark's account resembles Matthew's (28:1-8) more closely than it does the resurrection story as told by Luke or by John. The four reports vary with respect to several minor points. For the most part the variations can be easily reconciled. This holds with respect to such items as "when the sun was risen" (Mark 16:2), "a young man" (verse 5), and "they said nothing" (verse 8).

Matthew intersperses the story of the arrival of the women with a reference to the earthquake. The dramatic descent of an angel, and the terror experienced by the guards (28:2-4). In verses 9, 10 Matthew records the appearance of the risen Christ himself to the women.

To the names of the two women mentioned by Matthew and the three by Mark, Luke adds "Joanna . . . and the others with them" (24:10). He records the disbelief with which the apostles greeted the women's story (verse 11). In verse 12 he briefly summarizes Peter's experience at the tomb. John enlarges on this theme: Peter and John running to the tomb, after Peter had

---

839 Or: . . . the stone had been rolled away, for it was very large.
840 Or: greatly amazed; so also in the next verse.

677

been told by Mary Magdalene, "They have taken the Lord out of the tomb, and we don't know where they have laid him" (20:1-10).

1. Now when the sabbath was past, Mary Magdalene, Mary the (mother) of James, and Salome bought spices, that they might come and anoint him. [841]
The sabbath was ended. Accordingly it is now Saturday after 6 P.M. The bazaars are open again. So Mark relates that the three women who have been mentioned before (see 15:40), and two of whom were mentioned in the preceding verses (15:47), purchased spices in order that without any further delay they might go to the tomb the very next morning to anoint Jesus' body. It is true that Joseph of Arimathea and Nicodemus had already wound linen bandages around the body, strewing in a mixture of myrrh and aloes. But the dead body had not as yet been anointed. The living body had been anointed (14:3-9) but not the dead one. Besides, a week had gone by since that other anointing had taken place.

2. Very early on the first day of the week, [842] **when the sun was risen,** [843] **they were coming to the tomb.** They were evidently afraid that decomposition would take place if they should wait any longer.

As to the time when these women came: Mark says "when the sun was risen," Matt. 28:1 "at dawn," Luke "at early dawn," and John "while it was still dark." Probable solution: although it was still dark when the women started out, the sun had risen when they arrived at the tomb.

It is true that these women should have paid more attention to the Lord's repeated prediction that he would rise again on the third day. On the other hand, while we may criticize their lack of sufficient faith—a lack which they shared with the male disciples—let us not overlook their exceptional love and loyalty. They were at Calvary when Jesus died, in Joseph's garden when their Master was buried, and now very early in the morning, here they are once more, in order to anoint the body. Meanwhile, where were the eleven?

3, 4. And they were saying to each other, Who will roll away the stone for us from the entrance of the tomb? But looking up, they saw that the

---

841 διαγενομένου τοῦ σαββάτου, gen. absolute (literally, "the sabbath having come in between," hence, "having ended"). For ἠγόρασαν see on 11:15, footnote 538. ἐλθοῦσαι, nom. pl. fem. aor. participle of ἔρχομαι; ἀλείψωσι, third per. pl. aor. subjunctive of ἀλείφω; hence, literally, "in order that, having come, they might anoint him."

842 It makes little difference whether one conceives of the Greek plural for *sabbath* as referring *to the day* or to an entire *week* (the time from one day of rest to another). If the first is meant, then the idea is that this was the first day counting from the sabbath-day; hence, the first day after the sabbath-day. If the second is meant, the result is still the same; the day indicated is then not the last of the week but the first. In either case Sunday is meant.

843 ἀνατείλαντος, aor. participle of ἀνατέλλω. Cf. Mark 4:6; also Matt. 4:16; 5:45; 13:6.

stone had been rolled away. (They had been alarmed about the stone) for it was very large. [844]

On the way toward the tomb the women became worried about the huge stone in front of the tomb's entrance. They asked each other, "Who will roll it away for us?" But suddenly they saw—probably at a turn in the path—that the heavy stone had already been removed. What had taken place? Matthew, by divine inspiration, supplies the answer: "Suddenly there was a violent earthquake, for an angel of the Lord came down from heaven, stepped forward, rolled away the stone and was sitting on it. His appearance was like lightning, and his garment white as snow" (28:2, 3).

The interesting item about the alarm of the women before they saw that the stone had already been removed is found only in Mark's Gospel.

5. And as they entered the tomb, they saw a young man dressed in a white robe sitting at the right, and they were alarmed.

Why did the angel have to remove the stone? Not to enable Jesus to make his way out—for see John 20:19, 26—but to enable these women, and also Peter and John, to enter the tomb.

By the time the women had reached the tomb, the "angel" (thus Matthew) had entered the tomb. Here in Mark the angel is called "a young man dressed in a *white* robe." Compare this with Matthew's description "his garment *white* as snow." It is clear that Matthew and Mark are describing the same heavenly being. The fact that angels appear to humans in human form, so that an angel can also be called a man, and is even able to express himself in human language, is clear to every Bible student. See Gen. 18:2, 16;

---

[844] The words placed between parentheses are not found in the Greek, which reads, " . . . who will roll away the stone for us from the entrance of the tomb? But [or: And] looking up, they saw that the stone had been rolled away, for it was very large." A literal, word for word, translation into English would cause the reader to think either: *a.* that the stone had been rolled away because it was very large; or *b.* that the women were able to see the stone from a distance because it was very large. Neither of these interpretations sounds very natural. Far more reasonable is the explanation that the women were worried lest the size and weight of the stone and the probability that so early in the morning there would be no male friend or disciple around to help them, would make it impossible for them to remove this heavy object and to enter the tomb in order to anoint the body. This is the view that does justice to the context (verse 3). Besides, delayed explanatory clauses are not unusual in Greek. In English, however, the meaning might not be understood apart from the inserted parenthetical clause.

Note ἀποκυλίσει and ἀποκεκύλισται; the first form being the third per. s. fut. indic. active of ἀποκυλίω; the second form being the third per. s. perf. indic. passive of the same verb. Cf. *cylinder.* In Mark this word is found only in these two verses. It occurs also in Matt. 28:2 and in Luke 24:2. ἀναβλέψασαι is the nom. pl. fem. aor. participle of ἀναβλέπω. It may mean either *to look up* or *to see again,* that is, *to regain sight.* Here in 16:4 the meaning "looking up" is obviously indicated. Cf. 6:41; 7:34; 8:24. But in 10:51, 52 the verb means to regain sight. See also on 8:24, footnote 378.

19:1 f.; Judg. 6:12 f.; 13:3, 6; Ezek. 9:2. In connection with the story of Manoah (Judg. 13) does not even Josephus mention "an angel of God in the likeness of a comely and tall youth"? See *Antiquities* V. 277. It is therefore entirely unwarranted to see a contradiction here between Matthew and Mark. See also above, on 14:51, 52. And as to Luke's and John's "two angels," see N.T.C. on Matthew, p. 990.

If the shape and general appearance of the tomb, as described in N.T.C. on John, Vol. II, p. 444, is understood, the statement that the "young man" was sitting "at the right" will be clear. That the rolled away stone, the appearance of the inside of the tomb (in this connection see also John 20:6, 7), and the presence of "the young man" or "angel" caused the women to be "alarmed" or "greatly amazed" [845] is understandable.

6. **He said to them, Do not be alarmed. Y o u are looking for Jesus the Nazarene, who was crucified. He is risen. He is not here. Look, here is the place where they laid him.**

"Do not be alarmed," says the young man to the women. What he means is, "Stop doing what y o u are doing, and instead rejoice, for this is a day of cheer." He continues, "Y o u are looking for Jesus the Nazarene." [846] Yes, Jesus was indeed "the Nazarene," the One who had spent most of his earthly life in Nazareth and voluntarily humbled himself unto death, even death upon a cross. But now "He is risen." And to reassure the women who can hardly believe what they are seeing, the angel—for "the young man" was, after all, an angel—tenderly adds, "He is not here. Look, here is the place where they laid him."

We might have expected a different message, for example, a stern rebuke, in view of the fact that these women showed by their action of coming to the tomb in order to anoint a dead body, that they had not taken seriously enough Jesus' prediction of rising on the third day.

But now all is forgiven, blotted out by the risen Savior; for it must be borne in mind that it was not the heavenly messenger himself who had created this message of cheer. It was the risen One.

The place where they laid him, a declivity inside the huge tomb, is empty. This the women can see very well, for they have entered the tomb. Not only do they see how empty is this declivity but also how neatly arranged is everything around it: the linen bandages lying there, and the sweatband not lying with the linen bandages but neatly folded up and lying in a place by itself (John 20:6, 7).

The young man also conveys another message that had been given to him

---

845 See above, on 9:15, footnote 400.
846 For "the Nazarene" see above, on 1:24, footnote 41; also N.T.C. on Matt. 2:23; 26:71; and on John 1:46.

before he descended from heaven to earth. It reveals the same tender, forgiving love, namely, 7. **But go, tell his disciples and Peter, He is going ahead** [847] **of y o u into Galilee. There y o u will see him, as he told y o u.** Note: still "his disciples," even though in the hour of bitter trial they had all left him and fled. Also note "and Peter," and this in spite of those terrible denials, accompanied at times by curses. It is Mark, Peter's interpreter, who has preserved for us this beautiful little touch.

Thus, very clearly and emphatically, Mark prepared the reader for expecting a manifestation of the risen Lord to his disciples, a kind of reunion. It is going to take place in Galilee, according to the promise of 14:28, repeated here in 16:7.

How was this promise fulfilled? The beginning of that story—definitely only *the beginning,* however—is told in verse 8. **And they went out and fled from the tomb, for trembling and astonishment** [848] **were holding them in their grip; and they said nothing to anybody, for they were afraid.** What Mark clearly states and means is that these women were thoroughly scared, profoundly shocked. To interpret their *ekstasis* (thus the Greek) to mean anything else than astonishment, bewilderment, being "beside themselves" with terror, is hardly correct. Yet this is done at times, the aim being to harmonize Matthew and Mark. Not that these two evangelists are actually in conflict. They are not. But in this particular passage Mark is not thinking about the women's joy, [849] but of their fear and astonishment. And it was because of this inner disposition, this mental state, that they not only fled away from the tomb, but also did not stop along the way to relate the cause of their fright to anyone. They had been rendered speechless. It is true that they were also filled with joy, but it is not Mark who mentions this. It is also true that when they had somewhat recovered from their mental terror they ran to deliver to the apostles the message that had been entrusted to them. But again it is not Mark who says this. It is true that Jesus himself in person revealed himself to the women. But on this subject, too, Mark is silent. And it is true that Jesus, in fulfilment of his and the angel's message, actually met his followers in Galilee. However, *here again Mark remains silent!*

---

847 προάγει, third per. s. pres. indic. of προάγω; see on 14:28, footnote 714.

848 τρόμος, trembling, only here in Mark's Gospel. But see also I Cor. 2:3; II Cor. 7:15; Eph. 6:5; and Phil. 2:12. As to ἔκστασις (cf. *ecstasy*), Mark has used this word once before, and also in that case in connection with a resurrection from the dead; see above, on 5:42.

849 It is true that the Greek word ἔκστασις and the English "ecstasy" are etymologically related, but this does not make it correct to say that "the great joy" to which Matthew refers "is covered by" (thus Lenski) the ἔκστασις mentioned by Mark. In Scripture the meaning of ἔκστασις is rather "to be beside oneself with astonishment, amazement, or bewilderment" (Mark 5:42; Luke 5:26; Acts 3:10). At times the word indicates a trance (Acts 10:10; 11:5; 22:17).

Mark leads us to expect great things, a marvelous reunion in Galilee, but then all of a sudden his message breaks off. Are we now blaming Mark? Not at all, as will become clear. What we, along with many other interpreters of various theological positions, are saying is that we probably do not have all that Mark wrote. This will become clearer when we study "the long ending" (verses 9-20).

On the other hand, Mark has given us a most vivid portrayal of Christ's earthly ministry, death, and resurrection. Mark's Gospel is filled with unforgettable manifestations of Christ's power, mercy, and love. The great lesson which we learn from the present section is that not only did Jesus rise victoriously from the grave, but in addition he revealed himself to be the same thoughtful, kind, and loving Lord he had shown himself to be in earlier days. For that good news we should be very thankful.

THE PROBLEM WITH RESPECT TO MARK 16:9-20

Did Mark write verses 9-20? Though the Authorized (King James) Version of our English Bible contains them, modern translations all indicate in one way or another that there is considerable doubt about their authenticity. Thus, R.S.V. relegates them to a fine print footnote. Phillips calls them "an ancient appendix." Others add a note in which they call attention to the fact that "the two oldest and best manuscripts do not have Mark 16:9-20 but end Mark's Gospel with verse 8" (thus Beck).

Unanimity is lacking, however. Mark 16:9-20 also has its forceful defenders. The author of this commentary recently carefully reread the defense by J. W. Burgon, *The Last Twelve Verses of Mark,* reprint Ann Arbor, 1959; also R. C. H. Lenski's remarks, *op. cit.,* pp. 471-486; and E. F. Hills, *The King James Version Defended,* Des Moines, 1956, pp. 102-113. With what vigor these men argue in favor of their position! In reading Burgon one at times almost receives the impression that "orthodoxy" depends on saving these disputed verses.

If anyone would begin to think that the conflict of opinion is one between "orthodoxy" and "liberalism" (or "modernism"), he would be mistaken. Though it is true that those who cannot be counted among the conservatives reject the proposition that these twelve verses were written by John Mark, no one less than the thoroughly orthodox champion of the faith, the late Dr. N. B. Stonehouse, also rejected it. See his book, *The Witness of Matthew and Mark to Christ,* Philadelphia, 1944, pp. 86-118.

In a commentary there is no room for a discussion of the many positions held in connection with this topic. The main ones are two:
A. Mark wrote 16:9-20.
B. Mark did not write 16:9-20.

682

Those who defend B are again divided into two groups:

1. Mark intended to conclude his Gospel with the words of 16:8, " . . . for they were afraid." This is the view defended by Stonehouse and others. [850]

2. Mark did not intend to conclude his Gospel at this point. This is, perhaps, the predominant view. [851]

What, then, is the position of the author of this commentary? As to proposition A, I do not believe that Mark wrote 16:9-20. My main reasons are two:

a. *The external or textual evidence fails to support these verses.* They are lacking in the two earliest codices B and Aleph (Vaticanus and Sinaiticus), in codex K (codex Bobbiensis, the best exemplar of the earliest African Old Latin text), the Sinaitic Syriac, and other very early manuscripts. Early church fathers, such as Clement of Alexandria and Origen seem not to have known these verses. According to Eusebius, the famous church historian who was born about the year A.D. 260 and died about the year 340, "the most accurate copies" and "almost all the copies" of Mark's Gospel ended with the words of 16:8, ". . . for they were afraid." Jerome, probably born about the year in which Eusebius died, and like him dying at the age of approximately eighty, also writes that almost all the Greek copies lack the verses 9-20.

It cannot be denied that ever so many Greek manuscripts do contain these words, but when the manuscript evidence is properly *evaluated* instead of merely *counted,* the balance swings heavily toward the omission of the contested verses.

b. *The internal evidence also fails to support them.*

(1) *Argument based on diction* This evidence is rather strong. In order to feel the importance of it, one should carefully compare 16:1-8 with 16:9-20. In verses 1-8 he will probably find only four words that have not already been used by the evangelist in the rest of his book (1:1–15:47). Now study verses 9-20. Here one finds at least fourteen different words not found in the previous portion of the book. Since a few of these "new" words occur more than once in the disputed verses, the actual number of occurrences is

---

[850] Among those who have taken the same position are: E. P. Gould, *op. cit.,* pp. 301, 304; J. Behm, *Einleitung in das Neue Testament,* Heidelberg, 1963, p. 55 ff.; M. H. Bolkestein, *op. cit.,* pp. 364-366 (leans in that direction); E. Lohmeyer, *Das Evangelium des Markus,* Göttingen, 1937, pp. 356-360; A. M. Farrer, *The Glass of Vision,* London, 1948, pp. 136-146; R. H. Lightfoot, *The Gospel Message of St. Mark,* Oxford, 1850, pp. 80-97, 106-116.

[851] Included among those who hold it are: V. Taylor, *op. cit.,* p. 609; A. T. Robertson, *Word Pictures,* Vol. I, p. 402; B. M. Metzger, *The Text of the New Testament,* Oxford, 1964, p. 228.

about eighteen. There are also words used in a manner different than in the rest of Mark. And there are peculiar phrases. [852]

(2) *Argument based on style* However, it is the style of Mark 16:9-20, perhaps even more than vocabulary and phraseology, that points to an

---

[852]   New Words

Verse	Form here used (For the meaning of this form see the translation)	Basic Form	Meaning of Basic Form (First occurrences are in italics)
10	πορευθεῖσα	πορεύομαι	*to go*
10	πενθοῦσι	πενθέω	*to mourn*
11	ἐθεάθη	θεάομαι	*to see*
11	ἠπίστησαν	ἀπιστέω	*to disbelieve*
12	ἑτέρᾳ	ἕτερος -α -ον	*different*
12	μορφῇ	μορφή	*form*
12	πορευομένοις	πορεύομαι	*to go*
14	ὕστερον	ὕστερος -α -ον	*afterward*
14	θεασαμένοις	θεάομαι	*to see*
15	πορευθέντες	πορεύομαι	*to go*
16	ἀπιστήσας	ἀπιστέω	to disbelieve
18	ὄφεις	ὄφις	*serpent*
18	θανάσιμον	θανάσιμος -ον	*deadly*
18	βλάψῃ	βλάπτω	*to harm*
19	ἀνελήμφθη	ἀναλαμβάνω	*to take up*
20	συνεργοῦντος	συνεργέω	*to work with*
20	βεβαιοῦντος	βεβαιόω	*to confirm*
20	ἐπακολουθούντων	ἐπακολουθέω	*to follow, attend*

author other than John Mark. In the first *eight* verses of this chapter, verses definitely written by Mark, the conjunction "and"—Greek *kai*—, *at the beginning of sentences or of clauses* (we are *not* counting the other *kai*'s) occurs *eight* times, [853] but in the next *twelve* verses *kai* performs the same function only *six* or *seven* times. [854] This means that in the first eight verses *kai* occurs, on the average, once per verse; in the last twelve verses, on the average, only once (or slightly more than once) in every two verses. There is accordingly a transition from co-ordination of clauses to subordination, from paratactic to hypotactic style. The transition, to be sure, is not radical or absolute: even in the last twelve verses there is a degree of co-ordination. But the difference is, nevertheless, rather striking.

Moreover, speaking about style, in making the transition from 16:1-8 to verses 9-20, who does not sense the striking contrast between the graphic and colorful style of the former and the prosaic summarizing style of the latter?

(3) *Argument based on contents* If all this has failed to drive home the conclusion that he who wrote verses 1-8 did not write verses 9-20, the fact about to be mentioned surely should do so. In Mark 16:1-8 the "young man dressed in a white robe" tells the women to remind "the disciples and Peter" that Jesus, risen from the dead, will meet them *in Galilee*. One expects, therefore, that if any appearances of the Lord are going to be recorded, they will be those that took place in *Galilee*. What actually happens is the very opposite: verses 9-20 never even mention where the appearances there summarized occurred, whether in Judea or in Galilee. From the Gospel according to John (20:1, 2, 11-18) we learn that the appearance to Mary

---

As to words used in a manner different than in the rest of Mark note ἐκεῖνος in verses 10, 11, 13 (twice), and 20; and φαίνω in verse 9.

As to peculiar phrases, note μετὰ ταῦτα, "afterward"—literally "after these things"— (verse 12), which is found indeed in Luke (e.g., 5:27; 10:1, etc.) and in John (3:22; 5:1; 6:1; 7:1; etc.), but not elsewhere in Mark, nor even in Matthew.

"They will speak in new tongues" (verse 17) reminds one of Acts 2:4, 11; 10:46; 19:6; I Cor. 12:30; and of I Cor. 14.

And who, in reading "the Lord working with them" (verse 20) does not immediately think of Rom. 8:28? In the same verse (Mark 16:20) is not the phrase "confirming his word" an echo of the type of language found in such passages as Rom. 15:8; Col. 2:7; Heb. 2:3; 13:9?

[853] Once at the beginning of each of the following verses: 1, 2, 3, 4; twice in verse 5 and also twice in verse 8.

[854] I cannot follow Stonehouse when in his book *The Witness of Matthew and Mark to Christ*, p. 91, he finds not a single instance of this use of *kai* in the long ending. In my own tally I arrive at *six* by excluding the weakly attested *kai* at the beginning of verse 18. By including this *kai* also, the number increases to *seven*: once at the beginning of each of the following verses: 11, 13, 15; three times in verse 18 ("*and* they will pick up . . . *and* if they drink . . . *and* they will recover), and once in verse 19. I am in full agreement with Stonehouse's opinion that the style of 16:9-20 differs from that of verses 1-8.

Magdalene (Mark 16:9-11), mentioned first of all, took place in the Jerusalem region; from Luke (24:13-35), that the appearance to the two men who were walking into the country (Mark 16:12, 13) also occurred in that general vicinity. Next, Luke (24:36 f.) describes an appearance of Jesus to the eleven, etc., to which Mark seems to refer in verse 14. That, too, had nothing to do with Galilee. The only possible connection with Galilee is found in 16:15-20; for Mark's verses 15, 16 resemble Matt. 28:19, which records words spoken by the resurrected Lord in Galilee (Matt. 28:16). But even here whoever it was that wrote Mark 16:15 f. never mentions Galilee at all.

The fact that there is little if any connection between Mark 16:1-8 and verses 9-20 is also clear from the very nature of the disputed section's beginning. Mary Magdalene has just been mentioned twice (Mark 15:47; 16:1). Then, in verse 9, she is introduced as if she had not yet been mentioned at all: "Mary Magdalene, from whom he had cast out seven demons" (cf. Luke 8:2).

It has been established, therefore, that proposition A—Mark wrote 16:9-20—must be rejected. *Consequently proposition B—Mark did not write 16:9-20—has been accepted.* But which of its two branches?

According to the first—B 1—Mark *intended* to conclude his Gospel with the words of 16:8, " . . . for they were afraid." Along with many others I, too, do not feel happy with that solution. My objections are:

a. No other instance of a *book* ending so abruptly [855] has ever been found.

b. Not only is such an ending very abrupt, it is also very pessimistic. According to *Matt.* 28:8 the women departed from the tomb "with fear *and great joy.*" Did Mark, on the other hand, intend to end his story on a note of gloom?

c. The day of modern fiction writing had not yet arrived. Today in certain literary circles the fashion is to create an agonizing drama that leaves the reader hanging breathlessly on the edge of a cliff, wondering how things are going to turn out. Suddenly the story ends . . . minus any real denouement. Does Mark do something similar?

In reply it will be said that this objection is hardly fair, since even Mark has mentioned Christ's resurrection. But Mark has also promised a meeting of Jesus with his disciples *in Galilee* (verses 6, 7). Not unreasonably, therefore, the reader expects to hear about such a meeting. But nothing of the kind happens. To be sure, when we finally arrive at verse 15, the scene is

---

855 ἐφοβοῦντο γάρ.

probably Galilee, but, as pointed out previously, Mark's *ending* does not even say this.

The view endorsed by the writer of this commentary is, accordingly, B 2: Mark did not intend to conclude his Gospel at this point.

Questions now arise: "Did Mark ever finish his narrative? If not, why not? If he did, what happened to his concluding lines?"

All kinds of answers have been given to these questions, and every one of them has been immediately and devastatingly refuted. I have no desire to add to this confusion.

For theological reasons the objection may be raised, "But God would not allow his Word to remain unfinished!" The answer is: "Though it may well be true that the Gospel according to Mark lies before us in unfinished form, *the story itself* is brought to a most triumphant finish in Matt. 28:16-20.

What, then, must we think of Mark 16:9-20, that is, of *the ending?* It is an interesting summary of some of the appearances of the risen Savior and of his subsequent ascension and session at God's right hand. As such it is instructive, for it shows us an early church view—how extensively held cannot be precisely indicated—of these matters. *To the extent* in which this *ending* truly reflects what is found elsewhere inside the covers of our Bible it can be described as a product, however indirectly, of divine inspiration. Since it would be very difficult—perhaps impossible—to defend the thesis that every word of this *ending* is without flaw, no sermon, doctrine, or practice should be based solely upon its contents.

*   *   *   *   *

In addition to this "long ending" there is also a "short ending," which in some manuscripts is added after verse 8, as follows:

"But whatever they had been told they reported briefly to Peter and those with him. By means of them Jesus afterward sent out, from east to west, the sacred and imperishable proclamation of everlasting salvation."

Since this ending has found even less general acceptance than the longer one, and its spurious nature is evident even on the surface, additional remarks are unnecessary. This holds also for other endings.

*   *   *   *   *

BRIEF NOTES ON THE LONG ENDING (Mark 16:9-20),
which will be designated *the ending*

9 Now when he arose early on the first day of the week, he appeared first to Mary Magdalene, from whom he had cast out seven demons. 10 She went and told those who had been with him, as they were mourning and weeping. 11 But they, having heard that he was alive and had been seen by her, disbelieved.

16:9-11 *Christ's Appearance to Mary Magdalene*
Cf. Matt. 28:9, 10; John 20:11-18

The beginning is rather abrupt, for one has to go back all the way to verse 6 to find mention of Jesus by name. Also here in verses 9-11 his name never occurs. In fact, not until verse 19 is the identity of the One about whom such wonderful things are spoken finally revealed. Could it be that verses 9-11—or perhaps even verses 9-20—formed the conclusion of a lost account?

What we have in our present passage is a summary of John 20:11-18. See N.T.C. on that section. The summary here given is brief, to the point, comprehensive. The most important items are all included. Jesus arose on the first day of the week, and appeared first to Mary Magdalene, rewarding her loyalty and continuing to carry on the good work he had begun in her earlier (Luke 8:2; cf. Phil. 1:6). In obedience to Christ's command she told the disciples and those who were with them, "Jesus is alive, and I have seen him." The regathering of the previously scattered disciples is implied. She found the group mourning and weeping. That is easy to believe, for their hopes had been shattered. They were perplexed, baffled. And though the words they now heard were as precious as "apples of gold in a network of silver," they regarded them as being too good to be true. In the light of Luke 24:11; John 20:25, there is nothing in Mark 16:9-11 that is hard to accept as true to historical fact.

---

12 Afterward he appeared in a different form to two of them as they were walking into the country. 13 These went back and reported it to the others, but they did not believe them either.

16:12, 13 *His Appearance to Two Disciples*
Cf. Luke 24:13-35

Having summarized a section of *John's* Gospel, the report now turns to *Luke*. Having told what happened Easter morning, the events of Easter afternoon and evening are now related.

The summary is very brief; the section summarized is very lengthy (Luke 24:13-35). *The ending* presents certain difficulties. It informs us that Jesus appeared to the two men who were walking into the country—that is, to Cleopas and his companion (Luke 24:18)—"in a different form." We do not know exactly what this means. Does *the ending* wish to tell us that Jesus now appeared not as a "gardener" (John 20:15) but as a traveler or wayfarer?

The report that Jesus appeared to these men and joined them "as they were walking into the country" agrees with Luke's statement that these two were "going [clearly from Jerusalem] to a village named Emmaus." And *the ending's* further statement that the two men returned [to Jerusalem] and reported to the others what they had experienced is in harmony with Luke's story.

At this point, however, a real problem arises. *The ending* states that when the two men reported their exciting experience to Christ's assembled followers, their story met with unbelief. But Luke's version is, "They found the eleven and those with them, assembled together and saying, 'The Lord is risen indeed, and has appeared to Simon.'" A possible solution would be that some of Christ's followers had already accepted the glorious Easter truth, while others were still in doubt. Luke 24:37-41 (cf. Matt. 28:17) may give some support to that position. If this is not the answer, does this controversial item in *the ending* rest upon an erroneous tradition? We should bear in mind that *the ending* is not necessarily infallible, as is Luke's account.

---

14 Later he appeared to the eleven themselves, while they were reclining at table, and he rebuked them for their lack of faith and hardness of heart, because they had not believed those who had seen him after he had risen.

15 And he said to them, "Go into all the world and preach the gospel to the whole creation. 16 He who believes and is baptized will be saved, but he who does not believe will be condemned.

17 "Moreover, these signs will accompany those who believe: in my name they will cast out demons; they will speak in new tongues; 18 and they will pick up serpents with their hands; [856] and if they drink deadly poison it will not hurt them at all; they will place their hands on the sick, and they will recover."

16:14-18 *The Great Commission and The Signs*
Cf. Matt. 28:16-20; Luke 24:36-49; John 20:19-23; Acts 1:6-8

Again there is no indication of place or time; all we have is "later." It would appear, nevertheless, that in verse 14 the reference is still to Easter evening. It was then that lack of faith manifested itself, and this not only in the heart and mind of Thomas (John 20:24) but also on the part of the other ten disciples. See Luke 24:36-49. When Jesus suddenly appeared to his disciples in their Jerusalem gathering place, they thought that they saw a spirit, and even a little later they still "disbelieved for joy." Luke 24:42 may indirectly confirm the words of *the ending* that Jesus appeared to them "while they were reclining at table."

Now that *the ending* has summarized appearances recorded especially in John and in Luke, it is *Matthew's* turn. In verse 15 the scene shifts from Jerusalem to Galilee, as the parallel Matt. 28:16-20 indicates.

---

856 The phrase "with their hands" is omitted from some manuscripts.

Verse 15 of *the ending* is roughly parallel to Matt. 28:19, "The Great Commission" (see N.T.C. on that passage). The emphasis in verse 16 of *the ending* is not on baptism but on the exercise of faith, exactly as in Matthew; cf. also John 3:16, 18, 36. On the other hand, the person who by God's sovereign grace has surrendered himself to Christ will also gratefully accept the sacrament of baptism as a sign and seal of salvation. Thus baptism follows faith, as also in Acts 2:41; 16:31-34, and everywhere.

Verses 17 and 18 of *the ending* have given rise to much misunderstanding and grief. Jesus is here represented as having promised five signs that would accompany those who believed:

a. power to expel demons

b. ability to speak in new tongues

c. ability to pick up serpents, that is (implied), to pick up venomous snakes without being physically harmed

d. the gift of being able to drink deadly poison without being hurt

e. the power to place hands on the sick, who will then recover.

Now a. and e. present no special difficulty. Jesus did indeed impart such gifts to his disciples. They made use of them with good effect. See Matt. 10:1; Mark 9:38; Luke 10:17; Acts 5:16; 8:7; 16:18; 19:12.

Something similar is true with respect to b. the gift of tongues. See Acts 2:4; 10:46; 19:6; I Cor. 12:10, 28, 30; and the entire 14th chapter of I Cor.

In connection with such special gifts (a., b., and e. above) B. B. Warfield states, "These gifts were part of the credentials of the apostles as the authoritative agents of God in founding the Church. . . . They necessarily passed away with it." That with the passing away of the apostolic age these gifts ceased is also the testimony of Chrysostom and Augustine. It was also the view of Jonathan Edwards: "These extra gifts were given in order to the founding and establishing of the church in the world. But since the canon of Scripture has been completed, and the church fully founded and established, these extraordinary gifts have ceased." Among others who expressed similar views are Matthew Henry, George Whitefield, Charles H. Spurgeon, Robert L. Dabney, Abraham Kuyper, Sr., and W. G. T. Shedd. [857]

The ending mentions two more signs which Jesus supposedly promised to his disciples, namely, the ability without harm to pick up serpents and to drink deadly poisons (see c. and d. above). Those who accept *the ending* as fully inspired and infallible Holy Scripture find confirmation for c. in Luke 10:19 and Acts 28:3. See Lenski, *op. cit.*, p. 483. However, Luke 10:19 speaks about "treading on serpents," which is not exactly the same as

---

[857] For exact references to these statements, beginning with B. B. Warfield, see *The Outlook,* a journal of The Reformed Fellowship, published in Grand Rapids, Mich., the Oct. 1973 issue (Vol. XXIII, No. 10), pp. 22-24.

picking them up deliberately. According to Acts 28:3 Paul picks up a bunch of sticks and after he placed them on the fire a snake comes out and fastens itself on his hand. He shakes it off without physical harm to himself. But that surely is not what *the ending* says. Paul did not deliberately pick up a venomous snake! And as to drinking deadly poisons without harm, Lenski must confess that the New Testament offers no example of this. A. B. Bruce, *op. cit.*, 456, 457, is probably correct when he states that "taking up venomous serpents and drinking deadly poison seem to introduce us into the twilight of apocryphal story." Taking such risks is exactly what by implication Jesus condemned both by example (Matt. 4:7) and precept (Matt. 10:23; 24:16-18).

Ever so often newspapers report incidents of religious fanatics picking up venomous snakes and/or drinking deadly poisons, frequently with sad results. At times those who do this try to justify their strange behavior by appealing to Mark 16:18. It is high time that everybody be told that *the ending* is binding for faith and practice only to the extent in which its teachings are definitely supported by Scripture in general. In fact, they should be told that the items about picking up serpents and drinking poisons must not be considered Scripture at all!

It is possible, in fact, that in connection with four of the five items here mentioned the historical milieu is later than that of Christ's earthly sojourn. The following facts must be borne in mind:

Ability to speak in new tongues is never mentioned in the Gospels. Neither is ability to pick up venomous snakes or to drink poisons without incurring any harm. And even as to the gift of performing miraculous healings, though, to be sure, this is definitely mentioned in the Gospels, the possibility that the change from "anointing them with oil" (see on Mark 6:13) to "they will place their hands on the sick" (here in 16:18) is significant deserves consideration.

The public in general should become informed about the truth with respect to Mark 16:17, 18.

---

19 So the Lord Jesus, after he had spoken to them, was taken up into heaven, and took his seat at God's right hand. 20 Then they [the disciples] went out and preached everywhere, the Lord working with them and confirming his word by means of the signs that attended it.

16:19, 20 *Christ's Ascension*
Cf. Luke 24:50-53; Acts 1:9-11

The doctrine of Christ's ascension and particularly of his session at the Father's right hand was cherished highly by the apostolic church, and occupied a prominent place in its thought and confession (Acts 2:36; 7:55,

56; Rom. 8:34; Eph. 1:20-23; Col. 3:1; Heb. 1:3, 4; 2:9; 8:1; 10:12; Rev. 3:21; 5:5-14). *The ending* summarizes this doctrine beautifully. Note especially the following:

a. "the Lord Jesus." Lordship was ascribed to Jesus especially after his resurrection. Nevertheless, having taken note of Mark 11:3 (see on that passage) we do not find it strange to see this title in *the ending*.

b. "was taken up into heaven." Not here "he ascended into heaven," though this, too, would have been entirely correct (John 3:13; 6:62; 20:17; Acts 2:34; Eph. 4:8, 9), but "he was taken up" (cf. Acts 1:2, 11, 22; I Tim. 3:16; Rev. 12:5; and see also II Kings 2:3, 5, 11). In other words, the attention is here focused on the fact that it was the Father who drew his Son to himself, being eager, as it were, to reward him for his accomplished mediatorial work.

The eleven "went out" or "departed." This evidently means "from Jerusalem." This, however, is not in conflict with Mark 14:28; 16:7. *The ending*, as mentioned previously, is not interested in mentioning places. If some time after meeting with his disciples in Galilee Jesus made his final appearance in Jerusalem and then led them out until they were "over against Bethany" where he was parted from them (Luke 24:36, 50, 51), *the ending* does not contradict this in any way.

In obedience to Christ's command (verse 15; cf. Matt. 28:19) the disciples "preached everywhere," a statement which one would naturally associate with a period of church history considerably later than Pentecost.

However, their preaching would have been ineffective had it not been for the enabling power of the Lord, who was "constantly working with them" (cf. Rom. 8:28) and "confirming his word by means of signs that attended it" (see not only the reference to demon expulsions, new tongues, and miraculous healings, verses 17, 18, [858] but also Heb. 2:4).

On this high note *the ending* closes. Speaking in general, there is nothing in the entire *ending* (verses 9-20) that is more serene, uplifting, true, and beautiful than these final two verses. They point to "the Lord Jesus" as the One who, from his position at the right hand of God, tenderly watches over, guides, energizes, and governs his church.

Summary of Chapter 16

This chapter consists of two parts: verses 1-8 and verses 9-20. Mark himself was undoubtedly the inspired author of the first part. Arguments based on omission of the second part from the best Greek sources, and on

---

[858] If the author of *the ending* was thinking of all five "signs," then we cannot entirely agree with him.

vocabulary, style, and contents, have convinced most scholars that verses 9-20 are inauthentic, that is, of questioned origin, probably not written by John Mark. Who the real author was is not known.

A. verses 1-8

In verse 1 Mark relates what happened on Saturday evening, how three women, loyal to Jesus, bought spices with which to anoint his body.

In verses 2-8 he narrates what happened to these friends and disciples of Jesus very early Sunday morning: their worry about the huge stone in front of the tomb's entrance, their surprise upon the discovery that this stone had already been removed, and their entrance into the tomb where they were addressed by a young man in a white robe. By Matthew this "young man" is called an "angel." He conveyed Christ's message to the women. It was the glad Easter news: "He is risen. He is not here. Look, here is the place where they laid him." The "young man" also transmitted to them Christ's order. He said, "But go, tell his disciples and Peter, 'He is going ahead of y o u to Galilee. There y o u will see him, as he told y o u.' "

The actual reunion of Christ with his disciples in Galilee is, however, not reported by Mark. For that we must turn to Matt. 28:16-20. Mark's account closes with the words of verse 8: "And they [that is, the women] fled from the tomb, for trembling and astonishment were holding them in their grip; and they said nothing to anybody, for they were afraid."

B. verses 9-20

An unknown author briefly summarizes *John's* report of Jesus' appearance to Mary Magdalene (Jerusalem, early Easter morning). Cf. Mark 16:9-11 with John 20:11-18. *Luke's* story about Jesus' appearance to the two disciples who were on their way to Emmaus (Easter afternoon) is the basis for the next few lines. Cf. Mark 16:12, 13 with Luke 24:13-35. The events of Easter evening are reviewed in Mark 16:14: Jesus meeting with his disciples in Jerusalem. This is followed by a parallel to *Matthew's* account of The Great Commission. Cf. Mark 16:15, 16 with Matt. 28:19. A controversial report about certain "signs" which, it is claimed, Jesus promised to his followers, is found in 16:17, 18. Not all of these "signs" find support in the rest of Scripture, though some do. The final verses (Mark 16:19, 20) express the firmly rooted faith of the early church in Christ's ascension and session at God's right hand. The section closes with these words, "Then they [the disciples] went out and preached everywhere, the Lord working with them and confirming his word by means of the signs that attended it."

693

SELECT BIBLIOGRAPHY

Among the many works on this Gospel two are perhaps most widely known:

Swete, H. B., *The Gospel according to St. Mark*, London, 1913.

Taylor, V., *The Gospel according to St. Mark*, London, 1953.

Other titles that have a right to be included in a Select Bibliography are:

Bruce, A. B., *The Synoptic Gospels (The Expositor's Greek Testament*, Vol. I), Grand Rapids, no date.

Calvin, J., *Commentary on a Harmony of the Evangelists, Matthew, Mark, and Luke* (tr. of *Commentarius in Harmoniam Evangelicam, Opera Omnia*), Grand Rapids. 1949 ff.

Cole, R. A., *The Gospel according to St. Mark (Tyndale New Testament Commentaries)*, Grand Rapids, 1961.

Lane, W. L., *Commentary on the Gospel of Mark (New International Commentary on the New Testament)*, Grand Rapids, 1974.

Lenski, R. C. H., *Interpretation of St. Mark's and St. Luke's Gospels*, Columbus, 1934.

Stonehouse, N. B., *The Witness of Matthew and Mark to Christ*, Philadelphia, 1944. Though not strictly a commentary, the book sheds light on many passages of Mark's Gospel.

GENERAL BIBLIOGRAPHY

Alexander, J. A., *The Gospel according to Matthew*, New York, 1867.

Allen, W. C., *The Gospel according to Saint Mark*, London, 1915.

Ante-Nicene Fathers, ten volumes, reprint, Grand Rapids, 1950, for references to Clement of Alexandria, Irenaeus, Justin Martyr, Origen, Tertullian, etc.

Barclay, W., *The Gospel of Mark (Daily Study Bible)*, Edinburgh & Philadelphia, 1956.

Bavinck, H., *The Doctrine of God* (tr. of *Gereformeerde Dogmatiek*, Vol. II, "Over God"), Grand Rapids, 1955.

Behm, J. *Einleitung in das Neue Testament*, Heidelberg, 1963.

Berkhof, L., *Systematic Theology*, Grand Rapids, 1949.

Berkouwer, G. C., *Dogmatische Studiën* (the series), Kampen, 1949, etc.

Biederwolf, W. E., *Whipping Post Theology*, Grand Rapids, 1934.

Bolkestein, M. H., *Het Evangelie naar Markus*, Nijkerk, 1966.

Branscomb, B. H., *The Gospel of Mark (Moffatt New Testament Commentary)*, London, 1937.

Brown, D., *Bury My Heart at Wounded Knee*, New York, 1972.

Bruce, A. B., "The Baptism of Jesus," *Exp*, 5th series, 7 (1898).

Bruce, A. B., *The Synoptic Gospels (Expositor's Greek Testament*, Vol. I), Grand Rapids, no date.

Bruce, F. F., *Commentary on the book of Acts (New International Commentary on the New Testament)*, Grand Rapids, 1964.

Bundy, W. E., "The meaning of Jesus' Baptism," *JR*, 7 (1927).

Burgon, J. W., *The Last Twelve Verses of Mark*, Ann Arbor, 1959.

Burkill, T. A., *New Light on the Earliest Gospel: Seven Markan Studies*, Ithaca, 1972.

Burrows, M., *The Dead Sea Scrolls*, New York, 1956.

Burrows, M., *More Light on the Dead Sea Scrolls*, New York, 1958.

Burton, E. D., *Syntax of the Moods and Tenses in New Testament Greek*, Chicago, 1900.

Calvin, J., *Commentary on a Harmony of the Evangelists, Matthew, Mark, and Luke* (tr. of *Commentarius in Harmoniam Evangelicam, Opera Omnia*), Grand Rapids, 1949 ff.

Chadwick, G. A., *The Gospel according to St. Mark (Expositor's Bible)*, Grand Rapids, 1943.

Chiniquy, C., *Fifty Years in the Church of Rome*, New York, etc., 1886.

Cole, R. A., *The Gospel according to St. Mark (Tyndale New Testament Commentaries)*, Grand Rapids, 1961.

Dalman, G., *Jesus-Jeshua, Studies in the Gospels*, New York, 1929.

Deissman, *Light from the Ancient East*, New York, 1927.

MARK

Edersheim, A., *The Life and Times of Jesus the Messiah*, New York, 1897.

Edersheim, A., *The Temple*, London, 1908.

Elderkin, G. W., *Archaeological Paper VII: Golgotha, Kraneion, and the Holy Sepulchre*, Springfield, Mass., 1945.

Emden, C. S., "St. Mark's Use of the Imperfect Tense," *BTr* (July 1954).

Erdman, C. R., *The Gospel of Mark, An Exposition*, Philadelphia, 1945.

Farrer, A. M., *The Glass of Vision*, London, 1948.

Field, F., *Notes on the Translation of the New Testament*, Cambridge, 1899.

Finkelstein, L., *The Jews, their History, Culture, and Religion*, New York, 1949.

Flynn, L. A., *Did I Say That?*, Nashville, 1959.

Foster, R. C., *Studies in the Life of Christ*, Grand Rapids, 1966.

Geldenhuys, N., *Commentary on the Gospel of Luke* (*New International Commentary on the New Testament*), Grand Rapids, 1951.

Gould, E. P., *The Gospel according to St. Mark* (*International Critical Commentary*), New York, 1907.

Grant, F. C., *The Gospel according to St. Mark* (*Interpreter's Bible*, Vol. VII), New York and Nashville, 1951.

Greijdanus, S., *Het Heilig Evangelie naar de Beschrijving van Lucas* (*Kommentaar op het Nieuwe Testament*), Amsterdam, 1940.

Groenewald, E. P., *Die Evangelie volgens Markus* (*Kommentaar op die Bybel, Nuwe Testament*, Vol. II), Pretoria, 1948.

Grollenberg, L. H., *Atlas of the Bible*, New York, etc., 1956.

Grosheide, F. W., *Het Heilig Evangelie Volgens Mattheus* (*Commentaar op het Nieuwe Testament*), Kampen, 1954.

Halberthal, L., *The Plan of the Holy Temple of Jerusalem*, Montreal, 1967.

Hawkins, J. C., *Horae Synopticae*, Oxford, 1909.

Hendriksen, W., *The Covenant of Grace*, Grand Rapids, 1932.

Hendriksen, W., *The Meaning of the Preposition* ἀντί *in the New Testament* (unpublished doctoral dissertation), Princeton, 1948.

Hendriksen, W., *Bible Survey*, Grand Rapids, 1961.

Hendriksen, W., *More Than Conquerors, An Interpretation of the Book of Revelation*, Grand Rapids, 1970.

Hendriksen, W., *The Bible on the Life Hereafter*, Grand Rapids, 1971.

Hendriksen, W., *Israel in Prophecy*, Grand Rapids, 1972.

Hills, E. F., *The King James Version Defended*, Des Moines, 1956.

Hoekema, A. A., *The Four Major Cults*, Grand Rapids, 1963.

Hooke, R., *Discourse on Earthquakes*, 1668.

Hort, F. J. A., and Westcott, B. F., *The New Testament in the Original Greek*, Cambridge and London, 1882.

Huizenga, L. S., *Unclean! Unclean!*, Grand Rapids, 1927.

Johnson, S. E., *A Commentary on the Gospel according to St. Mark* (*Black's N.T. Commentaries*), London and New York, 1960.

Kollek, T. and Pearlman, M., *Jerusalem, A History of Forty Centuries*, New York, 1968.

Kraeling, E. G., *Rand McNally Bible Atlas*, New York, etc., 1966.

MARK

Lagrange, M.-J., *Evangile selon Saint Marc*, Paris.

Lane, W. L., *Commentary on the Gospel of Mark* (*New International Commentary on the New Testament*), Grand Rapids, 1974.

Lange, J. P., *Mark* (*Commentary on the Holy Scriptures*), Grand Rapids, no date.

Lenski, R. C. H., *Interpretation of St. Mark's Gospel*, Columbus, 1934. Full Title of volume is "The Interpretation of St. Mark's and St. Luke's Gospels." In this volume, pp. 1-486 are devoted to Mark's Gospel.

Lightfoot, R. H., *The Gospel Message of St. Mark*, Oxford, 1850.

Loeb Classical Library, New York (various dates), for The Apostolic Fathers, Eusebius, Josephus, Philo, Pliny, Plutarch, Strabo, etc.

Lohmeyer, *Das Evangelium des Markus*, Göttingen, 1937.

Machen, J. G., *The Origin of Paul's Religion*, Grand Rapids, 1947.

Mackenzie, J. G., *Souls in the Making*, New York, 1930.

Mackintosh, H. R., *The Doctrine of the Person of Christ*, New York, 1931.

Maier, P. L., *Pontius Pilate*, Garden City, New York, 1968.

Maier, W. A., *For Better Not for Worse*, St. Louis, 1935.

Manson, W., *Jesus the Messiah*, Philadelphia, 1946.

McMillen, S. I., *None of These Diseases*, Westwood, N. J., 1963.

Metzger, B. M., *The Text of the New Testament*, Oxford, 1964.

Meyer, H. A. W., *Critical and Exegetical Handbook to the Gospels of Mark and Luke*, Edinburgh, 1880. Comments on Mark are found in Vol. I, pp. 1-256.

Montefiore, C. G., *The Synoptic Gospels*, London, 1927.

Morag, S., "Ephphatha (Mark 7:34): Certainly Hebrew, not Aramaic?" *JSS* 17 (2, 1972).

Morgan, G. C., *The Gospel according to Mark*, New York, etc., 1927.

Mulder, H., *De Synagoge in de Nieuwtestamentische Tijd*, Kampen, 1969.

Mulder, H., *Spoorzoeker in Bijbelse Landen*, Amsterdam, 1973.

Müller, G. A., *Pontius Pilatus der fünfte Prokurator von Judäa*, Stuttgart, 1888.

Parmelee, A., *All the Birds of the Bible*, New York, 1959.

Pasternak, B., *Doctor Zhivago*, New York, 1960.

Plummer, A., *The Gospel according to Matthew* (*Cambridge Greek Testament for Schools and Colleges*), Cambridge, 1914.

Rawlinson, A. E. J., *St. Mark*, London, 1925.

Rice, E. W., *Pictorial Commentary on the Gospel according to Mark*, Philadelphia, 1882.

Ridderbos, H. N., *Zelfopenbaring en Zelfverberging*, Kampen, 1946.

Robertson, A. T., *The Pharisees and Jesus*, New York, 1920.

Robertson, A. T., *A Harmony of the Gospels for Students of the Life of Christ*, New York, 1922.

Robertson, A. T., *Word Pictures in the New Testament*, Vol. I, New York and London, 1930.

Robertson, A. T., *Luke the Historian in the Light of Research*, New York, 1923.

Robinson, H. W., *The People and the Book*, Oxford, 1925.

Rosenblatt, S., "The Crucifixion of Jesus from the Standpoint of Pharisaic Law," *JBL* 75 (Dec. 1956).

Russel, J. W., ed. *Teachers' New Testament with Notes and Helps*, Grand Rapids, 1959.

Schaff, P., *History of the Christian Church*, Volumes I-VII, New York, various dates.

MARK

Schmid, J., *The Gospel according to Mark* (*The Regensburg New Testament*), New York, 1968.

Schonfield, J., *The Passover Plot*, New York, 1965.

Schürer, E., *History of the Jewish People in the Time of Jesus* (tr. of *Geschichte des jüdischen Volkes in Zeitaltar Jesu Christi*), Edinburgh, 1892-1901.

Scroggs, R. and Groff, K. I., "Baptism in Mark: Dying and Rising With Christ," *JBL* 92 (Dec. 1973).

Smith, M., "Notes on Goodspeed's 'Problems of New Testament Translation,' " *JBL* 64 (1945).

Smith, W. C., *Islam in Modern History*, New York, 1959..

Speer, R. E., *The Principles of Jesus Applied to Some Questions of Today*, New York, etc., 1902.

Straton, J. R.-Potter, O. F., *Debates*, New York, 1924.

Streeter, B. H., *The Four Gospels*, London, 1930.

Stonehouse, N. B., *The Witness of Matthew and Mark to Christ*, Philadelphia, 1944.

Stonehouse, N. B., *Origins of the Synoptic Gospels*, Grand Rapids, 1963.

Swete, H. B., *The Gospel according to St. Mark*, London, 1913; Grand Rapids, 1956.

Talmud, The Babylonian (Engl. tr.), London, 1948.

Taylor, V., *The Gospel according to St. Mark*, London, etc., 1953.

Taylor, W. M., *The Parables of our Savior, Expounded and Illustrated*, New York, 1886.

Trench, R. C., *Synonyms of the New Testament*, Grand Rapids, 1948.

Trueblood, E., *The Humor of Christ*, New York, etc., 1964.

Turner, E. S., *The Astonishing History of the Medical Profession*, New York, 1961.

Turner, G. A., *Historical Geography of the Holy Land*, Grand Rapids, 1973.

Van Dellen, I., *The Ministry of Mercy*, Grand Rapids, 1946.

Van Leeuwen, J. A. C., *Het Heilig Evangelie naar de beschrijving van Markus* (*Kommentaar op het Nieuwe Testament*), Amsterdam, 1928.

Van Leeuwen, J. A. C., *Het Evangelie naar Markus* (*Korte Verklaring der heilige Schrift*), Kampen, 1935.

Warfield, B. B., *Christology and Criticism*, New York, Oxford, 1929.

White, W., "O'Callighan's Identification: Confirmation and Its Consequences," *WTJ* 35 (Fall 1972).

White, W., "Notes on the Papyrus Fragments from Cave 7 at Qumran" *WTJ* 35 (Winter 1973).

Wolff, M., "De Samenstelling en het Karakter van het groote συνέδριον te Jeruzalem voor het jaar 70 Na Chr.," *TT* 51 (1917).

Wood, J. G., *Story of the Bible Animals*, Philadelphia, no date.

Wright, G. E., *Biblical Archaeology*, London and Philadelphia, 1957.

Zahn, Th., *Introduction to the New Testament*, Engl. tr., Edinburgh, 1909.

Zondervan Pictorial Bible Dictionary, Grand Rapids, 1963.

Zwemer, S. M., *Across the World of Islam*, New York, 1929.